Hermann Lotze

Outlines of Psychology

Hermann Lotze

Outlines of Psychology

ISBN/EAN: 9783743314610

Hergestellt in Europa, USA, Kanada, Australien, Japan

Cover: Foto ©Thomas Meinert / pixelio.de

Manufactured and distributed by brebook publishing software
(www.brebook.com)

Hermann Lotze

Outlines of Psychology

OUTLINES OF PSYCHOLOGY

*BASED UPON THE RESULTS OF EXPERI-
MENTAL INVESTIGATION*

BY

OSWALD KÜLPE

Professor of Philosophy in the University of Würzburg

Translated from the German (1893)

BY

EDWARD BRADFORD TITCHENER

Sage Professor of Psychology in the Cornell University

LONDON
SWAN SONNENSCHEIN & CO., Lim.
NEW YORK: MACMILLAN & CO.
1895

TRANSLATOR'S PREFACE

The text upon which this translation is based differs only in a few minor points from that of Professor Külpe's *Grundriss der Psychologie* as published in 1893. The author has slightly modified passages in §§ 1. 9; 4. 6; 21. 2; 62. 4, and has added the footnote to § 21. 6, besides making some twenty verbal changes in the course of the work. Acting upon his suggestion, I have myself partially rewritten § 10. 4, to bring the paragraph into agreement with § 36. 4; have made slight additions to §§ 25. 2 (footnote); 30. 5; 35. 4, and 56. 1 (footnote); and have introduced a new paragraph, § 27a, on the experimental methods of the investigation of Memory and Association. For the form of these additions (which are indicated in the text by square brackets) I am responsible. But all of them were expressly indicated by Professor Külpe.

I have further (1) supplied an index of names; (2) filled in a very large number of cross-references, which the author had left in general terms; and (3) printed in small type the various passages in which he describes his own experiments. I hope that all three changes will be of assistance to the reader of the book.

The symbolic exposition of the measurement-methods in Part I. retains the German form in the translation. Many English writers on psychophysical questions have employed the German abbreviations; there are obvious difficulties in the way of an English terminology; and it is not probable that any proposals which could be made at the present time would find general acceptance. But, these reasons apart, I have thought it best to keep the German symbols as an aid to the student in his reading of German monographic literature. He may now familiarise himself with their explanation in the translation, or use the Sections in which they are discussed as a vocabulary of technical terms.

E. B. T.

Cornell University, Ithaca, N. Y.

CONTENTS

INTRODUCTION

PART I. The Elements of Consciousness.

SECTION I. SENSATIONS.

CHAPTER I. *The Analysis of Sensations.*

A. PERIPHERALLY EXCITED SENSATIONS.

CHAPTER II. *The Quality of Sensations.*

(1) The Quality of Cutaneous Sensations.

(2) The Quality of the Sensations of Taste and Smell.

(3) The Quality of Auditory Sensations.

(4) The Quality of Visual Sensations.

INTRODUCTION.

§ 1. Meaning and Problem of Psychology.

1. The business of all science is the description of facts. In any
particular description we employ a certain set of symbols, which serves
us as a means of expression of the facts which we wish to present.
Every science, therefore, constructs for its own use a system of symbols; and the *universal validity* of a scientific description depends in
part upon the accurate and consequent application of this system. In
part only: for it is a matter of experience that the individual fact
stands in definite relations to other facts, and that the existence and
specification of these are necessary to raise it above the level of mere
personal opinion and belief. Indeed, it would not be too much to
say, that any individual fact can be adequately defined by the
enumeration of all its relations to other facts. And while popular
thinking is usually content with a very incomplete statement of them,
it is the task of science to make their description exhaustive. So
that the universal validity of a scientific exposition depends in the
second place upon the progress made by the special science towards
the achievement of this end.

2. The facts with which science in general, apart from philosophy,
has to deal we term *facts of experience.* They are the ultimate and
original data of our experience: they constitute the subject matter of
reflection, although they are not in themselves reflection. Philosophy,
on the other hand, has to investigate the description of these facts;
our *reflection* upon experience is made the object of a separate inquiry.
Now it is evident that the ideas, passions, etc., which psychologists of
the most different schools agree in discussing in their treatises, must
be considered facts of experience. Hence it follows that psychology
belongs not with the philosophical disciplines, but with the special
sciences.

3. Our ordinary classifications of the special sciences are based
upon a number of divergent principles. Thus we distinguish botany

from zoology, jurisprudence from philology, by reference to the subjects which they treat. Or we express the degree of completeness, that is, the sphere of the validity of a scientific exposition, by the phrases 'descriptive' and 'explanatory science'. Or, again, we say that physics and chemistry stand to physical and chemical technology as theory to practice. And we speak further of inductive and deductive sciences,— the former characterized by progress from particular to general, the latter by that from general to particular.

Most of these principles of classification may be used to distinguish psychology from the other sciences. Psychology is inductive, for instance, while mathematics is deductive; it stands to pedagogy as theory to practice; it is still in the main descriptive, as compared with the 'exact' sciences, which are *par excellence* explanatory. The only principle of delimitation which cannot possibly be employed is that of the subject treated. The reason is, that there is no single fact of experience which cannot be made the subject of psychological investigation. Now since all the other rubrics specify the form and not the matter of the scientific work which they cover, and since the relation of psychology to natural science cannot be subsumed to any one of them in particular, it is clear that we must look for the distinctive character of psychological subject-matter not in the peculiar nature of a definite class of experiential facts, but rather in some property which attaches to all alike. This property is the *dependency of facts of experience upon experiencing individuals.*

4. We often express this by saying that psychology is a science of 'psychical' facts, facts of 'consciousness', or that the facts of psychology are 'subjective'. Such phrases are one and all misleading. Thus we may begin by restricting the term 'subjective' to the visual image of our own body: in which case everything else that is visible in space is objective. Or, going further, we may apply the term exclusively to states which cannot by any possibility be objectified, and which constitute an altogether peculiar department of psychology, such as thought, feelings of pleasure and pain, etc. In either case the object of psychological inquiry is wrongly or inadequately specified. In the same way, the word 'psychical' may be taken, in the light of certain well-known metaphysical doctrines, to denote a reality, entirely separable as such from the 'physical' processes. And the term 'consciousness' is equally ambiguous: it may mean simply what is experienced, it may mean our knowledge of that experience, or it may mean a state to which mental realities, otherwise unconscious, may somehow attain. Wherever in what follows we employ these equivocal expressions for the sake of brevity or

variety, we mean to indicate by them simply that part or aspect of the experiential fact which is dependent upon the experiencing individual. 'Subjective' or 'subjectified' processes, facts of 'consciousness,' 'psychical' or 'mental' states will mean for us no more than this; and 'consciousness' itself, or 'mind', will in our terminology merely denote the sum total of all these particular phenomena. We shall nowhere discuss anything like a 'transcendental consciousness', a 'substantial soul', or an 'immaterial spirit'.

5. But our definition of psychology as a science of the facts of experience in their dependency upon experiencing individuals is not altogether satisfactory. The term 'individual' is used in so many different senses that it itself requires discussion and definition. It might seem at first sight as though we were speaking of a psychical individual, and understanding by the phrase either a transcendent immaterial substance (soul or spirit) or a whole number of experiences and capacities that are ordinarily subjectified (feeling, attention, imagination, etc.). But we cannot, as a matter of fact, accept either of these interpretations. On the first no empirical psychology, on the second no scientific psychology is possible.—The latter statement requires some explanation; the former is self evident.

If psychology is to be scientific, its statements must possess universal validity, and particularly in the second of the two meanings which we attached to this phrase above. Now universal validity can only be obtained by a very complete description of the relations which hold between separate facts, and determine their special character. But no one would say that a musical chord was adequately defined by the statement that it was pleasant, or that it had drawn the hearer's attention to itself, or that it had called up the remembrance of a certain scene or of a certain composition. And not only are such statements imperfect as definitions, but there is no hint, in any of the constituents of our inner experience which are named in them, of that relation of dependency which we have made the *differentia* in our definition of psychology as a whole. Idea is not dependent upon emotion, nor emotion upon idea; a change in one is not necessarily followed by a definite change in the other. And ideas are not dependent solely upon one another; they come and go in our inner experience very much at random; their interconnections are for the most part not due to mutual influence, but obviously follow a law imposed upon them from without. Again, though the attention is frequently mentioned as one of the conditions of a subjective (psychical) process, we must remember, in the first place that it is only one condition out of many, and secondly that the use of the term, whose brevity and intelligibility render it a convenient mode of description, does not exclude the holding of diametrically opposite views as to the real nature of the phenomenon indicated. And finally it may be urged, that the objects of psychological inquiry would never present the advantages of measurability and unequivocalness, possessed in so high a degree by the objects investigated by natural science, if they could be brought into relation only with the psychical individual.

6. These brief remarks must suffice for the present to justify our rejection of the most obvious interpretation of the 'individual' in our definition. What we mean by the word will, of course, be shown in detail as the book progresses. But it is plain, even now, that the dependency of which we are thinking is a dependency upon the *corporeal* individual. No one has ever disputed its existence, except metaphysicians of a certain school: but the range of its validity has only become manifest as physiology and psychology have advanced. We know now that the bodily processes which stand in a direct functional relation to our experiential facts take place in man exclusively in the brain,— probably in the cerebral cortex. It is assumed that this dependency is always present, although in many cases its existence is merely hypothetical. At the same time, we are prevented from regarding the relation as temporally determined, that is, as causal, by two reasons: the facts do not require any such theory for their explanation, and the physical law of the conservation of energy appears to contradict it. Psychologists to-day are, therefore, accustomed to speak of a *parallelism* of psychical and cerebral processes: *i.e.*, the two are regarded as concomitant phenomena so related that any change upon the one side manifests itself in a corresponding change upon the other. This regulative principle is based upon experience, and we may expect that it will receive further confirmation from experience in the future. Whether in its metaphysical setting it be interpreted as a principle of the interaction of two substances (Dualism), or be thought to express the two aspects of the activity of a single being (Monism),—whether it be regarded as spiritualistic or materialistic, is scientifically indifferent. So that we, who represent an empirical psychology, may rightly dispense with any discussion of these possibilities.

7. But a dependency upon experiencing individuals may seem to imperil the universal validity of psychology and to increase the difficulty of the discovery of facts. However, *individual differences,* are always confronting us, and are important not only for the psychologist, but also for the zoologist and anthropologist. They do not constitute any danger to science, except in cases where it cannot transcend the particular description of an isolated fact. Wherever they can be

explained by an adequate specification of conditions, they can be readily subsumed to general rules. Anatomy and physiology are not hampered in the solution of their problems by the numberless individual differences in muscular structure, in nervous excitability, in the circulation of the blood. And in the same way, the fact of personal differences in regard to the subjectified facts of experience does not present any insuperable difficulty to psychology.

The second objection is more serious. What a man experiences himself, he rates as fact without any description; but he can never obtain more than indirect access to the experiences of others. The psychologist can only acquire knowledge of his neighbour's experiences by the aid of symbols, such as we have spoken of above; and the value of his results depends upon the correct use of these symbols on the one side, and the correct interpretation of them on the other. It is not given to every one either to use or to interpret correctly; and it follows that the right psychological disposition and special practice are indispensable both for observer and observed. The more difficult the symbols to interpret, the more equivocal the result:—think how hard it is to understand the gestures of a person speaking a foreign language, be their meaning never so simple! Such an illustration shows us how much hope there is of a psychology of the lower animals,—of the protozoa. Nevertheless, this difficulty in the ascertainment of facts is not in itself an absolute preventive of scientific knowledge. Language may, to a certain extent, be checked by experiment; and, as a generally intelligible means of expression of the similar experiences of different individuals, forms an extremely valuable aid to psychological inquiry.

8. It is plain from what has been said that the *problem* of psychology is a very definite one: it is the adequate description of those properties of the data of experience which are dependent upon experiencing individuals. The experiences to be examined include not only states which are altogether individual and which have no objective reference, such as emotions, impulses, and the like, but also facts which are, under certain aspects, independent of the individual, and which may consequently form the subject-matter of a natural science, such as the objects of our ideas, with their temporal and spatial relations. 'Sensible qualities' are regarded by the scientist as subjective processes, and their description relegated to psychology. But the temporal and spatial properties and relations of sensible objects are also matters of subjective experience and estimation; we compare distances and directions, movements and velocities, and contrast apparent magnitude and apparent duration with the real,—*i.e.*, with magnitudes and durations objectively

measured. So that while (1) all these phenomena must be depicted in detail, that we may see what property of our experiences it precisely is which indicates their dependency upon the corporeity of the experiencing subject, (2) the dependency itself must also be made the object of careful investigation.

9. The psychologist understands by a *theory* precisely what is meant by the term in natural science: the specification of the conditions of the appearance of a given phenomenon. A theory of psychical processes, in this sense, may be attempted in two different ways. (i) We may resolve the more complex phenomena into their elements, and trace the laws which govern the formation of the compound from the simple. The procedure here is similar to the qualitative and quantitative analysis of chemical method. It is especially useful in cases where psychology comes into connection with cognate and, in a certain sense, subordinate disciplines; *e.g.*, in the ethical and æsthetic judgments. (ii) But psychological theory may also consist in the proof of the dependency of mental phenomena upon certain bodily processes. Now this proof is peculiarly difficult. In the first place we have no means of directly examining the interrelations of the two sets of facts, the psychical processes and the central nervous excitations, during their course. It has sometimes been possible, after the removal by operation of a part of the skull, to note the parallelism of mass-movements of the brain and the appearance of sense-impressions, emotions, etc. But the value of such observations cannot be very great, as long as the determination and definite variation of the particular cerebral processes corresponding to particular mental acts remain impossible. And secondly the physiology of the central nervous system has not as yet been able to formulate the mechanism of cerebral activity in physical and chemical terms. We know nothing of the real nature of nervous excitation. The only thing done so far is the demonstration of areas of localisation in the cerebral cortex, that is, the demarcation of spheres, within which the nervous processes that run parallel to definite subjectified experiences take place.

10. It follows from this that we are not at present in a position to give a complete theory of psychical processes in the strict sense of the word. But we have two means of anticipating or indicating the complete theory, without having recourse to dubious or premature hypothesis. (1) We may discover a relation between experiences and certain bodily processes which stand in a causal connection with the unknown excitations in the cerebral cortex and admit of detailed examination. Psychology investigates in this way the dependency of sensation upon stimulus, and that of voluntary and involuntary move-

ments upon will and feeling. We may not, of course, argue from the relations of these widely remote links in a chain of causation to the relation between the parallel processes. But at least we are able to pave the way in some sense for the theory proper; and that is no small advantage. (2) The other mode of procedure is rather indicative than anticipatory. It consists in the introduction of general concepts for mental states or capacities,—memory, imagination, mental disposition, etc.,—concepts which indicate our ignorance of their actual conditions. These expressions were formerly employed on the analogy of the concept of force in modern natural science, to designate purely psychical dispositions or faculties, to whose existence or activity a particular experience might be referred. At the present day they serve simply as brief and intelligible expressions for the unknown conditions of certain peculiarities presented by single experiences or complexes of experiences. When we come to deal with sensations, for instance, we shall mention practice as one of the factors influencing their discriminability. We shall not mean by 'practice' a special psychical capacity, or even a new mental act, but merely a number of processes, not very exactly known, whose effect is to facilitate an operation which has been frequently repeated. And, as we shall see later, the same holds in a certain sense of attention.

11. We shall not deal in this book with *animal psychology* or with *social psychology*. Our material for the former would to-day be both scanty and unreliable; though we cannot doubt that there will arise in the future an independent science of zoopsychology, to which the psychology of man will bear the same relation as is borne by human physiology to the physiology of animals and plants. Social psychology treats of the mental phenomena dependent upon a community of individuals: it is already a special department of study, if not a fully developed science. But it is not difficult to see that the psychology of the individual man, as we must in strictness term our own psychology, forms the foundation both of animal and of social psychology. It must precede the former, because nothing but an accurate knowledge of the relations between the processes of consciousness and expressive movements in man can give us any solid basis for analogical inferences from movements to psychical states in animals: and it must precede the latter, because the mental processes dependent upon communities of men are only realized in individuals and only expressed by individuals. We might, therefore, also term our own psychology *general psychology*.

§ 2. Methods and Aids of Psychology.

1. The methods which psychology follows in the examination of
its subject-matter are of two kinds, *direct* and *indirect.* Direct methods
are applicable wherever an immediate apprehension and description
of the facts examined are possible. If we are investigating our own
sensations of colour, for instance, we employ a direct method by
immediately experiencing them and directly observing their details.
Indirect methods are used, on the other hand, wherever it is necessary
to infer the facts about which we wish to know from some group
of symbols which represents them. Thus we follow an indirect method
when we appeal to memory or communication by language to give
us knowledge of·particular experiences. It is evident that the direct
methods are greatly to be preferred to the indirect. At the same
time, psychology cannot dispense with the indirect, without reducing
itself to the nothingness of a purely individual science. Whenever
we attempt to study the mental processes of our fellow men, we are
compelled to proceed by indirect methods.

2. Each kind of method can be applied both objectively and purely
subjectively, since each can be used by outside inquirers as well as
by the experiencing individual alone. If we term the immediate
apprehension and description of mental processes ' inner perception '
or 'introspection', the subjective form of the direct method may be
named the *introspective method.* Its objective form will be the *experimental method,* since its objectivity depends upon the employment of
experiment. The indirect method may be similarly divided into a
memorial method, which is subjective, and a *linguistic method,* which
is objective. The two objective methods can never be applied apart
from the corresponding subjective methods, though the converse
procedure is quite possible. Experiment without introspection is no
more than a plaything borrowed from physics, and language without
memory is but a sound without sense. Language checks, strengthens,
and fixes memory, just as experiment increases the reliability and
generalises the significance of introspection.—We must look at the
nature and range of these methods somewhat carefully.

I.   Direct Methods.

3. (*a*) The *introspective method* is the simplest and most obvious of
all. It is common to science and to the ordinary self-observation of
practical life. But introspection can only be made a useful psycholog-

ical method if it is employed under special and favourable conditions. (1) Foremost among these is the state of *attention*. We understand here by this term that condition of mental processes in which they possess a peculiar vividness, duration, distinctness, associability, and reproductivity. Its importance in the examination of mental phenomena by the introspective method, then, needs no proof. We must only be careful to insure the direction of the attention upon these phenomena, and not upon their introspection, as otherwise the aim of the method is frustrated, or at least seriously diverted. The intentional self-observation recommended in various psychologies comes perilously near to such a distortion of method. It is really simply a question of 'attentively experiencing' a mental process. We may note the advantage accruing to the method from the fact that the attention can be concentrated exclusively or at least preponderantly upon particular sides and aspects of an experience, and so bring them into higher relief. (2) The other condition of methodically conducted introspection is *impartiality* as regards the facts. Even in natural science the investigator is apt to see what he desires to see; and this tendency is far greater and far more dangerous when the processes observed are subjective. If we approach the examination of consciousness with more or less definite expectations of what we shall find, whether these are theoretical or based upon a preliminary induction, we may depart very widely from actual fact. The only preventive, apart from a checking of introspection by experiment, is an extremely careful self-observation.

4. Introspection or attentive experience only becomes scientifically valuable when a description of its contents has been given. It is, therefore, necessary—we shall discuss the point more in detail when we come to deal with the linguistic method—that a system of intelligible and delicate symbols be built up, to meet this requirement of description as adequately as possible. And here again we obtain most assistance from a right direction and concentration of the attention. We have seen that in the condition of attention the various conscious phenomena are readily associable and easily reproduceable; and it clearly follows that the linguistic symbols, visual or auditory, which constitute a description, will be called up with especial facility and completeness by mental processes attentively experienced. But it is also clear that we are here, too, running a peculiar risk,—the risk of substituting for the facts cut-and-dried linguistic formulae, which as it were offer themselves for reproduction when the facts are presented. The description of an impartial observer must be altogether determined by his experiences. And it is a serious drawback to the introspective

method that it is not a trustworthy guide to this goal. Try as he will, it is hardly possible for the observer to nullify all the subjective tendencies which hinder his total self-surrender to the facts. To which we must add the further objections, that introspection is unable of itself to erect a theory of psychical processes, and that its results are apt to appear fortuitous and disconnected. Nevertheless, the method forms the basis of all the others, and is at the present day in many cases the only one which is directly applicable.

5. (*b*) *The experimental method.*—Experiment can no more take the place of introspection in psychology than it can that of observation in physics. It is only able, as it is only intended, to supplement the previous method, by filling up the gaps which remain when introspection is employed alone, by checking its descriptions, and by making it generally more reliable. The method is qualified for this task by six peculiar advantages. (1) It renders possible a *frequent repetition* of the process which is to be described. Psychical states are so transient and so complicated that a number of observations of the same phenomenon is the prerequisite of any exact analysis. The description becomes with repetition concrete and assured. One of the reasons for the stagnation of the older psychology was its over-hasty generalisation of observations based simply upon introspection, memory, and report. So that experiment helps us to ascertain what the facts of mind really are. (2) Experimental appliances enable us to *vary* particular constituents of the process under examination *separately*. Without this variation of details it is impossible to show the significance of the single factors and phases of a psychical event, and to establish their uniformities. It is our only means, for example, of informing ourselves about the temporal and spatial constituents of a perception, as distinct from its quality or intensity. And it is this property of experiment which the natural sciences have availed themselves of with such brilliant success. Here also, then, experiment goes deeper and extends further than introspection, with its liability to mistake, is able to do. Our knowledge of the facts is considerably enlarged, and the first steps taken toward their theoretical explanation.

6. (3) The ends of theory can be most effectively subserved by the discovery of *relations of dependency* between stimuli and the psychical processes which they evoke, or between subjective phenomena and the bodily movements which they occasion. Stimuli stand in causal connection with nervous excitations, up to and including the central processes, and the bodily movements which we see are the result of central innervations. We thus obtain functional relations between remote links in the chain, which may be expressed in the form of

laws, although they are not always simple and unequivocal. (4) And this leads us to another advantage of the experimental method. If we can prove these relations of dependency between subjective and objective processes, the latter will furnish us with a *measure*,—a permanent and reproduceable expression,—of the psychical. The value of such a measure becomes manifest as soon as ever we institute a comparison with the older psychology: whose statements were either so general that they covered all degrees of individual variation, or made no claim at all to universal validity. If we find to-day, by the experimental method, any divergence in the relations between objective phenomena and the subjective reaction of particular persons, we know where to look for the reason of the irregularity, and can refer the individual differences to their conditions, and thus bring them within the domain of science. In other words, the universal validity of psychological results is guaranteed by the measurability of mental phenomena, and measurability is assured by the experimental method.

7. (5) Experiment, again, supplies us with a means of securing the most favourable *disposition of the experiencing individual.* We have already mentioned attention and impartiality as the conditions of all useful introspection. But introspection itself did not provide us with means for the fulfilment of these conditions, or for the estimation of their better or worse realisation in a given case. On the other hand, it is perfectly easy to arrange an experiment in such a way that the observer remains wholly in the dark with regard to the value or correctness of his reports, and therefore has nothing but his experience to rely upon, while he is beyond the reach of influence by definite expectation of desired results. And it is equally easy to show, by the help of suitable experiments, what alteration in result is produced by such expectation, or in general by any predisposition of the observer. Moreover, a numerical comparison of the separate reports furnishes us with a quantitative determination of errors or influences, whose operation had escaped the observer's notice. So that the advantage of the experimental method here is, that it aids us, as it were, to force that disposition in the observer which is most favourable for our purpose, and acquaints us with all the influences and variations to which it is liable. This is sufficient to prove the injustice of a reproach often made to the experimental method,—the reproach that it posits an abnormal attitude, an unnatural mood, on the part of the observer. For, in the first place, the method gives us our only safe criterion of normal and abnormal; while, secondly, there is not the shadow of a reason for thus roundly terming the circumstances favourable for an

observation 'abnormal'. (6) Lastly, experiment has brought about a *community of psychological work* such as was previously impossible. This advantage has come with the observation of facts under rigidly definite conditions which can be reproduced by any and every investigator. Each psychologist can now enter into the methods and results of his colleagues, confirming or correcting; and so the stream of scientific knowledge flows steadily on. We shall soon give up speaking of 'the psychology' of this or that author as an individual system, and shall talk only of 'psychology' as a science resting on firm foundations, whose superstructure is so planned that the new fits in easily and harmoniously with what is already established.

8. Of the range of the experimental method in psychology we can say nothing more definite than that it is applicable in all cases where psychical processes stand in uniform relation to external bodily processes. Such a relation obtains, of course, not only between sensations and the stimuli which occasion them, but also between feeling and will and the movements of limb or feature, or the changes of circulation and respiration, which they produce; although the latter dependency has not as yet been so elaborately and successfully examined and formulated as has the former. But more than this: we have a number of ingenious devices for the experimental investigation of the connections of mental processes with one another. So that in principle there is no topic of psychological inquiry which cannot be approached by the experimental method. And experimental psychology is, therefore, fully within its rights when it claims to be the general psychology of which we propose to treat (§ 1. 11). If we compare the scanty harvest of facts reaped before the application of experiment in all the fields now open to experimental inquiry with the rich and steadily increasing store of laws and observations garnered since the experimental method has been followed, we cannot but look forward with hopeful anticipations to the time when the advantages of this most potent instrument shall be secured to every department of empirical psychology.

II. Indirect Methods.

9. (*a*) The *memorial method* is one of very frequent application in psychology, owing to the transitoriness of psychical phenomena. By 'memory' we understand here not a group of reproduced ideas or other mental processes, not, that is, the return to life of previous experiences, but a description or awareness of earlier experiences based upon certain present mental states. The conscious processes now present obviously serve as mere symbols of other processes previously

present. For instance, our memory of a considerable period of time does not enable us to reproduce that time with even approximate accuracy: we rather infer the length of the interval from the nature of the conscious processes now involved in our memory of it. In the same way, when we compare the intensity of a loud noise which we have just heard with that of another similar noise heard before, there is no recurrence of the latter in its original strength; we know how loud it was by certain indications afforded by the memory.—We are at present interested in memory, then, not as a psychological process, but as a means to the ascertainment of psychological processes.

10. The utility of the memorial method depends upon the reliability of the symbols from which we have to infer the various kinds of mental occurrences. It is hardly possible to give general rules for its use. *Attention* and *impartiality* are as necessary to a right conclusion here as they were in introspection. Concentration of the attention cements the union between symbol and symbolized at its inception, and keeps it firm and definite afterwards. And if introspection may be invalidated by the influence of extraneous suggestions, the danger is very much greater with memory, where the application of any direct check is usually impossible. Secondly, the *choice of appropriate symbols* is important. To a certain extent this is dependent upon the individual. Attention to it enables us to formulate a true memorial *method*, serviceable for psychological ends. For it is plain that our knowledge of previous experiences may be built up from the most various indications. Now it is the business of the psychologist to discover the significance of all these, and to estimate the value of results obtainable from the employment of any one in particular. The matter is one of especial importance when we are comparing successive conscious processes, since in such cases the experimental method must be combined with the memorial. Thus, we overestimate in memory sounds which are 'terrifically' loud, and underestimate weights which are 'surprisingly' small. Clearly, to ensure uniformity of experimental conditions, these sources of error must be as far as possible eliminated.—But when all is said, the memorial method remains purely subjective, and consequently very defective. It can only be raised to scientific importance by the employment of a system of intelligible and familiar symbols. Language furnishes the system required. So that it is only as related to language that memory becomes an objective psychological method, valid beyond the narrow limits of individual experience.

11. (*b*) *The linguistic method.*—Of all the symbols which have been employed in the service of description, those of language are the most widely diffused and the most highly valued. There are three principal

reasons for this exceptional position of language: (1) its flexibility and wealth of distinctions; (2) its constancy and accuracy; and (3) the ease and rapidity of communication through its channel. The advantages offered by it are naturally only relative: we may equally well regard these three rubrics as covering three distinct problems, which must be solved in the correct use of words.

(1) By the *flexibility* of language we mean its adaptability to the description of the most diverse facts, and its adequacy to the finest distinctions which they present. It is to be noted in this connection that new symbols or new combinations of the old can very readily be added to our current stock of words and phrases. We need hardly spend time upon the discussion of the advantage of this property of language for the psychologist: the fidelity and completeness of his depiction is evidently in very large measure dependent upon it. But just because it is so important we must insist that he makes exceedingly careful use of it. The experimenting psychologist in particular should have this brought home to him,—so that his description of results may be as detailed and comprehensive as possible. We may lay it down as a general rule that the larger his psychological vocabulary, the more extensive his psychological knowledge, the better equipped is he for his task. Individuals who are entirely unversed in the expression of experience in language can be used in but few psychological investigations, and those of minor importance.—The flexibility of language is essentially due to its *dependency upon the will* of the individual. The movements which subserve speaking and writing may be directed and varied at will. Their form and contents will, therefore, be regulated by the needs of the moment, for the most adequate expression of the facts which they are to describe. Nevertheless, there is one difficulty that we cannot hope entirely to overcome even by the most accurate use of our symbols: we cannot do complete justice to the continuity of the inner experience and its changes. Language is discrete. This is one reason why it is necessary, in psychological experiments, to collect a large number of judgments or reports.

12. (2) By the *constancy* of language we mean its independence of time. Of the subjective memorial method we may say in general that its trustworthiness is inversely proportional to the length of time which has elapsed between the occurrence of the original conscious states and that of the present processes which constitute our memory of them. The linguistic method is exempt from this variability; both symbol and meaning of symbol can be stereotyped. And this constancy secures the *accuracy* of language, an exact correspondence between the

symbol and the symbolized. We are all familiar with the advantages accruing to scientific description from the use of definitions. Logical rules ensure the permanence of these,—while dictionaries and encyclopædiæ protect the meanings of particular symbols from oblivion. The guarantee of these methodological advantages is afforded by the *constancy of the written character.* So that the best way of preserving introspective and memorial contents is to reproduce them in the visual figures which everyone uses and understands.

(3) The *easy and rapid communicability* of linguistic symbols is an advantage which we owe to the *practical needs of human intercourse.* Mental processes are quick to disappear and quick to change, and the account must keep pace with the facts. Besides which, our constant practice in the use of linguistic symbols gives us a kind of automatic accuracy in the right putting-together of words, while our attention remains directed with practical exclusiveness upon the experiences. We frequently increase this facility of expression still further, by agreeing to use simple or abbreviated symbols for certain classes of judgment: but it is to the interest of psychology to see that this procedure does not reduce the record of results to a mere schema, as it easily may. For, (i) the withdrawal of the attention from the record may lead to its partial withdrawal from the experience; and ennui is a fertile source of error. And (ii) it is inevitable that the conscious phenomena present be more complex than the processes which we are especially studying,—that they contain more than it is our primary intention to report upon. But we may require of the professional psychologist that he devote a certain interest to these secondary phenomena, and note them in his written record. Simple experiments upon just noticeable stimulus-differences, for instance, give us many valuable hints with regard to the association of ideas, the psychological basis of the judgment of comparison, etc. Looked at from this point of view, the simplest experiments become attractive to the student and fruitful for the science.

All these methods, the direct and the indirect, the subjective and the objective, can be best employed in combination, each serving to supplement and check the others. Their individual importance and uses we shall discuss in greater detail later on. The experimental method has had an especially rapid growth, and is now differentiated into a whole number of separate sub-methods.

13. We are able in certain cases to supplement the knowledge derived from the four psychological methods,—the introspective, memorial, linguistic, and experimental,—by *assistance from without.* Pathological changes in the mental constitution, the facts of mental

development, and the products of the various mental activities, all furnish some aid to the psychological inquirer. It need hardly be emphasized that this assistance is never more than secondary. For the beginnings and foundation of our knowledge of the facts and relations of consciousness we must always have recourse to the four methods, and in particular to a trained and adequately checked introspection. It is but very rarely either necessary or practicable to obtain from any of the three secondary sources information which we could not have acquired in a more direct way.

(1) *Mental pathology* is the most valuable of the extraneous aids. Just as current views of the physiological functions of certain portions of the brain and groups of nerve fibres are based upon pathological cases, in which the abrogation of special functions is correlated with the degeneration of special nervous areas, so our psychological analysis of complicated psychical processes and even more our knowledge of their dependency upon particular bodily organs or processes are materially furthered by the existence of certain diseases. When we move our arm, for example, we can judge fairly accurately, within certain limits, of the direction of the movement and of the altered position of the limb, even if our eyes are closed. What sensations constitute the psychological basis of these judgments? Cutaneous, muscular, tendinous and articular sensations are all involved in the arm-movement; and there is nothing in the nature of things to give any one set a preference over the others. Pathological cases have answered the question for us, by showing that abrogation of the cutaneous sensations is not followed by any considerable impairment of the judgments of position and direction. And pathological phenomena of this kind are useful to the psychologist wherever he is precluded from effecting a normal variation of the separate constituents of a psychical complex, and wherever he is investigating the dependency of conscious processes upon the more centrally situated nervous excitations. The various derangements of speech have given us invaluable assistance in the determination of dependency-relations; and a case of deaf-mute-blindness, like that of Laura Bridgman, may be termed an experiment from the hand of nature herself. The great importance of such pathological observations is plainly due to the fact that they enable us to distinguish operative factors from inoperative, or to compare mental defects with the anatomical abnormalities revealed by autopsy.

14. But it is useless to examine pathological states whose conditions and symptoms are not so clear and unmistakable, in the hope of reaching any definite result. The best illustration is, perhaps, afforded

by recent experiments in *hypnotism*. Hypnotism has been strongly recommended of late to the notice of psychologists. But apart from the danger to the subject which comes with repeated hypnotisation, however careful the method of induction, very many of the experimental results are rendered precarious by the scantiness of our knowledge of the state of consciousness in hypnosis. It would be foolish to deny that a good deal of interesting information has been gained by the help of intra-hypnotic and post-hypnotic suggestion; but it is almost entirely information with regard to curious powers and performances, such as would normally be found in but a few individual cases.—In the same way, we shall rarely have occasion to refer to other artificially induced alterations of the normal consciousness, the mental result of indulgence in narcotics, etc. It may be confidently asserted of these and similar conditions, that they are rather themselves problems demanding explanation, than the source of any increased knowledge of general psychology. The same holds of what are called 'mental diseases'. It seems more likely, as things are, that general psychology may be able to throw some light upon their rise, development, and causes, than that their study will afford any material aid to the student of psychology. The insane are usually incapable of introspection in the scientific sense.

15. (2) Assistance may be gained, further, from the study of *psychogenesis*. We understand in the first instance by this term the science which deals with the development of psychical phenomena in the human individual. It can undoubtedly teach us something of the origin of particular mental processes; we need mention only the origin of language, the development of memory, the formation of ascociations. But here, again, we are met by the difficulty that there is no guarantee of trustworthy and properly directed introspection. This makes inquiry into the psychology of childhood as uncertain as is the psychological study of animals. And it will hardly be maintained that important contributions to any question of general psychology have resulted from such inquiry. Nevertheless, it forms an indispensable supplement to our knowledge of the developed consciousness.

(3) Psychology gains least of all from the consideration of *mental productions*. Art, law, and language must primarily be regarded as subjects amenable to psychological interpretation and treatment, and only secondarily as matter for the illustration of certain mental connections or relations. We may perhaps find in the arrangement of linguistic forms and phrases rules which hold for the association of ideas in thinking. Or the artistic employment of the special senses and the reproductive mechanism may help us to express the uniform-

ities of relation which obtain for the association of sensations with one another and with feelings. But no one of these mental products is either wholly dependent upon psychological factors, or unequivocally referable to a particular psychical interconnection. And we must, accordingly, be circumspect both in accepting and applying information derived from them.

In this enumeration of external aids, we have made no mention of physics or physiology. The assistance which these sciences render to psychology is rather indirect than direct,—assistance in the obtaining of psychological material. (4) We must have *physical* knowledge and apparatus if we are to institute psychological experiments, and any advance in our understanding of the physical or chemical conditions of sense perceptions is of value for their psychological investigation; but the results of physics are not contributions to psychology. (5) It is a little different with *physiology*. The physiology of the sense-organs generally treats of sensations and perceptions, and the physiology of the central organs, of mental functions. And so we often find physiologists regarding psychology as merely a department of physiology. This view is based upon an epistemological error. Physiology does not deal with experiences in their dependency upon the individuals who experience them, but with vital phenomena which manifest themselves to our perception and which are dependent upon one another and upon their environment. But the psychical processes which accompany certain of these are valuable to the physiologist as indications of the presence of bodily functions. They are, therefore, not the strict object of his inquiry, but directions with regard to that object. There accordingly exists a very close relation between psychology and a certain portion of physiology; and similar tendencies and observations are apparently to be found in both. But a closer examination leaves no room for doubt that the ultimate aim and end of the two sciences are altogether different. Nevertheless, in the interest of psychological progress, it is desirable that, while the fundamental separateness of their spheres is recognised, there may still be in the future as much physiological research that can be turned to psychological account, as there has been in the past. The small number of psychological laboratories renders this neighbourly assistance doubly welcome.

§ 3. Classification and Literature of Psychology.

1. It has been customary ever since the days of Aristotle to classify the subject matter of psychology by grouping various psychical processes together, as those, *e.g.*, of knowing, feeling, and willing. Now the particular processes belonging to these different groups are introspectively all upon the same plane. It follows, therefore, that the principle of classification was not derived from psychological investigation in the strict sense, but was borrowed from certain familiar results of mental activity or modes of expression of mental attitude: the knowledge which the mind has acquired by the aid of sense and

understanding, the action which it executes under the stimulus of desire or resolve, etc. The classification itself is deficient for two reasons: the point of view is not consistent throughout, and the same psychical contents may subserve or belong to one mental product as well as another. If we wish to avoid these mistakes, we must (1) first of all subject the whole of conscious content to an exact analysis, and determine the ultimate elements of which it is composed. (2) We must then find a means of arranging these psychologically equivalent elements in a series,—and this we can only do, with the view which we hold of psychology, by discriminating between the relations in which they stand to bodily processes. (3) That accomplished, we shall be able to classify the complex processes, by distinguishing the modes of interconnection of the elements in consciousness. (4) And, lastly, we may make the state of consciousness itself—as presenting differences of a general character, cognisable by introspection, independently of the contents of the experience of the moment—the object of a special inquiry. It will be noticed that these four rubrics have a strictly psychological significance; *i.e.,* that they are directions either for the analysis of the subjective, or for its reference to the physical individual.

2. The *simplicity* which constitutes a psychical state an ultimate element of consciousness is not, as in physics, a spatial indivisibility, but merely a simplicity of quality or contents. The simplest mental processes, therefore, are·not comparable to physical atoms. The only analogous elements in natural science are those of chemistry. Just as it makes no difference to the nature of a chemical element whether its molecules are a hundred or a thousand, so it is indifferent to a conscious quality how great an extension—to take the first illustration that comes—we predicate of it. And just as the chemical element is a certain substance that resists further analysis, so are the simple contents of psychology experiences in which no parts are further distinguishable. Our instrument of psychological analysis is introspection, alone or assisted by experiment. If a given content which we call 'gray' shows no noticeable differences of shade, if its tone is entirely uniform, we term it a simple conscious content. It follows that a *compound* psychical state can only be distinguished from a simple process by our ability to perceive in it a number of separate simple states. A chord, for instance, a compound clang containing a number of simple tones, is a compound conscious state. Following Wundt's example, we shall make this difference the main principle of our psychological classification. Psychology will then fall into two main parts: the first treating of the *conscious elements*, and the second

of the *connection of the elements*. The number of chemical elements is very small, and efforts are naturally made to reduce it as far as possible,—if it may be, to one. The number of qualitatively distinguishable conscious states, on the other hand, is very large, and there is no reason for supposing that it can be diminished. The keener our psychological analysis, the more elements it finds to observe. Finally, certain peculiarities of state or attitude may be predicated of consciousness as a whole. These may be observed alike in simple and complex contents, and may, therefore, properly be made the object of a special investigation. A third part of psychology will accordingly be concerned with the *state of consciousness*. The principal subject of discussion in this part will be the state familiar to us as attention.

3. Any further classification of the simple conscious processes themselves must be based, as we have said, upon characteristic differences among the relations of dependency in which they stand to bodily processes. Applying this principle, we can distinguish two kinds of elementary psychical contents. (1) The first class is characterised by the dependency of the qualities which compose it upon the excitation of quite definite peripheral (and probably central) nervous organs. These elementary conscious contents we name *sensations*. The term 'sensation', therefore, does not denote a general mental capacity of reaction upon external impressions,—does not point to something above and beyond the separate experienced qualities, distinguishable from them as a particular conscious attitude, or what not,—but is simply the abstract generic name for a number of concrete elements which have the specific character just mentioned. The simple content of a given 'gray', that is, would be a sensation, since we know that its appearance depends upon an excitation of the retina and of various central organs lying between the eye and the visual centre in the cerebral cortex. (2) The second class is characterised by the absence of any determinable dependency of the qualities composing it upon particular external bodily organs:—of their relation to central organs we can at present say nothing definitely. These qualities we term *feelings*. For instance, the pleasure which we take in a pure tone, not too loudly struck, or the pleasure which we derive from a saturated colour, is a feeling; its particular quality being determined neither by the sense-organ nor by the specific excitations underlying the colour or the tone.

4. On the other hand, any further classification within the second part of psychology must be based, for the present at least, upon the results obtained by introspection. We should suppose a priori that the mode of interconnection of simple contents would not always be

the same. And we can, as a matter of fact, distinguish two principal modes: *fusion* and *colligation*. The former is a more close and intimate connection than the latter. Fusion occurs when the connecting qualities are thrust more or less into the background by the total impression which results from their connection,—when, that is, all or sundry of them lose in distinctness by combination. The total impression itself may be, as it were, the resultant of a balance of qualities, or may be dominated by one or more preponderant elements. A simultaneous connection of tones may stand as a typical example of fusion. Colligation occurs, on the other hand, when the cognisability of the separate qualities is either unaffected by combination, so that they retain their original independence, or is actually increased. The formation of a single qualitative impression is in this case more or less obstructed by the persistent individuality of the elementary constituents. Simultaneous colour contrast (the spatial combination of different colour sensations) may serve as a typical instance of colligation.

5. It is not necessary at this stage to go further into details of classification. But there is one other point to which attention must be called if we are to avoid misunderstanding of the character of the conscious elements. Just as in nature the various elements never occur alone, absolutely out of connection, but always in physical or chemical combinations with other elements, so the elementary phenomena of mind are never found except in fusion or colligation with their like. And just as natural science obtains its simple substances by analysis, so must we employ the analysis of introspection to make out our elementary qualities. By help of the attention we may, it is true, subject even the less intensive elements to special investigation or observation; but real isolation,—the actual experience of one single sensation, for instance,—can never take place. We may think that we have only heard a tone or seen a colour, but a closer inquiry shows that these were merely parts of a combination upon which the attention was concentrated with peculiar force. 'Sensation' and 'feeling' are not, therefore, different experiences, in the strict sense, but the results of a qualitative analysis of experience, of which we avail ourselves for scientific purposes. We cannot ascertain the uniformities of complex processes, without this preliminary analysis; and our first task is, accordingly, to examine separately every aspect or attribute which is at all obvious in the concrete mental state.

The tripartite division of mental faculties into those of knowledge, feeling, and desire, which obtained currency in the eighteenth century, is based upon the distinction (1) between objective states, referable to external objects, and subjective

states, expressive of the reaction of the ego, and (2), within this last, between a more passive and a more active reaction. These principles of classification were crossed by a division into higher and lower faculties. Such differences of standpoint were inevitable at a time when the exact conditions of the dependency of mental upon bodily processes were still unknown, and unassisted introspection was unable to establish universally valid results by its analysis of the more complex conscious processes. In particular, it had not been discovered that besides the 'five senses' we possess a number of sensitive bodily organs, which contribute nothing to our knowledge of the external world, and whose sensations cannot, therefore, be opposed to the feelings as objective to subjective. The distinction of higher and lower faculties is obviously altogether unpsychological : psychology cares nothing as to whether the ethical and æsthetic judgments ascribe a higher value to this conscious process or to that. Its introduction as a principle of classification is, however, very intimately connected with the depreciation of the sensuous which characterised an age and a philosophy of rationalism.—The tendency to divide up mental states into subjective and objective has persisted to our own day. It is the principal reason for the customary grouping of the sensations mediated by the internal organs of the body under the general name of 'common feeling'. The physiology of the senses still makes use of this objectionable phrase. And we often hear, too, of the 'sense of feeling', a current expression for 'touch' in ordinary conversation. Now inconveniences of terminology might be put up with in themselves; but unhappily they are apt to lead the investigator astray in method, if they do not land him in error upon matters of fact. While, again, if the only classification admitted be that of subjective and objective, psychology is altogether unable to cope with reproduced sensations and ideas, the 'images' of memory and fancy.—The principle of classification which we have followed was introduced into psychology, as is stated in the text, by Wundt; we have only carried it a little farther than he has done, in the hope that it will thus yield still better results. It is indicative of the confusion which obtains in psychology even at the present day, that this principle has not yet succeeded in gaining general recognition. Thus W. James, in his recently published *Principles of Psychology* (1890),—a work of large conception and much originality,—has argued from the fact that our mental life flows on in a more or less continuous stream of complex processes to the necessity of beginning with these, and not with simple conscious states which are the products of an artificial analysis. But by parity of reasoning the chemist and physicist and astronomer would be obliged to begin the exposition of their sciences with a depiction of concrete phenomena, instead of with mechanics or stoichiometry.

6. It is peculiarly difficult to give a survey of the most important psychological *literature*. The science has for centuries been dominated by philosophy, and has reflected all the many changes which metaphysics has undergone with the lapse of time. Even to-day psychologists are not at one concerning the problems which they have to solve. It is true that the union between philosophy and psychology has of late tended to become, more or less consciously, a union based rather

upon the interest of particular men than upon inherent relationship. But the development of that division of labour which is the one thing necessary for the successful progress of psychology, proceeds very slowly. We may be agreed upon particular experimental investigations, but there is small indication of a more general agreement as to principles. It is, consequently, hardly possible to cite from the literature, without giving some characterisation, however brief, of the standpoint of the various works. And it is necessary for the understanding of differences, as well as only just to the merits of the older psychologists, that any such characterisation should be prefaced by a historical retrospect, showing the origin of views and tendencies. We can distinguish two main directions in modern psychology; the first of which, though much the older, did not cease to exist when the second made its appearance. We may call it the *descriptive and metaphysical* direction, while the newer movement is *experimental and psychophysical.* The former makes exclusive use of the introspective, memorial, and linguistic methods; its descriptions are either purely individual or very abstract. The latter insists upon the application of the experimental method wherever it is possible, and aims at the establishment of general laws. Similarly, the theory of mental phenomena erected by the earlier school relies upon the assistance of metaphysics; while the later one regards knowledge of the relations of dependency obtaining between the conscious and bodily (especially cerebral) processes as the only practicable road towards a real explanation of the facts of mind.

7. German psychology before Herbart belongs entirely to the descriptive and metaphysical stage. Its principal exponent is Christian Wolff. To him is due the distinction between rational and empirical psychology,—the former principally concerned with the metaphysical foundation, the latter with the description of the facts of psychology. He also introduced the concept of mental faculty, not only as a principle of classification of psychical processes, but as a ground of explanation. His successors devoted most of their attention to empirical psychology; and there arose in the second half of the eighteenth century a whole series of treatises upon "Erfahrungsseelenlehre", which looked upon the description of interesting details as the principal aim of psychology. It may be said of all these works that they did not establish a single psychological uniformity of the concrete, *i.e.*, scientific kind. They are chiefly filled with accounts of special cases, general depictions, and hypothetical explanations. Nor did England and France do any better. Their psychologists busied themselves, for the most part, with psychological epistemology or the psychology of knowledge: psychology itself, that is, was only interesting for the

information it could give of the process of knowledge, the formation of concepts, of our ideas of external objects, etc. That is why the association of ideas is the one phenomenon of importance which attracted the notice of English philosophers at the time. Psychology as an independent discipline had a comparatively late birth in England.

8. Psychology being in this condition, we can understand how it was that Kant denied to it (as he did to chemistry for similar reasons) the rank of a science, and even attempted to demonstrate the impossibility of its ever becoming one. You cannot apply mathematics to conscious processes, he said, and the only scientific part of a study is its mathematics; nor can you make experiments upon other peoples' minds. The removal of the former objection is one of the services rendered by Herbart to psychology. Herbart pointed out that psychical phenomena vary not only in time but in intensity, and that in virtue of these two 'dimensions' they are amenable to mathematical treatment. His second great service is his annihilating criticism of the view that the specification of mental faculties and the reference of particular facts of consciousness to them were in any sense steps toward explanation. Nevertheless, the Herbartian psychology (Hartenstein's edition of the *Sämmtliche Werke*, vols. v. and vi.) belongs to the first of our two schools. It is based entirely upon a metaphysical foundation. Ideas are the only real states of the simple mind, which by their means maintains its integrity as against other simple existences. When they appear in consciousness, they do so in the guise of forces, reinforcing or inhibiting one another. The results of this interplay are changes in the intensity of mental contents. For these, Herbart has sketched the outlines of a statics and mechanics of mind, in which the ideas (certain hypotheses being granted) function as mathematical quantities. But the laws to which this most ingenious construction leads are purely theoretical, hardly admitting of application to any case actually realised in experience; and the whole attempt was naturally tentative and crude. It was left to one of Herbart's numerous disciples to bring the plan somewhat nearer completion (Drobisch: *Erste Grundlehren der mathematischen Psychologie*, 1850). He himself was but little concerned with the accurate analysis of subjectified experience, and his whole psychology stands and falls with his metaphysics. A far larger proportion of space is allotted to the discussion of empirical facts in certain of the most noteworthy works of the Herbartian school, some of which have also laid stress upon the importance of the relation of mental to bodily, especially nervous processes. These are:

M. W. Drobisch, *Empirische Psychologie*, 1842.

Th. Waitz, *Lehrbuch der Psychologie als Wissenschaft*, 1849.

W. Volkmann, *Lehrbuch der Psychologie*, third ed., 1884-5 ; fourth ed. in preparation. H. Steinthal, *Einleitung in die Psychologie und Sprachwissenschaft*, vol. I., second ed., 1881.

Volkmann's is the fullest of the four. It embodies many of the results of experimental and physiological psychology, contains elaborate historical excursus, and gives numerous references to the literature.— A very acute and suggestive book, written from a standpoint similar to that of Herbart, but expressly disclaiming any metaphysical parentage, is Th. Lipps' *Grundtatsachen des Seelenlebens*, 1883. The author has rigidly excluded physiology and psychophysics from his pages, though not upon ultimate theoretical grounds, and in place of them has made free use of the unconscious as a psychical value, without, however, attributing a metaphysical significance to it. He accepts the experimental method, and utilises the results of experimental inquiry.

9. Another reformer of psychology, besides Herbart, was Beneke (*Psychologische Skizzen*, 1825-7; *Lehrbuch der Psychologie als Naturwissenschaft*, fourth ed., 1877). Beneke aimed at giving an empirical account of the elements of mind, but found these not in qualitatively simple conscious processes but in certain formal capacities, which he called 'primal faculties'. The unconscious looms as large in his pages as in Herbart's, and his discussions are for the most part equally theoretical, without showing an equal regard to exactness and logical coherence. His work was, therefore, rather stimulating than fundamental.—The English psychology of this century is generally known as the 'association psychology', from its predominant interest in the processes grouped under the rubric of 'association of ideas'. It contains, however, little more than descriptions of complex states. In its most recent form, it is strongly influenced by the doctrine of evolution, the analogy of physical and biological differentation being carried directly over to the domain of mental phenomena. The principal English psychologists and their writings are as follows :

James Mill, *Analysis of the Phenomena of the Human Mind*, second ed., 1868.
A. Bain, *The Senses and the Intellect*, 1855 and later.
„ *The Emotions and the Will*, 1859 and later.
H. Spencer, *The Principles of Psychology*, 1855 and later.

An entirely different line has been taken by F. Brentano: *Psychologie vom empirischen Standpunkt*, vol. i., 1874. This author holds that the contents of sense-perception are physical phenomena, while ideation, judgment, and love and hate constitute the psychical processes. Such a psychology—though we must remember that no more than an introduction has as yet been published—cannot be either psychophysical or experimental; indeed, Brentano himself terms it descriptive. And we can see that ideation is certainly not a special psychical activity, experienced along with ideated contents, but a concept, which may cover processes of very different kinds. Moreover, the simplicity of the other two classes is more than doubtful.

10. The experimental and psychophysical movement in psychology began in Germany about the middle of the present century. Herbart had ascribed to the body a threefold influence upon psychical states: it exerted 'pressure' upon them, it developed a 'resonance' concomitantly with the occurrence of certain mental excitations, and it co-operated with the mind in action. But the thorough exploiting of the psychophysical principle began with H. Lotze and his brilliant work, the *Medizinische Psychologie* (1852). It is true that Lotze, following previous German usage, began his psychology with metaphysical prolegomena, and that he is still very far from the thought of a universal psychophysical parallelism. But, nevertheless, he speaks without any circumlocution of the nervous conditions of psychical processes, and is happy in hypothesis, where knowledge of the facts is not available. We need only mention his famous theory of local signs, which still possesses much more than a historical interest. Although the empirical portions of the work are for the most part antiquated, it may be strongly recommended to the student of to-day for its clearness, strictness of method, and suggestive manner. He should read with it the brief *Outlines of Psychology* (1881; dictated portions of lectures of a later period), which has seen several editions.— The deciding impulse to the experimental movement was given by E. H. Weber, chiefly by his valuable article, *Tastsinn und Gemeingefühl* (Wagner's *Handwörterbuch der Physiologie*, vol. iii., pt. 2; also published separately, 1851). This paper contains the first systematic experiments made in the psychology of the senses, and deduces from them a uniformity of general validity. The experiments themselves were carried out and partly published twenty years earlier.

11. But the actual foundations of an experimental psychology were laid by G. Th. Fechner, whose *Elemente der Psychophysik* (1860; second ed., 1889) was an attempt to carry through in detail the idea of a functional relation between physical and psychical processes. Though the particular mathematical form in which Fechner couched this relation is not now regarded as universally valid or even as possible of application to a complex of so many variables, we can hardly overestimate his services to scientific psychology. The concepts which

he introduced, the methods which he worked out in theory and applied in practice, his penetrating discussion of the empirical material already gathered, and his vast enrichment of it by personal observation and experiment, combined to give an extraordinary impetus to psychological study. Of his later works we may mention the *Revision der Hauptpunkte der Psychophysik* (1882), which supplements the *Elemente*, especially upon its methodological side.—Finally, the union of the experimental and psychophysical directions was effected by Wilhelm Wundt, less in his first important work, the *Vorlesungen über Menschen- und Thierseele* (1863; second ed., considerably altered, 1892; Eng. trs., 1894) than in the classical *Grundzüge der physiologischen Psychologie* (1874; fourth ed., 1893). Wundt's combination of the two movements, and his comprehensive discussion of all psychical facts,—which it lay beyond Fechner's power to give,—have resulted in what is ordinarily termed 'modern psychology'. His great work has thus become the text-book of the science, without having lost that individual character which such a book must present so long as we are referred to hypothesis upon so many matters of detail, and views of the classification and presentation of psychological subject-matter remain so divergent. Wundt further gave the most effective impulse to the systematic study of experimental psychology by his foundation of the Leipsic laboratory in 1879, and of the *Philosophische Studien* (an organ principally intended for the publication of researches made there) in 1883.

12. In conclusion we may enumerate certain quite recent works, whose general character places them within the domain of this modern psychology of which Wundt is the founder, however widely or radically the details of system and theory in any one may differ from those to be found in the *Physiologische Psychologie* or in the other books upon the list:

H. Höffding, *Psychologie in Umrissen*, 1887, second ed., 1893, in German. Eng. trs., 1891.

G. T. Ladd, *Elements of Physiological Psychology*, 1887.

  „   *Psychology, Descriptive and Explanatory*, 1894.

G. Sergi, *La psychologie physiologique*, 1888, from the Italian.

W. James, *The Principles of Psychology*, 1890.

Th. Ziehen, *Leitfaden der physiologischen Psychologie*, 1891, second ed., 1893. Eng. tr., 1892, second ed., 1895.

J. M. Baldwin, *Handbook of Psychology*, 1891.

J. Sully, *The Human Mind*, 1892.

The following periodicals are especially devoted to the interests of this psychological movement:

Philosophische Studien, edited by W. Wundt, 1883 ff.

The American Journal of Psychology, edited by G. Stanley Hall, 1887 ff

Zeitschrift für Psychologie und Physiologie der Sinnesorgane, edited by H. Ebbinghaus and A. König, 1890 ff.

The Psychological Review, edited by J. M. Baldwin and J. Mck. Cattell, 1894 f.

In the three last will be found a critical digest of current literature.

Special works, dealing with particular departments of psychology, will be named in their appropriate connection at the end of each chapter. We mention only the most important, or those which give full references to the literature of their subject.

PART I. THE ELEMENTS OF CONSCIOUSNESS.

Section 1. Sensations.

CHAPTER I. THE ANALYSIS OF SENSATION.

§ 4. The Attributes of Sensation. Sensitivity and Sensible Discrimination. The Classification of Sensations.

1. A sensation is a simple conscious process standing in a relation of dependency to particular nervous organs, peripheral and central (§ 3. 3). But despite its qualitative simplicity, a sensation may be compared with other sensations in respect of certain *attributes* which attach to it. A given pressure sensation, for instance, may be more vivid, more lasting, and more extended, than another, though it is of the same kind or quality. These attributes are characterised (1) by their inseparability from the sensation. Every sensation of pressure possesses, over and above its specific content, a certain strength and a certain temporal and spatial character. We need not necessarily pay particular attention to all the attributes in all cases; but they are never absent and can be noted and determined as circumstances require. (2) Further, the nullification of any of the attributes involves the disappearance or cessation of the entire sensation. A pressure sensation which is unextended, whose duration or intensity is zero, or from which the quality is abstracted, simply ceases to be a pressure sensation. Sensation, that is, is not something to which attributes are added; it does not imply a substrate or substantial nucleus, upon or around which they are grouped. It follows, accordingly, that a complete description of the attributes of sensation is equivalent to a complete description of sensation.

2. Applying this criterion to sensation, we have to predicate of it four attributes: quality, intensity, duration, and extension. *Quality* is, the property which characterises the simple conscious process as such,

and in this sense may be regarded as the most fundamental of all. It distinguishes 'blue' from 'red', 'sweet' from 'bitter', 'warm' from 'cold'. The other attributes all refer to it; intensity is the intensity of a certain quality, and so on. *Intensity* itself is the property of sensation which enables us to compare it with others in respect of vividness; and *duration* and *extension* designate respectively its elementary temporal and spatial character. Thus a taste may be 'very sweet' or only 'sweet'; a sensation of warmth may be of greater or less duration; a 'blue' may be a blue of greater or less extension. In general, it may be said that all four attributes admit of isolated variation, so that we can formulate their laws independently. Quality, however, is peculiar in this respect. For alteration in quality means transition to new sensations; while if quality is left intact, and the other attributes are altered, the sensation appears to remain the same. This is another proof that quality is of the very essence of sensation. It represents the solid foundation, so to speak, which underlies the variability of the other properties. When we come to ask how many sensations a sense-organ mediates, therefore, we shall simply inquire as to the number of qualitatively different sensations.

3. Not every sensation possesses all four attributes. Quality, of course, attaches to all alike; and duration, too, may be predicated of all. But extension belongs only to the visual and cutaneous sensations. If we speak of the 'extension' of tones, scents, or tastes, we are either using the term allegorically, to express the magnitude of the effect which they have upon us, or employing it in a secondary sense, to indicate the spatial character of the objective conditions of the sensations, or that of other sensations or ideas, visual or cutaneous, which we associate with them. And intensity cannot be ascribed to sensations of sight, since any alteration or modification, whether of the intensity of the physical stimulus or of any other of the elements in the determination of sensible intensity, brings with it an alteration in quality, *i.e.*, a transition to new sensations. The proof of this must come later (§§ 17 ff.); here we can do no more than note the fact. There is naturally no reason a priori why all the three attributes should attach to every sensation, over and above its essential and characteristic quality. We must appeal to experience, to discover whether variations in intensity, duration, and extension, occur in a particular case. As a matter of fact, cutaneous sensations form the only class which allows of isolated variation in all three directions.

4. Our analysis of sensations must extend to all the attributes which are capable of separate consideration. We must determine their quality, compare their degrees of intensity, investigate their temporal and

spatial characteristics. The instrument of this analysis was denominated by Fechner *sensible discrimination.* We speak, therefore, of a *qualitative, intensive, extensive,* or *temporal* sensible discrimination, according to the attribute which we are subjecting to analysis. It is impossible to arrive at an absolute determination of the various sensation attributes: recourse must always be had to their comparison with others. That is to say, our determinations of sensation can never be more than relative: and this is why sensible discrimination, the capacity of the intercomparison of sensations, is our sole instrument in the work of analysis. If we could obtain an exact account, in physical and chemical terms, of the nervous processes upon which we suppose sensations to be directly dependent, our results could be made absolute, *i.e.,* we could describe sensations independently of their relations to other sensations. As it is, we find some compensation for our ignorance in this respect, in the relation of sensations, under their various attributes, to the corresponding properties of stimuli. Such a relation presupposes, however, that the nervous excitations running parallel to sensation stand in a wholly unequivocal causal connection with the external stimuli; and the facts give only an approximate verification of this hypothesis. The modification of particular excitations consequent upon the state of the nervous tissue,—'nervous excitability', as it is called,—and upon the influence of other simultaneous excitations, is an important factor in the determination of any definite parallel process. The same stimulus may produce different central excitations, different stimuli the same central effect. So that, evidently, an objective measurement of psychical processes such as would allow of their absolute formulation in definite terms is, at present, out of the question, and could seldom be directly made in any case. We must, therefore, have recourse in the first instance to introspection, in our attempt to define our sensations. And we know that the results of introspection must necessarily be relative, because the psychologist cannot refer his conscious processes to a standard of comparison, like the metre-rod of the scientist. If we are trying to determine the different noticeable shades of a colour, we must compare them with one another or with remembered colours; if we wish to fix the intensity of a tone-sensation, our only standard of reference is other tone-sensations; if we attempt to describe the temporal or spatial character of a pressure sensation, we must have other pressure sensations with which it may be compared and contrasted.

5. The phrase 'sensible discrimination' must not be taken to denote a faculty of comparison, in the sense of a peculiar conscious process existing alongside of the various contents. It merely expresses, in the

first instance, the general fact that we have different experiences and experience them differently; in other words, it covers the introspection of different contents and the report of their difference. All the conditions which affect introspection in general will, therefore, affect sensible discrimination. But we also use the phrase to indicate our experience of like contents, and our report of their likeness. Our judgment of two colour sensations as like, *i.e.,* our ascription to them of the same quality, is just as much a function of our sensible discrimination as is our judgment that they are different because they occupy different places.—Sensible discrimination, then, has so far given us very general results: when we judge that two conscious processes are 'like' or 'different', we bring them, as it were, under the most comprehensive laws of thought stated by formal logic, the laws of identity and contradiction. But the mere determination of difference, without any exact specification of its nature and magnitude, would not take us very far. We therefore employ the experimental method to bring us to close quarters with the former question, and a number of special appliances (of which more later) to assist us to an answer to the latter.

6. Our definition of sensible discrimination comprised two processes: the experiencing of contents, alike or different, and the report of their likeness or difference. The first of these is plainly the prerequisite of the second. But it is a question whether we may assume that the report in language (we may abstract here from other means of description) is in every case a simple replica of the process experienced; whether, that is, the two forms of sensible discrimination, the *direct* and the *indirect*, may be taken as always equivalent. It is a question whether we may assume that the *judgment* 'equal' may be invariably trusted to reflect equality of sensations, and *judgments* 'greater' and 'less' corresponding relations between sensations. An analogy will make this clearer. Helmholtz has laid it down that sensations are symbols from which the student of nature infers the objective existence of natural processes, and not copies of these processes. He cannot assert, therefore, that like sensations are always the symbols of like objective facts, or that a particular difference in sensations necessarily signifies a corresponding difference of physical or chemical processes. Now the linguistic symbols which the psychologist employs might stand in a precisely similar relation to the facts of experience,—might, that is to say, be equally untrustworthy as means for their expression. If this is really the case, the further question arises, whether the psychologist can hope for as large a measure of success in his attempt to correct the errors of judgment as has fallen

to the lot of the scientist in so many phases of his struggle with the disparity of appearance and reality in nature.

7. Now there can be no doubt that deceptions of judgment occur, *i.e.*, that the contents of our knowledge of a given fact is not always adequate to the nature of the fact itself. Not only do we 'overlook' things in ordinary life, but we are not seldom the victims of illusion, due to the incongruity between the direct and indirect sensible discrimination. Besides which, the discrete symbols of language are often unable to cope with the continuity of mental occurrence (cf. §. 2. 11). And it happens to all of us quite frequently to halt for words which shall do full justice to an experience, and to end our description while we ourselves realise its insufficiency. These difficulties we can overcome very effectually by help of the experimental method, which is precisely adapted to meet such cases (cf. § 2. 5, 6, 7). But they do not exhaust the list of possible incongruities between experience and description of experience. For the relation of the latter to its original may be subsumed to a general psychological concept, usually spoken of as 'association' or 'reproduction': the linguistic symbols are 'reproduced' by the sensations, whether they appear in consciousness as visual ideas or auditory ideas or ideas of movement (*i.e.*, of the movements involved in speaking or writing). But the various relations set up in this way cannot, obviously, all be exactly alike. Some expressions will be readily reproduced, others with difficulty; we have in the literature a whole series of investigations in which these differences are clearly manifest. Moreover, it is exceedingly questionable whether any and every alteration in a sensation attribute can call up a corresponding judgment, or whether a certain amount of difference must not be present before the reproduction of the phrase appropriate to it is possible. These are difficulties, it is plain, which cannot be so easily overcome. Our only appeal is again to the experimental method, and up to a certain point the method responds to the appeal. We can obviate irregularity of reproduction by special practice, and we can tell when a defect in our record is due to such irregularity. But not even experiment can render the indirect sensible discrimination fully adequate to the direct. It would be well if this fact received, as it certainly deserves, more attention than it has hitherto attracted.

8. It is oftentimes necessary, if an investigation into sensible discrimination is to lead to the discovery of laws and uniformities of general validity, that it should be accompanied by an examination of *sensitivity*, that is, the bare capacity of experiencing and communicating sensations. We may subdivide sensitivity, according as it has reference to a whole sense department or to individual sensations. In the first

case it is known as *modal sensitivity*, and is measured by the number of sensations given with or possible to a particular sense. In the second, it may be termed *sensibility* (the word is current in this meaning in pathology), and is measured in terms of the attributes predicable of the separate sensations. We can, therefore, speak of a *qualitative, intensive, extensive,* and *temporal* sensibility, as well as sensible discrimination. To give an example: the modal sensitivity of the skin is determined when we have enumerated all the simple qualities or different sensations which can arise from cutaneous stimulation. When a sense embraces a large number of different qualities (sight and hearing, *e.g.*), it becomes necessary to preface this enumeration by a statement of the limits of stimulability. We have an 'upper' and 'lower limit' of sensations of colour and tone; *i.e.*, limits, beyond which in either direction stimulation is ineffective. The relation of sensation to stimulus is also turned to account in the determination of sensibility, and generally for the ascertainment of limiting values. Thus it would be a test of qualitative sensibility to inquire how many air vibrations are required for the perception of the pitch of tone to which their period corresponds. In the same way, we seek to discover the least intensity, duration, or extensity of a stimulus which can evoke a sensation. These just sensible minima of stimulation are called *limina* [1].

9. Our definition leads us to distinguish, further, a *direct* and an *indirect* sensitivity. What has been said above of the corresponding forms of the sensible discrimination holds equally of the two kinds of sensitivity. We find, as we should expect, an incongruity between them. It is to be remarked that we have as yet said nothing of what might seem to be properly termed 'indirect' sensitivity and sensible discrimination:—a judgment of sensations or differences between sensations formed not from the experiences themselves, but by the application of extraneous criteria, furnished, it may be, by other sensations, or by previous knowledge of the facts and their relations. The incongruity between this and the direct processes needs no demonstration. An illustration of it is afforded by our judgment of the distance of an object from the eye as inferred from the distinctness of its outline, which is empirically mediated, and not derived from any 'sensation of distance'; or by that of the direction from which a sound comes to the ear, which is not referable to any peculiar spatial characteristic of auditory sensation. There is great danger of confusing these judgments with those of the direct and indirect sensitivity and sensible discrimination in the strict meaning of the terms, and it can only be avoided

[1] Latin *limen*, a threshold.

by especial care and caution in analysis, whether observational or experimental.

10. Sensations stand in definite relations of dependency to certain peripheral and central organs of the nervous system. Their first arousal appears to be correlated, without exception, with the stimulation of the peripheral organs. Afterwards, however, they may enter consciousness by the central path. We may base our *classification of sensations,* then, upon this difference in their bodily conditions, and divide them into *peripherally excited* and *centrally excited.* The former obviously involve a central excitation as well, but the latter need no peripheral excitation to cause the central. The two classes must be treated separately, as they normally present characteristic differences. Within each class we shall examine the various sensation atributes in order. It will, however, be convenient to defer the consideration of extension to a latter period, since (1) only two senses possess the attribute (§ 4. 3), and (2) it is best to deal with all our spatial contents and judgments in connection. And for this latter reason we shall also postpone our discussion of duration, till we can examine all the temporal characteristics of consciousness in a single chapter. There remain two sub-sections, dealing respectively with the *quality* and *intensity of sensation.* Finally, it is desirable to arrange sensations according to *sense departments*, inasmuch as differences in the bodily organs must mean very considerable differences in the character of sensations. We shall, therefore, consider the cutaneous, visual, auditory sensations, etc., in turn, as separate classes. This is the only unequivocal principle of class-distinction among sensations, which has an indisputable foundation in the facts.

Our reasons for not co-ordinating affective tone, *i.e.*, the pleasantness or unpleasantness of a sensation, with the four attributes mentioned in the text, will be adduced at a later stage (§ 34. 4).—It may seem that the determination of sensations is not always so relative as we have made it. Thus it is undoubtedly possible to express certain qualities, as those of taste or of cutaneous sensations, in absolute terms; trained musicians sometimes possess an absolute memory for tones. Moreover, we can give an absolute designation of the spatial form in which visual sensations present themselves, provided that it allows of the application of some familiar geometrical name. And special practice culminates in a very great accuracy in the absolute determination of intensities, time-intervals, and distances. But (1) these are all exceptions, either falling within especially favoured sense-departments, in which there are but few qualities and no continuous transition from quality to quality, or forming only a comparatively small proportion of the whole number of available qualities, degrees of intensity, and temporal or spatial standards. (2) The capacity of absolute designation arose by way of comparison. Every system of names is based upon the determination of distinctive marks, and

that can only be based upon comparison. This does not mean, of course, that when the connection between name and contents has been firmly established the reproduction of the name must always be mediated by the original comparison. (3) Absolute designation is always assisted by relative, while the reverse is hardly ever the case. Thus the absolute denomination of the pitch of a tone is aided by its relation to other tones given in memory or perception; whereas the relative determination of two different pitches could scarcely depend upon the absolute denomination of either or both. (4) The capacity would be of little service for psychological purposes, for the following reasons. (*a*) It would always be necessary to provide a special check of its reliability in a particular case, since error is as possible here as elsewhere in association. (*b*) Its infrequent development would necessitate a special and elaborate training, which would, after all, prove useless in many cases. (*c*) There is simply no guarantee, so far as we can see, that the denominations of definite experiences by different individuals would have the same significance for all. With these considerations in our minds, we shall hardly be obliged to qualify the remarks made above (§ 4. 4). Sensitivity is the single rubric under which absolute determination can find a place. But sensitivity is ascertained and measured solely by its relation to stimulus-magnitudes; and this procedure makes only an indirect contribution to the analysis of sensation and its properties.

The classification of sensations by the external stimuli which evoke them, as sensations of 'light', 'sound', 'pressure', etc., cannot be accepted, for the reason that the sensations so denominated do not stand in any unequivocal relation to the exciting stimuli. 'Light' sensations, for instance, can be produced by mechanical or electrical stimulation of the optic nerve.

Even less tenable is the point of view which makes sensations the psychological symbols of objective facts or processes, and leads to their classification as sensations of 'movement', 'weight', 'time', 'space', and so on. Qualities of the most various kinds can do the psychologist this secondary service of symbolism for one and the same object. We do not deny that a psychology of knowledge would find the point of view valuable, and indeed be compelled to ask how far particular sensations or complexes of sensations have acquired or can acquire this significance for the denomination of objective facts. But where sensations are to be treated as simple conscious processes, it is indifferent, if not misleading.

It has sometimes been stated that sense-departments can be discriminated by the fact that sensations of any one sense form a continuous series, while the sensations of disparate senses are wholly unconnected. The statement is not quite correct. There appear to be no transition stages between the qualities of taste, or between those of pressure and temperature.

§ 5. General Conditions of Sensitivity and Sensible Discrimination.

1. The general capacities of sensing, and of experiencing like and different contents—that is, the direct sensitivity and sensible discrimi-

nation—may be supposed to be approximately the same in different individuals, provided that certain of their conditions (of which more in a moment) are kept constant. The capacity of reporting upon experience, on the other hand, will naturally vary very considerably. It is therefore commoner, perhaps, in psychological investigations of sensitivity and sensible discrimination than in any other department of scientific inquiry, that different observers reach quite divergent results. The discrepancy is not due, as a rule, to indefinable 'individual differences', but to differences in the object with which the various observers entered upon their research, and consequent differences in their observations of the same set of facts. The first great prerequisite of fruitful investigation into sensitivity and sensible discrimination is, then, a clear and precise formulation of the question to be answered, and a comparison or comparative evaluation of the reports in which answers obtained under similar conditions are given. E. H. Weber tested the 'cutaneous space sense' by applying the two points of a pair of compasses to the skin, and ascertaining how far apart they must lie for the two sensations to remain (descending series) or become (ascending series) just noticeable as two. Since his day, innumerable experiments of the same kind have been made for the same purpose, both with normal and pathological subjects. But what connection is there between the 'just noticeable twoness' of sensations, and the just noticeable cutaneous distance or extension? No satisfactory examination of the interrelation of these two judgments of noticeability has been made up to the present time; and until it has been made, we have no right to speak of the experiments as tests of the cutaneous 'space sense'. It would not be difficult to collect a large number of similar instances of incongruity between the direct and indirect sensitivity or sensible discrimination, due to inaccuracy of preliminary formulation or subsequent interpretation. The remedy, however, is in our own hands, and such cases have nothing in common with the difficulties discussed above (§ 4. 6, 7, 9).

2. There are three sets of conditions which affect the direct and indirect sensitivity and sensible discrimination alike. The first is that of

(1) *Attention.*—It follows from our definition of this state of consciousness (§ 2. 3) that its various degrees will influence both the direct and the indirect sensitivity and sensible discrimination. The greater or less vividness of sensations in consciousness will evidently affect our introspection of themselves and their differences; and their greater or less reproductivity will similarly affect the certainty and adequacy of their description. A general rule may, therefore, be formulated, to

the effect that, *the greater the attention, the greater are our sensitivity and sensible discrimination.* The influence of attention is so considerable that it is absolutely necessary, if observations are to admit of intercomparison, that we keep it constant throughout the series. Now the only degree of attention which can be experimentally maintained with anything like certainty, is that of complete concentration. Every observation, then, must be made under this condition: in all cases where the influence of attention is not itself the object of investigation, the rule will hold that *the direction of the attention must be constant and its degree maximal.* As a matter of fact, however, fluctuations both of direction and degree are inevitable. The attentive examination and careful judgment of like experiences at short intervals through a whole series of experiments are very fatiguing. Conscious distraction or diminution of the attention may be checked by accurate introspection on the part of the observer, who must put a special mark against judgments formed under unfavourable conditions, to distinguish them from the rest. On the other hand, the many unnoticed fluctuations of the attention will lead to accidental errors of observation, which can only be eliminated—as in the natural sciences—by mathematical treatment of a very large number of experiments. Unless the record shows a constant increase or decrease of sensitivity or sensible discrimination, it may be assumed that these accidental variations are equally grouped about the true, *i.e.*, the mean value. Let α, β, γ, ... be errors of observation due to accidental fluctuations of the attention, and causing the hypothetically true value B to vary in both the positive and negative direction; and let the sum total of the positive errors be equal to that of the negative. Then $B + \alpha$, $B + \beta$, ... will represent the experimental results actually obtained, and (n being the number of observations) we shall have

$$\frac{(B + \alpha) + (B + \beta) + (B + \gamma) + \dots}{n} = B.$$

In strictness, B should be termed not the true, but the probable value of the observation.

3. All states of consciousness which modify the attention will naturally exert an indirect influence upon sensitivity and sensible discrimination. Ill humour and depression generally mean distraction and diminution of the attention; and any physical discomfort, headache, etc., is apt to have the same effect. The greater the interest taken in the work, the more actively and exclusively will the attention be directed upon it; whereas a conviction of the fruitlessness or worthlessness of the observations brings with it an involuntary relaxation of the energy of introspection and a curtailment of description. Nervous

excitability capacitates a man for keen observation at the beginning of an experimental series, but makes him dull, and liable to all sorts of distraction, as the impressions are repeated. A conscientious observer will have to take account of all these elements in the inhibition or facilitation of his attention; and a skilful experimenter will gauge the quality of his experimental subjects by the judgments which they record for him. No specific directions can be given; and in any case, nothing but experience could show whether they were being followed. The extraordinary instability of the mental equilibrium is a factor with which the scientist has to reckon only as a source of accidental, not further analysable errors, but of which the psychologist must take very particular account. It presents itself to him both (1) as a sum of different processes affecting any given judgment and (2) as an independent object of scientific inquiry. A thorough analysis of its influence leads to a whole number of important results, of the kind to which we have already called attention in our protest against the mechanical treatment of special questions (§ 2. 12).

4. (2) *Expectation* and *Habituation.*—Both of these conditions consist in a predisposition of consciousness. ' To 'expect' a stimulus or stimulus-difference is to prepare its introspection or the judgment appropriate to it. This preparation can be accomplished in various ways: by a favourable attitude and adjustment of the sensory apparatus (direction of gaze, accommodation for a certain distance, etc.), by the central excitation of sensations which anticipate the expected impression (idea of the stimulus or stimulus-difference), by an especial readiness for the application of the appropriate judgment (mental rehearsal of the right sounds), and so on. Expectation, if directed upon the processes underlying the observer's report, must evidently increase sensitivity and sensible discrimination: for it is, in reality, simply a preparatory attention. It facilitates the prompt and full concentration of the attention upon the expected contents. Without it the attention, if the phrase is permissible, might easily come too late, and find the sensations already somewhat faded. To ensure its uniform co-operation in the observations of a series, it is customary to give a signal at some fixed interval before the appearance of the stimulus in each experiment, so that the subject's mind is prepared for its reception. The interval between signal (a spoken "Now!" or the stroke of an electric bell) and stimulus is made so short that expectation just reaches its maximum, without passing over into exhaustion, as it would do if the time were too long. The length of the interval is, of course, dependent upon the complexity of the necessary preparation, *i.e.*, of the experiment. The simpler the object presented to judgment, the shorter can

it be made. In many cases it has been found that 2 sec. is a good average time for the adjustment of expectation.

5. What has been said above of the distraction and diminution of the attention holds also of the distraction and weakening of expectation. The introspection of the observer must again furnish a check upon all conscious deviations from the norm; and the ingenuity of the experimenter must guard against such as would pass unnoticed. But since the contents of expectation may vary as well as its direction and intensity, we speak in experimental psychology of a *procedure with knowledge* (complete or incomplete) and a *procedure without knowledge*. In the former, the observer has or is given full or partial knowledge of the purpose of the investigation. This procedure is always followed, for instance, when the functions of observer and experimenter are combined in a single person. In the other case, the observer has no such knowledge. This procedure in its extreme form obviously implies that observer and experimenter are different persons. There are, naturally, a large number of gradations between the two; and neither can really be employed without some intermixture of its opposite. The procedure without knowledge, for instance, cannot entirely exclude knowledge of the circumstances of the experiment. We may vary the magnitude of a stimulus-difference, D, in a series of observations, in such a way that the subject is quite uncertain as to the direction and amount of its variation, but we cannot keep him in ignorance of the sense-organ to be affected and the kind of judgment to be made. The attributes 'with knowledge' and 'without knowledge', therefore, can only be predicated in the strict sense of the particular object of the individual judgment. Indeed, it is not desirable that the procedure without knowledge should overstep these narrow limits. For in that case, the important preparatory work of expectation would be rendered null and void.

6. It is impossible to make any general statement as to the comparative value of the two methods of procedure. Each is important in its own place; but the two sets of results must not be confounded. We may fairly assume that sensitivity and sensible discrimination will be greater in the procedure *with* knowledge. The more definite the contents of a correct expectation, the more easily must a stimulus be noticed and a stimulus-difference cognised. But both procedures leave the door open to certain errors. In that with knowledge, the impartiality of the observer may be more or less seriously affected. It is fatally easy to substitute knowledge for perception, and so lose sight of the actual facts. The result is an artificial regularity of judgment, an artificial value of the sensitivity and sensible discrimination.

In that without knowledge, on the other hand, it is not always possible to prevent the intrusion of some kind of definite idea of the character of the object of judgment. This idea may be right and may be wrong, and according as it is the one or the other will effect an abnormal increase or diminution of sensitivity and sensible discrimination. The observations will consequently vary within somewhat wide limits. And their variation will be rendered still greater by the *natural* uncertainty of the subject, who has purposely been left in ignorance of the precise character of the experiment. The method without knowledge, therefore, tends to rate sensible discrimination and sensitivity too low, just as the procedure with knowledge tends to put them too high. It is always needful to employ both, using each to check the other, and only deciding after very careful consideration which offers the greater advantages in a given case.

7. By *habituation* we understand a tendency, taking shape in the course of a series of similar observations, to experience and describe perceptions of similar character. All our voluntary actions become automatic after a certain number of repetitions, and both expectation and attention are dependent on the will. Within any series of psychological experiments, therefore, we are apt to find a certain direction and degree of the attention growing habitual, and a particular category of judgment becoming preferred. Or if the method employed for the investigation of sensitivity or sensible discrimination consists in the continuous gradation of stimulus-magnitudes, habituation is apt to manifest itself in another way,—in reversal of judgment after a certain series of 'equals' or 'differents'. A very simple experiment will show the magnitude of its influence. Let a number of comparisons be made with lifted weights, the second of each pair being kept constantly heavier than the first; and then let this heavier weight be replaced, in some term of the series—without the subject's knowledge—by one which is exactly equal to the first. The new weight will be judged to be noticeably lighter than the other. Here, as indeed in most cases, the process of habituation is unconscious. It has been technically termed *predisposition*, in the sense of a predisposition of sensory or motor centres for a particular excitation or impulse. But unconscious predisposition is plainly only a sub-heading of habituation, as we have defined it: there is no essential difference either between conscious and unconscious habituation, or between predisposition of the direct and that of the indirect sensitivity and sensible discrimination.— We cannot treat in detail of the long series of individual phenomena, all of the same general nature, which constitute habituation, any more than we could of the details of expectation; but we will speak of a

few points which bear unequivocally upon sensitivity and sensible discrimination.

8. An appreciation of the influence of habituation leads to two results. (i) A certain amount of habituation, such as is induced by a brief series of experiments, undoubtedly exerts a favourable influence upon the certainty of judgment, smooths the way for attention and expectation, and facilitates the report of essential facts. Provided, that is, that its direction does not bring it into conflict with objective conditions, it prevents any serious fluctuation of sensitivity and sensible discrimination. (ii) But with too great habituation, the activity of comparison tends to degenerate into a mechanical automatism, which practically nullifies the effects of attention and expectation, and dulls the subject's interest in the individual experiment. So that, if a certain amount of habituation is good, a larger amount is harmful.

The same two results come out, if we consider habituation from the point of view of the agreement or disagreement of its contents with the object of judgment. (i) A large measure of habituation to a particular perception or report leads us to substitute for the estimation or comparison of the stimuli, as such, a judgment based upon their relation to the disposition which their accustomedness has brought about. The incorrect judgment of the heaviness of the second weight, in the illustration given above, was largely due to the very natural comparison of the unexpected impression with that for which the subject was prepared. Under these circumstances we cannot, of course, obtain reliable information of the powers of sensitivity and sensible discrimination; we run the risk of basing our estimate of their normal function, or our general conclusions with regard to the comparative judgment, upon results which are wholly fortuitous, and due to the artificial conditions of the experiment. Such results are in all essential points incomparable with the others, and only valuable as indicating the great influence of habituation and predisposition. (ii) A small measure of habituation, on the other hand, is distinctly helpful to introspection, *i.e.*, increases the sensitivity and sensible discrimination, even in cases where the stimuli and stimulus-differences are variable. Here again, then, it rests with observer to take account of the source of error, and with experimenter to satisfy himself of its magnitude by a fitting disposal of his experiments. The procedure without knowledge furnishes a key to both problems.

9. (3) *Practice* and *Fatigue.*—We mean by these terms processes, which are ordinarily alike dependent upon the number of observations, but which exert diametrically opposite influences upon sensitivity and sensible discrimination. To practice is due a steady increase in

delicacy of perception and readiness of judgment; to fatigue a steady decrease in both. The words are so familiar and intelligible that it is unnecessary to define them. The processes have received a good deal of attention in physiology, muscular practice and fatigue, in particular, forming the subject of a large number of investigations. Practice expresses itself psychologically (i) in an increase of attentional concentration, with all its accompanying advantages, and (ii) in an increased capacity of reproduction. In both cases we may speak of it as general or special. *General* practice is equally valuable in all departments of inquiry. The subject who has rendered conscientious service in any set of psychological experiments will have gained in power of observation and of judgment, quite apart from the special facility which he has acquired. *Special* practice only applies to the latter. It is best, in embarking upon a new investigation, to secure the assistance of observers who have already had some general practice; special practice must obviously be gained in the course of the experiments. General practice in piano-playing, *e.g.*, does not by any means imply the capacity of rendering a new composition at sight. General practice increases in direct proportion to special; but the reverse is not necessarily true.

We shall not discuss general fatigue, since it is well to exclude persons who suffer from it from participation in an investigation; unless, indeed, it is one of the special objects of the experiment to ascertain what kind of report is made in a condition of general relaxation and exhaustion. A special fatigue, consequent upon continued occupation with the same problem, must show itself sooner or later, and is often operative before the subject has remarked its influence. It expresses itself in an increasing uncertainty and inaccuracy of judgment, and consists (i) in a weakening of attention, and (ii) in a diminished capacity of reproduction. Since certain muscles are essentially concerned in the reception of sense-impressions, it will be necessary to take account of their practice and fatigue, in accounting for increase or decrease of sensitivity and sensible discrimination.

10. The modification of sensitivity and sensible discrimination by practice and fatigue is very considerable. Hence it is important to be sure that only those judgments are compared which were obtained under similar conditions in each regard. And this holds of the judgments of different persons, as well as of those of the same observer. The question arises, therefore, as to how the two factors can be kept constant, or their variation checked, if variation is inevitable. (i) Fatigue can be combated with some measure of success, by judicious limitation of the length of the experimental series, and careful appor-

tionment of recreative pauses between the separate experiments which it comprises. (ii) Practice cannot be counteracted, and must, therefore, be accurately checked in every investigation. Its degree is estimated from a comparison of the particular experiments and experimental series, which show its progressive influence as more and more judgments are taken. It is now customary not to begin the experiments from which conclusoins are to be drawn with respect to sensitivity or sensible discrimination until the maximal degree of practice has been attained by the observers, and the different series and experiments have practically ceased to vary with its continuance. No general rule can be laid down as to the number of experiments necessary for complete practice. Where the problem is difficult and complicated it will hardly ever be safe to say that maximal practice has really been reached.

11. The last general condition of sensitivity and sensible discrimination, but a condition of their indirect forms only, is to be found in the *bodily* (physiological) *processes* which intervene between stimulus and sensation. Our previous discussion has involved some reference to these mediating processes; but the concepts of 'practice', 'attention', etc., include beside them influences of a more central nature. We have, however, already mentioned predisposition; the seat of which may possibly be looked for in the lower brain centres. There remain, therefore, only the manifold variations of nervous excitation which occur in the peripheral sense-organ. Observations of the effect of stimulation at one point of skin or retina may not be compared off-hand with those of its effect at other points: sensitivity and sensible discrimination are largely dependent upon the place at which the organ is affected by light or pressure. Again, the senses of sight, hearing, etc., evince a number of individual differences, peripherally conditioned, which are of great importance for theories of sensation, but which also serve considerably to modify sensitivity and sensible discrimination: the unmusical ear differs in both respects from the musical, the colour-blind eye from the normal. And, lastly, we must bear in mind all the uniformities of relation which have been established from the physiological side for stimulus and excitation. These facts would naturally enter into any appreciation of the capacity of sensitivity and sensible discrimination.—We shall speak of these conditions more in detail as occasion requires.

§ 6. The Measurement of Sensitivity and Sensible Discrimination.

1. The uniform dependency of sensitivity and sensible discrimination upon all these various conditions renders it necessary (1) to make a large number of observations, and (2) to follow a rigorous method, if we are to obtain valid results and successfully cope with distracting influences. The merit of having transformed the scattered experiments of previous investigators into *psychophysical measurement-methods* belongs to Fechner. The methods which we employ to-day for the experimental treatment of sensations are in principle the methods which he formulated, although they have naturally undergone modification and expansion. But Fechner's concept of psychical measurement, of the measurability of sensations, etc., gave rise to a controversy which still continues. We cannot discuss the points at issue in anything like adequate detail within the limits of the present book. It must suffice to give a brief indication of the position taken up in the following pages.

2. No one will maintain that we can *measure* sensations in the strict, *i.e.*, spatial meaning of that term. For (1) they cannot be divided up into parts,—this sensation of 'gray' is not two or three of that other sensation of 'gray'; and (2) there is no amount of sensation which can serve as the unit of measurement for all, since we can neither set up any such unit, nor could apply it with certainty if it were set up. We cannot, therefore, measure sensations by reference to or by means of other sensations. Neither can we, as things are, measure them by their functional relations to bodily processes (cf. § 4. 4). For (1) this would presuppose, at the very least, that we were able to conceive of sensations as divided into parts, and further to correlate these parts or degrees, which we had determined in idea, with physical measures. The sensation s would then correspond to a physical magnitude p; another sensation—say, $2s$—to the magnitude $2p$; and so on. But this method, however abstract we make it, is not applicable to sensations. (2) Again, sensations are not so entirely at our disposal that we can parallel them directly with external conditions, without any mediation of comparison and appreciation. If they were, we should not need to introduce such concepts as sensitivity and sensible discrimination, but could institute a direct comparison of sensations or sensation-differences and stimuli or stimulus-differences. There are two possibilities of measurement in natural science: the direct procedure, which formulates a process in terms of a conventional unit of its own kind, and the indirect, which gives it a quantitative expression by noting its functional relation to some directly measurable process.

Neither is applicable to sensations. If we call what can be measured a 'magnitude', we must say, then, that sensation is not a magnitude.— It may be remarked here that spatial magnitudes alone admit of direct measurement; and that the fundamental condition of exact measurement in natural science is, therefore, the establishment of unequivocal functional relations between spatial magnitudes and all other natural phenomena.

3. But the objections which hold against the measurability of sensations, at any rate at the present time, fall to the ground when urged against sensitivity and sensible discrimination. Direct measurement, of course, is impossible in their case: that is sufficiently obvious. But an indirect measurement is undoubtedly possible. There is no reason why we should not speak of a double or threefold sensitivity or sensible discrimination. And the judgments of sensitivity and sensible discrimination are, certainly, simple correlates of the objects judged. We measure a force by the velocity which it imparts; we measure sensitivity and sensible discrimination, not by sensations,—which are unmeasurable,—but by the stimuli or stimulus-differences which enable us to determine their capacity. This plainly implies that the verbal reports, which are to be correlated with the stimuli, possess a certain reliability. And experience shows that the condition is fulfilled in two cases only: (1) when the judgment is 'like' or 'different', and (2) when it is 'present' or 'absent'. Now, as a matter of fact, all the psychological measurement-methods are built up upon these two sets of judgments (and a few synonymous expressions), as passed upon stimuli or stimulus-differences. Upon their reliability, indeed, depend all kinds of measurement, including the direct procedure of natural science, however delicate and accurate be the instruments employed to assist observation. We need hardly, then, bring any special arguments to justify their application in experimental psychology. They correspond to the widest of all the logical categories, identity and contradiction, being and not-being, and must, accordingly, be postulated in every branch of thought and knowledge. It is often desirable, in view of the special object of an investigation, to give them a more concrete form; and this usually suggests itself without difficulty. It is customary, for instance, to indicate a definite kind of difference between two sensations by naming one of them 'greater' or 'less'. But this is no alteration in principle; since the judgment could just as well have been a simple 'different', if previous explanation had been given of the nature of the comparison.

4. The two terms in these two sets of judgments are not altogether upon an equality as regards contents. The predicates 'like' and 'absent'

are altogether unequivocal: their psychological meaning remains the same, whether they are asserted of sensations or of sensation-differences. But the judgments 'different' and 'present' may mean various things: sensations and sensation-differences can be present and different in all manner of ways. They are, therefore, incapable of furnishing a measurement of *definite* magnitudes. To obviate this difficulty, they have been employed in a very special form. The only 'difference' and the only 'presence' which it has been attempted to ascertain are those which may be termed 'just noticeable', *i.e.*, which constitute limiting values between 'different' and 'like', on the one hand, and 'present' and 'absent', on the other. In this way we obtain the concept of the just noticeable stimulus, as a measure of sensitivity (the mean between present and absent sensations), and the concept of the just noticeable stimulus-difference, as a measure of sensible discrimination (the mean between like and different sensations). It is clear that determinations of this kind cannot be made on the basis of the sensations themselves, but must be obtained indirectly, by special methods, from the indications of sensitivity and sensible discrimination. The sensations or sensation-differences which we characterise as 'just present' or 'just different' have no intrinsic advantage over others in introspection. If we should try to determine them, without more ado by appeal to introspection, we should be subject to the same mistakes and hesitations as we should if we attempted to determine the half or double or threefold of a sensation or sensation-difference It is only by the careful application of delicate methods that we can infer what is 'just noticeable' from general statements of the kind mentioned above.

A further measure of sensitivity and sensible discrimination is afforded by stimuli and stimulus-differences which evoke sensations or sensation-differences judged to be 'like'. In any given case of measurement, accordingly, we find the predicates 'like', 'different', and 'present' (the two latter in the special sense just explained) in direct application; while the judgment 'absent' is, naturally, apt to be applied only indirectly,—unless, indeed, it be synonymous with the term 'like', as referred to a sensation-difference. In other words, the use of the psychophysical measurement-methods means the obtaining of stimuli and stimulus-differences which appear 'like' or are 'just noticeable'.

5. The outcome of these considerations may be made clearer by a few concrete instances. If we find that a light of the intensity 1, directed upon the centre of the retina, produces the same impression as a light of the intensity $\frac{3}{4}$, directed upon some point in the lateral parts of the retina, we can formulate the result as follows: the sensitivity

in lateral stimulation stands to the sensitivity in central stimulation as
$1 : \frac{2}{3}$, or, is one-and-a-half times as great as the latter. The judgment
upon which this measurement is based is that of the apparent equality
(likeness) of the stimuli. We could have obtained that equality in a
different way,—by the determination of the just noticeable brightness
for the two retinal points. The higher the value of this brightness,
the smaller would be the sensitivity which it measured: in other words,
the magnitude of sensitivity is inversely proportional to the just noticeable or apparently equal stimulus-magnitudes. Again, we know that,
other things equal, the intensity of a sound decreases as the distance
of its source from the ear increases. If we determine the distance of
the just noticeable sound for different observers, and find that A can
just hear an intensity 1, while B only hears an intensity 3, we may
say that B's sensitivity for intensities of sound is only one-third as
great as that of A. To test sensible discrimination we proceed in
precisely the same way. Suppose that two weights of 100 and 120 gr.
are found just noticeably different when they exert a pressure upon
the palm of the resting hand, but that 100 and 104 gr. can be just
distinguished if they are lifted and 'weighed'. The stimulus-differences
stand in the ratio $5 : 1$, and the sensible discrimination in the first
case is, consequently, only $\frac{1}{5}$ as great as it is in the second. In
other words, the sensible discrimination is inversely proportional to
the just noticeable difference. Again, if we find that two brightnesses,
10 and 11, present the same apparent difference as the brightnesses
100 and 110, we may say that the sensible discrimination at 10 is
ten times as great as that at 100. In other words, the sensible discrimination is also inversely proportional to the magnitude of the
apparently equal difference.

6. The just noticeable stimulus is technically termed the *stimulus
limen*, and the just noticeable stimulus-difference the *difference limen*.
The stimulus is generally denoted by the letter r [1]; the stimulus-difference $(r - r_1)$ by the expression Δr (or D); the difference limen
by S [2]. For the stimulus limen we shall employ the symbol $\mathfrak{S}$. A
distinction is made—not very happily, as it involves the transference
of relations which obtain between stimuli to the sensible discrimination—between an *absolute* and a *relative* sensible discrimination.
The magnitude Δr or S, absolutely regarded, gives a measure of the
absolute sensible discrimination; its relation to the stimuli for which
the difference holds, $\dfrac{\Delta r}{r}$ or $\dfrac{S}{r}$, expresses the relative sensible discrimination. When two stimuli are compared, it is usual to keep

[1] *Reiz* = stimulus. [2] *Schwelle* = limen.

one constant while the other is varied. The former thus becomes, in a sense, the standard, to which the variable is referred for determination. It is accordingly termed the *standard stimulus*, N [1], as distinguished from the *stimulus of comparison*, V [2]. The relative sensible discrimination is usually expressed in terms of N, as $\dfrac{\Delta r}{N}$ or $\dfrac{S}{N}$.

The aim of all measurement of sensitivity is the ascertainment of $\mathfrak{S}$, or the apparent equality (likeness) of two r; the aim of all measurement of sensible discrimination that of S, or the apparent equality (likeness) of two Δr. This difference in the objects of the measurement of sensitivity and sensible discrimination is indicated by a difference in terminology. The ascertainment of $\mathfrak{S}$ is a *stimulus determination;* that of S a *difference determination.* So the procedure which consists in effecting an apparent equality (likeness) of stimuli is termed *stimulus comparison*; that which leads to an apparent equality (likeness) of stimulus-differences, *difference comparison.* /Stimulus determination and difference determination give absolute values; stimulus comparison and difference comparison relative./ Stimulus comparison by no means necessarily results in the correlation of subjective equality with objective equality of stimuli; and apparent equality of stimulus-differences is not an index of their objective equality. It may very well happen that an apparently equal stimulus-difference corresponds not to an equal difference between stimuli, but to an equality of their ratios: *i.e.*, that r and r_1 appear equally different with r_1 and r_2, not when $r - r_1 = r_1 - r_2$, but when $\dfrac{r}{r_1} = \dfrac{r_1}{r_2}$. This is, of course, in itself indifferent for the measurement of sensible discrimination. And it is, therefore, also indifferent whether in particular the absolute or relative sensible discrimination, *i.e.*, whether Δr or $\dfrac{\Delta r}{r}$ is constant.

7. All these expressions are expressions of the *magnitude* of sensitivity or sensible discrimination; *i.e.*, indicate their efficiency in face of absolute or relative values of determinate or compared stimuli or stimulus-differences. But when a physicist, *e.g.*, is reporting a scientific observation, he is not content to give merely the observed or calculated average of a series of experimental figures, but states how far the separate results agreed with one another before their average was taken. It is equally desirable that we, too, should indicate the fluctuations which sensitivity and sensible discrimination undergo in presence of the same stimulus and stimulus-difference. The mean value of these fluctuations furnishes a measure of the *delicacy* of sen-

[1] *Normalreiz.* [2] *Vergleichsreiz.*

sitivity or sensible discrimination. The necessity of the introduction of this second rubric of measurement is shown by the fact that small S have been found in various cases with relatively great variations, and large S with comparatively small variations. Knowledge of the 'magnitude' of sensitivity and sensible discrimination in such cases would obviously be but a part of the knowledge required.

No more is meant, here, by 'fluctuations' of sensitivity and sensible discrimination, than the vacillation which we have seen (§ 5. 2, *e.g.*) to result from the undulatory movements of attention. If we add together the errors ascribed to these in our previous equation, $\alpha, \beta, \gamma, \ldots$ without regard to their + or − signs, and divide their sum by the number of observations, we obtain the mean fluctuation or (as it is usually termed) the *mean variation*, *MV*. As related to this, the probable value of the observation, which we called B, becomes the *arithmetical mean*, *M*, of the series. M or B, then, affords a measure of the magnitude of sensitivity or sensible discrimination, while *MV* gives a numerical expression of its delicacy. Sensitivity and sensible discrimination are, here again, inversely proportional to the value obtained: the smaller the *MV*, the greater their delicacy.

The distinction of an absolute and relative sensitivity and sensible discrimination has an especial significance in this connection. As a general rule, it will be even more important to know their relative delicacy than their absolute, since the accuracy of an observation is gauged not by the absolute magnitude of its average error, but by the quotient of that error and M. It will, therefore, be necessary to determine the value of $\dfrac{MV}{r}$ or $\dfrac{MV}{\Delta r}$, etc., as well as that of MV.

8. Admission of the validity of a particular *MV* evidently presupposes the belief that the magnitude of sensitivity and sensible discrimination remained practically unchanged throughout the experimental series from which it was calculated. In the absence of this belief it would be useless to reckon out the *MV*, as it would arouse an altogether erroneous idea of the course of sensitivity and sensible discrimination. Suppose, *e.g.*, that the sensible discrimination increased twofold within a given series, *i.e.*, that the just noticeable stimulus-difference was at the end only the half of what it had been at the beginning: the mean variation might easily be disproportionately large. On the whole, it is safe to assume that magnitude and delicacy of sensitivity and sensible discrimination in the same individual are directly proportional to one another. To ascertain whether a series is unfitted to serve as a basis of calculation, owing to the influence of practice or habituation or what not, it is only necessary to divide

it up into a number of sub-series (say, of 5 or 10 experiments), and to compare the averages obtained from these. If their differences are merely fortuitous and irregular, the series may be treated as a whole.

We distinguish these purely accidental fluctuations of judgment, due to the operation of variable factors which cancel or compensate one another, from variations which show a definite tendency, *i.e.*, a continuous increase or decrease of sensitivity and sensible discrimination. Such *constant* variation furnishes a very simple measure of the influences which occasion it; the amount of increase or decrease of sensitivity or sensible discrimination is a direct indication of the extent of their power. They cannot be really avoided or eliminated (cf. what was said of practice above, § 5. 1*c*).

9. This constant variation is not to be confused with what are called *constant errors*, which can be eliminated by the proper methodical means. They constitute positive or negative increments of the probable value of an observation, consequent upon differences in the temporal or spatial position of the stimuli compared, that is, upon differences in the external conditions under which these stimuli affect the organism. If the two stimuli in question are r and r_1, and r regularly precedes r_1, we have a *time error;* if r and r_1 are presented simultaneously, but r is always to the right and r_1 to the left, or r always above and r_1 below, we have a *space error*. Both errors can be quite simply eliminated. When observations with a particular temporal or spatial arrangement have given a particular mean value, M_1, an equal number of observations is taken with the precisely opposite arrangement (r following r_1, r to the left, r below, and so on), and gives the value M_2. The arithmetical mean of M_1 and M_2 is free of constant errors. If both kinds of error are operative in the same investigation (as where pressure stimuli are applied successively at different points of the surface of the skin), four series of observations must be made, and the arithmetical mean of M_1, M_2, M_3 and M_4 calculated. In either case the magnitude of a special error can be separately determined. Both elimination and determination are, of course, only possible if the conditions of judgment have been kept constant in all other respects.

The reasons for the errors cannot be stated with any degree of certainty. The different sensitivity of the points of skin or retina stimulated may partly account for the space error; the difference in the conditions of nervous excitation for the two stimuli may partially explain the time error. But both may be affected also by the difference in the circumstances under which the standard stimulus and stimulus of comparison are judged. In any event, we can make no general statement as to their direction and magnitude.

10. The methods which can be employed for the formulation of the magnitude of sensitivity or sensible discrimination in terms of stimulus or difference determination, or stimulus or difference comparison, may be denominated *gradation methods* and *error methods*. In the abstract, any method can be employed for any object; but, as a matter of fact, theoretical foundation and practical application differ in different cases. The gradation methods make use of small and uniform changes in stimuli and stimulus-differences to obtain the value required: they measure the magnitude of sensitivity and sensible discrimination in a relatively direct and simple manner. The error methods deduce the probable course of sensitivity and sensible discrimination from a large number of judgments, on the assumption that the errors made in the production or estimation of given stimuli or stimulus-differences bear a uniform relation to the delicacy of sensitivity and sensible discrimination: the measurement of their magnitude is here attended with certain difficulties. The methods remain essentially the same, however different the problems which they are called upon to solve. Our discussion can, therefore, most usefully be based upon this cardinal difference in procedure.

Our space does not admit of a more detailed examination of the individual psychophysical measurement-methods. The reader may refer to Wundt, *Phys. Psych.*, I; Fechner, *Elemente der Psychophysik*, and *Revision der Hauptpunkte der Psychophysik;* and Müller, *Zur Grundlegung der Psychophysik*, 1878.

The following table of the symbolic expressions explained in the previous paragraphs, and of some others which will be used in what follows, may be of service to the student.

$r, r_1, r_2, r_3 \ldots$	= stimulus. (Any of the possible modifications of stimulus may be thus represented; stimulus form or stimulus intensity, stimulus duration or stimulus [spatial] magnitude.)
$\Delta r = D = r - r_1, \ r_1 - r_2 \ldots$	= stimulus-difference.
S = just noticeable Δr	= difference limen.
$\mathfrak{S}$ = just noticeable r	= stimulus limen.
$\Delta r, S$	= absolute magnitude of sensible discrimination.
$\dfrac{\Delta r}{r}, \ \dfrac{S}{r}$	= relative magnitude of sensible discrimination.
N	= standard stimulus.
V	= stimulus of comparison.
M	= arithmetical mean.
MV	= mean variation.
$\dfrac{MV}{r}$	= relative delicacy of sensitivity.

$\dfrac{MV}{\Delta r}, \quad \dfrac{MV}{N}$ = relative delicacy of sensible discrimination.

$\overset{v}{r}$ or $\overset{v}{\Delta r}$ = subliminal (unnoticeable) stimulus or stimulus-difference.

$\hat{r}$ or $\overset{\wedge}{\Delta r}$ = supraliminal (more than just noticeable) stimulus or stimulus-difference.

Subjective or apparent equality (likeness) of stimuli or stimulus-differences we shall denote by the sign $|||$; subjective or apparent difference in the sense of 'greater' ('stronger', etc.) by $\overline{>}$; and subjective or apparent difference in the sense of 'less' ('weaker', etc.) by $\overline{<}$.

§ 7. The Gradation Methods.

(1. Characteristic of all the gradation methods is the continuance of small, unnoticeable changes of stimuli or stimulus-differences in a constant direction, until a corresponding change takes place in the judgment of the observer. (Thus, if we set out from an objective and subjective equality of stimuli, and seek to discover at what point one of them becomes just noticeably different from the other, we shall take a large number of short steps in the direction of difference, and note at what objective point of change the subjective cognition of difference arises. It is not necessary to bring reasons in support of this slow advance, since the accuracy of determination must obviously be proportional to the number of values bordering upon the required value which the observer has opportunity to judge. The delicacy of physical measurements enables us to make our steps comparatively very small. Their number and magnitude are, as a rule, inversely proportional to each other. How large they must be, or how numerous they may be, in a particular case, will depend upon the magnitude of sensible discrimination or sensitivity. To minimise the influence of expectation, fatigue, and habituation, it is usual to interpolate but few steps,—perhaps five,—between two different judgments. The steps are best made fairly large at first, and afterwards diminished, so that the level at which the change of judgment takes place is defined as accurately as may be. The judgments themselves should be recorded at once, under the immediate influence of the impressions, since they are meant to be simply a reproduction of these, and must not admit any modifying or reinforcing extraneous processes,—or, in other words, since the indirect sensitivity and sensible discrimination are meant to be, as far as possible, a true copy of the direct. If an assured judgment is for some reason impossible, the experiment must be repeated, and no reliance placed upon the recovery of the lost assurance by reflection and memory.

2. But the limiting value which we obtain in this manner cannot be regarded as furnishing in itself an adequate measure of sensitivity and sensible discrimination. For every fresh step in the direction of the required change of judgment adds to the probability of its occurrence, so that, as a general rule, it will take place earlier than might be expected under normal conditions. The chief psychological cause of this phenomenon must be sought in expectation. The subject knows that the stimuli are undergoing continuous alteration, and that the object of the experiment is to bring about a change of judgment. He naturally inclines, therefore, to let his judgment change. In certain cases this tendency can be compensated by the antagonistic influence of habituation. But we can never be quite certain that the change of judgment really corresponds to the just noticeable alteration. It was, therefore, proposed by G. E. Müller that this method should always be combined with a reversal of procedure; that when the first change of judgment had been effected, the experimenter should work in the opposite direction, from a supraliminal value of the object of judgment back to its original value. If, for instance, we began with the subjective equality of r and r_1, and brought about a noticeable difference between them by a gradual alteration of r, we should afterwards begin again with a clear difference between them, and gradually diminish it until it became unnoticeable. The new judgment of equality in the latter case must, for the reasons alleged above, come somewhat too soon, *i.e.*, the objective difference be too large. Then, by taking the mean of the two Δr, we may hope to have obtained a probable expression of the sensible discrimination. If this combination of procedures is to be of any real worth, however, the number and magnitude of the steps must be the same in both directions. To ensure this similarity, in cases where the method begins with a supraliminal stimulus or stimulus-difference, Wundt proposed further that the experiments should be continued beyond the point at which the judgment changed to one at which the stimulus-difference was quite clear, and that the reversed procedure should start from this latter. Under these circumstances the number and size of the steps can be regulated with a fair degree of certainty.

3. It will easily be understood that a procedure by gradation, such as we have here sketched, is equally useful for stimulus determination and stimulus comparison, for difference determination and difference comparison. It is, therefore, an undesirable usage which distinguishes a method of just noticeable differences or of least differences from a method of supraliminal differences or mean gradations and a method of just noticeable stimuli and equivalents. For these

differences of name do not correspond to differences of method, but merely to differences in the object of inquiry. The procedure is precisely the same in all the special methodical developments. The method of just noticeable or least differences consists simply in its application to difference determination, the method of supraliminal differences or mean gradations in its application to difference comparison. In the same way, the method of just noticeable stimuli applies it to stimulus determination, that of equivalents to stimulus comparison. The titles in ordinary use are further undesirable, for the reason that they make it appear as if values like S, $r \parallel\!\mid r_1$, etc., could not be determined in other ways, by means of the error methods. We shall, therefore, in what follows, treat of the procedure by gradation under the single rubric of the *method of minimal changes* (Wundt), and indicate its applicability in different departments of investigation under the four headings explained above,—stimulus determination, stimulus comparison, difference determination, and difference comparison.

I. The Method of Minimal Changes in its Application to Stimulus Determination (Method of Just Noticeable Stimuli).

4. Fig. 1 gives a schema of this method. Magnitudes of the stimulus employed in the investigation are supposed to be arranged in ascending order along the vertical AB, extending from the subliminal (at A) to the supraliminal (at B) through all possible intermediate stages. The experiments begin at $\overset{\cdot}{r}$. The stimulus r is changed, by very small positive increments, until the judgment is made that a sensation is present to consciousness. The corresponding stimulus value ($\mathfrak{S}_o$) is entered in the experimenter's record. From this point on the increase is continued, by quick removes, not specially noted in the schema, until a stimulus $\hat{r}$ is reached, which is clearly supraliminal. Now begins an alteration of r by

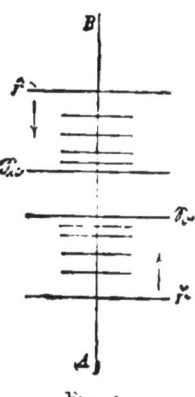

Fig. 1.

very small negative increments, which is continued to unnoticeability, *i.e.*, until the judgment is made that there is no longer any sensation present. The corresponding stimulus value ($\mathfrak{S}_u$) is again entered in the record. Taking the mean of the two values $\mathfrak{S}_o$ and $\mathfrak{S}_u$, we have:

$$\frac{\mathfrak{S}_o + \mathfrak{S}_u}{2} = \mathfrak{S},$$

the stimulus limen for the particular series of observations. The number of constant and accidental errors to which sensitivity is liable renders it desirable to repeat the series several times over, and to calculate the average of the various limina,—provided that they do not show any constant increase or decrease. Moreover, the method must begin alternately with $\overset{v}{r}$ and $\hat{r}$, in these series, for the elimination of a possible constant error attending the choice of either.

This method of stimulus determination admits of application to all those limina of sensibility which we have already mentioned (§ 4. 8), as well as to the limits of modal sensitivity. Suppose, *e.g*, that we are determining the intensive stimulus limen for pressure sensations at the tip of the finger. We begin by placing a weight of 1 mgr. upon the surface of the skin; then 3 mgr.; and then 4 mgr.,—at which point the subject notices a gentle pressure. We then pass to 7 and 9 mgr., with which latter the sensation of pressure is tolerably clear. Travelling in the opposite direction from 9 to 7 and onwards, we find that 6 mgr. are not noticed. The pressure limen is then $\frac{6 + 4}{2} = 5$ mgr. The magnitude of sensitivity for pressure stimuli at the tip of the finger would consequently be $\frac{1}{5}$: since sensitivity in general may be regarded as $= \frac{1}{\mathfrak{S}}$.

II. The Method of Minimal Changes in its Application to Stimulus Comparison (Method of Equivalents).

5. The schema of this method, given in Fig. 2, is very similar in appearance to that of the former. The stimulus magnitudes here,

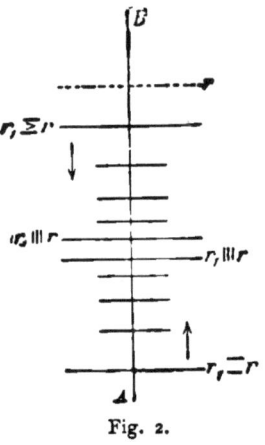

Fig. 2.

however, need not be restricted to the limen, but may be all supraliminal. We denote by r the standard stimulus, which remains constant throughout the experiment, by r_1 the stimulus of comparison, which is to be made equal to r. The method begins with a value of r_1, which is clearly smaller than r; then passes, by the familiar short steps, to a judgment of equality (ascending); proceeds by quick removes to an r_1, which is clearly greater than r; and there turns back, continuing until a second judgment of equality (descending) occurs. The mean of the two corresponding stimulus magnitudes is taken, and may be looked upon as the true $r_1 \ ||| \ r$. For the elimination of constant errors it is necessary not only to vary the starting point of the whole procedure, but also the temporal or spatial position of the two stimuli.

This method may also be employed to test all kinds of sensibility, and to measure the modal sensitivity in the case of different observers. We may put the matter in the form of an equation:

$$\text{Sensitivity} : \text{Sensitivity}_1 = r_1 : r,$$

which expresses the fact that the sensitivity of one observer (or of one portion of the skin, under certain circumstances) stands to the sensitivity of another observer (or of another portion of the skin, under other circumstances) inversely as the apparently equal stimuli in corresponding experiments. Suppose, *e.g.*, that the pressure sensitivity with stimulation of the finger-tip is to be compared with the same sensitivity with stimulation of the back of the hand. Let a pressure of 5 gr. on the former serve as standard stimulus. The application of the method as described above may give a pressure of 2 gr. as its equivalent. The sensitivity of the back of the hand is then 2½ times as great as that of the finger-tip. From this we can calculate that the stimulus limen, which we found to be 5 mgr. for the finger-tip, will be 2 mgr. for the back of the hand; in other words, that the sensitivity is here ½, while it was previously ⅕.—The production of minimal stimuli and of minimal changes in them is often so difficult that stimulus comparison, with its application of supraliminal magnitudes, has been very extensively employed to test sensitivity. It must, however, be remembered that only those stimuli should be chosen for comparison which can be readily and certainly judged, and which can claim the relatively largest noticeability for the relatively smallest alterations. Stimuli which are too weak or too strong, too small or too large, too short or too long, must be avoided; though no more definite rules can be laid down.—It is customary, in physical photometry, to make the subjective equality of two uniformly variable light intensities the criterion of their objective equality. In such work, the method of minimal changes might serviceably be employed, and the precautions which it suggests profitably observed.

III. The Method of Minimal Changes in its Application to Difference Determination (Method of Just Noticeable or Least Differences; also termed Method of Minimal Changes, in the narrower sense).

6. The just noticeable difference between two stimuli can be determined in two ways, by a gradual increase and by a gradual decrease

of the stimulus of comparison. This twofold procedure (schematised in Fig. 3) gives two difference limina, which are termed the *upper* ($V = r_1$ increased) and the *lower* ($V = r_1$, decreased) respectively. The usual starting point of the experiment is the apparent equality of the two stimuli ($r ||| r_1$). The increase and decrease of r_1 must be regularly alternated, for the elimination of constant errors.

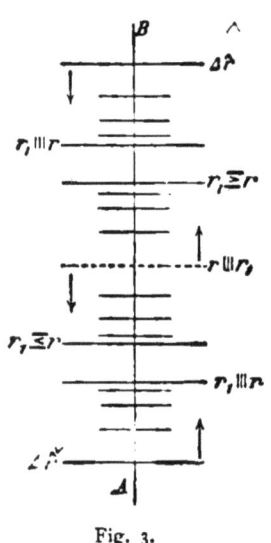

Fig. 3.

Suppose that we first of all make $r \gtreqqless r$: the stimulus difference is recorded as $\triangle r'_o$ [1]. We then increase r_1 to $\triangle'_r$; and from that point return to $r_1 ||| r$, or the apparent disappearance of the difference (recorded as $\triangle r''_o$). We thus have

(1) $\dfrac{\triangle r'_o + \triangle r''_o}{2} = \triangle r_o = S_o$; the *upper difference limen.*

We then go on to decrease r_1 still further, to the apparent difference $r_1 \lesseqgtr r$, which we record as $\triangle r'_u$ [2]. From that we proceed to a $\triangle'_r$; and then again return to an apparent equality, at the difference $\triangle r''_u$. We thus have

(2) $\dfrac{\triangle r'_u + \triangle r''_u}{2} = \triangle r_u = S_u$; the *lower difference limen.*

From these two we can determine

(3) $\dfrac{S_o + S_u}{2} = S$; the *mean difference limen.*

If we make $r + S_o = r_o$, and $r - S_u = r_u$, we obtain

(4) $r_o - S = r_u + S = R$; the *estimation value* of the stimulus r, and

(5) $\pm (R - r) = \triangle$; the *estimation error* or *estimation difference.*

Substituting in equation (4) the original expressions for r_o or r_u and S, we get the following for R and $\triangle$:

(4 a) $R = r + \dfrac{S_o - S_u}{2}$;

(5 a) $\triangle = \dfrac{S_o - S_u}{2}$.

If $\triangle = 0$, *i.e.*, $S_o = S_u$, we have found constancy of the absolute sensible discrimination: if $\triangle$ is positive, *i.e.*, $S_o > S_u$, a decrease of the absolute sensible discrimination with increasing r: if $\triangle$ is negative, *i.e.*, $S_o < S_u$, an increase of the absolute sensible discrimination with

[1] o = 'over'.   [2] u = 'under'.

increasing r. In the first case $R = r$, *i.e.*, r is correctly estimated; in the second $R > r$, *i.e.*, r is overestimated; in the third $R < r$, *i.e.*, r is underestimated. Sensible discrimination can, therefore, be expressed in terms of R and Δ, as well as by S_o, S_u, and S.

7. But the method can be employed in still more ways, and gives still other test-values. Thus, in cases where it is desirable to ascertain by a rapid procedure the dependency of sensible discrimination on the magnitude of the stimuli, it is sufficient to determine the upper difference limen only. Again, it is not necessary to begin at $r^1 \parallel\!\mid r$; a supraliminal Δr may be made the starting point. This will be especially convenient where $r_1 \parallel\!\mid r$ does not correspond to $r_1 - r$, owing to constant errors or other circumstances. Again, to eliminate constant errors, the experimenter must vary not only the temporal or spatial position of standard stimulus and stimulus of comparison, but also the direction in which r_1 is altered. If he starts out from $r_1 \parallel\!\mid r$, *e.g.*, he must begin by increasing r_1 as often as he begins by decreasing it, and arrange the order of his determinations by reference to the beginning. Further, the course of sensible discrimination can be expressed not only by S_o, S_u, S, Δ and R, but by $\dfrac{r_o}{r}$ and $\dfrac{r}{r_u}$, which are termed *limina of relation.* If $\dfrac{r_o}{r} = v_o$ is the *upper* limen of relation, and $\dfrac{r}{r_u} = v_u$ the *lower*, then

$$\sqrt{v_o \cdot v_u} = \sqrt{\frac{r_o}{r_u}} = v$$

is the *mean* limen of relation. These values are used in particular, with $\dfrac{S_o}{r}$, $\dfrac{S_u}{r}$ and $\dfrac{S}{r}$, to characterise the relative sensible discrimination.

An illustration will serve to make the matter clearer. Suppose that we have a standard stimulus of 90 gr. given us, and that we are required to find the stimulus of comparison which is just noticeably different from it. We apply first standard weight and then variable weight to the surface of the skin, and note that at $r_1 = 90$ gr. the two stimuli are judged to be subjectively equal. Gradual increase of r_1 then leads to a $r_1 \gtreqless r$ (*i.e.*, to r'_o) at 95 gr. A further increase, to 100 gr., makes the difference very apparent. Gradual decrease of the 100 gr. leads to a $r_1 \parallel\!\mid r$ (*i.e.*, to r''_o) at 97 gr. We thus have $\dfrac{r'_o + r''_o}{2} = r_o = 96$, and $\Delta r_o = r_o - r = 6$. Continuing to decrease r_1 beyond the limits of the judgment of equality, we obtain a $r_1 \lesseqgtr r$

(*i.e.*, r'_u) at 85 gr.; and then, returning from 80 gr. upwards, a $r_1 \,|||\, r$ (*i.e.*, r''_u) at 84. We thus have $\dfrac{r'_u + r''_u}{2} = r_u = 84\cdot5$, and $\Delta r_u = r - r_u = 5\cdot5$. Averaging, we get $\dfrac{\Delta r_o + \Delta r_u}{2} = S = 5\cdot75$, while $r_o - S = R = 90\cdot25$, and therefore $\Delta = \pm(R - r) = +0\cdot25 = \dfrac{S_o - S_u}{2}$.

The absolute sensible discrimination is therefore not constant, but decreases with increase of the stimulus magnitude. Whether the relative sensible discrimination is constant cannot be inferred with certainty, as Δr_o and Δr_u lie too near together. A calculation of the limina of relation gives $v_o = \frac{18}{16}$, $v_u = $ approximately $\frac{18}{16}$, and consequently $v = $ approximately $\frac{18}{16}$. This makes a constancy of the relative sensible discrimination probable.

IV. The Method of Minimal Changes in its Application to Difference Comparison (Method of Supraliminal Differences or Mean Gradations).

8. To determine directly the apparent equality of two stimulus differences $r_1 - r = \Delta r_1$ and $r_2 - r_1 = \Delta r_2$, it is best to employ the method of minimal changes in the manner schematised in Fig. 4. Two of the three stimuli (those farthest apart from one another, r and r_2)

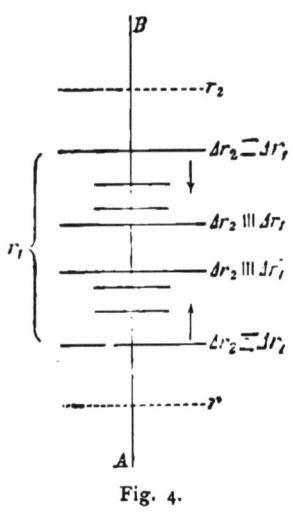

Fig. 4.

are kept constant, and the third (the intermediate r_1) varied. A clear difference of Δr_1 and Δr_2 (say $\Delta r_2 \gtreqless \Delta r_1$) is chosen as the starting point of the experiment, and r_1 increased, in the familiar way, until $\Delta r_2 \,|||\, \Delta r_1$. This r_1 is then further increased, until a difference in the opposite direction is quite distinct ($\Delta r_2 \lesseqgtr \Delta r_1$); and then again decreased until the difference becomes unnoticeable. In both cases the gradation can be extended to apparent inequality of the differences. The procedure gives four values of r_1, the average of which is taken. If the two values obtained in the direction A to B are termed r'_o and r''_o, and the two obtained in the direction B to A are termed r'_u and r''_u, the quotient

$$\frac{r'_o + r''_o + r'_u + r''_u}{4}$$

is the magnitude of r_1 which corresponds to

the probable subjective equality of the two differences. If $\Delta r_2 > \Delta r_1$, the absolute sensible discrimination has decreased with increasing magnitude of the stimuli; if $\Delta r_2 < \Delta r_1$, it has increased; if $\Delta r_2 = \Delta r_1$, it has remained constant. In the latter event (*i.e.*, when $\Delta r_2 ||| \Delta r_1$ corresponds to $\Delta r_2 = \Delta r_1$), r_1 must be the arithmetical mean between r and r_2. If, on the other hand, the relative sensible discrimination is constant, Δr_2 must be $> \Delta r_1$, when the two are apparently equal: the proportion being $r : r_1 = r_1 : r_2$, or $r_1 = \sqrt{r . r_2}$. The dependency of sensible discrimination upon the magnitude of the stimuli can, therefore, be very simply tested by the calculation of r_1 as the geometrical and arithmetical means of r and r_2, and the comparison of these calculated values with the r_1 obtained by experiment.

9. Difference comparison was introduced into psychophysics by Plateau. It bears the same relation to difference determination as is borne by stimulus comparison to stimulus determination. It can be used with difference determination to measure sensible discrimination, just as the two stimulus methods can be used together to measure sensitivity. As a general rule, it is the more direct path to knowledge of the course of sensible discrimination. Moreover, since two just noticeable differences may be regarded as two subjectively equal differences, its results can be employed to check one another. Constant errors, dependent upon the direction of the experiments and the temporal or spatial position of the stimuli, must be eliminated here, as always, by a regular alternation of conditions. With regard to the choice of stimuli, it is usually best to take such as present a considerable difference. For (1) the relative accuracy of estimation is thereby increased:— it has been found that the *MV* does not increase proportionally to the stimulus differences; and (2) the greater the distance from r to r_2, the greater are the technical accuracy and the possibility of variation in the procedure by gradation. The statement made above, that it is desirable to keep r and r_2 constant, and to vary r_1 until the two differences $r_1 - r$ and $r_2 - r_1$ are subjectively equal, is based upon the obvious consideration that the sensible discrimination can be more exactly determined if the limiting stimuli remain unaltered. The two differences thus become mutually regulative; change in one means simultaneous change in the other. Lastly: It has sometimes been objected to the method, that the magnitude of supraliminal sensation differences cannot be experimentally adjusted to allow of comparison either as between different observers, or for the same observer at different times. But a similar objection might be urged with regard to just noticeable sensation differences. And it is altogether irrelevant to the measurement of sensible discrimination. Sensations and sensation differences cannot

be measured at all (§ 6. 2—5); and any possible change that they may undergo is, consequently, wholly indifferent to us.

We may again conclude with an illustration. Suppose that we have given us the pressure stimulus $r = 15$ gr., $r_2 = 135$ gr.; and that we are required to find by gradation an intermediate stimulus r_1 of such a magnitude that the difference $r_1 - r = \Delta r_1$ is apparently equal to the difference $r_2 - r_1 = \Delta r_2$. We begin with $r = 15$, $r_1 = 30$, $r_2 = 135$. The r_1 is gradually increased, until subjective equality $(\Delta r_1 \parallel\mid \Delta r_2)$ is reached at $r_1 = 42$ (r'_o). It is then still further increased, till $\Delta r_1 \geqq \Delta r_2$ at $r_1 = 49$ (r''_o). The same procedure is now repeated from $r_1 = 60$; and r'_u found at 48, and r''_u at 41. We thus have $\dfrac{42 + 49 + 48 + 41}{4} = 45$; *i.e.*, the stimulus differences are subjectively equal when $r_1 = 45$ gr. In this case $\Delta r_1 = 30$, $\Delta r_2 = 90$: there is no constancy of the absolute sensible discrimination. The same result is reached by comparing r_1 with the arithmetical mean of r and r_2,—75; it is too small by 30 gr. On the other hand, the decrease of the absolute sensible discrimination is directly proportional to the increase of the stimuli. It decreases in the ratio 3 : 1, while the stimuli form a geometrical series with the exponent 3. But if the absolute sensible discrimination decreases as the stimuli increase, the relative sensible discrimination must be constant. We find, as a matter of fact, that not only $\dfrac{\Delta r_1}{r} = \dfrac{\Delta r_2}{r^1}$, but $r_1 = \sqrt{r \cdot r_2}$. Now we know already that a pressure of 96 gr. is just noticeably different from a pressure of 90 gr. It follows at once, that for 15 gr. S must $= 1$, for 45 gr. $S = 3$, and for 135 gr. $S = 9$. The quotient $\dfrac{S}{r}$, which expresses the relative sensible discrimination, is therefore constant, at $\frac{1}{15}$. This result is in complete agreement with the value previously obtained for $v - \frac{18}{8}$.

10. There are still one or two general considerations which must receive attention before our presentment of the procedure by gradation can be regarded as complete. (1) It must be emphasised, in the first place, that the method of minimal changes always implies the *procedure with knowledge*. It is true that the direction of the first series of changes in difference determination, *e.g.*, may not be clear to the subject. But since the further course of the method is perfectly plain to any one familiar with it, when once this initial direction has been made out, it is better to secure uniformity of experimental conditions by following the procedure with knowledge from the outset. All that the observer has to do, under these circumstances, is to

express the contents of his introspection as impartially and conscientiously as possible. (2) It is further desirable to keep the *direction of judgment constant,* wherever the comparison of two or more stimuli is involved. By constancy of the 'direction of judgment' we mean constant adherence to the rule that the second stimulus or stimulus-difference is to be judged in its relation to the first; so that, if r_1 is the second stimulus, *e.g.*, the expressions 'greater', 'less', 'equal' always signify $r_1 \gtrless r$, $r_1 \lessgtr r$, $r_1 \mid\mid\mid r$. This constancy is valuable in two ways. (*a*) It greatly facilitates the naming of the introspective contents, and secures definiteness and steadiness of attention and expectation. (*b*) It is a condition of any real elimination of constant errors. An increase of r_1 as second stimulus corresponds to the judgment 'greater'; its increase as first stimulus to the judgment 'less'. Now since the time error is certainly dependent, in part, upon this direction of judgment, it could not be really eliminated, unless the rule of constant direction were applied in turn to each of the stimuli. We know nothing with any certainty, however, of the influence of the direction of judgment. Systematic experiments upon the subject would be welcome.

11. Our account of the method of minimal changes has not included any special reference to its applicability to the measurement of the *delicacy* of sensitivity and sensible discrimination. The delicacy of sensitivity and sensible discrimination is measured by the inverse value of the *MV*; and this is obtained by the calculation of the average divergence of a number of similar observations from their arithmetical mean (§ 6. 7, 8). Thus the *MV* in Method I. can be determined by the combination of the various $\mathfrak{S}_o$ or $\mathfrak{S}_u$ of the particular experimental series, and the $\mathfrak{S}$; in Method III., by that of the corresponding values of S_o, S_u and S: always provided that no constancy of variation is discoverable. A very interesting question arises in this connection,—that of the relation between the (absolute and relative) delicacy and the (absolute and relative) magnitude of sensitivity and sensible discrimination. No systematic attempt to answer it has as yet been made.

It will easily be seen that in a procedure with knowledge, such as is presupposed by the method of minimal changes, the *magnitude and number of the gradations* introduced must exercise a considerable influence upon judgment. The most characteristic effects are those produced upon expectation and habituation. It has been found, *e.g.*, in experiments by Method IV., that alteration of the starting point of the variable r_1 is regularly followed by alteration of the values r'_o, r'_u, etc., if the subject has become habituated to a definite number of gradations. This shows two things: the very great influence of habituation, and the importance of strict adherence to the procedure with knowledge which the principle of the method of minimal changes requires, if any valid results are to be gained by an examination of sensitivity or sensible discrimination. If the observer knows that the number and size of the steps will vary irregularly, he will naturally make allowances for the fact in attention and expectation. This would seem to indicate that it is well not to accustom him to a regularly recurrent number of gradations. But at present we have not enough experimental material to enable us to decide with any degree of confidence upon the best method of working, or to say anything definite as to the range and character of the influences to which we have drawn attention.

§ 8. The Error Methods.

1. The foregoing consideration of the gradation methods has shown us that the accuracy of sensitivity and sensible discrimination falls very far short of the accuracy of measurement or production of stimuli in physics or chemistry. One and the same judgment of equality, for example, may correspond to a whole zone of stimulus differences; a complete series of unnoticeable changes may have taken place on the objective side, before there is any awareness of their existence or direction on the subjective. It has shown us, further, that our observations are liable to accidental variation, as a result of which the same judgment does not always recur at the same level of stimulus alteration in different experiments. It is natural to regard these incongruities between the judgments of sensitivity and sensible discrimination and the objective stimulus values as 'errors', in the sense in which the word is used in natural science; and to make their magnitude or number the basis of an estimation of the magnitude or delicacy of sensitivity and sensible discrimination. Thus the analogy has given rise to the two error methods: the *method of right and wrong cases* and the *method of average error*. In the former, a constant stimulus or stimulus-difference is made the object of judgment in a large number of experiments, each judgment recorded, and the proportions of the various judgments calculated. In the latter, a stimulus or stimulus-difference is presented to the subject, and he is required to reproduce it; and the differences between standard stimulus and stimulus of comparison in a series of experiments are employed for the determination of the sensitivity. The range of applicability of the first method is plainly greater than that of the second, which

presupposes two or more stimuli, and admits no judgment except that of equality.

2. If we assert that the formulæ employed in the mathematical theory of errors of observation are capable of direct application to psychophysical investigations, we obviously do so upon the assumption that the deviations from the most probable value in psychophysics are of the same kind as the deviations from the probable value with which mathematics is concerned. The latter are subject to the following general rules. (1) The errors must occur in continuous gradation from o to $\pm$ a; or, since the a-limit cannot be defined with certainty, from o to $\pm$ ∞. (The extension is indifferent in practice.) In other words, the errors must not be of one definite magnitude, or fall within a series of definite magnitudes, but must appear in all the different magnitudes possible within the stated limits. (2) The larger errors must occur less often than the smaller, and the maximum of frequency must be attained by the error o. (3) Positive errors must appear as often as negative; *i.e.*, the sum of the positive must be equal to the sum of the negative. We may take it for granted that these conditions are realised in what we have called the 'accidental variations' of sensitivity and sensible discrimination: if only for the reason that the errors of observation with which the mathematical theory has principally to deal are really nothing else than accidental variations in the judgments of this same sensitivity or sensible discrimination. If, then, we are able to abstract from constant variations, we may have recourse for our special purpose not only to the general law of the distribution of errors, but also to the special formulæ for the probability of an error of definite magnitude or of the errors within certain fixed limits.—We need do no more than glance very briefly at the values and formulæ which the mathematical theory of errors of observation employs.

The relative frequency of the various errors can be best indicated by a curve of the form shown in Fig. 5. The abscissæ give the magnitude of the errors (δ), the ordinates their relative frequency or probability. The curve reaches its maximum at the value $\delta = o$. From this point it falls on either side,—symmetrically, since the probabilities of positive and negative errors are equal; and approaches the axis of the abscissæ asymptotically by a comparatively quick descent. The relative frequency of an error of definite magnitude α is expressed by the equation [1]

$$W_\alpha = \frac{h}{\sqrt{\pi}} \cdot e^{-h^2\alpha^2},$$

where h denotes the 'measure of precision' of the observation (Gauss), a constant

[1] W = *Wahrscheinlichkeit*, probability.

5

bearing in general an inverse ratio to the magnitude of an error, π is Ludolf's number, and e the base of the natural logarithms. For $\alpha = 0$, $W'_\alpha = \dfrac{h}{\sqrt{\pi}}$. For our purposes, it is of more importance to know the probability of errors which

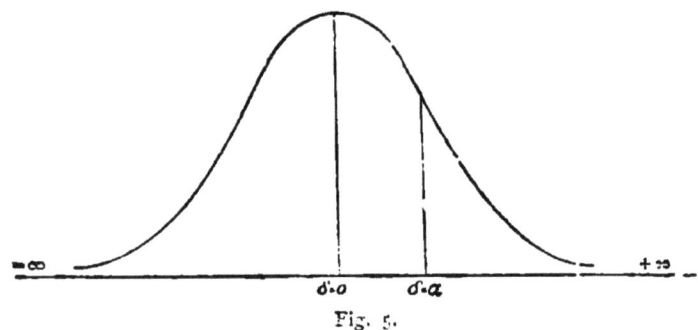

Fig. 5.

lie between certain fixed limits. Since they constitute a series with continuous gradations, their sum can only be expressed by an integral. If we make $h\delta = t$, the probability of the errors between the limits o and $+\infty$ is:

$$\overset{+\infty}{\underset{0}{W'}} = \frac{1}{\sqrt{\pi}} \int_0^{+\infty} e^{-t^2} dt.$$

In the same way we obtain:

$$\overset{+\infty}{\underset{-\infty}{W}} = \frac{2}{\sqrt{\pi}} \int_{-\infty}^{+\infty} e^{-t^2} dt.$$

And similarly, the relative frequency of the errors between the limits o and $+\delta$ will be:

$$\overset{+\delta}{\underset{0}{W}} = \frac{1}{\sqrt{\pi}} \int_0^{h\delta = t} e^{-t^2} dt.$$

This integral may be regarded as the expression of an area, which in Fig. 5 is bounded by the ordinates upon $\delta = 0$ and $\delta = \alpha$. Its value has been calculated, and a table of the various values of t constructed, in which the values of W from $t = 0$ onwards are given. Thus, if 100 observations have been taken, we have, according to the table,

for values from $t = 0$ to $t = 0.5$ a $W = 0.52$ or 52 errors,
   „ „ „ $t = 0.5$ to $t = 1.0$ „ „ $= 0.32$ „ 32 „
   „ „ „ $t = 1.0$ to $t = 1.5$ „ „ $= 0.13$ „ 13 „
   „ „ „ $t = 1.5$ to $t = 2.0$ „ „ $= 0.02$ „ 2 „

How quickly the probability decreases as the errors increase is shown by the fact that for the range of values $t = 2 \cdot 0$ to $t = \infty$ there is only one error left in the series of 100 observations $(52 + 32 + 13 + 2 = 99)$.

Fechner has somewhat modified the table given in the text-books of probability, for the special purposes of psychophysics, where we are concerned to determine the $t = h \delta$ from the relative frequency of judgments made, and $t = 0$ is assumed for a certain relative number of right cases. Cf. *Elem. d. Psychophys.*, I., 108-111; *Revision der Hauptpunkte der Psychophys.*, 66 ff.; *Abhandlung. d. Königl. Sächs. Ges. d. Wiss.*, XX., 206 ff.

Gauss' law of error is strictly valid only for an infinitely large number of observations. A large number of experiments must always be made, if it is to be fruitfully applied. It is very necessary to prevent the co-operation of external physical errors of any magnitude.

In place of the mean variation (MV), many experimenters prefer to use the more exact value of the *average error* (MF) [1], of the particular deviations from the arithmetical mean. The formula is:

$$MF = \sqrt{\frac{\delta_1{}^2 + \delta_2{}^2 + \delta_3{}^2 \ldots}{n}} = \sqrt{\frac{\Sigma (\delta)^2}{n}},$$

where δ_1, δ_2 .... are the various deviations from the arithmetical mean, used irrespectively of their $+$ or $-$ sign; n the number of observations; and Σ the sign of summation. If n is small, it is usual to introduce a correction into the formula, by writing $n - 1$ in the denominator instead of n.

The measure of precision, h, and the MF stand in the simple relation:

$$h = \frac{1}{MF\sqrt{\pi}}, \text{ or } MF = \frac{1}{h\sqrt{\pi}}.$$

Lastly, the probable error (w) is defined as that magnitude of error which is as often exceeded as not reached; *i.e.*, for which the error integral has the value $0 \cdot 5$. The corresponding value of t in the table mentioned above is

$$t = 0 \cdot 476936 = hw.$$

We can also determine w by the following formula:

$$w = \frac{0 \cdot 674489}{\sqrt{n}} \cdot MF, \text{ or } w = \frac{0 \cdot 845347}{\sqrt{n}} \cdot MV,$$

which presupposes the relation obtaining when the number of experiments is very large,—

$$\frac{MF}{MV} = \sqrt{\frac{\pi}{2}} = 1 \cdot 2533 \ldots$$

I. The Method of Right and Wrong Cases.

3. The method of right and wrong cases can be employed in as many ways and for as many purposes as that of minimal changes. So far, however, the theory of it has been worked out only for the three rubrics of stimulus determination, difference determination, and

[1] $F = Fehler$, error.

difference comparison; and in practice it has been principally used for difference determination. Psychophysicists are, moreover, not so unanimous in their views of the mathematical treatment of the experimental data, the measure of sensible discrimination which the method affords, etc., as they are with regard to the essentials of the method of minimal changes. It is not too much to say that the theory of the method is still an open chapter, and that experiments by it have not yet been made in sufficient numbers to permit of our passing any confident judgment upon the trustworthiness of the values obtained or the true functions of the method in general. We cannot attempt in the present connection to fill out these lacunæ, to appreciate the various points of criticism, or to modify the principles of the method in accordance with our own opinions. We shall only refer to the most important discussions in the literature, and indicate the course which the method ordinarily follows in practice. The reader who desires fuller information may turn to the works already cited, and in particular to the articles by J. Merkel in the *Phil. Studien* (VII., 558; VIII., 97): *Theoretische und experimentelle Begründung der Fehlermethoden*. We shall further restrict our present discussion to the single case of difference determination, since this has received the largest share both of theoretical consideration and practical illustration.

4. Suppose that we have a stimulus difference $D = r_2 - r_1$, which is very little $\gtrless S$; *i.e.*, which cannot always be cognised, even with apparently equal concentration of the attention and under similar objective conditions. (If we have no idea at all of the value of S, the D required can easily be found in a series of preliminary experiments.) The subject is allowed to judge of this D, which is kept constant, say 100 times. In a certain proportion of cases the judgment will be correct, *i.e.*, we shall have $D\,|||+(r_2-r_1)$; in a certain proportion it will be incorrect, *i.e.*, the estimate will be $r_2 \lessgtr r_1$ or $D\,|||-(r_2-r_1)$; and in yet another proportion we shall obtain $r_2\,|||\,r_1$ or $D\,|||\,0$. Besides these three categories of judgment, the first few series of experiments generally require a fourth, for 'doubtful' cases; *i.e.*, cases in which the subject cognises a difference, but is unable to characterise its direction,—in which $D\,|||\pm(r_2-r_1)$. No special rubric is made for them, however; since (1) they disappear as practice advances, and (2) can obviously be counted, while they occur, half to the correct and half to the incorrect judgments. If n is the number of observations, then $r+f+g = n$ [1], and

(1)
$$\frac{r}{n} + \frac{f}{n} + \frac{g}{n} = 1.$$

[1] $r = richtig$, correct; $f = falsch$, incorrect; $g = gleich$, equal.

The question now is: how we can obtain from the relative proportions of right, wrong and equal cases, a measure of sensible discrimination, which will give us numerical statements of its magnitude and delicacy analogous to those furnished by the method of minimal changes; how, equation (1) being given, and the size of D known, we can arrive at a general formulation of this magnitude and delicacy. Fechner has answered the latter part of the question, and G. E. Müller the former.

5. The sensible discrimination in difference determination can be measured either by S, the difference limen, or by the mean fluctuation, MV or MF. The first thing to do, then, is to discover from the values of $\frac{r}{n}$, $\frac{f}{n}$ and $\frac{g}{n}$ for some particular D, the value of $D = S$. In the same way, a value must be found, which stands in a definite relation to the MV or MF. Now when we were calculating S_o and S_u by the gradation method, we were led by the consideration of certain sources of error to make them the mean between the first noticeable difference and the first unnoticeable difference; and we accordingly defined S as that stimulus difference which constitutes the limiting value between the noticeable and the unnoticeable (cf. § 7. 2, 6). Applying this definition in the present case, we may say that S is that stimulus difference which is just as often cognised (correctly judged) as not cognised (incorrectly judged). The probability of a correct estimation of S is then equal to the probability of its incorrect estimation: each $= \frac{1}{2}$. We can, therefore, designate S (on the analogy of the probable error) the probable difference limen. And this gives us the first relation required,—that between S and the three classes of judgments. For $D = S$, we must have $\frac{r}{n} = \frac{f+g}{n} = \frac{1}{2}$.

Again, we have just seen (§ 8. 2) that MF and h stand in the simple functional relation of inverse proportion. The delicacy of sensible discrimination can, therefore, be measured directly by h as well as inversely by MF or MV. It is only necessary to be quite sure, in this case also, that there has been no considerable interference of errors independent of sensible discrimination; in other words, that h really expresses sensible discrimination, and not possible irregularities of a technical and physical kind. The same caution applies, for that matter, to the measurement of the magnitude of sensible discrimination; the ratio $\frac{r}{n} = \frac{1}{2}$ must be wholly ascribable to accidental sources of error which are internal and not external.

6. At this point we make the assumption that the occurrence of

r, f, and g cases is subject to the law of error; that it is due to accidental errors that a constant D is sometimes cognised, sometimes incorrectly judged. We may imagine that positive or negative errors are algebraically added to D, making it a $+ D$, o, or $- D$ for sensation, according to circumstances. Every error is, therefore, expressible by a D magnitude, and the probability function of the r, f, and g cases is formulable as though hD, and not $h\,\delta$, were the t for the relative number of cases in question. We thus obtain the relative number of r, f, and g as a function of $t = hD$; and by the aid of the equation found above for $D = S$ and of equation (1), reinforced by two other determinations, are able graphically to represent the course of the r, f, and g cases according to the law of probability. For $D = o$ we have to assume an equal probability of r and f, i.e., $\dfrac{r}{n} = \dfrac{f}{n}$. Now for $- D$ the f cases become r cases; for $+ D$ the r become f. It follows that the relative number of f for a negative D obeys precisely the same law as the relative number of r for a positive D,—an f case being defined in general as that in which $D \,|||\, - (r_2 - r_1)$. The curves of the r and f cases will consequently intersect at $D = o$, pursuing symmetrical paths in opposite directions. Lastly, the g cases are found by the equation $\dfrac{g}{n} = r - \dfrac{r + f}{n}$.

The three curves are accurately represented in Fig. 6. The ordinates represent the numbers of the particular cases, the sum of which

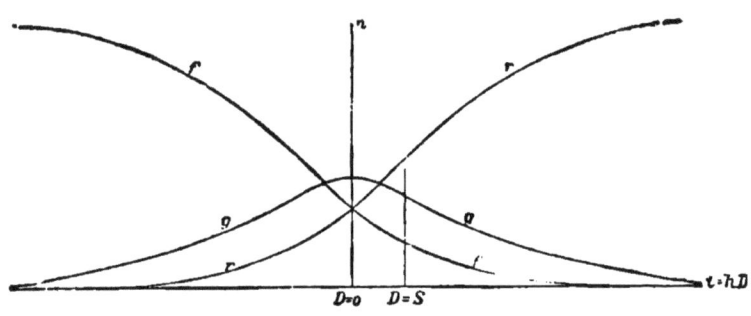

Fig. 6.

is n; the abscissæ denote the $t = hD$ given in Fechner's fundamental table. To avoid disturbance of the regular course of the curves of r and f cases, the term r is employed for all cases in which $D \,|||\, + (r_2 - r_1)$, and the term f for all in which $D \,|||\, - (r_2 - r_1)$.

7. If we grant the hypothesis that the foregoing discussion is in

place when referred to sensible discrimination and its expression in the three classes of judgments, we may call in the aid of the law of probability, and shall find no difficulty in constructing formulæ from which to calculate the S and h for a given stimulus and a definite D.

Suppose that $D > S$,—as can be seen at once by the increase of r cases over 50 p. c. For the observer, $D = D \pm \delta$; where δ indicates the positive or negative error which occasions the different judgments. An r case will obviously occur when D is positive, or negative and in absolute magnitude $< D - S$. The relative number of r cases is, therefore, = the probability of all positive $\delta +$ the probability of those $-\delta$ which are smaller than $D - S$: that is—

(2)
$$\frac{r}{n} = \tfrac{1}{2} + W = \tfrac{1}{2} + \frac{1}{\sqrt{\pi}} \int_{0}^{h(D-S)=t_1} e^{-t^2} dt.$$

An f case will occur, when δ is negative and in absolute magnitude $> D + S$. The relative number of f cases is, therefore, = the probability of all $(-\delta)$ — the probability of those $-\delta$ which are smaller than $D + S$: that is—

(3)
$$\frac{f}{n} = \tfrac{1}{2} - W = \tfrac{1}{2} - \frac{1}{\sqrt{\pi}} \int_{0}^{h(D+S)=t_2} e^{-t^2} dt.$$

Finally, a g case will occur, when δ is negative and in absolute magnitude $> D - S$ but $< D + S$. The relative number of g cases is, therefore, = the probability of negative δ within the limits $D - S$ and $D + S$: that is—

(4)
$$\frac{g}{n} = W_{D-S}^{D+S} = \frac{1}{\sqrt{\pi}} \int_{h(D-S)=t_1}^{h(D+S)=t_2} e^{-t^2} dt.$$

In Fechner's fundamental table the appropriate $t = h D$ is given for every $\dfrac{r}{n} > 0.50$. For $\dfrac{f}{n}$, the value of t for the equivalent $\dfrac{r + g}{n}$ must be looked for in the table. If the first t is written t_1, as in equation (2), and the second t_2, as in equation (3), we have:

$$h(D - S) = t_1, \text{ and}$$
$$h(D + S) = t_2; \text{ and, therefore,}$$

(5)
$$h = \frac{t_1 + t_2}{2 D}$$

$$2 S = \frac{t_2 - t_1}{h}$$

(6)
$$S = \frac{t_2 - t_1}{t_2 + t_1} \cdot D.$$

8. The practical application of the method is a very simple matter. We will again have recourse to pressure sensations for our illustration. Suppose that two pressure stimuli, whose magnitudes are to be compared, are given successively upon the same portion of the skin 100 times over. Let $r_1 = 90$ gr., $r_2 = 99$ gr., and D, therefore, $= 9$ gr. We obtain 65 right, 10 wrong, and 25 equal cases: *i.e.*, $\dfrac{r}{n} = 0\cdot65$, $\dfrac{f}{n} = 0\cdot10$, and $\dfrac{g}{n} = 0\cdot25$. For $\dfrac{r}{n}$ (in this case $> 0\cdot50$, *i.e.*, $D > S$) we find $t_1 = 0\cdot2725$; for $\dfrac{f+g}{n}$, $t_2 = 0\cdot9062$. Hence $h = 0\cdot07$, and S (approximately) $4\cdot8$ gr. Constant errors, dependent on the temporal or spatial arrangement of the compared stimuli, can be eliminated by a regular alternation of their positions in an equal number of experiments within each experimental series. The elimination is most successfully accomplished if the mean of the t_1 and t_2 values is taken, instead of that of the individual r, f, and g cases occurring under the different spatial and temporal conditions.

The method admits both of a procedure with knowledge, and a procedure without knowledge. The extant investigations seem to show that either can be followed with good results, though a half-way procedure leads to great irregularities of judgment. To secure a procedure without knowledge in regard to the D of the inquiry, it is customary to interpolate blank experiments, with $D = 0$ or a negative D, whose frequency and position in the series are unknown. The judgments made in these blank experiments can be treated by themselves, apart from those which constitute the principal object of the investigation. It is always imperative that the number of experiments be large, since there is otherwise no justification for the distribution of judgments in accordance with the law of probability.

For the application of the method to *stimulus determination*, cf. G. E. Müller, *Ueber die Massbestimmungen des Ortsinnes der Haut mittels der Methode der richtigen und falschen Fälle* (Pflüger's *Archiv für die ges. Physiologie*, XIX., 191 ff.), and Fechner, *Ueber die Methode der richtigen und falschen Fälle in Anwendung auf die Massbestimmungen . . . . des Raumsinnes* (*Abhandl. des Kgl. Sächs. Ges. d. Wiss.*, XXII., 111 ff.). For its application to *difference comparison*, cf. C. Lorenz, *Untersuchungen über die Auffassung von Tondistanzen* (*Phil. Studien*, VI., 26 ff.), and F. Angell, *Untersuchungen über die Schätzung von Schallintensitäten nach der Methode der mittleren Abstufungen* (*Phil. Studien* VII., 414 ff.).

It has often been said that the method of right and wrong cases is the best of all the psychophysical measurement-methods. The statement cannot be accepted as it stands: and that not only because of the very large number of experiments required. It is true that mathematical ingenuity it most strikingly evidenced in the development of the theory of this method; but it is still an open question whether the application of the law of probability is justifiable. Even now we can point to certain facts and arguments which cast doubt upon the validity of that law for the magnitude of sensitivity and sensible discrimination.

(1) No account has been taken of the important difference between direct and indirect sensitivity and sensible discrimination. If our assumption is that the apparent stimulus-difference is produced by the co-operation of positive or negative errors, that can only mean that the *sensation*-difference is positive, negative, or o, and that accordingly *r*, *f*, and *g* judgments occur. But there can be no question that any one of these judgments may be recorded in consequence of an accidental inclination towards or preparedness for a certain judgment category, without the sensation difference having necessarily undergone a corresponding change. As a matter of fact, instances of a habituation of judgment have been observed: and it needs no proof to convince us that they cannot be subsumed off-hand to Gauss' law. But there is one fact in particular which points to this incongruity between the direct and indirect sensitivity and sensible discrimination. We should expect, on the law of probability, that with increase of D there would be effected, besides an increase of $\frac{r}{n}$, a more speedy disappearance of $\frac{f}{n}$ than of $\frac{g}{n}$. For the errors which are supposed to occasion the f judgments, are greater than those which cause the judgment g. In practice, however, and especially in the procedure without knowledge, it has been found, not only that $\frac{g}{n}$ is ordinarily smaller than $\frac{f}{n}$, but also that as the stimulus-difference increases $\frac{g}{n}$ disappears earlier than $\frac{f}{n}$. This fact must be taken in connection with that of the occurrence of the 'doubtful' cases, mentioned in the text: judgments, in which the subject is clearly conscious of a difference between the sensations compared, but is unable to determine its direction. Although these equivocal difference judgments do not figure in the report as a special category after a certain stage of practice, their influence does not by any means cease to make itself felt. On the contrary, the relative preponderance of the f cases clearly indicates it. The probabilities that an equivocal difference judgment is transformed into a definite r or f are about equal; the probability that it is registered as g extremely slight. That is to say, f cases may be looked for wherever the equivocal difference judgments are possible, *i.e.*, with all stimulus differences which are too large to evoke judgments of equality. These considerations have led to the proposal of two limina —a limen of right cases, and a limen of undecided cases. At any rate, the fact has nothing to do with any alteration in the magnitude of a sensation-difference by accidental errors of observation.—The determination of the proposed limen of

the general cognition of difference cannot be really carried out, if only for the reason that the 'doubtful' judgments occur in practice rarely and irregularly.

The only way of coping with this incongruity between the g cases and the r and f cases is that followed by Merkel in his *Methode der Gleichheits- und Ungleichheitsfälle.* Unfortunately, the procedure is not worked through with logical consequence. The inequality cases are identified with the r, and possible f included in the g judgments. S can only be determined on this method if experiments are made for at least two different D, and then the S obtained from the resultant values by interpolation.

This modification of Merkel's is, however, psychologically regarded, an improvement upon the method of r and f cases as ordinarily understood. Besides which, it does away with the inappropriate and misleading terms 'right' and 'wrong'. But it still leaves the question of the relation of the direct to the indirect sensitivity and sensible discrimination open, and so fails to meet the objections urged against the applicability of the law of error. Their incongruity gives the reason for another fact—that the employment of different D has led to the ascription of different values to S. This result is not due to a dependency of sensible discrimination upon the magnitude of the D (r_1 remaining the same), occasioned perhaps by a different degree of strain of the attention, but is an artifact of the method. If with increase of D the g cases decrease more rapidly than the f cases—the disproportion beginning from somewhere about the point at which $D = S$,—it is clear that the value of S for a larger D cannot be the same as its value for a smaller D. But that makes it quite doubtful, in what relation the calculated S really stands to sensible discrimination. In any event, the conclusion of our present discussion must be that the method of right and wrong cases is not to be placed on a higher plane than the gradation methods, which furnish us with direct information of an incomparably more reliable kind as to the magnitude of sensitivity and sensible discrimination.

(2) Gauss' law postulates an equal distribution of positive and negative errors, and a maximal probability for the error o. It is again only in certain cases, not by any means always, that these postulates hold for sensible discrimination. For instance, it is not invariably true that with a $D = o$ the g cases are the most numerous. And sensible discrimination for a stimulus decrease is by no means invariably the same as sensible discrimination for a stimulus increase. If the relative sensible discrimination, and not the absolute, is constant, the probability of negative errors must be greater than that of positive, it being assumed that the r, f, and g judgments are dependent upon their co-operation. In the same way, the increase of $\frac{r}{n}$ on either side of the limit where $\frac{r}{n} = \frac{1}{4}$ will obviously be conditioned by the absolute (or relative) sensible discrimination in a manner which can hardly be brought to light at all by the method of right and wrong cases. The various modes of overestimation and underestimation, which can be so simply demonstrated by the gradation methods, are more or less concealed under a general law of error, which is made the principle of distribution of the separate judgments. All this shows, again, that the method of minimal changes, with its freedom from postulates of a law of error, etc., is not only more simple, but also better applicable to

the determination of the magnitude of sensitivity and sensible discrimination, than is the method of right and wrong cases.

(3) We must note, too, that the theory of errors of observation explicitly confines the notion of 'accidental error' to those deviations from the most probable, mean value, the causes of which are unknown, or at least indeterminable as regards their separate degrees of influence. Thus it is quite usual to speak of the imperfection of instruments, or the uncertainty of perceptions, without going into details concerning the reasons for this imperfection and uncertainty or their comparative importance, and without drawing any accurate distinction between external sources of error in the apparatus, and internal sources in sensation. The only secondary hypothesis involved is, that the number of sources of error and of their possible connections remains constant. But sensitivity and sensible discrimination are not subject to 'accidental errors' in this sense of indeterminable variations. On the contrary, the conditions under which they exist, and the influences which these conditions exert upon them, are made the object of elaborate investigation; and the procedure which gives us the most unequivocal and untheoretical information regarding them is, therefore, absolutely the best. It is accordingly advisable to postpone the examination of the *magnitude* of sensitivity and sensible discrimination by the method of right and wrong cases, until we have acquired such a measure of positive knowledge respecting its laws and conditions as will enable us to work out, in theory and practice, a reliable error method; one which, while taking account of all these phenomena, shall be adequate to the accidental variations that still remain.—The measure of precision, h, is, as a constant, independent of such variations. This simple mathematical fact makes it probable that the above considerations do not apply to h. And in practice it has been found, that h remains unchanged with increase of D, provided that the other experimental conditions do not vary. A measure of the *delicacy* of sensitivity and sensible discrimination can, therefore, be obtained from the method of right and wrong cases, even as ordinarily employed. For this purpose, h may be determined by the simpler Fechnerian procedure: the appropriate $t = hD$ is found in the fundamental table for the particular $\dfrac{r}{n}$ or $\dfrac{r + \frac{s}{2}}{n}$, and h made $= \dfrac{t}{D}$. Cf. Kämpfe: *Beiträge zur experimentellen Prüfung der Methode der richtigen und falschen Fälle* (*Phil. Studien*, VIII., 511 ff.); Bruns, *Ueber die Ausgleichung statistischer Zählungen in der Psychophysik*, (*Phil. Studien*, IX., I ff.).

II. The Method of Average Error.

9. The procedure in the method of average error consists in the repeated reproduction by the subject of a given stimulus or stimulus difference; *i.e.*, in the collection of records of $r_2 \,|||\,$ (a given) r_1 or $\Delta r_2 \,|||\,$ (a given) Δr_1. It is, therefore, only applicable to stimulus comparison and difference comparison. A stimulus determination or difference determination in the absence of the stimulus or difference to be determined—if the phrase is permissible—would scarcely be possible, as the just noticeable stimulus

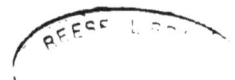

and the difference limen are limiting values, not to be obtained by any voluntary predisposition, however frequently repeated. Hitherto, the method of average error has been applied only to stimulus comparison; so that nothing more can be said of its applicability to difference comparison than that an affirmative judgment is warranted on general grounds. Its sphere is still further limited by the fact that it can only be profitably employed in cases where the union of subject and experimenter in one and the same person is easily practicable and the results of the union sufficiently trustworthy. This second condition is best realised by the choice of stimulus magnitudes which allow of continuous alteration, passing through all possible gradations within certain fixed limits; a finite number of steps may very well give occasion to constant errors of predisposition. It is further desirable that the stimulus alteration be effected not only without trouble, but mechanically, without making any demand upon the attention, and that no particular adjustment be consciously or unconsciously given an advantage over the rest. In other words, care must be taken that the subject's judgment is altogether dependent upon sensitivity or sensible discrimination, and is not affected by secondary circumstances. We see at once that the fulfilment of such a condition cannot always be assured; and thus have further reason for our opinion that the method of average error can only be employed without suspicion in certain special cases.

10. The procedure in stimulus comparison is exceedingly simple. A stimulus, r_1, is given. The subject is required to make a second stimulus, r_2, exactly equal to r_1 in sensation, n times. These n 'error stimuli' present certain differences, in virtue of which they can be subjected to mathematical treatment. If the separate error stimuli are f_1, f_2, f_3, ..., and we take their average

(1)
$$\frac{f_1 + f_2 + f_3 + \ldots f_n}{n} = F,$$

F is the *mean error stimulus* or the *average crude error*. It helps us to determine (*a*) a constant error

(2)
$$F - r_1 = \pm C,$$

which measures the divergence of the apparent from the objective stimulus equality. This constant error may be referred partly to the temporal or spatial position of the stimuli compared, partly to differences of sensitivity. To ascertain the facts underlying the two possibilities in the particular case, we must eliminate the time or space error in the usual way, by an appropriate variation of the arrangement of the stimuli. If a constant difference between F and r_1 is still left, we know that the sensitivity for r_1 and r_2 was different, *i.e.*, that r_2 was overestimated or underestimated as against r_1. The magnitude of sensitivity is then measured by r_1 and r_2 ($= F$), just as in the corresponding gradation method, by aid of the equation

$$\text{Sensitivity}_1 : \text{Sensitivity}_2 = r_2 : r_1$$

(§ 7. 5). But F is also employed (*b*) for the determination of a variable error. The mean variation or average error (*MV* or *MF*) of the separate error stimuli is calculated :

(3)
$$\frac{(F - f_1) + (F - f_2) + \ldots (F - fn)}{n} = \triangle m, \text{ or}$$

$$\sqrt{\frac{(F - f_1)^2 + (F - f_2)^2 + \ldots (F - fn)^2}{n}} = \triangle m_1.$$

This $\triangle m$ (or $\triangle m_1$) is *the mean variable error* or *average pure error.* Like the corresponding *MV* (or *MF*) of the method of minimal changes, it furnishes a measure of the delicacy of sensitivity.—It has been the custom to look upon this mean variable error as the peculiar measurement-value afforded by the method. But Wundt has shown, that in the value of F after the elimination of the time and space errors, which he terms the *true constant error* ($F - r_1$), we have a measure of the magnitude of sensitivity, analogous to the $\triangle$ of minimal changes proper (§ 7. 6).

11. The simplicity of the procedure just described renders a Figure needless. We may, therefore, proceed at once to consider an instance of its application. Pressure stimuli will hardly serve our purpose, since a continuous increase or decrease of pressure intensity could only be effected by the help of special and complicated apparatus (cf. 9 above). We will take the comparison of distances by the eye. Suppose that two horizontal distances are marked off by fine, smooth lines. The left-hand distance, N, remains constant at 50 mm.; the right-hand distance, V, can be altered by means of a finely threaded screw, the turning of which moves the limiting line in or out. V is made apparently equal to N ten times; and its values are $f_1 = 52$, $f_2 = 49, f_3 = 50, f_4 = 51, f_5 = 52, f_6 = 50, f_7 = 49, f_8 = 51, f_9 = 51$, $f_{10} = 50$. We then have $F = 50.5$ mm., $C = + 0.5$, $\triangle m = 0.9$. To ascertain whether the constant error is not merely accidental, *i.e.*, due to a chance fluctuation of sensitivity which the small number of experiments would not suffice to compensate,— to a defect in the experimentation, rather than to any particular attitude of sensitivity,—we calculate out the probable error, by the formula already given (§ 8. 2). This proves to be 0.24, *i.e.*, is < C. We may, therefore, suppose that what we have discovered is a true constant error; and we proceed to determine its special nature by elimination of the space error.— With regard to the right regulation of predisposition, we may note that the variable stimulus must not be always changed in the same direction,

that its equality to N must not be obtained always from a higher or always from a lower value, but that the direction must be varied, so that equality is as often reached from one as from the other. Another way of avoiding the error that might arise from alteration in a single direction is to move the variable stimulus to and fro in each experiment, until the point of equality seems to have been found with absolute accuracy. This latter procedure may, perhaps, diminish the value Δm, i.e., educe a greater delicacy of sensitivity (of which Δm is an inverse measure); but it has the disadvantage of making the determination of equality tedious and more fatiguing.

12. We may conclude by giving a comprehensive table of the values furnished by the various methods, which are principally employed in the measurement of sensitivity and sensible discrimination.

Stimulus and Difference			Determination	Comparison
Sensitivity	Magnitude		$\mathfrak{S}$	$r \,|||\, r_1$ ($Sensitivity : Sensitivity_1 =$ $r_1 : r$)
	Delicacy		$MV;\ MF$	$MV;\ MF$
Sensible Discrimination	Magnitude	Absolute	S	$\Delta r \,|||\, \Delta r_1$ ($Sensible\ Discrim. : Sensible$ $Discrim._1 = \Delta r_1 : \Delta r$)
		Relative	$\dfrac{S}{r}$	$\dfrac{\Delta r}{r},\ \dfrac{\Delta r_1}{r_1};\ r : r_1 = r_1 : r_2$
	Delicacy	Absolute	$MV;\ MF;\ h;\ \Delta m$	$MV;\ MF$
		Relative	$\dfrac{MV}{r};\ \dfrac{MF}{r};\ h\,.\,r;\ \dfrac{\Delta m}{r}$	$\dfrac{MV}{r};\ \dfrac{MF}{r};\ \dfrac{MV}{\Delta r};\ \dfrac{MF}{\Delta r}$

§ 9. Stimulus and Nervous Excitation.

1. The physiological definition of *stimulus* is too wide for psychological purposes. The physiologist means by stimulus the cause of a change in the state of the organism; the psychologist means by it the condition of a change in consciousness. As every condition of a change in consciousness is at the same time an affection of the organism, the psychological stimulus is simply a special form of the

physiological. There is one particular class of physiological stimuli to which all psychological stimuli (at least in man) may be subsumed; the stimuli, *i.e.*, which produce an alteration in the nervous system, an 'excitation'. We can, therefore, make our definition more concrete, and say that by a psychological stimulus we mean the cause of a nervous excitation which is attended or followed by a change in consciousness. The cause of a nervous excitation of this kind may be (1) another nervous process, (2) any other organic process connected with it, or (3) a physical or chemical action external to the organism. In any event, the word 'stimulus', in psychological as in physiological nomenclature, always signifies a physical, measurable process, whose nature we more or less completely understand. Our own use of the term so far has not been altogether unequivocal. We have spoken in the usual way of a 'just noticeable stimulus' or 'stimulus-difference'; and this usage may have suggested to the reader that the observer in the experiments from which these magnitudes are derived, directly determines or compares the stimuli or their differences. Really, of course, the only objects of the observer's estimation and perception are the sensations which he experiences, not the stimuli within or without his body. The phrases in question, then, must refer to the result of the observation, which is common property, not to the observer. The same holds of the expressions 'stimulus determination' and 'stimulus comparison'. We prefer not to speak of 'just noticeable sensations' or 'sensation-differences', because we do not wish to embody in the terminology of empirical measurements any particular hypothesis of the relation between the direct and indirect sensitivity or sensible discrimination. To assert the noticeability or unnoticeability of a sensation-difference would be to assume at once an incongruity between the direct and indirect sensible discrimination (cf. § 4. b). The measurement terminology in ordinary use is based simply upon the correlation of judgment and stimulus, the only links in the chain of dependency to which the objective investigator has access.

2. We distinguish stimuli as *external* and *internal* according to their place of origin. The former are physical or chemical processes outside of the observer's body, the latter corresponding processes within it. Thus, a concussion of the air which produces an auditory impression, or a weight which exerts a noticeable pressure upon the skin, would be an external stimulus. External stimuli are the peculiar instruments of experimental investigation, and the measurement methods which we have hitherto discussed employ them almost exclusively. Internal stimuli are originated, *e.g.*, by the constant processes of

metabolism, in the most different parts of the body. But as a general rule, these stimuli do not give rise to conscious phenomena, unless the nervous excitations which they set up are abnormal or especially strong. Internal stimuli are, further, occasioned by movements of the body or parts of the body: these appear to possess an extreme facility in the evocation of sensations and feelings. And lastly, nervous processes, central or peripheral, which are not directly due to some external cause, may be regarded as internal stimuli. 'Reproduced' sensations are referable to internal stimuli of this kind.

External stimuli are generically classified as *physical* and *chemical*. The former admit of subdivision into *mechanical* (pressure, impact, pull), *acoustic* (periodic and aperiodic concussions of the air), *thermal* (heat, cold), *optical* (homogeneous and mixed light), and *electric* (galvanic and faradic currents). Magnetic stimuli, as such, have no more effect on consciousness than on the organism. The process of organic stimulation which all these external stimuli initiate,— the process, that is, which precedes the arousal of a nervous excitation in a particular sense-organ, may also be either physical or chemical We, therefore, speak of mechanical and chemical senses, the former including those of pressure and hearing, the latter those of temperature, taste, smell and sight.

3. External stimuli are further divided, according as their effect is special or general, into *adequate* (homologous) and *inadequate* (heterologous) stimuli. It is characteristic of the former that they can only affect a particular sense-organ, and set up the excitatory process peculiar to it. Thus, optical stimuli are ineffectual for the production of visual sensations unless they act on the eye (retina); acoustic stimuli are ineffectual, except for the ear. Stimuli are inadequate, on the other hand, when they do not bear any such definite relation to the sense-organ. The one fact of importance underlying this classification is that 'adequate' stimuli form a continuously graded series, with which the corresponding scale of sensations can be directly compared. The entire system of visual sensations (as we shall show later) can, *e.g.*, be correlated with ether undulations; whereas pressure on the eye-ball, or galvanic stimulation of the optic nerve, though an 'inadequate' stimulus for light sensations, cannot be brought into functional relation with vision over its whole range. Each sense-organ has its own adequate stimulus; the skin, pressure and temperature; the ear, concussion of the air; the eye, rays of light: although it must be admitted that for taste and smell the adequate stimulus, which we must suppose to exist, has not as yet been defined in terms of physics or chemistry. Any other stimulus which can excite the sense-organ or

the sensory nerve will then be 'inadequate': mechanical pressure and impact for vision, electrical processes for the skin, etc. Psychophysical measurement of sensitivity and sensible discrimination presupposes, of course, the employment of adequate stimuli ;—of stimuli whose form, strength, duration and extension correspond more or less directly to the quality, intensity, duration and extension of sensation. Defined in this way, the notion of stimulus 'adequacy' is not only sufficiently unequivocal, but acquires an especial value for experimental psychology. We shall, therefore, in what follows, make almost exclusive use of adequate stimuli in reviewing the functions of the various sense-organs. How these unequivocal relations between particular stimuli and particular sensations originated,—how their origin is to be explained,—is a question which we cannot attempt to answer here.

4. The *nervous excitation*, which we have to regard as the proximate condition of a conscious process, is a process of whose objective nature, physical or chemical, we cannot give any exact description in the present state of physiology. But this very obscurity has been a powerful incentive to the investigation of its dependency upon stimulus. There is only one kind of nervous excitation which leads directly to an alteration in consciousness, and which is therefore of primary psychological importance,—that of the *sensory* nerves. The excitation of a *motor* nerve results in a movement, *i.e.*, a muscular contraction. The significance of movements is secondary for psychology: they are interesting simply as expressive of emotion, as voluntary or automatic, as internal stimuli to the sensory nerves, as objects of perception, etc.—Nerves are further classified, topographically, as *central* (running their course within the spinal cord or brain, the two 'central' nervous organs) and *peripheral* (running their course outside these, toward the periphery of the body).—It is misleading to speak of *centrifugal* and *centripetal* nerves, since no nerve has its faculty of conduction limited to a single direction. As a rule, however, the sensory nerves conduct centripetally, the motor centrifugally, as the terminus of the former is the centrally situated organ of consciousness, and that of the latter the peripherally situated organ of movement.—The principal morphological constituents of nervous substance are *nerve cells* and *nerve fibres*. The cells (nerve cells, ganglion cells, ganglia) are found almost exclusively in the central portions of the nervous system, combining with the granular matrix (itself made up of ganglionic processes and the finest branches of the nerve fibres) to form the *grey substance*. The strands of fibres in the central parts compose what from its different appearance is called the *white substance*.

5. We cannot here discuss the histological structure of the nervous

6

system. The reader may consult Wundt's *Physiol. Psychologie*, vol. i., or the standard treatises upon anatomy and physiology. We shall refer in brief to the minute structure of the sense organs, as occasion demands: but our discussion will not be intended as a substitute for anatomical and physiological study, with books or in the laboratory. And the particular facts of nervous physiology necessary in other connections to our explanation of psychological phenomena will be set forth in their proper places. For the present, we shall speak only of certain general facts or concepts which play some considerable part in the theory of mind.

First and most important of these is the *law of specific sensory energy*. It is not easy to give a precise formulation of the law. The phrase 'specific energy' originally meant what we have indicated by our distinction of adequacy and inadequacy of stimuli: the eye was the specific organ of vision, the ear of hearing, etc. But when it was discovered that the excitation of a sensory nerve aroused the sensations peculiar to the sense, in the absence of direct stimulation of the peripheral organ, the specific part of the physiological function was transferred from that to the nerves. This gave a specific energy of the optic nerve, another of the olfactory, and so on. Later, the energy was specialised still further, and a specific fibre or terminal organ assigned to each of the sensation qualities discriminable within a sense department. Thus the sensory cutaneous nerves were divided into nerves of pressure, cold, heat, and pain; the fibres of the optic nerve into red-sensitive, green-sensitive, and violet-sensitive (!). The most recent observations, however, render the specific energy of nerve fibres an altogether improbable hypothesis; and the physiology of to-day is, therefore, inclined to look for specialty of function not in the nerve, but in the peripheral or central termini of the nervous apparatus.

6. This view attempts to explain the fact that general or heterologous stimuli arouse in a nerve fibre the excitation specific to its peripheral organ, by emphasising the effect of adaptation to particular forms of excitation. The sensory nerve becomes accustomed to the function imposed upon it by its connection with peculiar terminal organs. On this theory, that is, we should not speak of a specific energy of the sensory nerve, but only of a specific function of it under given circumstances. But that phrase, again, is hardly admissible, since a nerve which is brought into different connections appears to give up its previous function at once, and to take on that which the new connections dictate. We are, therefore, compelled to regard the fibre as a perfectly indifferent conductor, capable of quite different functions, *i.e.*, of propagating or evoking quite different excitations,

according as it terminates in one organ or another. It has not inaptly been compared to a telegraph wire, which will ring a bell, move a pencil over paper, or decompose chemical substances, just as we connect it. The effect of inadequate stimulation may now be explained in one of two ways: we may suppose either that a peripheral organ is somehow directly affected,—that when we are stimulating by the electric current there is an escape of electricity towards the periphery,— or (and this is more probable) that the excitation set up in the nerve is propagated to the terminal organs. The mere fact that an inadequate stimulus is able to excite the nerve between centre and periphery, while many adequate stimuli apparently cannot do so, can hardly be urged in support of the doctrine of specific energies. For (1) we do not find in general that every physical or chemical process affects others in the same way, and, therefore, must not expect that every stimulus will necessarily set up a sensitive excitation in a nerve fibre; while (2) we cannot allow that the statement possesses anything like the universal validity to which it lays claim. It has been recently discovered, *e.g.*, that the acoustic nerve is excitable by waves of sound, after the extirpation of the peripheral organ.

7. Looked at in this way, the doctrine of specific energy is plainly no more than the regulative principle of psychophysical parallelism—which says that a peculiar physiological process corresponds to every distinguishable conscious quality—applied in a particular department. Now there is nothing in the principle which requires these peculiar processes to have separate anatomical substrates. Its formulation in particular cases will be entirely dependent upon the actual phenomena presented by consciousness and the facts of bodily organisation as ascertained by natural science. Since we are able to analyse a clang, *e.g.*, we must assume that there are special instruments of analysis to be found in the ear. But since we are unable to analyse a complex of visual qualities, we shall satisfy the demands of theory by assuming that the changes which we remark in colour-tone and brightness are occasioned by a differentiation of excitatory processes within a single anatomical organ. It would, therefore, be quite wrong to imagine that the principle of psychophysical parallelism posits a specific nerve or a specific peripheral or central organ for each individual conscious quality. The principle simply requires the correlation of peculiarities in psychical processes with peculiar properties of nervous processes; the exact determination of these latter it leaves to the necessities or discoveries of the special case.

As to the localisation of the 'specific', in its first beginnings,—of the condition of the peculiarity of a nervous process,—we can hardly be in any doubt. The latest anatomical investigations show that the sensory centres are very uniform in structure; whereas the peripheral sense organs present obvious differences, which are plainly of importance for the differences in the conscious processes which they mediate. If we continue to speak of specific energies, we must consequently localise them in the peripheral sense organs. Look at the two higher senses, and see how admirably the structure of the eye is adapted to its spatial duty, and the structure of the ear to its qualitative function! The specific significance of the external organs is also evidenced by the fact, that their removal absolutely prevents the appearance of sensible qualities in consciousness, while extirpation of the corresponding central organs may to a certain extent be compensated by the activity of others.

8. We are, therefore, justified in supposing that the nerve fibres and their central terminations are physiologically indifferent structures, capable of the most diverse functions; and that their specific character is imposed upon them from without. In other words, the excitations of the central organ are functions not intrinsically localised, but altogether dependent upon internal or external stimulation. But it is sufficiently clear that their connections must give them a definite form; and that practice, the repetition of the same function, must bring about a predisposition, more or less strong, to the performance of that function. This explains the large measure of success that has crowned the attempts of physiologists to determine the particular cortical areas with which the sensations of the various senses and the different motor impulses are correlated. Such an area, or *localisation centre*, is not to be regarded as the inevitable substrate of a class of sensations or of a sensation quality, on the same plane with the peripheral organ, but only as a condition of its appearance which has acquired importance in consequence of the accustomedness of certain connections. An illustration is afforded by right-handed writing; the right hand may be considered as a localised complex of conditions, but is not the inevitable substrate of the movements subserving penmanship.

We shall, then, in what follows, briefly indicate the cortical local-isation centres of the various conscious functions. But we shall make no reference to the particular paths of conduction, since a knowledge of the nuclei with which a sensory nerve is connected within the brain is psychologically unnecessary, however interesting from the stand-point of anatomy and physiology.

9. There is, however, one recent discovery of which mention must be made, as it seems to throw light upon many points of diffi-culty in the theory of sensation,—the discovery of sensory nerve

fibres with centrifugal conduction. These have been carefully examined in the case of the optic nerve, and may be presumed to exist in all the sensory nerve trunks. Side by side with the sensory fibres, in the usual meaning of the term, which take their origin in the peripheral organ and terminate in the brain, there will then be another set of sensory fibres, originating in the brain and ending in the sense-organ. This fact helps to explain (1) the effect of inadequate stimulation upon the nerve stem. We may suppose that the excitation is propagated along centrifugally conducting fibres to the periphery, and at that point makes itself known in consciousness by the ordinary channels. At the same time there is no difficulty in the alternative hypothesis, that the accustomed excitation is directly set up in the centripetal fibres. (2) The phenomena of after-sensation, which have only lately become known to us in detail, may also be brought into connection with this anatomical discovery. It has been found, *e.g.*, that an exclusively monocular stimulation gives rise to a sensation in the unstimulated eye. This suggests the existence of a kind of sensory reflex-arc in an optical brain centre. (3) It has been noticed, in almost all the sense departments, that a brief stimulation of the peripheral organ gives (*a*) a 'primary' sensation, (*b*) then a short pause, occupying a fraction of a second, and (*c*) finally, a 'secondary' sensation, of the same quality as the other. The succession becomes readily intelligible, if we conceive of the first, centripetal excitation, as arousing a second, centrifugal. We have no need of the special hypothesis proposed for the sense of pressure, and mentioned below (§ 10. 7). (4) Lastly, we may imagine that the 'centrally excited' sensations,—memorial images, as they have also been very inappropriately named—are at least in many instances correlated with a co-excitation of the peripheral organs. We thus have a comparatively simple explanation of the fact that in certain cases these sensations may take on the character of peripherally excited mental processes (cf. hallucinations and illusions).

10. The nervous excitation is not exclusively dependent upon the stimulus, but also upon the nature of the nervous substance itself. We speak in this connection of the *excitability* of nerves, and of their peripheral and central organs. A high degree of excitability denotes a quick and ready reaction upon stimulation; a low degree, slowness and difficulty of reaction. These differences of excitability are partly individual, and so (apart from definite pathological disturbances) inexplicable in the present state of our knowledge; partly the result of the variation of certain conditions. Thus we are familiar with the influence upon excitability exerted by age, surroundings, mode of life,

and period of the day. Any extended psychological investigation should, therefore, be carried out at the same daily hour, with individuals of regular habits of life, and in the same surroundings. Again, excitability depends upon the character of the stimuli which affect the nervous substance. Physiology teaches us that as a general rule weak stimuli increase and strong stimuli decrease excitability; while a diminution is also brought about by long duration and frequent repetition of stimulation. To secure the greatest possible uniformity of nervous disposition, therefore, the relations of intensity and duration of stimulus must be carefully adjusted.—Many psychological phenomena might be called upon to illustrate these statements, as, *e.g.*, the time error in the comparison of successive stimuli (§ 6. 9, § 31. 5), the affective results of stimulation, etc.

A. PERIPHERALLY EXCITED SENSATIONS.

CHAPTER II. THE QUALITY OF SENSATION.

(1) The Quality of Cutaneous Sensations.

§ 10. The Sensation of Pressure.

1. By peripherally excited cutaneous sensations we understand sensations produced by stimulation of the sensory nerves which terminate in the skin. Our every-day experience tells us that these sensations are of three kinds—sensations of *heat*, *cold*, and *pressure*. The object of their scientific examination is to discover (1) whether they are the only qualities correlated with stimulation of the cutaneous nerves, and (2) in what relation they stand to one another and to physiological processes: or, in other words, (1) what is the course of the qualitative sensitivity and sensible discrimination in the sphere of cutaneous sensation, and (2) what are the principal conditions of the results which they furnish. By 'qualitative sensitivity' we mean, of course, only the modal sensitivity; since the qualitative stimulus limen coincides in cutaneous sensation with the intensive (or extensive and temporal), and therefore sensibility cannot be dealt with till we come to the chapter on Intensity of Sensation. And our investigation of sensible discrimination need be only of a quite simple nature, cutaneous sensation apparently presenting a very limited number of qualitative differences.

Of the special literature of cutaneous sensation we may mention the following works:

E.H.Weber, *Der Tastsinn und das Gemeingefühl.* Wagner's *Handwörterb. der Physiol.*, III., Pt. 2, pp. 481 ff.

O.Funke and E.Hering, *Tastsinn und das Gemeingefühl; Temperatursinn.* Hermann's *Handbuch d. Physiol.*, III., Pt. 2, pp. 289 ff.

M.Blix, *Experimentelle Beiträge zur Lösung der Frage über die specifische Energie der Hautnerven. Zeitschr. f. Biologie*, XX., pp. 141 ff.; XXI., pp. 145 ff.

A.Goldscheider, *Neue Thatsachen über die Hautsinnesnerven. Arch. f. Anat. u. Physiol.*, 1885. *Physiol. Abth. Supplementbd.*, pp. 1 ff.

M.Dessoir, *Ueber den Hautsinn. Arch. f. Anat. u. Physiol.*, 1892. *Physiol. Abth.*, pp. 175 ff.

2. That pressure sensations are evoked by the contact of foreign bodies with the skin, and temperature sensations by its heating or cooling, everyone will agree. But it is a matter of dispute, whether we can distinguish differences of quality, within the category of 'pressure.' Certain observers have enumerated, as qualities of cutaneous sensation, sensations of touch, contact, tickling and itching, besides those of pressure proper, heat and cold. In discussing such a view, we must apply two criteria: (1) that of the simplicity of the conscious process denominated 'sensation', and (2) that of accuracy (freedom from extraneous suggestive influences) of sensitivity and sensible discrimination.

(*a*) The distinction of sensations of contact and pressure is based upon two observations: that contact is not referred by the subject to excitation by external stimuli, whereas pressure conveys to him the idea of his affection by some external object; and that gentle contact leaves the sensitive organ wholly passive, whereas pressure occasions a certain resistance, a certain degree of tension in the muscles subjected to it. Now the first argument forsakes the direct report of sensible discrimination, and seeks to establish the difference by emphasising points which are wholly irrelevant. It therefore proves nothing. That a sensation serves as the symbol, or brings us knowledge, of external stimuli, may be due to its intensity, duration, etc., just as well as to its quality. Nor is the second observation in any better case. That a strong pressure excites with conscious effect the sensory nerves in the deeper-lying organs, muscles or tendons, as well as the nerves of the skin, does not make any difference in the cutaneous sensation, but simply combines it with muscular or tendinous sensations into a complex, the separate qualities of which are, it is true, sufficiently difficult to analyse.   •

3. The same objections may be urged against the other apparently distinguishable qualities. (*b*) We speak of sensations of touch, when the organ which receives the stimulus, *e.g.*, the hand, moves towards or over the object; *i.e.*, when the application of the stimulus is to some extent active or voluntary. There is then a combination of pressure sensations with the sensations evoked by movement—sensations of muscular contraction, tendinous strain and articular friction. It is again not easy to analyse the complex into its elements, and we are accustomed to judge of it as a whole. But the pressure sensation involved does not undergo qualitative change.—The principal judgments of touch are 'hard', 'soft', 'rough', and 'smooth'. These include a

reference not only to pressure and to the sensations occasioned by movement, but to temporal and spatial relations and attributes of these sensations, which we cannot now discuss.

Similarly, the 'sensation of double contact', which arises when a movable object (stick or pencil) is thrust or pressed by the touching hand against a second object, or passed over its surface, is merely a complex of qualities: the pressure of the stick and the resistance of the object touched excite the organs of movement at the same time with the skin.

We find the same explanation to hold of (c) tickling and (d) itching. They contain no new sensation, above and beyond the qualities of pressure and temperature, but consist in a combination of these, characterised by rapid alternation of contents or of intensities of contents.

Moreover, a thorough examination of the surface of the skin by means of a needle or horse-hair gives no other result than the determination of points more or less sensitive to pressure, cold and heat. The points of peculiar sensitivity to contact have been named *pressure spots*. Weakly stimulated, they give rise to a delicate sensation, often accompanied by tickling; strongly affected, to a 'granular' sensation. Tickling appears to be due to a diffusion of stimulation, and the consequent production of concomitant sensations. The sensation aroused at points of the cutaneous surface which are not specially sensitive to pressure is dull and indefinite. So that direct experimental investigation gives no support to the view that pressure sensations present really qualitative differences.

4. But there is a further point. (e) Our sensible discrimination enables us to localise cutaneous impressions with a considerable degree of accuracy, although we have no outside knowledge of the place at which they originate. Thus at the tip of the finger we can cognise the spatial separateness of two impressions, if the stimuli which produce them are no more than 1 mm. apart. It is tempting to refer this accuracy of localisation to qualitative differences within the scale of pressure sensations. There would be no need to assume that these differences increased with the distance of cutaneous areas from one another; it would be sufficient for the hypothesis if every cognisable local difference corresponded to a difference of quality. An approximate calculation of the number of distinct pressure sensations which this view renders necessary gives 1100 for the head alone, and at least six times that amount for the whole body. But if we try to abstract, as far as possible, from the local value of the impressions which affect different parts of our skin, we seem to find nothing like

a really qualitative difference in the sensations. We should surely expect, if all the many local differences depend upon qualitative peculiarities, that some sort of clear gradations would be discoverable within the system of pressure sensations. As this is not the case, we must refer localisation to other conditions, and accept the qualitative simplicity of sensations of pressure. Further evidence is afforded by the localisability of impressions of temperature (produced by radiant heat, without contact). No one would ascribe to our sensations of heat and cold a number of specific qualities, corresponding to their cognisable space differences.

Finally, (*f*) *pain* has been held to be a special quality of cutaneous sensation, and pain nerves put alongside of the nerves subserving heat, cold, and pressure. The hypothesis has found its chief support among physiologists. We cannot accept it, as it stands: for pain is produced in all cases where the stimulation of a sensory nerve passes a certain limit of intensity. At the same time, pain may, perhaps, be regarded as a general quality of sensation, distinct from the specific qualities which are always involved in it (whether as intense heat or excessive pressure or grating tone or blinding light), and from the unpleasant feeling with which it is combined. The qualities which cutaneous pain contains, besides that of pressure, are therefore, a specific feeling and a general sensation quality, which may be originated by the excitation of any sensory nerve (cf. § 36. 4).

5. We conclude, then, that in all probability the name 'pressure sensation' denotes a single sensation quality. We have now to raise the question of the *place* of its peripheral origination. It may be laid down in general that both the external skin and the 'skin', as it is ordinarily called, which lines the internal passages of the body can mediate pressure sensations. But whether this skin can function as a sense organ over its whole extent must be left undecided. Some observers have asserted that the cold and heat spots are not sensitive to pressure and contact, and that certain parts in the interior of the body are incapable of pressure sensation. But the truth contained in these views appears rather to be that sensibility to pressure suffers marked diminution at certain places. Pressure excitations can be set up at any point of the skin, provided only that the stimuli are strong enough. Of course, there is the possibility that the stimulation extends, until it involves sensitive parts.—No single proposition of universal validity can be formulated, for the reason that the nature of the skin itself differs appreciably from point to point, and its nerve supply, the thickness of the epidermis, and other circumstances, may shift the limen of pressure sensations very considerably.

An observation which has been quite recently made deserves mention here. It has been found that after brief contact, *after sensations* make their appearance. They are separated from the primary pressure sensation by a blank interval, just as are the after-images with which we have long been familiar in the sense of sight. They can be best obtained from a gentle tap with the point of a needle, and seem to move in the opposite direction to the primary sensation, welling up from within. If the stimulus is electrical, the break-shock of an induction coil, they do not occur unless at least two shocks have been given in quick succession.

6. A *theory* of pressure sensation must state the special conditions, upon which the appearance of the quality of pressure in consciousness is dependent. These conditions must necessarily be sought in specific bodily dispositions and functions: since (1) it is impossible to derive the individual fact of a particular sensation quality from a definition of mind, or from general faculties and dispositions ascribed to it, and (2) the adequate mechanical stimuli are by no means the sole factors in the origination of pressure sensations. We may look for the excitations which are functionally related to these either in a peripheral organ and the nerves connected with it or in a central organ. Sensations have been obtained by direct electrical stimulation of cutaneous nerves as well as by stimulation of the external skin. It would seem, therefore, that the nerve concerned in their production is only capable of the single reaction to which its connection with definite terminal organs has accustomed it. These organs, then, are the most essential constituents in the complex of bodily conditions forming the substrate of the quality of pressure.

The skin consists of two layers, the *epidermis* above and the *cutis* below. The former is divided into the *stratum corneum* and the *stratum Malpighii*, the latter into the *corium* and the *subcutaneous connective tissue*. The corium is the part most richly supplied with nerves. It is probable that fine nervous processes penetrate into the epidermis. The nerve endings are partly free, *i.e.*, composed of very fine fibrils, partly enclosed in special cells. These latter have various forms, and are classified as the touch cells of Merkel, the touch corpuscles of Meissner, the end bulbs of Krause, and the corpuscles of Vater and Pacini. The thickness of the epidermis varies between 0·03 and 3·75 mm.

7. The anatomical facts suggest a relation between pressure sensation and some one of these kinds of nervous termination. It was formerly thought that the free endings were only sensitive to general nervous stimulation, while the specific terminal organs were reserved

for the effects of pressure and temperature. But such a view is negatived (1) by the fact that the corpuscles of Pacini, touch corpuscles and end bulbs have a much more limited range of distribution than the cutaneous sensations; (2) by the observation that the cornea, which is sensitive to pressure and temperature, contains only free nerve endings; and (3) by the result of a direct comparison of cold, heat, and pressure spots with the nervous structures underlying them, which showed that they bear no uniform relation to the terminal organs in question. The corpuscles appear, therefore, to have no definite reference to the quality of sensation, but to be intended either for the protection of the nerves or for the more accurate distribution and isolation of stimulation. On the other hand, Goldscheider believes that he has discovered a difference in the character of the nervous terminations underlying pressure spots and temperature spots respectively. In the former case, the fibrils are spread over a larger cutaneous area, innervating a relatively extensive portion of the corium. It may be that this plate of interlacing fibres is the specific substrate of the perception of pressure.

The sensory nerves of the skin pass into the posterior columns of the spinal cord, and there ascend in the white masses by a fairly direct path to the cerebral cortex, which they reach in the neighbourhood of the central convolutions. A certain proportion of their fibres, however, enters the gray substance of the cord, where the origination and propagation of an excitatory process is in general slower and more difficult. This fact has been used to explain the appearance of the after sensation. The excitation of the gray substance gives rise to a second sensation, but the relations of excitability and conduction obtaining there are such as to defer its appearance until a noticeable interval has elapsed after the passing of the primary sensation, mediated by the white substance. (Cf., however, § 9. 9.)

§ 11. Sensations of Temperature.

1. Temperature sensations differ from pressure sensations, which we have found to possess but a single quality in consciousness, in including a duality of qualities, *heat* and *cold*. We need make no detailed inquiry as to whether these are the only forms of temperature sensation possible, since the fact is universally admitted. And there is equal . agreement with regard to the general designation of the stimulus adequate to the sensitive organ. All bodies which give out or take up heat in the physical sense, in other words, all thermal stimuli, are adequate to the excitation of sensations of heat or cold,

whether by way of direct contact or (as in the case of radiant heat) of operation from a distance. But difficulties arise when we come to ask for the special conditions of sensations of heat and cold. A simple increase or diminution of temperature can change either sensation into its opposite, the path of change lying through a *point of indifference* or *zero point.* (There is no analogy to this fact in the sphere of sensation, though there is a very complete one in that of feeling.) Any temperature above this zero point will thus be a heat stimulus, any temperature below it a cold stimulus; and the determination of the zero point is, consequently, the first step towards the definition of particular adequate stimuli. The physics of heat speaks of an absolute zero point (the temperature at which the tension of gases = o) and of a conventional zero point, established in reference to a particular substance (the temperature at which water freezes). Neither of them has anything to do with the point of indifference between sensations of cold and heat. We shall, therefore, speak of this indifferent temperature as the *physiological zero point,* to distinguish it from the limiting values employed in physics.

2. Our most obvious course would now be to take as our physiological zero point the neutral normal temperature of the nerve endings which mediate thermal sensation, and to regard every increase of this normal temperature as a heat stimulus and every decrease of it as a cold stimulus. But, apart from (1) the difficulty of a direct determination, we have to remember that (2) the epidermis, a poor conductor of heat, intervenes between the external source of heat or cold and the terminal nervous apparatus, and that its normal temperature, which is variable, is algebraically added to that of the stimulus. Then, again, (3) it is a familiar experience that the point of indifference between sensations of cold and heat depends upon the present temperature of the skin; or, in other words, that the neutral normal temperature of the nerve ending is capable of adaptation, within wide limits, to the superficial temperature. And (4) it is questionable whether the thermal stimuli as such give rise to the corresponding nervous excitation, or whether the stimulation process proper is not rather to be looked for in the mechanical effects which warming or cooling of the skin produces upon the nervous apparatus. Taking all this into consideration, we shall probably do best to make the neutrally sensed, normal temperature of the skin our physiological zero point. It will average about 34° C. Increase of this normal cutaneous temperature is sensed as heat, decrease as cold. Each sensation can be obtained in two ways; by increase (diminution) of the heat supply, or by inhibition (facilitation) of the output of heat.

3. Temperature sensations, like pressure sensations, cannot be excited in the same degree at all points of the skin. Thus there appears, as a rule, to be no direct sensation of cold or heat producible by direct stimulation of the mucous membrane throughout the œsophagus and downwards to the excretory passages. Temperature sensations which we localise in the interior of the body must be regarded as due to a change of temperature propagated from within to the external skin. Nor is that uniformly sensitive. A careful examination of those portions of it which are accessible to experimentation has led to the discovery of points particularly sensitive to cold and heat, as well as to pressure. They can be found not only by thermal stimulation (hollow metal cylinders, pointed at one end, filled with a liquid of the required temperature); but by electrical (weak induction current) and mechanical (pointed piece of cork) as well. Blix and Goldscheider, accordingly, speak of *heat* and *cold spots*, and regard them as the peculiar terminal organs of the temperature sense, and as independent of the pressure spots. The heat spots, in their opinion, are locally distinct from the cold spots. No cold sensation can be produced in the former, no heat sensation in the latter. These observations, however, were not confirmed by Dessoir, and are theoretically so improbable that we may decline to accept them. It is difficult to know what to think of a cold spot, which when affected by a thermally indifferent mechanical stimulus mediated a noticeable sensation of cold, and when carefully touched with a point of heated graphite gave a vivid sensation of heat. The familiar fact of the adaptation of the nerve to the momentary normal temperature of the skin can hardly be brought into harmony with the existence of special apparatus for the two qualities of the temperature sense. It is, therefore, quite possible,—indeed, it seems to be shown by pathological observations,—that the sensations of pressure and temperature are dependent on different nervous organs; but it is probable that the sensations of cold and heat are referable to different forms of the excitatory process within one and the same nerve.

4. Not much can be said at present of the anatomical substrate of temperature sensations. There is no proof that any of the four forms of the terminal organs of the cutaneous sensory nerves (§ 10. 6) has as its specific function the taking up of thermal stimuli. Goldscheider's histological examination of fragments of skin upon which cold, heat, and pressure spots had been determined, led him to declare that a characteristic difference obtained between the nerve ending beneath a pressure spot and the nerve ending beneath a temperature spot (§ 10. 7), but did not indicate the existence of any difference

between the cold terminations and heat terminations assumed by his theory. This is noteworthy. Dessoir attempts to show that the 'free' nerve endings are the specific organ of temperature sensations. It is certainly not without significance that the compact bundles of nerve fibres beneath cold and heat spots are found in the immediate neighbourhood of blood vessels.

Not much is known, again, of the further course of the nerves which conduct thermal excitation, towards the centre. They probably ascend to the brain, like the pressure nerves, through the posterior columns of the spinal cord. The cortical centre, which was formerly thought to be in the gyrus fornicatus, is now placed in the gyrus sigmoideus.

After sensations of heat have been observed, of a kind similar to those of pressure. The blank interval between primary and secondary sensation amounted to about 1 sec. It is, therefore, conjectured that the thermal excitation also undergoes dispersion into the gray substance of the cord (§ 10. 7), and that there summation and retardation of stimulation take place.

5. Presupposing that a single nervous organ serves for heat and cold sensations alike, we may entertain various ideas as to the excitatory process within it. According to Hering's theory of the temperature sense, two opposed processes, assimilation and dissimilation, run their course in the sensitive nervous substance. If they are in equilibrium, they cancel one another: but the preponderance of one or the other means the appearance in consciousness of a definite sensation. The sensation of cold corresponds to assimilation, which is produced by the sinking of the neutral normal temperature of the skin; that of heat to dissimilation, produced by the rising of this temperature. As Hering has assumed the existence of antagonistic nervous processes in other nervous structures, *e.g.*, the visual substance, he should evidently have mentioned the specific characteristics, which explain their present function for temperature sensations. At the same time, the general idea fits in most easily to a theory of temperature,—since temperature sensations do pass into each other through a point of indifference, and do cancel one another to a certain extent. Their analogy with the feelings (§ 11. 1) explains how it is that the same idea recurs in connection with affective theory (§ 41. 4).

Passing over general hypotheses of this nature, we may suppose that the rise or fall of the cutaneous temperature produces a contraction or expansion of the terminal nervous apparatus, and so sets up an excitatory process, which corresponds to the sensation of heat or cold. On this view, there would be nothing surprising in the occurrence of separate heat and cold spots, since the different character of the tissue in different parts might be expected to offer mechanical conditions favourable sometimes to heat and sometimes to cold. Any attempt at further detail in this connection would lead us into idle conjecture.

The physiology of the sense-organs usually attributes to the skin, besides the senses of pressure and temperature, those of space, locality and touch; and tends to regard pain (which it designates a common feeling, § 3. 5) as essentially a cutaneous quality. We must enter a protest, in the interests of clearness and logical consistency, against this extension of the meaning of the word 'sense'. The cognition of spatial relations is not the exclusive privilege of the skin;—we estimate extent and distance, we perceive form and locality, by the aid of eye and movement of our limbs, to say nothing of sensations of smell and hearing. The term 'sense', as ordinarily understood, and as used in psychophysics, can be employed only to cover the system of sensations correlated with a definite organ. As the sensations of pressure and temperature cannot, in the present state of our knowledge, be referred to special organs, it is best to speak of the 'cutaneous sense' in general, as inclusive of both classes of sensations. Dessoir's proposed terminology sets up a haptics alongside of the temperature sense, and distinguishes within it a sense of contact and a sense of touch (pselaphesia). Here is displayed the tendency, which we previously condemned (§ 4. 10), to name sensations in accordance with the external processes of which they are the symbols, or from their physical conditions. The only unequivocal principle of nomenclature is that based on the reference to the peripheral organ.

(2) The Quality of the Sensations of Taste and Smell.

§ 12. The Qualities of Taste.

I. The mucous membrane which lines the cavity of the mouth, and the upper surface of the tongue are not only adequately excitable by pressure and temperature stimuli, but contain organs for the mediation of sensations of an entirely new order—sensations of taste. In popular parlance we call all the sensations that are produced in the mouth 'tastes', and speak of a 'hot' or 'pungent' taste as we do of a 'sweet' or 'salt' flavour. And since there is such an intimate local connection between sensations of smell and the sensations of the buccal cavity, and both may be excited by the same stimuli, we are apt to attribute to gustation the far more numerous qualities of olfaction; we talk in conversation of the 'taste' of fish or wine, and declare that we can 'taste' nothing, when the olfactory mucous membrane has been rendered anæsthetic by an inflammation. Even in chemistry and mineralogy, in which a statement of the gustatory properties of substances forms part of their scientific description, it is not infrequent to find this confusion of the functions of different sense-organs.

The first problem which psychology has to solve, therefore, is that of the qualities of taste proper. Since this problem was formulated, there has been a steady reduction in their number. Linnæus distinguished ten, later observers six, while there is general agreement at the present time that four are all that can be claimed : *sweet*, *bit-ter*, *acid* and *salt*. There are, however, some psychologists who would add *alkaline* and *metallic* to the list.

2. There are two principal methods for the determination of modal sensitivity, which we may term in brief the *physical* and the *physiol-ogical*. The physical method consists in the running through the whole scale of adequate stimuli, and accurate observation of the parallel alterations in conscious quality. In the senses of sight and hearing it has led to a relatively exact determination of the number of possible sensation qualities. Unfortunately, it has so far proved altogether inapplicable to the senses of taste and smell, for the reason that we cannot define stimulus adequacy for either sense-organ. We are ignorant of the physical and chemical basis of taste; and when we speak of a substance as 'sweet' or 'bitter', we simply state the fact that its effect upon the organ of taste is to arouse that sensation, not denoting by the adjective a property capable of objective definition, independently of the sense-organ, like that of weight or heat. All that we know at present of the objective nature of gustatory substances is that they must be in a fluid condition, to produce an effect upon the sensitive surface. But there is no definite relation between degree of solubility and gustatory value. Solubility would seem to be merely a mechanical condition of the occurrence of a taste excitation, the nervous structures being set very deeply in the tissues. Not every fluid or soluble substance can excite gustation; while two substances of very different chemical constitution, like cane sugar $[C_{12} H_{22} O_{11}]$ and lead acetate $[Pb (C_2 H_3 O_4)^2]$, may give precisely the same taste.

3. More has been done for taste by the physiological method, though much still remains to be done. The method has two forms. It consists (1) in the examination of the entire sense-organ by means of delicate and cleanly cut stimuli. Such an examination is only possible for certain organs. As applied to the skin, the method has led to the discovery of pressure and temperature spots. In the domain of taste, it has shown that differences of perceptive power exist as between the various parts of the tongue and buccal cavity, and has enabled us to map out the areas excitable by taste. No nervous organ, however, has as yet been found, which serves ex-clusively for the mediation of one particular taste. (2) In its alternative

form the method consists in the excitation of the nerves by general, inadequate stimuli. A gentle mechanical pressure on the root of the tongue will arouse the sensation of bitter, while electrical stimulation gives rise to acid and alkaline tastes,—probably simply in consequence of the electrolytic decomposition of the saliva. Recently, however, the induction current has been reported as exciting sweet and bitter also. Neither of the physiological methods has been able to furnish us with a complete list of all the possible taste qualities.

My own observations lead me to think that there are only four gustatory qualities. If I apply a metallic or alkaline substance to my tongue, I never obtain anything more than a salt or acid flavour—apart, of course, from sensations of temperature and of different degrees of pressure. I should refer the astringency of a 'taste' to these latter.—No investigator has been able to discover a variety of qualities within any of the four principal categories. A very large number of experiments has been made, always with negative result. As different sweet, bitter, acid and salt substances were applied, the sensation either remained unchanged, or, if it altered, did so only in respect of taste intensity or the cutaneous and olfactory elements involved in it.

4. There is no indication of a continuous transition between the four qualities which tastes appear to present, as there is between the qualities of tone sensations. They form, not a one-dimensional manifold, but a discrete system of unknown relations. Ordinary language, it is true, opposes sweet to the other three qualities, but evidently only for the reason that sweet is pleasant, even at a considerable intensity, while the rest (and especially bitter) become unpleasant when they have reached a very moderate degree of strength. Relations of contrast, however, appear to be made out. The effect of an acid is enhanced by a previous sweet; and if salt and sweet are simultaneously applied to different parts of the tongue, each sensation is noticeably strengthened by the other. On the other hand, if two substances of different flavour are mixed, and the mixture tasted, the discrimination of the two original qualities, though possible, is not so easy as if they affected different parts of the tongue at one time or the same part in succession. Such experiences are not as convincing as they would be if the possibility of chemical change in the gustatory substances were excluded. Still, they may be allowed to modify our original statement, that the directions of relation within the system of tastes are unknown, to some extent: we may suppose that the four sensations do not come and go in complete independence of one another, but that there is some sort of connection between them, or rather, between their physiological substrates. These facts, however, rightly belong in the second main chapter of psychol-

ogy, which deals with the connections of the conscious elements.

5. The parts of the buccal cavity sensitive to taste are the tongue, the hard and soft palate, the uvula, and the palatal arches. Not all of these are sensitive in all cases, and not all that are sensitive in an individual case are equally so. On the whole, the most sensitive part seems to be the root of the tongue. It is an every day experience that if we wish to bring out the full taste of a substance, we take it back to the root of the tongue, and execute certain movements which place it in contact with the greatest possible number of the nerve endings there situated. The tip of the tongue is for many persons almost exclusively excitable by sweet, and altogether insensitive to bitter. The middle of the tongue is wholly irresponsive to gustatory stimuli. The edges are only sensitive in certain cases. The statements made in the literature as to the sensitivity of median surface and edge are extremely conflicting.

It seems that certain substances can destroy our sensitivity for particular excitations of taste. Thus a solution of cocaine hydrochlorate inhibits the sensation of bitter, while leaving sweet and salt intact; and *gymnema silvestre* inhibits sweet in the same way.

Nausea, which was formerly looked upon as a gustatory sensation, is probably an unpleasantness arising in connection with muscular sensations, which precedes vomiting and is especially noticeable when there is a tendency to the vomiting movements. It has been found that an antiperistaltic reflex movement is necessary for the appearance of nausea, so that it can only be caused by stimuli which excite that reflex. Such would be the mere idea of unpalatable food, an unpleasant taste, or a simple mechanical pressure upon the root of the tongue. Any one of these can arouse the sensation of nausea. If, however, the unpleasant stimulus is removed by swallowing, there is no nausea. It cannot, therefore, be a quality of taste.

6. A *theory* of the qualities distinguishable within the sense of taste must in its turn begin with the consideration of anatomical and physiological facts. The terminal organs of the nerve of taste (the glossopharyngeal and the chorda tympani of the facial) are the taste buds or taste beakers, structures consisting of cover cells and taste cells proper. These organs lie in peculiar folds of the mucous membrane, the circumvallate, fungiform, and foliate papillæ. The former are confined to the posterior portion of the surface of the tongue, the other two occur both at the tip and on the edges. Taste beakers have also been found in the soft palate, the larynx, and the vocal chords. Their distribution accords tolerably well, therefore, with the results of experimental determination of the sensitive parts of the buccal

cavity. It is doubtful whether the taste cells possess a specific sensitivity to particular qualities; their small size and close packing render experimentation exceedingly difficult. Oehrwall stimulated his own fungiform papillæ separately, by the aid of delicate pencils, and states that all proved to be sensitive to pressure, heat, and cold, but that some showed a taste reaction only to certain stimuli.

We cannot decide at present for or against the hypothesis of special terminal apparatus for sweet, bitter, acid, and salt. The contrast phenomena mentioned above do not favour it. In any event, we must assume that the excitations underlying these qualities have physiological differences,—although we are unable, as things are, to say wherein these differences consist, or what is the actual course of the process of stimulation.

The central organ for excitations of taste was formerly placed in the gyrus hippocampi and the gyrus uncinatus. Recently it has been transferred to the neighbourhood of the coronal suture, on the convex surface of the longitudinal fissure.

Literature:—

M. von Vintschgau, *Physiologie des Geschmackssinnes*. Hermann's *Handb. d. Physiologie*, III., *Abth.* 2, pp. 145 ff.

H. Oehrwall, *Untersuchungen über den Geschmackssinn. Skandinav. Arch. f. Physiol.*, II., pp. 1 ff.

§ 13. The Qualities of Smell.

1. The organ of smell is situated in the upper portion of the nasal cavity. Important as the sense is—it has been termed the guardian of respiration, and it certainly shares with the sense of taste the wardship of digestion—we have but little positive knowledge of its functions. Gustatory qualities are so few that they can be determined even without the aid of a scale of adequate stimuli: but the qualities of smell are so numerous that a similar lack of guidance has hitherto prevented us from ascertaining their number and interconnection. Psychology can hardly go beyond the experience of every day life, which gives to the qualities of smell the names of the substances that occasion them. It is significant that language, which distinguishes sweet and acid, hot and cold, heavy and light, white and red, has no special names for odours, but uses descriptive terms,— the fragrance of the rose, the scent of the violet, the perfume of the carnation, etc. Smell is, in this respect, analogous to hearing, and Jean Paul has somewhere spoken of a 'harpsichord of scents'. It seems that the particular qualities of olfactory sensation are not correlated

with groups of different substances or bodies, but stand in a specific relation to their sources; so that the fragrance of the rose, *e.g.*, can be obtained only from the rose, and not from anything else. Here again, we have an analogy with auditory sensation, and the peculiar relation existing between clang colour and the particular source of sound. In the case of smell we have no explanation of the phenomenon to offer. The division of olfactory qualities into agreeable and disagreeable smells merely indicates their close connection with the feelings of pleasantness and unpleasantness.

2. It was thought until recently that only gaseous substances could serve as stimuli to the sense of smell. This opinion was based upon a single experiment, originally made by E. H. Weber and but a few times repeated. Weber poured into his nose a mixture of water and eau-de-cologne (in the proportion of 11 : 1), and found that a sensation of smell occurred only in the first moment, before the liquid had reached the olfactory membrane. Aronsohn, some forty years later, discovered that the whole experience was so unpleasant, and the blunting of the sense of smell so lasting, that it was impossible to say whether the liquid after contact was smelled or not. But by considerably reducing the concentration of the mixture, and using an indifferent salt solution of 0·73 p.c. to dilute the olfactory substances, Aronsohn obtained, at a temperature of 40⁰ C., distinct sensations of smell in himself and others during the contact of the liquid with the sensitive surface. However, results arrived at in this unusual and uncomfortable way are less reliable (in the author's observation) than those gained in the ordinary manner by inspiration, while they also indicate a decreased sensitivity of the organ. We are, therefore, no better off than before as regards the nature of the olfactory process. Aronsohn further attempted to classify smells by the aid of a special form of the physiological method. He found that our sensitivity to certain substances can be blunted, while others are still able to excite sensation. But the lack of objective guidance naturally prevented him from turning this interesting phenomenon to its full account.

3. We can at present, then, say nothing definite of the number and order of the olfactory qualities. It is probable (from the author's observations) that continuous transitions exist between them : at least, the ethereal oils have been arranged in series the terms of which are very similar. It seems, too, that no chemical element can excite smell. Electrical stimulation of the sense-organ has lately been found effective ; whether mechanical stimuli can excite an olfactory sensation is doubtful.

The theory of olfactory qualities is correspondingly incomplete. The upper portion of the nasal cavity is lined by the olfactory mucous membrane, characterised by a special thickness and a brownish colour. In it are distributed the terminations of the olfactory nerve, the first cerebral nerve. Physiologists distinguish between supporting cells and smell cells proper, and conjecture that both forms are connected with the terminal fibrils ot the nerve. Nothing is known of the character o. the excitation or of a specific reaction of particular cells to particular qualities. The cortical centre is placed in the gyrus hippocampi.

Literature :

M. von Vintschgau, *Physiologie des Geruchssinnes.* Hermann's *Handbuch der Physiologie,* III., *Abth.* 2, pp. 225 ff.

E. Aronsohn, *Experimentelle Untersuchungen zur Physiologie des Geruchs.* Du Bois-Reymond's *Arch. f. Physiologie,* 1886, pp. 321 ff.

(3) The Quality of Auditory Sensations.

§ 14. Auditory Stimulus and Auditory Quality.

1. Hearing is, after vision, the richest and most important of all the senses. It plays the largest part in our daily intercourse with one another, and forms the almost exclusive condition of one great department of artistic activity,—music. But the sounds employed by speech and music are of a complex kind; and we must, as psychologists, seek to determine the elementary qualities, thus variously combined to satisfy some of the supreme interests and necessities of our lives. We are assisted in this endeavour by the customary and popular classification of auditory impressions into *musical chords* and *noises,* which at once suggests the existence of two corresponding classes of simple qualities. The suggestion is borne out by the facts of physical acoustics. They show that *sound,* the objective cause of auditory sensation, may appear in the form of a *periodic* or an *aperiodic* concussion of the air; and that a compound periodic concussion,—the peculiar cause of a musical chord or clang,—can always be analysed into a number of simple periodic movements, bearing a definite numerical relation to one another. The stimulus of the sensation complex given in a noise is an aperiodic concussion of the air, analysable either as a highly complicated combination, or as an irregular alternation of simple movements. It does not follow from this, of course, that the elementary qualities must be different in the two cases, and, as a matter of fact, it has been maintained that every noise, like every clang, is capable of resolution into tones. But a

tone invariably passes into a noise, if the duration of the stimulus which occasions it is reduced to a certain minimum. We may accordingly divide the elementary qualities of audition into two groups, the first of which embraces *tones*, and the second *simple noises*.

2. The concussions of the air set up by the movement of a sounding body are called *vibrations*, if they present a steady alternation of condensation and rarefaction, and *periodic* vibrations, if each wave (movement to and fro, complete or double vibration) occupies the same period of time. A periodic vibration is completely definable in terms of *duration*, *magnitude*, and *form*. The simplest form is that of a pendular vibration (curve of sines) in which the distance of the vibrating particle from the position of equilibrium is proportional to the sine of the time occupied by its movement. Every complex form of periodic vibration can be analysed, as stated above, into a number of simple vibrations, whose periods are a half, a third, a quarter, etc., of the duration of the total vibration. The mathematical discovery of these relations dates back to 1822; but the knowledge that the analysis of clangs performed by the ear accords with their theoretical reduction did not come till much later. Simple vibrations differ in duration and magnitude, but not in form. The duration of their period (wave length) determines the *quality* or *pitch* of the tone heard, its magnitude or amplitude the *intensity* of the tone. We do not speak, however, of the duration of a vibration, but use the inverse value of the number of vibrations in the 1 sec. The greater the number of vibrations in the 1 sec. or the shorter the wave length, the higher is the pitch.

3. We cannot give equally positive definitions of the physical equivalents of the sensation of noise. An aperiodic vibration of the air may be compounded of shocks of the most different kinds; and in the case of a quick, single concussion or non-periodic shock nothing can be said of the form of the wave, although we may know something of its amplitude and duration. In the case of complex noises, however, we have the physical possibility of a certain combination of pendular vibrations as well as that of non-periodic concussions. The whistling of the wind, or the musical imitation of flowing water, is referable to the former cause, the crack of a rifle to the latter. The elementary qualities involved are respectively *tones*, plus the beats produced by their interference, and simple noises. The physical basis of the simple noise will accordingly be a non-periodic atmospheric concussion of a certain velocity. Whether its form shows any characteristic differences we cannot tell: its quality and intensity, like those of the tone, are dependent upon the duration and amplitude of movement. The simple noise undoubtedly has quality, height or

depth, besides intensity: we will call it *noise pitch.* Periodic concussions of the air which are not vibrations excite a series of discontinuous noises; if they pass into vibrations, and attain a certain rapidity of succession, we have clangs or tones. No strict distinction can be made in physics, therefore, between what we call noise and what we call clang or tone.

4. The fact that the air vibrations are longitudinal, while those of the sound producing body are transverse, is not of importance in the present connection. It is, however, worthy of remark that these transverse vibrations may take on very different forms. The clangs of a violin differ essentially from those of a flute and an organ, even when their pitch is apparently the same. The difference is expressed in the term *clang colour.* Every musical instrument has its own clang colour. The explanation of this fact is due to Helmholtz, who found that a special character is given to the fundamental in each case by the different number and intensity of its overtones. It is, therefore, necessary, in investigating the elementary qualities of clangs, to employ instruments which are as far as possible free of overtones. The best instruments of the kind are tuning forks: when placed upon a resonance box, or exciting the ear through a resonator, they give a pure, clear tone; and their vibration rate can be minimally changed by a simple movement of running weights along their prongs. The experiments quoted in what follows were almost exclusively made with tuning forks. And in all of them the compared tones were given to the observer successively. This has two reasons: (1) the sensible discrimination of simultaneous tones is considerably less than that of successive; and (2) vibration rates which differ but a little from each other are liable to fluctuations in intensity (owing to the interference of the sound waves), which render appreciation and judgment of the impressions exceedingly difficult, and at the same time furnish an indirect criterion of their difference.

§ 15. The Pitch of Tone and Noise.

1. Qualitatively regarded, tones constitute a one-dimensional manifold. The position of a given tone within the series is ordinarily indicated by the words 'high' and 'low'. This determination, however, is not absolute, and cannot be made so. For we have no names for the individual qualities; even those used in music are not the hard and fast equivalents of definite vibration rates, but relative terms, enabling us conveniently to establish or indicate some particular interrelation of tones. For the composer it is, within fairly wide limits, a

matter of indifference with what vibration rates the notes upon his score are imparted to the ear, provided only that their relations, *i.e.*, the intervals are rightly rendered. Whether an instrument is tuned to an $a = 435$ or an $a = 440$ is irrelevant for musical rendition in general, although it means very considerable absolute differences of pitch in the higher parts of the scale. There are two chief reasons for uniformity: (1) the limited range of certain instruments, and in particular the human voice, makes it desirable that the physical interpretation of musical symbols should not be too variable, while (2) the orchestral combination of a number of instruments naturally demands that their differences of attunement are not so large as to be noticeable. Nor is there anything in the whole construction of the musical scale to call attention to the absolute significance of the separate qualities. This connects with the fact that very few persons possess the power to recall accurately a tone of definite pitch. The practically universal lack of 'absolute tone memory' compels music to give up any presumption of a knowledge of the absolute qualities which she employs, if her influence is to be at all extensive. For the comparatively few musical intervals, on the other hand, most of us possess a memory which is adequate to their sensible recognition, if it does not always extend to names.

2. In the absence of names, recourse might be had to the various characteristics of tone pitch,—the harshness and fullness of the bass, and the shrillness of the treble. But as these, too, are insufficient aids to scientific inquiry, experimental psychology must seek help from special instruments. As regards modal sensitivity, we have to ask first of all whether the air vibrations on either side of the range of tones employed in music (about 40 to 40,000 vibrations) are capable of exciting sensation. A careful examination by means of tuning forks, vibrating rods, etc., has shown that the lower limit of tone perception lies at about 16, the upper at about 50,000 vibrations in the 1 sec., but that individual differences may largely alter these values,—especially the latter. Sensible discrimination, also, decreases considerably towards the upper limit of the scale. The number of tones audible within these limits has been determined by a systematic test of sensible discrimination by the method of minimal changes as applied to difference determination, and that of right and wrong cases as applied to difference comparison (cf. § 7. 6 and § 8. 3, 8). As the two modes of determination have given practically the same result, we may look upon this as fairly certain. For the region 64 to 1024 vibrations (C to c^3 in musical terminology), the just noticeable difference (S) remains approximately $= 0.2$ vibration. The absolute sensible discrim-

ination is, therefore, constant over this part of the scale. At 32 and 2048 vibrations, S was found to be = 0·4. Above and below these pitches the absolute sensible discrimination appears rapidly to decrease. Practice has a marked influence upon the cognisability of differences. The absolute delicacy of sensible discrimination is also constant for the region 64 to 512 vibrations, and decreases on either side of it.

3. We thus have data for a rough calculation of the number of distinguishable tones. It is only a matter of the summation of an ordinary arithmetical series. If we call the first term a, the final term l, and the difference between successive terms d, the number of terms $n = \dfrac{l - a}{d} + 1$. We will put the average difference limen for the region 16 to 64 vibrations at 0·5, for the qualities from 65 to 1024 at 0·2, and for those between 1025 and 4096 at 0·5. For the tones beyond this latter limit, we have only a few occasional observations. Thus it has been found that the most practised subjects are unable to cognise the objectively large difference between 12,288 and 16,384 vibrations. We will, therefore, assume no more than 23 distinguishable tones on the far side of 4096. The number of terms in the first part of the scale is 97, in the second 4800, in the third 6144; *i.e.*, 11,064 in all. We may, accordingly, say that a practised ear can distinguish some 11,000 elementary qualities of tone. The number of notes employed in music is curiously small in comparison. Similar attunement presupposed, all the requirements of melody and harmony are satisfied by the scanty total of 85 (more or less) tones or clangs. It is evident that sensible discrimination did not furnish the principle upon which they were chosen. In asking what that principle was, we must be careful to keep two things apart: the arrangement of the notes, and the distance between them. (1) The arrangement is by intervals, which stand in definite relations to one another. The scaffolding consists of a division into octaves, within each of which is found a recurrence of precisely the same harmonic connections. This arrangement is altogether independent of sensible discrimination: it is based upon facts of tonal connection, which we shall discuss in Pt. II., and is most intimately connected historically with the development, of polyphonic music. (2) But the distance of note from note might have been anything, whatever the principle of arrangement. That the smallest difference is as much as a semitone must have its special reasons. The first that suggests itself is the fact, that differences even of a quarter tone in the lower portions of the scale would mean very small differ-

ences of vibration rate. More important, perhaps, is the consideration that the most original and one of the most valuable of musical instruments, the human voice, is unable to render with any degree of certainty differences smaller than those which music employs,—a fact authenticated both by observation and experiment. Unfortunately, we are ignorant of the law which governs the voluntary adjustment of the larynx to increasing height of pitch. The conjecture that apparently equal differences of adjustment correspond to equal relative increments of the vibration rates of the tones produced, deserves investigation. If it accords with the facts, the equality of the same intervals in different octaves, which appears self-evident to many musical persons, could be referred to the sensible discrimination of the singing organ. And we should have a very simple explanation of a seeming paradox,—that unmusical persons often possess a very accurate sensible discrimination for the tones which they have heard.

4. We have no direct means of determining the number of qualities of noise. The most obvious mode of procedure is to diminish the duration of an air vibration to the minimum at which tone ceases, and only a noise, a dull or sharp shock or stroke, is heard. Investigations of this kind, to discover the qualitative limen of tonal sensitivity, have often been carried out. It has been found that on the average sixteen vibrations are necessary for the hearing of a quality in its fully determinate tonal character,—that this number marks the near limit of best possible discriminability; and that below this limit the distinctness of pitch decreases for all vibration rates, until at about two vibrations the tone passes over into noise. These two vibrations do not, however, constitute a sharp line of division; they are subject to increase, and also to decrease, with different individuals and with the same individual at different times. Now at the dividing line, two qualities have been found to be distinguishable, whose vibration rates were in the proportion 48 : 49. This would give an average difference limen of some 4 vibrations for the region investigated (80 to 250 vibrations). Sensible discrimination for simple noises would consequently be twenty times less than that for tones; and we should have—presupposing the same range of sensitivity—only about 553 discriminable qualities of noise. The total number of auditory qualities discriminable under the most favourable conditions (of individual endowment, of attention, and of external experimental conditions) would then amount in round numbers to 11,600.

5. It has been suggested that the sensation of silence is a special auditory quality,—the sensation normally mediated by the ear in the absence of external stimulation, and analogous to the intrinsic retinal

light familiar to those possessed of normal vision. The sensation is said to occur 'in the African desert, on the Alpine glacier, on fields of desolate lava, on the unmoved ocean'. The difficulty of realising these conditions prevents the experimental examination of the phenomenon; but we are probably justified in supposing that the sensations intended are those excited by internal auricular stimulation. Closure of the external auditory meatus often produces a high tone, and regularly occasions a kind of humming or buzzing, which becomes disagreeably insistent in certain pathological cases even when the meatus is left open. The same high tone appears in what is called 'singing in the ear'. It has been carefully investigated, and appears to be the resonance tone of the middle ear, the cavity of which would emit a sound in response to vibrations of this particular pitch [1].

Inadequate stimulation of the acoustic nerve by the galvanic current gives the sensation of the same high tone. It is probably always present, therefore, but only perceived under especially favourable conditions. The humming or buzzing proves to be dependent upon respiration, and varies in intensity synchronically with the heart beat. It seems to be due to the inrush of blood, which, also, becomes audible only in favourable circumstances.

§ 16. Theory of the Qualities of Audition.

1. The nerve of hearing, the eighth cerebral nerve, divides into two branches, the cochlear and the vestibular. Only one of these, the cochlear, appears to subserve the functions of audition; the vestibular is connected with an organ for the preservation of the equilibrium of head and body (§ 23. 5). The peripheral auditory apparatus is extremely complicated. It has three principal parts, known as the external, middle and internal ear. (1) The *external ear* consists of a slightly bent tube, the external auditory meatus, of the pinna, and of the tympanic membrane, which forms the boundary line between it and the middle ear. The sound waves set up in the air traverse the meatus, and set the tympanic membrane in transverse vibration. The membrane is funnel-shaped, and pointed inwards: when relaxed, its peculiar tone is one of some 700 vibrations in the 1 sec.; with tension, this tone becomes higher. Hence deep tones are as a rule heard under less favourable conditions of discrimination than high tones. (2) The *middle ear* consists of the tympanic cavity, the auditory ossicles, and the internal auditory meatus. By the latter, the Eustachian tube,

---

[1] In my own case the tone is generally $\natural$ g^3, though I have sometimes found it to be $\flat$ c^4 or $\natural$ g^4.

the cavity of the middle ear is placed in communication with the pharynx and the atmospheric air. The tension of the air within it can thus be kept approximately constant, and any interference with the function of the tympanic membrane avoided. The ossicles conduct the vibrations of the membrane onwards to the internal ear. In their passage across the tympanic cavity, the sound waves, which possess at the outset a relatively great amplitude and a relatively small force, are transformed into excursions of relatively small magnitude and relatively large force. This is plainly of advantage for the stimulation of the internal ear and the delicate nerve endings which it contains. All three auditory ossicles—malleus, incus, and stapes—stand in close articular connection. The handle of the malleus is affixed to the tympanic membrane, the plate of the stapes to the membrane of the oval window of the labyrinth, a membrane which divides the middle from the internal ear. The pull exerted on the tympanic membrane by the malleus facilitates its adaptation to waves of different form and duration, and accelerates the damping of its vibrations. Two muscles of the middle ear deserve mention: the tensor tympani and the stapedius. Contraction of the former draws the tympanic membrane inwards; that of the latter probably lessens the pressure of the stapes upon the oval window. The main function of both seems to be the protection of the organ against too violent concussions of the air.

2. (3) The *internal ear* or labyrinth consists of the vestibule, the semi-circular canals, and the cochlea. Nervous terminations are found in all three divisions; but it is probable, as mentioned above, that only those of the cochlear nerve in the cochlea are connected with hearing. The cochlea is a hollow tube of two and a half turns, divided along its length by a bony shelf (lamina spiralis) upon which rests a membrane, the basilar membrane. The two sections of the cochlea are called the scala vestibuli and the scala tympani. The former is again subdivided by a cuticular wall, which forms an acute angle with the basilar membrane, and is known as Reissner's membrane. This triangular portion of the scala vestibuli, called the cochlear canal, contains the essential parts of the whole structure,—the arches of Corti, arranged along the basilar membrane, and the reticulated membrane supported by them, through which the bristle-like continuations of the cells of Corti project. According to the results of the most recent investigations, the terminal fibrils of the cochlear nerve lie around and between these cells, but do not enter them. The scala vestibuli starts from the oval window already mentioned; the scala tympani from a round window, similarly closed by a membrane, on the other side of the labyrinth. The labyrinth is filled with a liquid, the endolymph or

water of the labyrinth, which transmits to the nerve endings the vibrations carried along the chain of ossicles to the oval window.

3. The mechanical cause of the excitation of the auditory nerve is, undoubtedly, the impact of the total mass of endolymph upon the membrane of the round window, which follows from a push of the stapes against the oval window. To explain the obvious dependency of tone sensations upon the properties of the external stimulus we must suppose further, that the differences in the form, duration and intensity of the movements of the endolymph, corresponding to similar differences in the atmospheric sound waves, give a special character to the final nervous reaction. And lastly, the fact that we can analyse compound periodic vibrations into their simplest components, *i.e.*, that we can hear out, from a clang or compound clang, the tones which correspond to the simple vibrations discoverable by mathematical physics in the complex movement, requires us to assume the existence of a peculiar nervous apparatus, adapted to the purposes of acoustical analysis. Now all that we know of acoustics in other connections leads us to believe that this analysis can only be performed by a set of instruments, adjusted within certain limits for sympathetic vibration to definite wave lengths. We must, therefore, imagine that the cochlea contains instruments of the kind, whether it be that there are special structures for the transmission of special stimuli, or that the fibres of the auditory nerve themselves possess a selective excitability. We may put the alternatives somewhat more concretely. In the former case, the nerve would have its excitation simplified by the interposition of a graduated system of vibratile masses, each of which would be set in motion purely mechanically by the wave length to which it was attuned,—just as a compound wave might be analysed into its components for our ear by the help of a number of appropriately adjusted tuning-forks. In the latter, the separate fibrils, *i.e.*, the separate nervous conduction paths, would have the property of being excitable only by vibrations of a certain wave length.

4. The only psychophysical theory of audition elaborated up to the present time has chosen the first of these alternatives. Helmholtz originally supposed that the analysers required were to be looked for in the arches of Corti. The hypothesis proved inadequate, however, since (1) these structures do not differ sufficiently in size, (2) there are too few of them (about 4000), and (3) they are absent in the ears of birds, whose hearing of tones and words cannot be doubted. Hensen accordingly suggested that the basilar membrane is the important structure in auditory sensation. He regards it as a graduated system of vibratile fibres. There are two reasons which support his view :

(1) the membrane is tightly stretched radially, while the longitudinal connection of its fibres is not at all close; and (2) it increases in breadth, from base to tip of the cochlear canal, in the proportion of 1 : 12 (0·041 to 0·495 mm.). It may, therefore, be regarded as a stringed instrument, the separate strings of which vibrate only to certain wave lengths. The excitation of the fibres is, perhaps, mediated by the bristles of the cells of Corti, which must be particularly responsive to the impact of the endolymph. The number of cells is said to be between 16,000 and 20,000: and we saw that there were some 11,000 distinguishable tones. The differentiation of the nervous apparatus is, therefore, amply adequate to sensation.

At the same time, it is not difficult to see that the theory fails to answer certain questions, and leaves room for doubt at certain points. It has been recently found that the auditory nerve itself is excitable by sound (cf. § 9. 6). This would seem to indicate that the mediation of the cells of Corti is not necessary for audition, and that vibratility or selective excitability may be ascribed directly to the nerve fibres.

5. It follows from our discussion of the simple noise above (§ 14. 3, § 15. 4) that its theory will not constrain us to posit an especial anatomical and physiological substrate, over and above the cell of Corti. The non-periodic air concussions forming its physical basis must excite a large number of fibres, and consequently blur the perception of pitch. Indeed, we have a continuous transition from tones of perfectly definite quality to noises of practically indefinable pitch. In speaking of the quality of a noise, we shall, as a rule, take account of the relatively strongest excitation. The duration of a non-periodic air-concussion will, consequently, not always be proportional to its perceived pitch. Thus the quality which we ascribe to the snap of the electric spark does not appear to approach at all nearly to the upper limit of tone perception, although its duration has been calculated to be only 0·00001 sec.

The Helmholtz-Hensen theory of auditory qualities has received confirmation from pathological cases of the abrogation of hearing over a certain part of the scale. There are persons who are insensitive for particular tones. The easiest explanation of this phenomenon can be given in terms of specific terminal apparatus or of a selective excitability of the separate nerve fibres.

The cortical centre for the impressions of each ear is situated in the temporal lobe of the opposite side.

Literature:

II. von Helmholtz, *Die Lehre von den Tonempfindungen.* Fourth ed., 1877.

V. Hensen, *Physiologie des Gehörs.* Hermann's *Handbuch der Physiol.*, III., *Abth.* 2, pp. 3 ff.

C. Stumpf, *Tonpsychologie.* Vol. I., 1883.

(4) The Quality of Visual Sensations.

§ 17. Light and the Visual Qualities.

1. So far, whenever we have been able to compare the adequate stimulus with the sensations occasioned by it, we have found a certain parallelism between the two : the simple in stimulus has corresponded to the simple in sensation, and the objectively compound to the compound in experience. Intensive graduation of qualitatively similar pressure stimuli, and of temperature stimuli above or below the point of indifference, gave a parallel alteration of intensity in cutaneous sensation, without change of conscious quality ; and complex sound waves were correlated with a complex in audition, simple periodic or non-periodic air-concussions with a simple tone or a simple noise. There is no such correspondence between light and vision. Our examination of visual qualities must, therefore, be prefaced—all the more necessarily, as the point is neglected in many psychological treatises—by an inquiry into the actual relations existing between sen-/sation and the various forms of light stimulation.

It is indifferent for the present purpose whether we adopt the elasticity theory of light, or the more recent electromagnetic hypothesis. For convenience' sake we will employ the usual terminology, and refer the physical process of visual stimulation to transverse vibrations of the ether particles. On this view, the velocity of the individual wave is very great, and (as with the sound wave) very different in different cases. The difference is expressed either in wave lengths or in the number of vibrations in the 1 sec. Thus, a light wave of 0·000589 mm. length vibrates in the customary medium, atmospheric air, 509 billion times in the 1 sec. Simple undulatory movements of this kind can only be obtained, as a rule, by the analysis of ordinary mixed light, which contains waves of the most various lengths. It is usual, there-fore, to distinguish *mixed* light from *homogeneous* light, which consists of waves of approximately the same length and vibration rate.

2. In determining the qualities of visual sensation, however, we have to consider not only the difference between homogeneous and mixed light, but the variations of both in intensity, duration, and extension, and the results of the combination of homogeneous with mixed light, and of particular homogeneous lights with one another. There

is a subjective effect corresponding to all these phases of the objective process. But as duration and extension of stimulus, if they affect the quality of sensation at all, affect it in practically the same way as does stimulus intensity, we need not discuss the influence of all three factors in detail.

(a) *Mixed light*, in which no particular wave length has a noticeable predominance, excites the sensation of light or of *brightness*. Intensive graduation of white light gives rise to a series of sensation qualities which constitutes a one-dimensional manifold analogous to the tonal scale, and extends from the deepest black to the most brilliant white. There are two peculiarities in this correlation: (1) an intensive alteration of stimulus produces a qualitative alteration of sensation, and (2) a highly complex physical process corresponds to an entirely simple psychological experience. Brightness sensations can be obtained in the greatest purity by the reflection of mixed light from a dead surface of the right absorption capacity. White and black or gray papers are, therefore, generally used for experiments on brightness sensations. The sources of mixed light have all some trace of colour, due to the relative preponderance of certain rays for sensation.— We reach two conclusions, then: (1) that brightness qualities do not possess intensity as a separate, variable attribute; and (2) that an analysis of the qualities contained in mixed light requires their spatial or temporal isolation.

3. (b) *Homogeneous light* gives rise to *colour sensations*, the second series of visual qualities. Alteration in wave length or vibration rate produces alteration in colour tone. Homogeneous light, in the strictest sense of the term, has never been seen, so that we cannot say how it would be sensed. Approximately homogeneous light can be artificially produced: most conveniently by the refraction of mixed light. Thus, a pencil of white light falling upon a glass prism issues as a band of colours, in consequence of the different refrangibility of rays of different wave length. The more intensive the source of light from which this pencil proceeds, the more luminous are the colours. The pure colours of the solar spectrum are, consequently, the most beautiful that we know.

Here, the physically simple appears to be correlated with the psychologically simple. But, whereas the vibration rates steadily increase from red to violet, becoming invisible outside both these limits, the colour sensations begin by growing more and more unlike, and end with tones more nearly resembling the first of the series. An analogy has often been drawn between the solar spectrum and the musical scale, in particular the course of tone sensations within

8

the octave: but it is incorrect. Moreover, we can produce colours intermediate between the visible qualities of the two ends of the spectrum, which are not represented by simple physical undulations. So that here, too, there is no exact correspondence between stimulus and sensation.

It must also be noticed that what we call colour tone or colour sensation is always a brightness sensation also. This fact is best demonstrated by a gradual alteration of the intensity of a homogeneous light. We obtain a graduated series from black (or dark gray) to white, within which the colour sensations occur from their darkest to their lightest shade, with and without qualitative alteration. As the ends of the series are occupied by brightness sensations alone, we cannot doubt that these sensations are also present in the middle portion, where the colour is still visible. We thus have the curious result that what we call a colour is really a connection of two simple qualities, colour tone and brightness. It is not infrequent to find the brightness of a colour referred to as its intensity. But as it is simply a sensation, which, under appropriate conditions, can be perceived alone, without any intermixture of colour, this terminology leads to the paradoxical conclusion that brightness is a mere intensity, a non-qualitative sensation. It is one of Hering's services to psychology to have restored the black-white series to its rights as a qualitative system. Indeed, to speak of an intensity of sensation because the corresponding variable quality of stimulus is called intensity, involves a quite unjustifiable transference of terms from physics to psychology. Our previous discussion of the attributes of sensation (§ 4) makes it indubitable that the brightness sensation, whether with or without colour, must be regarded as a quality. The connection of colour tone and brightness is the most intimate connection of qualities that we know: in fact, in one sense it is inseparable, since a colour sensation cannot occur without a brightness quality. We have, then, in visual sensation, a direct contradiction between the physical and the psychological: the physically simple (homogeneous light) corresponds to the psychologically compound (colour tone + brightness), and the physically compound (mixed light) to the psychologically simple (brightness).

4. (c) A *mixture of two mixed lights* of different intensities, each of which would give rise to a simple sensation of brightness, produces on the physical side a mean intensity, and on the psychological a brightness sensation lying midway between the two primary sensations. The physical mixture can be replaced for vision by a quick succession of the two brightnesses; *e.g.*, by the rapid rotation of a circular

disc composed of black and white sectors. The after duration of the visual excitation is so great that we obtain the same psychological effect as if we had brought about an objective (compensatory) mixture of the components.

(*d*) The psychological result of a *mixture of homogeneous lights* can be stated in three propositions:

(1) A mixture of two homogeneous lights of very similar wave length produces a colour sensation, which occupies an intermediate place in the series of spectral colours between the sensations of the two primary lights. The nearer the homogeneous lights are to one another, the more vivid or more saturated is the intermediate colour; and the more remote their vibration rates, the paler or thinner the colour. A mixture of red and yellow gives orange, of blue and green bluish green.

(2) A mixture of two homogeneous lights of a certain difference of wave length (not the same for all observers or all colours) produces a sensation, not of colour at all, but of brightness. These lights are termed *complementary colours*, and are psychologically characterised by the fact that their sensations present the greatest differences, *i.e.*, form the greatest contrast to each other. Hence, the complementary colours are also termed *contrast colours*. Red and greenish blue, yellowish green and violet, orange and cyan blue are complementaries.

If the difference of wave length is still further increased we again obtain a colour sensation of more or less saturation, belonging in the series of purples, which is not represented in the spectrum.

(3) A mixture of more than two homogeneous lights can always be reduced to a mixture of two, and so does not require any special discussion. There are three homogeneous lights—red, green, and violet—the mixture of which produces a simple brightness sensation. This result becomes intelligible, if we substitute yellowish green + greenish blue for green. We then have two pairs of complementaries: violet + yellowish green, and red + greenish blue. These will excite a colourless gray whether taken singly or together. It is plain that they are the only three homogeneous lights which can excite the sensation of brightness, since no other three can be resolved into two complementary pairs. The peculiarity has gained for them the name of *primary colours*.

5. These laws of mixture are only valid on the assumption of a definite intensity of the homogeneous lights which are to be combined. In the solar spectrum, the complementary colours possess a different luminosity; but even apart from that, the amount of homogeneous light necessary to complete complementariness differs in different

cases. We say, therefore, that the various spectral colours have different colouring power. Violet is strongest, yellow weakest; red and cyan blue have approximately the same power, approaching that of violet, orange and green are about equal and stand nearer to yellow. The rules for the mixture of homogeneous lights can be put in the form of a geometrical figure,—most conveniently in that of a triangle. The three angles are formed by the primary colours, and in the centre is a point, *B*, denoting the sensation of brightness. There are two other properties of the primary colours which we may mention here: (i) all the other colours can be obtained, at the relatively greatest degree of saturation, by their intermixture, and (ii) no primary colour itself can be produced by the mixture of the other two. If we mark the angles of the triangle *R* (red), *G* (green), and *V* (violet), the side *RG* will contain orange, yellow, and yellowish green, the colours intermediate between red and green; and the side *GV*, the colours greenish blue, cyan blue, and indigo blue, the

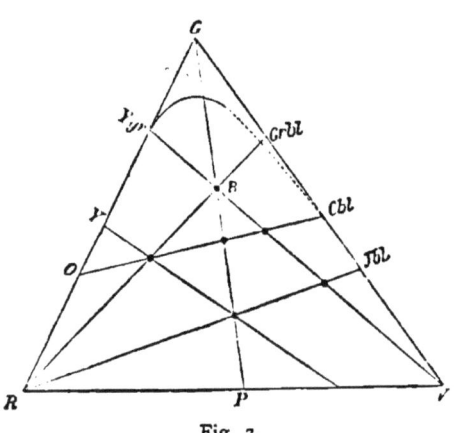

Fig. 7.

colours intermediate between green and violet. The base *RV* will contain the tones intermediate between red and violet, *i.e.*, the purples, which are absent from the spectrum. The lines of connection between angles and sides of the triangle, which intersect at *B*, or at other points not specially marked in the Figure, indicate possible mixtures of remote terms of the colour series; and their length is proportional to the colouring power possessed by the various colours (Fig. 7).

6. This figure, however, is not entirely satisfactory. It gives no indication of the fact that comparatively few mixtures of different wave lengths produce the sensation correlated with the mean wave length. Really, that is, the lines *RG* and *GV* ought not to be straight, but somewhat curved. The point *G*, in particular, with the neighbouring qualities on the prismatic spectrum, should lie lower, and the side *GV* follow a course similar to that marked in Fig. 7 by the dotted line. But apart from these defects, the schema gives an instructive and simple demonstration of the incongruity between the physical and psychological series. One and the same sensation may be obtained by the most various combinations of physical processes;

every point of the area enclosed by the three sides of the triangle has passing through it an infinite number of lines of connection between pairs of homogeneous lights. In consciousness, there is no trace of this unlimited wealth of sensation components; each separate degree of saturation which a colour presents is as much a simple quality as the colour sensation originated by a definite, homogeneous spectral light. On the psychological side, the series of possible variations is covered by the parallel processes adduced under (*a*) and (*b*). Under (*a*) we have a series of pure brightnesses, under (*b*) a connection of colour tone and brightness in all possible degrees and proportions, with the single exception of a zero value of brightness. The mixture of mixed lights, and the mixture of homogeneous lights, (*c*) and (*d*), give us no new sensation. Colour tone and brightness are, after as before, the sole kinds of simple visual qualities. But on the physical side, the list of possible variations is by no means concluded.

7. (*e*) The *mixture of a homogeneous light with mixed light* produces a series of double sensations, rising from the most saturated colour tone to simple brightness, according to the relative intensity of the components. Such a mixture gives us another physical means of varying the relation of colour tone and brightness within the colour sensation. The mixture of two complementary colours, or the simple illumination or darkening of a homogeneous light, serves the same purpose. The customary definition of the degree of *saturation* of a colour by the amount of white light mixed with it is, therefore, psychologically incorrect: (1) because the alteration of depth or vividness of a colour tone may have very different physical causes, and (2) because the most saturated spectral colour contains much more than a minimum of brightness,—the psychological equivalent of mixed light. We shall, accordingly, employ the term saturation to designate simply the degree of distinctness with which a colour can be perceived as a particular quality over and above its brightness. The greatest saturation is afforded by a certain homogeneous light of a moderate intensity; and its degree is diminished, not only by the addition of mixed light, but by an alteration of intensity, and (under certain circumstances) by the intermixture of other homogeneous lights.

On the assumption that a colour tone suffers no qualitative change in its different degrees of saturation, we might look upon these as constituting the real intensity scale of colour sensation. The same may be said of the saturation of brightness sensations, except that it is obviously not to be regarded as a variable intensity.

This concludes what we had to say of visual sensations, by way

of preface to their special investigation. Our result can be very simply
formulated: it is necessary to draw a sharp line of distinction between
the physical and psychological. Physical optics has already banished
the laws of sensation from the science of light: psychology must now,
in its turn, decline to apply physical ideas in the analysis of its facts
and in its theory of visual qualities. Complementary colours, primary
colours, mixture—these are all physical concepts, which bear a certain
relation to the phenomena of sensation, but which must not be transferred bodily into psychology. Sensations do not mix, and sensations
are not complementaries. Whether these concepts have a physiological validity, whether, *i.e.*, we can find in the nature of the optical
nervous excitations an explanation of the lack of strict parallelism
between stimulus and sensation, is another question. We shall seek
to answer it later (§ 21), when we come to deal with the theory of
visual qualities.

§ 18. The Sensation of Brightness.

1. The scale of colourless sensations is very difficult to obtain in
absolute purity, owing to the influence of impressions in the physical
environment, and to empirical habits of judgment. Our notion of
'white', in particular, is very fluctuating and uncertain. Brightness as
such, *e.g.*, a colourless sensation occupying the entire field of vision
with complete uniformity, is only given under rare conditions. It
may be realised by the deep black of a lightless space, provided that
no subjective qualities are present to interfere with it. As a general
rule, the terms 'black', 'white', 'gray', which we usually employ to
designate sensations of brightness, are altogether relative. Writing paper,
newly fallen snow, linen fresh from the laundry, etc., appear white,
although their objective brightnesses are extremely different, and are seen
to be different as soon as directly compared. In their ordinary surroundings, the colour tone of these substances (otherwise distinctly perceptible) is forced so far into the background, and their brightness
so prominently brought out, that for lack of any absolute standard of
reference in sensation we place them all in the indeterminate category
of 'whites'. Our memory for absolute light intensities is very unreliable, and its development has been prevented by the constancy
of the relative sensible discrimination, of which we shall speak
presently (5 below). On the other hand, our memory for spatial
form is exceedingly accurate. This explains how it is that we come
to attribute definite apparent brightnesses to particular objects as
permanent predicates, which we ordinarily apply in speech, although,

as a matter of fact, they do not remain constant. The closeness of the association of a definite spatial image of an object with a judgment expressive of its brightness (under certain conditions, which are taken as normal) comes to be a convenient indirect criterion of the applicability of the predicate. Under these circumstances, it is not strange that 'brightness' and 'whiteness' should not always mean the same thing in popular parlance. The term 'white' is used in the first instance to indicate absence of colour, the lack of any self-insistence on the part of a colour tone, or of its recognition on our part: it is the analogous concept to what we have called 'saturation' in colour. It consequently denotes the degree of dinstinctness with which brightness as such is perceived, while it covers very different degrees or gradations of brightness. Thus the snow may be whiter than the gray sky, and yet darker. That is, the snow is more colourless, and under the influence of its surroundings may even appear brighter, although a direct comparison would prove that it is less bright.

2. As all this is equally true of 'gray' and 'black', it might be imagined that the brightness sensation has two attributes attaching to it, besides its spatial and temporal characteristics,—quality, expressed by the words 'white', 'gray', etc., and intensity, expressed by 'dark', 'bright', and intermediate names. But the two sets of terms are in reality very far from being independent of one another. The degrees of 'black' and 'white' are meant to express degrees of brightness, just as much as those of 'dark' and 'light'. It is not as if one and the same black or gray or white could run through all degrees of brightness, and possess different intensities at different times. / The two sets of judgments are passed upon the same material, the same sensations. Their distinction depends not upon the existence of quality and intensity as variable attributes of brightness sensations, but upon the double relation in which every such sensation is naturally placed. ⌊A brightness sensation is related on the one hand to all the rest of the brightness sensations, on the other to colour tones (by way of its purity, *i.e.*, the absence of any intermixture of colour). The terms 'white', 'gray', and 'black', are principally used in the latter connection; 'dark' and 'light' in the former. It is, therefore, quite allowable to speak of a saturation of colourless sensations, on the analogy of colour saturation, if we mean by it the degree of their distinctness. Only, the greatest saturation of a brightness quality is given by the total absence of colour tone, and the minimum of saturation with the maximum of colour. It may be that the connection between colour tone and brightness is so intimate, that it is as impossible for brightness to occur without colour, as for colour to appear without brightness:

the maximal saturation of brightness would then be a limiting case, never actually realised. It is at least conceivable that what we call pure gray or pure white would appear different if we had an absolute standard of reference and more accurate means of comparison. But we should still be compelled to regard the black of a lightless space and similar depths of darkness as pure qualities of brightness sensation, simply because in such cases there is no objective possibility of the origination of a colour tone.

3. Our sensible discrimination of brightnesses is diminished (as will be shown later: § 49) by their connection with colour tones. It is, therefore, difficult to determine the number of distinguishable brightness qualities, as the analogy of previous Sections requires us now to do. Indeed, even the upper and lower limits of the scale can hardly be defined. Sunlight, the brightest light known to us, is dazzling and painful; but we cannot say whether the brightest artificial lights, at a corresponding distance, would show a noticeable difference from the brightness of the sun. Every day experience seems to prove that our sensible discrimination of intensive brightnesses, absolutely measured, is exceedingly small; and that consequently, when once a certain degree has been reached, we shall not find many more distinguishable qualities. As to the lower limit of perceptible brightness we are in equal uncertainty. The dark which we sense after a lengthened stay in a blackened chamber, from which every source of light has been cut off, is little different, if at all, from a less scientifically produced darkness, such as that of deep black velvet, upon which no direct light of any considerable intensity is allowed to fall; although the objective brightness is very different in the two cases. The reflected brightnesses which we ordinarily compare, vary between the limits of 3700, that of brilliantly white paper, directly illuminated by sunlight, and 1, that of a dead black paper, seen in the twilight. If the same two papers are uniformly illuminated by diffuse daylight, the ratio of their brightnesses is about 60 : 1.

We cannot here discuss the various photometric methods. As those that are in use at present are still based upon the comparison of sensations, for which some employ the procedure of minimal changes and others that of average error (§§ 7, 8), their results are not altogether comparable. Besides which, the physical formulæ on which these results are calculated (the law of decrease of light intensity with the square of the distance from the source of light, the laws of polarisation, the Talbot-Plateau law) are not by any means necessarily a true reflection of relations which obtain in the sphere of sensation comparison.

4. When it is further considered, that the brightness stimuli employed

in the investigation of our sensible discrimination for brightness have been possessed of different degrees of 'colourlessness', some observers having worked with varying intensities of artificial light and others with daylight, some having chosen shadows as the objects of comparison and others gray papers, etc., it will not be found surprising that the results are as divergent as they are. Not only the magnitude of the difference limen, but the laws of the course of sensible discrimination in general, are differently given by different observers. A certain proportion of these differences is undoubtedly attributable to the influence of a number of variable sources of error, of more or less significance, which have not received their due (or even, an equal) measure of attention from every experimenter. One of these would be the adaptation of the eye for brightness, the importance of which is borne in upon us by the familiar experience of passage from the light into a dark room. Until the eye has become adapted to the new environment, we cannot distinguish the separate objects about us; *i.e.*, perceive the differences of brightness which they present to vision. Another is the accommodation of the eye for distance. If the outlines of the objects to be compared are not sharply drawn, but appear vague and blurred, our ability to remark their brightness differences is considerably impaired. Yet others of these variable factors are the magnitude of the bright surfaces compared, their relative positions, the duration of stimulation (the influence of which varies with variation in the intensity of the mixed light employed), the character of the surroundings, rest or movement of the eyes, monocular or binocular regard, etc., etc. Of the general conditions of sensible discrimination, discussed above (§ 5) fatigue plays a principal part in the present connection.

It is no wonder, then, that some observers have found a constancy of the relative sensible discrimination, others a variation of it with variation in the absolute intensity of light; and that where constancy of the relative difference limen is maintained, its magnitude is variously given as $\frac{1}{80}$, $\frac{1}{100}$, $\frac{1}{120}-\frac{1}{230}$. At the same time, there seems to be no doubt that, within certain limits, the constancy of the relative sensible discrimination is an established fact. The essential thing is, that the experiments be made with similar retinal adaptation. Below and above these limits, $\frac{S}{r}$ steadily increases. Difference comparison has also given a relative equality of apparently equal differences, for certain regions of difference. But in this case, the results are crossed by the effect of contrast, to an extent which we are at present unable to determine with any accuracy. Its increase is certainly not directly proportional to increase of the stimulus differences.

5. Where results are so extraordinarily divergent, our 'calculation' of the number of distinguishable brightness qualities cannot be much more than a guess. We will assume that between the limits 1 and 1000 (1 being a black situated towards the lower end of the brightness scale, but 1000 a white still comparatively far removed from its upper boundary) the relative difference limen is constant at $\frac{1}{100}$. That is a fair average value. The scale of discriminable degrees of brightness may then be regarded as a geometrical progression, whose first term $a = 1$, final term $t = 1000$, and exponent $e = \frac{101}{100}$. If n is the number of terms, $t = a \cdot e^{n-1}$; *i.e.*, $n = \dfrac{\log \dfrac{t}{a}}{\log e} + 1$, = approximately 696.

Adding to this total another 104, for the degrees of brightness on either side (but especially above) the limits chosen, we have the number of distinguishable qualities = 800. Not more than the half of these are at the disposal of the painter or etcher, who seeks to reproduce the brightnesses presented in nature. The whole series of brightnesses obtainable by brush or needle is included within the limits expressed by the ratio 1 : 60 (cf. 3, above). That both are able, nevertheless, to produce a successful imitation of the reality they copy, is plainly due to the constancy of the relative sensible discrimination, or, as it is called, to Weber's law. This law (§ 26) says that differences are apprehended as equal, whether they hold between weak or strong stimuli, provided that their relation to one another remains the same. Thus a brightness difference of 200 between 1200 and 1000 has the same effect upon us as one of 20 between 120 and 100, or one of 2 between 12 and 10. The painter must only avoid the attempt to reproduce brightness differences which lie very far indeed outside the limits imposed by his art. We, therefore, rarely find the midday sun, or any other extremely intensive source of light, introduced into a picture.—We can understand, if Weber's law is valid, how it is that shadows and contours on canvass or in the objects which form our daily environment do not vary with every alteration in the strength of illumination, but seem to remain practically constant. A memory for absolute brightnesses, analogous to the memory for absolute tone pitch, which we occasionally discover, or to that for spatial forms and colour tones, which we all possess in a greater or less degree, could not be developed under the circumstances.

6. The foregoing discussion of our sensible discrimination for brightnesses is based upon observations made with direct vision, *i.e.*,

with the centre of the retina, or the 'spot of clearest vision'. We are not accustomed to employ the lateral portions of the retina for the cognition of objects: if we wish to get an exact visual idea of anything situated on the periphery of the field of vision, we bring eyes or head or the whole body into a position which renders a direct regard possible. Nevertheless, there are many ordinary experiences which should teach us that the lateral parts of the retina are by no means less sensitive to brightness than the central portion. A uniformly gray surface, such as a white-washed wall or a cloudy sky, does not appear to grow darker from the centre outwards, but makes the same qualitative impression over its whole visible extent. Since, as a matter of fact, the light which falls upon the peripheral regions of the retina is weaker, other things equal, than that which stimulates the centre, the truer conclusion seems to be, that the brightness sensitivity of the former is greater than that of the fovea centralis. And there are many other indications that this view is correct. Stars of small intensity can be more quickly and easily remarked in indirect vision than in direct. It has been shown, by elaborate experiments, that the retinal sensitivity for brightnesses increases from the centre outwards and inwards to about $25°$, where it is some $1 \cdot 2$ times as great as in direct vision ; and from the centre upwards and downwards to about $15°$, where it is some $1 \cdot 04$ times as great as at the spot of clearest vision. Beyond these limits it appears to decrease again. The teleological significance of the arrangement is obvious, since the movements of the eyes are reflexly regulated by the strength of stimulation, and the limit of their excursion in different directions, while the body remains unmoved, is approximately given by these angular values. Some bright object or sudden change of brightness in the lateral parts of the field of vision impresses us, and we are able at once to direct the eyes upon it and obtain an exact perception of its nature. No systematic investigation has been made of the magnitude of sensible discrimination in indirect vision.

7. We cannot speak of a stimulus limen in the case of brightness, since even when the eye is at complete rest there is present in consciousness a colourless sensation, the subjective black or 'intrinsic retinal light'. We can, however, determine the brightness which is just noticeably different from this black. It is given, *e.g.*, by the weak shimmer of a platinum wire heated by the electric current, estimated at $\frac{1}{300}$ of the intensity of the light of the full moon. Unfortunately, the intensity of moonlight was here considerably underestimated.

There are still other sources of error involved in the examination of our sensitivity and sensible discrimination for brightness, which call for a passing mention. We have already remarked (§ 17. 2) that spatial and temporal variations of the mixed light employed modify sensations in the same way as variations in the intensity of stimulus. It has been experimentally demonstrated that within certain, fairly narrow limits, an increase of stimulus duration or of the magnitude of its retinal image has the same subjective effect as the increase of its intensity. Both duration and magnitude must be conceived of as absolutely very small. If the extension of the object of observation increases beyond a certain magnitude, differences of sensibility are involved (6 above), while the sense-organ may very well be unable to comprehend the object in its entirety. And when once a certain limit of duration has been exceeded, the qualitative change in sensation ceases, just as it did with tones : in physiological language, the maximum of excitability has been reached. The only result of persistent stimulation is an apparent diminution of the stimulus brightness, due to fatigue, or the appearances of a phenomenon which we shall come to know later under the more general rubric of 'fluctuation of the attention' (§ 75. 6). Lastly, eye movements serve to increase the sensitivity and sensible discrimination for brightnesses. A small difference can be more quickly and certainly remarked, if the eyes are allowed to travel to and fro from the one brightness to the other.

§ 19. The Sensation of Colour.

1. If it was difficult to obtain a pure brightness, it is still more difficult to obtain a pure colour. Indeed, as we have seen, no colour sensation is ever given except in connection with a certain degree of brightness, so that the preparation of colour tones cannot even be looked upon as the goal of scientific experiment, approachable by degrees, however incapable of actual attainment. The only course open to us is to investigate colour sensations by abstracting as far as possible from the brightness quality fused with them. The abstraction can evidently only be successful, if at all, when the colour tones are relatively distinct, *i.e.*, the colours very saturated, and when they allow of variation independently of the brightness attaching to them. But as we do not know of any source of light, whose refracted rays are all of equal intensity, a simultaneous fulfilment of these two conditions is impossible. In the solar spectrum, *e.g.*, the green and yellow light is considerably brighter than the red and blue, while the saturation of the two latter qualities is greater than that of the former. If we diminish the intensity of the yellow and green rays, we diminish their saturation at the same time. In experimenting upon the sensible

discrimination of colour tones, observers have, consequently, been content as a rule to eliminate one of the two inevitable sources of error in the particular case, the diminution of saturation, and have assumed that in little different homogeneous lights the brightness differences are negligible as compared with the alteration in colour tone. But no reliable information can be obtained in this way as to the number of discriminable colour qualities, for the reason that there is absolutely no guarantee that the differences noticed are really differences of colour tone, and not merely (or partly) differences of brightness. On the other hand, if we seek to eliminate the brightness error, by keeping all the colour tones investigated at the same brightness level, there is the consideration that increase or decrease of the brightness of a colour tends to reduce it to a pure brightness sensation, *i.e.*, forces the specific character of its tone into the background. This method would, therefore, in all probability, give fewer distinguishable colour tones than there really are. The observations recorded in the literature do not furnish sufficient material for an estimation of the relative effect of these two factors, colour purity and colour brightness, as they cross one another in the given case.

2. A second difficulty in the way of an investigation of colour qualities can be best put in the form of a question. May we suppose that we have obtained the complete series, when we have worked through as pure a spectrum as we can produce, and determined all the discriminable tones within it? It is quite possible that the various transition colours between remote qualities, such as can be got by the mixture of the appropriate rays, and the various degrees of saturation of the same colour, might give us new simple qualities, not represented in the spectrum. And the existence of the purples raises this possibility into certainty. But, apart from purple, there do not seem to be any colour tones not in the solar spectrum. All the other intermediate or mixed colours prove to be familiar qualities, differing from the spectral only in their degree of saturation. Brown, *e.g.*, finds a place in the series from red, orange, and yellow to a darkish grey; and some one of these three spectral qualities is cognisable in every variety of it. Rose, again, is a purple of diminished saturation and increased brightness. There is nothing antagonistic to our view of colour sensation in the fact here brought out, that the saturation and brightness of a colour are neither identical nor directly proportional to one another. A high degree of purity and distinctness may be combined with a low degree of brightness, and a less degree of purity with a greater degree of brightness. There seems to be a most favourable brightness for every colour tone, *i.e.*, a particular brightness at which it is purest or most

saturated. Red, blue and violet are more saturated in the spectrum than are green and yellow: and we accordingly ascribed to them a greater colouring power, in the formulæ of colour mixture (Fig. 7). Saturation cannot, obviously, be increased beyond a certain limit; and therefore, under given conditions of illumination, there must inevitably be differences of saturation in the different colour tones, even with the most favourable brightness.

3. We were able to define a colourless sensation in two different ways: by stating the degree of its colourlessness, and by assigning it to its position in the brightness scale. The same applies to colour tone. It is capable of modification in two ways, more or less independent of each other: as regards saturation (purity, distinctness), and as regards position in the scale of colour qualities (measured by vibration rate). But while we could conceive of the various brightnesses as arranged along a straight line, beginning with the deepest black and ending with the most brilliant white, we must place the series of colour tones along a line which returns upon itself, *i.e.*, a curved line, inasmuch as we have transition tones between the terminal red and violet of the visible spectrum, which are not identical with any of the qualities contained within it. It is, therefore, customary to represent the series of colour tones as a circle. This has the disadvantage that it ignores the different colouring power of the separate qualities, their saturation or weight (if the term is permissible). The various tones discriminable in this continuous colour series,—any point of which may be taken equally well as end or as beginning,—are all upon an equality in respect of simplicity. It is erroneous to say, as has sometimes been done, that certain of them are simple and others compound. Language has done much to further the error: we have no expression for many of the tones, except a connection of the names of the two neighbouring colours. When we wish to designate, *e.g.*, the quality intermediate between green and yellow or blue and green, or produceable by their mixture, we must speak of yellowish green, bluish green, etc. But there is no such connection in the sensation of this quality; and if we find that only certain colours—red, yellow, green, blue—have special, simple names, that is not because they are the only simple colour tones, but because they are the colours of familiar and particularly interesting objects. Purple, violet, and orange, which the same mistaken view regards as compound colours, have nothing even in their names to indicate their composition from blue and red or red and yellow. And within the range of colours which each name covers, there are many discriminable tones, all of equal simplicity.

4. After all this discussion, we may attempt to determine the number

of distinguishable colour qualities, in terms of the difference limina obtained from a colour continuum of the greatest possible saturation, by a method which abstracts from the changes of brightness attending alteration of colour tone. It has been found, in investigations made under these conditions, that there are two 'terminal regions' in the spectrum, which show a difference of brightness only—not of colour. One of these extends from the beginning of the visible spectrum in red (under favourable circumstances, 0·000762 mm. = 762 $\mu\mu$) to about 655 $\mu\mu$; the other from about 430 $\mu\mu$ to the end of the violet (311 $\mu\mu$). Our sensible discrimination for colour tones need, therefore, be tested only over the middle portion of the visible spectrum; the terminal tracts may be disregarded. Examination of this range of colours has always given the same result: the course of sensible discrimination is not uniform. The difference limen is comparatively large in red and violet, reaches a minimal value in yellow and blue, and has an intermediate magnitude in green. Thus in red an S has been found = 4·7 $\mu\mu$, in yellow = 0·88 $\mu\mu$, in green = 1·88 $\mu\mu$, in blue = 0·72 $\mu\mu$, and in violet = 3·0 $\mu\mu$. No determination has been made of our sensible discrimination for the purples. Calculating from these data, we may put the number of discriminable colours at about 150. The delicacy of sensible discrimination (measured by the magnitude of the average error in the method of that name) runs parallel, with few deviations, to its magnitude (measured by the difference limina).—Neither of these results is absolutely conclusive, however, as we do not at present know enough of the undoubtedly very considerable influence of the variation of brightness.

5. The duration of stimulus modifies colour sensation (cf. § 18. 7). But here, too, it is difficult to be sure as to what is due to saturation and what to the brightness of the colour. At a certain lower limit of duration, all homogeneous lights alike seem to produce a brightness effect only, *i.e.*, to affect the eye as would a mixed light, or an exceedingly strong or weak homogeneous light. With a somewhat greater duration of stimulation, the whole spectrum is seen in two colours, red and blue—just as happens with increased intensity of light. On other points, the records of different observations are not in entire agreement. Some make the cognisability of a colour, the just noticeable colour tone, dependent exclusively on brightness, others on brightness and saturation. This contradiction is attributable partly to differences in the colour stimuli selected (solar spectrum, spectra of artificial sources of light, coloured glasses), and partly to individual differences between observers and methods of experimentation. It is reasonable to suppose that saturation, which exerts a distinct influence upon the character

of the colour tone, when the intensity of the light is varied, must also exert an influence when duration is the variable factor. Blue, which is usually much darker than green, is consequently seen earlier than green. Violet, which is generally but very little luminous, is, on the other hand, cognised last of all. Yellow has been seen first in experiments with coloured glasses. But (1) these do not by any means give pure tones; and (2) the source of light employed (lamp light) was in itself predominantly yellow in colour. Here again, then, the two influences of brightness and saturation cut across each other, in a way which we cannot at present explain.

We meet with the same result, when we seek to determine, not the temporal limen, but the length of time necessary for the distinct and adequate perception of a colour, *i.e.*, for the attainment of the maximum of excitation. If this time were simply dependent upon the brightness of the different colours, yellow and green should become distinct before red and blue. It has been found, however, that, if brightness differences are checked and as far as possible eliminated, red is seen clearly before blue, and blue before green.

6. One of the most surprising facts and most important problems in psychophysical optics, the 'phenomenon of Purkinje', apparently belongs in the present connection. If we alter the intensity of the light illuminating the series of spectral colours, we obtain a remarkable change in their relative brightnesses. In the normal solar spectrum, *i.e.*, with a relatively high degree of saturation of the different colour tones, yellow and green are seen brightest, blue and violet darkest, and orange and red midway between these two groups. If the light is reduced in strength until the colours disappear, the order of brightnesses is somewhat as follows: green, blue, yellow, violet, orange, red. The experiment can easily be made with coloured objects, and its result is, perhaps, most striking when red or yellow is compared with blue or violet. By lamp light or day light there can be no doubt but that yellow makes an impression of greater brightness than blue; in the twilight, at dusk, there can be just as little doubt that the blue object is the brighter. Red is most effectually darkened by the disappearance of its colour tone: it may readily be confused with black.

The interpretation of these facts is exceedingly difficult, as we shall see when we come to discuss them in detail (§§ 49, 50). At present it is enough to point out (1) that the Purkinje phenomenon illustrates certain peculiarities of optical fusion, and (2) that it shows the divergence between the relations of saturation and brightness or intensity in the various colours, of which we have already spoken.

7. The magnitude of the coloured surfaces has, within certain

limits, an influence upon sensitivity and sensible discrimination, analogous to that exerted by the duration or intensity of stimulation. There is, consequently, a 'most favourable magnitude' for the cognition and discrimination of colour tones, just as there are a most favourable intensity and duration of the coloured light. But, apart from this, the colour sensitivity of the retina is different in different parts of its area. While the brightness sensitivity increases up to a certain limit of deviation from direct vision, the colour sensitivity is generally greatest and most delicate at the fovea centralis, and steadily decreases both in magnitude and delicacy from centre to periphery. The order of disappearance of the various spectral colours, as the angle of inclination to the sighting line of direct vision increases, is somewhat as follows: violet, green, red, yellow, blue. The magnitude and brightness of the coloured surfaces employed are here of primary importance. It is, therefore, intelligible that the results of different observers should differ both as regards the order of disappearance of the colours, and the extent of the area over which they are visible. The only point of really universal agreement is this, that the nasal portions of the normal retina are sensitive to all colours at a greater distance from the centre than the temporal, and the upper portions at a greater distance than the lower. The teleological value of this arrangement is evident. The two monocular fields of vision are partly coincident. The outlying portions of the two retinæ, therefore, mutually supplement each other: their colour sensitivity need not extend very far. But the inner, nasal portions are intended to function for the most part independently, and are accordingly so organised as to possess, each in its own right, an extended colour sensitivity. Similarly, it is as a general rule far more important for us to survey a large section of the lower portion of the field of vision, and cognise the colour qualities in it, than to have the power of overlooking an equally large section of its upper portion.

§ 20. After-images and Anomalies of Vision.

1. After sensations, regarded as direct after effects of stimulation, are nowhere so strong and so characteristic as in the domain of sight. The after sensations of pressure, which have but recently been discovered (§ 10. 5), would seem to appear only under very special conditions, hardly realised by normal stimulation. The effects of temperature stimuli may persist for a certain length of time, but always (so far as we know) in the quality of the original sensation. An after taste and an after smell are also known, but have not been made the subject of any systematic investigation. As a rule, they are probably

simply a more or less tardy remainder of the sensation excited by the stimulus. Lastly, an auditory after sensation has been observed, which is precisely analogous to the after sensation of pressure: it is separated from the primary sensation by a brief interval, and then appears as a reproduction of it at a less intensity. But on the whole, the after effects of auditory impressions are very weak and transient; and we have, therefore, made no special mention of them.

Visual sensations are exceptional in this respect. The visual *after-image* may differ in quality from the original impression. And it presents during its course a number of phenomena which are of interest in various connections, and have consequently been often examined. Thus the after-image is *continuous* (follows directly upon the primary impression, and constitutes a continuation of it) or *discrete* (separated from the impression by a brief interval, blank for sensation), according as the stimulation has lasted for a long or a short time. Again, it may be *positive*, resembling the primary impression in brightness, or *negative*, differing from it to a considerable degree. Again, the after-image of a colour can be *same-coloured*, *i.e.*, repeat the colour of the stimulus, or *other-coloured*, *i.e.*, exhibit a different colour. These other-coloured after-images are usually termed *complementary*, as they are most commonly of that quality. But the more general title is the more correct, since stimulation by mixed light with a predominant colour tone may give rise to other-coloured images whose quality is not complementary to that of the preponderant stimulus. Lastly, monocular stimulation can occasion an after-image not only in the excited, but also in the unstimulated eye (§ 9. 9). We must accordingly distinguish the *direct* image, of the stimulated eye, from the *crossed* image, of the other.

2. Discrete after-images are only obtainable from stimuli of very brief duration ($\frac{1}{100}$ sec. and less), such as the flash of a not too intensive electric spark. The primary image usually disappears with extraordinary quickness, and the appearance of the after-image occurs after an interval of some $\frac{1}{8}$ sec. Between sensation and after sensation, it is said, there not infrequently intervenes a negative (or complementary) after-image of exceedingly short duration [1]; and the positive is sometimes succeeded by a second, weak negative. If the duration of stimulation is increased, the positive (or same-coloured) image follows directly upon the primary sensation, to be followed in its turn, without noticeable interval, by the negative (or other-coloured). If the duration of stimulation is still further increased, a negative (or other-

---

[1] I have found confirmation of this statement in monocular observation, never in binocular. Binocular contrast (§ 68. 6) is possibly involved in the phenomenon.

coloured) image appears at once upon its cessation, *i.e.*, continuously with the original sensation. It appears, therefore, as if the characteristic course of the after-image could be studied most fully and with best result in its first form, as discrete; whereas the continuation of stimulation led to the omission of certain of its stages.

It is evident, then, that the phenomena of the after-image are essentially dependent upon the duration of stimulation. But of very great importance for its quality and the succession of its phases are, further, the quality, intensity, extension, and visual surroundings of the stimulus. If we stimulate the eye with apparently colourless light, the after-image will also be colourless—unless certain colour tones were really contained in the seemingly gray or white surface. If the mixed light is very intensive, and of not too brief duration, it gives rise to a whole series of coloured after-images [1]. This effect is known as the *flight of colours* in the after-image.

3. Stimulation with light of a single colour is usually followed (1) by a same-coloured positive, and (2) by a complementary, generally negative after-image. If the illumination of the retina is sufficiently intensive, and especially if the field of projection is dark, the complementary image may also be positive. The greater the intensity of stimulus, the greater is the duration of the after-sensation and the quicker the appearance of its negative (or complementary) phase. If the stimulation is sufficiently weak, on the other hand, there may be no second phase at all. A light of considerable intensity and little duration or extension has the same effect in after sensation, within certain limits, as a light of small intensity and greater duration or extension. The visual surroundings of the stimulus (of which we shall treat in detail when we come to speak of the phenomena of contrast: § 68) may enhance or diminish the vividness of the after-image, coloured or colourless. The nearer they approach to the colour or brightness of the stimulus, the less distinct is the after-image; simply because the whole of the light falling upon the retina will be effective for after sensation, and the same laws of phase and quality will hold for the area which we term 'the stimulus' as for all

---

[1] Thus, after looking at the sun for at most ½ sec., I have seen (1) a bright (positive) after-image, which (2) took on a red border; (3) then the centre became green, and a violet area appeared beyond the red border; (4) then the violet became dark gray and the red and green centre pure blue; (5) then the blue changed to white, with a red border; (6) then came a rose-violet centre, with dark blue border, while the dark gray area beyond took on a greenish colour; and finally, (7) the whole image was blue, with bright green border, upon a white field. This succession of phases occupied several minutes, and others would undoubtedly have followed if I had not interrupted the observation.

the rest. The brightness of the negative image of a black object will, therefore, be proportional to the brightness of the surroundings of the object and the darkness of the field upon which it itself is projected. Again, the brightness and colour tone of the after sensation are largely dependent upon the nature of the *primary* light, the original stimulus, and of the *reacting* light, the illumination of the field in which we see it. If we fixate a green object on a white background, the after-image on white is reddish, on green whitish, on red red. The same green object seen on a purple background gives in the dark field of vision a deep purple image with a broad green border. Finally, it must be mentioned that the excitability of the after-image differs greatly in different individuals. The stimulability of an eye can, to a certain extent, be measured by its after sensitivity, *i.e.*, the qualitative and temporal course of its after-images.

All these statements refer either to the binocular or the direct after-image. Proof has recently been adduced of the existence of a crossed image, which in temporal and qualitative regard is a weaker copy of the direct. Its total duration is less, the complementary phase appears later and is less saturated, its form is less distinct, sometimes it does not attain to the complementary stage at all, etc. Special practice is required for its observation: the two monocular fields of vision must be sharply separated, either by the help of instruments constructed for the purpose, or by squinting, or by exclusive concentration of the attention upon one field.

4. Corresponding in vividness and variety to the phenomena of after-images are a number of subjective visual sensations, which cannot be referred to the mere after effect of stimulation. We abstract here from the centrally excited sensations (which will be discussed in Ch. IV.), and shall mention only the light dust or light chaos, composed apparently of finely sifted specks of light, which is seen in the dark field of vision of the rested eye. If the eyes are quickly moved, there sometimes appear weak flashes of light, probably due to the mechanical shock imparted by movement to the optical apparatus. They occur, too, under inadequate stimulation,—pressure, pull upon the eye-ball, section of the optic nerve, electrical excitation. In all these cases a flash of bright light has been observed, indefinite in outline, and localised at the place of stimulation.

A leading part among subjective sensations is also played by entoptic perceptions, *i.e.*, the observation of objects within the seeing eye itself. Under favourable conditions we can see threads and granules moving in the vitreous humour, or an image of the retinal vessels. We need not go into these phenomena in detail, as they have no significance for psychological optics. Their quality is always some one of the familiar series of colours or brightnesses; and it has not been found possible to turn them to account for a theory of the physiological conditions of vision.

5. More important in this connection are the various anomalies of vision. We mean by the phrase not disturbances of visual space perception, but the abrogation of certain visual qualities. It is noteworthy (1) that a more or less complete colour blindness *(total* or *partial colour blindness)* is found, without impairment of the brightness sensitivity, but that there is no such thing as a separate brightness blindness, and (2) that in cases of total blindness, *i.e.*, of abrogation of sensitivity both for colour and brightness, the intrinsic retinal light or retinal black (§ 18. 7) also disappears. Total colour blindness is rare, and generally implies a diminution of the sensible discrimination for brightness: but partial colour blindness is quite common, and presents a number of varieties. Occasionally the blindness is confined to one eye, so that the visual qualities remaining can be checked by those of the normal retina, and the correctness of their definition assured; but this is not often.

Three classifications of colour blindness may be mentioned. (1) Visual systems have been divided, in terms of the phenomena of colour mixture (§ 17), into *trichromatic, dichromatic,* and *monochromatic.* The normal eye is trichromatic; the totally colour blind monochromatic; and the partially colour blind, all of whose sensations can be produced by the mixture of two primary colours, dichromatic. There is further a special class of anomalous trichromates, who react to three primary colours, but to three which differ considerably from those of the normal type. This classification is based upon one particular theory of the visual qualities: the second upon another. (2) It is assumed that red, green, and violet are not only primary colours (*i.e.*, of primary importance in colour mixture), but also primary sensations, corresponding to definite elementary nervous processes. There are then three possible forms of dichromatism: red blindness, green blindness, and violet blindness. (3) A third theory, finally, looks upon red-green and blue-yellow blindness as the only possible forms of partial colour blindness.

All these classifications, however, are merely schematic. Each rubric covers a number of demonstrably different forms. And even as schemata they are inadequate. Thus a case of insensitivity for violet, green and yellow has recently been observed, in which all varieties of visual quality could be obtained by the mixture of red and blue, and these two were actually complementary.

6. We cannot devote more space here to the diagnostic methods

or special forms of colour blindness. It will be sufficient to note certain important results of its observation, which lead us to the subject of the next Section. If it is true, as has lately been asserted, that hardly any two instances of colour blindness are precisely alike, the simplicity of the classifications hitherto proposed can only be defended on the ground that it allows of a general survey of the whole field. In other respects it must be regarded as altogether prejudicial to the detailed investigation of the facts. Assuming (as we did in § 19) that every discriminable quality in the closed series of colour tones is equally simple for sensation, we must accept a very large number of possible varieties of colour blindness. It must be emphasised, in particular, that the disappearance of particular colour qualities does not, on this view, necessarily involve the abrogation of their complementaries. And the scale of brightness sensations, an otherwise independent series of visual qualities, must also be considered as not necessarily affected by disturbances within the colour scale. This position has recently received confirmation in the course of careful investigations of total colour blindness. The brightness of the monochromatic spectrum proved to be precisely the same as that of the normal spectrum in Purkinje's experiment (§ 19. 6). A colour blind individual is, therefore, in much the same condition as one afflicted with partial deafness. It has been found that the sensitivity for tones can be diminished, while that for noise remains unimpaired. The analogy between this case and that of total colour blindness cannot, of course, be pressed; but we may reasonably compare insensitivity for deep tones (bass deafness) with, say, red blindness, or insensitivity for high tones (treble deafness), which is especially common, with, say, violet blindness. An abrogation of certain portions of the middle region of the tone scale is also known, though it is far more rare. Just as in psychophysical acoustics these facts have been held to support the theory of a cochlear key-board, an anatomical and physiological instrument reacting selectively upon sound waves of different vibration rates, the parallel facts of colour blindness have been appealed to, in psychophysical optics, to prove the existence of nerve fibres specifically sensitive to red, green, and violet, or of a red-green and blue-yellow visual substance.

§ 21.   Theories of Visual Sensation.

1. The optic nerve, the second cerebral nerve, connects the peripheral organs for the reception of light stimuli with the central termini of visual excitations, situated in the occipital lobes of the cerebral

cortex, and especially in the neighbourhood of the calcarine fissure. Whether centre or periphery is physiologically responsible for the different visual qualities is a question which we cannot at present answer with any degree of certainty. Some observers regard the peripheral terminal apparatus of the optic nerve in the retina as structures sufficiently differentiated in form or excitability to serve as the substrate of all the variety of our visual sensations. Others prefer to place the anatomical or functional differences of optical excitation, required by the facts of consciousness, in the central organ. Some, again, have had recourse to both—making the retina discriminate colours, and the cortex brightnesses; while others explicitly decline to refer the hypothetical differences in nervous process to particular localities within the optical nervous system. The differences between psy-/chophysical theories of vision and of the other senses, and between the visual theories themselves, are thus obvious from the very first. It seemed self-evident that the qualities of sensations of hearing, taste and pressure should be brought into relation with peripheral organs. In the case of sight, not even this preliminary point has been finally settled: and under such circumstances the translation of theoretical ideas into the concrete is plainly impossible. It is not surprising, then, either that the psychophysical theories of vision should be different, or that they should be abstract. Until the facts which we have passed in review in the previous Sections can be explained in definite physiological and anatomical terms, their 'theory' must necessarily remain a mere conceptual formulation of postulated physiological processes, more or less happily adapted to the psychical phenomena which it has to cover. We can here only sketch in briefest outline the most recent attempts made to cope with this difficulty.

2. In this condition of affairs it is not incumbent on us to give any very elaborate description of the optical apparatus,—more especially as we shall discuss certain parts of it in detail when we come to treat of visual space perception (§ 58). Of the path of light rays through the refractive media of the eye, *e.g.*, we shall say nothing. The essential facts are as follows. The optic nerve, on entering the eye-ball, radiates in all directions over the internal ocular membrane, the retina. It is insensitive to light at the place of entry, where we find none of the peculiar terminal organs, the rods and cones. The light ray must penetrate fairly deeply into the retina, before it can excite these terminal organs. At the spot of clearest vision, the yellow spot or fovea centralis, are set cones only; over the remaining area of the retina is spread a mosaic of rods and cones, the latter becoming more and more sparse as the periphery is approached. What change

is produced in the substance of these structures by illumination we do not know. The length of time required for the origination of a visual sensation, and the long duration of the after effect of stimulation, suggest, however, that the process of retinal excitation is of a chemical nature. The significance of the change of form of the cones (they become thicker and shorter under illumination) has not been ascertained. Light has a visible effect upon the visual purple, which is found in the external members of the rods, and causes a migration of the particles of pigment in the pigment layer: but though it is not improbable that both processes are in some way related to sensation, whether of brightness or colour, nothing positive can be said upon the question. Nor has any tenable hypothesis been proposed of the possible significance for the visual qualities of the extraordinarily delicate electrical stimulability of the ocular apparatus, and in particular of the idio-retinal currents. Even less can be said of the processes set up in the cortical visual area and the lower centres, such as the corpora quadragemina. So that in the sphere of vision we are unfortunately altogether unable to correlate anatomical and physiological facts with psychological data. Psychology, therefore, furnishes at once the only real criterion of validity and the exclusive factual support for the three theories which we shall now set forth.

3. (1) Regarded from this standpoint, the first theory—originally propounded by Young, and extended and specialised by Helmholtz— is certainly the least probable. It starts out from the existence of the three primary colours. From the fact that there are three homogeneous lights, the mixture of which in the right proportions gives all the colour tones, at a relatively maximal degree of saturation, and all the colourless sensations, it is argued that there are also three elementary excitations, and three primary sensations corresponding to them. The three excitations are conceived of as peculiar to three differently functioning nervous apparatus, whose peripheral terminations are endowed with different kinds of photochemically decomposable substances. Stimulation of one gives rise to the sensation of red; stimulation of another, to that of green; of the third, to that of violet. Objectively homogeneous light excites all three apparatus, but with different degrees of intensity, according to its wave length. Thus the red substance (if the phrase may be used for the sake of brevity) is intensively excited by red light, less intensively by yellow rays, and very weakly by violet. Every peripherally excited colour sensation depends, therefore, on a mixture of the three elementary excitations. Lastly, white arises in sensation from the simultaneous stimulation of all three substances at an equal degree of intensity.

(*a*) The most serious objection to the theory is the indubitable independence of the series of brightness sensations. We have only to
remember the existence of total colour blindness, the pure brightness
quality which results from very brief, very intensive or very weak stimulation with homogeneous light, and the phenomenon of Purkinje, to
be fully convinced of this. The secondary hypothesis of a qualitative
variability of the elementary excitations, which has been set up to explain, in particular, colour blindness and the decrease of the sensible
discrimination for colour tones towards the periphery of the retina, is
inadequate to meet the objection, apart from the fact that it leads to
extremely difficult and indeterminate ideas of the actual character of
the three primary sensations. (*b*) Moreover, the phrase 'primary sensation'
seems to be altogether inadmissible. Considered as sensations, all the
colour tones intermediate between red, green and violet are as simple
and elementary as these themselves. And the principle of psychophysical parallelism does not by any means require that all sensations be
correlated with equally elementary nervous processes. (*c*) Finally, the
theory does not take account in a satisfactory way of the incongruity
between the physical and the psychological (emphasised in § 18), and,
more especially, of the connection between colour tone and brightness,
of the complementariness of colours, and of the psychological equivalence of intensive homogeneous and mixed light.

4. (2) Hering's theory of vision improves upon the Young-Helmholtz hypothesis in most of the points to which we have taken exception. It, too, starts out from the assumption of three visual substances, though it expressly declines to localise them. Each of these
substances, however, is capable of serving as the substrate of two antagonistic nervous processes, dissimilation and assimilation, corresponding
respectively to the loss to the living organism occasioned by the excitation, and to its subsequent repair (cf. § 11. 5). The six hypothetical
processes thus obtained are the physiological correlates of six sensations,
which are, by the verdict of introspection, the only simple visual
qualities. They are the colour tones red, yellow, green and blue, and
the colourless sensations black and white. A gray, Hering says,
bears evident marks of its composition from black and white, and
orange, violet, etc., show as evidently that they are derived from the
mixture of two principal colours. The four colour tones are so chosen
that red and green, blue and yellow are complementaries: a condition
which shifts the 'primary red' in the direction of purple. We have,
accordingly, blue-yellow, red-green, and black-white substances. Red,
yellow and white are sensations of dissimilation; green, blue and black
sensations of assimilation. Every light stimulus stimulates the black-

white substance, while the other two substances are affected only by mixed light with a preponderant colour tone or homogeneous light of a visible wave length. If assimilation and dissimilation are in equilibrium, we have no colour sensation, but only one of brightness: and if the equilibrium occurs in the special black-white substance, it gives rise to a sensation of gray intermediate between the two extremes. Mixed colours and degrees of brightness arise from the preponderance of assimilation or dissimilation in various proportions.

5. There can be no doubt that Hering's theory does fuller justice to the facts described in our previous Sections than that of Helmholtz. Its ideas are, it is true, for the most part too abstract to furnish a real explanation of the facts, but at least they accord better with experience than do those of the foregoing hypothesis. (*a*) The most serious objection that can be urged against the theory is, again, an objection to the relation into which it brings the two series of coloured and colourless sensations. The complete analogy between the processes in the black-white substance and the two colour substances, assumed by the theory, does not really exist. Complementary colours pass into each other through a point of indifference, but the passage from the deepest black to the most brilliant white is along a continuous series of colourless sensations. It is impossible to suppose that an equilibrium of assimilation and dissimilation can in one case give rise to an intermediate gray, when in other cases it corresponds to the point of indifference between complementary colours, *i.e.*, to an abrogation of excitation in the particular colour substance. The peculiar nature of the brightness scale is unrecognised, therefore, in this theory as in the other. We must demand that the idea of antagonistic nervous processes be given up, either for colour or for brightness: it cannot possibly hold of both. (*b*) Again, an introspection which distinguishes by direct analysis the red and yellow, *e.g.*, in the transition tones lying between those qualities, and finds in every shade of gray a mixture of pure black and pure white, is certainly not characterised by that 'impartiality as regards the facts' (§ 2. 3) which we have seen to be a necessary condition of its psychological application. That a sensation differs more or less from certain other sensations must not be interpreted to mean that it is a mixture of these. The only qualitative analysis of which we are capable, when a retinal element is simultaneously stimulated by two or more colours, is the discrimination of colour tone and brightness. (*c*) We may pass over other difficulties, such as the inadequate explanation of certain forms of dichromatism. It need only be briefly remarked, in conclusion, that it is extremely improbable that the blue and green

rays, which are just as much stimuli as the red and yellow, exert an assimilative influence upon nervous substance.

6. (3) Wundt's theory of the visual qualities is, perhaps, the most abstract, but at the same time the theory which accords best with the facts of observation. According to it, the normal retina, when free from stimulation, is in a condition of permanent excitation from within. The correlate of this excitation is the sensation of black. Every light stimulation sets up two excitations, a chromatic and an achromatic. The former is an approximately periodic function of wave length, the most extreme visible differences of which produce similar physiological effects. The effects of certain intermediate differences are of opposite characters, so that they can entirely cancel one another. The achromatic excitation is dependent upon wave length only as regards its relative intensity. The two are, further, affected in different ways by the intensity of light. The achromatic begins at a very low degree of stimulus intensity, and increases continuously with it; the chromatic is greatest at moderate intensities of stimulus, and loses in weight, relatively to the achromatic, both with increase and decrease of the strength of stimulation.

If we translate this view into the current phraseology of 'visual substance', we obtain two substances, one of which reacts to light somewhat as the pupil does, *i.e.*, responds only to its intensity, and even when affected by homogeneous rays seems to be dependent simply upon their strength [1], while the other stands in an equally exclusive functional relation to the quality of coloured light, *i.e.*, to wave length. The apparent dependency of chromatic excitation upon stimulus intensity is readily explicable from the number of degrees of fusion of colour tone and brightness, as is the analogous apparent dependency of achromatic excitation upon wave length. We then only need to make the further assumption, for the chromatic substance, that the excitations set up by any two complementary lights cancel each other when they originate in the same retinal element, and that the different colours attain the maximum of saturation or distinctness at different degrees of light intensity. With these simple postulates it is possible, on Wundt's hypothesis, to give an unforced explanation of all the phenomena of vision.

7. In conclusion, we may notice one or two facts which must be regarded as important, whichever of the extant theories of vision we may accept or reject. (1) The superior sensitivity of the periphery of the retina for brightnesses is usually ascribed to the increase in the proportion of rods from the centre outwards. The rods are consid-

---

[1] According to Sachs, the pupillar reaction to colours is determined by their *apparent* brightness.

ered to be catoptric structures. (2) The colouring of the yellow spot seems to exert an especially weakening influence upon the blue rays, by absorption; and the fluorescence of the retina to be somewhat prejudicial to the approximation of the colour tones of the red and violet rays at the ends of the spectrum. (3) Fechner proposed, and Helmholtz and Wundt have adopted a theory of after-images, according to which the positive and same-coloured phases correspond to the after effect of the original excitation, while the negative and complementary are to be looked upon as phenomena of retinal exhaustion. The theory needs revision, in face of the pause in sensation between primary excitation and positive after-image, observed with stimuli of short duration. Hering regards after sensation partly as a continuation, partly as a reaction, of assimilation or dissimilation in some one of the visual substances.

Literature:

H. von Helmholtz, *Handbuch der physiologischen Optik*, 1867. Second ed., 1885 ff.

H. Aubert, *Grundzüge der physiologischen Optik*, 1876.

E. Hering, *Grundzüge einer Theorie des Lichtsinns und des Farbensinns. Sitzber. d. Wiener Akad. d. Wiss., Abth.* 3, vol. 69.

J. von Kries, *Die Gesichtsempfindungen und ihre Analyse*, 1882.

W. Wundt, *Die Empfindung des Lichts und der Farben. Phil. Studien*, vol. 4, pp. 310 ff. 1887.

(5). The Quality of the Organic Sensations.

§ 22. The Muscular, Tendinous and Articular Sensibility.

1. By 'organic sensations' we mean the sensations adequately stimulated by changes in the condition of the bodily organs,—muscles, joints, etc. Thus the sensation evoked by the movement of a limb or arising from muscular fatigue, and that which follows from a diminution of the amount of moisture in the mucous membrane of the pharynx, are organic sensations. In every case, the adequate stimulus consists of a change in the condition of the particular organ, and the organ itself is the peripheral seat of origin of the nervous excitation which is thus set up. The fact that the stimulus acts within the body, —indeed, is a bodily process, and that the organic sensation itself is not referred, as a rule, to any external cause, has led to the belief that a sharp line of distinction must be drawn between the internally excited and externally excited sensation contents. The latter are the sensations of the 'five senses'; the former constitute 'common feeling',— although an exception has sometimes been made in favour of the 'muscle sense', which has been accounted the sixth of the special

senses. But there is nothing in the phenomena to justify this principle of classification.

(1) Sensation qualities may be essentially similar, however great the differences in their localisation. (2) Localisation is not a safe criterion in any case. Thus, if it is to serve as *differentia*, the subjectified visual sensations must be included in common feeling. If on the other hand the name is used to denote complexes, fusions of sensations, it must be remembered that these cannot be co-ordinated with the simple qualities of the external senses. Our present investigation of organic sensation will be confined to the discussion of the question whether they present new qualities, not contained in any of our previous lists, and to the explication of their peripheral origination, where that is possible.

2. The heading of this Section enumerates the most familiar, and perhaps the commonest of the organic sensations. The three classes are still not infrequently grouped together under the name of the *muscle sense*. But now that we know that not only the muscles, but the ligaments, tendons and articular surfaces mediate sensations, which would all fall within the group covered by this term, we must evidently give it up as inadequate. It is more usual at the present time to find the sensations classed as *movement sensations* or kinæsthetic sensations, for the double reason that they are most effectually excited by movements, and serve as our principal means of estimating movement. But this very ambiguity of application has proved to be a fruitful source of error, and is sufficient to condemn the proposed title. Since we are now able, within certain limits, to determine the special parts played by the various organs in 'movement sensation', it seems best to employ the particular rubrics given above—muscular, tendinous and articular sensibility. We thus escape the danger of a confusion of the visual or cutaneous 'movement sensations' with the organic.

The analysis of organic sensations has not been an easy matter. The organs are not exposed, isolated excitability can only be predicated in rare cases, and the stimuli are not sufficiently well known. The two methods of qualitative analysis, which we have previously described (§ 12. 2, 3) as the physical and physiological, cannot, therefore, be called upon to assist in their determination. Again, the normal indistinctness of the qualities and their very high degree of fusion prevent any exact discrimination by introspective analysis. Our knowledge of the sensations is, in fact, entirely due to experiment and to anatomical, physiological and pathological observation. It is only since the sixties, to speak roughly, that a special muscular sense has been recognised, while the significance of tendinous and articular sensation is a discovery of the past few years.

3. If we move our hand slowly to and fro with fingers outspread, while the eyes remain closed, we have (1) an extraordinarily accurate visual idea of its changes of position, (2) a number of fairly distinct cutaneous sensations, due to changes in the tension of the skin, and (3) very vague and weak sensations from subcutaneous organs,—so little intensive that, in certain positions, we are conscious only of those residing in the wrist-joint. If, again, we hold our hand out as though we were firmly grasping some small object, the internal sensations are very vivid; preponderant in the complex being a certain sensation of strain, which quickly becomes unpleasant. We observe similar sensations if we let our arm hang down while a heavy weight is held in the hand, only that the strain sensation is now distributed over the whole arm. These facts seem to show that the sensations arising from the friction of the articular surfaces are brought into special clearness by movement, and that they are specifically different from the strain sensations, which are not necessarily excited to a noticeable degree by the simple movement of a limb or organ. We can convince ourselves still more positively of the existence of articular sensations by moving a finger which is strongly pressed down in its socket, *i.e.*, under conditions of unusual proximity of the articular surfaces concerned. Strain sensations, on the other hand, appear most intensively in consciousness after exhausting bodily exercise or in muscular cramp. When the limbs are not moving, the excitations set up in the joints are exceedingly weak and, as a rule, no more remarked than the cutaneous excitations due to the pressure of our clothes. We may, accordingly, suppose that movement is the adequate stimulus for the articular sensibility, and the contraction of muscle and tendon indirectly dependent upon it the adequate stimulus for the sensations excited in those organs. As both muscles and tendons are involved in every contraction, we may for the present employ the general term *strain sensation* to cover all the sensations derived from them, distinguishing this class from that of the articular sensations. It is evident that only the articular sensibility can furnish exact information of extent of movement; that it alone can arouse an accurate visual idea or a direct judgment of change of position. Indeed, this is a universal rule of sensation. While it is characteristic of adequate stimuli that they stand in the most comprehensive functional relation to the sensations which they excite, we also have in them, conversely, the best criterion of the existence and quality of particular sensations. The adequate stimuli for articular sensations are movements, the positions of a limb from moment to moment; the adequate stimuli for strain sensations are the greater or less degrees of contraction of muscle and tendon.

4. Anatomy and physiology have proved the existence of sensory nerves in joint, ligament, and tendon as well as in muscle. The articular surfaces are richly supplied with the Vater-Pacini corpuscles, familiar to us from the external skin (§ 10. 6), and the sinews contain peculiar terminal apparatus, the sensory terminal plates and the spindles of Golgi. The nervous terminations in the muscles are, for the most part, free fibrillar processes: nuclei are sometimes found. The existence of sensory nerves has also been demonstrated in the fasciæ and sheaths of muscle and tendon. We may, perhaps, conjecture from these facts that strain sensations are mediated by the peculiar terminal organs of the tendon nerves, while the free nervous terminations or Vater-Pacini corpuscles are excited in the same way as the cutaneous pressure nerves, and give rise to qualitatively similar sensations. The articular sensations are, undoubtedly, very closely related to those of pressure. Of muscle sensations proper we know hardly anything. Goldscheider rendered the skin over a muscle anæsthetic by a subcutaneous cocaine injection, and then produced a slight muscular contraction by electrical stimulation. There was no sensation. With increased strength of current and stronger contraction, he obtained "a dull sensation of peculiar character", which was qualitatively entirely similar to a sensation caused by pressure on the muscle, was subcutaneously localised, made an impression of 'diffusion', and did not at all suggest the idea of movement. The same observer has shown that our judgment of the heaviness of lifted weights, when the cutaneous pressure factor is as far as possible eliminated, is founded not upon sensations of muscular innervation, but upon impressions proceeding from the strain exerted on the tendons. It seems certain, therefore, that the strain sensations, in the strict sense, which may play so large a part in consciousness, are peripherally excited in the tendons and the tendons alone. On the other hand, the muscle sensations, which were formerly accorded the leading rôle in the cognition of weight and the estimation of the magnitude and direction of movement, do not really appear at all, except as the result of intensive stimulation, great fatigue, or in the form of muscular pain; and, consequently, are only useful as informing us of the functional capacity of the organs.

5. This view is confirmed both by psychophysical experiment and pathological experience. (1) It has been proved (a) that our sensible discrimination for the heaviness of weights is much more delicate when they are lifted, than when they exercise a merely passive pressure upon the skin. (b) We know, too, from everyday observation, that the weight of an object in sensation is proportional to its distance from the point of rotation of the moveable limb. This illustration of the

law of the lever could not be explained in terms of simple cutaneous sensation. (*c*) And, lastly, sensible discrimination and sensitivity for weights remain unimpaired when the sensibility of skin and muscles has been very greatly reduced by artificial means, *e.g.*, by faradisation; whereas the same sensitivity is proportionally lessened by diminution of the tendinous sensibility. We may conclude from these observations that strain sensations produced by weighting a moveable limb are of independent origin, and that the place of their origination is the tendinous nerve termination. On the other hand, there are numerous investigations and experiences which speak for the importance of the articular sensibility. (*a*) It may be conjectured *a priori* that muscular and tendinous sensations cannot form the ground of our judgment of the position and movement of our limbs in the absence of visual perception. We saw above that movement is not to be regarded as the adequate stimulus for strain sensations. We may now add to this the fact that it is impossible to postulate a uniform relation between amount of contraction or degree of extension of muscle or tendon and magnitude of movement. Not the mere change in length of muscle or tendon would appear to produce a sensation, but only the intensity of the strain accompanying contraction and extension. It plainly follows that a considerable movement may be correlated with an insignificant strain, and a slight movement with a severe strain, *i.e.*, that there is no proportionality between extent and direction of a movement and the possible concomitant sensory excitations in muscle and tendon. On the other hand, the relation between the positions of the articular surfaces as regards each other and positions or movements of the limb is just as simple as that between the different parts of skin or retina and the points from which they are stimulated. (*b*) If the arm is supported by a rest, its position can be judged as correctly as though it were held out freely, in spite of the extremely different amounts of muscular activity involved in the two cases. (*c*) Experimental diminution of the cutaneous and muscular sensibility by the interrupted current does not impair the judgment of position and movement, whereas a similar disturbance of the articular sensibility affects them very considerably. We see, therefore, that the articular sensibility furnishes the real basis of our perception of the position and movement of our limbs, where an appeal to vision is excluded.

(2) Pathological observation is in complete agreement with these results. (*a*) In cases of complete anæsthesia of the external skin, the judgment of the position of the limbs is perfectly normal, and even where the anæsthesia involves the muscles it is not inadequate.

If, on the other hand, the whole limb is insensitive, the patient lets an object fall which is given him to hold,—unless he can look at it,—and has no idea at all of the position of the diseased limb. (*b*) It has also been noticed that patients suffering from anæsthesia of skin and muscles give the most accurate judgment of movement if the articular surfaces of the moved limb are pressed closely together, and become very uncertain in judgment if the joint is pulled as far as possible apart.

6. The inference to be drawn from this discussion is very simple. (1) The quality of articular sensations is, in all probability, quite similar to the quality of pressure, mediated by the external skin. (2) The strain sensations derived from the sensory nerve terminations in the tendons present a new quality. (3) The muscular sensations, which become noticeable only when the change of organic condition which stimulates them is of some magnitude, are also, it seems, of a peculiar kind, although we cannot give any definite account of their quality.

The qualitative similarity of articular and pressure sensations can be illustrated in another way. Besides their importance for space perception, the articular surfaces furnish us with information of the resistance which we encounter in touching, grasping, striking, etc. Our judgment is based, in particular, upon the intensity of the sensations aroused, which are exceedingly responsive to variation in the amount of the resistance offered, the density and solidity of the object touched. That it is really a specific function of the articular sensibility has been shown by Goldscheider, in a series of experiments devised for this express purpose. The phenomenon which he names 'the paradoxical resistance sensation' is very striking. Suppose that a weight, not too light, attached to the hand or finger by a thread, is dropped with moderate quickness till it strikes suddenly, but as noiselessly as possible, upon some soft surface. There at once arises a fairly distinct sensation of resistance, due to the persistence of the contraction of the antagonists after the weight has ceased to act, and the consequent increase in the counterpressure of the articular surfaces against each other.—It is very misleading to term the same sensations sensations of resistance or of position and movement, according as they mediate an idea of resistance or a spatial perception. We might equally well name the cutaneous pressure sensations sensations of pressure, place, or movement, as circumstances suggested, and so appear to imply the existence of three different qualities. That two classes of judgments or ideas should originate in the same sensations does not present any real difficulty. In the cognition of the magnitude of a pressure or resistance, their intensive differences are the important thing: in space perception we rely not upon this intensive gradation, but rather upon their local difference. The character of the dependency involved cannot be further discussed here.

It is impossible at present to attempt a detailed theory of the muscular, tendinous, and articular sensibilities. We will only mention in conclusion that all the sensory nerves concerned probably ascend to the brain in the posterior columns of the cord, and radiate in the cerebral cortex for the most part in the neighbourhood of the posterior central convolution. It is noteworthy that these columns, whose chief function is to inform us of the condition of our own body, attain their full growth particularly early in the development of the individual organism.

Literature :

G. E. Müller and F. Schumann: *Ueber die psychologischen Grundlagen der Vergleichung gehobener Gewichte.* Pflüger's *Archiv f. d. ges. Physiol.*, vol. 45, pp. 37 ff.

A. Goldscheider: *Untersuchungen über den Muskelsinn.* Du Bois-Reymond's *Archiv f. Physiol.*, 1889. pp. 369 ff. Supplement. Pp. 141 ff.

E. B. Delabarre: *Ueber Bewegungsempfindungen.* Dissertation. Freiburg. 1891.

§ 23. Analysis of the Common Sensations.
The 'Static Sense.'

1. We employ the expression common sensation, in place of the usual physiological term 'common feeling', to designate certain compound mental states, which are the result of the combination of various sensory excitations from the periphery of the body, and whose elements, so far as they can be determined by analysis, are to be regarded as sensations. This definition excludes two special elements which play an important part in common feeling as ordinarily understood, *i.e.*, the pleasurable and painful constituents of the complex. It is a fact of continual experience that these processes (which in our terminology must be denominated feelings) are apt to attain a high degree of intensity when compounded with sensations of the internal organs. Peripheral pain appears almost exclusively in company with sensations of this kind, and the most intensive sense pleasure, the sexual, also occurs in connection with certain organic sensations. Since the presence of a strong feeling conceals the quality of its concomitant sensations, the analysis of a class of sensations which hardly ever make their appearance except under this condition will obviously be exceedingly difficult. Moreover, the experimental appliances, which render such good service elsewhere in facilitating the isolation of the constituents of a complex, by specially directed variation and modification, for purposes of observation and judgment, are here almost entirely useless.

Our description of the common sensations must, therefore, be incomplete and hypothetical. We can do no more than review their most familiar forms, and determine their presumptive elements. With this intention we will deal as briefly as possible with hunger and thirst, tickling, itching, tingling, and shivering, exertion and fatigue, the sensations attending the cardiac and respiratory activities, and physical well-being and its reverse.

2. *Hunger* and *thirst* are the common sensations which more particularly subserve the nutritive impulse. Their localisation is comparatively definite: hunger is usually referred to the interior of the body, and thirst to the buccal cavity. But the causes of their appearance, proximate and remote, are still obscure. We may suppose that their localisation is correct, *i.e.*, tallies with their peripheral origination, since thirst can be quenched, at least for the time being, by moistening the soft palate and the root of the tongue with citric or acetic acid, and hunger has been removed by the direct introduction of food into the stomach through a fistula. The condition of thirst would thus appear to be a decrease of the amount of moisture in the mucous membrane of the mouth. That the acids can generally quench thirst is due to their special action upon the secretion of the salivary glands. The quality of the sensations noticeable in thirst must be regarded as cutaneous, and preponderantly as that of pressure (the tongue 'cleaves to the roof of the mouth'). But that some part is played by temperature sensations is shown by the well known phenomenon of feverish thirst, which may rise to the point of pain. The proximate cause is again, in all probability, a drying of the mucous membrane, which thus loses in its power to conduct heat. The conditions of hunger are more difficult to determine. It might be thought that continued inactivity of the muscular system of stomach and intestine would result in a state of stimulation giving rise to this complex of sensations. More probable is the assumption that the formation of acid, which takes place on an increased scale immediately after the completion of digestion, acts as a stimulus upon the mucous membrane of the stomach, and so provokes hunger. On this theory the quality of the sensations involved would again be cutaneous.

3. The second group of common sensations are also, undoubtedly, complexes of cutaneous sensations. *Tickling* is produced by weak and intermittent stimulation of the skin, or sometimes even by a mere light touch upon some part of it. The unpleasant factor in these sensations shows itself in reflex or voluntary movements of defence, rubbing of the stimulated area, etc. The expressive movement of laughter, which often accompanies tickling and stands in apparent

contradiction to the movements of repulsion, is probably not the effect
of the common sensation but of feelings arising from the comicality
of the situation. *Itching* appears (to the author and others) to be a
complex of the same sensations as tickling, except that it generally
arises from some internal cutaneous change, without the operation of an
external stimulus. We may accordingly suppose that the causes of these
two common sensations are the same. And it seems reasonable to imagine
that alterations of circulation are the proximate conditions of tickling
and itching alike. It has been found that gentle pressure or blowing upon
a portion of the skin is followed by a considerable increase of arterial
blood pressure, while intensive and even painful stimulation is often
unable to influence it in any way. [1] We may, therefore, believe that
certain processes (not at present definable) in the vessels which supply
the skin serve as the substrate of the cutaneous impressions of weak
pressure, and especially of more or less vivid heat, which occur in
quick alternation in tickling and itching. The qualitative constituents
of *tingling*, pricking, pins and needles,—complexes which are sensed
in their full character during weak faradisation of the skin or the
'waking up' of a limb which has 'gone to sleep',—are altogether
similar, except that the special intermittent sensations are stronger than
they are in tickling. Here, again, we may refer the common sensation
to excitations of the sensory cutaneous nerves, due to change in the
metabolism of the tissue. *Shivering* and goose-flesh seem to originate
in diffuse excitations of the nerves of temperature, as certainly as fever-
ishness and parchedness. They may all be ascribed, once more, to
vasomotor changes.

4. *Exertion* and *fatigue* are qualitat. ly most nearly related to strain
sensations and muscular sensations. Both are among the most familiar
of common sensations to those who are intensively engaged upon
physical or mental work. The peculiar sensations of this kind, often
passing the limit of pain, which are aroused by persistent mental activity, are the result (1) of the continuance of a definite bodily position
during a long period of time, (2) of the unvarying accommodation and
fixation of the eye, and (3) of involuntarily arising strain of the superficial muscles of the head. According to the general law that a
nervous excitation of a given intensity can be produced either by an
intensive stimulus of short duration or by a weak stimulus of long
duration, we may assume that the continued action of the weak stimuli
involved in such cases will in the long run lead to these common

---

[1] I have also noticed that when the blood is confined within the finger by a liga-
ture round the lowest joint, the sensitivity of the isolated phalanges for tickling is
entirely destroyed.

sensations just as infallibly as a brief experience, say of the carrying of a heavy load. The common sensations which accompany alterations of the activity of the *heart* and of *respiration* are of a similar nature. Like most impressions of the same class, they only become noticeable as a general rule when the stimuli are intense and the disturbances they cause unpleasant, or when a change of some magnitude takes place in the organs which mediate them. We are for the most part conscious only of the cutaneous sensations excited by the movements of heart or lungs, or of secondary phenomena connected with the greater or less degree of uniformity with which these organs supply the tissues. At the same time, the original sensations of strain and exhaustion in heart and lungs sometimes make themselves known in an unusually strong heart-beat and respiration. Lastly, the states which lead us to say that we are 'all right' or the contrary furnish a particularly good illustration of the ordinary vagueness of the common sensations. If we abstract from the feelings of pleasure and pain, which are certainly of primary importance for both conditions, it is hardly possible to point with assurance to any group of definite sensations, to which the feelings are attached.

5. So far, then, we have found no new qualities among the common sensations. But this does not affect the multeity of their total impression: spatial and temporal relations, the intensity of the different qualities, and their connection with feelings are sufficient to endow them with great variety. We now pass to the consideration of another common sensation, *giddiness,* which has lately come to be regarded as the function of a particular sense organ, that of the *static sense.* This organ consists of the nervous apparatus of the vestibule and semicircular canals of the labyrinth; and the nerve which conducts its excitations to the centre is the vestibular, one of the two main branches of the eighth cerebral nerve (cf. § 16. 1). The vestibule is divided into two sacs, one of which, the utriculus, communicates with the canals, while the other, the sacculus, is connected with the cochlea by the cochlear canal. In both divisions are certain small elevations, the maculae acusticae, into which the nervous terminations penetrate, and from which they issue in the form of bristle-cells or hair-cells. A very delicate membrane rests upon these hairs and supports the otoliths, minute white crystals of carbonate of lime. The nervous stimulation is, in all probability, set up by a mechanical concussion of the points of the bristles in the endolymph. The fibres of the vestibular nerve which enter the canals terminate in a very similar way. The canals themselves are three bent tubes, filled with endolymph, and placed at right angles to each other in the three planes of space.

Each of them as it leaves the vestibule swells out to form an ampulla, which contains the nerve endings. These again take the shape of fine bristles or hairs, projecting fanwise from a ridge, the crista acustica, and covered with a delicate membrane. The excitation will, therefore, be a similar mechanical concussion of the liquid of the labyrinth, such as would be produced, *e.g.*, by a movement of the head.

6. It was formerly thought that the excitations of these organs had to do with hearing, and, in particular, with the perception of noise. Recently, an attempt has been made to use them for the explanation of our cognition of the direction from which a sound comes to us, *i.e.*, to give them a functional significance as organs for the localisation of auditory stimuli. But despite its apparent support by the spatial arrangement of the three canals, the hypothesis is exceedingly improbable, for the reason that there is absolutely no proof of a uniformity of relation between the spatial positions of the sound producing body and the various points of excitation of the vestibular nerve. On the other hand, an alternative theory, which makes canals and vestibule the organ of a static sense, is steadily gaining ground. It embraces, however, two distinct views which are liable to be confused. The first is, that the vestibular nerve endings constitute an organ for the maintenance of the bodily equilibrium; the second, that they mediate sensations, or more correctly ideas, of rectilineal movement and rotation of the body, and especially of the head. The two hypotheses are not mutually exclusive, but they do not either necessarily imply one another. The condition of bodily equilibrium can be conceived of as regulated entirely by reflexes, without any participation of consciousness. And just as we should not think of making the constant arousal and government of the respiratory and cardiac activities dependent upon sensations, so we need not suppose that the sensory excitations proceeding from vestibule and canals effect the delicate and accurate adjustments of the muscles of body or head, which maintain equilibrium in the most different movements and positions, simply and solely by way of sensation intermediaries. We must, therefore, separate the question of a reflex mechanism for equilibrium from that of special conscious processes due to the same bodily organ. We shall find that the existence of the former is well attested, while that of specific sensations is still *sub judice*.

7. The result of (1) anatomical investigations has been to show that the principal connection of the vestibular nerve is with the cerebellum, although it also has a centre in the medulla oblongata. No path to the cerebral cortex has as yet been made out. (2) A large number of physiological observations on animals have put it beyond question that

the canals constitute an important organ for the maintenance of equilibrium, exciting and sustaining a permanent muscular tonus, *i.e.*, a certain active tension of the muscular system. The more delicate and varied the functions of a particular muscle, the more completely subject it seems to be to this organ. (3) These facts obtain valuable support from pathology, from observations made on deaf-mutes. In a certain percentage of cases, the peripheral organ of the vestibular nerve is found to be destroyed as well as that of the cochlear. A similar proportion of patients undergo characteristic disturbances of equilibrium when blindfolded. Many of them, also, show no trace of the 'compensatory' eye movements, which appear under normal conditions after rotation of the body, and which point to a reflex connection between the nerves supplying the muscles of the eyeball and sensory excitation of the vestibular terminations. (4) Lastly, Mach's psychophysical experiments on the objective and subjective phenomena produced by passive rotation and rectilineal forward movement of the body, render it probable that our judgment of the position and movement of the body is derived only in part from the indications afforded, *e.g.*, by the articular and cutaneous sensibilities and visual perception, and that there must be a special organ in the head affected by change of position and acceleration of movement. All these results, as we can see, furnish evidence for the existence of a reflex mechanism, the sensory portion of which is placed in canals or vestibule. The character of its peripheral excitation has been variously conceived. Some observers refer it to a concomitant movement of the endolymph, others to simple change of pressure in the endolymph, and others again to active ciliary movements of the hair-cells, which must meet with a different resistance from the water of the canals in accordance with the position and movements of the head. However this may be, the situation of these structures is such that an alteration of the position of the head can at once effect a change in the excitation of the entire organ.

8. But the question of the mediation of peculiar sensations by vestibule and canals does not admit of any such definite answer. Animal vivisection, of course, leaves it entirely open,—all the more as the particular motor disturbances which follow removal or blocking of the canals or electrical and mechanical stimulation of the ampullary nerves appear with the same (or even greater) regularity after extirpation of the cerebrum as when the cortex is left intact. Moreover, an impartial introspection of our non-visual ideas of bodily position and movement does not give any new sensation qualities besides the cutaneous, tendinous and articular. The only psychical process which appears to represent the activity of the organ in consciousness is that of *giddiness,*

which may also make its appearance, as we know, after rotation, in the form of 'rotatory vertigo.' But this process has such a variety of causes—it can arise, *e.g.*, without any movement of head or body—that it is dangerous to make it exclusively dependent upon an affection of the canals. It is difficult to say what the common element in sensations of giddiness is, when we have abstracted from the objective disturbance of the co-ordination of movements and its various concomitant phenomena. If we describe it as 'an illusory perception of the spatial relations of our surroundings,' the specific character of the common sensation is left entirely unmentioned. The nature of the excitation in vestibule and ampullæ suggests that the sensations produced there may be regarded as pressure sensations; but, under ordinary circumstances, we do not appear to localise qualities of this kind in the neighbourhood of the organ. The argument that deaf-mutes are often found to be incapable of sensations of giddiness is weakened by the consideration that individual differences in inclination or disposition to attacks of vertigo are normally very great. We must, therefore, suspend our judgment with regard both to the origination of the common sensation and the possible qualities mediated by the 'static sense.' We shall return to the subject in brief when we are dealing with the idea of space (§ 62. 6).

Literature :

C. Richet, *Recherches expérimentales et cliniques sur la sensibilité*, 1877.

E. Kröner, *Das körperliche Gefühl*, 1887.

E. Mach, *Grundlinien der Lehre von den Bewegungsempfindungen*, 1875.

J. R. Ewald, *Physiologische Untersuchungen über das Endorgan des nervus octavus*, 1892.

§ 24. The Intensive Sensibility.

1. The problems to be solved by the psychology of sensation in connection with its second general property, that of intensity, are simpler than those presented in the sphere of quality. We have not now, as in the previous Chapter, to devote most of our attention to the discrimination of a large number of conscious contents, each and all demanding special description and theory. Intensity is a more abstract sensation attribute, and can, therefore, be much more easily dealt with from general points of view, valid for all qualities alike. The differences of numerical result which are naturally found again in intensive sensitivity and sensible discrimination do not affect this statement. For in our consideration of the intensive sensible discrimination we shall come at once upon a general uniformity, which will be of great service in facilitating our survey of the facts. And the differences which we shall discover in intensive sensibility, where they are not due to the incomparability of determinations in various sense departments, find their explanation in certain peculiarities of the external sensory apparatus and not in the nature of particular qualities. We shall, therefore, be able, after a brief discussion of the general problems and methods of this part of our subject, to give a simple tabulation of the most important results obtained for all the classes of sensation discussed in the foregoing Chapter.

2. The intensity of a sensation is an attribute of finite extent and one-dimensional character, defined by its upper and lower limiting values. The lower limiting value is that of the weakest or minimal sensation; the upper, that of the strongest or maximal. We can, again, give a numerical expression of these values only by translating them into terms of the stimuli which correspond to them. The just noticeable stimulus is, therefore, the equivalent of a sensation just discriminable from no-sensation; and the *terminal stimulus* the equi-

valent of the strongest sensation, *i.e.*, of one which is not susceptible of further intensification. As there are just noticeable sensation stimuli or stimulus limina in other connections than the intensive, we shall speak in this Chapter of the *intensive stimulus limen.* The expression 'terminal stimulus', on the other hand, has been restricted to denote the upper limit of sensation intensity. It is certainly possible to employ it, too, in reference to the other sensation attributes. Thus we might use the expression 'qualitative terminal stimulus', when we are giving the number of vibrations required for a perception of tonal quality incapable of further increase of distinctness (cf. § 15. 4). And we might conceive of an 'extensive terminal stimulus,' as marking the limit of comprehensibility of a spatial complex in the field of vision or of regard. But we need not attach any weight to these possibilities, since the terminal stimulus, in whatever reference it is meant, cannot be of very great importance. In the present connection of intensity, in particular, we must remain content with the name, and the belief that it corresponds to a fact: we are precluded from undertaking any special or detailed investigation by regard for the integrity of the organ experimented on. The ordinary measure of sensibility, in all the sense departments, is consequently afforded by the stimulus limen. The only other determination which yields useful results is that of relative sensibility by the method of stimulus comparison.—The sensible discrimination for intensities is also subjected to measurement. The methods employed are those of difference determination and difference comparison (cf. § 6). In every case, the affection of stimulus correlated with change of intensity in sensation is of great importance. We have no right at all to assume an exclusive functional relation between strength of stimulus and intensity of sensation. Sensation intensity is also dependent upon the temporal and spatial character of the stimulus. At the same time, the strength of stimulus bears a similar relation to intensity of sensation, as is borne by the adequacy of stimulus to its quality. It accordingly furnishes us with the only means of a complete determination of sensitivity and sensible discrimination for intensity over their whole extent.

3. (1) Intensive sensibility in the sphere of *cutaneous* sensations.— (*a*) The adequate stimulus for *pressure* sensation is the presence upon the skin of some ponderable body. The intensity of the sensation is dependent upon the weight of this body. The intensive sensibility is tested by the aid of thermally indifferent objects, *e.g.*, small cork pellets. It has been found in this way by the method of stimulus determination that ⴹ varies within wide limits according to the part of the skin which is stimulated. Thus it is 2 mg. upon forehead,

nose, and cheeks, 5 mg. on lips, upper arm, and nape of the neck, 10 mg. on the fingers, and 1 g. on the nails. Moreover, the limen on the extremities is somewhat lower over the whole left side of the body than over the right. The differences in these values are certainly more than the expression of a varying sensibility in the cutaneous nerve endings: they point to the influence of the very considerable differences in the thickness and resistance of the epidermis. We do not know how far they are referable to the special forms of nervous terminations in the skin (§ 10. 6). Another noteworthy fact is, that cold weights seem heavier than warm weights of the same magnitude. Its explanation must be looked for in the mechanical effects of thermal stimuli upon the skin. We know nothing definite about these: but it is not improbable that they are connected with the diminution of sensibility which is observed to accompany hyperæmia, and the increase which attends anæmia of a cutaneous area. (*b*) An examination of the intensive sensibility of *temperature* sensations presents peculiar difficulties, owing to the variability of the physiological zero-point and the uncertainty attaching to its determination. We cannot at present make any positive statement of the magnitude of the just noticeable stimulus of heat and cold. Some measure of information is afforded, however, by the results of stimulus comparison in this department. It has been ascertained that the sensitivity for cold is on the whole greater than that for heat; that the increase or decrease of the two sensitivities at different parts of the body follows parallel lines; that sensitivity in general is more weakly developed in the median line of the body than over its lateral surfaces; and that as a rule it increases from the periphery towards the trunk. The explanation of these phenomena is afforded partly by the more frequent occurrence of cold spots, partly by the different conductivity of the epidermis, partly by variation in nervous and vascular supply, etc. Lastly, it is interesting to remark that temperature stimuli appear more intensive, the larger the cutaneous area which they affect. A bowl of warm water seems warmer to the whole hand than when only a single finger is dipped into it. Whether this fact is to be considered a summation effect, or is merely dependent upon the different sensitivity of the different parts of the skin, cannot at present be decided.

4. (2) Intensive sensibility in the sphere of sensations of *taste* and *smell*.—We have already seen (§§ 12, 13) that the adequate stimulus for these sensory qualities cannot yet be defined in terms of physics or chemistry. The customary statements of the relative quantities of gustatory or olfactory substances which constitute the stimulus limen are, therefore, of but doubtful value. For we are not justified in concluding from them that the sensitivity for the particular taste or smell

stimuli is different. Thus the assertion that a strychnine solution in the proportions of 1 : 2,000,000 is just noticeably bitter, or a saccharine solution of 1 : 200,000 just noticeably sweet, does not necessarily imply that the sensitivity for bitter is greater than that for sweet. We have no measure of bitter or sweet; so that the results possess simply an empirical value for particular known substances. Precisely the same holds of the sense of smell. It is true that the acuteness of taste and smell in different individuals can be compared in this way, and that such comparison will always be useful in clinical investigation. But it is more important for the psychologist to know that different parts of the tongue possess a different sensibility. Unfortunately, there are no exact quantitative determinations of this fact (for which cf. § 12. 5) extant. The intensity of gustatory sensation is further dependent, like that of temperature, upon the magnitude of the area excited. It can be increased by movement and pressure of the gustable substance within the buccal cavity. The intensity of olfactory sensation is dependent upon the rapidity of respiration of the current of air charged with the olfactory substance. Sensitivity seems also to be increased by a quick succession of inspiratory movements ('sniffing').

5. (3) Intensive sensibility in the sphere of *auditory* sensations.—The intensity of a sound stimulus is represented by the amplitude of the vibrations or concussions occurring in the ordinary medium (atmospheric air) or in some moveable solid body, etc. This amplitude is merely the expression of the kinetic energy of the movement of the vibrating masses. We have no adequate objective method of ascertaining the intensity of the non-periodic and aperiodic concussions which form the substrate of simple or complex noises, independently of the statements of the observer whose sensibility we are testing. The phonometric determination of sound intensity in psychophysical experiments is, therefore, usually carried out upon a principle similar to that employed in photometry: the objective stimulus values in the apparatus employed,—say, elastic balls falling from a measurable height upon a resisting plate,—are determined by way of a subjective comparison. The results are, then, purely empirical, valid only for the material used, the special circumstances of the observation, etc. Thus it has been found that a cork pellet of 1 mg. weight falling from a height of 1 mm. upon a glass plate at a distance of 91 mm. from the ear is just audible under favourable external conditions. A similar attempt at an absolute determination for tones with a pipe of 181 vibrations gave the amplitude of vibration of an air particle at the limiting distance of audibility as 0·00004 mm., and the mechanical work

performed on the tympanic membrane as $\dfrac{1}{3\ \text{billions}}$ kgm. This illustrates the extraordinary acuteness of hearing. On the whole, the sensitivity for tones appears somewhat greater than that for simple noises. This is explicable on the assumption that a noise excites a large number of auditory fibres weakly, and a tone a small number relatively strongly (§ 16. 4, 5). Interesting is another fact of frequent observation,—that the sensitivity for high tones is, in general, greater than that for deep tones. We are reminded, in this connection, that the tympanic membrane in its relaxed condition has a tone of its own, of some 700 vibrations, which necessarily becomes higher as the tension is increased; that the other sound-conducting portions of the middle ear possess high tones; and that the resonance tone of the tympanic cavity itself belongs in the upper region of the scale (§ 15. 5). We cannot here discuss pathological disturbances of the intensive sensibility, which are especially common in audition.

6. No adequate test has been made of intensive sensibility in the sphere of *organic* sensations. The difficulties which it presents are, for the most part, due to the normal impossibility of varying the sensations in isolation. Even the articular sensibility admits of intensive gradation (§ 22. 6) only to a very limited extent.

A further interesting question which falls under the rubric of intensive sensibility is that of the waxing and waning, or the *rise* and *fall* of sensations. The qualities of the different senses show peculiar differences in this regard. A sensation of temperature, taste, or smell, attains only gradually to an intensity corresponding to the intensity of the given stimulus, whereas a sensation of pressure or hearing seems to reach its maximum at once. The same holds for the disappearance of sensation. The difference must be referred not to the special nature of the nervous process, but to difference in the mode of stimulus transmission. The epidermis is a poor conductor of heat, so that a temperature stimulus must act for a certain length of time before it can produce its effect upon the terminal nervous apparatus, while the excitation cannot either disappear at the movement of the removal of the stimulus. And the purely mechanical transmission of pressure to the skin or of sound through the auditory organ renders possible an apparently instantaneous origination and evanishment of the corresponding sensations. On the other hand, the transmission of a taste or smell stimulus to the organ which it is adequate to excite must be conceived of as retarded by circumstances of which we are still ignorant.

We saw above that a quantitative determination of the *terminal stimulus* was impossible. We should not, perhaps, go very far wrong if we made the appearance of pain the criterion of maximal sensation intensity. At least, the quality of a sensation generally becomes more or less seriously blurred at this point.

§. 25. The Intensive Sensible Discrimination.

1. The principal problem which we attempted to solve by the aid of sensible discrimination in the sphere of sensation quality was that of the number of distinguishable qualities within a given sense department. The nature of the functional relation which we might there find obtaining between qualitative change in sensation and its equivalent change in stimulus was in itself indifferent to our inquiry. And we found, as a matter of fact, that the relation took on very different forms: for tone sensations, there was a constancy of the absolute sensible discrimination within certain limits, beyond which it decreased, but not in such a way that we could formulate a definite law, valid for any considerable portion of the sensation scale; for visual sensations of brightness, a constancy of the relative sensible discrimination within certain limits, beyond which it decreased; and for visual sensations of colour, a variation of the absolute sensible discrimination between high and low limits, with an irregular distribution of its values. It seemed inadvisable to draw theoretical conclusions from these differences of result, until we had arrived at some positive idea of the nervous processes corresponding to the changes in sensation. On our original definition of quality, a discriminability of qualities was equivalent to the discovery of separate sensations; and for each particular quality we required a particular structure or function in the sensory organs. The laws of qualitative sensible discrimination, therefore, were valuable for a theory of sensation in general: they pointed out the way, so to speak, which we should follow in order to attain to a general theory. But there was, plainly, no special problem involved in the functional relation between sensation change and stimulus change. We had simply to suppose that every noticeable stimulus change must be paralleled by a difference in the nervous process underlying sensation, a difference obtained, perhaps, by the aid of specific, peripheral terminal structures in the service of perception. In the different theories of visual sensation, *e.g.*, we can trace the effort made to take adequate account of the acknowledged differences of the simple qualities. That done, the relations between stimulus and sensation, which experiment has established, are at once explained, or, at least, described.

2. The case is different with the intensive sensible discrimination.

For when we attempt to mark off the separate degrees of intensity of a sensation, we are always occupied with the same quality; and the functional relation which we find to hold as between sensation intensity and stimulus intensity is then a special problem requiring special explanation. We might, here again, seek to determine how many distinguishable intensities exist between stimulus limen and terminal stimulus. But to use the uniformity of sensible discrimination for the purposes of such a calculation would render us no material assistance. (1) The number is of no interest, because we are unable to give any absolute description or definition of the particular degrees of intensity, at least over so wide a range of variation. (2) The discreteness of these degrees might suggest or even demand the misleading hypothesis that the continuous alterations of stimulus intensity are paralleled by a discontinuous series of intensities of sensation. This view obviously implies a definite interpretation of the facts, which has no place at the outset of an inquiry. When we were dealing with analogous phenomena in our discussion of the qualities of vision and audition, we took especial care not to adopt a hypothesis of the kind, whether as the only possible, or as the correct expression of our results. We spoke simply of the number of *distinguishable* qualities, and made no attempt to decide whether this number should be regarded at the same time as that of the *sensible* qualities [1] (cf. § 15. 3, 4; § 18. 5; § 19. 4). This very question forms the central point of a most difficult controversy, which we shall have to mention later (§ 26). (3) The calculation of the number of distinguishable degrees of intensity of a sensation does not lead to any theoretical conclusions worthy of notice. If we find that 300 degrees of intensity can, under favorable conditions, be distinguished within a definite sensation quality, from stimulus limen to terminal stimulus, we can easily explain the fact by supposing that the different degrees of intensity of the equivalent nervous excitation can reach as high a number. So that, in the case of intensive sensible discrimination, it is the course of discrimination, *i.e.*, its uniform relation to stimulus, which is the real object of investigation. And when we find authors speaking in absolute terms of the relation between stimulus and sensation, where they are really only referring to the intensive sensible discrimination, we can explain the phraseology by the particular interest attaching to this relation in this special department of inquiry.—The question, then, which we have to answer here, is: what is the increase of sensation reported by sensible discrimination when we increase the objective intensity of the stimulus?

[1] In all probability, qualitative sensation changes are continuous.

We will first glance briefly at the facts, and then proceed in the next Section to their theoretical discussion.

3. (1) Intensive sensible discrimination in the sphere of *cutaneous* sensations.—(*a*) Experiments can be made upon *pressure* sensations in two ways. Weights may be either simply placed upon the portion of the skin to be examined, as in investigations of sensibility (cf. the exposition of the methods in §§ 7, 8), or their application may be regulated by a special apparatus (most serviceably constructed on the principle of the balance). It is best that the weights to be compared should be laid successively on the same cutaneous area at suitable, regular intervals. The simultaneous affection of different parts of the skin complicates the method by the necessity of compensation of differences in sensibility, and seems, also, to increase the difficulty of comparison,—probably by way of dividing the attention. Sensible discrimination has accordingly always proved to be somewhat less in this case than when the same cutaneous area has been stimulated successively. It is best, again, to make the area of application of the stimulus weight as small as possible. With a greater extent of stimulus the sensible discrimination is liable to variation, due both to changes in sensibility, which differs very considerably even as between closely neighbouring parts of the skin, and to the uneven, more or less rounded character of the cutaneous surface. A test of intensive sensible discrimination at the pressure spots, which possess a maximal sensibility, would be extremely valuable; but no systematic investigation of them has yet been carried out. The experiments made hitherto refer either to the course of sensible discrimination with increasing stimulus, or to its dependency upon the place of stimulation. In the former connection, the relative sensible discrimination has been proved to be constant within the limits set by weights of 50 and 2000 g. With an area of contact of 1 mm. diameter, the difference limen $\dfrac{S}{r}$ on the index finger of the right hand was $\frac{1}{18}$ to $\frac{1}{20}$. With an area of contact of 7 mm. diameter, sensible discrimination fell to $\dfrac{S}{r} = \frac{1}{13}$ to $\frac{1}{18}$. For weights smaller than 50 g., the relative sensible discrimination was less (*i.e.*, the quotient $\dfrac{S}{r}$ greater), and for weights larger than 2000 g., greater (*i.e.*, $\dfrac{S}{r}$ smaller). The dependency of sensible discrimination on the place of stimulation has not been examined by an unexceptionable method. The same initial pressure has been used for both of the compared areas, and no attention paid to its different value for sensation. (*b*) Sensible discrimination in the sphere of *temperature* sensations can be

tested either by plunging the cutaneous area to be examined into a liquid, whose temperature is determinable with an accuracy of less than $\frac{1}{10}^0$ Cels., or by bringing it into contact with bodies which are good conductors of heat. The procedure of successive stimulation of the same surface has, again, given better results than that of simultaneous excitation of different. The sensible discrimination for degrees of temperature has always been found to be greatest with normal stimuli of 27^0 to 33^0 C. (where $S = \frac{1}{10}^0$). Beyond these limits, it decreases, at first slowly (to 14^0 below and 39^0 above), then more quickly. There can plainly be no question, therefore, of a constancy of the sensible discrimination, whether absolute or relative. We can only say that it is greatest in the neighbourhood of the physiological zeropoint; and as this lies, as a rule, a little above 33^0 (§ 11. 2), that it is better in its judgment of divergences from the zeropoint in the direction of cold, than of those in the opposite direction,—a fact of obvious teleological significance. It must be further remarked that noticeably cold or hot stimuli blunt the nervous excitability. The dependency of sensible discrimination upon the place of stimulation appears to run parallel to that of sensibility.

4. (2) Intensive sensible discrimination in the sphere of sensations of *taste.*—While no investigation at all, under this rubric, has been made upon sensations of *smell*, but very little, and that inadequate, has been done for those of *taste.* Since a real comparison of the different qualities is out of the question (for the reasons alleged in § 24. 4), we could do no more than make a separate inquiry for each quality into the empirical course of sensible discrimination as dependent upon the degree of saturation of the gustable solution. Even this determination would remain problematical, as long as our ignorance of the physical or chemical meaning of 'gustable' continued.

(3) Intensive sensible discrimination in the sphere of *auditory* sensations.—(*a*) Experiments upon *tonal* intensities, which might be suggested by the relative simplicity of the physical conditions of the sensation, and, more especially, by the approximate constancy of its quality, are very few in number, the reason being that the necessary quantitative gradation of the objective intensity of simple periodic vibrations presents great difficulties. Occasional tests have given a constancy of the relative sensible discrimination; but we know nothing positively of the limits of this constancy or the magnitude of the relative S. (*b*) Investigations of the intensities of *noise*, on the other hand,—although these cannot be considered to attach to simple qualities, which do not alter with increase of intensity,—have demonstrated the constancy of the relative sensible discrimination within wide limits, by the procedures of difference determination and difference comparison.

$\dfrac{S}{r}$ is approximately $\frac{1}{3}$. The method of right and wrong cases has been employed in addition to that of minimal changes, and the constancy of the product $h.r$ shows that the delicacy of the relative sensible discrimination also remains unchanged within wide limits.

5. (4) Intensive sensible discrimination in the sphere of *organic* sensations.—We cannot attribute any great possibility of intensive gradation to the articular sensations. They need hardly be considered in connection with the intensive sensible discrimination. On the other hand, the strain sensations, which in all probability are aroused by sensory excitations in the tendinous nerves, are shown by facts of ordinary experience to be quite capable of intensive gradation to an extent sufficient for experimental purposes. E. H. Weber noticed that the sensible discrimination for lifted weights was about twice as great as that for intensities of pressure, and argued from this fact to the existence of a special 'muscle sense'. Since Weber's time elaborate series of experiments on the comparison of lifted weights have been made, in particular by Fechner, according to the method of right and wrong cases. They have given an approximate constancy of the relative delicacy and magnitude of sensible discrimination within certain limits, both for successive lifting with one arm and for simultaneous lifting with the two arms. Sensible discrimination is appreciably greater in the former case than in the latter (cf. the result obtained for pressure intensities: 3 above). The limits of constancy of the relative sensible discrimination are approximately set by the values 300 and 3,000 g. $\dfrac{S}{r}$ is $\frac{1}{30}$ to $\frac{1}{40}$; sometimes even less. This *direct* estimation of the heaviness of lifted weights, in terms of the intensity of the strain sensations caused by their downward pull, is often employed on every day occasions when we are comparing the portableness of objects in common use. There is also possible an *indirect* judgment, to which we have recourse when the lifting is done quickly and the procedure without knowledge rigidly followed. It is based upon the greater or less velocity of the lifting movement. As a general rule, the lighter the weight, the more quickly is it raised,—a definite impulse to movement being presupposed. Experiments upon predisposition (§ 5. 7, 8) have brought out the significance of this indirect criterion with great clearness. Its applicability plainly involves the presence of a certain motor predisposition to a light or heavy weight. So that the more effectually the tendency to predisposition is checked, the less important is the part played by this secondary criterion. Conversely, its application may lead to a serious deception of judgment, since the

over or under estimation of the lifted weight will be proportional to the magnitude of the impulse to which the arm has been predisposed by the foregoing experiments. The same effect can also be produced voluntarily, by the brace taken in preparation for a heavy weight: the intensity of the preparation shows itself in that of the strain sensations arising from the active contraction of the muscles. It follows that an exact comparison of the strain sensations aroused by the stimulus is only possible when the arm is allowed to hang down, motionless and relaxed, and the weights to be compared are properly attached to it while in that position. Attempts to test the sensible discrimination of the 'muscle sense' by active pressure against a resistance of variable intensity, such as a spring, are so ambiguous, that we cannot devote space to them here.

§ 26. Weber's Law.

1. This brief survey of the facts of the intensive sensible discrimination shows clearly enough the recurrence of one definite uniformity throughout the various sense departments. With pressure, auditory, and strain sensations we find, within fairly wide limits, a constancy of the relative sensible discrimination. When we remember (1) that the question of the validity of this law in the sphere of taste and smell is still entirely open, (2) that temperature sensations are peculiarly situated (physiological zero-point, etc.), and that nothing positive can be at present said as to whether or not they form an exception to it, and (3) that the same rule holds for the sensible discrimination of intensities of light, we cannot hesitate to affirm that the constancy of the relative sensible discrimination for stimulus intensities is the expression of a general law. Fechner named it 'Weber's law', because E. H. Weber was the first to call attention to its far-reaching significance. We cannot here do more than briefly summarise the numerous discussions to which Weber's law has given rise. We have already met the fundamental objection urged against the measurability of sensation (§ 6), and will only remark now that the functional relation between subjectively compared and objectively measured stimulus intensities is capable of several different interpretations, and that the customary classification of explanations of Weber's law as physiological, psychological, and psychophysical is quite rough, each type readily admitting of further subdivision. For it is evident that the fact of Weber's law simply asserts a relation between stimuli and reports of the sensations excited by them, and that between these extremes there lies a whole series of mediating processes, all of which, theor-

etically considered, may co-operate to give the relation its special character.   The restriction of theory, hitherto, therefore, to a psychological, psychophysical, and physiological interpretation of the law, has led to the setting up of merely classificatory rubrics (except in the special case of psychophysics, where only one form of explanation is conceivable), which may cover very different concrete opinions.

2.   E. H. Weber regarded the existence of the law which has received its name from him as an interesting psychological fact.   (1) Fechner, on the other hand gave it a *psychophysical* significance, and maintained this position in various discussions with the representatives of opposing views.   He makes the law an expression of the quantitative interrelation of physical and psychical magnitudes.   Within the physical world and within the psychical the law of simple proportionality obtains: but the relation which the two worlds bear to each other is more complicated.   In order to obtain an exact formulation of this relation, Fechner assumes that equally noticeable sensation differences (all just noticeable differences, *e.g.*, or all subjectively equal supraliminal differences found by the method of difference comparison) are equal magnitudes, or form equal increments of a given sensation intensity.   That is to say, equal absolute sensation differences (ΔE)[1] correspond to equal stimulus relations or equal relative stimulus differences $\left(\dfrac{\Delta r}{r}\right)$, and we have

(1) $$\Delta E = C . \frac{\Delta r}{r},$$

where C is a constant, regarded as dependent upon the quality of the stimulus, etc.   If sensation itself is to be expressed as a function of stimulus, the equation (1) must be changed into a differential equation and then integrated.   We thus obtain the *fundamental formula:*

(2) $$d E = C \frac{dr}{r}$$

and by integration

$$E = C . \log r + c.$$

The integration constant c can be determined from the fact that, when the stimulus becomes liminal, $E = 0$.   If we denote the stimulus limen by ϱ,

$$0 = C . \log \varrho + c,\ \text{or}$$
$$- c = C . \log \varrho,$$

from which we obtain the *measurement formula:*

(3) $$E = C (\log r - \log \varrho):$$

sensation increases proportionately to the logarithm of stimulus.   This

[1] $E = Empfinding$, sensation.

formula, which is not a necessary consequence of Weber's law, is termed *Fechner's law* or the *psychophysic law*. It is really valid for the relation of sensation to central nervous excitation, *i.e.*, for the two directly parallel psychical and physical magnitudes. This cannot be explained: it is a fundamental fact. On the other hand, it is only approximately valid for the relation of stimulus to sensation, of which it was primarily intended as the empirical expression: only, *i.e.*, where stimulus and central nervous excitation are proportional. That this proportionality does not hold outside of certain limits is shown by the upper and lower deviations from Weber's law. Fechner is thus compelled to make the assertion, that in *external* psychophysics, which exhibits the relation of sensation to stimulus, all manner of physiological conditions interfere to prevent an exact verification of his law; but that in *internal* psychophysics it holds serene and undisputed sway, manifested in particular in the adjuvant and inhibitory effects of attention. Having adduced this positive argument, Fechner is content to meet the physiological explanation of Weber's law with a simple indication of the inconceivability of a logarithmic dependency between physical magnitudes.

3. (2) The chief representative of the *physiological* interpretation of the law is G. E. Müller. Hitherto, this interpretation has generally found its expression in the view that Weber's law gives the relation of stimulus to the central nervous excitation, which is directly proportional to sensation; although it might equally well substitute for this correlation that of stimulus and peripheral nervous excitation, or stimulus and any other member of the total series of nervous processes. No direct and irrefragable proof of the existence of any such physiological uniformity has as yet been brought. But it is well within the range of possibilities, and there are enough corroborative facts of nervous physiology to raise it at least above the level of mere speculation. We know, in the first place, that weak stimuli increase the excitability of nervous substance, and that strong stimuli diminish it. We may, therefore, suppose that it remains constant within certain limits. We know again, that the nervous centres offer a resistance to the propagation of an excitation, which can only be overcome by frequent repetition, long duration, or high intensity of stimulation. And we know lastly, that a peripherally originated nervous excitation may take different paths within the central organs, and that the area of its dispersal is probably proportional to its intensity. Thus a brilliant light gives rise to a reflex closure of the lids, as well as to a visual sensation, and a sudden, loud noise is not only heard, but answered with the start of surprise which involves the entire body. It can be shown that in cases like these the sensation does not come first and

cause the movements, but that they appear simultaneously with or even noticeably earlier than the sensation. The whole category of involuntary motor phenomena consequent upon sensory stimulation is evidence that the effects of stimulus upon the nervous system are manifold, and that only a fraction of the physical energy transformed into a sensory excitation is used for the central nervous process correlated with sensation. If we assume that this fraction always bears the same relation to the magnitude of the stimulus, we obtain Weber's law. The upper and lower deviations from it, and the fact of the stimulus limen could then be explained partly by reference to the variations in excitability mentioned above, partly by the resistance offered within the central organs, and partly by the consideration that certain weak excitations, such as the idio-retinal light, appear to be constantly maintained as a result of internal stimulation.

4. (3) (*a*) The *psychological* explanation of Weber's law, of which W. Wundt is the principal representative, also assumes that sensation and central nervous excitation are directly proportional, but asserts further that both are proportional to the intensity of stimulus. It, therefore, refers the facts embraced by Weber's law to the process of comparison of sensations or sensation differences. Equally noticeable sensation differences, which the physiological theory can interpret most simply, with the psychophysical, as equal magnitudes, are here regarded as differences which represent the same value for our comparison. Equation (1) is consequently regarded not in the light of the *difference hypothesis* (which makes equal, absolute sensation differences correspond to equal relative stimulus differences), but in that of a *relation hypothesis* (which makes equal relative sensation differences correspond to equal relative stimulus differences), and accordingly written,

$$\frac{\Delta E}{E} = C. \frac{\Delta r}{r}.$$

This psychological explanation is based upon the general psychological fact that we do not possess an absolute measure of the intensity of our conscious processes, but can only measure them by one another, *i.e.*, by comparing the intensity, say, of a sensation, with that of another present at the moment. This fact is designated by Wundt a general law of relativity. Weber's law thus becomes merely a special case of the wider uniformity, which manifests itself in our inability to transcend a relative estimation of intensity, extension, and duration in other connections, *e.g.*, in the investigation of the feelings and of temporal and spatial magnitudes. And since, further, the principal part in all comparison is played by attention or apperception (§ 72. 4, etc.), Weber's law becomes for Wundt an expression of the relation of stimulus (or sensation) intensity to apperception. (*b*) The psychological interpretation may, however, assume a different form,—in which it is represented by Ziehen. On his view, Weber's law is a law of association. The ideas of 'greater' and 'less' are associatively connected with the stronger and weaker sensation. Not every sensation difference reproduces such an idea, but only a difference which stands in a definite relation to the absolute sensation intensity. Weber's law may·therefore be written as follows: two or more sensation differences reproduce the same judgment 'different', when the relative stimulus differences corresponding to them are equal.

5. The most improbable of all these interpretations is, evidently, the psychophysical. Its basal assumption of the equal magnitude of equally noticeable sensation differences is exceedingly precarious. The point is wholly missed that the relation obtaining between sensation and the account given of sensation is too complicated to admit of our entertaining any hope of sensation measurement. And no explanation is given of the form of dependency expressed by Weber's law, other than an arbitrary and undemonstrable assertion that it is a remarkable fundamental fact. Indeed, it is not too much to say that psychology has given her final verdict in the case of Fechner's law. While we cannot deny the importance of the underlying idea of a functional relation between psychical and physical phenomena, we cannot admit the necessity of a logarithmic proportion in this relation or the validity of the metaphysical reflection which suggested it. The many differences in the observed facts, and the limited range over which experiment has proved Weber's law to hold have not received their due share of attention, and the assumption of extraneous influences preventing an exact verification of the law in external psychophysics is inadequate to its task. The two other interpretations are preferable to the psychophysical, in that they attempt to furnish a real explanation by bringing Weber's law into connection with known facts of physiology or psychology. The physiological view has the advantage of the psychological in its ability to meet particular facts with particular explanations; the psychological has the advantage of the physiological in its explicit recognition of the peculiar relations involved in the comparison of sensations. It is obvious that the psychological theory does not exclude a physiological, since the central nervous processes which run parallel to apperception or association must stand to the physical processes running parallel to sensations in the relation required by the law. It is, probably, too early to attempt a decision. The more generally Weber's law is confirmed in cases of quantitative comparison of conscious processes, the greater

will be the likelihood of the psychological interpretation. On the other hand, the more limited the domain within which the law is found to apply, the greater will be the reason for the adoption of the physiological explanation with its adaptability to the individual fact.

6. The question of the psychological significance of Weber's law is quite different from that of its interpretation. We have spoken more than once of the connection between memory and the laws of sensible discrimination (cf. § 15. 1; § 18. 1, 5). The recognition of sense impressions we have seen to be dependent not upon their absolute but upon their relative likeness. It is for this reason that a musical composition may be rendered without suffering any considerable change not only by orchestras or choirs of different strength, but even upon the piano, the dynamic capacities of which fall very far short of orchestral production. It is for this reason that we can orientate ourselves in our surroundings with approximately equal facility under very different conditions of illumination : the equal relative brightness differences are taken to be equally great. It is for this reason that a landscape painting does not displease the eye; but may even deceive it by producing an illusion of reality. And it is for the same reason that our memory of something seen or heard may be extremely accurate although the absolute intensities of the impressions are altogether impossible of reproduction. All this is evidence of the importance and purposiveness of Weber's law in our daily life. The thought accordingly suggests itself that a law of its character, a rule of perception, must have been developed in the course of organic evolution : and, as a matter of fact, experiments on the lowest organisms have given a similar formulation of their reaction upon external stimuli. This result does not do away with the need of a detailed explanation, but it at least sets the law in the perspective of a genetic treatment. We must be especially careful, however, to avoid supposing that observations on the sensitivity of lower organisms to stimuli prove the correctness of the physiological theory of Weber's law, because, *e.g.*, these creatures are unable to compare and to judge. Weber's law is the law of a relation between stimulus and judgment and not of one between stimulus and reactive movement; and the difference between the organic processes in a differentiated nervous system and a homogeneous protoplasmic mass is too great to allow of translation of one into the other, or of inference from the protozoon to ourselves.

Literature :

J. Delboeuf : *Examen critique de la loi psychophysique*, 1883.

A. Grotenfelt : *Das Weber'sche Gesetz und die psychische Relativität*, 1888. Cf. also the references given in §§ 6, 10—23.

B. CENTRALLY EXCITED SENSATIONS.

CHAPTER IV. REPRODUCTION AND ASSOCIATION.

§ 27. Memory, Imagination, Reproduction.

1. The guidance afforded us in our discussion of peripherally excited sensations by the existence of adequate stimuli is not continued in the present Section. A special investigation of the nature of centrally excited sensations is, therefore, exceedingly difficult. And the stumbling blocks which beset the path of inquiry enable us to understand how it is that all the terms employed to designate the phenomena, some of the commonest of which are named in the heading of this paragraph, are still loosely defined and variously applied. We must, therefore, begin by clearly stating the problems, principles, and concepts, with which such an inquiry has to deal. What partially replaces the guidance previously furnished by stimuli is really a dogma, which we may formulate, almost in the words of a famous philosophical dictum, as follows: nihil est in memoria, quod non prius fuerit in sensu. In our own terminology the proposition would run: there is no centrally excited sensation which has not previously been peripherally excited. The English philosophy and psychology have declared with a persistency which has given repeated assertion the appearance of axiomatic truth that memorial images are of the same kind as perceptions, only weaker—with the occasional addition that fancy images are in their turn weaker than memorial. A proposition like this obviously makes it superfluous to undertake an especial investigation, at any rate of the quality of centrally excited sensations. But its correctness has never been demonstrated, and its constant assumption has perhaps done as much as anything else to render this department of psychology barren and schematic. We shall enter upon its examination in detail in the next Section: first of all we will attempt a critical estimate of the value of the

concepts of memory, imagination, reproduction, etc., and of their correspondence with the facts.

2. The fact implied in the terms *memory* and *reproduction*, and in part also in *recollection*, is simply this: that an impression which has been produced in the past by a particular stimulus does not disappear outright with the cessation of that stimulus, but is somehow conserved, and, under certain conditions, has the power of again becoming a noticeable part of conscious contents, without any renewal of the original peripheral stimulation. We often explicitly recognise it on its reappearance as the same impression, and are frequently able to describe the circumstances of its original production. From these facts it is conjectured that even in the not very uncommon cases where there is no *recognition*, general or special, the centrally excited sensations are still merely 'reproductions,' 'memorial' or 'fancy images' of previous peripherally excited sensations. If we abstract from the metaphysical ideas which have clustered round the phenomena (one theory consigns the images to the care of an unconscious mind, another makes the brain deposit its sensory excitations in particular ganglion cells), we have in this view a generalisation of experiences of whose reality there can be no doubt. The word 'memory' lays particular stress upon the latency of the 'conserved' impressions; 'reproduction' and 'recollection' upon their recurrence in consciousness. *Imagination* differs from all three in admitting the possibility of a dissimilarity between the peripherally and centrally excited contents. The fancy image is, in a certain measure, something new, not a mere copy of a foregone perception. The activity of memory is reproductive: that of fancy or imagination seems in contrast to it to be productive, creative. What is ordinarily regarded as new in imagination, however, is not the occurrence of peculiar elementary qualities, which have never made their appearance in peripherally excited sensation, but simply the arrangement or connection of conscious elements, already given in sense perception. This hypothesis, again, has its exclusive factual support in the frequent recurrence of a recognition of the elements. Memory, then, as the storehouse of peripherally excited impressions, is the root both of recollection and imagination; but while recollection repeats the connection which obtained between the elements of a perception, imagination arranges them with some degree of freedom.

3. It is evident that the psychological processes comprehended under these terms are all centrally excited sensations, and that the function of the terms is to fix and describe their relation to sensations peripherally excited. Recognition, which acts as intermediary, appears to be simply a special function of the sensible discrimination. When

we are comparing peripherally excited sensations with one another, we determine their qualitative likeness or difference. And recognition merely covers the special cases in which a centrally excited sensation is judged to be qualitatively identical with another sensation, peripherally excited on some former occasion. But the matter is really not so simple. (1) We are ordinarily unable to institute a direct comparison of memorial image with perception. Even though comparison be possible, it is rendered exceedingly difficult by the great differences in intensity, duration or extension. (2) Apart from this, however, the conditions are as unfavourable to comparison as they well can be. In all other instances of the investigation of the sensible discrimination for successive stimuli, we take care that only a few seconds shall elapse between the compared impressions, and attempt to limit the number of judgments of equality by all kinds of variation of experimental conditions and stimulus magnitudes. Here, on the other hand, the interval between peripherally excited and reproduced sensation may be of any length, and an exact gradation of the objects of comparison or isolated variation of their conditions is out of the question. We can, therefore, understand why it is that recognition as a general rule refers not to a memorial image, but to a perception, which is judged to be equal or similar to a previous impression peripherally excited. Now in the view of certain physiologists, and in particular of Munk, this fact can only be explained on the assumption that the memorial image of such a previous impression is reproduced. When, *e.g.*, we judge a colour to be of a familiar quality, the process involved is that of the reproduction of the same colour as previously seen. This recognition would, accordingly, be a simple reversal of the case described above; the comparison is seemingly instituted between a given peripheral impression and a memorial image called up by it.

4. We are thus led to the special problem of the process of recognition itself. Recognition may take place in two very different ways: either in the form of a judgment, general or particular, expressive of familiarity with an object or an occurrence, without a reproduction of the sensations involved in its previous perception; or by the intermediation of reproduced sensations, which connect with the object of present perception or ideation, and repeat certain circumstances of the original situation. The first is *direct*, the second *indirect* recognition. The reproduction of memory images which correspond to the previous perception and represent it with more or less of fidelity seems to occur but seldom. [1] Direct recognition has recently come to receive the

---

[1] This is my own experience. And I cannot but think that it must be the experience of others, although reproduction is so often made the *differentia* of recognition in

attention which it deserves, and a theory has been propounded that a 'quality of knownness' attaches to immediately recognised sensations. It is true that such a theory merely introduces a new word, instead of proceeding by way of careful analysis and detailed explanation—a word, moreover, which may very well carry with it the erroneous suggestion that familiar ideas as such possess a peculiar attribute, *i.e.*, that of familiarity: but at least it admits by implication that a judgment of familiarity can be passed without the intermediation of particular memorial images, and thus raises the question of the real basis of this judgment. In our own view, its foundation consists (1) in the especial effectiveness for central excitation of familiar impressions or memorial images, and (2) in the characteristic mood which they ordinarily induce, and which embraces both pleasurable (or at least comfortable) affective states and the corresponding organic sensations.

5. (1) No argument is required to prove that the effectiveness of the known for central excitation is essentially different from that of the unknown. While the former more or less quickly arouses the most various local, temporal, conceptual, etc. ideas, showing all degrees of relation to the perceived or remembered impression, the unknown stands in isolation, and can only be brought into connection with our existing mental furniture by definite judgments of reference and comparison. Of course, for the developed consciousness there is hardly any such thing as an absolutely unknown. Some concept or other will always admit of application to the impression, however novel; or, in psychological phraseology, every sensation will reproduce at least a verbal idea. But recognition does not, as a rule, consist in a mere general determination of this kind, but rather in the wholly specific judgment that a given impression has been already experienced. It is sufficient for direct recognition, in this connection, that the effectiveness of a known impression (in the present sense of the word) for central excitation is noticeably different from that of the impression not yet individually experienced, without there being any clear idea of the particular elements which justify or underlie the judgment. For the most part, the judgments of this direct recognition are not further specialised; there is only an immediate reproduction of the name 'known'. It is facilitated by the working of a psychological law, absolutely valid within certain limits,—the law that general denominations are more easily reproduced than special. (2) The mood into which we are thrown by familiar impressions, again, is essentially different from that induced by unfamiliar. If we abstract from the particular

psychological treatises. It appears as if schematism had here gained an easy victory over the presentment of facts as they really are.

character of the two in the given case, and from the differences in the state of consciousness preceding them (expectation and unprepared attention), we may say that the known, as known, has a reassuring or pleasurable effect, while the unknown, as unknown, is disquieting or unpleasant. This is intimately connected with the indisputable biological and practical importance of the distinction between the known and the unknown. Every impression produces a certain reaction on the part of the living organism: but while known phenomena reproduce a sensory and motor reaction, previously employed and tested, with relative ease and certainty, unknown must be assimilated, and an appropriate form of reaction discovered. It is readily intelligible, therefore, that feelings and organic sensations are aroused and moulded in a distinctive manner by a recognisable impression.

6. Two objections may be urged against this view of direct recognition. (*a*) It may be said that it only pushes the real problem one step further back, in referring the recognition of an impression to the mood reproduced by it, or to its especial effectiveness for central excitation,—*i.e.*, to something which itself constitutes the object of recognition, and only in that way can furnish the basis of the recognitory judgment. If this objection held, there would be no such thing as direct recognition, but only indirect; and the mediation which it posits must be conceived of as continued to infinity. The recognition of the mood must in its turn be mediated by the recollection of particular elements, and so on. We may abstract from this *reductio ad absurdum*, and consider only the denial of the fact of direct recognition. If the fact is substantiated, as we believe it is, a simple difference in the effectiveness of the known and the unknown is plainly adequate to its explanation, in as much as these quite general determinations are all that are involved in it. (*b*) It may be urged that we have asserted the possibility of a judgment of familiarity in cases where the various reasons which justify it are not reproduceable. This objection, however, is simply the expression of a logical postulate; not a rule of psychological reaction. On the contrary, as we remarked just now, the psychological law is that the denominations of general concepts are more quickly and easily reproduced than those of special. This law is itself only a particular case of the universal rule that the frequency of excitation exerts an influence upon the reproductivity of impression. Since the name of a logical category must, in general, occur in consciousness far more frequently than the name of the individual subsumed to it (it can be referred to a far greater number of reproducing stimuli), it will appear more easily and more quickly in the given case. This fact has an important bearing upon the

significance of concepts, and more especially of general concepts, and upon the explanation of scientific development. It is further confirmed by the experience that when memory begins to fail in consequence of age, concrete names, and particularly the names of individual persons or things, are forgotten before abstract. Another illustration of the law is afforded by the result of experiments by the procedure without knowledge. The existence of a difference between the compared sensations is earlier remarked than the direction which it takes, or the nature of the objects between which it obtains.

7. It follows from this conception of direct recognition that its judgments will not seldom be erroneous. Two kinds of wrong judgment are possible. We may regard something as known which has not been individually experienced, and we may declare something to be unknown which has been a matter of individual experience. (i) We can explain the first error, by assuming that the effects which we have described above may be produced not only by precisely identical processes or objects, but also by those which are simply more or less similar, *i.e.*, which are either partially coincident with the contents of the original sensations, or evince no noticeable difference to a sensible discrimination so unfavourably circumstanced. Thus we may imagine that we have previously been in some place which it can be proved we have never seen before, or that we know an individual whom we have certainly never met, etc. It may be that Plato in his doctrine of ἀνάμνησις and pre-existence was thinking of experiences of this kind. (ii) The second error is due, on our theory, to the fact that the unrecognised impression was too transient, or appeared too seldom, or was separated by too long an interval from its revival, to be able to produce a noticeable effect upon reproduction or mood.— Lastly, the question arises, whether one of these two factors which we regard as the basis of direct recognition is to be considered fundamental, or whether the two are to be looked upon as altogether coordinate resultants of the operation of the known, however different the value of each may be in a given case. Unaided introspection can hardly return a satisfactory answer to this question. But certain pathological observations in cases of *mental blindness* and *mental deafness* (Munk) seem to admit of a definite interpretation which throws light upon it. By mental blindness and mental deafness is meant the incapacity of cognising an object of sense perception in its true significance, or of naming it and making use of its experientially known properties. Thus, if a patient be given a spoon, he may see it and even declare that it is familiar, but be unable to name it or to put it to any use, etc. Such cases may rise to the extreme of logical

paradox. Thus, a patient has been known to describe a fork exactly, and yet not to cognise it as a fork when it was shown her. Here we obviously have an abrogation of the reproducing effect of impressions. That these may, nevertheless, appear familiar must be due to the power of what we have called mood to exert an influence independently of their effectiveness for central excitation, *i.e.*, as a co-ordinate factor in the recognitory process.

8. It is plain that direct recognition supplies no foundation for the statement that memory images are merely revived perceptions. No comparison of the two is carried out. But it may, perhaps, be otherwise with indirect recognition. In certain cases, and especially when a recollection requires time and trouble for its full development, we can observe a real comparison of the reproduced and peripherally excited impressions. Two general types of indirect recognition can be distinguished. In the first, the environment of the recognised object (not only in the spatial sense, but regarded as the sum of attendant and simultaneously perceptible processes) is noticeably the same as before; in the second, it is noticeably different from that of the previous perception. In the former case, indirect recognition admits of resolution into a series of acts of direct recognition: not only the individual definite object, but the individual circumstances are successively judged to be familiar. But it will deserve the name of indirect recognition, whenever the object itself, even if nothing else, is recognised solely upon the ground of the familiarity of its attendant circumstances. If on the other hand, the environment is noticeably different, indirect recognition will be effected when the object reminds us of its previous surroundings, *i.e.*, reproduces sensations which represent them, or knowledge about them, etc. In virtue of this effectiveness for central excitation, which plainly assumes a quite definite form in consciousness, the object itself is here placed in the category of the known. That the same object is compared with its own memorial image for purposes of recognition can happen but rarely, and then only under the unfavourable conditions already referred to. It is evidently impossible to assert on this basis that qualitative likeness is established by the direct comparison of perception and memory image. The assumption of their identity rests, therefore, not upon any adequate empirical induction, but upon the old sensualistic idea that the mind can store in memory nothing which it has not received through the senses, and upon the view, which has found many representatives in modern times, that the same nervous centres form the substrate of perception and memorial image.—Munk's contrary argument from the facts of mental blindness and mental deafness to a physiological and

anatomical separateness of these centres is shown by the outcome of the present discussion to be altogether insufficient.

9. The same holds of fancy images. Here again, the recognition of the elementary constituents is no proof of the agreement of their contents with those of the perception and memory image. Direct comparison with the perceived object is so far facilitated, that there is no coincidence at any rate in the arrangement of qualities, *i.e.,* that one series cannot completely overlay the other. But the conditions of comparison in general are just as unfavourable as before. Moreover, memory and imagination show great individual differences, which are by no means necessarily paralleled by corresponding differences in perception. We speak of a special development of the auditory or visual memory,—of a special tendency to reproduce verbal images in contradistinction to a predominant inclination to recollect in terms of concrete pictorial images. We cannot say that these cases present equally clear differences in the accuracy and ease of auditory or visual perception, etc. Few persons appear to have the power of reproducing colours with any degree of clearness, and the recollection of tones or series of tones is at least very largely assisted by the motor excitations of the vocal organs, which, if they do not make reproduction possible in the first place, are able considerably to increase its clearness. But it has not been found that recognition is particularly deficient in persons with poor visual memory, *i.e.,* that because they are unable to imagine a colour tone, it is, therefore, impossible for them to recognise a definite colour which they have previously seen. We are, therefore, again led to the conclusion that recognition does not consist essentially in a comparison of reproduced and perceived qualities.

I have made observations upon several persons with a view to determining their power of the recollection (reproduction) of colour tones. We sat in a darkened chamber, and I required my subjects to reproduce definite colours, which I named to them in any order: yellow, green, red, etc. In most cases the reproduction was effected with more or less vividness in some 10 Sec. But one observer was absolutely incapable of forming a sensory idea of any coloured object. He saw nothing, in spite of all his efforts, and although plenty of time was allowed him. His visual perception was quite normal, and he stated that he had never had illusions. I had no opportunity of testing his auditory reproduction. The process of recognition, so far as I could discover, was entirely normal. Here then, we have a person who recollects and remembers without memory images, and has thoughts and ideas without images of imagination. It is certainly difficult to bring his case within the schema of association and reproduction current in psychological treatises.

10. Two results follow from these considerations; that what we

call recollection is by no means identical with the reproduction of that which we recollect, but that, on the contrary, reproduction plays a relatively unimportant part in the total process; and that if we give up the dogma quoted at the beginning of this Section, we have absolutely no adequate knowledge of the nature of centrally excited sensations, while we have facts which appear to show that their relation to peripherally excited sensations is not a simple one. If, in conclusion, we enquire what are the conditions of the origination or the phenomena of centrally excited sensations, we are invariably referred to *association*, a form of connection between sensations or ideas characterised by the fact that the appearance of one term of it is followed by the revival of the other. It will now be our task (*a*) to examine the properties of centrally excited sensations in the light of the few experimental investigations which have hitherto been made, and (*b*) to discover what we can of their conditions, and so pave the way for their theory. Where recollection is involved in these inquiries, it too will occupy our attention. We may, however, remark at once that the most important thing for recollection in general is the possibility of movements which can be guided by the will to imitate the contents of perception. The repetition of words and tones which we have heard spoken and sung, and the drawing and painting of lights and shades and colours seen, not only facilitate and strengthen recollection, but furnish an opportunity which is independent of the contingency of perception for the repetition of the impressions to be remembered. We can accordingly understand how it is that we so often recollect by merely noticing the movements or impulses to the movements which would serve to produce a particular impression, and that some psychologists believe that all recollection takes place in this way.

[§ 27 *a*. The Investigation of Association and Memory.

1. Galton appears to have been the first to apply an experimental method to the investigation of the 'association of ideas'. His earlier and cruder procedure was to walk leisurely along a busy thoroughfare for a distance of some 450 yards, attentively scrutinising every successive object (some 300 were viewed) that caught his eyes, and holding the attention upon it until one or two thoughts had arisen by way of direct association. Out of the observations taken in this way grew the following method. A list of 75 words was written out on separate sheets of paper. They were exposed one by one; and a chronograph was started as each was cognised, and stopped as soon as "about a

couple of ideas in direct association with the word had arisen " in the mind. These associative ideas were written down, and the experiment then resumed with the next word. The results were subjected both to quantitative and qualitative analysis (cf. § 71. 7).

2. Galton's method has been developed on its quantitative side in experiments upon the duration of the association reaction (cf. §§ 70. 6, 71. 6). It has been turned to qualitative account, in various forms, by Scripture and Münsterberg. (1) Scripture's experiments were made in a darkened chamber, completely protected from external disturbances. Internal sources of error were also as far as possible eliminated. The observer was not hurried by the thought that his association-time was being measured; and the " Now! " of the experimenter induced an approximately constant state of consciousness. The "Now!" was called out two seconds before the experiment (§ 5. 4). In the visual series a white card, on which was pasted a word, picture, symbol, etc., was illuminated for four sec. The subject might name his associations at any time during this exposure limit; but was required to arrest the train of associated ideas on the disappearance of the stimulus. Some visual experiments were also made with a large coloured surface as stimulus; and other series were taken with sounds, tastes, and tactual impressions. (2) Münsterberg's earlier inquiry is directed upon the more special question whether there is any qualitative difference between the apperceptive and associative connection of ideas (§ 77. 4). The reaction method was employed throughout. There are two groups of experiments. The first seeks to show that the final psychical results of voluntary ideation can be produced without conscious activity of the will; the second to relate acts of choice or judgment with cases of mere association, under conditions which prove that the same psychophysical explanation must hold for both alike. The former procedure is described and criticised by the author below (§ 70. 2). In the latter, the hypothesis that, in the compound reaction, process follows process in serial order is tested by a progressive complication of reaction conditions (from " Name the associate of gold! "—"Silver!" to, *e.g.*, " Which is more impressive: the finest drama of Shakespeare or the finest opera of Wagner? "—" Lohengrin ! ") and a direct intercomparison of the numerical results obtained.—One of Münsterberg's later studies is discussed below (§ 28. 1, 2).

3. Turning from investigations of association to those of memory, we have to mention, in the first instance, the work of Ebbinghaus (§§ 30. 5, 8; 31. 7). In this research memory (learning, retention, reproduction) is measured in terms of two of its external conditions: time and the number of repetitions. Some 2300 'nonsense' syllables

were formed, each containing two consonants and one of eleven vowels and diphthongs. These were mixed together, and series of different length drawn from them in the order of chance. The separate series were read aloud repeatedly, until they could be voluntarily just reproduced, *i.e.*, until they could be said 'by heart,' when the first term was given, without hesitation, in a definite tempo, and with the consciousness of accuracy. The method has four advantages. The material is comparatively simple (though eye, ear and vocal muscles are concerned in the learning of the syllables); it is comparatively uniform (though certain differences of ease and difficulty were noticeable); it furnishes an inexhaustible supply of combinations of the same character; and it readily admits of quantitative variation. Constancy of experimental conditions was secured by the observance of several rules. The separate series were always read completely through from beginning to end; reading and repetition were performed at a uniform rapidity; a single rhythm was introduced; the interval between experiment and experiment remained the same; learning was done as quickly as possible, *i.e.*, the attention was held at the highest level of concentration; all artificial aids to memory were excluded; and the external circumstances of experimentation (time of day, previous work, etc.) strictly regulated. Four sources of error appeared to be incapable of absolute elimination; neither material nor external circumstances could be made absolutely uniform; predisposition varied; and as Ebbinghaus was at once experimenter and experimentee, theories and interpretations might be expected to take shape in the course of the investigation, and, though unremarked, to exert an influence upon the experimental results.—The points considered in the enquiry are as follows: the dependency of the rapidity with which a series is learned upon the number of syllables contained in it; the dependency of retention upon the number of repetitions, upon the frequency with which the series has been brought to the limit of just possible reproduction by repeated learning, and upon the succession of terms in the series; and the dependency of retention and forgetfulness upon time interval.

The method followed by Ebbinghaus has recently been discussed in an elaborate monograph, on the basis of new experiments, by Müller and Schumann. We cannot here enter upon the question of the mathematical treatment of the results, with which these authors (as well as Ebbinghaus himself) deal at some length. They suggest the following methodological improvements: that experiments should always be made by two persons; that the syllables should be presented to the observer by a special rotation apparatus; that they should be

made more uniform than in Ebbinghaus' series; that the interval
between experiment and experiment should be objectively regulated
by definite rules, valid for all observers; and that the observers should
be carefully chosen, and work begun only with those who can devote
a considerable period of time to the research. The advantages of the
amended method are demonstrated in detail, and exact directions
given for the construction of syllables, etc.

4. Wolfe (§ 31. 6, 7) remarks that Ebbinghaus' material is not
the simplest possible, since memory need not demand the co-operation
of three senses. He separates the special problem of tonal memory
from that of memory in general; and employs the procedure by recognition (stimulus repeated, and judged as 'same' or 'different') in preference
to that by reproduction in the ordinary sense. Two sets of experiments
were taken, under slightly different conditions, by the method of right
and wrong cases (§ 8. 3). In the first, five standard tones were used.
These were varied, within narrow limits, during the experimental series.
The compared tones might differ from the standard by 4, 8, or 12
vibrations in the 1 sec., and were given after intervals of 1 to 120
sec. In the second set, eleven standard tones were used, and kept
constant throughout a series. The compared tones might differ by 4
or 8 vibrations, and were given after intervals of 1 to 75 sec. The
investigation deals with the dependency of tonal memory upon time
interval, upon pitch, and upon general conditions (practice and fatigue).
Both musical and unmusical observers took part in it.

5. Lehmann (§ 31. 5, 6) attacks the problem of recognition itself,
in two investigations, making it the touchstone of the validity of the
two 'laws' of association, similarity and contiguity (§ 29). His experiments fall into four groups. (i) First paper: Visual experiments on
'simple' recognition. —These form a pendant to the auditory experiments
of Wolfe. The observer sits in a dark room. A standard gray (black and
white sectors) disc, *n*, is shown him. After a certain interval, *t*, either
n is exposed, or a brighter disc, *l*, or a darker, *m*. This second gray
is judged to be equal to or different from that of *n*. The experiment
is repeated, after an interval, with the same *n*, *l*, and *m*, given in
different order. This is done 10 times; and then a new series is
taken, with different *n*, *l*, *m*, and, perhaps, *t*. Lehmann investigated
the dependency of recognition upon the difference between the sensations, and the number of impressions; upon the time interval; and
upon general conditions (individual disposition and practice). (ii) Visual
experiments upon recognition 'by definition'.—Three series of
grays were formed, between the extremes of black and white; one
consisting of 5, one of 6, and one of 9 equal sensation differences.

A full series was shown to the observer, arranged in the order from black to white. After a brief interval, the 5, 6 or 9 terms were exposed singly, in any succession; and the observer was required to state the place in the series which each occupied. These experiments were supplemented by others, similar to those of (i), except that two discs were displayed simultaneously in the first instance, and one of them again after the lapse of t; and that the observer was asked to judge whether this isolated disc was the darker or lighter of the original two. The dependencies investigated were those upon the differences of the sensations, the time interval, and disposition and practice. (iii) Second paper: Olfactory experiments on 'direct' recognition.—A series of 62 scents was prepared. The observer was asked to decide, first of all, whether the sensation was familiar; and if it was, to write down all the ideas called up by it. Some 10 or 20 experiments constituted a series. No time limit was set to the separate experiment. The observers were not chemists, and could not recognise the stimuli by their appearance. The scents were not intensive, nor was a series long enough to fatigue the organ. (iv) Auditory experiments on 'prepared' recognition.—Two series were taken. In the first, a standard stimulus (dropping of a steel ball from a known height) was followed at variable intervals by a stimulus of comparison, whose intensity was varied in both directions until subjective equality was reached. In the others, the second stimulus was kept constant, and judgment made in terms of the first (variable) sound. Three intervals, (2, 4 and 6 sec.) were investigated.

6. Binet has recently published the results of an investigation into the development of visual memory in children. Some 300 boys from the primary schools of Paris were examined by classes (average age 7 to 9, 9 to 11, and 11 to 13), the experiments being made upon groups of four. (i) Method of recognition. (α) A standard vertical line (1.5, 4; 16, 40 or 68 mm.) was shown for 5 or 6 sec. After an interval of 4 or 5 sec., a series of vertical lines (single point to 1 cm., differences of 0.5 mm.; point to 8 cm., differences of 4 mm.) was displayed, and the subject required to indicate the line which appeared equal to the standard. (β) The standard was directly compared with the series. It was placed below the latter, at a distance of about 10 cm. from it. (ii) Method of reproduction. (α) The standard lines, shown horizontally, were drawn by the subjects from memory, or (β) were copied, the standard remaining exposed during the experiment.

The same author has further examined the 'typical' memories of blindfold chess players (visual) and professional calculators (visual and auditory), and has compared the number memory of the latter with the simulated number memory acquired by mnemotechny (cf. § 30. 5).

Binet distinguishes four methods of memorial investigation. (i) The method of *description* consists simply, as the name implies, in the characterisation of an object 'from memory.' (ii) The method of *recognition*. (iii) The method of *reproduction*. (iv) The method of *comparison*. A given impression is compared with the memory image of a previous impression (cf. the sensation method of right and wrong cases). The last three methods are the more important. They can be employed (α) where the functions of experimenter and experimentee are combined in the same individual (Münsterberg); (β) where two persons serve alternately as observer and experimenter; and (γ) where experiments are made by a single experimenter upon a large class (Binet and Henri, Jastrow, Bourdon). They are of assistance for the investigation of individual memories (typical, professional, etc.); of 'mental span', or the number of objects which can be fixed in memory in a given time; of the persistence of memory; etc., etc.

Literature:

G. E. Müller and F. Schumann, *Experimentelle Beiträge zur Untersuchung des Gedächtnisses. Zeitschr. f. Psych. u. Physiol. d. Sinnesorgane,* vol. vi., pp. 81 ff., 257 ff. Also published separately.

A. Binet and V. Henri, *Introduction à la psychologie expérimentale,* Chapter V. 1894.

„   „   *Le développement de la mémoire visuelle chez les enfants. Revue générale des sciences,* March 15, 1894.

„   „   *Simulation de la mémoire des chiffres. Revue scientifique,* June, 1894.

A. Binet, *Psychologie des grands calculateurs et joueurs d'échecs,* 1894.

F. Galton, *Psychometric experiments. Brain,* vol. ii., pp. 149 ff. *Inquiries into Human Faculty and its Development* 1883, pp. 185 ff.

Cf. the literature cited under § 33, 11.]

§ 28. The Attributes of Centrally Excited Sensations.

1. Centrally excited sensations, like peripherally excited, must be accredited with quality, intensity, and a temporal and spatial character. The exact determination of these attributes, however, is exceedingly difficult, since they do not stand in a simple functional relation to external stimuli, and are only occasionally distinct or persistent enough to allow of detailed description. Important as the question of their definition is, therefore, it cannot be experimentally approached except by indirect methods. The first point of interest is, the relation which they bear to the corresponding attributes of peripherally excited sensations. Its elucidation has been attempted in two experimental researches: by Münsterberg (who employed printed words to produce illusions) and the author (who obtained judgments of subjective and objective illumination of a dark surface). Illusions, *i.e.*, subjective per-

versions of the contents of objective perception, occur very frequently, unless deliberately guarded against, and especially when the outlines of the perception, the differences of the objective brightnesses, etc., are indistinct. Most of us have mistaken a tree trunk in the twilight for a living person. Poets have often described the changes in a dead face that seem to follow the mood of the watcher, and the power of a strained expectation to deceive eye or ear. But it is not easy to ascertain how much in such effects is due to a mistaken judgment, and how much to centrally excited sensations. In many cases the illusory judgment comes first, and the impression is then transformed into agreement with it. But the fact of importance in all phenomena of the kind is that centrally excited sensations can apparently take the place of peripherally excited, that to the judgment of the observer they are of equal value with perception. The inference is, perhaps, allowable, that in certain circumstances they are qualitatively similar to peripherally excited contents. And, as a matter of fact, Münsterberg has found that if a word is displayed for a brief time which presents some slight difference from another word, it is read as though this difference were not visible, provided that a word is previously called out to the observer which stands in intimate association to the other, but has nothing to do with the actual impression. Thus 'part' is read as 'past', if 'future' is suggested; 'fright' as 'fruit', if 'vegetable' is given.

2. The limits of possible variation of conditions in these experiments are plainly restricted; and the experiments themselves cannot be considered as wholly free from objection. For the number of changed or absent letters was so small, that the high degree of effectiveness of the remainder (which belonged to a word related to the word called out) for central excitation could not be very greatly diminished; and the time of exposure was so short, that a really clear perception was impossible, and it might have been precisely the region of change or absence which was indistinctly remarked. Again, there is the danger that the spoken word helps to form the impression which should have been produced by the word seen. And the observer's statement that he clearly saw the whole word is hardly a sufficient guarantee that errors of this kind were eliminated.—The author's experiments were primarily intended to show that there might be impressions, even for the developed consciousness, whose character as objective (referable to an external stimulus) or subjective (attributable to the condition of the subject) could not be established a priori, by the aid of criteria of general applicability; and that, consequently, the predicates, subjective and objective, are always secondary and

empirical determinations, suggestible in a great variety of ways. The experiments served at the same time to extend our knowledge of the relation of reproduction to perception. The procedure was, of course, altogether without knowledge. The observer sat at his ease in a darkened chamber, and was required to say whether he saw anything, and if so, what it was like, and whether he thought 'that it was objective or subjective. The only objective phenomenon introduced was a faint illumination of the dark wall facing the subject, given at irregular intervals, for various periods of time, and at different degrees of intensity. Nearly all the observers were liable to confusion when the stimulus approached the limen: an objective was very seldom subjectified, but a subjective frequently objectified. The number of erroneous judgments differed within fairly wide limits for the different subjects. One observer (the same who is mentioned above, § 27. 9) invariably cognised the objective as objective, and saw nothing else.

3. It may be objected that there is here no proof of the occurrence of centrally excited sensations, but that the 'subjective' phenomena were due, perhaps, to the idio-retinal light dust. The objection is answered by the character of what was seen, the length of time allowed for the adaptation of the eye to the dark, and the fact (previously referred to) that the individual capacity of voluntary ideation of required colour tones showed a quite parallel development to that of the capacity of discrimination in the present case. It is hardly possible that the retinal light dust could have been confused with an objective illumination. One of the facts which the experiments brought out most strongly was the dependency of the cognition of the objective light upon the manner of its appearance and disappearance, its duration and immobility, etc. What is of most interest to us just now, however, is the extent of stimulation over which confusion is possible. The experiments showed that it is very small, embracing only stimuli in the near neighbourhood of the limen. The normal intensity of centrally excited visual sensations is, therefore, exceedingly weak. It is true that the observer sometimes expressed the belief that he had seen a strong illumination; but as all the visible stimuli employed were very faint, and the surroundings entirely dark, the absolute intensity of the light seen cannot, probably, be put very high. At any rate it is noteworthy that no confusion was made when once the stimuli had passed somewhat beyond the limen: they were then invariably declared to be objective. It must be admitted that the conditions were not favourable to an extension of the range of confusability. The stimuli used in the investigation were all of the same kind, and the part of the wall illuminated remained the same throughout. Under

these circumstances, even with the procedure without knowledge, special criteria of objectivity must have been easily discoverable. And this hypothesis is borne out by the fact that as a rule errors were most frequently made in the first experimental series, *i.e.*, before any such criteria could be applied. For the same reason, the experiments do not add very much to our knowledge of the quality of centrally excited sensations. There is, however, no indication of any really novel and especial quality; and the judgment of subjectivity or objectivity was never based upon the fact of a peculiar qualitative difference between the two sets of sensations. So that in theory it is not impossible to obtain stimuli which shall make an exactly similar impression in consciousness to that of the memorial or fancy image. The principal distinction between perception and reproduction seemed to lie in their spatial and temporal relations and properties. It is not easy to imitate the oscillation and migration, the shrinking and expanding of the subjective images, when they are the result not of a voluntarily directed recollection, but of the free and fortuitous play of imagination; and these peculiarities often secured their cognition. It not infrequently happened, again, that an impression was at first regarded as objective, but immediately afterwards declared to be subjective, for the simple reason that the curious changes which it underwent could not be ascribed, in the observer's experience, to an objective cause.

4. We may assert, without fear of contradiction, that the number of discriminable qualities of centrally excited sensations in general is less than that of the peripherally excited qualities. While we can distinguish the quality of two tones, whose vibration rates differ by only half a vibration, it is impossible for us to imagine two tones of such slight difference in pitch. And it seems equally impossible to recollect the minimal differences of colour tone which we find just noticeable in the visible spectrum. In the sphere of brightness, the functions of the centre lag far behind those of the periphery in every respect. But apart from cases in which there is no qualitative reproduction at all, we may assume that centrally excited sensations present the same qualities as peripherally excited, *i.e.*, that they contain no quality which is not found among the latter. At the same time, they cannot be regarded as simple revivals of peripherally excited contents, if only for the reason that their remaining attributes are very rarely indeed identical with those of perception. The most striking evidence of disparity is, perhaps, afforded by intensity: at least, this would explain why it is that intensity is ordinarily considered to be the distinguishing characteristic for the separation of perception from

memory. It has often been remarked that an imagined tone does not sound, or a remembered pain burn, or a colour impression thought of illuminate. And it has, presumably, been said also that the idea of an intensive noise is not the same as an intensive idea of the noise. It is only in special cases that centrally excited sensations can rise from their accustomed faintness to the vividness of sense perception. We then speak of them as *hallucinations*; and they enter into a disastrous competition with the real material of perception, completely transcending the boundary line which so usefully divides it from the material of imagination. The normal gradations of intensity of memorial images are very few. As regards their temporal and spatial determination, we again find large differences between the results of peripheral and central excitation. Let the reader attempt to construct by recollection the image of a town, which a brief glance. from a suitable distance can comprehend in all its spatial complexity. It is difficult to reproduce with any pictorial distinctness and adequacy even this or that part of the image; and the part thus reproduced is but a minute fraction of the whole. And with the duration of the centrally excited idea it is even worse. If the perception was a matter of a few seconds, its reproduction may be possible, although it is difficult to hold a centrally excited sensation unchanged even for a few seconds. But any considerable duration is simply unreproduceable. Succession, too, cannot be imagined as of more than a certain rapidity; whereas in some sense departments the rate of sequence of perceived impressions may be very much greater.

5. It follows from these considerations that memorial and fancy images are as a rule sufficiently different from perceptions to be readily and certainly distinguished from them. Indeed, this difference is necessary, if recollection on the basis of reproduction is to be possible at all. It is of the greatest importance, biologically and practically, to know whether an impression has been already sensed, experienced, or whether it is altogether novel. Only peripherally excited sensations have this property of novelty, and we are, in most cases, quite sure as to its applicability. This difference of character, then, is necessary, if a recollection is to be judged at once as recollection and an imagination as imagination. On the other hand, a *definite* recollection contains always an unequivocal reference to the experience which it recalls. Thus a photograph will remind us of a scene or a person, despite its unmistakeable differences from the original, because of the expression which it gives to individual and characteristic features. And a memorial image of an object or occurrence will recall that particular object or occurrence, because of

its unequivocal relation to it. The unequivocal reference of the photograph is due to its apparent identity in spatial arrangement and distribution of light and shade with the object which it represents: that of the memorial image to its essential agreement with the previous perception as regards quality and temporal and spatial disposition. Centrally excited sensations are thus seen to be merely convenient signs and symbols of perception, but not its only possible representatives, and not a priori given in that character. We must learn to utilise the relation of memorial images to peripherally excited sensations, just as we learn to understand the relation of photograph to original. The process is enormously facilitated by the likeness of the qualities of perception and memory, and by our habit of describing experience without reference to the special attributes and properties which differ considerably as between image of recollection and image of perception, *i.e.*, intensity, extension, and duration.

6. But it is important to emphasise what has just been said, that reproduced sensations are by no means the only aids to recollection. Any fortuitous perception may excite the idea of a situation in which a similar impression had a part to play. Written and spoken words, seen and heard, symbolise experiences of the most varied kinds in characteristic ways. Moreover, certain properties of peripherally excited sensations we have seen to be altogether impossible of reproduction: such are the extension, intensity, and long duration of an impression. As we are, nevertheless, able to recollect these facts with more or less of accuracy, there must be a number of special indications in addition to the reproduced sensations, enabling us to cognise their existence in the original perception. And, indeed, there is no lack of signs from which we can infer duration, extension, and intensity. When, *e.g.*, we wish to reproduce the time occupied by a certain process, we are accustomed to estimate the number and duration of the individual experiences contained within that time. We follow precisely the same method, only reading space for time, in forming an idea of a distance which we have previously seen. Very intensive impressions are usually sensed not only by way of the organ to which they are adequate, but by others as well. The common sensation which is thus originated may assist us in the ideation of a brilliant light or a loud sound, etc. Movements are everywhere important (cf. § 27. 10). It is perhaps not too much to say that a voluntary recollection never takes place without their assistance. When we think of intense cold, our body is thrown into tremulous movement, as in shivering; when we imagine an extent of space, our eyes move as they would in surveying it; when we recall

a rhythm, we mark its rise and fall with hand or foot. Most important of all, however, are the movements of speech, which stand in unequivocal relations to the perceptions of every sense department. The principal reason for our forgetfulness of most of the events of our early childhood is that they occurred before speech was fully developed, that they were not fixed in memory by unequivocal phrases. Our recollection of an event often consists simply in its description in language. And this helps us to understand how it is that a practised speaker owes comparatively little to the conscious guidance of reproduced sensations, when developing his views in the steady flow of his oration.

7. It will now be seen why we have spoken in this Chapter of centrally excited sensations and not of memorial or fancy images. Both of these expressions are, to say the least, liable to misunderstanding. No mental process is intrinsically a recollection or an imagination; no special class of sensations has the exclusive privilege of subserving memory. A certain content becomes recollection by a judgment connected with it, and this judgment can be produced by extremely different causes. Imagination, in the same way, is characterised not by the appearance of particular series of sensations or ideas, but by the realisation that the given ideas present something new, never before experienced in this form, but possibly to be perceived in the future. The actual psychology of recollection and imagination will, therefore, vary within wide limits; *i.e.* both the conscious contents which serve as motives to recollection or which are realised to be fancies, and the specific judgments which attribute this significance to them can be entirely different. We also avoid the use of the term reproduction in this connection. In the first place, it fosters the incorrect opinion that centrally excited sensations are simple revivals of peripherally excited,—or, at least, implies this particular theory of their origination. But it also lays exclusive emphasis upon the qualitative similarity between centrally excited and peripherally caused sensations, and takes no account of their generic or specific differences. We may claim to have proved that, especially in the case of recollection, the differences are not less essential than the similarities. Moreover, it must not be forgotten that likeness of quality is only noticeable, apparent likeness,—that it is simply a relation of contents, in which they evoke the same judgment. The judgment of likeness may be passed, when, as a matter of fact, the sensations judged are not like one another, and the range of this objective unlikeness will be greater, the more unfavourable are the general conditions of comparison. Now we know that the certainty of cognition of qualitative differences is proportional to the coincidence

of all the other attributes of the compared sensations. So that the great differences which we find in intensity, and in spatial and temporal character, must of themselves make it very doubtful that apparent likeness is here even an approximation to actual likeness. But, for the process of recollection, it is merely apparent likeness which is necessary. And the numberless mistakes to which our recollection is liable are only too clear proofs of the difference between the asserted and real identity of the contents of perception and memory.

§ 29. Critique of the Doctrine of Association.

1. Aristotle found the conditions of the reproduction of ideas in certain relations, which he classified under the four heads of similarity, contrast, succession, and contiguity. In modern times the English psychologists, and especially Hume, have carried out the Aristotelian doctrine in detail, and applied it in various directions. Thus the belief that *association* is the sole condition of reproduction has come to be one of the cardinal articles of the psychological creed. J. S. Mill declared that the law of association was co-ordinate with the law of gravitation, ruling the psychical world as gravitation governs the physical. Sometimes, it is true, another view has cropped up : Herbart, in particular, speaks of a direct reproduction by way of *spontaneous ideas.* Hartley, too, developed a physiological theory of association, to which recent pathological observations and anatomical investigations have given a more definite form. Experimental psychology has hitherto concerned itself but little with the association question, though a few valuable contributions have been made to our knowledge of the intimate nature of the particular processes involved. Lastly, Wundt has distinguished between associative and apperceptive connections. The former are the result of given relations between ideas, *e.g.*, their contiguity in space or immediate succession in time ; the latter require a comparative and selective activity of the subject, *i.e.*, the aid of apperception. Wundt also considers association in its technical sense of the condition of reproduction to be only a special case of ideational connection in general. And it is his merit to have denied the fundamental value of the distinction drawn in psychology previously between perception and recollection, which we have ourselves disputed in the two foregoing sections.

2. The law of association in its most general form asserts that two ideas, *a* and *b*, under certain circumstances connect with one another in such a way that the appearance of one of them, *a*, effects the reproduction of the other, *b* (§ 27. 10). Now it can be shown that

this is not the only possible formulation of the uniformity in question; and, what is more, that its content does not command universal assent. Mill's proud comparison with the law of gravitation is, therefore, in somewhat sorry case. The law of gravitation can be stated simply and accurately in a mathematical formula. But (1) every psychologist of standing has his own laws of association. This fact alone would decide us to analyse and scrutinise narrowly the facts upon which the laws are based. Moreover, (2) the strict school of association requires that every reproduction be brought about in the same way, *i.e.*, that the only reason for the return of a reproduced sensation to consciousness be an association previously formed with another sensation. There are two experiences which appear irreconcilable with this requirement. (*a*) The first is one which we have just referred to: direct reproduction, or the spontaneous origination of ideas. It is not seldom that a complex of centrally excited sensations suddenly 'occurs' to us, without our being able to find any associative origin for it. The difficulty of this exception to the rule that association is the sole condition of reproduction is usually met by the assumption of unnoticed or unconscious connective terms. Special circumstances, it is said, combine to prevent the conscious appearance of any but the final link in the chain. Now it cannot be denied that resolution of direct into indirect reproduction is often confirmed by a subsequent analysis of experience. But whether indirect reproduction is the only possible form remains an open question. And its answer will depend not upon particular observations, which are incapable of deciding it, but upon the theoretical ideas by which their explanation is attempted.

3. (*b*) But there is another experience which speaks more decisively than the spontaneous origination of ideas against the doctrines of the strict school of association psychologists. It is the indisputable occurrence of indirect recognition without any precedent association of the reproduced and reproducing ideas—without any previous implication in an associative connection of the conscious processes concerned. We do not come with vacant minds, helpless and heedless, to the reception of new impressions: the novel, like the familiar, sets up a movement in the train of our ideas, perhaps, more or less universal, perhaps unequivocal and definite. It makes no difference whether the qualities are simple or complex. But as it may be affirmed of the latter that at least their simple constituents, the truly excitatory or reproductory processes, have been already experienced, it is better for our purpose to establish the fact at issue first of all by reference to simple qualities and separate sensations. No one can say that he has seen every discriminable degree of brightness, that he knows every possible 'gray', and has set it in an especial

association. And yet, any quality of brightness which becomes the object of attention will at once excite a name, if nothing else, and quite possibly other individual ideas. The same argument may obviously be extended to all sense departments in which the number of qualities is large, *e.g.*, to smell and hearing. But the reasoning holds equally well of complex impressions which reproduce in their totality, and not by way of particular constituents already experienced and connected. A painting, a musical composition, a landscape, may be effective as a whole to produce centrally excited sensations; and it cannot be asserted that in every case certain individual factors of the total impression have formed the starting point of reproduction. The psychological explanation of a subsumption of concrete processes under a general concept is that the processes given in perception reproduce the name that represents the concept But the subsumption by no means involves an association of all the given processes with the name in question.

4. But we have not yet exhausted our supply of factual objections to this form of the doctrine of association. So far we have spoken only of qualities as reproducing factors. But each of the other attributes of sensation may be effective in its own way for the production of central excitation. All degrees of the intensity, all gradations in the spatial and temporal character of an impression may give occasion to reproduction, and still only belong in part to the category of the experienced and associated. Here again, then, is a refutation of the assertion that all indirect reproduction must be preceded by an association. We are at least compelled to admit an indirect reproduction which is not a simple repetition of an earlier connection formed in perception and memory. But we can go farther. When we remember the results of the foregoing discussion, we shall not hesitate to affirm that a repetition of the latter kind can hardly take place at all. Psychology cannot say absolutely, even of perceived impressions, that they remain the same in spite of changes in time and circumstance: still less can it assert that the centrally excited sensation is an exact replica of the peripherally excited. And the question of the relation between association and reproduction turns essentially upon cases in which the connection between two perception contents is given as the explanation of the fact that the revival of one of them arouses or excites the memorial image corresponding to the other. If, then, we term the partial identity of memory image and peripherally excited sensation 'similarity', we can only say, in strictness: a perception content *a* reproduces an idea β, which is similar to a *b* previously connected with it.

5. Again, the current distinction of the four laws of association contains an admission of the possibility of indirect reproduction without precedent connection of conscious contents. Reproduction on the ground of temporal or spatial contiguity certainly presupposes that the ideas associated have been previously experienced in that connection. But the recollection of an impression similar to or contrasting with the object of perception as certainly does not imply that the two contents thus related either have or have not been experienced together in the past. The representatives of the strait doctrine of association which we are here opposing have, naturally, proceeded now and again to draw the logical conclusion that contiguity is the sole incentive to association, and that all apparent cases of reproduction by similarity or contrast must really be referred to it. We cannot ourselves admit the necessity of this reduction, as we have, in the course of the present discussion, found other reasons for believing in the possibility of a reproduction which is not dependent upon association. The only question for us, then, is whether the allegation of similarity and contrast as causes of an indirect reproduction not associatively effected, can be regarded as a correct and adequate description of the facts. The similarity of two simple qualities may consist (*a*) in the slightness of the difference that obtains between them. Thus two just discriminable shades of indigo blue in the spectrum may be termed similar colour tones. (*b*) Or similarity may be defined as partial identity. Two colour tones of different saturation, extension, or duration, but of the same quality, would then be similar. (*c*) Or, lastly, similarity may be predicated of two qualities which stand in one and the same relation to a third. Thus red and green are similar, because both reproduce the word 'colour'. It is easy to see that these definitions may cross in various ways, and, in certain cases, may contradict one another. We cannot, therefore, allow the term 'similarity' as the name of a law to pass unchallenged: it is far too ambiguous. And the same is true (it is not necessary to go into details) of 'contrast'. Moreover, it is suggestive, that only the second of the three possible meanings of similarity can be at all precisely formulated; and that even here there is the danger of forgetting partial identity, and falling back again upon a vague similarity. Under these circumstances, anything can plainly be looked upon as similar to anything else, and in particular a relation of contrast translated forthwith into a relation of similarity.

6. It has accordingly been attempted to eliminate contrast altogether, and to explain all cases of contrast association by the similarity which contrast implies. But then we have an equal right to press the extreme

instability and relativity of 'similarity' still further, and to draw the conclusion (highly satisfactory to a mind dominated by the craving for unification) that there is only one incentive to reproduction—similarity. As a matter of fact, all the terms of a relation of temporal or spatial contiguity are similar. On the other hand, if psychology and not logic is to furnish the criterion, the only road to a knowledge of the conditions of the appearance of centrally excited sensations, to a determination of the incentives to reproduction, lies through an analysis of the facts. We will not here anticipate the results of this analysis, but will merely remark that experience undoubtedly demonstrates the effectiveness of associations based upon the contiguity of their terms, whereas there is no clear proof at all of reproduction by similarity or contrast. (*a*) It will hardly be asserted that a tone, odour, or colour, which is but little different from another, will arouse that other in virtue of the slightness of its difference. Or at least, it will not be found that this fact alone, apart from other incentives to reproduction, gives it any noticeable advantage for memory over sensations whose differences are more considerable. (*b*) We pass to the partial identity of similar contents. As referred to sensations, this can only mean that one attribute is the same, while the rest are different. But as referred to sensation complexes it may also mean that certain constituents are identical, or that certain relations (temporal, spatial or intensive) make the same impression in spite of absolute divergences. Now 'reproduction by similarity' presents no difficulty in the case where an absolutely identical or at least apparently identical quality is common to both sensations or sensation complexes. When the two ideas *ab* and *ac*, which are 'similar' in this sense of the word, reproduce each other, the process of recollection is plainly mediated by a *substitution;* i.e., the identical part *a* reproduces its former surroundings, which as it were step into the place of those given in the perception of the moment. But this is a reduction of reproduction by similarity to association by contiguity. It is worth while to emphasise the fact that the term 'substitution' covers a real process, and is not a mere figment of theory. The idea *ab* does not function as a whole to reproduce *ac;* *a* is not duplicated, but remains unchanged, while *c*, which it excites, attaches itself to it. Sensations, again, do not seem to reproduce and be reproduced in this simple way. A green square does not as a matter of course call up a green triangle or a red square. On the other hand, the process is of very frequent occurrence among sensation complexes, the common constituents of which can initiate reproduction in their own individual right. Thus some secondary *motif* in a piece of music heard for the first time

13

may remind the auditor of a familiar composition in which it also occurs; or an odour which is now sensed in a particular connection may arouse the idea of a previous situation in which it played a part.

7. Much more difficult of explanation is the other case of partial identity: that due, not to an absolutely identical factor, but only to a relative identity. A favourite instance of reproduction by similarity is the suggestion of a person by his picture, or of an extensive and variegated landscape by a small monotone photograph. In these cases contour and light and shade make the same impression, but there is no really common constituent,—absolutely regarded, qualities are as different as forms. There can, therefore, be no question of the occurrence of a simple substitution, such as we have just described. But in all such cases recollection only takes place (in the author's experience) if we already possess a knowledge of the significance of picture and photograph. We have to learn (cf. § 28. 5) that a relation exists between them and the objects which they represent. When that is understood, the knowledge that what we have before us is simply a copy of an object will guide reproduction into the right path. As a general rule, the concrete name of the represented impression appears first of all in consciousness, and then follows, perhaps, its memorial image, with all the circumstances of the previous perception. But the portrait (in the author's observation) does not arouse the idea of its original directly, for the simple reason that the two contents cannot possibly subsist side by side, and that it suffices for recollection to think of the circumstances and name which attach to the original. There is no more a revival or duplication of perception here than there is in recognition (§ 27. 8). The similar does not recall the similar, but has the same effect as the similar, *i.e.*, reproduces the same words, ideas, etc. The problem which this instance presents is, therefore, the same as that offered by similarity (*c*) in its third meaning. Two impressions, we said, are similar, when they stand in the same relation to a third. Here again, it cannot be asserted that similarity works as an incentive to reproduction, but only that similar contents can arouse the same ideas. We shall return to this point, which is of especial importance for the psychology of the concept, in the following Section (§ 30. 9, 10, 11. Cf. § 31. 2).

8. We have been unable to discover any confirmation of the hypothesis that similarity is a law of reproduction. In many cases its influence is not demonstrable in experience at all, in others it may be reduced by careful analysis to a particular form of contiguity, to substitution, and to a peculiar psychological phenomenon which does not appear to have been described hitherto with any minuteness. It could

easily be shown that experience speaks with equal decision against reproduction by contrast. But we need not spend time in defence of this assertion, as the theory of reproduction by contrast is hardly taken seriously by modern psychology. We have not attempted to answer the fundamental question as to how similar ideas come to have the property of effectiveness for central excitation, since we have not been concerned so far with theoretic explanation, but only with the ascertainment of the facts accessible to introspection. But at the conclusion of our inquiry, we can hardly avoid raising the general issue. Similarity and contrast are capable of quantitative gradation. At least, in its first and simplest meaning of a slight difference, similarity may be regarded as of various degrees. And the same is true by analogy of contrast, which would indicate a very high degree of difference. Now if similarity and contrast are put forward as incentives to reproduction, we should expect that their degrees would be referred to as affording a quantitative determination of their reproducing power. It is curious that the literature of association (so far as the author can discover) is silent upon this point: it is nowhere stated, *e.g.*, that a greater similarity is more effective than a less. This is only another indication of the uselessness of the two concepts for the expression of a law of reproduction. On the other hand it must be admitted that the experiences upon which our analysis has been based are both incomplete and uncertain. The deficiencies of psychological investigation when unassisted by experiment are only too manifest throughout.

9. We have not, even yet, said all that there is to say in criticism of the doctrine of association. (1) For the word association is not always employed in the sense in which we have used it. It often signifies reproduction itself and not a condition of reproduction. The phrase: 'the idea *a* associates with the idea *b*' then simply means: '*a* reproduces *b*.' In this sense, the term has been made to cover every form of connection of ideas or sensations which occurs in consciousness. In principle, no objection to the usage can be made: it is only regrettable that more has not been done over the whole field of sensational connection. For the connection of a peripherally excited sensation with a centrally excited is only one of a number of possible and actual connections. That it has attracted such exclusive attention is due to a purely material cause, the great interest that attaches to it as one of the most important factors in cognition and volition. (2) Association has often been interpreted as a causal link between ideas. Herbart has employed it in this sense for the construction of a real mechanics of ideas and their relations, their rise and fall. It would be foreign to our purpose to discuss this construction, which, largely

conceived as it was, is devoid of all practical significance, and has never been carried to its full completion. The metaphysical postulates which Herbart required in order to subject the course of ideation to mathematical treatment are not reconcilable with the recent observations of nervous physiology and pathology, and must, therefore, be declared invalid. There can be no doubt at all that reproduction is influenced in quite definite ways from the physiological side. But if the associated ideas are dependent upon cerebral conditions, we need not assume a particular causal connection between the ideas themselves. The facts which seem to point towards its existence are much more simply explained by the causal interconnection of certain localised physiological processes. And this reference is especially valuable as enabling us to understand the variations which experience, unaided by metaphysics, cannot but notice, and find adverse to the theory of the causal character of the supposed mental relations. (3) Lastly, the association psychology, as a rule, takes no account of the marked influence exerted upon reproduction by temporary mood, direction of the attention, etc., *i.e.*, by general and special conditions of a central nature. We shall endeavour in what follows to tabulate the conditions of centrally excited sensations with some degree of completeness.

§ 30. Incentives to Reproduction and Liability of Reproduction.

1. Centrally excited sensations differ from peripherally excited in that the proximate condition of their origination is not the excitation of a sense organ, but a purely central process. This distinction implies that they, too, stand in a functional relation to physiological processes. We cannot give any more precise description of these than we could in the case of peripherally excited sensations: and we cannot, of course,—as in their case we could,—bring specific quality and the other sensation attributes into a relation of thorough-going dependency upon particularities of sense organ or external stimulus. The central nervous processes which run parallel to sensation admit at present only of local definition. We must, therefore, dispense in our investigation of centrally excited sensations with the valuable assistance which an exact variation of physical conditions renders to psychology in other connections. The results of experiments upon living animals might be appealed to: but (1) we cannot reason without hesitation from the animals to man; and (2) the established facts are too few in number to have added much to our stock of knowledge, and are inadequate to overcome the many difficulties of the problem.

One conclusion, in particular, which has been drawn from physiological experiment,—that the 'perception cells' are different from the 'memory cells', *i.e.*, that the locality of the central process underlying peripherally excited sensation is different from the physical counterpart of centrally excited sensation,—is based upon a very insufficient analysis of recognition (§ 27. 8). The various pathological observations of disturbance of memory, intelligence, etc., furnish a greater number of useful and reliable facts. But for the most part, we have to depend upon the results of introspection, which is indicative of the conditions of reproduction, at least in the frequent cases in which they are accompanied by conscious phenomena.

2. The appearance of a centrally excited sensation is declared by introspection to be dependent (1) upon *general* conditions, *e.g.*, upon attention, feeling, will. These conditions do not, as a rule, give rise to definite centrally excited sensations, but constitute a complex of causes adequate to determine their general character in consciousness. Why this reproduction, and no other, takes place at a particular moment, cannot be explained either by attention or by the feelings as such. (2) The second class of conditions of the appearance of centrally excited sensations is composed of other (peripherally or centrally excited) sensations. We term these *special* conditions, because they stand in an exclusive relation to definite reproductions. They fall into two clearly distinguishable groups, which we may term *incentives to reproduction* and *materials of reproduction*. The former comprehends the sensations which give occasion to the formation of a reproduction, *i.e.*, covers practically the same ground as the current term 'association.' When a centrally excited sensation β appears in consequence of a peripheral sensation *a*, *a* is the incentive to the reproduction of β. The relation which must be assumed to hold between *a* and β we will call *liability of reproduction;* and it will be part of our problem to discover the circumstances upon which it is dependent. The second group of special conditions embraces the peripherally excited sensations, which (experience tells us) must have been produced for centrally excited sensations similar to them to be possible. We must have seen, if we are to be able to experience visual memory images : there are no centrally excited visual sensations in congenital blindness. These materials of reproduction are, therefore, always peripherally excited sensations. The relation which obtains between them and the centrally excited sensations dependent upon them we will call the *fidelity of reproduction ;* and we shall have to inquire into the circumstances which influence it. In the present Section we will deal, first of all, with the incentives to reproduction.

3. If we are seated in a darkened chamber and suddenly catch the scent of a rose, we shall be apt to think of the rose as an object of visual perception, *i.e.*, the scent will call up the image of some rose previously seen. There can be no doubt that this reproduction could not have been effected without experience. We must at some time or other have had both contents in consciousness, the characteristic fragrance and the visual idea of the flower. But it does not necessarily follow that this definite flower was connected in our minds with this definite scent; nor is it necessary that the visual image arise at all. A judgment may be formed: "there are roses in the room"; or we may recall a situation in which the scent of roses particularly attracted our attention, and so on. Which of these different possibilities is realised does not depend upon the sensation of smell; where that exerts any influence at all upon the character of the reproduced ideas, it does so only within certain limits. If our sensible discrimination for scents is highly trained, the centrally excited visual sensation of a rose will be restricted to a definite variety of the flower; but even in this case the differences of form, of size, and of surroundings are so great that the reproduction cannot be said to be really definite and individual. So that, on the assumption that we have seen not only one but a whole number of rose blooms, that these perceptions occurred under different circumstances, and that we have sufficient knowledge to name them, there is a fairly large range of variation for the conscious contents aroused by the olfactory sensation. Conversely, perceived roses of very different colour, form, and size may excite the same olfactory image or olfactory judgment. The same holds of every other sensible quality. A tone does not necessarily recall definite tones or definite auditory perceptions, nor a colour definite objects. The individual quality of a centrally excited sensation is, therefore, by no means always guaranteed by the quality of the sensation which excites it. The character of the reproduced idea has a range of variation proportional to the experience of the subject.

4. Sensations only obtain an individual significance when they enter into connection with one another or combine to form ideas. But not every connection possesses an equally high degree of individuality. Thus the common chord of C-major, $c - e - g - c'$, is but little capable of arousing an idea of entirely definite character. The capacity is most strongly developed in cases where the sensations have a temporal or spatial arrangement. A very brief musical *motif*, *e.g.*, may give occasion to the unhesitating reproduction of a series of tonal ideas, and the idea of a human figure recall a definite situation of which it was part. We shall probably not go far wrong in regarding

this individual significance of spatial juxtaposition and temporal succession as the principal reason for the exceptional importance attached to them in the traditional doctrine of association and reproduction (§ 67. 3). In their case, we certainly do often discover an entirely individual dependency of idea upon idea, and can clearly trace the influence of previous experience upon later reproduction. Moreover, it is characteristic of spatial and temporal colligation that its separate constituents have their independence and peculiarities emphasised, *i.e.*, the distinctness of their apprehension essentially furthered, by combination (cf. § 3. 4, and § 42). And lastly, it is only possible to perceive and to retain any considerable complex of sensations as a distinctive whole, when its components are contiguous in space or time. Such a whole may be termed an 'intuition'; and we can understand why it is that space and time are then designated the 'forms of intuition', under which our sensible knowledge is comprised. But it cannot be asserted that temporal and spatial colligations are the only connections which condition reproduction. They occupy an exceptional position in the series of possible connections, simply because they present particularly favourable circumstances. Any conjunction of sensations in consciousness can, however, function as an empirical condition of reproduction. Thus our own instance of the reproduction of a visual idea by an olfactory sensation is a connection of psychical states which need not have originated by way either of spatial or temporal colligation.

5. This brings us to our first general result. *Sensations, which have at some time been together in consciousness, establish a liability of reproduction,* so that when one of them is re-excited, a sensation like the other (cf. § 29. 4) ordinarily arises. This 'being together' in consciousness, however, requires further explanation. It is not absolutely necessary that it be conscious, *i.e.*, that the connection be itself perceived; but the more nearly the sensations present in consciousness approach to a unitarily perceived total impression, the greater is the liability of reproduction. This explains the fact that comparatively few of the large number of sensations simultaneously present possess or acquire a noticeable liability of reproduction. Here again, spatial and temporal colligation has a distinct advantage, in that the character of its total impression facilitates the comprehension of its contents. And this is of itself sufficient to prove that liability of reproduction can present very different *degrees*. We have found here (1) that its intensity depends upon the *nature of the conjunction* or connection of sensations in consciousness, as making for or against a unitary apprehension and judgment. This unitary apprehension, however,

is furthered by a number of circumstances besides (*a*) spatial and temporal colligation Thus, (*b*) the distance of the impressions from each other in space and time is of very great importance. The greatest liability of reproduction is correlated with a direct contiguity or succession. This law has been experimentally established by Ebbinghaus, in his excellent investigation into the laws of memory for nonsense syllables. (*c*) The fact that impressions belong to the same or to different sense departments naturally influences their comprehensibility. Other things equal, the connection of homogeneous impressions means a greater liability of reproduction than that of disparate. (*d*) The nature of the surroundings is to be mentioned. The more it differs from the group of contents, the easier will be their unification, and the greater the liability of reproduction which it sets up. (*e*) The character of the temporal succession of connected sensations has an effect upon their liability of reproduction. It is a familiar experience, to which Ebbinghaus' experiments have given a quantitative definition, that impressions which were received in a particular order of succession can be reproduced very much more easily in this than in the opposite order. (*f*) The existence of a name for the whole complex, or its independent reproductivity, is naturally of great importance for the interconnection of the separate constituents and their mutual effectiveness for central excitation. It is this which, in part at least, gives a special significance to the *thing*-idea, the idea of an *object*. Despite the complexity of qualities psychologically contained in it, its liability of independent reproduction renders the union and cohesion of these elements very close. [(*g*) And lastly, individual differences of 'memory type' (*types auditif, visuel,* etc.) are of considerable importance (cf. §§ 69. 2; 71.7).]

6. (2) The degree of liability of reproduction inherent in a connection of sensations is further dependent upon the *attributes of the sensations* themselves. (*a*) The more individual the *quality* of the connected contents, the stronger is the liability of reproduction of each by the others. The simple sensation, which (as we saw just now) can occur in the most various connections, does not as a rule possess any considerable effectiveness for central excitation. But more complicated processes, ideas, are often quite individual in character, and endowed with a correspondingly high degree of liability of reproduction. A distinction has been drawn, in experimental investigations of the rapidity of reproduction, between *free* and *constrained* associations, the difference being in essential that of the degree of definiteness of the connection. Taking the rapidity of association in this sense as the criterion of liability of reproduction, we find that unequivocally definite, *i.e.*, wholly

individual reproductions are effected most quickly, while ambiguously defined reproductions, which have a limited range of variation, require a longer time, and free reproductions are the slowest of all. The limit of variation is set for a particular experiment by a previous statement of the kind of reproduction required. Thus a visual impression of colour can be made individually excitatory by the condition that the observer names or reproduces in imagination the colour which lies to the left hand side of it in the spectrum. This arbitrary limitation of effectiveness for central excitation is also useful as throwing light upon the fortuitous definiteness of a reproduction. That a given sensation actually arouses one single conscious content, out of the many possible, is not due to anything in the sensation itself. The principal reason for the determinateness of the reproduction is that all the other processes present in consciousness combine to further the excitation of the content in question. The result is, therefore, always individual, even though the special incentives to it are neither obvious at the time nor discoverable by subsequent analysis. The degree of liability of reproduction in these apparently free, but really constrained associations is, however, not so high as in the typically constrained form, because the intensity of the secondary influences in their fortuitous co-operation is apt to be far less than that of a condition expressly imposed, and because the influences themselves may cut across one another, *i.e.*, tend to divert reproduction into different channels.

7. (*b*) The degree of effectiveness for central excitation is dependent, again, upon the *intensity* of the reproducing sensations. Not only do the more intensive members of a sensational connection acquire a greater liability of reproduction, but the intensity and distinctness of the reproduced sensation are dependent upon the intensity and distinctness of the reproducing. We do not readily forget the time and place at which we were 'so bitterly cold' or 'in such intense pain'. The authority of many teachers over their scholars is mainly due to the intensity of the sound waves issuing from their vocal organs. In psychophysical experiments we find that the promptness and certainty of judgment increase with increase of the magnitude of stimulus difference or of the clearness of stimulus quality, etc. Here, too, belongs the fact that centrally excited sensations as a class are less liable to reproduction by one another than peripherally excited sensations, and that the peripheral sensations have a much more preponderent influence upon consciousness. A striking instance of the latter statement is afforded by 'Strümpell's case'. The patient showed a complete anæsthesia of skin and internal organs, and his remaining senses were so seriously deficient that the entrance of external stimuli

into consciousness could easily be prevented. If under these circumstances he was debarred from making any extensive movements (although these again did not evoke sensations), he inevitably fell asleep after a few minutes. Since Strümpell observed and described this case, many similar experiments have been made on other persons with the same result. It is noteworthy that Strümpell's patient came in time to object to the experiment, because, as he said, there was 'nothing left of him.'[1] We could not have a more convincing illustration of the importance of peripherally excited sensations for ideation.—Evidence of the correctness of the general statement at the head of this paragraph is furnished in abundance by our everyday experience, so that we need not spend time in substantiating it here.

8. (c) The *temporal* and *spatial character* of sensations affects their liability of reproduction in the same way as intensity. We have found it to hold elsewhere, within certain limits, that the extension, duration and frequency of a stimulus are psychological equivalents of its intensity (cf., *e.g.*, § 17. 2; § 18. 7; § 19. 7). Duration and frequency are of especial importance in the present reference. The longer a connection of sensations is continued in consciousness, the greater will be the liability of reproduction of its terms. And the frequency with which a connection is repeated has a precisely similar effect. We stand for a long time looking at a famous picture, because we wish to be able to recall it in all possible distinctness of detail; and we fix a poem in memory by 'learning' it, *i.e.*, by reading and repeating it over and over again. This influence of duration and frequency manifests itself in two ways, like that of intensity. Not only do the more permanent and more frequent members of a sensational connection acquire a greater liability of reproduction, but the effectiveness of an impression for central excitation is proportional to the length of its stay in consciousness and the frequency of its presentation to perception. It is true that ideation gradually becomes exempt from modification by events of everyday occurrence, which sink to unconsciousness or (in physiological language) affect only the lower centres. But it is precisely when they have become automatic or reflex-like that the effectiveness of these persistent peripheral stimuli for central excitation is most certain and reliable.—The influence of frequency upon liability of reproduction in the first sense of the term has received quantitative expression in experiments by Ebbinghaus. A series of 7 nonsense syllables could be repeated without a mistake after a single attentive perusal; a series of 12 had to be read over some 17 times. The number of readings necessary for accurate repetition increased at first

[1] "Dann bin ich ja nicht mehr da."

quickly, and afterwards more slowly, with increase of the number of syllables comprised in a series. The experiments show, further, that the length of a series is inversely proportional to the degree of liability of reproduction of any one term by the next following. It is interesting to note that, when the series of syllables 'makes sense', the number of readings necessary for learning it by heart is reduced about tenfold. Apart from the influence of rhyme and rhythm (the words learned were six stanzas of Byron's *Don Juan*), the increased liability of reproduction under these circumstances is mainly due to the definiteness of the interconnection of the separate terms of the series.

9. We have now surveyed, with approximate completeness, the whole domain of *empirically incited reproductions, i.e.,* of what are usually termed simultaneous and successive associations. It may not be amiss here to repeat our previous statement that neither the reproducing nor the reproduced sensation need be identical with its empirical conditions,—that all that is required for its relation to previous sensations is a similarity, in the sense of partial identity or of slight difference. If we denote this similarity, as before, by the correlation of Latin and Greek letters, we can say, therefore, that a connection of the sensations a and b may be the incentive to the reproduction of b by a and of a by b, to that of β by a and α by b, or to that of β by α and α by β. No accurate determination has been made of the influence of the degree of similarity upon liability of reproduction. It is hardly necessary to enter a special caution against the confusion of this use of similarity with the meaning which it has in the phrase 'association by similarity' (§ 29, 7).

The second class of reproductions, besides the empirical, includes what we may call *free reproductions.* We have already given some account of them (§ 29. 2, 3). They consist (1) of spontaneous ideas, the reality of which is vouched for by introspection, and can scarcely be disputed; and (2) of centrally excited sensations which can be shown never to have been together in consciousness with the process that excites them, and which are not either similar to any process which has been connected in the past with the reproducing sensation. (1) The special conditions of spontaneous ideas have not been investigated, even where they might seem to be accessible to introspection. Indeed, it would probably be difficult to subject them in any way to systematic experimentation, since they owe their very existence to accident, and introspection can hardly be adequate to define their peculiarities. On the other hand, our consideration of the materials of reproduction of centrally excited sensations will bring to light a number of more general conditions valid for spontaneous ideas, as for all other similar processes.

10. (2) The second group of free reproductions embraces all those cases in which a new quality or a new complex of qualities is effective for central excitation. Our investigation of them is greatly simplified by the fact that we may assume the possibility of their inclusion under the general schema to which we have referred the empirically conditioned reproductions. When we were formulating this, we found that not only sensations identical with those which had formerly been in consciousness, but also sensations which were similar to previous sensations, were capable of reproducing one another. No other postulate is needed for free reproductions, as we have defined them. They, too, are shown by experience to be excited simply by sensations similar to others which have been at some time connected with them. No impression is absolutely strange to consciousness; every new impression, that is, will be somehow similar to one or more past experiences. To give explicitness to this aspect of free reproductions in our schema, we will use indices to denote similarity to the processes symbolised by our original letters. Let a_1, a_2, a_3, be peripherally excited sensations, similar to a previously experienced sensation a, and b_1, b_2, b_3 sensations related to an earlier sensation b; and let α and β be the centrally excited sensations similar to a and b. Then β can be excited not only by a or α (empirically incited reproduction), but also by a_1, a_2, a_3 (free reproduction); and α in the same way, not only by b and β, but also by b_1, b_2, b_3. All that we have said of the influence of the attributes of sensation upon liability of reproduction will now hold, with slight modifications which need not here be particularised, of these cases of free reproduction. Since centrally excited sensations show a less degree of qualitative differentiation than peripherally excited (§ 28. 4), it is not surprising that the same α or β can be reproduced by a whole number of discriminable peripheral impressions. Moreover, it is not impossible that α be transformed into α_1, α_2, α_3; and it can then happen that the same b reproduces different α. This is the more likely, as the total surroundings of a centrally excited sensation may exert an influence upon its character (§ 30. 5).

11. The degree of similarity which must or may be assumed for the occurrence of a free reproduction cannot at present be estimated. But it seems indubitable that a certain similarity must exist between the effectual incentive to a free reproduction and other previous experiences, related to the centrally excitable processes in question by some liability of empirical reproduction. For when once this similarity sinks below a certain (not definable) lower limit, what may seem to be the occasion of the appearance of definite reproductions proves not to be their actual incentive. Instances are sufficiently common.

I requested an observer to look into a spectroscope, with the remark that he would see violet, when, as a matter of fact, only yellowish green was visible. He at once stated that he saw bluish green, but immediately corrected himself, and declared that it was yellowish green. The incentive to reproduction in the judgment 'bluish green' was certainly not exclusively the yellowish green actually seen: the difference between the two colour tones is too considerable for the same specific name to be reproduced by them. The judgment, then, was plainly due in part to the precedent suggestion of 'violet'.

This distortion of recorded judgment in consequence of subjective prepossession or other circumstances, is not infrequently noticeable in psychophysical experiments, and constitutes another reason for the employment of trained and careful observers (§ 2). Many illustrations are afforded, also, by the phenomena of the recollection of complex processes. It is, of course, doubtful how far the judgment of the observing individual may be regarded as an adequate criterion of the effectiveness or significance of a sensation as an incentive to reproduction. Certain cases of 'spontaneous' ideation may, perhaps, be referred to empirically incited or free reproductions; the really excitatory sensations or ideas having escaped cognition or recognition as incentives to reproduction. We have seen that recognition is by no means always reliable (cf. § 27. 7): so that the hypothesis is not altogether improbable.

§ 31. Materials of Reproduction and Fidelity of Reproduction.

1. The materials of reproduction constitute the factual basis of the dogmatic belief which we referred to above (§ 27. 1), that the memorial attribute, reproductivity, always implies a repetition or revival of a previous perception. Experience seems to justify the inference that there would be no centrally excited sensations, if there were none peripherally excited. But the process of reproduction is nothing so simple as a mere renewal of a precedent excitation. We have seen (§ 28. 5 ff.) that recollection, for which this hypothesis was thought to be necessary, is explicable without it. And there is at present no proof that it accords with the facts (§ 27); while there are very definite indications that centrally excited sensations are not immutable weaker copies of earlier peripheral sensations. (1) First and foremost of these is the familiar phenomenon of *forgetfulness.* We 'forget', when we are incapable of recollecting an experience. This incapacity need not depend upon an abrogation of 'memorial images': recollection is an ambiguous term (§ 27. 9). For us, how-

ever, it is only interesting when really based upon an alteration of
the centrally excited sensations themselves.

2. There can be no doubt that complex impressions undergo
alteration of this kind. Psychologists have often described the breaking
down of ideas, their fading away, their passage into vague and blurred
contents. These terms certainly do not express a mere weakening
of the same impression: they denote a concomitant, more or less
radical change of its quality. But simple qualities also lose their
individuality, in this process of forgetting; fine shades of difference
become incognisable, and fusion with other qualities takes place.
There results what we may call an *abstract idea*—however dubious
the term may seem after Berkeley's trenchant criticism. It would, of
course, be wrong to assert the possibility of an abstract idea which
had absolutely no specific characters, no quality, no form, etc. But
there undoubtedly are abstract ideas in the sense of centrally excited
contents which can call up a large number of peripherally excited
sensations, *i.e.*, which lack the definiteness and distinctness characteristic
of these latter. They have peripheral analogues, which can be produced quite easily under suitable experimental conditions. If a colour
stimulus, *e.g.*, is allowed to act upon the eye for a brief instant of
time, what is seen is no more than 'a flash of light', which it is wholly
impossible to define further; if the duration of the stimulus is somewhat increased, it is cognised as a colour tone, and not merely as
brightness, but its quality may be quite widely mistaken, *i.e.*, it may
be very differently interpreted. This want of individual clearness is
found in all centrally excited sensations which fall a prey to the
change involved in forgetting; indeed, in a certain measure, it is one
of their regular attributes in the normal consciousness. And it is this
which we mean when we speak of an 'abstract' idea. The importance
of the process for the formation of *concepts* is obvious (cf. § 29, 7).

3. (2) There is another fact to mention, besides that of forgetfulness,
in evidence of the independent variability of centrally excited sensations.
It is, the manifold influence exerted upon them by other conscious
contents. Here again, complex impressions show the clearest traces
of central modification. New combinations are constantly being formed
among reproduced processes: connections are severed, and separate
ideas connected; elements are exchanged, and forms remodelled.
The pranks of the dream imagination furnish a sufficiency of striking
instances. But simple qualities do not either remain unaltered by
their new connections; they adapt themselves more or less to their
changed significance; and the result may be, that a sensation of really
peripheral origin, which at first imprinted a clear image upon our mind,

is believed to have never formed part of our previous experience. It is obviously difficult to bring examples; but careful introspection will hardly fail to reveal cases of the kind. They cast no doubt, however, upon the general dependency of centrally excited on precedent peripherally excited sensations. The congenitally colour blind have no idea of the colours which they do not see; and the deaf-mute who has never spoken or heard has no 'images' of speech or hearing, The converse fact, that the child who is accidentally blinded in the first years of its life retains certain visual ideas through manhood and old age shows for how long a time the after effects of peripheral excitations may be reproduced with some degree of fidelity. In what follows, then, we shall attempt to enumerate the conditions of this *fidelity* of the memorial image, meaning by 'greater' or 'less' fidelity its greater or less similarity to the peripherally excited sensation upon which it appears to be directly dependent. Connected with this is, probably, the greater or less facility of the particular reproduction, or (to use another phraseology) the degree of our preparedness or disposition for certain ideas.

4. (*a*) The first of these conditions is the *quality* of the peripherally excited sensations. The more widely a peripherally excited sensation differs from sensations already experienced, the more nearly will its reproduction resemble it. This proposition is plainly analogous to that which we formulated above (§ 30. 6) with reference to the degree of liability of reproduction. We there found that individuality of character of the sensational connection (*i.e.*, a slight degree of liability of confusion with other connections) carried with it a comparatively high degree of liability of reproduction. Here, in the same way, the distinctness of a quality, its sufficient difference from other qualities, implies that the centrally excited sensation which it originates has but slight tendency to vary from it. A 'striking' impression leaves a true image of itself in memory. Connected with this is the fact that qualities of the same sense run but little risk of serious alteration, if they differ considerably among themselves: pressure and temperature, *e.g.*, or the specific qualities of taste, or sensations of brightness and saturated colours. Where, on the other hand, the qualities are closely related, passing into one another by gradual transition (green and greenish blue, or tones of nearly similar pitch), the centrally excited sensations possess but little fidelity or permanence. (*b*) *Intensity* has an effect upon these attributes. The more intensive a peripherally excited sensation, the greater is the fidelity of the coresponding centrally excited sensation. It is an everyday experience that, other things equal, memory is more retentive of intensive than of weak impressions,

whatever their character. (*c*) The *temporal* and *spatial* character of the peripherally excited sensation exerts a similar influence. Wide extension or peculiar form increases the reproductivity of a quality. The effect of duration and frequency upon fidelity of recollection is well known. Every lesson that we learn shows the importance of repetition for the retention of a memorial image. And apart from the intensification of the liability of reproduction which occurs in 'learning', an impression will 'fix itself' better in the mind, when its imprint is the result of repetition. In practice it is, naturally, difficult to separate the two processes. Ebbinghaus found by experiment that the capacity to reproduce a series of attentively read nonsense syllables increased, within certain limits, in approximate proportion to the number of repetitions.

5. No other systematic experiments than these of Ebbinghaus have been made upon the dependency of fidelity of reproduction on the character of the peripherally excited sensations which reproduction presupposes. We have valuable researches upon recognition and various functions of memory; but they all deal with something quite different from the laws and processes whose outlines we have sketched in the present discussion. Thus, the experiments of A. Lehmann upon direct and indirect recognition tell us something of the permanence and degree of liability of reproduction in different cases. It was found, *e.g.*, that those brightnesses were best cognised which possess definite names (light gray, dark gray, etc.); that only 7 p.c. of a large number of judgments of 62 different scents showed a direct recognition in its pure form, etc. But to assume that in all cases, where a sensation *a* of peripheral origin is to be judged as like or unlike a previously experienced sensation *b*, *a* is compared with the memorial image of *b* (in our terminology, β), and the relative certainty and correctness of the judgment depends upon the fidelity with which β reproduces *b*, is to set up a hypothesis which, so far as we have been able to find, does not really express the facts. The judgment 'like' or 'different' is generally passed quite as directly as the judgment 'known' in (technically) direct recognition. In neither case is a comparison instituted with a centrally excited sensation,—the quality of which, moreover, in the sphere of brightness sensation, is usually very different indeed from the quality of the peripheral excitation. If we reserve the term 'indirect' for comparison mediated by reproduction, or involving any other conscious application of empirical criteria, this particular form of recognition must be referred in most cases to a direct comparison. Direct comparison occurs, again, in experiments upon sensible discrimination for successive stimuli, which

has also been wrongly interpreted to consist in the comparison of the present impression with the memorial image (all that is left) of the preceding. This view explains the time error of the experiments (cf. § 6. 9) as due to the natural weakness of the memorial image in comparison with the vividness of the sensible impression. But if the explanation held, the error must be least with weak and greatest with strong stimuli, and always take the same direction. The facts are otherwise. It is only with weak stimuli that the time error has the significance which the theory ascribes to it, *i.e.*, that the second impression appears the stronger; it then decreases, and with very strong stimuli changes its direction entirely, so that the second stimulus actually appears the weaker. It follows, therefore, that there is no mediation of a comparison by the memory image, but that judgment is passed immediately after the perception of the second stimulus, just as in direct recognition.

6. It seems, therefore, that neither Lehmann's experiments upon recognition nor those of Wolfe (carried out by quite similar methods) upon tonal memory can tell us anything of the fidelity of centrally excited sensations. The judgments are passed altogether independently of them. We have rather to explain direct comparison and direct recognition somewhat as follows. (1) In many cases, the direct form is a derivative of the indirect. The transformation is due to the working of a *law of exclusion* of intermediate terms, which plays a large part in the determination of ideational connection in general. It may be formulated in this way : when a simultaneous or successive connection of three contents, *a*, *b*, and *c*, has established a liability of reproduction between *a* and *c*, *c* gradually comes to be excited directly by *a*, without the intermediation of *b*. This 'short cut' through experience is of immense importance both theoretically and practically for the rapid advance of knowledge. And we have an instance of it in the passage of indirect recognition and comparison into the direct forms. (2) 'Like' and 'different', 'known' and 'unknown' are all concepts of relation. They can never be predicated of a content as such, but only of it as related to other contents. As, however, no other contents play a conscious part in direct comparison and recognition, we must imagine that equivalent physiological processes, not at present definable, combine with the perceived impression to reproduce the judgments. In other words, we have always to presuppose the co-operation of a central excitation, which may either be already present when the stimulus of comparison is given (as in anticipated and purposive recognition or comparison), or is excited by it (as in unanticipated recognition and comparison).

This central excitation need not be a residuum of the sensation caused by the standard stimulus or object of reference; it may be the equivalent of other contents subserving comparison and recognition. It will, therefore, hardly be disputed that experiments involving an intentional comparison of a given impression with an impression previously experienced can tell us nothing of the fidelity of memorial images but for the most part simply indicate the liability of reproduction existing between sensation and central excitation (the after effect of the previous impression or of any other indirect criterion) on the one hand, and a particular judgment on the other.

7. On the other hand, these experiments, as well as certain series taken by Ebbinghaus in the course of his investigations of memory, may be appealed to for information upon another point,—the influence of *time* (*i.e.*, of the time interval) upon the liability of reproduction. We know from experience, that the longer the time which has elapsed since a particular event, the more uncertain and incorrect is our recollection of it. It is with this law and its exact formulation that experiments upon recognition, memory, etc., are principally concerned. If we term the weakening of recollection 'forgetfulness', and measure forgetfulness either by the work necessary for the complete restitution of the recollection, or by the number of correct judgments formed in the process of determinate recognition or direct comparison, we may say in general that forgetfulness increases at first quickly and then more slowly. Ebbinghaus and Wolfe discovered a logarithmic relation for it, which is stated by the former as follows: the quotients of retention and forgetfulness (of the time saved in and required for relearning) are inversely proportional to the logarithms of the times passed since the first learning. [1] This agreement in experimental results shows clearly, as against the various opinions of philosophical psychology, that forgetfulness really exists, and that its existence cannot be invalidated by the allegation (supported merely by an indefinite 'experience') that what seems to be forgotten only needs the right occasion to reappear with entire fidelity. But nothing can be inferred from the experiments as to an obscuration and weakening of memorial images, or a crumbling of their connections, for the simple reason that these 'images' are neither the materials of judgment in direct comparison nor the necessary incentives to motor activity in subsequent repetition. Here again, we must rather emphasise the variety of the processes actually involved, as we did before in the case of recollection (§ 28. 7).

---

[1] $\dfrac{b}{v} = \dfrac{K}{(\log t)c}$, where $b =$ *Behaltenes* (retained), $v =$ *Vergessenes* (forgotten), $t =$ time-interval, and k and c are constants.

§ 32. The General Conditions of Centrally Excited Sensations.

1. (1) The most important of the general conditions of reproduction is, undoubtedly, the state of *attention*. Unfortunately, its significance for special acts of recollection, reproduction, etc., has not been thoroughly made out. We do not know, in particular, how far what is ordinarily called 'association', and what we ourselves have somewhat inconsistently termed reproduction, can be brought about without the co-operation of attention. We find, however, that its action is two-fold: it renders the incentives to reproduction more effectual, and gives the materials of reproduction a greater consequence. In other words, it enhances the *associability* and *reproductivity* of sensations. Instances of this influence are sufficiently common: all the rules which we have laid down for the special conditioning of centrally excited sensations are based upon the implicit assumption that the processes which they cover are experienced in the state of attention (cf. § 5. 2, 3). Hence it is impossible, at present, to say with any degree of certainty, how associability and reproductivity would be affected if we abstracted from the influence of attention. That it is not the only condition operative is indicated by two sets of facts: (*a*) the familiar experience of 'not catching' a question, and then recollecting and being able to answer it after some interval of time, or of 'overlooking' a constituent of the field of vision, and yet reproducing it with more or less fidelity; and (*b*) the impossibility of the reduction of all the different effects of the special conditions of centrally excited sensations to their effects for attention alone. In any case, however, it is desirable to collect observations, and if possible make special experiments upon a point of such importance for the theory of centrally excited sensations. It is certain that the influence of attention can hardly be exaggerated. Everyone knows how little the inattentive repetition of a lesson does for its retention. Fechner observed that the *memorial after-image*, as he called the voluntary reproduction of a recently perceived impression, only appeared if the object of perception had also been the object of attention, and only contained those constituents of the perception on which the attention had been particularly directed. In psychological experiments upon association, again, it is often remarked that the associability of two visual objects which are perceptible together for a short time is essentially dependent upon the degree of attention with which the connection of the impressions was regarded. We cannot here enter into the special factors comprised

under the general name of attention: we shall treat of them in the
third Part of the book (§§ 72 ff.)

2. (2) Besides attention, *practice* and *fatigue* have a general influence upon associability and reproductivity. We discriminated above
between general and special practice and fatigue (§ 5. 9), and can
apply the distinction again in the present connection. The facts which
belong under this rubric are those of the 'trained,' 'overstocked,'
'worn out,' etc., memory. The more general practice we have had in
learning by heart, the easier is our retention of a particular lesson; but
different qualities and different arrangements require a further and more
special practice. The various 'types' of memory, memory for names and
figures, for colours and tones, etc., are in great measure referable to
special practice in these classes of centrally excited sensations, itself
due to inclination or opportunity. The schoolboy who whistles every
melody that he hears does not thereby improve his memory for
colours or forms, words or odours. The various types of sensible memory
(§ 10, 5) require altogether individual development, just as physical
training can be exclusively directed to a particular part of the body.
It is the same, again, with the influence of fatigue. The general
relaxation which we experience after a sleepless night weakens associability and reproductivity in all sense departments alike. But the
fatigue of memory produced by persistent occupation with a particular
object need not extend to other objects; indeed, it may change to an
undiminished vigour, when attention is turned to a wholly different
complex of processes, dependent upon other conditions. The more
extensive the draft made upon the sensible memory by a given
occupation, the more general is its consequent fatigue. Mental work,
which involves the most diverse conscious processes, is, therefore,
productive of general fatigue. It is again impossible to say with
certainty whether these processes influence associability and reproductivity directly, or only indirectly, *i.e.*, by way of attention. The
abnormal increase of central excitability at a certain stage of fatigue
(evidenced by vivid dreams, multiplication of illusions, etc.) seems to
indicate that the diminution of associability and reproductivity resulting
from fatigue does not affect the central sensations themselves so much
as the arrangement, connection and direction which are normal to
them under the guidance of voluntary attention. An analysis of the
influence of practice leads to a similar conclusion. We must, therefore, suspend judgment upon the question whether practice and
fatigue are conditions of centrally excited sensations co-ordinate with
attention.

3. (3) The same holds of the *feelings* of pleasantness and unpleas-

antness. We can, it is true, lay down the general rule that the associability and reproductivity of sensations are greater, the more vivid the feelings connected with them: but we cannot say with certainty whether a direct functional relation obtains between feelings on the one hand, and associability and reproductivity of centrally excited sensations on the other, or whether the feelings are simply concomitant processes, implied in every high degree of attentional concentration, and in that way acquiring an apparent influence of their own upon association and reproduction. It must, consequently, remain doubtful, whether the feelings which accompany, *e.g.,* a peripheral impression, are themselves the conditions, promoters, or mediators of its influence upon the train of ideas, or whether the increase of attention which an affectively toned impression regularly commands is the really important factor. The facts are familiar enough. Pleasure and interest in an object increase the capacity of memory both in the child and in the adult, and unpleasant impressions leave a deep imprint and are recalled with great fidelity. The influence of the two qualities of affective tone upon the reproductivity of sensations would seem, therefore, to be the same. Their effect upon associability, on the other hand, is different, pleasantness being a decided incentive to association, and unpleasantness a hardly less decided preventive of connection. A sensation of strongly unpleasant tone elbows its way into consciousness, so to speak, and leaves no standing ground for other ideas.

The most indelible impression of melancholy which I received from a visit to a lunatic asylum was made by a middle-aged woman afflicted with *melancholia.* She sat motionless upon a chair, her features wearing a look of intense sadness and bitterness, her head sunk, the eyes seemingly fixed upon the one inevitable horror which she could not even name. But instances are not wanting in ordinary life. The mourner prefers to dwell upon his grief in solitude, where he is not compelled to struggle against exciting impressions, but can nurse his sorrow unhindered until the spell is broken by a salutary exhaustion.

Pleasurably toned sensations show something of the same character. A very intensive feeling of pleasure may bring about a temporary paralysis of consciousness, though the condition lasts only for a very short time. As a general rule, however, pleasure means communicativeness and enlivens the course of thought, hurrying it from image to image, from scene to scene, from action to action. The flight of ideas in *mania*, due to an excessive cheerfulness of mood, is thus the precise opposite of the insistent brooding of *melancholia.*

4. A question of especial importance in this connection is whether the feelings of pleasantness and unpleasantness may of themselves determine the course or the quality of a train of ideas, *i.e.,* are to be

classed among the processes directly subserving ideational excitation. It is generally held that the associability and reproductivity of a sensation are modified by its attendant feelings, but that these cannot be looked upon as independent causes of reproduction. It is, again, hardly possible to decide the matter at the present time. But there are certain observations which point to the necessity of the recognition of feeling as a real incentive to reproduction. (*a*) It is an everyday experience that a cheerful impression recalls other cheerful impressions, and depressing circumstances others like them. (*b*) In mania and melancholia the predominant mood (pleasure or pain) determines the course of the train of ideas; nothing is reproduced which does not stand in connection with the affective disposition.

This fact showed itself very strikingly in a case of hashish poisoning which I had opportunity to observe. The emotions of the moment seemed to have usurped the actual direction of the course of ideas in consciousness. The patient was not at all incapacitated for introspection, and his subsequent recollection of the details of his case was very accurate. He himself noticed and emphasised the importance of the affective disposition. The excitement under which he generally laboured gave occasion to a whole series of more or less incoherent reproductions, originating (as he said) simply and solely in the affective state. Fits of depression and intervals of keen anxiety, by which it was interrupted, immediately changed the course of the ideational movement. The observation is, of course, by no means unequivocal. For (α) we might analyse this 'reproduction by feeling' as we have already analysed 'association by similarity'. It might be referred, in particular, to the category of reproduction mediated by substitution (cf. § 29, 6). In this event, feeling would undoubtedly possess an importance of its own for the origination of centrally excited sensations; it would be the persistent identical element, which arouses a new idea whose similar has previously been together with it in consciousness, and which is thus the reproducing factor in the complex. But (β) we might also imagine that not the feelings, but the concomitant movements which are so accurately adjusted to express them, and which are correlated with definite organic sensations, were the reproductory agents. (γ) Both explanations assume that the reproduction was not effected by way of some secondary character of sensation or idea; but the correctness of the assumption is not by any means certain.

5. (4) Lastly, there is to be mentioned the dependency of centrally excited sensations upon the *will*. By 'will' we understand here not a new elementary quality of consciousness (the evidence for which we shall discuss in § 40), but what is called 'will' in the language of everyday life and of modern psychology alike—the capacity which the individual possesses to determine his own attitude and action, internal and external. Wundt has shown that will and attention are intimately related, and has employed the term *apperception* to denote their common constituent. We cannot now enter into the details of the apper-

ception controversy: it is sufficient for our purpose to point out that apperception itself is obviously not a speculative construction, or a metaphysical faculty, or any other of the objectionable things which hostile critics have represented it to be, but an expression for undeniable facts of consciousness. If we did not possess the capacity of will or attention or apperception, whichever we call it, consciousness would be at the mercy of external impressions (which we have found to be ordinarily stronger than any class of reproduced sensations), thinking would be made impossible by the noisiness of our surroundings, etc. The normal individual must, therefore, be able to open a free path to certain ideas and movements, while he inhibits certain others; *i.e.*, to determine the direction and character both of his thoughts and of his bodily movement. But the question as to the influence of this capacity, will, on the origination of centrally excited sensations, can hardly be answered without a more precise statement of the particular processes comprised under the general name, and a more concrete definition of the name itself. We may, therefore, briefly remark that we regard the activity of will as the expression of the totality of previous experiences, in all the degrees of authority and consequence which they have acquired in accordance with universal psychological laws, and with all the weight of influence which distinguishes the old and proven from the new and strange. It is for the most part but a small and fragmentary measure of this that finds its way into consciousness: the reserve of energy which gives efficacy to will lies below the conscious limen. Even this short account (the detailed investigation and exposition follow in §§ 40 and 77) will be enough to put it beyond doubt that will—a capacity which sums up in itself the whole course of individual development—must be a condition of exceptional importance for the course of centrally excited sensations. As a matter of fact, we can by its assistance reproduce an idea or suppress a reproduction or divert associability into a definite channel. The product of volition is, of course, not a creation out of nothing, though it may sometimes present this appearance to introspection, when the particular determinants of will and of the ideas willed do not emerge from the limbo of the unconscious, of physiological processes. This bare statement must suffice in the present connection. We need only add that what are called the *mental dispositions* [logical or mechanical memory, inductive or deductive intellect, receptive or constructive imagination, talent, etc.: cf. § 39. 6] may also be looked upon as ultimate general conditions of centrally excited sensations. They, too, are forces, which appear in the course of individual development, but which are only fragmentarily accessible to introspection; though the name is further used to indicate special inclination for certain classes of internal and external activity. Whether they require individual mention, over and above the special conditions, is a question which it is impossible to answer.

§ 33. Theory of Centrally Excited Sensations.

1. There are three considerations which convince us that the conditions enumerated in the two previous sections do not constitute an adequate theory of centrally excited sensations. (1) 'Spontaneous' ideas cannot be explained by any of the special conditions hitherto formulated. For they are distinguished from other reproductions by the absence of a conscious incentive to their arousal; and all the conditions which we have mentioned have been explicitly gained by abstraction from introspection. (2) The process of direct sensational comparison shows that the dependency of reproduction upon precedent conscious impressions must not be interpreted to mean that the origination of centrally excited ideas is the exclusive function of peripheral stimuli whose effect is discoverable by introspection. This and many other instances of 'unconsciously' mediated reproductions prove that our 'special conditions' (§ 30) are not absolutely necessary presuppositions of centrally excited sensations. (3) And the last few decades have fairly overwhelmed psychology with cases of pathological derangement of memory, association and reproduction, in a large number of which direct anatomical and physiological disturbances have been demonstrable, while the general character of all prevents their explanation in any other way. If we refuse to admit the validity of physiological interpretation, we shall be compelled either to give up the facts as enigmatical, or to take refuge in metaphysics or mysticism. In neither event is justice done to the scientific problem. We must, therefore, face the consequences to which these facts lead, although we can only state them in outline.

2. Disturbances of memory are of very various kinds. We may classify them under the heads of *general* and *special* derangement. The former illustrates the effectiveness of the different materials of reproduction of centrally excited sensations (§ 31); the latter serves to explain and elucidate the special conditions of reproduction (§ 30). General disturbances of memory are not limited to any single sense department, but bring about a diminution of recollective capacity in all. This diminution appears under normal circumstances with advancing age, and runs its course in obedience to definite laws. At first, the newest impressions are the most easily forgotten; then the store

of ideas gradually disappears, in the order from more recent acquisition to more remote. The subject's vocabulary is also narrowed in a peculiar way: substantives are forgotten more quickly than verbs and adjectives, proper names more quickly than common, concrete terms more quickly than abstract. All these stages of forgetfulness appear also in transient or permanent derangements of memory caused, *e.g.*, by violent concussion of the brain. The facts tell us nothing new: they are simply fresh instances of the special and general conditions of centrally excited sensations which we discussed above (§§ 30—32). They are especially indicative of the influence of frequency of reproduction, the individual significance of the impression, attention, etc. There is, however, one point which, if not explained by reference to attention or fatigue (and the explanation is doubtful), takes us at once to conditions not accessible to introspection: the point that in old age the latest and newest impressions are worst reproduced, while in childhood, other things equal, they have the advantage over all others. We will group these conditions together under the general heading of a retardation of nervous processes correlated with decay of the organic functions. The retardation, which may depend upon a reduction of metabolism, must obviously be greatest where the excitations are following wholly new paths, and will gradually affect more accustomed processes, inhibiting always that which offers the least resistance.

3. Another instance of general derangement of memory is furnished by the phenomenon of double consciousness or the divided self, observed in cases of hypnosis, hysteria, etc. It is characterised by the existence of a more or less complete separation of two aggregates of conscious processes, which alternate at certain intervals or can be called up in irregular sequence by favourable conditions. The two aggregates are oftentimes of entirely opposite character. An individual whose behaviour is normally serious and decorous shows himself, in his new circle of ideas, frivolous and impudent. The 'two minds' succeed each other without conflict; frequently they know nothing of each other. All those factors in the mental and physical attitude and conduct of the individual which we call conscience, taste, principles, etc., seem to persist in the one self with unchanged intensity and unimpaired influence, while in the other they are either destroyed or transformed into their opposites. We cite these facts in the present connection, because from the purely psychological standpoint they are in the last resort simply phenomena of memory. It has been suggested that the importance of the common sensations and of the general mood or temper of mind which reflects the

state of the whole body is such as to mark them out as the nucleus or substrate of these conscious aggregates. Attention has also been called to analogous divisions of the normal consciousness occurring, *e.g.*, when we carry on a conversation while composing a letter. However it may be with these hypotheses, the two selves constitute two more or less independent circles of ideas, mediation between which is prevented by some reason inaccessible to introspection. Here again, then, we are forced to the assumption of physiological conditions. But we cannot at present make any probable conjecture as to their character.

4. The general disturbances of memory which extend merely to experiences subsequent to a particular event or comprised within a definite period are absolutely inexplicable by a psychology which refuses to pass beyond introspection into physiology. These temporary obscurations of memory have been not infrequently observed. Sometimes they are confined to the sense impressions received and the knowledge acquired during the particular time, while the actions which had become automatic are not affected; at others, they include every acquisition whose date falls within it. Sometimes again, a previous experience intervenes between new impressions, but is not judged as familiar. All these cases of more or less complete loss of the capacity to recollect precedent experiences require for their scientific explanation a dependency of the reproductivity of sensations and ideas upon some set of nervous processes. The lost memory is often fully restored after a certain lapse of time, so that there can be no question of serious anatomical derangement. Indeed, in the majority of instances the disturbance must be regarded as purely functional. This view is confirmed by the number and variety of special symptoms in amnesia. Disturbances of speech, in particular, have been very carefully studied, and show almost every conceivable type of isolated inhibition of the recollective capacity. Besides pure motor *aphasia*, which is of no interest to us here, there is a great diversity of sensory forms. One patient (alexia) will be more or less completely incapable of translating written words into speech movements, *i.e.*, of 'reading' in the ordinary sense of the word, although he can repeat what he hears quite correctly; while another suffers from more or less complete abrogation of the connection between audition and speech, although he can read without trouble. Or again, audition and vision may be convertible into spoken words, while there is more or less lack of understanding of what is read and repeated. Yet again, pathological cases are known where wrong letters or words are constantly employed, consciously and uncon-

sciously, in reading or repeating what has been heard, and in voluntary speaking. All these disturbances appear to be also possible in the translation of vision, audition, or speech into the movements subserving writing. And within each of the larger groups we can discriminate highly specialised individual cases, in which the derangement is limited to definite classes of words, definite words, definite letters, etc.

5. We find analogous phenomena in other departments of memory. Thus memory for the forms of visible objects, and the musical memory under all its different aspects seem to be capable of isolated derangement. But we can pass fairly easily from the normal consciousness even to these deep-seated pathological inhibitions, (i) because similar disturbances of less intensity sometimes occur in ordinary life, and (ii) because individual inclination or education usually leads to a preference for definite kinds of ideation and centrally excited sensations. Putting all the facts together, we may draw (1) the general conclusion that memory is not a unitary force, equally and always at the disposal of every mind for every mental process, but takes on a special form for the separate groups of centrally excited sensations and their combinations; so that what we call 'memory' consists in a number of special memories, and is not a peculiar capacity above and beyond them (§§ 30.5; 32. 2). We may also assert, without hesitation, that (2) the conditions of centrally excited sensations determinable by introspection are not their real conditions, but only symbols or indications of the reality. If we attempt to explain all the facts upon no other data than those of introspection we are compelled, in cases like those which we have just mentioned, either to dispense with an explanation altogether, or to introduce vague and indefinite concepts of unconscious ideas, mental faculties, dispositions, tendencies, etc. If, on the other hand, we make up our minds to consider nervous processes as the actual conditions of centrally excited sensations, we have, in the first place, the advantage of being able to explain all the facts, in principle at least, without putting pressure upon them or shifting our own point of view, while we also reap the benefit of basing our theory upon a universal law of nervous structure and function, which obtains whether or not there are psychical phenomena to accompany excitation. It cannot be charged against an explanation of this kind that it is either arbitrary or merely hypothetical.

6. When we come to details, however, we can offer little more than hypothesis. Our present ideas of the nature of these nervous processes, which we take to be the conditions of centrally excited sensations, are quite vague and general. A current physiological view

regards the cells of the cerebral cortex as differentiated organs, sub-serving particular perceptions and recollections. It is thought that each separate idea has its seat in a separate cell; and a calculation has been made of the number of ganglion cells, with the comforting result that there are enough of them to hold the stock of ideas accumulated in the lifetime of the individual. This theory dates back in principle to the seventeenth century. However imaginatively worked out, it is too crude to be accepted as even an approximation to the true explanation. Besides, there is nothing in the facts, normal or pathological, to suggest its selection from the list of pos-sibilities, apart from the purely physiological or purely physical diffi-culties which it presents. An attempt has been made to amend it by correlating the elementary conscious processes with the element-ary constituents of the cerebral cortex, and thus making sensation the specific energy of the cortical ganglion cell. But nothing is gained by the new formulation. The old difficulties remain practically as they were, and new ones are added. For instance, even the revised cellular hypothesis can hardly explain how it happens that sensation complexes which contain the same elements and differ from one another only in the arrangement of their contents can be possessed of such various importance for memory. And it is hardly conceiv-able (though this objection holds as against the older form of the theory as well) that visual sensations of any considerable extension can be represented on the physiological side by the excitation of a single cell. Both views, however, are put out of court by their inability to show us how or why a newly arrived sensation or idea selects a particular cell out of the whole number at its disposal.

7. This hypothesis of the seat of the separate associable elements finds its complement in the further hypothesis that incentives to the reproduction of centrally excited sensations, or (to use the commoner expression) associations, are anatomically and physiologically mediated by the tracts of fibres connecting the various sensory centres. Hence we hear of *association paths*, along which the excitation is propagated from centre to centre, and by whose means the idea which has previously been connected with an impression is reproduced when the impression is repeated, in accordance with the laws of temporal and spatial contiguity. Now there can be no doubt that the fibre masses which can be anatomically demonstrated to run from quarter to quarter of the cerebral cortex stand in relation to the association of ideas. Lesion or degeneration of the one is followed by disturbance of the other. But this relation is both inadequately and mislead-ingly expressed by the hypothesis. For (1) association is possible not

only between ideas of different sense departments, but between impressions of the same sense. The explanation consequently requires the assumption of connecting fibres between the cells of the individual sensory centre. (2) We must also suppose that, as the specific substrates of definite ideas, the cells possess specific association paths. But our present knowledge of the structure of the cerebrum, so far from giving support to this view, tells directly against it. Besides which, all the difficulties of the cellular theory recur again in connection with the theory of specific association paths. (3) Moreover, the phrase 'association path' suggests that the fibres, or their function, are the actual equivalent of 'association', in the psychological sense of the connection of sensations in consciousness. We need hardly give reasons for the contrary belief, that the function of the paths is merely a condition of empirically incited and free reproduction (§ 30. 9), and not the special topographical substrate of the simultaneity of associated sensations in consciousness.

8. It is obvious that all these ideas are closely connected with that of the law of specific sensory energies and the strict doctrine of localisation of cortical function. Indeed, if the operation of the law is transferred from periphery to centre, there is no difficulty in assigning every discriminable conscious quality its particular seat in the cerebral cortex (cf. § 9. 5 ff.). It will then depend simply upon the view of the individual psychologist, whether he make the single cell the depository of a simple or complex mental process. How far the bias of this individual psychology may lead is shown by the distinction drawn between perceptive and recollective cells on the basis of the facts of mental blindness and mental deafness (cf. § 27. 3, 7, 8), and by the localisation of a special *conceptual centre* alongside of the various sensory centres. But there is a further development to mention. As the cerebral cortex contains motor as well as sensory centres, recourse has been had of late to schematic drawings, to illustrate the connection which introspection finds to hold between idea and movement. We shall dispense with this convenient mode of illustration here, for two reasons: (1) because it would reflect the opinion of only one group of psychologists, and (2) because we regard the schematic figures ordinarily employed not only as premature, but as wrong in their essential implications. Besides the adherents of the strict localisation doctrine, there is a school of physiologists which holds that all motor centres are also sensory; another (to which Goltz belongs in particular) which keeps more or less consistently to the view of Flourens, that the cerebrum as a whole is the substrate of all mental function; and yet others which adopt neither

of the extreme theories, but accept the localisation of sense departments and motor impulses, while they reject the hypothesis of specific cells and refuse to posit a different cellular substrate for perception and recollection or an independent conceptual centre. In face of this divergence of opinion, the author may be permitted to present his personal standpoint.

9. In the first place, it is at least exceedingly misleading to speak of a 'seat' of sensation or idea. There can be no doubt that the term, with the incorrect metaphor which it embodies, must share the responsibility of many epistemological and psychophysical difficulties. When we 'localise' a sound heard, we do not make it spatial: we merely determine the part of space which is the seat of its visible source or condition. In the same way, when we distinguish local cortical centres, we are not placing sensations or ideas within a limited spatial area, but simply defining the locality of the visible conditions upon which they are dependent. All that a localisation of cortical centres can do, then, is to furnish a topography of the central nervous conditions of psychical processes. The real question at issue in the conflict of opinions is, therefore, simply this: are the central conditions of sensation referable to distinct localities, as its peripheral conditions admittedly are? To this question we may probably reply in the affirmative, appealing to the most reliable observations of pathological anatomy for facts upon which to base our answer. As the course of particular sensory nerves has been traced again and again to definite areas of the cerebral cortex, it is reasonable to suppose that the central processes are locally restricted, as are the processes in the peripheral sense organs. At the same time, this does not necessarily mean (*a*) that the sensory centres are the ultimate conditions of sensation. It is entirely conceivable that they are only links in a serial chain of conditions, which begins with the peripheral sense organ, and is continued beyond the sensory centre (since in every case paths lead from this to the frontal brain region) to reach its final conclusion, possibly, in the frontal cortex. And (*b*) this local differentiation of sensory centres does not by any means imply the validity of the cellular hypothesis criticised above. We attempted to show in a previous connection (§ 9. 7) that the law of specific sensory energies was only tenable if the specific function was brought into connection with the peculiar structure of the sense organs, and its extension to the individual qualities of sense made altogether dependent upon the special character of the experiences and observations comprised within a given sense department (*cf.* vision with audition).

10. It is noteworthy that while the motor centres of the cerebral

cortex, more especially in the neighbourhood of the anterior central convolution, are markedly different in histological structure, the sensory centres (the visual in the occipital lobes, the acoustic in the temporal, etc.) present a very similar appearance in microscopical preparations. We find, accordingly, that central disability of a motor area is overcome with extreme difficulty, whereas a sensory derangement is comparatively easily and quickly compensated. Similarly, the extirpation of a motor portion of the brain is followed by permanent local disturbance of movement; whereas an animal deprived of a sensory portion will very soon show every sign of complete recovery, provided that the exsected area was not too extensive, *i.e.,* that connection was not entirely severed between cortex and sensory nerve. All these phenomena are evidence that the specific function of a nervous excitation is as a rule dependent upon its normal place of origin: the peripheral organ in the case of sensory nerves, the central in the case of motor. It would seem, therefore, that we may compare the unknown processes of the sensory centres with the known phenomena of the motor periphery, and attempt in this way to gain a more definite idea of their nature. We must then correlate the particular sensation not with the excitation of a single cell, but with that of a larger or smaller cortical area, according to the range of the peripheral stimulation. Moreover, we shall find no difficulty in conceiving of a 'superposition' of the different cortical functions; since this only requires that each particular form of movement occurring in the cerebral cortex be independently renewable, without disturbance or abolition of others. And lastly, we may designate the state of the nervous substance, in which the various cortical areas are capable of reproduction,—employing a phrase proposed by Wundt,—*functional disposition.* Just as the piano player uses hands and fingers for the most varied combinations of movements, so the same parts of the cortex may be concerned in very different forms of excitation. The view which we oppose to the cellular hypothesis may, therefore, be termed a dynamic hypothesis. It takes account of the comparatively rapid compensation of limited brain injuries, while it also recognises local differences within the cortex.

11. If we suppose, further, that these central excitations can be originated not only by a peripheral stimulation (which, of course, is the *conditio sine qua non* of excitation in general, on our own theory as well as on the others), but also by purely central causes, we have in these last the physiological equivalent of centrally excited sensations. We must take it for granted that the mechanics of nervous substance realises the necessary special condition of empirical reproduction, simultaneous occurrence in consciousness (§ 30. 5), and responds to

all the influences which introspection showed to be determinants of the effectiveness of this condition. As we might lay down quite similar rules for combinations of movements of our limbs, we may conjecture that they are general laws of nervous excitation. We can at present form no positive idea of the physiological equivalent of conscious simultaneity. We might, perhaps, conjecture that the parallel process was a confluence of the separate sensory excitations in a supreme central organ, which seems anatomically given in the frontal lobes. As the existence of such a central organ is also vouched for by the phenomena of attention and will (§ 76. 5, § 77. 7), and as we were compelled to give attention the most important place among the general conditions of centrally excited sensations, if not to regard it as the inevitable condition of reproduction and association (§ 32. 1), it will be seen that our present hypothesis is not a mere analogical construction.

The occurrence of free reproduction, again, presents no difficulty on our theory. Introspection is unable to discover any condition for the spontaneous origination of ideas. We must, therefore, suppose that the central causes of the origination of the parallel excitations are not represented in consciousness. Nor is the other group of free reproductions any obstacle in the way of a physiological explanation, when we remember the general corollary of the law of causation, that similar causes produce similar effects. The schema to which we reduced these phenomena (§ 30. 10) can be applied directly, from this point of view, to the central nervous excitations. The conditions of centrally excited sensations enumerated above (§§ 31, 32) also admit of a physiological interpretation in accordance with our dynamic theory. Indeed, we have already shown, in certain instances, that this translation offers no special difficulty (cf., e.g., § 31. 6; § 32. 5). Coming, lastly, to the pathological observations which have been so largely influential in suggesting a physiological explanation, we can say that our hypothesis is able to do them full justice, even though it cannot state in detail how precisely this or that derangement of memory is produced.

Literature:

H. Ebbinghaus, *Das Gedächtniss*, 1885.

Th. Ribot, *Les maladies de la mémoire*. Fifth ed., 1888.

C. Hauptmann, *Die Metaphysik in der modernen Physiologie*, 1892.

B. Bourdon, *Les résultats des théories contemporaines sur l'association des idées*. *Revue philos.*, vol. xxxi., pp. 561 ff.

M. Offner, *Ueber die Grundformen der Vorstellungsverbindung. Philos. Monatshefte*, vol. xxviii., pp. 385 ff., 513 ff.

The experimental articles by Wolfe, Lehmann, and Scripture: *Phil. Studien*, vols. iii., v., and vii.; and by Münsterberg: *Beiträge zur experimentellen Psychologie*, pts. i., **iv.**

Section II. Feelings.

§ 34. Sensation and Feeling.

1. It is beyond question that we owe the richness and complexity of our conscious experience to sensation. We found that there are some 13,000 distinguishable sensation qualities (§ 15. 4, § 18. 5, § 19. 4); and this number is far exceeded by the various combinations of sensations, and the discriminable differences of intensity, etc., in which each quality can be given. The qualitative differentiation of feeling is poor indeed in comparison. Nevertheless, the feelings occupy a far more important place in popular opinion than sensations. They pass for real states of the experiencing subject, his most intimate possession, the expression of his personality and activity; while sensations seem to be something foreign to the self, imposed upon it from without, passively received by it. This divergent estimate of the two classes of conscious elements is well founded. It is based (1) upon the observation that the interrelations of feelings can never be independent of the subject as those of many sensations can, *i.e.*, that feelings have no objective significance over and above their psychological. Feelings, in other words, appear as something purely subjective, while sensations are only partially subjective [1]. But it also (2) finds support in the fact that feelings are comparatively much less dependent upon external stimuli than sensations, and are consequently much more independent of the objective influences to which the subject is exposed. This means that the attitude of the individual himself is a determining factor in the origination and course of feeling, and the impression is produced that the sole condition of its appearance and character at any given moment resides in him as experiencing subject.

2. But the view of the relation between feeling and sensation implied in these suggestions is not definite enough to be psychologically satisfactory. Psychologically regarded, both processes alike are dependent upon the experiencing subject; and external stimuli exercise a real influence upon the feelings, although it is less than in the case of sensations. The relation of the two elements, then, calls for a closer

[1] A reference to the subjective side of experience is, of course, implicit in the name *Empfindung*; but this is irrelevant to the present discussion. [No such reference seems contained in the English *sensation*].

examination. We find, first of all, an important difference, which may be regarded as characteristic for the special laws governing feeling and sensation. We divided sensations into two great groups, peripherally excited and centrally excited, and found that this distinction, so far from being unessential for consciousness, was normally recognised in every case by introspection. But there is no difference of moment between peripherally and centrally excited feelings. The centrally excited are usually as vivid as the peripherally excited, and can compete with them successfully for the determination of the will. It is curious that the representatives of eudaemonistic ethics seem one and all to have overlooked this fact, which is really the necessary presupposition of their theory. If centrally excited feelings resembled centrally excited sensations, a present pleasure, satisfaction of the senses, would inevitably be victorious over an expected pleasure or a merely imagined satisfaction. Moral action, which on the eudaemonistic view always requires an imagined pleasure as its determinant, would then only be possible if the present condition were that of sensuous dissatisfaction or of peripherally conditioned indifference. The immense importance of this equivalence of centrally and peripherally excited feelings for instruction and education, indeed, for the general progress of humanity, is obvious. Only the very highest degrees of sense pleasure and sense pain are now able to overpower the centrally excited, 'higher' feelings. Even here, the advance of civilisation has effected a partial emancipation, although the pangs of hunger and the rage of lust are still all too frequent causes of crime. On the other hand, the faintness of centrally excited sensations as compared with peripherally excited is of great importance for an unimpeded knowledge of the external world, for the progress of empirical investigation. We distinguish memory from perception, the product of imagination from the presentation of sense, so easily, that there can be no serious disturbance of the course of objective knowledge; and the growth of naturalism in art and of object-teaching in education affords a sufficient guarantee that the capacity of imaginative interpretation of perception or of vivid reproduction of (or reconstruction from) description · finds no encouragement to further development.

3. These phenomena furnish at least a partial explanation of the relatively slight dependency of feeling upon external stimulus. If centrally excited feelings are of equal value with peripherally excited, an affective state which results from the combination of peripheral and central causes will evidently show but little trace of the influence of external stimulation. Consciousness will hardly ever, one might say never, be exclusively determined by a peripheral stimulus, even

though attention place no obstacle in its path. There will always be centrally excited sensations more or less clearly present; and as they, too, are ordinarily connected with feelings, the affective influence of an external stimulus will always be modified by a pre-existent affective state. It will depend upon circumstances whether a particular stimulus is pleasant, unpleasant, or neutral, although the sensation which it arouses remains practically the same in every case. It is, therefore, in general, wholly indifferent for the investigation of sensitivity and sensible discrimination whether the stimuli are agreeable, disagreeable, or neither, provided only that their affective value does not divert the attention. We may leave it for the present undecided whether this modification of the affective influence of a peripheral stimulus may not be due in some measure to other peripheral excitations. The facts alleged put it beyond doubt that feelings obey different laws from those of sensation, and that other processes and other conditions are involved in their origination. A systematic inquiry into the relation of sensation to feeling leads to the same result. Three forms of this relation are theoretically possible. We may regard feeling (1) as an *attribute* of sensation, co-ordinate with quality and intensity; (2) as an effect or *function* of sensation or of a sensation attribute; or (3) as an *independent conscious process*, which accompanies sensation under given conditions, but which requires separate description and explanation. We will pursue our investigation under these three heads.

4. (1) *Feeling as Attribute of Sensation.*—We reject this possibility, for three principal reasons. (*a*) We can discriminate the same attributes of feeling which we previously obtained by our analysis of sensation,—quality, intensity and duration. Extension does not attach to feeling; but neither does it to all sensations (§ 4. 3). It is logically inadmissible to count a process, itself possessed of these different attributes, as one among the corresponding attributes of sensation. At the very least, we should be compelled to look upon it as an attribute of quite different rank or character; and for this there is no reason. It would be equally justifiable to consider sensation an attribute of feeling. (*b*) We made it a criterion of the attributes of sensation that, if they applied at all, they were inseparable characteristics of the content. If any one of them = 0, the whole sensation = 0 (§ 4. 1). Measured by this standard, feeling cannot be called an attribute of sensation. For the affective tone of a sensation may very well disappear, without the cessation of the sensation itself. We actually find sensations present where feeling is absent, *i.e.*, we have sensations which are neither agreeable nor disagreeable; and we further find (such, at least, is the author's experience) feelings present where sensation is

absent, *i.e.*, we have feelings which are not accompanied by or attached to a definite sensation, or which arise where the nervous conditions of sensation are debarred from the exercise of their ordinary influence on consciousness. When cases like these exist, it is evidently wrong in principle to speak of feeling as an attribute of sensation. (*c*) Sensation, as we saw above (§ 4. 1), is not something beyond or beside the attributes of quality, intensity, extension and duration. It is adequately defined by the definition of all these characteristics. But the feeling which belongs to a sensation is not a necessary factor in this definition, one without which a complete characterisation is impossible. The relation between the two is precisely similar to that between the sensations of pressure and temperature. Pressure may be warm or cold or thermally indifferent. But its own quality is not more fully or accurately defined by the statement of this secondary fact; the statement is simply a description of a new phenomenon, whose occurrence or non-occurrence in consciousness depends upon special circumstances. Sensation, in the same way, is something beside or beyond the present or absent feeling, and feeling is something beside or beyond sensation.

5. (2) *Feeling as Function of Sensation.*—Feeling may be considered a function of sensation, (*a*) if the attributes of sensation directly condition its course, *i.e.*, if a parallelism obtains between the two processes similar to the functional relation which we found to obtain between sensation and stimulus, or (*b*) if certain connections of sensations exercise a determining influence upon it. The second of these views, stripped of its metaphysical wrappings, is represented in the history of psychology by Herbart. In its exclusive form, it is plainly negatived by the verdict of introspection. We constantly find ourselves attributing agreeableness or disagreeableness to sensations absolutely, without basing our judgment on their relation to other sensations. Toothache remains disagreeable, although the other sensations in consciousness are neither of the same nor of the opposite affective quality. An attempt has been made to meet this objection by drawing a sharp line of distinction between the affective tone of sensation and the feeling originating in the mutual relations of ideas. But the distinction, again, entirely disregards the testimony of introspection, which declares that the pleasantness or unpleasantness attaching to a simple sensation does not differ in any essential point or attribute from the feeling attaching to a relation between sensations. And the other view, which makes feeling a function of particular sensations, is equally one-sided, since feelings can undoubtedly attach to their interrelations as well as to themselves. There remains the question whether, perhaps,

a combination of both views is introspectively possible. In endeavouring to answer this, it will be sufficient for us to examine one of them only,—that which can be the more summarily treated. This is the hypothesis of the dependency of feeling upon the particular sensation, or (what is the same thing) upon the attributes of sensation.

6. It is evident that no one of the attributes of feeling is dependent (i) upon the *quality* of sensation. There are no sensation qualities which are everywhere and always pleasant or unpleasant, strongly toned or weakly toned, provocative of long continued or transient affective result. Nor can it be maintained (we shall discuss the question in detail in § 36) that every sensation quality possesses a specific affective tone, distinct from the pleasantness or unpleasantness peculiar to other sensations. This would mean that we had in consciousness at least twice as many affective qualities as sensational — a wealth of contents of which introspection reveals no trace. We often speak, again, of 'warm' and 'cold' colours, of 'grave' and 'cheerful' tones, etc., but the phrases need not be interpreted to imply that qualitative differences of feeling are correlated with certain sensation qualities. The view that feeling is dependent upon sensation is, therefore, usually narrowed down, (ii) and feeling becomes a function of the *intensity* of sensation. It is certainly true, as a general rule, that weak to moderately intensive sensations are pleasant, more intensive unpleasant. But it is not the greater or less intensity of the sensation as such which gives this law its real or general significance. Different sensations in different sense departments, and even within the same sense department, fall under it at very different absolute intensities. Thus a very slight intensity of organic sensation is distinctly unpleasant (a stomachic derangement, *e.g.*, which is represented in consciousness by hardly any definite sensations at all), while sensations of pressure, sight and hearing must reach a fairly high intensity before they can produce a similar effect upon feeling. And while deep tones are rarely unpleasant, even when they are intensive enough to excite the nerves of touch as well as those of hearing, weak tones from rods or tuning forks of very high pitch are exceedingly disagreeable. Pathological evidence can be adduced in support of these observations. Cases are known in which a gentle contact is painful, faint noises unbearable, and dim light very disturbing; and although they usually show a general increase of sensitivity, the increase is never sufficient (as is demonstrated by the value of the stimulus limen) to explain the alteration of the affective reaction. We are forced to conclude, then, that the intensity of sensation is not the determinant of the course of feeling, and that the law laid

down above holds only under certain circumstances, *i.e.*, when the changes in sensational intensity coincide with changes in other processes which constitute the actual conditions of feeling.

7. The same holds (iii) of the *temporal* and *spatial* character of sensation. The relation of duration and extension to feeling is precisely similar to that of intensity: long duration and wide extension have the effect of high intensity. We have found this rule to obtain for sensation (cf., *e.g.*, § 18. 7), and it has been confirmed by investigations into the physiology of the nervous system (cf. § 9. 10). So that what we have said of the relation between feeling and intensity of sensation applies of the analogous relation between feeling and duration and extension of sensation. But the spatial character of sensation includes form or shape, as well as extension; and this seems to have a special effect upon feeling, more particularly in the sphere of sight. Certain forms are pleasing, others displeasing. The feelings thus originated have been termed *elementary æsthetic feelings*, and the phrase used to cover every degree of pleasantness or unpleasantness correlated with the temporal arrangement and spatial form of sense impressions, apart from their qualitative or intensive contents.

But here again it can be shown that form as such is not provocative of feeling. Not only do different individuals give very different affective reactions (and we cannot refer the differences here, as we could in the case of sensation, to peculiar dispositions or functional differences of the perceptive organs), but the same individual is very differently affected by the same form at different times. In other words, we are again unable to discover a parallelism between feeling and sensation. And as the same arguments may be applied to the alternative hypothesis, that feeling attaches to the relation between sensations, we are driven to the conclusion that there is no simple functional relation between the two contents.

(3) There remains only the last of the three possible views of the relation of feeling to sensation, that which makes feeling an independent conscious process. All the objections which we have urged against the other two tell in its favour. We will, therefore, accept it as a correct interpretation of the facts, without intending for a moment to deny the normal connection of feeling with sensation in consciousness.

§ 35. The Investigation of the Feelings.

1. It follows from the foregoing Section that an investigation of the feelings will demand special methods; that we cannot make direct

application of the rules which we have found to hold for sensation Experiment in particular, which did such good service for sensation analysis, must now be employed in a different way, to suit the changed conditions. But we cannot either *classify* the feelings on the lines laid down for the classification of sensations (§ 4. 10). For (*a*) there is no essential difference between peripherally excited and centrally excited feelings (§ 34. 2) ; and (*b*) the quality of feeling is not dependent upon the character of the perceptive organ—so that we have no classes corresponding to the 'cutaneous', 'visual', etc., sensations (§ 34. 6). It will be easily seen that the classification of the feelings must, under these circumstances, present peculiar difficulties. For introspection is no more able to suggest an independent principle of arrangement here than it was in the case of sensation (cf. § 3. 1). (1) Feelings are very commonly divided into *higher* and *lower*. The pleasantness of a colour or a taste, *e.g.*, is a lower feeling; pleasure in a picture or in a piece of good news a higher. But the criterion which gives these values to particular contents is plainly derived from a definite theory of life, a more or less complicated and individual systematisation of the rules of action, thought and sensation. What is valueless, in the first instance, is not the feeling, but the sensation or idea which underlies it. This distinction of higher and lower feelings is, therefore, simply an offshoot of a more general distinction, which ranks sense impressions, the whole domain of sense perception, as 'low', in comparison with concepts, the activity of reason or understanding. Such an appraisement belongs to rationalistic metaphysics, not to scientific psychology. As a matter of fact, there is no qualitative difference discoverable [1] between the pleasantness of a colour and that of a successfully concluded argument, when careful abstraction is made from the very wide differences in all their attendant circumstances. It cannot serve, then, as the basis of a classification of the feelings.

2. (2) A very similar classification of feelings groups them as *sensible* and *intellectual*. The latter are further subdivided into logical, ethical, religious, and aesthetic. It is evident that the line of separation here practically coincides with the line of separation in the previous classification, into 'higher' and 'lower'. The sensible feelings are identical with the lower. But it is a distinct advance to have exchanged the irrelevant criterion of metaphysical value for the simple dependency of feeling upon its excitatory processes. The sensible feelings are aroused by sense impressions, more especially by their quality and intensity ; the intellectual are produced by ideas and interrelations of ideas. At the same time, this classification, like the other,

[1] In my own experience and, I imagine, in that of others also.

pays no regard to the qualitative differences within feeling itself. And where that is the case, it is the conditions of the feelings, and not the feelings as such, which are really classified.

(3) It has been proposed to employ the term 'feeling' not for simple conscious processes, but for those more or less complex contents which we should regard as connections of sensation (idea) and feeling. The suggestion finds support in popular German and in popular and scientific English phraseology; and its adoption naturally carries with it the possibility of a very extensive classification. Bain, and more recently, Lehmann, have given us classifications under this head. But it can hardly be asserted that any useful result has been attained by them. For if we assume that pleasantness and unpleasantness are the only 'emotional' elements, then they may obviously connect with all possible sensations and sensation complexes; and there is no need of a special classification of the connections, since sensations and sensation complexes have been already classified. If we believe, on the other hand, that these emotional elements, pleasantness and unpleasantness, are themselves capable of qualitative gradation, then it is before all things desirable, in the interests of scientific inquiry, that their various simple qualities be exhibited in the greatest possible purity. We say nothing at all of the transference of popular phrases into scientific terminology, and its doubtful value for the analysis and comprehension of the facts.

3. (4) Lastly, it might be thought that the scientific discrimination of *emotion, mood, impulse,* etc., furnishes a basis for a corresponding classification of feelings. And it is not uncommon to find the emotions of anger, joy, etc., regarded as 'feelings', upon precisely the same plane as satisfaction or dissatisfaction in a given complex of sensations. But again, when we raise the fundamental question whether the pleasantness and unpleasantness in all these cases are as such specifically different, or whether the experiential difference between, *e.g.,* an unpleasant feeling and an unpleasant emotion is not rather referable in its entirety to concomitant conscious processes, there seems to be no escape from an answer in the sense of the latter alternative. Emotions and moods obtain their peculiar 'colouring' principally from organic sensations. On the other hand, it is doubtful whether the characteristic quality of impulse, which appears again in voluntary action, in desire and in longing, can be reduced to organic sensations, or is an irreducible elementary content, an elementary volition or feeling of effort. (We shall discuss this point at length in § 40.)

We cannot, then, accept any classification of the feelings. We are left with the simple qualities of pleasantness and unpleasantness,

which refuse to admit of further subdivision. This is additional
evidence of the independent position which feeling occupies with
regard to sensation (§ 34. 7). All the more imperative, therefore, is
the necessity of discovering a reliable method for the investigation
of feeling, irrespectively of simultaneously present sensations. Two
affective methods are now beginning to be employed: the first and
older of which we may term the *serial* method, the second the method
of *expression*. The former consists in the systematic application of
stimulus series, the latter in an accurate registration of the centrifugal
manifestations of feeling.

4. (1) The serial method attempts to overcome the difficulty
which the relation of feeling to sensation (§ 34) puts in the way of
an experimental investigation of the affective consciousness by the
aid of external stimuli. For it is evident that a functional relation
to external stimulus is open to very similar if not to the same
objections as a functional relation to sensation. We may, it is true,
assume that the stimulus will exercise a special influence on feeling,
apart from its effect for sensation; and this is so far an advantage.
But feeling is, as a matter of fact, no more an exclusive function of
external stimulus than it is an exclusive function of sensation. At
the same time, this is not inconsistent with a certain degree of
dependency,—the determination of which is the object of the serial
method. It sets out from the fact that although the affective result
of stimulation differs absolutely within wide limits under different
circumstances, yet relatively the origination or modification of feeling
by particular stimuli may remain constant. If, *e.g.*, we are in the
mood to find all colour tones indifferent, we shall still be able, when
a number of coloured objects is placed before us, to discriminate
between their effects upon our affective state. Some will please us
more than others, or at least some will displease us less than others;
and so we may arrange them in a series from the relatively most
pleasing to the relatively most displeasing, independently of the
absolute affective value of each separate impression. The regard or
disregard accorded to the various terms of a series of this kind is
then an expression of the dependency of feeling upon the stimuli.
Experiments can, of course, be made with all attributes of stimulus,
with that which corresponds to sensation quality, as well as with
those underlying, the intensity, duration and extension of sensation.
The method has not as yet received any quantitative formulation;
and, in particular, no real measurement of affective change has been
obtained, such as we possess in the measurement of sensitivity and
sensible discrimination. It remains to be seen whether a just notice-

able affective change or apparently equal affective changes can be produced with any degree of constancy, even where the absolute affective disposition is subject to considerable fluctuation. [1]

5. A comparison of the results of the serial method with those of similar modes of procedure in certain sense departments at once suggests itself. (i) Thus we might compare the relative judgment of tone pitch with the relative regard or disregard expressed in the affective series. But we may be sure that a tone under normal conditions will be heard, if at all, at the definite pitch which is physically characteristic of it, and will therefore appear higher or lower only as related to other similarly fixed and definite tones; whereas we have no right to expect a definite affective result as such from a stimulus as such, but only a result more or less constant in the relative way indicated above. Our ordinary inability to give the quality of a tone a specific name must be ascribed to the lack of a well developed liability of reproduction as between tonal pitch and denomination, not to any relativity or mutability attaching to the sensations themselves. On the other hand, the bare judgment that a stimulus is pleasant or unpleasant is very simple and easy; but it follows from the very nature of feeling that it will vary greatly even for the same stimuli. (ii) Or again, we might (as we did above, § 11. 5) compare the feelings with the temperature sensations. They share with feeling this variability of reaction to external stimulus. But in their case, too, the difference between sensation and feeling is unmistakable. The occurrence of a sensation of heat or cold is, in general, determined by quite definite peripheral conditions, *i.e.,* the temperature of the skin. This we saw to be algebraically added, whatever its degree, to the thermal attribute of the stimulus; so that, when it is taken into account, a parallelism of stimulus and sensation, though difficult, is nevertheless possible (§ 11. 2). But feelings are not thus regulated by peripheral apparatus. At the same time, the analogy holds to the extent that 'warm' and 'cold' mean very different things as predicated of the external stimulus; and that this difference has its root, not in the relation between sensation and judgment, but in sensation itself. We can speak, too, of a given impression as 'warmer' or 'colder', without there being a sensation of heat or cold present in consciousness.

6. The general dependency of feeling upon stimulus, in the serial method, can evidently only be represented by a curve showing the subjective changes which answer to a determinate form of change in

[1] And the necessary distinction between constant and variable errors is yet to be drawn.

the stimuli. The values of this curve have no absolute significance, but must merely be conceived of as varying between the relatively highest and relatively lowest degrees of pleasure. If all the curves obtained for the same form of stimulus change have an entirely similar course, they may be accepted as giving a reliable expression of the dependency under investigation. We cannot predict a priori what will happen; but certain sets of experiments, taken by the serial method, on the æsthetic effect of figures seem to show that the course of the curve is not only constant for the same individual, but approximately similar for different individuals. An attempt has been made to bring these curves into relation with the absolute affective tone, by ascribing positive and negative values to the ordinates that express the degree of feeling, the pleasantness values being made positive, the unpleasantness values negative, and the o-ordinate the point of affective indifference. But it follows from the foregoing discussion that this procedure is not only dangerous, but, in view of the facts, incorrect. The judgments of different individuals and of the same individual at different times are, in their absolute affective value, exceedingly variable. It is, therefore, altogether irrelevant for the application of the serial method (until we obtain an accurate measure of affective change: cf. 4 above) how high above the abscissæ we place beginning and end, maxima and minima of the curve: they must only be brought as far as possible into accord with the verdict of introspection. From this point of view, we may regard affective change itself as a purely quantitative process, the maximum of which is given by the relatively most pleasant, the minimum by the relatively most unpleasant feeling. The various degrees of feeling intermediate between these limiting values will then form an unbroken chain, and we shall be able to pass continuously from one to the other, as we can in the colour triangle from a saturated colour to a pure white (§ 17. 5, 6). The discovery and exact formulation of these interrelations of the various feelings are most valuable. But it is equally desirable to be able accurately to determine the qualitative significance of pleasurable and unpleasurable states. This seems to be rendered possible by the method of expression; which thus supplements the serial method, as the test of sensitivity supplements that of sensible discrimination.

7. (2) The serial method was first employed by Fechner, in his experimental investigation of æsthetics; the method of expression in its systematic form is due to Mosso. The various 'expressive movements', voluntary and involuntary, possess so obvious an importance as means for the expression of emotion, mood, impulse,—everything, in short, which can be called an affective process, that it is natural

to make them the starting point of an experimental inquiry into the internal states of which they are the bodily manifestations. Good results have been obtained from observations of the change of pulse and respiration, of the variation in the volume of a limb, and of the extent of voluntary movements, under the domination of different feelings. No use can be made, on the other hand, of the various forms of gesture and of the manifold play of feature which serve to express affective disposition, for three reasons. (*a*) It is difficult to turn them to experimental account. They can be (and often have been) photographed, and so made permanent: but that is all. (*b*) Their dependency upon the will gives them a certain independence of feeling. And (*c*) they are indicative not only of pleasantness and unpleasantness, but of concomitant ideational contents as well (cf. § 54). The facts which have hitherto been collected by the application of the method of expression render it probable that the changes in power and rapidity of pulse and respiration (indicated by the registration apparatus), the variation in volume dependent upon the supply of blood to the tissues, and the extent of voluntary movements (read off directly from a special instrument) stand in a quite uniform relation to states of pleasantness and unpleasantness (§ 37. 1). It appears, if we take the state of indifference as normal and regard pleasantness and unpleasantness as diverging from it in opposite directions, that all deviations from the corresponding physiological norm which we see reflected in these different processes, really give direct and simple expression to the affective state of the moment. (i) It is, therefore, necessary for an accurate employment of this method (and this is an undeniable difficulty), that the norm be determinable not only in a general way, but for every individual case and for every experimental series, as representing the indifference of affective disposition of the particular subject at the particular time.

8. This difficulty has hitherto received too little consideration. The method has been employed for the determination of the more obvious expressive differences, whose existence could be demonstrated irrespectively of a strict standard of reference. But it can evidently only give us absolute values for pleasantness and unpleasantness under the condition that the 'normal' reaction denotes an affective indifference of consciousness. We must trust to future investigators to establish its claim to rank with the other psychophysical methods more securely, by as accurate as possible a comparison of objective and subjective, and of the various objective results with one another. (ii) But there is a second difficulty in the way of its application. The changes which have been registered by observers so far are dependent not

only upon the affective state, but partly also upon other circum-stances. We know, *e.g.*, that the rapidity of the pulse is liable to a certain increase with increase in the rate of succession of auditory impressions, while consciousness may be affectively neutral, or the precedent pleasantness or unpleasantness remain stationary. It has been found, again, that quick movement shortens the period of pulse and respiration; and a whole series of other physiological conditions of their variation might be given. If the method of expression is to furnish a trustworthy account of the feelings, we must be able to distinguish certainly between the physical changes due to affective fluctuation, and those produced by other causes, of whatever kind. No general rules can be laid down at present, except that all external sources of error, accidental sounds, etc., must be as far as possible eliminated. (iii) Again, the method has hitherto been developed only along qualitative lines; it tells us nothing of the degree of pleasant-ness or unpleasantness. (iv) And lastly, it is still an open question, how the feelings can be best evoked for examination. Two modes of procedure are possible. We can obtain the desired effect by ex-ternal stimulation, or we can suggest the reproduction of certain sensa-tions or ideas, and so excite the pleasantness or unpleasantness which attaches to them. In neither case (certainly not in the first) have we any means of determining a priori how much of the changes registered is the result of feeling, and how much the result of other processes set up by the stimulus or central excitation. It is clear, then, that much preliminary work is necessary, before the method of expression can be regarded as a safe and adaptable instrument for the experimental investigation of the affective consciousness. The serial method seems to have the advantage as regards perspicuity and reliability on nearly every count. But it, too, requires to be carefully checked on one point. It is hardly possible for the devel-oped consciousness, in presence of a series of forms, qualities, etc., to abstract entirely from the relations in which one or other of them must inevitably stand to its general stock of ideas (cf. § 75. 4). It may, therefore, very well happen that an affective reaction is called forth not merely by the particular impression whose value in the series we wish to determine, but partly also by the recollection into which it is absorbed. A green colour, *e.g.*, may be pleasing not in itself, but because of the ideas of pleasant meadows and shady trees which it excites. If the curve which represents the affective value of a colour series is made to include judgments of this kind, it will plainly bring together a medley of very heterogeneous states. Fechner has drawn a useful distinction between *intrinsic* and *associative* affective value, which serves to keep the two classes of judgment separate. The only direct means of preventing the interference of associative factors is to keep a careful introspective watch upon the process of judgment. Secondarily, however, the comparison of different experimental series, taken from the same or from different subjects, may perhaps suffice for the detection of extraneous influences.

Fechner distinguished three methods: the method of *selection*, the method of *producti·n*, and the method of *usage*. The first is identical with that which we have termed the serial method. In the second, the most pleasing impression (visual figure, *e.g.*) is 'produced' by the subject himself (in the form of a drawing). The third consists in the comparison and measurement of the pleasing or displeasing relations actually presented by nature or art. It is plain that only the first of these, our serial method, has any general claim to rank as a real experimental method. But no exact formulation has as yet been obtained even for it. We do not know, in particular, whether we may combine the judgments of different individuals to an average result, whether they can be employed simply for the determination of the relatively most pleasant impression, or can be used for the construction of a continuous curve of affective values, whether in this latter case the particular degrees of pleasingness should be specially defined, etc., etc. The method of production is a useful supplement to the serial method, if the conditions for the application of the allied method of average error (§ 8. 9, 11) are observed.—While the methodology of sensation has already attained a certain measure of finality, that of feeling is still lamentably deficient. But there is good hope that the feelings, variable as they are, can now be subjected in their turn to an accurate and detailed examination, with similarly successful result.

§ 36. The Attributes of Feeling.

1. We use the phrase 'attributes of feeling' in precisely the same sense in which we spoke of attributes of sensation (§ 4. 1). That is, we understand by them certain inseparable characteristics, which attach to every individual feeling, and whose disappearance implies that of the feeling itself. All feelings have the attributes of *quality, intensity* and *duration*. The terms are identical with those employed to designate the attributes of sensation, except that extension, which we ascribed to visual and tactual sensations, cannot be predicated of any class of feelings. 'Quality' is, again, the name of the most important and fundamental attribute; the qualitative definition of feeling consists in its cognition as pleasantness or unpleasantness. 'Intensity' denotes the degree of vividness at which a pleasantness or unpleasantness is given in consciousness, and 'duration' is the elementary temporal character of a feeling. In view of the facts of the previous Section, we cannot hope to determine these attributes as positively and comprehensively

as we could those of sensation, or at least of sensations of peripheral origin.

(1) This expectation is confirmed at once when we enter upon the consideration of the *quality* of feeling. Psychologists agree that pleasantness and unpleasantness are qualitative differences, but they are by no means at one upon the question whether the terms are simply classificatory concepts, covering a variety of qualitative differences, or individual concepts, expressive of an ultimate qualitative divergence. An unlimited number of qualities of pleasantness and unpleasantness is as axiomatic to one as a simple duality of affective tone is to another. It is hardly possible at the present time to reach a final solution of this basal problem. From the point of view of method, however, preference must be given to the second view: it is the more simple, and it avoids the unscientific use of 'feeling' as denoting a content which the observer cannot or will not subject to a careful analysis. In ordinary phraseology everything may be a 'feeling' or depend upon a 'feeling'; we have a 'feeling' that something is right or true, we 'feel' for ourselves and others, etc. If we introduce into psychology this custom of terming everything a 'feeling' which is not obviously something else, we run the risk of stopping short in our analysis whenever we come upon a process which in any way suggests the word. This source of error is eliminated where pleasantness and unpleasantness are regarded as the only qualities of feeling.

2. From this point of view it seems fair to say that the *onus probandi* in the question at issue lies with the psychologists who accept a multeity of pleasant and unpleasant tones. Those who simply assert that the difference between pleasantness and unpleasantness is a difference of quality, need have no fear of contradiction; this fact is fundamental for any hypothesis as to the nature of the feelings. But those who pass beyond it to the assertion of an unlimited number of qualitative varieties, may reasonably be called upon at every step to bring evidence for their position from the facts. It will, therefore, only be necessary here to examine into the validity of the arguments by which the second view is supported. What follows is simply supplementary to what was said above (§ 35. 1, 2, 3) of the classification of the feelings.

(*a*) The most obvious theory attributes a peculiar affective quality to every quality of sensation (cf. § 34. 6). The feeling of a 'blue' would then be different from the feeling of a 'red', and the affective reaction to colours in general different from that to sounds. But this would mean that every sensation had two different affective tones, one bearing a general character of pleasantness, the other a general character of unpleasantness. For every sensation quality may be either pleasant or unpleasant, according to the intensity of stimulus and the total state of consciousness. Now it is hardly credible that there are twice as many qualities of feeling as there are of sensation. If there were, the difference between extreme terms within the affective system would surely be so distinct that no doubt could exist in regard to it. The most unmusical ear, *i.e.*, an ear of the lowest discriminative capacity, finds a difference between a note in the bass and a high tone in the treble. If there really are so many different feelings, and if they are so much alike in different individuals as they appear to be, it is impossible that their difference should not manifest itself, of its own accord, in introspection. It may be objected that the sensation differences, which undoubtedly exist, obscure the finer divergences of feeling. But colours, as we saw (§ 17. 3), are always connections of simple qualities, brightness and colour tone ; and yet we are none the less able to estimate the separate variation of either constituent. Lastly, it is scarcely conceivable that, with so many separate qualities of pleasantness and unpleasantness, what must be regarded as the abstract difference between pleasantness and unpleasantness in general should be so much more distinct than any instance of difference given in the concrete.

3. (*b*) If we restrict the discriminable pleasantnesses and unpleasantnesses to certain groups of sensations, we obtain no more support from the facts, while we have absolutely no principle upon which to rely for guidance. It cannot be said, *e.g.*, that high tones possess a different affective character from deep tones : (i) because the musical representation of a particular mood is not effected by the employment of tones of any particular pitch, and (ii) because all the differences that really exist are easily explicable from certain temporal and intensive peculiarities of the sensations. We know that high tones can be given in more rapid succession, without fusion, than low tones; hence they are in general better adapted for quick rhythms. The impression of gravity and dignity made by deep tones is, therefore, a consequence of the relative slowness with which they must succeed one another, in order to be distinguishable. This dignity or gravity, however, does not point to any specific feeling, but rather to a certain carriage of the body (with its concomitant organic sensations) and a preponderant disposition towards unpleasant feelings. In the same way, the 'cheerful' character ordinarily ascribed to high tones indicates their frequent employment in quick passages, a corresponding attitude and mobility of the body, and a predominant disposition to pleasant feelings. But, as we said just now, either region of the tonal scale may be drawn upon for the representation of either mood. Brahms, the greatest of

modern composers, often makes use of very high intervals, combinations of the highest and lowest tones, for the expression of a deep seriousness. The distinction of 'grave' and 'cheerful' tones, then, cannot be accepted as implying a distinction of specifically different affective qualities. And the same is true of the 'warm' colours of the long-wave end of the spectrum, and the 'cold' colours of the short-wave end. There is a tendency to connect red and yellow with passionate excitement, and blue with a quiet circumspection. But apart from the fact that this interpretation of the 'warm' colours is by no means constant, we cannot admit that a 'mood', here or elsewhere, denotes a specific affective quality. It is not a simple conscious process at all, but essentially a complex of organic sensations, *plus* a disposition towards certain feelings occasioned by (or correlated with) them. The excitement into which we are thrown by warm colours is principally due to the more mobile attitude of the body; and this is connected with a disposition towards pleasurable feelings. In presence of cold colours, on the other hand, we experience a certain evenness of mood, resulting from the steadiness of bodily carriage, and indicative of an indifference of affective disposition.

4. (*c*) The attempt to prove the diversity of pleasantnesses and unpleasantnesses by purely formal argument is still less successful. Thus it has been asserted that the abstract concept, pleasantness or unpleasantness, must of necessity be discriminated from the concrete experiences which fall under it. But such a statement merely begs the question, whether the two concepts, as qualitatively regarded, are classificatory or individual. (*d*) Again, it has been urged that both intensity and quality of stimulus exercise an influence upon the feelings, and that every feeling is therefore variable in two directions. Now this inference can only be made the ground of acceptance of the 'diversity' theory, if the variability attributed to feeling transcend the indisputable qualitative duality, accepted by all theories alike (cf. 2, above). But a twofold dependency upon stimulus does not necessarily carry this implication with it. We were obliged to correlate the qualities of the brightness series, in visual sensation, and the qualities of heat and cold, in temperature sensation, with a stimulus series capable of only intensive or quantitative gradation. So here, the relations obtaining between character of stimulus and attributes of feeling may be of the most various kinds. As a matter of fact, we find that pleasantness and unpleasantness are correlated not only with different qualities, but with different intensities: a simple increase of stimulus intensity will change pleasantness into unpleasantness. An aprioristic determination of the number of affective qualities on

this basis, is, therefore, altogether impossible. (*e*) Lastly, the fact that we can distinguish pains which arise in the internal organs of the body as stabbing, gnawing, burning, etc., has been looked upon as evidence of qualitative differences within the state of unpleasantness. The evidence is not convincing, however, because the organic sensations which are also excited within the body (cf. §§ 22, 23) furnish sufficient explanation of the distinction. At the same time, it is possible that pain must be recognised as a special category of sensation, distinct from unpleasantness which is contained in and expressed by it, and originated as a rule by very intensive stimulation of any sensory nerve (cf. § 10. 4). But even in this case, there would be no qualitative differences within unpleasantness, but only within the specific pain sensation which combines with it in the concrete pain.

5. For the present, then, we have no choice but to adopt the view that the feelings possess no more than two different qualities, and that other differences must be referred to changes in duration, intensity, or concomitant sensations. The two qualities stand in a peculiar relation to each other: they are separated by a state of indifference, a neutral point. A stimulus on either side of this point will excite pleasantness or unpleasantness according to its character The existence of the state of indifference can hardly be doubted in face of a long series of observations which support it. For instance, any impression, pleasing or displeasing, is apt to become indifferent if long continued. Very weak stimuli are naturally indifferent, unless we make them disagreeable by giving ourselves especial trouble to apprehend them. If an originally pleasant stimulus intensity is slowly increased, there will be a gradual decrease of pleasantness, and, following that, a gradual increase of unpleasantness. Introspection is not so clear, however, in this case, as to the line of demarcation between pleasantness and unpleasantness, the stage of indifference. It has even been argued, from an experiment of the kind (the gradual heating of a vessel of water in which the hand is plunged) that the neutral point is altogether imaginary. The argument does not hold. For (i) the whole process is, in all probability, too short for the determination of a period of such narrow limits. (ii) Again, the different portions of the hand have not an equal sensitivity to temperature; so that one part may still be mediating a pleasant warmth, while others have become unpleasantly hot. And (iii) we may observe the transition from cold to heat in a similar experiment, without noticing the interval of indifferent temperature [1]. On the whole then,

[1] I myself, at least, have been unable to verify the occurrence of a neutral temperature in such an experiment.

we may regard the indifference of feeling as an established fact. This implies, of course, that there are sensations which are neither pleasantly nor unpleasantly toned,—a statement which is sufficiently justified by a reference to the indifferent ideas and actions of every-day life. It is hardly necessary to emphasise, in conclusion, the theoretical importance of affective indifference. We saw that the method of expression is dependent upon its determination (§ 35. 7, 8), *i.e.*, that the experimental investigation of the feelings is largely based upon the assumption of its reality and graphic representability. But besides this, a certain direction is given to our theoretic ideas of the origin of the feelings by the fact that pleasantness and un-pleasantness cannot appear or subsist side by side, like two colours or tones or tastes, but are antagonistic to each other, arising from a change of the 'normal' process in opposite directions (cf. § 39. 7).

6. (2) The *intensity*, like the quality, of feeling can only be exactly defined by its relation to indifference. The greater the distance from this in either direction, the greater is the pleasantness or unpleasant-ness. Neither can be increased indefinitely; so that we can speak of a maximal pleasantness and unpleasantness, as the analogues of the terminal stimulus in the sphere of sensation (§ 24. 2). We may also introduce the concept of the limen, defining the just noticeable devi-ation from indifference as a liminal pleasantness or unpleasantness. Any change in the position of the neutral point carries with it a change in the relation of affective intensity to stimulus, but, so far as we can judge from the observations extant, produces no alteration in the mutual relations of the particular pleasantness or unpleasantness intensities. We may, therefore, conceive of the course of feeling as dependent in its totality upon external and internal conditions. This means a considerable simplification of affective investigation: for a single determination will be sufficient to indicate the course of feeling in general. If we find, *e.g.*, that a stimulus excites pleasure to a definite noticeable degree, it is at once possible (provided that this degree is capable of numerical expression) to calculate the position of the neutral point and of the various degrees of unpleasantness. The most useful determination for an exact definition of the pleasant or unpleasant character of a given conscious process is plainly that of the underlying affective indifference. At the same time, the determination of the relation of affective intensities to one another does not seem to require any reference to the point of indifference, any more than to pleasant-ness or unpleasantness absolutely regarded. At present, we can only speak in the abstract of an affective limen or of maximal pleasantness or unpleasantness, since no experiments have been made with a view

to their quantitative expression, and the pain limen (which has been frequently determined) cannot be considered either as the limen or maximum of unpleasantness.

§ 37. Results of the Method of Expression. Dependency of Feeling upon the Attributes of Stimulus.

1. (1) The results of the method of expression furnish practically all the material available for an experimental treatment of affective quality. There are four bodily processes, which appear to stand in a functional relation to pleasantness and unpleasantness: voluntary movements, which can be read off from the dynamometer; changes of pulse, which are registered by the sphygmograph; the rise and fall of the chest in inspiration and expiration, registered in a very similar way by the pneumatograph; and variations in the volume of a limb, recorded by the plethysmograph. The employment of the plethysmograph has the advantage that the instrument registers the periodic oscillations of pulse and respiration, at the same time that it records the alteration of volume due to blood supply; though it does not render the use of sphygmograph and pneumatograph superfluous. Now the amount of work done by a muscle is entirely dependent, other things equal, upon the intensity of the motor central innervation; the height of the curves of pulse and respiration upon the innervation of the cardiac and respiratory muscles; and the blood supply of a particular organ upon the dilatation of the peripheral blood vessels and so upon the innervation of the vascular muscles. This shows, that all the phenomena which have been taken as expressive of feeling are conditioned by some group of central influences, governing central motor innervation. These influences, then, will be the real physiological correlates of the feelings. The phenomena evidently owe their especial value for the expression of feeling to the fact that they are capable of variation from a norm (itself variable) in two different directions. On the one hand, innervation may be intensified, and the curve of respiration or pulse heightened or quickened, or muscular work increased; on the other, innervation may be inhibited or diminished, and pulse, respiration and muscular force weakened. We may accordingly conjecture that the feelings will find more or less simple and direct expression in these opposite tendencies.

2. As a matter of fact, the experimental results go far to confirm this conjecture. Unfortunately, however, they (*a*) wear an appearance of complexity, due to the very different character of certain of the primary and secondary phenomena, and (*b*) are not altogether

unequivocal, some of the effects observed under the four rubrics being referable to different causes. For instance, the innervation of the cardiac and respiratory muscles may be mediated by excitatory or inhibitory nerves, the blood vessels may be arterial or venous, their nerves vasodilator or vasoconstrictor, while the excitation of the different centres for the motor nerves concerned may be directly or reflexly set up. To take a concrete case: increase in the blood supply of the arm, recorded by the plethysmograph, may proceed from a dilatation of the veins and arteries; it may be produced directly by innervation of the vasomotor centre (perhaps from higher centres) or reflexly, *e.g.*, by alteration of the cardiac activity; it may result from an inhibition or diminution of excitation of the vasoconstrictors or a special excitation of the vasodilators. The facts as observed do not warrant a positive decision in favour of any one of these possibilities; and consequently no statement of the central conditions of the phenomenon can be anything more than hypothetical. So that although we spoke just now without qualification of an intensification and inhibition of motor innervation, it cannot be assumed at the outset that these opposites are definitely correlated with the qualitative opposites of feeling. The method of expression must at any rate be much more fully investigated, before we can say anything positively of the conditions of the processes directly recorded and observed. Moreover, the differences between the primary and secondary phenomena represented on a curve of unpleasantness render the interpretation of the facts additionally difficult.

3. The experimental results are as follows. (i) Pleasurable states are regularly accompanied by increase of the force of voluntary muscular action, and unpleasurable states as regularly by its diminution. If we may assume that the conditions here are of a purely central kind, the result is relatively unequivocal; the first case apparently presupposing an increased, and the second a diminished excitability of the motor centres. (ii) Pleasurable feelings are regularly evidenced by increased power, though not by any constant acceleration of pulse. The first effect of unpleasant feelings is generally a weakening of the pulse, without any necessary reduction of its rapidity; and this is followed, not by a simple return to the normal, but by increase beyond it. The difference between the primary and secondary phenomena of unpleasantness seems to be proportional to the strength of the excitatory impressions. Whether this depends upon the unpleasantness or upon the intensity of stimulus can hardly be decided. (iii) The respiratory curves show a similar divergence. Pleasurable feelings usually mean an increased depth of respiration, shown by

the greater amplitude of the curve. Unpleasant feelings, again, give somewhat more complicated and ambiguous phenomena. If the stimuli are weak, they first of all effect a diminution of the depth of respiration, which is afterwards replaced by an abnormal increase. If the stimuli are more intensive (*e.g.*, very disagreeable tastes or smells), this stage of increased depth of respiration appears suddenly as the almost immediate result of stimulation, its permanence and amplitude being proportional to the strength of the stimulus: then follows a relaxation indicated by a lowering of the respiratory curve. Here again, we do not know how much is the consequence of the intensive stimulus as such, and how much is to be ascribed to the unpleasantness. So that it is no more than conjecture to make the relative decrease of depth of respiration the real functional expression of the feeling of unpleasantness. In all probability, pleasure has the same two stages of expression (only in the contrary direction), and it is merely due to the small intensity of the pleasurable feelings experimentally aroused that they have not been remarked. (iv) Pleasurable states are ordinarily attended by an increase of volume, *i.e.*, a dilatation of the peripheral blood vessels, and unpleasant states by a diminution of volume, *i.e.*, a constriction of the peripheral vessels.

4. We cannot here enter upon a detailed discussion of these phenomena, and the various possibilities of their interpretation; but we may endeavour to formulate a general hypothesis from which the experimental results can be deduced with some degree of simplicity and probability. It would seem that the universal concomitant of a pleasurable state is an increased excitability of the sensory and motor areas of the cerebral cortex. This appears to be a necessary inference from the fact that weak or moderately intensive stimuli, which increase the excitability of the nervous centres, ordinarily give rise to pleasurably toned sensations (§ 34. 6). It would seem, on the other hand, that the universal concomitant of an unpleasurable state is a diminution of central excitability in the motor and sensory spheres. This view is supported by the familiar fact that more intensive stimuli, which are ordinarily unpleasant, bring about a reduction of nervous excitability. Introspection affords a confirmation of the general hypothesis. In a pleasurable state, we usually find an acceleration of the train of ideas, an increased tendency to movement, a greater facility in the apprehension and estimation of perceptive material; in an unpleasurable state, a retardation and restriction of the course of ideation, a diminished disposition to voluntary and involuntary movement, and a difficulty of discriminative perception. And lastly, observations upon mania (in which there is excess of pleasure) and melan-

cholia (in which there is constant unpleasantness) point to the fact that the ultimate physiological equivalent of a pleasurable state is the increase of excitability following from a dilatation of the blood vessels which supply the brain, while the ultimate physiological equivalent of an unpleasurable state is the lasting diminution of excitability connected with constriction of the central vessels. We must, therefore, suppose that the increase of cardiac and respiratory activity and of voluntary movement, observed in the experiments, is a simple consequence of the heightened excitability of the pleasurable state, while the corresponding decrease of these motor phenomena is the direct consequence of the lowered excitability in the unpleasurable state. The increase or reduction of volume, on the other hand, may be regarded as a reflex result of the increase or reduction in cardiac activity; and the secondary phenomena in unpleasantness as the reflex motor effects of intensive stimuli. It must be remembered, however, in the latter connection, that the first effect of a diminution of blood in the capillaries of the brain is probably an increase of excitability, which passes later into a more or less marked decrease.

5. (2) The serial method has been employed hitherto only in connection with the temporal and spatial aspects of stimulus. No really systematic experiments have been made on the relation of its quality and intensity to feeling. We must therefore attempt to determine this from the more occasional observations of everyday experience. (*a*) The *quality* of stimulus seems to be of some importance for feeling in all sense departments; certain qualities are distinctly preferred to others of the same sense, quite apart from individual variation. Deep tones are ordinarily more pleasant than high tones, *e.g.*, and the very highest are as a rule positively disagreeable. Many persons find the colours of greater refrangibility than green more pleasant than those of less refrangibility (red and yellow). Yellow in particular is almost universally regarded as the least agreeable colour. Sweet is usually considered the relatively most pleasant taste, and bitter the relatively most unpleasant. Scents are so closely connected with feeling that they are commonly divided into agreeable and disagreeable. As we have no scientific principle of classification of the olfactory qualities (§ 13. 3), it is impossible to state with any further degree of accuracy which are pleasant and which unpleasant. In the sphere of cutaneous sensation, warmth is generally more pleasant than cold; pain is decidedly unpleasant; and smoothness and bluntness are preferred to roughness and sharpness. The organic sensations, again, are so intimately and constantly connected with feeling, that the resultant complexes (moods and emotions) have only recently been analysed into their components. We

have no means at present of drawing up a scale of qualities, and cannot therefore reduce the complicated interrelations of the two to any simple schema. It appears, however, that all the qualities of organic sensation, but those of the common sensations in particular, can combine with relatively vivid feelings, and that the more intensive the sensation, the more distinct is its affective colouring. The articular sensations are perhaps less markedly affective than the tendinous and muscular, and these again, perhaps, than hunger, thirst, etc.

6. We cannot say at present why it is that a particular quality calls forth a particular affective reaction, since we have no knowledge of the physiological effects of the different stimuli. But the fact that no stimulus is absolutely and always a stimulus of pleasantness (§ 34. 3; § 35. 4) seems to show that the differences in the affective influence of particular stimulus qualities must be referred in the last resort to differences of quantity or intensity. In other words, the dependency of the feelings upon the quality of stimulus must probably be narrowed down to a dependency of the point of indifference or of the affective limen. A high tone will produce the same effect upon feeling as a low tone, on this view, if it is given at a certain difference of intensity from the low tone. Or a very large dose of sweet will produce the same unpleasant effect as a very small dose of bitter. It should, therefore, be possible, by suitable gradation of stimulus intensity, to obtain affective equations expressive of the influence of quality. And it might then be conjectured that the various qualities at the same intensity set up quite different physiological processes. Unfortunately, the hypothesis cannot be applied in detail, as there are no observations extant upon the point, either psychological or physiological. We will therefore assume, for simplicity's sake, that the different stimulus qualities have different effects, positive or negative, upon the excitability of the cerebral cortex ; and that the intensity necessary for its increase or decrease, is very different for different stimuli. There is no need to justify this particular formulation (cf. 4, above).—Only one stimulus, again, can be regarded as absolutely and always a stimulus of unpleasantness—that of pain. But the stimulation is, of course, very intensive ; consisting either in a direct alteration (mechanical, electrical, thermal, or chemical) of the sensory nerve fibres, or a very strong excitation of the sense organ itself. Nevertheless, it may run its course also without unpleasantness, if the excitability of the central nervous substance is artificially diminished (*e.g.*, by chloroform) or has been reduced by disease (*e.g.*, *tabes dorsalis*). We then have analgesia, a state of painlessness, in which an ordinarily painful impression, say, a needle prick, is sensed simply as pressure or contact.

7. (*b*) The great importance of stimulus *intensity* for pleasantness and unpleasantness is vouched for by the result of the foregoing discussion of the relation between feeling and stimulus quality. It is usually summed up in the following rule : weak to moderately strong stimuli excite pleasantness, stronger stimuli unpleasantness (§ 34. 6 ; cf. 4, above). But this law cannot lay claim to universal validity, since it says nothing of the influence of quality ; and is very variously applicable in different circumstances, being crossed by the more general conditions of the affective consciousness (§ 39). It is radically wrong in correlating the appearance of the two feeling qualities with particular stimulus magnitudes, however relative their definition. We can only repeat here what we have said before, that no stimulus intensity is in itself provocative of pleasantness or unpleasantness ; and that consequently difference in intensity can be accredited only with a relative importance as determining the degree of feeling under otherwise equal conditions. If a weak stimulus excite pleasantness, at a greater intensity it may either increase pleasantness, or decrease it and ultimately change it to unpleasantness, according to the position of the neutral point. It cannot be said that a stimulus, to produce increase or decrease of pleasantness, must be of this or that particular strength or weakness in the particular case.—The ordinary course of the affective reaction, as depicted in the psychologies, is as follows : a very weak, but sensible stimulus has no noticeable effect upon

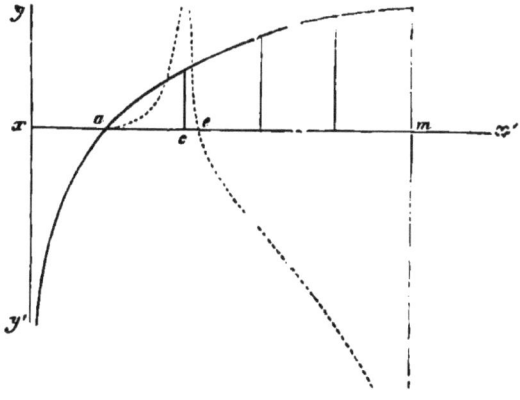

Fig. 8.

feeling ; as its intensity increases, the limen of pleasantness is reached and passed, and maximal pleasure attained ; from this point the intensity of feeling decreases up to the stage of indifference ; and this in turn gives way to a liminal unpleasantness, increasing by degrees to maximal unpleasantness. Wundt has represented this course by a curve, which is reproduced in Fig. 8. The various points of the line *xx'* denote stimulus intensities, from the zero-value, *x*, to an intensity beyond that of the terminal stimulus, *x'*. The ordinates *yy'* give the intensity of pleasurable (calculated in the positive direction, above *xx'*) and unpleasurable (negative, below *xx'*) feeling. The continuous curve shows the increase of sensation intensity; a is the stimulus limen, e the neutral point, c the cardinal sensation value (the value at which sensation increases in direct proportion to stimulus intensity). Wundt conjectures that maximal pleasure coincides with this cardinal value of sensation. The dotted curve, lastly, indicates the course of feeling.

8. The validity of this schema and the interrelations of the various affective stages have never been subjected to a thorough experimental test. We may hope that the serial method in particular will assist us to a more accurate formulation of the dependency of feeling upon intensity of stimulus. An absolute estimation of the affective value of a stimulus intensity leaves too much to the temporary disposition and purpose of the individual, and so cannot be relied upon as an index of its pleasantness or unpleasantness. That intensity of stimulus is of great importance for feeling is put beyond all doubt by facts of everyday occurrence in ordinary life. And certain effects of (c.) the temporal relations of stimulation are reducible to it. We have more than once remarked that the duration of a stimulus may produce the same result in consciousness as its intensity (§ 17. 2, etc.). We may now bracket with duration the frequent repetition of stimulation, intermittent excitation. Both duration and frequency exert an influence upon sensation, but to nothing like the same degree as upon feeling. A weak stimulus, which at first is hardly pleasurably toned at all, may if it persists call forth every form of the affective reaction, up to maximal unpleasantness. And the influence of intermittent stimulation is even more marked. It accounts, *e.g.*, for the unpleasantness of tickling (§ 23. 3), of flickering lights, and of beating tones (§ 14. 3). The stimulus may at first be pleasant (as is often the case, *e.g.*, with tickling); but this primary effect of weak stimulation very quickly changes to the opposite quality. It is noteworthy that all these modifications of stimulus—intensity, frequency and duration—are familiar to nervous physiologists as conditions of central excitability. As a general rule, stimuli which are weak to moderately strong, of short duration, and of infrequent recurrence, increase excitability, while those which are very strong, which persist for a long time, or which recur at brief intervals, decrease it (cf. 4, above). Here is further evidence, then, of the importance of central excitability for the affective consciousness.

§ 38. The Elementary Æsthetic Feelings.

1. The temporal relations of stimulation produce a quite different effect upon feeling, when the temporal attribute as such is the object

of perception and judgment, *i.e.,*, when pleasantness and unpleasantness are their direct, and not simply their indirect results. Their affective influence is then altogether independent of that of the other stimulus attributes. The same is true of the spatial relations of stimulation, which also serve within certain limits (§ 17. 2) merely to increase or replace intensity. The sphere of this special influence is that of the elementary aesthetic feelings; the sphere in which the serial method has found its most extensive application (§ 37. 5). Ever since there have been works of art, paintings and statues, capable of exciting pleasure by the arrangement and proportion of their constituent parts, and ever since the preference of one time order over another has shown itself in the rhythmical succession of movements, words and tones, the aesthetic judgment has been mainly founded upon the mind's appreciation of the temporal and spatial relations of its impressions. Both lie beyond the limits which we have set hitherto to our treatment of affective variation—the limits of a purely sensible dependency of feeling upon stimulus. A perfect square is more pleasing than a slightly imperfect square, although the area of the two figures, the quantity of light which they reflect, the duration of their action upon the retina—in a word, all the sensible attributes in virtue of which they could produce a difference in sensible excitation—are precisely the same. And a rhythm in ¾ time with accentuation of the first quarter note is generally more pleasing than an exactly similar rhythm with accentuation of the second or third, altogether irrespectively of the sensible effect of the total interval or the separate intervals, of the intensity of each note, etc. The variation of feeling in these cases cannot, then, be referred to the power of stimulus directly to increase or decrease the degree of central excitability. Important as that may be secondarily, in particular instances, the ultimate basis of the aesthetic judgment must be sought elsewhere.

2. A further reason for this conclusion is given by the fact that aesthetics, the aesthetic attitude and judgment, is a historical development, not necessarily implicit in the sensible organisation. The pleasurable or unpleasurable effect of stimulus qualities and intensities can be traced in the animal mind as certainly as in our own, by the aid of unequivocal expressive movements; but aesthetic effect presupposes a certain degree of human civilisation. Again, the conditions of the aesthetic judgment differ widely from time to time, from nation to nation, from individual to individual; but this has no analogue, even approximately, in the sphere of sensible feeling. And lastly, the internal dispositions or conditions are of absolutely decisive import-

ance for the appearance of æsthetic pleasure or displeasure, while
they are far less significant for the feelings which depend upon
stimulus. Everything points, then, to the origination of the æsthetic
feelings in central relations. Some light is thrown upon the nature
of these relations by the slow development of the æsthetic feeling:
it is not often that it arises at once, like the sensible, as the simple
and direct consequence of the impression. If we look a little closely
into the contents of this interval of development, we find comparison,
reflection, vacillatory judgment—in a word, a manysided activity of
reproduction. We may accordingly conjecture that the æsthetic feeling
originates in a *relation of the perceived impression to the reproduction*
which it excites. Our schematic representation of the course of feeling
under the influence of stimulus intensity will then be applicable in
the present connection. Too little effectiveness for reproduction will
produce no affective result; a greater, pleasure; too great, unpleasantness. Now if the relation between sensation and judgment (to put
it briefly) is the source of origin of the æsthetic feelings, the degree
of facility and certainty with which judgment is passed must naturally
have a part to play in their arousal; *i.e.*, they may be brought into
connection with sensible discrimination. And this origin would serve
to explain further why pleasure in the beautiful is 'disinterested'.
The reproductory effectiveness of a sensation has plainly nothing to
do with a desire for the possession of the object which excites it.

3. Before proceeding to discuss still other consequences of our
hypothesis, we will give a short summary of the results obtained by
the serial method as regards the effect of the spatial relations of
stimulus upon feeling. Only one general remark needs to be made by
way of preface. We are dealing here not with absolute spatial magnitudes, but with the relations of spatial magnitudes to one another.
The former topic has already been discussed by implication: extension and duration (or frequency) produce the same impression as
intensity (cf. § 37. 8). This fact is also of importance as indicating
the distinctive position in which the æsthetic feelings stand. But the
category is wider than we have hitherto made it. We are able to
appreciate the relations of qualities and intensities (more especially of
qualities), quite apart from their absolute and separate significance.
The feeling which is expressed in a judgment of this kind is also
denominated an æsthetic feeling. Thus our judgment of the beauty
of a picture may be essentially determined by the qualitative factor,
as well as by the spatial; indeed, the artist may even be led to disregard the latter in his striving for qualitative effect, as we see in the
works, *e.g.*, of Arnold Böcklin. Unfortunately, no systematic experi-

ments have been made on this point. A serial investigation of the two great classes of visual quality, colour tone and brightness, independently and in their mutual relations, would be especially valuable. —In the same way, a connection of tones in a compound clang or a melody is the object of pleasure or displeasure, quite irrespectively of the affective value of the individual tone or clang. When we speak of a melody as 'voluptuous', etc., we have in mind the peculiar æsthetic effect of the qualitative relations which it employs, an effect which may persist unimpaired though the sensible clang stimulus as such is very greatly weakened. We may conjecture that the basis of the æsthetic feeling is the same in all these cases, as in those cited above. The conjecture is certainly borne out by the rules of æsthetic practice in painting and music, so far as anything to the point can be learned from them.

4. We may now enter upon a discussion of the uniformity discovered for simple spatial relations. The first maximum of pleasantness in the division of a straight line is given with the apparent equality of the two parts, *i.e.*, with the apparent proportion 1 : 1. Our visual sensible discrimination of length is relatively very accurate, and the æsthetic feeling is very sensitive to noticeable deviations from symmetry. Thus, an objective bisection, which is not judged as a bisection, in consequence of optical illusions or other constant sources of error, is not felt as pleasing, but as relatively very unpleasing. A second maximum of pleasantness in the division of a straight line occurs at the golden section. In the proportion of the golden section, the smaller part (minor) stands to the larger part (major) as the larger to the whole line. If we call the minor 1 and the major x, we have a simple expression for the golden section in the proportion $1 : x = x : 1 + x$, which gives an irrational number, $x = \dfrac{1 \pm \sqrt{5}}{2}$. The sign of the square root is positive for a positive major, negative for a negative. The ratio of minor to major is approximately 1 : 1.618. Arithmetically, the right proportion is more closely approached, the farther the series 2, 3, 5, 8, 13, 21, 34, 55 .... (in which each term forms the sum of the two next before it) is continued. This series renders it quite easy to divide a line according to the golden section with practical accuracy, even without the aid of the construction familiar from elementary geometry. The interesting mathematical properties of the golden division have frequently been discussed; but no one has called attention to its most important psychological characteristic, *i.e.*, to the fact that the ratio which it expresses is simply a special case of the constancy of the relative

sensible discrimination, or of Weber's law (cf. § 7. 8; § 26). If this law holds for visual measurement, it is demonstrated that the division of a line at the golden section produces apparently equal differences between minor and major on the one hand and major and whole line on the other.

5. As a matter of fact, Weber's law has been found to hold for visual measurements within certain limits (cf. § 59). Unfortunately, sensible discrimination has not been investigated by the method required for a strict comparability of results: there has been no comparison of the relations of three lengths to one another, and, more particularly, no testing of sensible discrimination by the division of a total magnitude. But we have seen (§§ 6,7) that a difference limen determined by one of the methods of error or gradation may be regarded as a difference which is apparently equal to all other difference limina. And if the relative S's remain approximately constant, it may be assumed that apparently equal differences of supraliminal magnitude will correspond to equal objective relations. In that case, we have in the pleasingness of the golden section simply the pleasingness of apparently equal differences. It represents, so to speak, a symmetry of a higher order. It is not surprising to find that deviations from an accurate division at the golden section are not so quickly or certainly felt to be displeasing as deviations from apparent equality. For (a) the estimation of the equality of differences appears always to be made with less assurance than the estimation of the equality of stimuli. And (b) in the case of the division of a line, the conditions are peculiarly unfavourable to an estimation of the former kind. This explains why a deviation from Weber's law, which has frequently been found in investigations of sensible discrimination, has but little effect upon the pleasingness of the golden section for feeling.

The same two maxima of æsthetic effect have also been observed in figures in which the proportions of symmetry and of the golden section somehow recur. Thus, the most pleasing rectangles are the apparent square (*i.e.,* 1 : 1) and the figure whose vertical and horizontal sides stand in the ratio of the golden section; the most pleasing ellipse is that whose two axes stand in this ratio, etc. Constant errors of overestimation or underestimation of distances, such as always attend, *e.g.,* the comparison of horizontal and vertical lines, must, of course, be eliminated before the proportions are calculated. It is easy to determine the relative pleasingness of other linear divisions by intercomparison, and so to construct a curve, the ordinates of which express degrees of pleasingness, and the abscissæ stimulus proportions. We need not here go into further detail, especially as the experimental investigations extant are by no means complete. We will only call attention to two other points: to the noteworthy fact that variation of the absolute magnitude of the separate terms of a proportion does not influence the æsthetic judgment, provided that it does not noticeably disturb comparison, and to the observation that if complicated figures are employed, presenting various proportions for estimation, one or another is very apt to have no share in the æsthetic impression, or to be overlooked in the æsthetic judgment. It is therefore, necessary for the experimenter to be extremely careful to define the real object of æsthetic appreciation.

6. After this summary of the results of experiment upon the elementary æsthetic feelings, we may return to our attempt to group them under an explanatory rubric. (*a*) We notice, in the first place, that the observations lend every support to our conjecture that these feelings are not due to simple sensible excitation, but to a relation between sensation and judgment, impression and reproduction. It may, perhaps, be objected that the pleasingness or unpleasingness of the division of a line is determined by its influence upon eye movement. The pleasantness of apparent equality, we must admit, might possibly be conditioned in this way; but the hypothesis breaks down in face of the ordinary preference of division at the golden section to apparent bisection, and is obviously altogether inadequate to explain the occurrence of similar proportions in rhythm. We must rather suppose that the conditions of æsthetic effect are not particular influences, valid for a single sense organ, but influences of a general nature, valid for sense impressions in general. There seem to be three principal factors in the production of the elementary æsthetic feelings. The first (i) is the *determinateness of the reproductory effect* of a sensation. The more definite the effect, the more pleasing will the impression ordinarily be. The second (ii) is the degree of *facility* with which reproduction is consummated. Here we have the three familiar stages: the too easy, which does not excite any noticeable feeling; the moderately easy, which excites pleasure; and the too difficult, which excites unpleasantness (cf. 2 above). And the third (iii) is the *relation between the reproductory effect of the total impression and that of its separate constituents.* The greater the agreement between the two, the pleasanter does the impression appear. The co-operation of all three in the concrete case is sufficiently obvious. (i) The judgment of the apparent equality of stimuli and stimulus differences (as we have remarked in another connection: cf. § 6. 4) is psychologically simple, unequivocally conditioned. The judgment 'different,' on the other hand, can only be put into definite form by a special and laborious con-

nection of several judgments, which implies an extreme vacillation and
uncertainty of reproduction on the part of the observer. Slight deviations from apparent equality are, therefore, particularly unpleasing.
(ii) Again, it is easier to cognise the apparent equality of stimuli
than the apparent equality of stimulus differences. In the first case,
cognition is on the borders of the 'too easy,' in the second it usually
corresponds exactly to what we have called the 'moderately easy,'
i.e., the pleasurable. At the same time, this relation is not constant.
If the figures are very complicated, the judgment of apparent equality
of differences may be too difficult. In that case, division at the golden
section is not always found pleasant, or pleasanter than the apparent
equality of the magnitudes or their complexes. (iii) And lastly, with
apparent equality of differences, the effectiveness of the total impression for reproduction is entirely coincident with that of its separate
constituents, inasmuch as these are reproductively active only in their
mutual relation, and not in their own right. With the golden section,
the single judgment 'equal' covers all proportions. But with the
apparent equality of the distances, the judgment 'equal' holds simply
of the relation of the separate parts, while the relation of each of
them to the total distance is expressed by the ratio $1:2$. The
required agreement is, therefore, less with apparent equality of distances than with apparent equality of their differences. This, again,
serves to explain the customary preference of the latter in the affective judgments. (*b*) And, finally, our general theory is confirmed by
the fact that the constant error in the comparison of spatial magnitudes
is of determining influence on æsthetic appreciation. This clearly
shows that it presupposes a relation of the sensations to sensible
discrimination or sensitivity.

7. The view here presented has one obvious advantage: we obtain
from it a quantitative formulation of the degree of pleasantness or
unpleasantness, which can always be tested by a direct appeal to the
facts. Another of its good qualities, not so evident, perhaps, but none
the less real, is that it can be put in the form of a psychophysical
theory, and co-ordinated with the physiological interpretation which
we gave above of the results of the method of expression and the
influence of stimulus intensity upon the feelings. This appears most
plainly with regard to our second principle. It is natural to posit the
same differences of central excitability for the relative facility of a reproduction as for the relative intensity of an impression. The dynamic
revival of previous excitations must also stand in intimate relation to
the excitability of the nervous substance, and restriction to a limited
area and a slight expenditure of energy will produce a different

central effect from that of extension over a wide range and intensive action upon numerous centres of excitation. But the analogy with the effect of stimulus extends further, to the relative determinateness of a reproduction (our first principle). Indeterminate reproduction may be conceived of—and the interpretation is supported by introspection—as an intermittent process, a vacillation between different judgments or reproductions. But intermittent stimuli excite unpleasantness; and the disagreeableness of an impression which gives rise to indeterminate reproductions may very well have its source in the alternation, the restless oscillation of the activity of reproduction. We have a similar intermittence of reproductory impulses, combined with oscillation of impulses to movement, in uncertainty, hesitancy, doubt, etc.; and all these states are unpleasant moods or emotions. Lastly, the third principle, the relation of the reproductory effect of the total impression to that of its separate constituents, points to an adjuvant or inhibitory function of different reproductions, exercised when they are given in juxtaposition. We cannot at present form any definite conception of the actual mechanism of this reinforcement or inhibition. Apart from it, unpleasantness may be excited here, too, by an intermittence of reproduction, due to a divergence of the judgments suggested by the total impression and by its separate constituents.— In this way we obtain a simple psychophysical interpretation of the elementary æsthetic feelings, which is again couched in terms of increase or decrease of excitability in the central organs (cf. § 37. 4).

8. Something must be said, in conclusion, of the applicability of our three principles to other relations than the temporal and spatial. Where qualities and intensities of sensation are the factors in affective excitation, the absolute character of the various stimuli will always play a large part in the result. But some importance must be attributed, at least in many cases, to the relation obtaining between impression and reproduction. We prefer, *e.g.*, a series of colours whose brightness is evenly graduated to a series which shows irregular differences of brightness. This judgment contains an æsthetic appreciation, based upon the difference of reproductory effect in the two cases. Again, some tones are pleasant in combination, others unpleasant or indifferent. This is also due (apart always from the sensible effect of the separate tones, or the possible occurrence of beats) to the relation of their reproductions, and more especially to the relative intensity of the excitation of the activity of reproduction by the total impression, as compared with its excitation by the individual tones or clangs. The affective result has nothing to do with

17

the degree of harmony. The most harmonious tones are those whose vibration rates stand in the proportion $1 : 2$, *i.e.*, which constitute the octave. But this interval hardly excites feeling at all; it is indifferent. The most pleasant interval for most persons is the major third, which is not so perfect a harmony. The reason must be, that the reproductory effect of the total impression is here approximately equal to that of the separate clangs. In some cases the affective judgment is further influenced by the apparent equality of the differences in chords or tonal series. No one of these phenomena has been adequately investigated.

The principles are also applicable, *mutatis mutandis*, to the activity of memory and imagination, to the moral, logical, and religious feelings. The pleasurable feeling aroused in us by a valid judgment, a good action or a settled conviction, is capable of reduction to the relation between impulse to reproduction and reproductory effect: we cannot here enter into details. The more complicated the object of affective appreciation, the less possible, of course, is it to decide a priori what aspects of it will be effective, and, consequently, what will be the nature of the resultant feeling. Moreover, as we have already remarked (§ 35. 8), the associative factor is largely concerned in all the 'higher' feelings. This means that the agreeableness or disagreeableness of an experience is determined by the affective value which the ideas, judgments and actions excited by it possess for the individual.

§ 39. The General Conditions of Feeling.

1. By the general conditions of feeling we understand, in the first place, the processes indicated by the terms attention, expectation, habituation, fatigue, etc. (cf. § 5). In connection with the attention we must also take account of the influence of will, and of the various individual dispositions of the affective consciousness. And lastly, we must examine into the apparent dependency of the feelings upon one another.

(1) (*a*) We begin with *attention*. The relation of attention to sensitivity and sensible discrimination has already been discussed (§ 5. 2, 3). We found that its influence was distinctly favourable: it increased the clearness, vividness, and reproductivity of sensations. We shall, therefore, be justified in supposing that a definite influence upon feeling accompanies these effects upon sensation. And we find, as a matter of fact, that attention is equivalent in its effect to an intensification of external stimulus. A weakly pleasurable feeling is intensified by the direction of the attention upon its concomitant sensations, and an

impression which stands on the borderline between pleasantness and unpleasantness may be made unpleasant by an intense concentration of the attention upon it. In a certain sense, then, attention is a favourable condition for the feelings as it is for sensation. But, curiously enough, the result is quite different if attention is turned upon the feeling itself. It is a familiar fact that contemplation of the feelings, the devotion of special attention to them, lessens their intensity and prevents their natural expression. This diminution of intensity does not consist in a reversal of the course of feeling under intensificatory influences (§ 37. 7), but in a tendency of the affective contents to disappear altogether, to make way for the state of indifference. It would seem that attention never transforms an unpleasantness into a pleasantness. Such, at least, is the author's experience.

2. Attention, then, is adverse to the feelings, when concentrated directly upon them, *i.e.*, produces quite different results upon feeling and sensation. The fact needs further investigation, preferably by the method of expression   It is of great importance for a theory of the feelings. There appear to be only two possible explanations of it, and they are closely related.   (i) We might suppose that the direction of the attention upon the feeling accompanying a sensation is equivalent to its diversion from the sensation. The further consequences would then follow of themselves, if we assume that feeling is in some way dependent upon sensation. The diversion of attention from the sensation renders it less vivid and distinct, etc.; the feeling, which is dependent upon these attributes of sensation, must therefore undergo a similar modification. (ii) If, on the other hand, feeling is regarded as a product of the co-operation of sensation and attention, it is plain that diminution or alteration of the second factor will have the same effect upon feeling as obscuration or alteration of the first. The only difference (it will be noticed) between the two hypotheses is that the latter gives attention a definite share in the origination and direction of the feelings. In neither case is it meant, of course, that sensation and attention as such, *i.e.*, as experiences, condition feeling; the words are merely used to cover psychophysical processes which stand in a determinate relation to the psychophysical process of feeling. It is difficult to decide, at present, between the two views, as the facts can be brought equally well under either. But as within certain limits (defined by the intensity, number, and reproductory effect of sensations: § 75) we can concentrate the attention upon any one sensation to the exclusion of others, it is certainly fair to infer from its relation to feeling that the feelings stand in a closer connection with sensations than these with one another.

3. A decision can only be reached by way of an exact determination of the effect of the direction of the attention upon feeling.

I made a series of sphygmographic experiments upon this point, which seem to throw some light upon it, although they have no claim at all to be regarded as final. The attention curve (I use this expression for the sake of brevity to denote the sphygmogram obtained when the attention was directed upon a feeling) showed a constant approximation to the normal curve (curve of indifference, taken before the experiments) only in the case of pleasurable feelings. On the other hand, the slowing of the pulse during the course of an unpleasant feeling was increased by an affective direction of the attention. The subject often insisted that the feeling had altogether disappeared under attention, and that it was very difficult, in any case, to attend to pleasantness or unpleasantness. Feeling has too little objectivity and substantiality for the attention to be directed and held upon it. It is focussed for a moment, and then other processes, especially organic sensations, interpose and take possession of the conscious fixation point. This fact, again, is easily explained on the assumption that attention is adverse to feeling.

The first of the alternative views given above asserts that the direction of attention upon feeling is always equivalent to a weakening of sensation or of the stimulus which occasions it. But, in that case, it must be possible, under certain circumstances, for unpleasantness to be transformed into pleasantness; diminution of an intensive and consequently unpleasant impression may make it pleasant. Now if, as a matter of fact, the direction of the attention upon feeling always results in indifference, its effect is plainly not simply that of a weakening of stimulus or sensation, and it must, therefore, have a special part to play in the origination of the feelings,—as the second hypothesis maintains. Presupposing that pleasantness is connected with increase and unpleasantness with decrease of excitability in the central organ, we are thus led to the conclusion that the effect of attention is to compensate these functional modifications. The result is only produced, however, when the attention is concentrated upon the feeling and not upon its attendant sensation. In the latter case, the psychophysical process in sensation is allowed free scope as a determinant of excitability. This conclusion is borne out by the consideration that attention is, in all probability, not a positive process, which adds something to the conscious contents already present, but a process of inhibition (§ 76. 5).

4. Whatever may be the true interpretation of the facts, there can be no doubt of their great practical importance. Attention gains a new significance as the *fons et origo* of circumspection, sobriety, coolness of judgment. It illuminates the obscurity of feeling, and allows a clear and just view of the question at issue: or, to change

the metaphor, it puts the reins of conduct in the hands of reason. We speak of an 'emotional' mind, when we mean one that is too exclusively subject to the guidance of its feelings, one which does not make these feelings themselves the object of observation and examination; of a 'rational' mind, where we see evidence of a developed capacity of active, inhibitory resistance of feeling. We shall not be far wrong in regarding the difference as due in the main to the special direction of the attention, which in the first case is wholly devoted to the sensations accompanying feeling, in the other is, often at least, diverted to the feelings themselves. The difference between the naïf or impulsive and the reflective or calculating dispositions is of a precisely analogous character.

(*b*) It will be readily understood that the influence of *expectation* upon feeling is practically the same with that of attention. If it is directed upon the concomitant sensations, pleasantness and unpleasantness attain their full force, while its concentration upon the feelings effects a noticeable reduction of their intensity. It is a familiar experience that the unpleasant is more disagreeable, and the pleasant more delightful in anticipation than in reality. A long expected pleasure is often disappointing in its realisation. There may, of course, be other reasons for this: there may be aspects of the reality which were not foreseen and expected and which, nevertheless, contribute largely to the affective result; or hope deferred may have brought relaxation and exhaustion, with a consequent lack of appreciation when the hoped-for happens. But quite apart from these secondary phenomena, the influence of expectation as preparatory attention may be conceived of as similar to the influence of attention itself.

5. (*c*) The effect of *habituation* on feeling is very like that of attention, *i.e.*, under its influence both pleasantness and unpleasantness approach indifference. Here again, there is no evidence that unpleasantness passes into pleasantness (cf. 1, above). Observations that seem to point towards any such process are referable to other causes. At least, the reverse passage, of pleasantness into unpleasantness, will be found to be of hardly less frequent occurrence; and no one would attempt to explain it by habituation. The organism adapts itself to constantly repeated excitations, on the same principle that the mind is reassured by the occurrence of the known (cf. § 27. 5). Habituation has the same compensatory power in the sphere of feeling which we ascribed to attention (cf. 3, above).

(*d*) The effect of *fatigue* is the same with that of an intensification of the internal or external stimulus. It weakens what would otherwise be a pleasure, and increases what would normally be a moderate unpleasantness. If fatigue is continued to exhaustion, this increased stimulability is changed to an equally well-marked dulness. In the first stage, quite weak stimuli may be very unpleasant, in the second, stimuli of considerable intensity exert no noticeable influence. This agrees with the general characterisation of unpleasantness, as correlated first with an increased, and then with a greatly diminished excitability (§ 37. 4). Now if we set out with an abnormal degree of excitability, as in the first stage of fatigue, even a weak stimulus must be unpleasant, since it will necessarily bring about a still further increase. The influence of fatigue is, therefore, explicable in terms of the underlying central nervous excitability.

(e) *Contrast* has sometimes been included among the general conditions of feeling. But it is not a simple principle, and its influence cannot be unequivocally defined. If we understand by it merely the effect of the unaccustomed and novel, we may say that it gives rise to unpleasantness. The unknown is disquieting and exciting, and arouses unpleasantness in its primary stage (§ 27. 5). If, on the other hand, we mean by affective contrast that an unpleasantness is greater, the greater the previous pleasantness, and *vice versa*, the principle cannot claim universal validity. A pleasurable excitation coming after a long period of suffering is not, as a rule, particularly pleasurable in feeling. Contrast effects are not found, that is, at any rate in the second stage of unpleasantness, that of diminished excitability. Nor is the proposition *variatio delectat* universally valid. Everything depends upon the character of the variable. So that the particular cases in which feeling is referred to the effect of 'contrast' must be carefully kept separate, and the special conditions of excitability examined.

6. (2) (a) It is usual to deny the dependency of the feelings upon the *will*. It is quite true that no feeling is directly produced by the intention of the subject. And it is also true that a present feeling cannot be changed at will,—destroyed, or transformed into its opposite. But an indirect influence of will upon feeling, and the education of the affective consciousness which this implies, are not only possible but must be admitted as well authenticated facts. Reproduction, attention, and movement (in part: cf. § 77. 1) are dependent upon will; and as these are all factors in the determination of feeling, will must plainly be counted among its conditions. Nowhere, we may think, is the task of self-education more severe or its results more wonderful than in the sphere of feeling. Especially important is the control· of expressive movements. The course of feeling seems to be least disturbed and the conditions of its development most favourable when these movements are given full play; and their suppression, by

voluntary inhibition, *e.g.*, may perhaps be looked upon as a means of weakening and destroying feeling.

(*b*) The existence of special individual *dispositions* towards the origination and direction of feeling has long been recognised. They find expression in such words as 'temperament,' or in the phrases 'emotionally minded,' 'rationally minded,' 'capricious,' 'reliable,' etc. Not all of these terms, it is true, have exclusive reference to the development or state of feeling in an individual; but, whatever else they may mean, all alike tend in this direction. It is customary to distinguish four temperaments, the sanguine, choleric, melancholy, and phlegmatic. The concepts are not properly co-ordinate; and only one of them (that of melancholy) contains any direct implication of a disposition toward a particular affective quality (unpleasantness). The others (with the possible exception of sanguineness) are indicative not of an inclination to definite feelings, but only of the normal rapidity and constancy of conscious processes. They are, *i.e.*, formal definitions, which we may very well refer with Wundt to the contrast of strong and weak on the one hand, and quick and slow on the other. But these formal definitions are as valid for the feelings as for other contents. In the sanguine mind, pleasantness and unpleasantness arise quickly and easily, and as quickly and easily disappear. In the phlegmatic, there seems to be a predisposition to the state of indifference. In the choleric, we find a comparatively slight susceptibility to change, and a high degree of constancy in the retention of certain feelings and incentives to feeling. We have already discussed the terms 'emotionally minded' and 'rationally minded' (§ 39. 4). They may, however, be interpreted in another way, the former to denote a disposition favourable to the origination of feelings, and the latter a predisposition to the contrary. Again, we say that a character is 'capricious,' when we see that similar impressions give rise to very different feelings at different times, *i.e.*, when the mood is very variable, and changes without allegeable external cause. Capriciousness of character and sanguineness of temperament are thus very closely related,—unless, indeed, we define sanguineness (as is sometimes done) with special reference to pleasure. It can hardly be doubted that there are also specific affective dispositions. We speak of 'cheerful' and 'gloomy' natures, and have a pathological exaggeration of the two in mania and melancholia. And we contrast 'dulness' with 'liveliness,' 'evenness' of temper with 'excitability,' meaning to oppose a customary affective indifference to an unusual susceptibility for feelings. We may conjecture with some degree of confidence that all these distinctions have reference to central excitability.

7. (3) Lastly, we have to discuss the apparent *dependency of feelings on one another.* The facts are as follows. An impression that would excite pleasure, if we were indifferent, leaves us cold if we are out of humour; or an impression that would excite unpleasantness, if we were indifferent, has no effect upon us if we are cheerful and in good humour. This holds also when a single impression has its agreeable and disagreeable aspects. We may, of course, alternate between the two, directing our attention first upon one and then upon the other; but if we regard only the total impression, the two feelings cancel each other in proportion to their intensities. We may accordingly say that pleasantness and unpleasantness are antagonistic, or that they can be added together algebraically. These facts appear to contradict the effects of contrast (mentioned above, 5); since contrast points to an intensification of pleasantness by precedent unpleasantness, and *vice versa.* But a somewhat closer consideration of the two cases shows an important difference between them: contrast effects are successive, the others simultaneous. A pleasantness is increased by contrast, it would seem, only after the cessation of the precedent unpleasantness, and not during its continuance. We can explain the influence of contrast by supposing that the neutral point is shifted (cf. Fig. 8, § 37. 7), and find at least a temporary support for this assumption in the analogy of the alteration of the physiological zero point, under similar conditions, in the sphere of temperature sensation (§ 11. 2). We suppose, *i.e.,* that a continuance (not too long) of pleasant or unpleasant stimulation shifts the neutral point in the direction of pleasantness or unpleasantness, and that, consequently, a feeling of the opposite quality, if it occurs, appears more intensive than it otherwise would appear. The algebraical addition of feelings, on the other hand, takes place only if we are exposed to the simultaneous influence of a number of excitations, in themselves of various affective value. It becomes intelligible when we recall the physiological equivalents of the two affective qualities, and assume that increase and decrease of excitability cannot exist peaceably side by side, but somewhere and somehow seek to compensate each other. This hypothesis is quite plausible, as it stands; but it admits of different interpretations, and, moreover, contradicts an often repeated observation. Many observers have recorded the occurrence of *mixed feelings,* feelings in which pleasantness and unpleasantness arise and exist in consciousness side by side. It is hardly possible in the present state of our knowledge to decide positively for or against the reality of these mixed feelings. The position taken up in regard to them is ordinarily determined by theoretical ideas of the nature of the feelings. If we imagine that the physiological conditions of feeling are localised where sensations have their probable central substrate, the possibility of mixed feelings cannot be doubted. But if we imagine that they are unitarily localised, or not localised at all, mixed feelings must be regarded as improbable. In our own view, mixed feelings are certainly less well authenticated than cancellation of feeling. This we explain by the hypothesis that when a stimulus to pleasantness and a stimulus to unpleasantness meet, neither can produce its normal effect; so that the resultant total feeling does not originate in definite partial feelings, but is the sole and simple affective result of the conditions of excitability.

§ 40. The Question of an Elementary Quality of Will.

1. Very different meanings attach to the word 'will' in different psychological treatises. Some writers use it to denote what is meant by 'will' in the language of everyday life, while others believe that it designates special conscious processes, distinct from sensation and feeling. In the former sense, will is a general attitude of the subject, co-ordinate with automatic or impulsive and reflex reaction; in the latter, it is regarded as a specific concrete conscious content, capable under certain circumstances of combining with ideas and affective processes. And theory is naturally as widely divergent as interpretation. In the one case, it consists in a tabulation of the conditions of a state of consciousness, upon which not only particular mental processes but the movements of the subject are dependent. In the other, it seeks to furnish the definition and explanation of a new element in mental life in general. There is no necessary contradiction between the two.—We must defer the examination of the first and more important question as to the nature of the will until we come to our third Part (cf. § 77); but we may here approach the special problem of an elementary will quality.

The psychologists who assert the validity of this third element of mind have generally been led to do so by their analysis of certain complex states or processes. The most obvious material for an analysis of the kind is furnished by the experiences which we call in ordinary life voluntary actions, resolutions, etc. [1] No one doubts that sensations are concerned in a voluntary action, or that its course is commonly attended by feelings. The point at issue is, whether we can discover, besides these familiar processes, a specific act, an elementary will. It may be looked for in the decision for one particular action

[1] *Willenshandlungen, Willensentschlüsse.*

in face of all the many possibilities; or in an internal initiative, significant of the active interference of the subject in the mechanical course of events; or in an effort, such as is present also in impulse, in unsatisfied and unexpressed desire, in longing and aspiration.

2. It must be fully understood that however the issue is decided, whether, *i.e.*, we accept or reject this elementary will quality, nothing is thereby gained for the explanation and analysis of voluntary action itself. The psychophysical question, in particular,—the question whether the physiological substrate of the voluntary action is anything other than the sensory excitations underlying the automatic succession of ideas, and a motor innervation directly determined by them—is not touched at all. The two inquiries, as was hinted just now, must be kept entirely separate; not only because their subject matter is different, but because the elementary quality, if it existed, could not possibly be the distinguishing characteristic of voluntary action. There is obviously no invariable connection between them: for voluntary action assuredly does not necessarily imply a 'feeling' of internal initiative, the 'sensation' of an effort of decision, or the intensity of desire or aspiration. We may, therefore, for the time being, abstract altogether from the significance for voluntary action of a possible simple conscious content, over and above sensation and feeling. This granted, we believe that all the empirical observations of internal initiative, as given in impulse, longing, etc., are explicable in terms of one definite phenomenon, which we may, perhaps, most adequately and objectively describe as *effort*. We understand by it an urgency from within outward, a mental strain, an activity of the self. If stress is laid on the analogy of this state, in its subjective aspect, with the feelings, it is termed the 'feeling of effort'; if its analogy with sensations is to be emphasised, the 'sensation of innervation.' A special relation to the feelings seems indicated by the fact that effort is opposed to reluctance [1] in the same way as pleasantness to unpleasantness. On the other hand, the quality of effort bears a very close resemblance to those of the organic sensations, and especially the tendinous and articular sensations. The question arises, then, what the psychology of the process really is.

3. There are two experiences in which effort plays a particularly distinct part. The first is that of resistance to an opposition, of struggle under a physical or mental burden, and the second is the wish for a change in a given state, which may be conceived of as indifferent. In both cases, effort appears to be a complex of more or less vivid organic sensations, composed of tendinous (strain) and arti-

[1] *Streben, Widerstreben.*

cular sensations, peripherally and centrally excited. Evidence for this analysis is furnished by two sets of facts: the relative intensity of effort runs parallel to the relative intensity of the organic sensations; and wherever we find effort, we find motor innervations, actual or ideal. Moreover, effort can be voluntarily aroused by the thought of a pleasant change of locality. The pleasantness in this instance simply acts as an effective stimulus to the origination of ideas of movement, and the sensations occasioned by the imagined movement of the limbs. The elementary will quality, therefore, would seem to reduce to definite sensation qualities. This conclusion helps us to understand the distinctness of effort in so many voluntary actions, where it is not essential: the organic sensations involved are for the most part those attending ideal or real movement. In desire and longing, where it is also distinct, the conditions are again favourable for the origination of these sensations. The analogy with the feelings is not difficult of explanation. The difference between effort and reluctance is not referable to a specific difference of sensations, but to the opposition of affective quality on the one hand, and to that of the direction of movement, made or intended, on the other. The idea of movement towards the object of effort is connected with a feeling of pleasantness; while reluctance is characterised by intended or actual movement from the repellent object, and an unpleasant feeling which attaches to it.—The phrase 'sensation of innervation' may be understood to mean that the process of central motor innervation itself is accompanied by sensations; which is not the case. It is, therefore, best to avoid the expression altogether.

§ 41. Theory of Feeling.

1. All the difficulties which we have encountered in our discussion of the laws of feeling recur when we attempt to elaborate a theory of pleasantness and unpleasantness. This is plainly not included in the theory of sensation, since the feelings, as we have shown (§ 34. 7), must be regarded as specific and independent conscious processes. It will, however, resemble the theory of sensation in its psychophysical formulation: the phenomena of the dependency of feeling upon stimulus, of expressive movements, etc., refer us directly to physiological processes. Any theory, therefore, which, like that of Herbart, derives the feelings from the interrelation of sensations may be rejected at the outset. We can distinguish three different forms of the psychophysical theory of feeling: a teleological, a peripheral physiological and a central physiological. The first attempts to explain the feelings

by reference to the various effects of stimuli upon the organism. The second ascribes the origination of feeling to certain processes in the peripheral nerve or sense organ. And the third finds the conditions of pleasantness and unpleasantness in certain central processes, which may be modified but are not wholly determined by peripheral influences.

(1) The *teleological* theory brings pleasantness and unpleasantness into connection with the useful or harmful effect of stimulation upon the organism. It is based upon the evolutionary view that this difference of effect arose through adaptation, selection, and heredity. In its more general form it emphasises the effect upon the organism as a whole, in a more special formulation; the hurt or advantage of the directly stimulated organ. Now it is indisputable that there is a wide reaching correspondence between the useful and hurtful on the one side, and pleasantness and unpleasantness on the other, so that there is some ground for regarding the quality of feeling as a criterion of the nature of stimulus. But it is equally indubitable that the parallelism is not coextensive with the facts. The teleological theory in its more general form is thus obliged to have recourse to quali- fication or subsidiary hypothesis to meet, *e.g.*, the unpleasantness of many wholesome foodstuffs and the pleasantness of many that are deleterious. In its special form it can always say that the hurt or advantage does not extend beyond the directly stimulated organ; in the instance given, that of taste.

2. The reasons which have led to this explanation of the origin of feeling are intelligible enough. (*a*) It illustrates the all-pervading tendency of biology to regard the course of organic development as purposive, and every form of organic reaction upon or reception of external influences as preservative of race or individual; and (*b*) it is in complete accordance with the popular conception of feeling, which makes pleasantness a symptom of health and unpleasantness a sign of ill health, pleasure the final goal of all activity and mutation, and pain a preliminary or transition-stage necessary to its achievement, and consequently the almost invariable stimulus to action. But there is obvious danger that the biological analogy or the adoption of the views of ordinary life will obscure the real task of a psychophysical theory; and the fact that many psychologists are content with a bare statement of the parallelism shows that it is not always escaped. It is no explanation of the winking reflex to say that it is of use for the protection of the eye. We must demand of a theory that it enter more fully into details, showing what sensory nerves are stimulated, how and where the excitation is transferred to motor centres and thence to the muscles of the eyelid,—in a word, that it reveal the

mechanism of the whole process. Neither can the practical value of pleasantness and unpleasantness serve as a starting point for a theory of the feelings. For all that it tells us is that the useful and harmful are really identical with the (sooner or later) pleasurable and unpleasurable. An unpleasantly bitter medicine is termed useful, because its effects are satisfactory; and a sweet poison harmful, because its ultimate consequences are exceedingly painful. If the teleological theory made no attempt to go behind these statements, it could never arrive at any real explanation or transcend the simple enumeration of the conditions of pleasantness and unpleasantness. For as the useful is the pleasurable, and the hurtful is the unpleasurable, the theory would be a mere restatement of its own problem. It follows, therefore, that until 'useful' and 'harmful' have been defined in other terms than those of their relation to feeling, we cannot speak of a teleological *theory* in any strict sense of the word.

3. The general form of the teleological theory makes no difficulty of this definition. Everything which destroys or deranges the organism is harmful; everything which secures or furthers its life and growth is useful. But such propositions are evidently far too indefinite to meet the requirements of a psychophysical theory. (i) In all probability, feelings, like sensations, are correlated with excitation processes in the cerebral cortex. It would, therefore, always be in place to raise the further question of the relation between organic furtherance or derangement and the central nervous processes which presumably underlie pleasantness and unpleasantness. (ii) Again, it is at least exceedingly difficult to define the usefulness or harmfulness of the excitatory factors in the case of centrally excited feeling (æsthetic, moral, etc.), independently of their affective result. (iii) And the whole theory is too crude to be adequate to all the finer gradations of feeling. That pain is deleterious to the organism is obvious on the surface; but the result of a less intensively unpleasant stimulus is far more easily determinable in its affective aspect, than in its detrimental. And the same holds of pleasantness in general. (iv) Lastly, there are certain facts which the general teleological explanation cannot cover. There are very serious organic derangements (phthisis, *e.g.*) which are hardly unpleasurable at all; and the degree of pleasantness and unpleasantness does not stand in any sort of uniform relation to the extent of organic furtherance or derangement. The pain of a diseased tooth is one of the worst that we can experience, and is certainly out of all proportion to its detrimental effect upon the organism.

Certain of these objections hold also as against the special form of the teleological theory. This can always, of course, be brought into formal agreement with the facts; it is always possible to assume that pleasantness goes with sustentation of the stimulated organ, and unpleasantness with its impairment,—since there is at present no objective criterion to which these processes can be referred independently of the feelings. But we are no more justified here than we were before in speaking of a theory, until 'use' and 'harm' have been objectively defined, in principle at least, as specific phenomena. And if this definition involves their translation into physiological terms, *i.e.*, the distinction of processes within the stimulated nerve or its central terminations, which are conceived of as advantageous or detrimental to these organs, the special form of the teleological theory passes at once into a peripheral physiological or central physiological hypothesis. It is, therefore, best to avoid the use of the misleading expressions 'useful' and 'harmful' altogether.

4. (2) The common element in the peripheral physiological and central physiological theories is their assumption of a special 'affective' nervous process, or at least of a definite modification of sensory excitations, as the equivalent or excitatory condition of pleasantness and unpleasantness. They differ only in their localisation of this process; the former placing it in the peripheral nerve, while the latter refers it to the central organ. The *peripheral physiological* theory regards the state of nutrition of the stimulated nerves as the sole condition of the origination of pleasantness and unpleasantness. Every stimulus, besides setting up a specific excitation in a sensory nerve (the conscious correlate of which is sensation), must, evidently, make a more or less extensive draught upon its store of energy; and the force required for the restoration of the original conductive capacity will vary in proportion to the intensity or duration of stimulation. These processes of the distribution or consumption of stored energy and its subsequent restitution are regarded by the theory as the physiological equivalents of the feelings. The more intensive the stimulus, the greater is the demand made on the latent nervous energy, and the more difficult and uncertain the return to the original state. The weaker the stimulus, the more adequate is the reserve of energy to cover the loss due to excitation. The stimulus is accordingly felt as pleasant, (or a pleasurably toned sensation arises) under favourable conditions of supply and expenditure, *i.e.*, (to phrase the matter in Hering's terminology: cf. §§ 11, 21) as long as the dissimilation which it has caused is not in excess of the subsequent or simultaneous assimilation. On the other hand, the stimulus is unpleasant (or there arises an unpleasurably toned sensation), if the dissimilation is so great that a

complete restitution is impossible at the moment. The neutral stage of feeling will then be correlated with the equilibrium of assimilation and dissimilation.

5. The first objection (*a*) to be urged against the peripheral physiological theory of feeling is that it is at best not a theory of feeling in general, but only of the sensible feelings. It is difficult to see how the division of a line at the golden section, *e.g.*, should make less demand on the energy of the peripheral optic nerve than any other division. And the homogeneity of the affective quality makes this objection a strong one. (*b*) But the theory can be justly criticized even as an explanation of the sensible feelings. If the excess of demand over supply in the sensory nerve can be carried to greater and greater lengths, and unpleasantness increase in proportion, it is only logical to suppose that the excess of supply over demand will in turn manifest itself in a corresponding intensity of pleasantness. The facts are otherwise. We must, therefore, choose between a conclusion which satisfies the hypothesis but violates the facts,—that the weakest stimuli are the most pleasant; and a conclusion which, though adequate to the facts, is apparently irreconcilable with the hypothesis,—that assimilation increases within certain limits with dissimilation, so that the excess of supply over demand grows constantly larger, up to a certain intensity of stimulus. (*c*) Again, it is difficult to harmonise this theory with the well authenticated physiological fact of the inexhaustibility of the nerve. The presupposition of an excessive consumption of energy is hardly borne out by the observation that the capacity of a nerve is not noticeably diminished by continued and intensive stimulation. (*d*) And lastly, the theory makes no attempt at all to account for the various indications of a definite state of the central nervous substance which we found in the course of our discussion of the method of expression and its results (§ 37), the influence of attention on the feelings (§ 39), etc.

On the other hand, the objection that the processes of nutrition within a nerve have no possible claim to rank as the specific nervous substrate of feeling cannot be recognised as valid. If the process of 'excitation', the real nature of which is altogether unknown, is accepted as the equivalent of sensation, there seems no reason why the consumption and restoration of nervous energy which it involves should not be the equivalent of feeling. No one except Hering (in his theory of the antagonistic nervous processes underlying visual and temperature sensations) has suggested that the restoration of the loss of energy consequent upon excitation is in any way reflected in sensation. It would appear, then, that the process may quite well be regarded as an expression or condition of feeling.

6. (3) The peripheral physiological theory is obliged to take some account of the central conditions of feeling. But it regards them as the simple consequences of the peripherally initiated process. The *central physiological* theory, on the other hand, asserts that the excitations set up at the periphery produce their due intensive or temporal effect upon feeling only under certain circumstances, *i.e.*, that they are merely stimuli, whose affective result is entirely dependent upon the state of the nervous substance. The real conditions of the origination of pleasantness and unpleasantness are found in the central organ. It will be remembered that we adopted a general view of this nature in our preliminary discussion of the results of the method of expression and their interpretation ; we came to the conclusion that pleasantness and unpleasantness are correlated with differences in the excitability of the central substance (§ 37. 4). A central theory has one great and obvious advantage : it enables us to explain all the facts of the affective consciousness. It helps us to understand why there is no radical difference between peripherally excited and centrally excited feelings, as there is between the corresponding categories of sensation (§ 34. 2). And it certainly furnishes the simplest explanation of the facts obtained by the combined application of the serial and expressive methods (cf. § 37. 8), and of the homogeneity of feeling, *i.e.*, the impossibility of a simultaneous experience of more than one pleasant or unpleasant state (§ 39. 7). But the theory may take, and has actually taken, very different forms. In what follows we shall mention only two of these : the theories of Meynert and Wundt. According to Meynert, the physiological equivalent of feeling is to be looked for in the variation of the nutrition of the cerebral cortex; on that of Wundt, pleasantness and unpleasantness arise from the reaction of apperception (cf. § 32. 5) upon sensations, or (in physiological terms) from the reaction of a special apperceptive centre upon the sensory excitations set up in the various sensory areas. The two theories are essentially different; the former regarding the affective processes as distributed throughout the cerebral cortex, and the latter giving them a determinate localisation in a particular brain centre.

7. (i) Meynert supports his theory by a reference to the physiological processes which are observed to follow from intensive (painful) and weak (pleasant) stimuli. In the former case, (α) the excitation is greatly retarded in its conduction through the gray substance. Pain only arises, if the stimulation can reach the gray matter of the spinal cord, and this offers much more resistance to the propagation of an excitation than does the white matter (cf. § 10. 7). (β) Intensive

(painful) stimuli are followed by a reflex constriction of the arteries. Intense bodily pain may in this way produce a swoon, and the tortures of the rack have sometimes put the victim to sleep. (γ) This arterial constriction implies a reduction of metabolism in the nervous elements, and must, therefore, produce a change in their chemical relations, a dyspnœic phase of their nutrition, which in its turn may give rise to definite movements, *e.g.*, deep inspiration or even convulsions. The phenomena of weak and pleasant excitation are the exact contraries of these. They are (α) an unimpeded nervous conduction, *i.e.*, a quick and certain propagation of excitation to particular nervous centres; (β) a dilatation of the arteries, *i.e.*, a functional hyperæmia; (γ) and, lastly, an increased metabolism in the nervous elements, *i.e.*, an apnœic phase of their nutrition. The feelings are thus an expression of the state of nutrition of the cerebral cortex. The cortex itself on Meynert's view has two active functions: the innervation of trains of thought and the movements associated with them, and the innervation of the muscles subserving arterial constriction. Inactivity of thought means increased innervation of these muscles, *i.e.*, is correlated with functional anæmia; while activity of ideation and energy of the movements which it conditions bring with them a dilatation of the arteries, *i.e.*, a functional hyperæmia. In the former case we have unpleasantness, in the latter pleasantness.

8.　(ii) Meynert's theory sets out from purely physiological phenomena, the movements of seizure and avoidance which follow the action of pleasant and unpleasant stimuli. Wundt, on the other hand, is primarily concerned to explain the observed facts of the affective consciousness. The ordinary view of feeling as a more subjective process than sensation (cf. § 34. 1) he regards as indicative of the central character of its physiological substrate. Again, the contrary direction of the will in effort and reluctance points to its relationship to feeling, in whose qualities the same opposition recurs (§ 40. 3). Hence it would appear that feeling is most correctly defined as the *mode of reaction of apperception upon sensations.* Pleasantness and unpleasantness, that is, appear only when sensations are apperceived, *i.e.*, the attention directed upon them. This view is further supported by the fact that increase of feeling appears to follow a similar law to that of the intensity of sensation (Weber's law), *i.e.*, that feeling increases proportionally to the logarithm of the affective stimulus (cf. § 26). For Wundt, as we have seen, regards this law as a law of apperception.—The assumption that feeling arises in the apperception of sensations carries with it a localisation of its physiological substrate. Wundt places the activity of apperception in a special cerebral organ (certain areas of the frontal lobes); and we must, therefore, suppose that feelings originate in the interaction of this organ and the sensory centres. Wundt does not say how this interaction is to be brought into connection with the two qualities of feeling. He calls attention to the fact that the various physical phenomena which accompany feeling are readily explicable upon his theory.

9. It must be admitted that Meynert's theory of feeling has many advantages, despite the extremely hypothetical nature of certain of its arguments. It enables us to determine the physiological equivalents of pleasantness and unpleasantness with some degree of accuracy, and brings the affective qualities into a simple relation with the results of the method of expression and other facts which we have mentioned above. The general increase of excitability in pleasurable states, and its general decrease in unpleasurable, in particular, may very well be referable to functional hyperæmia and anæmia. And the primary stage of unpleasantness (an increased capacity of function, at least upon the motor side, which shows itself in deep inspiration and even in convulsions) can be easily explained from the point of view of the theory, if we take into account the familiar fact that a stage of overstimulation, of abnormal excitability, precedes the stage of exhaustion, of decreased excitability (§ 37. 3). But there are two facts which seem hardly reconcilable with it. In the first place, pleasantness and unpleasantness appear immediately, as the effects of stimuli, simultaneously with the sensations which the stimuli evoke. It is not easy to believe that their condition is a functional hyperæmia or anæmia produced by stimulation. The alteration of volume, pulse, and respiration which the method of expression shows to result from pleasant or unpleasant stimuli is produced comparatively slowly, whereas pleasantness and unpleasantness (apart from the primary stage of unpleasantness) arise far more quickly. We shall, therefore, rather incline to regard these changes as the consequences of feeling or of its psychophysical conditions. The second fact is the homogeneity of feeling. Functional anæmia or hyperæmia need not by any means necessarily extend over the whole cortex or to all the sensory centres, but may be strictly localised. Nevertheless, pleasantness and unpleasantness appear unable to subsist side by side; and we have no simultaneous experience of different pleasantnesses and unpleasantnesses (cf. 6, above). Neither of these observations presents any difficulty to the alternative theory. The homogeneity of feeling agrees excellently with the homogeneity of apperception; and the feeling which accompanies a sensation in consciousness may be

conceived of as originating at once with its apperception. All that this theory leaves to be desired is a more exact determination of the substrate of the specific affective qualities.

Literature:

A. Lehmann, *Die Hauptgesetze des menschlichen Gefühlslebens,* 1892.

T. Ziegler, *Das Gefühl.* Second ed., 1893.

J. W. Nahlowsky, *Das Gefühlsleben.* Second ed., 1884.

G. T. Fechner, *Zur experimentellen Aesthetik. Abhandl. d. mathemat.-phys. Classe d. kgl. Sächs. Ges. d. Wiss.,* vol. ix., 1871. Pp. 555 ff.

L. Witmer, *Zur experimentellen Aesthetik einfacher raümlichen Formver-hältnisse. Phil. Stud.,* vol. ix., pp. 96 ff., 209 ff.

PART II. THE CONNECTIONS OF CONSCIOUS ELEMENTS.

§ 42. Definition and Classification of Connections.

1. Our concrete experiences are always made up of connections of the conscious elements. Simple qualities, insolated sensations and feelings, are products of scientific analysis (§ 3. 5), and their separate investigation is only possible by the aid of special methods and under favourable general conditions. Even so, the actual experience is practically always complex in character.

We cannot, however, pass at once to the consideration of these actual experiences. Our discussion of conscious connections must also travel, for some time at least, along abstract lines. Psychology (i) has to show that (and how) the connections arise from the elements, and to distinguish between the total impression and its elementary constituents; and (ii) has to inquire whether the connections are all of a single kind, or show characteristic differences, and in the latter case to give the reasons for the divergence. We have, *i.e.*, a further series of problems for analytical treatment, whose solution is necessary for the understanding of the concrete mind.

2. The elements of consciousness are of two kinds, sensations and feelings. We may therefore, have connections of sensations with sensations, of feelings with feelings, and of sensations with feelings. It is evident a priori that these three types of connection cannot be of equal importance in consciousness. The qualitative differences of sensation are very numerous (§ 34. 1), those of feeling very few (§ 35. 3); and the forms and laws of the interconnection of sensations will accordingly be various and complex, while those of the other two categories of connection are correspondingly simple. This is in itself sufficient evidence that we should be ill advised to discuss the subject matter of the second Part of our psychology under three co-ordinate rubrics. But there is another and a more important reason for the rejection of a classification by contents. The doctrine

of conscious compounds is mainly occupied with an exact investigation of the formation and attributes of connections. Our task will be very greatly simplified, therefore, if we can discover in these certain general peculiarities (irrespectively of the quality of the connected elements) which may serve as the basis of their broad distinction into definite groups. The best classification of connections, *i.e.*, is a classification in terms of certain distinguishing characteristics of the connections themselves,—provided always that no violence is done by it to the alternative classification in terms of the quality of the connected elements. We have already stated (§ 3) that connections, regarded from this point of view, fall into two great classes, and have termed them *fusion* and *colligation*. It is characteristic of the fusion that the elements contained in it are more difficult of analysis, of the colligation that they are easier of analysis, in connection. Or, to put it in different terms: other things equal (apart, *i.e.*, from the general conditions of sensible discrimination, and its special laws within the given sense department), the character of the connection of compared qualities is of determining influence upon the magnitude and delicacy of sensible discrimination. In both aspects, it is relatively diminished by fusion and increased by colligation.

3. A close examination of the conditions under which the two kinds of connection appear in consciousness leads to two important results. We find (*a*) that the quality of sensations or feelings is unessential for fusion and colligation alike; *i.e.*, that the terms really indicate general peculiarities of conscious connection, and are not mere classificatory names, applicable only to definite elements. And (*b*) we discover a simple rule for the cognition of the particular form of connection in a given case. The rule is couched in terms of the three (or four) attributes of sensations and feelings. It is plain that we have no right to speak of a connection unless we can, directly or indirectly, analyse it into its elements. If, *e.g.*, two sensations are temporally and spatially indistinguishable and qualitatively identical, we actually have but *one* sensation, though two stimuli may be acting upon consciousness. Nor can we speak in strictness of a connection of two sensations where the two stimuli differ merely in intensity; since stimuli which are identical in all other respects will ordinarily give rise to a single sensation. Connection, that is, presupposes a noticeable difference in the quality, extension, or duration of its elements. Our rule now runs as follows: if the connected elements are temporally and spatially identical, but differ in quality, their connection must be termed fusion; if they differ in duration or extension, colligation. Fusion, *i.e.*, may be briefly defined as a qualitative, and colligation as a

temporal or spatial connection. The rule has a further formal value, as transcending the relativity of our general definition of fusion and colligation. This relativity has no practical significance, however: for, given equality of conditions, the different facility of analysis of the two connections is constant and well marked. The general definition is really relative only in the sense that it restricts the discrimination of fusion and colligation to cases in which their elements are the same. It tells us that we may compare tonal fusion with tonal colligation, the fusion of colour tone and brightness with their colligation, etc., but that we have no means for the comparison of the fusion of certain elements from one sense with the colligation of certain elements from another.

4. This limitation is another proof of the dependency of conscious processes upon sensible conditions (§ 3. 3). The differences in the sense organs and their adequate stimuli prevent any quantitative comparison of the sensations of different sense departments. Hence it was impossible to determine the course of the intensive sensible discrimination as between sense and sense (§ 25). It follows that we must here treat of fusion and colligation with special reference to the forms which they assume in different sense departments; we must examine separately the fusion of auditory sensations, the fusion of visual sensations, etc. Many of these departments have been but very imperfectly explored, and we shall often be obliged to content ourselves with the demonstration of a few typical cases of the phenomena, while reviewing the rest in more summary fashion. Again, it will be necessary, when we come to deal with colligation, to set forth *in extenso* the psychological doctrine of time and space, since we postponed the consideration of the temporal and spatial attributes of the conscious elements (§ 4. 10) in order to bring them into relation with more complicated phenomena of the same order. We shall also, of course, have to discuss the connection of sensations of different senses and of different classes of elements (sensations and feelings). Connections of the former kind were named by Herbart *complications*; the sense impressions which enter into them we term *disparate*. As feelings are ordinarily attached to sensations, the connection of sensations and feelings will take the shape of fusion. Special forms of this connection are denoted by the abstract terms emotion, impulse, mood, and passion. A comparison of these fusions with corresponding colligations is, directly at least, impossible. We must, therefore, be satisfied either to prove that they have all the characteristics of fusion in general, or to ascribe them without proof to this class of connections, in order to bring them into agreement with our schema. In the Sections on colligation, besides the problems of time and space

mentioned just now, we have to discuss the qualitative relations of the elements given in temporal or spatial connection, and especially the phenomena of visual contrast and of what is popularly called 'action.' The doctrine of compounds, like that of elements, must begin with peripherally excited sensations. Our remarks upon centrally excited sensations may in any case be made very brief, since their connections have been, for the most part, already considered in the special Sections devoted to them in our first Part.

5. It only remains, after this hasty survey of the contents of our second Part, to explain how we distinguish a connection of conscious elements from a concrete mental experience. A musical *motif* or a melody has as much right to be called a connection of elements as a chord or a clang; and we can form an idea of a room, or a house, or a street, as well as of a chair or a table. In other words, we must attempt to define a 'connection of conscious elements' as regards number of components, spatial extent, and period of duration. If we do not draw a fixed line of demarcation, the term connection will be very vague and ambiguous, and may even, under certain circumstances, be coextensive with consciousness itself. Now (α) in the first place, our sensible organisation and our capacity of attention prevent the number of elements simultaneously present in consciousness from exceeding a certain finite limit. (β) The normal restriction of the field of vision sets a certain finite limit to the spatial extension of connected visual qualities. And (γ) the normal interruption of consciousness by sleep (§ 78) divides the temporal course of our experiences into sections of definite length. But it is plain that these are not the only limits set to conscious connections. We distinguish special combinations, particular groups of elements, within the total consciousness of the moment, within the field of vision, and within the waking day. The melody, and the chord, and the chair, are relatively small parts of the possible whole. There must, then, be some special reason for the further limitation of conscious connections. It appears to be this: that certain combinations of elements are effective for reproduction, *i.e.*, can serve as incentives to or as materials of reproduction (cf. § 30). On this view, all the various forms of particular connections can be readily explained. As we have already seen (§ 30. 4), the associative coherence of elements is greatly strengthened by the reproductory value of their total impression. Provision is, therefore, made for the discrimination of these separate connections in consciousness.

6. Our investigation of the processes of fusion and colligation is not greatly affected by these considerations. We shall have to inquire, in the particular case, into their possible dependency upon the number,

duration or extension of the connected elements. But the difference between them persists independently of any such influence. The question of the origination of separate connections, therefore, does not further concern us, since we have already discussed the relations of centrally excited sensations to each other and to peripherally excited sensations (§§ 27, 29—31). For the same reason, we shall not use the current term *idea* to denote a connection of sensations, as it merely indicates reproductory value and contains no reference to the actual process of connection. A qualitative fusion and a temporal or spatial colligation of elements may equally well be termed ideas, provided that they can reproduce or be reproduced as wholes. It is evident that this qualification does not necessarily attach to either of the connective processes. The factors upon which the degree of liability of reproduction and the effectiveness of materials of reproduction are dependent, do not include character of the attributive interconnection of elements in consciousness. The word 'idea', therefore, contributes nothing to the definition of the actual connection of elements, but merely expresses a consequence of connection which is important for the course of thought.—Wundt has distinguished between *apperceptive* and *associative* connections (cf. § 29. 1), according as the active apperception is or is not involved in the origination of the particular processes. But we may defer their consideration, on similar grounds, until we come to our Section upon the will (§ 77).

Section 1. Fusion.

CHAPTER I. THE FUSION OF AUDITORY SENSATIONS.

§ 43. The General Phenomena of Tonal Fusion.

1. There are several reasons for the choice of tonal fusion as the principal illustration of sensation fusion in general. (1) In the first place, it comprises a great variety of special processes, all of which have been investigated with some degree of thoroughness. (2) Again, successive, as well as simultaneous connections of the separate elements are of familiar occurrence within the sphere of tonal sensations. (3) And lastly, there is a close relation between tonal fusion and the tonal connections whose æsthetic effect is displayed in music. We are thus in the fortunate position of having the results of centuries of artistic practice to compare with the outcome of psychological experimentation. Since the introduction of polyphony into music, a more or less sharp line of distinction has been drawn between consonant

and dissonant compound clangs (chords), between harmonious and inharmonious tonal connections. It is reasonable to suppose that this distinction is based upon a definite psychological effect; and successful attempts have been made, more especially since the work of Helmholtz, to discover the psychophysical foundations of musical forms. As a rule, however, the affective value (pleasant or unpleasant) of the compound clangs, and the phenomena of the sensible connection itself have not been differentiated with sufficient clearness. We shall see that consonance is not identical with agreeableness, or dissonance with disagreeableness (§ 48. 2; cf. also § 37. 8).

2. The physical result of the meeting of two simple periodic sound waves, under favourable conditions, is their combination to a third, resultant wave, whose period of vibration is equal to that of the longer of the two component waves, and whose amplitude is represented by the algebraic sum of their amplitudes. If this resultant wave strike the ear, it is not, however, transmitted to the auditory nerve as a total movement of definite form, duration, and intensity, but is again separated into its primary constituents by the analysing apparatus which we have found to exist in the cochlea (§ 16. 4), and so comes to consciousness as a complex of individual sensations [1]. When a compound clang is sounded, we always hear, as a matter of fact, a number of individual clangs; and with practice even a simple clang (a connection of fundamental and overtones) can be analysed up to the first few overtones. But the instance of the simple clang shows us that the subjective analysis of a complex sound wave is not always possible, and, indeed, we must say in general that the connection of simultaneously sounding tones is highly prejudicial to their separate discriminability and cognisability.

3. It has been argued from this fact (which is characteristic of fusion in general: § 42. 2) that a simultaneous connection of tones is really sensed, not as a multiplicity, but as a unity. The action of a complex sound wave upon the ear would then give rise to a sensation quality as simple as that excited by a simple periodic vibration. The older view of the clang colour (§ 14. 4) of different musical instruments led, it is true, to the interpretation of the influence of vibration form upon consciousness as due to a special qualitative colouring. It would, therefore, be necessary to attribute to auditory sensations a second series of qualities beside the familiar differences of pitch, and to include within this new schema of qualitative variation not only the simple clang, but all the compound clangs as well. And we should

---

[1] We abstract for the moment from certain secondary effects (beats or combination tones) which are ordinarily produced by the combination of simple sound waves.

further be compelled by the theory to assert that a purporting analysis of tonal connections merely presents the appearance of a perception of several sensations without its reality, and is based upon familiar associations which presuppose a knowledge of the character of particular clangs or compound clangs.

4. But this view, which we may briefly term the doctrine of unity, stands in direct contradiction to a whole number of facts. Musicians are unanimous in declaring the analysis of tonal sensations to be original and not simply mediated by association. We can resolve into its separate constituents a compound clang which we hear for the first time as easily as we can resolve a familiar chord. And overtones, if heard at all, are heard in absolute purity, *i.e.*, not at all as they are really given by instruments of 'equal temperament.' All these reasons tell decisively in favour of the occurrence of a direct analysis of tonal connections, at least in certain cases. Besides which, the doctrine of unity as such is untenable, while it is no difficulty to the theory of direct analysis that tonal connections sometimes give the impression of unitariness or simplicity. The combination of a number of simultaneously present qualities into an unanalysed total impression is a possible phenomenon in every sense department. Simplicity would accordingly be a limiting case, referable to an exceptional intimacy of connection or a high degree of fusion. We are thus brought to realise that there are different *degrees* of fusion. The lowest degree of fusion is that which presents the least difficulty of analysis, and the highest degree that which offers the greatest resistance to a discrimination of its primary constituents.

5. The degree of tonal fusion is obviously dependent on very different conditions. (α) In the first place, it is subject to certain general conditions of introspection; attention, expectation, practice, fatigue, etc. (β) But it is also conditioned in special ways by the character (quality, intensity, number, etc.) of the connected tones. All these influences manifest themselves in increase or decrease of the degree of fusion. We must, therefore, endeavour to trace their effect in detail, illustrating it as far as possible by reference to experiment. But before we enter upon this task, we may briefly consider the peculiarity of what must be called the fusion whole, the total impression as contradistinguished from the separate and separately cognisable tones. If the doctrine of unity were in the right, this total impression would of necessity be essentially different from the elements contained in it. The fact is otherwise: the fusion whole appears always either in the quality of its predominant constituent (as, *e.g.*, is the case with clangs, where the fundamental is usually

taken to be the quality of the whole impression), or as a simultancity of several tones (as in the compound clang, where the separate simple clangs exert an equal influence upon consciousness). It follows, there-fore, that we need not undertake a special investigation into the quality of tonal fusion. It will be sufficient, when we are discussing the various degrees of fusion, to indicate their individual importance for the total impression. It follows also and more particularly that fusion cannot be regarded as the analogue of chemical combination, the properties of which are, of course, essentially different from the properties of its elementary components. Intensity forms the only exception to this rule.

6. We do not make any general distinction between intensive and qualitative fusion, because the connection of two or more sensations, which differ in intensity but are in all other respects identical, gives rise to what is really a single sensation, incapable of resolution into its components by any refinement of analysis (cf. § 42. 3). But a high degree of fusion of qualitatively different sensations carries with it a resultant intensity, which may be considered as the intensity of the fusion whole. It is conjecturable a priori that this resultant inten-sity will stand in a definite relation to the intensities of the primary impressions. We may expect, in accordance with Weber's law, that the total intensity will be noticeably greater than the intensity of a given component, only when the intensity of all the rest taken together is at least equal to the upper difference limen of that component. As a matter of fact, it has been found in experiments upon the inten-sive suppression of a sound sensation by another simultaneous sound, that the stimulus intensities must stand in the ratio 1 : 3 if the weaker is to be just audible beside the stronger. If we translate this result into terms of sensible discrimination as determined by the aid of suc-cessive stimuli, it tells us that two sound intensities must be just noticeably different when they are in the proportion of 3 to 4, or when $\dfrac{S}{r} = \frac{1}{3}$. But this is the exact value of the relative difference limen obtained in previous experiments on the sensible discrimination for sound intensities (cf. § 25. 4). This relation to sensible discrimin-ation enables us to state at once the general law governing the total intensity of a tonal fusion, wherever the conditions of a total intensity are realised. The lower the degree of fusion, the more difficult does it become to say anything positively of its total intensity.

7. It might be imagined that the phenomena of tonal fusion itself can be simply explained as instances of the intensive suppression of

component by component; that as a total intensity is not equal to the sum of the intensities of the separate elements (Weber's law), the intensity of each of the connected tones must suffer, and analysis be consequently rendered more difficult. The hypothesis would be inadequate, if only for the reason that it leaves altogether out of account the influence of sensation quality upon tonal fusion, which is demonstrably very considerable. But it is wrong in principle. Difficulty of qualitative analysis is not by any means identical with diminution of the intensity of the sensations. In certain circumstances, a complex of weak sensations may very well be easier of analysis than a connection of intensive elements. The distinctness of a conscious content is not the same thing as its intensity. Unfortunately, we have no systematic investigation into the analysis of sensations under unfavourable intensive conditions. But the difference between the clearness or distinctness and the intensity of an impression has been clearly brought out of late in experiments upon the attention. We shall find frequent occasion, in our review of the various degrees of fusion, to make use of this factor of distinctness, and it will be seen that intensity is only one, and not the sole condition of fusion.

8. We have at present no reliable methods for the measurement of the degrees of tonal fusion. Stumpf, who was the first to turn the concept of tonal fusion to general account in psychological acoustics, bases his inferences (a) partly upon his own observation of the total impression of different musical intervals, (b) partly upon the results of experiments made with unmusical subjects. But subjective analysis, here as elsewhere, furnishes too uncertain a standard for quantitative discrimination; and experiments upon the apparent number of tones contained in a tonal connection are limited to unmusical persons, if the intervals are simple, and furnish at best a merely external criterion of the degree of fusion. Recourse should be had, therefore, to other methods of inquiry. ⁻ (c) An attempt has been made to utilise the reaction method in this regard (cf. §§ 69 ff.). Two series of experiments were taken, with the major and minor chords as stimuli; the reaction movement following the cognition of the special character of the chord. The reaction-time with the minor was constantly though but slightly shorter than that with the major. It remains to be seen whether this method is capable of wider application for the determination of degree of fusion. The general rule would obviously be, that the chord which is more quickly cognised is the worse fusion. (d) Another method of investigation which suggests itself is that of the reduction of the duration of the compared inter-

vals to the point at which analysis is impossible. If this limiting duration proved to be different for different intervals, it might be made a measure of the degree of fusion, on the assumption that the longer the time required for analysis, the higher must be the degree of fusion of the particular interval. But experiments of the kind made with tuning-fork tones upon musically educated subjects have not given any satisfactory result. Plainly, then, there is great need in this department of psychology of the elaboration of delicate and trustworthy methods. Especially would it be desirable (e) to employ the qualitative sensible discrimination for the testing of degree of fusion.—The facts and laws given in the following Sections are, for these reasons, derived rather from occasional observations and the rules which obtain in music than from any exact experiments.

§ 44. The Dependency of Tonal Fusion upon the Quality of the Components.

1. We have only to compare two intervals like the octave and the major seventh to see that the quality of the tones contained in a tonal connection is not indifferent for the unitariness of the impression. The analysis of the octave, where the vibration rates of the two tones stand in the ratio 1 : 2, is extraordinarily difficult,—not always possible even for musically educated persons; while the presence of two tones in the seventh, where the vibration rates are in the ratio of 8 : 15, is usually cognised even by unmusical subjects. Treatises upon harmony distinguish between consonant and dissonant intervals, and divide the consonances into perfect and imperfect. Perfectly consonant intervals are the octave, the fifth, and the fourth; in which the ratios of vibration rates are 1 : 2, 2 : 3, and 3 : 4. Imperfectly consonant are the major and minor thirds and the major and minor sixths, whose vibration rates stand in the relation 4 : 5, 5 : 6, 3 : 5, and 5 : 8 respectively. All other intervals are dissonant; more particularly the major and minor seconds and the major and minor sevenths, whose ratios are 8 : 9, 15 : 16, 8 : 15, and 4 : 7. The different intervals have different affective values; dissonances are certainly less pleasant than consonances. But if we refer their discrimination not to relative pleasingness or unpleasingness, but to the degree of unitariness of the total impressions, we may conjecture that the musical order is in essential an arrangement by degree of tonal fusion.

2. Stumpf's observations are in complete agreement with this hypothesis. He distinguishes five different degrees of fusion within

the limits of the octave. The highest (α) is that of the octave itself; then follow (β) the fifth, (γ) the fourth, and (δ) the pure thirds and sixths; worst of all (ϵ) are the minor seventh and the remaining intervals. It is especially important to note that these degrees of fusion recur independently of the absolute pitch of the components. We may, accordingly, lay it down as a general rule that *the degree of fusion of two tones is constant, if the ratio of their vibration rates is constant.* The rule can be easily verified by a comparison of the same intervals in different regions of the tonal scale. It must not, of course, be confused with the law of sensible discrimination for tone pitch. In the one case we have a constancy of the absolute sensible discrimination within certain limits (cf. § 15. 2); in the other an independence of the degree of tonal fusion as regards absolute differences of vibration rate, which rather suggests an analogy with Weber's law (§ 26). But these facts of tonal fusion are only indirectly related to sensible discrimination, even as determined by the aid of successive tonal stimuli; and Weber's law is not applicable to them, if only for the reason that the different intervals present such varying difficulty of analysis. There is, however, one point of analogy, in the existence of upper and lower deviations from the fusion law. Owing to the decrease of the absolute sensible discrimination, the equality of degree of tonal fusion in the same interval does not extend to the extreme regions of the scale in either direction. The same reason accounts for the restriction of ordinary musical usage to a range of some seven octaves, embracing the vibration rates between (approximately) 32 and 4,000.

3. The degree of a fusion is not noticeably changed by slight deviation of the component vibration rates from their strict proportion. But it seems that the magnitude of the noticeable change is less, the higher the original degree of fusion, *i.e.*, that a slight misadjustment is more quickly and easily cognised in the octave than in the fifth, and in the fourth than in the sixth. This law of the inverse ratio of the noticeable deviation to the degree of fusion is confirmed by the results of experiments upon sensitivity for the purity of intervals. These were made with tuning forks, and the two tones of each interval given in succession. In the order from greatest to least sensitivity, the series for one observer, *e.g.*, was as follows: octave, fifth, fourth, major sixth, major third, minor third, second, minor sixth, minor seventh, major seventh. The only important difference between this list and the series of fusion degrees is the comparatively high position occupied by the second, which may, perhaps, be explained from the frequency of this particular interval in musical usage. Further investiga-

tion may, possibly, show that we have here a key to the quantitative definition of the degrees of fusion (cf. § 43. 8). It should be noticed that the fall of a fusion degree from a higher to the lowest level, in consequence of gradual alteration of vibration rate, appears to take place at once, *i.e.*, does not involve a transition through all the intermediate stages.

4. There remain the intervals beyond the limits of the octave. Stumpf asserts that the degree of fusion outside the octave remains the same, if the vibration rates of the primary tones stand in the ratio $\dfrac{v}{v_1 \cdot 2^x}$; where v is the vibration rate of the lower tone, v_1 that of the higher, x a simple whole number, and $\frac{1}{2} > \dfrac{v}{v_1} \geq \frac{1}{4}$. With $x = 0$, the interval becomes an octave.—If this law holds, the double octave (1 : 4) has the same degree of fusion as the octave, the twelfth (1 : 3) the same as the fifth, the tenth (2 : 5) the same as the major third, etc. But, in the author's observation, these results do not accord with the facts. While the relative degree of fusion remains the same for intervals beyond the octave that it is for corresponding connections within the octave, all the intervals of the former kind stand upon a somewhat lower level of fusion than their less remote correlates. In other words, the double octave possesses a higher degree of fusion than the twelfth, the twelfth than the tenth, etc., but the double octave in its turn fuses less well than the octave, the twelfth than the fifth, etc. No more positive statement can be made at present of the relation between the fusion degrees of intervals beyond the octave and those of connections within the octave.

The difference between the various discriminable degrees of fusion seems to increase with increase of the fusion itself. The difference between the fusion of the octave and that of the fifth is considerably greater than the fusion difference of the fifth and the fourth.

As the different degrees of fusion do not appear to stand in any uniform relation to the relative differences of vibration rate, it is impossible to explain the phenomena of this Section by reference to the physical composition of the sound waves, differences of tonal pitch, or other extraneous facts. Hence we have no choice but to conclude that the dependency of tonal fusion upon the quality of the components is a problem for purely psychological or psychophysical solution.

§ 45. The Dependency of Tonal Fusion upon the Intensity of the Components.

1. Two questions fall to be considered under this heading: that of the influence of the absolute, and that of the influence of the relative intensity of components upon tonal fusion. As a general rule, alteration of the *absolute intensity* of the primary tones does not appear to affect the degree of fusion, provided that their relative intensity remains constant. If two tuning-forks, whose tones constitute a definite musical interval, are sounded at approximately equal intensities, and allowed to 'die away', there is no noticeable alteration in the fusion. The same result is obtained if the resonance boxes upon which the two forks stand are closed, or alternately opened and closed by a sliding shutter, care being taken that the closure is equally effective in both cases: the absolute diminution and reinforcement of the intensity of the tones are indifferent for the total fusion effect. The law is, then, that tonal fusion is independent of the absolute intensity of the components. There are, however, upper and lower deviations from it (cf. § 44. 2); if the two components are very intensive or extremely weak, the clang makes an impression of greater unitariness, and analysis is rendered more than usually difficult.

2. On the other hand, tonal fusion is to a very considerable extent dependent upon the *relative intensity* of the components. This is easily proved by experiments with tuning-forks; if one resonance box is closed, while the other remains open, the clang becomes distinctly more unitary, *i.e.*, the degree of fusion is increased. And the character of the total impression alters at the same time. If the intensities stand in the ratio 1 : 1, *i.e.*, if the components are of equal absolute intensity, [1] the two tones contained in the interval are of equal importance in perception; but if the components are of unequal absolute intensity, the total impression inclines to the side of the more intensive tone, so that the weaker is more or less effectually reduced to the condition of a mere attribute of the stronger. It gives a certain colouring, if the expression be allowable, to the predominant tone of the complex, and the unitariness of the resultant fusion is inversely proportional to the distinctness of its specific quality within the tonal connection.—The most favourable conditions of analysis are, therefore, given with equal absolute intensity of the components. We cannot at present, however, obtain any exact formulation of the law of change

---

[1] It must be remembered in this connection that equal intensities of tonal stimuli are not necessarily correlated with equal intensities of sensation: cf. § 24. 5.

of fusion degree with variation of the relative intensity of the component tones. Two questions in particular must be left for the future to decide. We cannot say whether Weber's law exerts an influence upon the course of fusion change, or how it is affected by the qualitative differences already mentioned (§ 44).

3. (1) The best illustration of an alteration of tonal fusion with variation of the relative intensity of the components is furnished by *clang colour* (§ 14. 4). The fundamental in a simple clang is ordinarily more intensive than the overtones, while these again differ intensively among themselves. Every musical instrument possesses a specific clang colour, and it has been demonstrated that the peculiarity is due to differences in the number and intensity of the overtones contained in the clang. It can be easily shown that the fundamental is not the exclusive determinant of the character of the total impression. A clang which is rich in overtones, especially if it belongs to the lower region of the scale, seems higher than a simple tuning fork tone whose pitch is the fundamental of the clang. And it sometimes happens that the first overtone of a clang is subjectively more intensive than the fundamental; we have seen that higher tones in general are sensed as more intensive than lower tones of the same vibration amplitude (§ 24. 5). Moreover, the overtones of a clang are not all equally easy of analysis. Certain of the higher overtones are often particularly distinct: thus in the clang of a flue-pipe, whose fundamental is the c of 128 vibrations, the fourth overtone (the e'' of 640 vibrations) is more easily cognised than the third (the c'' of 512 vibrations). It is evident that we have in this fact a reference to the qualitative degree of fusion. Hence it may be laid down as a general rule that the odd numbered overtones, other things equal, are easier of analysis than the even numbered immediately before them (cf. § 46. 4).

4. The unitariness of the clang has been variously explained. (i) Helmholtz, in the first three editions of his *Lehre von den Tonempfindungen*, attempted to account for it by customary association. We are accustomed, he said, to look upon a sum of sensations as the sign of a single object; and the ability to resolve this sign into its elements only comes with special practice and a gradual acquisition of knowledge. The clang of the violin is characteristic of the violin, the clang of the piano characteristic of the piano, and the unitariness of the object suggests a unitary apprehension of its clangs. This view is certainly incorrect. For (*a*) it has never been observed that the reference of a clang to an object ceases at the moment when some one of its overtones becomes audible. (*b*) Again, the musician, who is familiar with instruments, is better able, as a general rule, to analyse

their clangs than the unmusical person, whose ignorance may entirely prevent him from referring a given clang to a particular instrument. (*c*) Again, it does not follow that because one overtone is audible, all the rest are at once perceived, although the connection of the clang is broken by the first step in its analysis and its reference to an object thereby made impossible. (*d*) And lastly, the principle is in any case inadequate to the unitariness of total impression in a compound clang, in which, nevertheless, precisely the same phenomena recur, with a simple difference of quantity. (ii) Helmholtz subsequently gave up this view for another, in which the problem of the clang is inverted. Instead of seeking reasons for the unitariness of the impression, he now attempts to explain the possibility of its analysis. The explanation hinges upon the alleged empirical fact, that if overtones are to be analysed out of a clang, they must previously have been perceived separately. But it follows from what we have already said of the purity of overtones when heard (§ 43. 4) that this rule is not without exceptions; and in any case it would apply only to a portion of the phenomena under consideration (§ 47. 8).

5. (iii) Another view makes the clang the psychical resultant of simultaneous nervous stimuli, one or other of which may be brought to perception by a special direction of the attention. We need not here enter into the question whether this interpretation of the facts is adequate as a theory of tonal fusion itself. It is preferable, in any event, to consider the clang simply as a particular form or degree of the general phenomenon of fusion. (iv) And lastly, an attempt has quite recently been made to explain clang colour by the ascription of an analogous characteristic, tone colour, to simple tones. The difference between a dull and a clear clang can only be explained, it is urged, by the attribution of a certain clearness or dulness to the separate tones. Tone colour varies with tone pitch, and the resultant of the colours of the individual tones is clang colour. Such a view obviously gives up all the advantages of the concept of fusion. The character of the total impression is necessarily different from that of the separate components; and a unitariness of certain clangs is implicit in the very idea of fusion, since fusion, according to circumstances, has all degrees, up to a complete impossibility of analysis. But the fact that a sensation cannot be qualitatively analysed out of a complex of impressions can never be interpreted to mean that it is not present: each of the components must be imagined to contribute a certain share to the total impression. All the separately imperceptible overtones of a clang contribute something, as their intensity and quality allow, to the perception of the whole; and

the sum of these contributions constitutes what we call clang colour.

6. We are thus led by our discussion of the clang to the consideration of an important fact of general psychology, that of the co-operation of unnoticed components in the total effect of a connection of conscious processes. We might, perhaps, use the word *unconscious* to denote these components, and so find a place for the term, which we have hitherto avoided, in our description of psychical phenomena. Nothing could be objected to this usage if the observations which we are here describing had furnished the sole reason for the origination and application of the concept. As ordinarily employed, however, it includes processes, whose very existence is not attested by introspection, but which are merely the results or the postulates of certain philosophical reflections. Some authors, *e.g.*, have urged the necessity of a 'pure' psychology,—and 'pure' psychological exposition and discussion require the aid of unconscious intermediaries; others have interpreted the principle of psychophysical parallelism to mean that an unbroken chain of psychical processes must be correlated with the uninterrupted continuum of physical. The 'unconscious' which is reached in this way is not only unknown to introspection as a specific process, but does not either betray its existence by any sort of modification of the material of perception. For ourselves, who believe that an empirical psychology must and can hold aloof from the acceptance of any such metempirical concept, an 'unconscious' is only possible in the sense of a constituent of a connection of elements, which contributes something to the total impression, but is not separately perceptible. The 'unconscious', in this meaning of the word, is characteristic of the activity of two processes, fusion and attention (§ 76. 3). Just as in the clang the various overtones which accompany the fundamental combine to form a total impression (clang colour), the cognition of whose individual constituents presents more or less of difficulty, so in the consciousness of a given moment all those various processes upon which the attention is not directed constitute an unanalysed whole, the background, as it were, of the favoured process placed at the fixation point of attention.

7. Clang colour is not the only normal instance of a dependency of tonal fusion upon the relative intensity of the components. The same phenomenon can be observed (2) in compound clangs, in which the simple clangs that carry the melody are made especially intensive. When an air is sung to a continuous harmonic accompaniment, the voice stands out most clearly in virtue of its relative intensification, while the tones accompanying it combine to form a

total impression which is comparatively little analysed. We may, therefore, lay it down as a general rule that a fusion is more complete, the greater the relative difference of the component intensities. (3) Another instance is furnished by what are called *combination tones*, which are of two kinds: *difference* tones and *summation* tones. The vibration rate of the former is given by the difference between the vibration rates of the primary tones, that of the latter by their sum. Thus, if two tones are given whose vibration rates are 256 and 384, we shall have a difference tone of 128 and a summation tone of 640. Both, and the summation tones in particular, are relatively weak. Hence they were not discovered until very late,—the difference tones in the eighteenth and the summation tones in the present century. Nothing is known with certainty of their objective origination. Helmholtz, it is true, has shown by calculation that both kinds of combination tones are produced by the interference of two different tone waves. But we do not know in what relation these secondary waves stand to the auditory apparatus; and the fact that difference tones can be fairly distinctly heard where the primary tones are relatively weak is an indication that the condition of their production is not to be looked for simply and solely in the formation of resultant vibrations,—which are only set up when the primary sound waves are intensive. It has, therefore, been recently suggested that the difference tones are in reality *beat tones*, *i.e.*, tones arising from the recurrence of beats at a certain rapidity. *Beats* (§ 14. 3) are intensive fluctuations, which are perceived with especial clearness when the difference between the vibration rates of the primary tones is but slight. Their number tallies exactly with this difference of vibration rate, since the maxima and minima of intensity, the waxing and waning of the tone, are dependent for their frequency upon the periods of the two sound waves. If the difference is increased, the rate of succession of the intensive fluctuations will also be increased, and we may ultimately have a third tone whose pitch is defined by the number of beats in the second.

8. If the vibration rates of the two beating tones are but slightly different, we ordinarily hear a single tone which sounds alternately stronger and weaker. With a more considerable difference of vibration rates, we sense the separate tones, their beats, and also a new, third tone. This tone cannot be termed either a beat tone or a difference tone, as its vibration rate lies midway between the rates of the primary waves. It appears to suffer most of all from the fluctuations in intensity. We may conjecture (and the conjecture is in accordance with auditory theory) that the tone arises from a co-excitation of the parts of the

auditory apparatus lying midway between the sensory fibres which subserve the perception of the primary tones.

In all probability, difference tones are differently originated from beat tones. There are various reasons for this view. (*a*) Difference tones are relatively distinct in consonant intervals which give no perceptible beats. (*b*) Difference tones require for their production an equal absolute intensity of the primary tones, whereas a difference of this absolute intensity is the most favourable condition for the formation of beat tones. It has been similarly conjectured that summation tones are simply high overtones, and not new formations. But the most recent observations seem to show that they are clearly audible under circumstances which hardly admit of the origination of noticeable overtones. Thus, if the primary tones stand in the ratio 1 : 10, the tenth overtone of the lower clang will be hardly perceptible, and yet a tone corresponding to its relative vibration rate, 11, is heard with comparative distinctness when the two are sounded together. There are also summation and difference tones of the second, third, etc., order, in addition to those of the first order which we have mentioned hitherto. A difference tone of the second order is produced when the difference tone of the first order forms a difference tone with one of the primaries. The combination tones of these higher orders are not always weaker than those of the first order. We cannot here enter into the further details of the subject.

§ 46. The Dependency of Tonal Fusion upon the Number of the Components.

1. In the previous Section we confined ourselves as far as possible to cases of the fusion of two components, although the instances of a fundamental with its overtones, and of two primaries with their combination tones, took us beyond the limit of composition of the simple musical interval. So far, however, we have only been interested to determine the influence of intensity in these connections. We must now enter upon a systematic investigation into the changes of fusion degree caused by the addition of a third tone, of approximately equal absolute intensity, to the two tones constituting an interval. A tonal connection which consists of more than two simultaneously sounding tones is called a chord. It is of especial importance to discover whether the influence of the number of components is dependent upon the purity of the selected tones, in other words, whether it is modified in any way by clang colour. It seems to follow from the observations of Stumpf and

of the author, as well as from the facts of musical practice, that the clang colour of the fundamentals contained in a chord is ordinarily indifferent. The rule is at least so far true, that the relations obtaining between fusion and number of components in different compound clangs remain relatively the same; although the degree of fusion, absolutely regarded, is usually higher in clangs than in simple tones. This fact simplifies our investigation very considerably. The problem reduces itself to that of the relative modification of the various degrees of tonal fusion by the number of components. In particular cases, where certain overtones are very intensive, the degree of fusion will be dependent, of course, upon the quality of these overtones, as well as upon the number of the fundamentals; but such cases are exceptional.

2. If we strike on the piano the notes *c-g-c'* in the middle region of the tonal scale, we have fusions of octave and fourth for the upper *c'*, of octave and fifth for the lower *c*, and of fifth and fourth for the *g*. Each of the tones seems more distinct in this connection than in the simple intervals *c-c'* or *c-g*. On the other hand, *g* and *c'* are heard more distinctly in the interval *g-c'* than in the chord. It is the same with the connection *f-g-d'*. Here we have fusions of second and sixth for *f*; the tone is less distinct than in the interval *f-g*, and more distinct than in the interval *f-d'*. For *g* we have fusions of second and fifth; the tone is clearer than in the fifth *g-d'*, and less clear than in the second *f-g*. From these and similar facts we may draw the general conclusion that where more than one interval is given *a mean degree of fusion* is the result. The better fusion seems able partly to compensate the worse, and the worse partly to offset the better. This fact is of great importance for musical effect; the dissonant intervals are made far less harsh by combination, and can thus be employed with greater æsthetic advantage. For instance, the chord of the sixth, *d-f-g-b* (the ordinary inversion of the chord of the seventh) shows but little trace of the unpleasant roughness of the fusion of the second.

3. The same law obtains beyond the limits of the octave that holds within it. The combination of several tones or clangs gives rise to a mean degree of fusion, the resultant of the fusion degrees predicable of the component intervals as such. If the number of components is at all largely increased, an extraneous factor intervenes to prevent analysis,—the narrow range of our attention, *i.e.*, our inability to observe and judge a large number of simultaneous processes with any degree of uniformity. We therefore restrict our inquiry into the influence of the number of components upon fusion to the simplest case of a con-

nection of three tones or clangs. Here, too, we can naturally hope to discover really valid laws only when we have made accurate quantitative measurements of the degrees of fusion. In all probability the number of components will then be found to admit of very considerable increase, since the capacity of analysis must be specially tested for all the separate constituents of the connection. A procedure which might be serviceable in this regard would consist in the determination of the intensity which a component must possess if it is to be heard out from its connection. At present, the application of any such method is prevented by the difficulties in the way of a practicable objective measurement of tonal intensity.

4. The clang, again, furnishes one of the best illustrations of a fusion of several tones. We have already spoken of the influence of relative component intensity in the connection of fundamental and overtones (§ 45). But it is beyond all question that the difficulty which certain of the latter present to analysis is not wholly attributable to their relative weakness, but is partly due to the high degrees of fusion which occur among the overtones themselves, or at least among the first few of them. The ratios of the vibration rates of fundamental and successive overtones are expressed, of course, by the series of simple whole numbers, $1 : 2 : 3 : 4 : 5 : 6$, etc. (cf. § 14). The first half-dozen overtones obviously stand upon a high level of fusion: we have the octave, fifth, fourth, major and minor thirds, twelfth, etc. This also explains the fact that certain overtones can be more distinctly heard than others: they fuse less perfectly with the fundamental, the predominant tone in the clang (cf. § 45. 3). Stumpf asserts that the degree of fusion of two clangs is the same with that of two tones, whose pitch is that of the fundamentals of the clangs. But the view is not borne out by facts. (α) A simple comparison of an interval as given by the tuning forks with the same interval as composed of the clangs of two flue-pipes shows that clang fusion is greater than tonal fusion. (β) Moreover, the fusion of two clangs of equal pitch of fundamental but different clang colour is by no means identical with the fusion of two clangs of the same fundamental and like clang colour, or with that of simple and qualitatively similar tones. In the two latter cases, the fusion is simply intensive, and it is altogether impossible to analyse the total impression into its components, or at least (in the instance of the clangs) to separate the two fundamentals; in the first case, the fundamentals can be easily held apart in perception. In a unison of instruments of different clang colour the individual clangs may quite well be distinguished, despite the likeness of their fundamentals. And a clang octave, in the same way, seems to fuse

decidedly better than a tone octave. [1]   All these examples tell against Stumpf's view.

5. Compound clangs are said to be 'related' when the fundamental of one constituent coincides with an overtone of the other, when both contain one or more identical overtones, or when both are referable to a common fundamental. In the first two cases we speak of a *direct*, in the latter of an *indirect clang relationship*. The degree of direct clang relationship is proportional to the number and intensity of the coincident overtones. As the intensity of the overtones decreases with increase of the number denoting their place in the series, direct relationship will be noticeable only in clangs the vibration rates of whose fundamentals are expressible by small whole numbers. And as the number of coincident overtones decreases with increase of the distance of the first coincident pair from their fundamentals, the degree of direct clang relationship will be here determined by the nearness of the common overtones, *i.e.*, again, by the smallness of the numbers expressing the vibration rates of the two fundamentals. Indirect clang relationship is proportional to the nearness of the common fundamental to the fundamentals of the two related clangs. This definition, again, makes the degree of relationship dependent upon the magnitude of the numbers giving the vibration rates of the fundamentals ; a common fundamental must obviously lie nearer to clangs whose ratio is 2 : 3 than to clangs whose ratio is 5 : 6, etc. It is evident that the series of degrees of clang relationship, obtainable by these criteria, is very similar to the series of grades of tonal fusion referred to above (§ 44. 2).

6. Indeed, the earlier theorists (Helmholtz [2] and Wundt in particular) have used the principle of clang relationship to explain the musical value of consonance and dissonance, harmony and disharmony, with or without simultaneous reference to the unpleasantness of the beats in dissonant intervals (cf. § 48. 2, 3). But there are several indications that it is not adequate to the phenomena. (i) The consonance or dissonance of simple tones, and of clangs of different clang colour, is precisely analogous to that of clangs of the same instrument.

---

[1] If tuning forks are used, I am always able to cognise the two tones in the interval of the octave, while I am sometimes deceived by clangs with numerous overtones. This is perfectly natural, since the first overtone in a clang is the octave of the fundamental, so that when the octave clang is given, this overtone is merely intensified, and no new quality introduced with the total impression.

[2] It is irrelevant to the course of the present discussion that the two degrees of clang relationship recognised by Helmholtz are only partially identical with those distinguished by Wundt (who is followed in the text), and that Helmholtz employs them principally for the explanation of clang sequence.

This can hardly be explained by the rules of clang relationship. We should expect, according to them, that intervals composed of pure tones, and consequently containing no common overtones, would either not be consonant or dissonant at all, or would differ radically from clang intervals in their musical effect; and that clangs of different clang colour, whose overtones differ in number, quality and intensity, would vary very considerably in their harmonic or disharmonic character. As was said above, this is not the case. (ii) The series of fusion grades is not in complete agreement with the series of degrees of clang relationship; and if the intervals about which they differ are judged by the standard of musical importance, the fusion series undoubtedly has the advantage. Thus the clangs of the twelfth are more closely related than those of the double octave. In the former, the first and second overtones of the higher clang coincide with the third and sixth of the lower; in the latter, the first and second of the higher with the fourth and eighth of the lower. On the other hand, the double octave possesses a higher degree of fusion than the twelfth. And there can be no question that it is regarded in music as the more consonant interval. Or again: there is scarcely any difference in clang relationship between the clangs of the minor third and those of the minor seventh. In the former, the sixth overtone of the deeper clang coincides with the fifth of the higher; in the latter, the seventh overtone of the deeper with the fourth of the higher. But the minor third is a distinctly better fusion than the minor seventh. Here again, musical harmonics are on the side of fusion. (iii) Lastly, the degrees of clang relationship, and more particularly those of indirect relationship, seem to be intellectual constructions rather than sensible relations. As there are no such things as undertones, the common fundamental, the nearness or remoteness of which determines the degree of indirect clang relationship, can only be given as a difference tone or as a concomitant tone sensation associatively excited. These tones are invariably too weak, as the common overtones also very frequently are, to furnish a satisfactory theoretic basis for the obvious differences of harmony and disharmony.

7. An especial importance attaches to the two great chord systems at present employed in polyphonic music, the major and the minor, or, as they were originally called, hard and soft (Germ. *dur* and *moll*). As at first applied, these names did not refer to a difference in the compound clangs, but were simply different terms in musical nomenclature, indicating a difference of scale. The sequence *f-g-a-♮b* (*b durum*) was designated hard; and the sequence *f-g-a-♭b* (*b molle*) soft. It is evident that the two words were primarily used in quite

different meanings from those which they bear in modern music; and
it is important to keep this fact in mind when we are tempted to
draw an inference from the original names to the character and
musical effect of the chords. If we compare the pure sensible relations of the major chord, c-e-g, with those of the minor chord,
c-$?e$-g, we find as a matter of fact, that the total impression is harsher,
less 'soft', in the latter case than in the former. The minor chord is
evidently a worse fusion than the major (cf. the results of experiments
upon their reaction times, quoted above, § 43. 8). On the relationship theory, this difference of major and minor is referred to the
differences of direct and indirect relationship. The first common
overtone of c-e-g is the ninth overtone of g, *i.e.*, lies three octaves and
a third above the fundamental of the highest clang. The first common
overtone of c-$?e$-g is the third overtone of g, *i.e.*, lies a double octave
above it. The distances of the common fundamentals of the two
chords from c stand in the reverse relation. As the degree of direct
clang relationship is ordinarily more important than that of indirect,
it would follow that the minor chord, whose clangs are more closely
related directly, is the better harmony. This conclusion, again, is not
borne out by the facts. At the same time, the laws of tonal fusion
do not either furnish any valid explanation of the difference of major
and minor, except on the assumption (which is no more than an
assumption) that the serial order of the degrees of tonal fusion, *i.e.*,
the pitch of their separate components, has a determining influence
upon the total impression. For we have precisely the same grades of
fusion in the connection c-$?e$-g that we have in the major chord
c-e-g. The only difference is, that the minor third comes first in the
minor, and the major third first in the major. The assumption
would, therefore, be that the degree of fusion of a chord varies with
the position of its constituent degrees of fusion within the tonal
scale; decreasing when the worse degrees are the lower, and increasing
when they are the higher.

§ 47. Other Conditions and Phenomena of Tonal Fusion.

1. (1) (*a*) The analysis of a connection of two tones is so far
dependent upon the *distance* which separates them upon the tonal
scale that their discriminability ceases at a certain lower limit of difference of vibration rate. It is noteworthy that the difference limen
is considerably larger for simultaneous than for successive tones. In
this regard, however, individual differences are especially marked. Unmusical persons have been found who were incapable of analysing

an interval composed of two tones more than an octave apart. It cannot, of course, be said without qualification that the facility of analysis of two tones is directly proportional to the difference between them. Such a rule would not be reconcilable with the existence of qualitative degrees of fusion (§ 44. 2, 4). Here as elsewhere, different factors cross one another (cf. § 46. 4), and their special influence cannot always be traced in the particular case. At the same time, the fact that the qualitative sensible discrimination is diminished when the stimuli are simultaneously given points unequivocally to the validity of the general concept of fusion.

2. Many persons hear the same tone differently with the two ears, although they remain ignorant of the fact as long as the difference of quality does not exceed a certain limit. The abnormality (*diplacusis*) may be restricted to a single ear, may be transitory or chronic, and may be confined to definite parts of the tonal scale or co-extensive with it. Stumpf found that the difference between two tuning forks held to the two ears might be increased to twelve vibrations, if beats were avoided (*i.e.*, if the tones were kept at a comparatively low intensity), before the difference of pitch became noticeable. The purity of the impression was not markedly impaired until the difference had reached twenty vibrations. The limen in the middle region of the tonal scale (where the experiments were made) would accordingly amount to some sixteen vibrations, *i.e.*, would be about fifty times as great as the limen for successive tones. The absolute sensible discrimination appears to decrease continuously under these conditions with increase of pitch, while the relative increases from the lower to the middle region and decreases from the middle region upward. It is very desirable that the observations should be systematically repeated. [1] A curious point which they have brought to light is the fact that the discrimination of simultaneously sounded tones which lie near one another on the scale is easier with clangs containing numerous overtones than with simple tones. This divergence from the rule (§ 46. 4) must probably be referred to the mediation of noticeable differences by the more intensive overtones of the clangs.

3. (*b*) Under the head of *spatial relations* we may consider the dependency of the analysis of a tonal fusion upon the localisation of its separate components. We have, of course, no auditory space in the sense that we have a visual and tactual space (§ 4. 3); the spatial element in an auditory perception is simply an associatively aroused idea of the direction and distance, *i.e.*, of the locality, of the source

---

[1] Occasional experiments of my own have afforded a general confirmation of Stumpf's results.

of sound. This idea may be definitely visual or tactual; or it may be the unanalysed substrate of an 'immediate judgment' (cf. § 62. 2). As difference of localisation does not carry with it an actual spatial separation of the tones, its influence may very well be investigated, without prejudice to the character of the fusion as such. The result of inquiry is to put it beyond all doubt that the analysis of a tonal fusion is greatly facilitated by a different localisation of its components. Thus, we can follow the separate clangs in orchestral music much more easily if we have our eyes fixed upon the instrument from which they proceed, while in the absence of any such artificial aid to analysis, *e.g.,* if the eyes are closed, the harmonic impression of the whole is far more vivid and distinct. Stumpf had an unmusical subject, who almost invariably judged two piano tones to be one, however wide their separation on the scale and however dissonant their character; though with successive stimulation by tones taken from the middle region he could generally form a correct estimate of the difference of pitch. If two forks were held to his two ears, he could cognise the separate tones in all intervals greater than the major third. It seemed, therefore, that sensible discrimination was assisted by divergent localisation. We cannot, however, say with any degree of certainty how far this whole phenomenon was due to direction of the attention, or, consequently, how far it is attributable to divergent localisation.

4. (*c*) Two points call for notice under the rubric of *temporal relations.* (i) In the first place, simultaneity of the components in consciousness is the *conditio sine qua non* of fusion in general. (ii) The dependency of fusion upon the duration of the tones has not been thoroughly investigated. We know that the qualitative sensible discrimination is essentially determined by the duration of the tonal stimulus (§ 15. 4). As a general rule, two vibrations are necessary if the impression is to be anything more than that of a mere noise, and about sixteen if the clearness of the tonal perception is to be maximal. These facts must certainly be of importance for fusion and analysis. (*d*) The influence of *partial tonal change, i.e.,* of continuous or discrete intensive and qualitative variation of a tone or clang within a connection of tones or clangs, is similar to that of differences of localisation. Everyone must have noticed how strongly the attention is attracted in a concert by the voice which carries the melody. The singer's voice, even if comparatively weak, can be heard without special effort above a full orchestral accompaniment, in passages where it alone has to rise and fall, to execute trills and runs. The fact that the same voice is obscured at once, if it is allowed to rest upon a single note, shows that the phenomenon is not wholly explicable by the

mere alteration of the degree of fusion. Nor is it a simple consequence of the analysing function of the attention. It is hardly possible to single out the particular voice from a steadily continuous compound clang with the utmost strain of the attention. But let the voice move, while the accompaniment remains stationary, and the attempt will be immediately successful. Partial tonal change, then, must be regarded as an independent factor in fusion analysis.

5. There is, therefore, a good psychological reason for the musical rule that the voice which carries the melody shall move differently from the clangs which form the accompaniment. Where, for some cause, the tempo of both is precisely similar, the melody is marked off from the concomitant harmonies by a relative intensification of its tones.—Another observation which belongs here is the following. The *reflected tones* which we notice in passing by an echoing wall or walking through an avenue of trees, etc., are more distinct if the distance of the reflecting surface varies, *i.e.*, if the tones themselves are subject to slight alteration of intensity and quality. It is a probable conjecture that the Oreads and Dryads of mythology had their origin in the observation of these reflected tones. Difference tones also become more distinct when the primary tones are subject to slight fluctuation, and they themselves consequently undergo qualitative alteration.

This influence of partial change makes itself felt in other sense departments: the relatively mobile constituents in a visual idea, *e.g.*, are more easily noticed than the relatively stationary components. We may, therefore, look upon it as a principle of general psychological importance. It is not improbable that the conditions of its origination lie far back in the course of organic evolution.

6. (2) We pass now to a brief discussion of the *general* conditions of tonal fusion. (*a*) Most important of these is the *attention*. The influence of attention upon the perception of a sensation complex is ordinarily stated as though its function were exclusively analytical. Now there can be no doubt that the direction of the attention upon the particular tones in a compound clang is the most favourable and the most frequent condition of their individual analysis. But attention will serve equally well (in the author's observation) to intensify or focus the total impression of the fusion, to bring the given interval as such more vividly before consciousness. It is, therefore, as incorrect to ascribe a purely analytical function to attention as it would be to look upon all analysis simply as its effect. The question before us is accordingly the question of the actual nature of the influence of attention. We will look at a few typically different cases, and attempt

to abstract from them a general idea of the operation of this factor.

7. (i) The first case to mention is that of the analysis of particular tones or clangs. We make an effort, perhaps, to distinguish one of several equally intensive clangs. If all are weak, we notice that the constituent to which the attention is turned is intensified. If all are moderately strong, it is again relatively intensified, though not absolutely: it seems rather that the other tones or clangs, upon which the attention is not directed, are weakened. Where the constituents are of unequal intensity, it is possible by concentration of the attention upon a weaker component to make it stand out against the stronger,—again by way of a marked intensification. In this manner, individual overtones can be analysed from the clang which contains them, and successively brought to consciousness. The analysis is facilitated by the choice of a definite order in which the overtones shall be taken. (ii) The second case which we have to mention consists in the attentive perception of a tonal connection. If a note is struck upon the piano, it is possible (in the author's experience) by a suitable direction of the attention to single out whole intervals and chords from among the overtones of the clang. Here again, the tonal complex which is specially distinguished seems to be relatively intensified. On the other hand, it is exceedingly easy to bring out the total impression of a fusion by aid of the attention, if any special direction of it upon particular constituents is avoided. The most striking fact here is that the whole as such obtains an increased capacity of reproduction, *i.e.*, that it becomes effective for reproduction as a unitary idea. The influence of attention is thus seen to be exercised in two directions: it may either relatively intensify the particular constituent upon which it is directed, or increase the capacity of a constituent or of the total connection reproductively to determine the course of ideation.

8. (*b*) The influence of *practice* and *fatigue* must also be noticed. Practice, like attention, may be operative in either direction—to facilitate the analysis of a fusion or to prepare the way for the apprehension of the total impression. We have already spoken of the great importance of experience, of familiarity with the individual tones, for the analysis of a clang or compound clang, and of the hypothesis suggested by it—that the constituents of a tonal connection, if they are to be distinguished at all, must previously have been perceived separately (§ 45. 4). This theory is no more adequate than another, which refers ease of analysis to a reproduction of similar sensations. It is rather true, as a general rule, that practice assists the apprehension both of sensations and of their connections, the separate or conjoint perception

of simultaneous impressions. The assistance consists, primarily, in an increased facility and accuracy in the assignment of the material of perception to its place within the circle of ideas, present or available (cf. § 5. 9). We must distinguish between general and special practice. General practice does not of itself qualify the hearer to understand and accept the novel and strange chords which modern composers not infrequently employ to the surprise even of the musical ear. *Fatigue* is apt to retard the work of analysis. It is far more difficult to distinguish the individual tones in a clang or to reduce a compound clang to its simpler constituents when the mind is fatigued than when it is fresh. The effect of fatigue, therefore, seems to be restricted to the increase of fusion degree, to the reinforcement of the unitariness of the total impression.

9. (*c*) *Expectation* and *Habituation.*—*Expectation*, in the sense of a preparatory attention to particular components of a coming total impression, is a further aid to analysis. It very frequently takes the form of internal song, *i.e.*, the soundless innervation of the larynx to the position required for the production of a certain tonal quality. Some psychologists have supposed that the recollection of tones is altogether dependent upon the occurrence of this motor excitation. The hypothesis affords another instance of the exaggerated emphasis of a single important condition (cf. 8, above). We find no difficulty in recollecting tones whose pitch far exceeds the limits of our own singing voice; and tones are far less accurately discriminated by help of the voice than they can be by memory. Equally untenable is the view which makes the function of the *tensor tympani* or *stapedius* of determining importance for expectation. It is quite true that strain sensations of more or less distinctness are aroused in the ear under the influence of expectation. But an accurate preparatory attention to tones of determinate quality is found to be compatible with absence of the tympanic membrane. Expectation also serves to bring the impression of the harmony as such into clearer relief. Here again, *i.e.*, it manifests itself as a particular form of the attention; capable, like attention itself, of influencing the perception of a tonal fusion in both directions. *Habituation* has a precisely similar effect. It lends an added distinctness to the total impression or to the individual constituents of a connection, according as one or other has been the object of repeated judgment or perception. A particular consequence of habituation is the formation of a tendency to mediate judgments. If we know the composition of a compound clang, we say at once that it is a combination of simple clangs, without having actually analysed the sensible relations in the particular case.

10. (3) It only remains to call attention to certain *peculiarities of the impression* produced by a tonal fusion which have not been referred to in the previous Sections. Stumpf asserts that the pitch of a steadily continuous compound clang is the pitch of its lowest tone, even though this is not absolutely the most intensive constituent. Thus, if the deeper tone in the octave be suppressed, perception seems to spring across to the higher tone, whereas the silencing of the higher note makes no essential difference in sensation. The phenomenon recurs, though less distinctly, in other intervals, in direct proportion to their fusion degree.—As a matter of fact, the rule only holds (in the author's experience) for stimulation by clangs containing numerous overtones. The suppression of the fundamental clang is naturally far more prejudicial to the total sensation effect than the silencing of a higher clang, whose fundamental coincides with some more or less distinct overtone of the lower. It is, however, noteworthy in this regard that where high and low tones are sounded together, the high suffer more by a relative intensification of the low than *vice versa*.

Again, the apparent difference of pitch between the components of a connection varies with the nature of the interval which it represents. As a general rule, the distance between two tones seems to be lessened when they are sounded together; but an interval of low fusion degree and of slight difference of vibration rate may appear larger than one of a higher fusion degree and a greater objective difference of components. To an unmusical ear, *e.g.*, the second may appear larger than the third, and the third than the fifth. It is plain that ease of analysis is here made the criterion of difference.—The influence of fusion upon sensible discrimination is also seen in the ease with which clangs or noises of indefinite pitch accommodate themselves to other impressions of more definite character which are given with them. Orchestral music employs only two kettledrum clangs, which are a fifth apart. The dissonances which inevitably arise (as they do with the triangle and the bass drum, for similar reasons) are rarely remarked, because the compensatory influence of fusion reduces the differences for perception.

§ 48. Theory of Tonal Fusion.

1. Very different principles have been adduced in explanation of the facts set forth in the present Chapter. Before it was recognised that the musical relations of consonance and dissonance, harmony and disharmony could be brought under the general rubric of fusion, theory was simply concerned to account for the agreeableness or dis-

agreeableness of the various intervals, or to deduce the differences of musical concord from purely intellectual conditions. Thus Euler spoke of an unconscious counting by the mind, and believed that the simplicity of the numbers expressing the relative vibration rates of the tones in different intervals exercised a definite influence upon their perception, their harmonic or inharmonic impression. This view has been recently revived by Lipps, who seeks to give it a psychological foundation by instancing the facility with which two movements can be executed together when the rapidity of one is a simple multiple of that of the other, and the rapidly increasing difficulty presented by more complicated ratios. The nature of an interval as harmonic or inharmonic is thus determined by some sort of unconscious mental reaction upon the simple or complex relations of its component vibration rates.·

2. It is evident enough that the affective value of the different musical intervals was the first consideration in the framing of this theory. But it does not enable us to give any quantitative expression to that value. The analogy of the execution of movements in different rhythms breaks down as soon as we attempt to apply it. For if it held, very considerable difficulty ought to be experienced even with the ratio 2 : 3, and this considerable difficulty should quickly become excessive with increasing complication. This is not confirmed, of course, by the actual pleasingness or displeasingness of the intervals. And the hypothesis is inadequate on other grounds. It makes no attempt to explain the different sensible relations of the perfect and imperfect consonances and of the dissonances. The connection between ratio of vibration rates and musical effect, upon which it insists so strongly, is at most the postulate of a theory, not the theory itself.

Very much the same may be said of the theory proposed by Helmholtz, who makes the presence or absence of beats in a fusion of different tonal qualities the cause of dissonance or consonance. A flickering light, an intermittent cutaneous stimulus, and the recurrence of beats in more or less rapid succession are all unpleasant. The objection has often been made that even if the explanation hold for dissonance, the definition of consonance remains purely negative. It is a more fundamental objection that the real problem has been altogether missed. Consonance and dissonance are not used primarily to denote the pleasant or unpleasant effect of a compound clang, but to specify the peculiar interrelations of sensations, *i.e.*, the unitariness or diversity of their total impression.

3. It was soon realised that explanations of this kind were inadequate to the great variety of musical effect. Subsequent theories have

for the most part drawn a sharp line of distinction between consonance and dissonance, on the one hand, and harmony and disharmony on the other, and have applied the principle of clang relationship in their explanation of the latter. It cannot be denied that the principle affords a real theory of musical harmonics, and a theory which covers a large proportion of the facts. But we have already shown that it, too, must be pronounced inadequate (§ 46. 6). Stumpf was the first to suggest that the musical categories had their psychological basis in the phenomena of tonal fusion (§ 43. 8). On this view, it is unnecessary to emphasise the distinction between consonance and harmony or dissonance and disharmony: both may be regarded as simultaneous connections of tones.—The influence of beats, again, cannot be disputed. They lessen the affective value of a compound clang and destroy the unitariness of its total impression. But they are not necessarily implied in dissonance, as is shown by the simple observation that equal degrees of dissonance may be connected with a very variable number and intensity of beats. And where a tone is heard differently by the two ears (*diplacusis*), the degree of dissonance is not diminished, although beats are altogether absent.

4. We find mention of the fusion of tones in Herbart's psychology. But the Herbartian concept is of metaphysical origin, and has a quite different meaning from that which we have given to the word fusion. When sensations which belong to a single continuum meet within the mind, Herbart says, they fuse with one another more or less intensively according to their degree of opposition. This degree of opposition is defined in terms of the semi-tones of the tempered scale (§ 43. 4). In the octave the relation of the components is that of complete antithesis, and the degree of fusion $1/12$ (the chromatic scale contains twelve tones within the octave). The degree of opposition in the remaining intervals is expressed by a fraction, whose denominator is the number of semi-tones from the fundamental to the limiting tone of the interval, and whose numerator is the number of steps between this tone and the octave of the fundamental. Herbart is thus led to the curious result, *e.g.*, that the degree of opposition in the fifth (expressed by $7/8$) is seven times as great as that in the second ($2/10 = 1/5$). Since fusion is inversely proportional to opposition, the octave is the worst and the second the best fusion. It is unnecessary to bring evidence for the statement that this entire view is in direct contradiction to the facts. Herbart has obviously confused two processes which we have learnt to keep sharply distinct,—sensible discrimination and fusion. It is true in general that the discriminability of successive tones increases with increase of the distance separating the qualities upon the tonal

scale. But in fusion other influences are at work, which largely compensate the differences of vibration rate.

5. It might be conjectured, from a purely psychological standpoint, that the similarity of two tones or clangs is the condition of their fusion. The rule would then be that the separability of two contents simultaneously present in consciousness is inversely proportional to their degree of similarity. There can be no doubt that this view is implicit in the principle of clang relationship: community of fundamental or of certain overtones simply expresses a certain similarity between the related clangs. But the theory of similarity, in this sense of partial identity, cannot account for the fusion of simple tones. Similarity may, therefore, be given a different meaning, which can be best illustrated, perhaps, by reference to the octave. No one will deny that two tones whose vibration rates stand in the ratio 1 : 2 make a very similar impression on consciousness. Whether a succession of clangs be played in a higher or lower octave makes very little difference to their perception. But on the other hand, there are no distinct degrees of similarity within the octave. And if it is suggested that the degree of fusion is a key to the degree of similarity, the question arises whether similarity is the condition of fusion or fusion the cause of the impression of similarity.

6. In view of the difficulty which thus attaches to a purely psychological explanation of the phenomena of fusion, Stumpf has insisted upon the necessity of a psychophysical theory. And the dependency of tonal fusion upon the quality of the components seems to justify his contention. The effects of attention, the influence of relative intensity, etc., refer us to conditions which obtain for all forms of conscious contents as simultaneously presented. But we have seen that the influence of the component qualities is shown in the appearance of wholly specific differences of fusion with alteration of the ratios of the vibration rates of the exciting stimuli in a definite direction. Stumpf has accordingly set up a hypothesis of *specific synergy*. There is a specific synergy for the octave, the fifth, the fourth, in short for all the different degrees of fusion, and its condition is given with the simultaneous occurrence of two specific excitations subserving the sensations of the tones composing the interval. Nothing more is gained by this formulation than the embodiment of the postulate of a psychophysical theory in a single phrase. In the existing state of our knowledge it seems impossible to read a concrete meaning into the notion of 'specific synergy'.

Literature :

C. Stumpf, *Tonpsychologie.* Vol. ii., 1890.

Cf. the literature cited under § 16.

CHAPTER II. THE FUSION OF OTHER THAN AUDITORY SENSATIONS.

§ 49. The Fusion of Colour Tone and Brightness.

1. The view that a colour impression is at least as simple a matter as an impression of white or gray or black, which we find current in the older psychologies, has in modern times given way to the conviction that every colour contains two qualities, a chromatic and an achromatic. Still more recent is the recognition that alteration in the brightness of a colour cannot be termed an alteration of its intensity, except by an application of the word intensity in a sense foreign to its usual meaning. There are three facts in particular which oblige us to regard a colour impression as a fusion of the two components colour tone and brightness. (*a*) The first is the peculiar modification of sensation by the continuous increase of the intensity of a homogeneous light." At the lowest degrees of intensity we have a brightness sensation, free from any trace of the stimulus colour. As the intensity increases, we get the impression of the colour." This colour sensation becomes increasingly clearer in tone, reaching the maximum of saturation at a certain intensity of stimulus. After this it grows less clear, and ultimately, at extreme degrees of intensity, loses its colour tone altogether, so that only a brightness sensation remains. The phenomena are practically the same for all colours, except that the tone varies in certain cases: continuous increase of brightness is accompanied at first by an increasing and then by a decreasing distinctness of the colour tone. There is no escape from the conclusion that colour tone and brightness are two different qualitative components in the total impression of a colour. And the inference is confirmed by the observation that the qualitative changes of brightness under these conditions are precisely the same as those which occur in pure brightness sensations.

2. (*b*) The second fact of importance is the comparability of the brightness of a colour with a pure brightness. As a general rule, it is very difficult to compare the intensities of different sensations (§ 42. 4). But recent experiments on the determination of the apparent brightness of a colour have shown that the selection of a gray of equal subjective brightness with a given colour is neither impossible nor so uncertain as might a priori be conjectured. This fact again points to the conclusion that what we call brightness in a colour is the same for sensation as the brightness of a white or gray. (*c*) And lastly, Purkinje's phenomenon (cf. § 19. 6) shows that colour tone and brightness are subject to different conditions in the different colours, and

that the total colour impression can hardly be explained except on the assumption of a fusion of the two qualities. Certain quite recent experiments, it is true, have given occasion to a different interpretation of this phenomenon,—to the notion of a specific brightness of colours, or to the hypothesis of an influence of the colour processes upon the brightness processes. At all events, the difference in the apparent brightness of different colours with objectively equal stimulus intensities again suggests that we are in the presence of a connection of different qualities.

3. The investigation of visual fusion is rendered especially difficult by our inability to separate out one of the components, colour tone, from its attendant brightness. Our inquiry into its facts and laws is, therefore, confined to the comparison of colour brightness with colour brightness or of colour brightness with brightness proper. The latter method tells us nothing of the alteration which a colour tone certainly undergoes even at the brightness most favourable for its saturation. The alternative method, on the other hand, can be applied in various directions: (α) we may determine the sensible discrimination for change in colour brightness with variation in the intensity of (as far as possible) homogeneous lights; (β) we may determine the sensible discrimination for the degrees of saturation of a colour with increase of the amount of its brightness component; or (γ) we may determine the relative brightness of colours with change of the absolute intensity of illumination. Experiments have been made in all three directions, though least extensively by the second method. The first and second methods have given results which can be assigned at once to a place within our doctrine of fusion; but the observations so far taken by the third method are of a character which does not allow of their subsumption with any degree of certainty to the general rules of fusion. It will be noticed that the facts with which we deal in the present section would be ordinarily discussed partly under the heading of 'intensity of colour sensation', and partly under that of 'colour saturation'. Our reasons for departing from the customary procedure have either been stated already (§§ 17—19) or will appear in the course of the Section itself.

4. (α) The sensible discrimination for the brightness of spectral colours has been found within certain limits to follow Weber's law. There is an approximate constancy for all colours of $\dfrac{S}{r} = \frac{1}{60}$. This value is considerably larger than the $\dfrac{S}{r} = \frac{1}{100}$ or less obtained under the most favourable circumstances for brightness sensations proper (cf. § 18. 4, 5).

We may, therefore, infer that the sensible discrimination for brightness is diminished when the compared brightnesses are connected with colour tones. It is also noteworthy that $\frac{S}{r}$ remains approximately the same for all colours. The fact affords confirmation of our hypothesis that the brightness factor in colour is identical throughout,—is the brightness sensation proper. The magnitude of $\frac{S}{r}$, on the other hand, seems to confirm the view that colour tone and brightness fuse with each other. At least, the reduction of sensible discrimination for brightnesses, when connected with colour tones, stands in complete accord with the results of qualitative fusion in other departments (§ 42. 2). Here, too, upper and lower deviations from Weber's law have been discovered, of the same character as those which occur in the pure brightness series: there is increase of the relative difference limen in either direction.

5. (β) Unfortunately, no systematic investigation has been made into the sensible discrimination for the degrees of saturation of a colour. All that has been attempted is a determination of the angular magnitude of a coloured sector sufficient to give a just noticeable colour tone to a rotating disc of black, gray, or white. These experiments contribute nothing definite to the solution of the fusion problem. It is especially desirable that the question be made the subject of an accurate and detailed experimental inquiry, for two reasons. (i) In the first place, the method allows of a direct determination of the clearness of colour tones. Tests of the sensible discrimination for colour brightnesses (the former method) have as their primary object the definition of the just noticeable change of brightness; and although the clearness of the colour tone may change with its brightness, the conditions of the experiment are too complicated to allow of any certain inference as to the dependency of, colour saturation upon intensive variation of the homogeneous light. Experiments should, therefore, be carried out on a different plan: a gray of the same brightness with that of the colour under examination must be added to the colour in increasing amounts, and the just noticeable degrees of saturation change recorded. In this way the apparent brightness would be kept constant, while the clearness of the colour tone itself or of the brightness sensation connected with it was altered step by step in a definite direction. (ii) But there is another purpose to be served by a detailed experimental investigation of sensible discrimination for degrees of colour saturation. The system of visual sensations is ordinarily represented by the figure of a double cone, a double

pyramid or a sphere. The equational plane of the sphere, *e.g.*, is formed by the colours circle, the periphery of which contains the saturated colours in their spectral order together with the purples connecting red and violet (cf. § 19. 3); the two poles correspond to the most brilliant white and the deepest black; and their line of junction passes through all degrees of the pure brightness sensation between its two limiting values. The meridians then represent the various changes produced in sensation by a simple intensive variation of a homogeneous light, or the degrees of saturation of a colour tone under the increasing influence of a very dark or very light colourless sensation. The lines connecting points upon the equator with various points on the line of junction of the two poles give the different degrees of saturation of brightness or colour tone between the two values taken. The double cone and double pyramid are used in precisely the same way. The base of the two cones is the colour circle, and their apices represent the most brilliant white and the deepest black. The base of the pyramid is formed by the triangle ordinarily employed to illustrate the phenomena of colour mixture (cf. § 17. 5, 6; Fig. 7) with the three primary colours at its three angles, and the points of the two pyramids denote the two limiting values of the brightness series. Now it is evident that these figures can have no concrete meaning until we know something positively of the laws governing degree of saturation. We cannot say anything of the length of the various lines, or even of the form of the whole tridimensional figure, until we have ascertained (by a test of sensible discrimination) the number of distinguishable degrees between any two limiting values. In any case, however, the figure could not represent the complete system of visual sensations, but would merely be a convenient illustration of the dependency of the analysis of colour tone and brightness upon the relative weight of either component.

6. It is sufficiently clear from these remarks that we cannot at present isolate the various factors which are of influence for visual fusion so accurately and completely as we could the conditions of tonal fusion. In the latter case, we could trace the individual influence of quality, intensity, and number of components. We cannot speak here of an influence of intensity, because there is no such thing as an intensity of visual sensation; and we cannot speak of the influence of number, because simultaneous light impressions which are spatially co-incident present but two qualities to analysis,—a colour tone and a certain brightness. The 'mixed' colours, as we saw above (§§ 17, 19), are just as simple in colour tone as the 'principal' colours.

There is, therefore, only one method by which an influence of visual quality upon fusion can be determined: we must ascertain the relation of different colour tones to the different degrees of the brightness series. (γ) A beginning has been made in this direction by experiments on the change of apparent brightness in different colours under the influence of change in the absolute intensity of illumination (the third method). Purkinje's phenomenon must be regarded as one of the observations which belong here, as it shows the brightness of different colours with a reduction of absolute illumination to the point at which the specific quality of the colour tone ceases to be cognisable.

7. We have already given a brief description of Purkinje's phenomenon (§ 19. 6). If the absolute brightness is reduced to the point just mentioned, the relative brightnesses of the different colours follow a quite different order from that in which they stand while the colour tone is perceptible. At a relatively high intensity of illumination the maximal brightness is reached by a yellow of about 605 $\mu\mu$; as the illumination decreases, it travels in the direction of green, up to about 535 $\mu\mu$. We may lay it down as a general rule that the more refrangible colours, from green onwards, gain, while the less refrangible colours, from red to yellow, lose in relative brightness with diminution of the absolute illumination, and *vice versa* if the absolute illumination is increased. Or, if we wish to express the fact in another way, we may say that red, orange and yellow have a positive, and green, blue and violet a negative brightness coefficient, while between yellow and green there must be a point of indifference at which brightness is independent of its attendant colour. Beyond a certain limit of illumination there is but very slight apparent alteration of colour brightness. It might be inferred from this that colour brightnesses are relatively constant at a certain maximal intensity: although the obscuration of Purkinje's phenomenon under these conditions may also be referred to the diminution of the absolute sensible discrimination with increasing stimulus intensity. It is noteworthy that the distribution of brightness in the spectrum at the lowest degree of intensity differs very little with different individuals, and in particular holds for the monochromatic (cf. § 20. 5) as well as for the normal eye, whereas the determination of relative colour brightness at higher intensities of illumination shows considerable differences as between different subjects.

§ 5o. Theory of Visual Fusion.

1. Certain of the facts which we have outlined in the foregoing Section have always been of crucial importance for the formulation of a general theory of visual sensation. The Purkinje phenomenon in particular cannot be interpreted on the Young-Helmholtz theory (§ 21) except by the aid of very complicated and improbable hypotheses of the nature of the primary sensations and their dependency upon the absolute stimulus intensity. We have already mentioned (§ 20. 6) that to a totally colour-blind eye the brightness of the various spectral colours at all degrees of absolute illuminative intensity are the same with those of the normal spectrum in Purkinje's experiment, *i.e.*, at the lower limit of intensity, at which the colour tones as such disappear. An unbiassed consideration of this fact cannot but lead to the conclusion that the brightness component in a colour impression is an independent factor, subject to special conditions. The theories of Hering and Wundt are both able to take account of it. Hering, indeed, finds one of the principal supports of his hypothesis in the coincidence of the monochromatic brightness sensations with the distribution of colour brightness at the lowest intensity in the normal spectrum. But Wundt's theory, with its distinction between the chromatic and achromatic excitations, is also adequate to the phenomena. It assumes that the intensive course of the two excitations is governed by different laws : the achromatic begins earlier than the chromatic, and rises approximately in a straight line, while the chromatic increases rapidly up to a certain limit, and then remains practically constant at the same level of intensity. Hence the chromatic excitation must reach a relative maximum at a certain moderate degree of intensity, on either side of which it grows relatively weaker. It is clear that this view is also adequate to the fact of a gradual increase in the intensity of homogeneous rays (§ 17. 3; § 49. 1).

2. Hering, however, goes on to assert that green and blue (the colours of assimilation) obscure the brightness of the total impression, while red and yellow (the colours of dissimilation) increase it. He does not offer any explanation of the manner in which this result is brought about. We might, perhaps, imagine that the assimilatory colours checked the dissimilation of the black-white substance, and that the dissimilatory enhanced it. The mutual independence of the two kinds of visual substance would then be given up for a partial dependency of the black-white upon the colour substances. As a matter of fact, an attempt has recently been made by Ebbinghaus to

remodel Hering's hypothesis upon these lines. On the new theory, all stimuli are dissimilative, *i.e.*, have a decomposing action upon the sensitive substance of the retina. But the brightness of a gray is not exclusively determined by its pure brightness component; it is the resultant of this and of the brightness values of simultaneous chromatic excitations, whatever they may be. The view is supported by a very remarkable observation. It is found that a gray which is procured by the mixture of complementary colours shows the same dependency upon the absolute intensity of illumination as is displayed by the two constituent colours under the conditions of Purkinje's experiment. Thus, if a gray obtained from red and green is made equally bright with the gray obtained from blue and yellow at a certain low intensity of illumination, it will appear distinctly darker than the second gray when the absolute illuminative intensity is increased. And the reverse effect is produced, if the two grays are made equal at a comparatively high intensity, and this is afterwards diminished. Ebbinghaus declares that the phenomena can only be understood on the assumption that the chromatic values, even when they are not perceptible as such, exert an influence upon the intensity of excitation of the achromatic. In his own words, the brightness of a gray is "originally derived from two sources: from the decomposition of the white substance, and from the decomposition of the (in some respects antagonistic) chromatic substances."

3. But even in this modified form the Hering theory is not altogether satisfactory. Ebbinghaus has furnished a possible explanation of the brightening effect of red and yellow; but his view does not account for the contrary influence of green and blue. If there is summation of the decomposition processes in all the visual substances, we can understand why the decomposition of a chromatic substance should make a certain positive contribution to the excitation of the white substance; but there is no ground for the assumption of a negative contribution, such as is required by the observations with blue and green. Indeed, if we probe a little deeper, it is not easy to see how either result is really explicable by the presuppositions of the theory. A ray of homogeneous light has but two attributes, period (wave length or vibration rate) and amplitude (energy or intensity). The most reasonable hypothesis would seem to be, then, that the chromatic excitation is dependent upon the former, and the achromatic upon the latter. It is hardly conceivable that the excitation in both kinds of visual substance is dependent upon both of the stimulus attributes, *i.e.*, as the theory declares, that increase of the decomposition process in one necessarily implies its greater or less increase in

the other. In other words, we cannot form any definite idea, in terms of physics and physiology, of the reinforcement of the brightness sensation by chromatic stimulation. Of course, this only adds to the difficulty of the observation of the brightness of complementary colours (cf. 5, below). But the point to be made here is, that the Hering theory as remodelled by Ebbinghaus is still inadequate to its explanation.

4. In the author's view, the Purkinje phenomenon is simply a phenomenon of fusion. The different colours have very different effects upon the perceptibility of the brightness connected with them. Unfortunately, we cannot say how their own cognisability is influenced by this attendant brightness (§ 49. 3), since brightness is as invariable in the colour impression as intensity in the ray of light. On the other hand, we know the nature of the pure brightness component in the colour impression from our own observation of colours at a low intensity of illumination and from the distribution of brightness in the colour-blind spectrum. As the apparent brightnesses are differently distributed in the spectrum when the separate colour tones are visible, we must suppose that the intermixture of colour quality exerts a definite influence upon the brightness of the total visual impression. Red and yellow are relatively bright colours, green and blue relatively dark; *i.e.*, in our own terminology, the impression of yellow or red enhances the quality of the pure brightness component in the fusion, while green and blue diminish its apparent brightness. Visual fusion is, accordingly, of an altogether different type from tonal fusion. The addition of colour to brightness not only renders the analysis of brightness more difficult, but alters the quality of the brightness component in a definite direction.

5. The difference between this view and that of Ebbinghaus is sufficiently plain. We regard the actual brightness of an impression as exclusively dependent upon the intensity of the homogeneous light; Ebbinghaus speaks of a contribution made to it by the colour components. We, therefore, are under no obligation to accept the physical and physiological difficulties which arise upon the other theory. Visual fusion would rather be analogous to those instances of tonal fusion in which fusion degree conditions an apparent alteration of quality (cf. § 47. 10). We found that an unmusical subject judged the interval of the second to be greater than the interval of the third, and the third greater than the fifth; a low degree of fusion was interpreted as a considerable difference of quality. So here, a brightness appears greater than it is, when connected with red and yellow, and less than it is, when combined with green and blue. There is one fact, however, which requires a definite physiological explanation,—the

constancy of the apparent brightness of the individual colours under constant conditions. The simplest hypothesis is furnished by Wundt's theory. Following it, we suppose that the different colours increase in colouring power and attain their maximal saturation at different rapidities, with equal increase of stimulus intensity. Red and yellow, *i.e.*, attain their maximal clearness at a relatively low intensity, while a relatively high intensity is necessary for the maximal saturation of green and blue. This view receives support from observations on the time required for the perception of the various colours with perfect clearness (cf. § 19. 5). And it is an obvious corollary that a gray obtained from complementary colours cannot remain constant with alteration of the absolute stimulus intensity, but must incline in the direction of one of the colour tones. We thus have a very simple explanation of Ebbinghaus' observation (2 and 3, above).

§ 51. The Fusion of Other Sensations.

1°. (1) We find instances of qualitative fusion in other sense departments than those of vision and audition. (*a*) We can hardly doubt, *e.g.*, that olfactory sensations fuse, though not so completely as to prevent analysis of the individual components. But no exact observations, to say nothing of experimental investigations, have as yet been made upon the question. The first requisite for the understanding of olfactory fusion, as for the theory of olfaction in general, is a knowledge of the adequate stimuli for the various olfactory qualities. (*b*) Certain phenomena of gustatory fusion have been observed. Thus a mixture of salt and sweet substances in solutions of appropriate saturation renders the analysis of either component difficult (or prevents it altogether) under conditions which exclude the possibility of chemical interaction. The same rule seems to apply to other gustatory substances, but the observations extant are not sufficiently numerous to prove its general validity. It is interesting to notice that contrast effects frequently occur when different gustatory stimuli are simultaneously applied to different parts of the tongue. Salt, *e.g.*, is relatively intensified by acid, and *vice versa*. It would appear, therefore, that both forms of sensible connection are possible within the sense of taste; a contrast, or at least an independence of the component sensations appearing with their spatial or temporal separation, and fusion arising with identity of spatial and temporal conditions. Quantitative results, however, must remain of doubtful value until we can attach an objective significance to the amount of gustatory substance contained in a solution (§ 12. 2, 4; § 24. 4).

2. (*c*) Fusion is impossible within either of the principal classes of cutaneous sensations, for two reasons: their spatial attributes admit of no other connection than colligation, and their qualitative unitariness prevents any combination of different qualities. There is only one fact to mention under this head: the preponderance of pain over the sensation qualities which it accompanies. If a pressure, cold, or heat stimulus is increased to the point of painfulness, the resultant impression is essentially the same. Pain is here regarded, of course, not as affective tone, but as a special quality of sensation (§ 10. 4).

(*d*) That there is something analogous to fusion in the sphere of the organic sensations is shown by the difficulty of their introspective analysis. We have seen that special experiments were required before anything positive could be discovered as to the quality and physical origination of the sensations of the 'muscle sense' (§ 22. 2). Even now we are by no means certain of the specific qualities of common and organic sensation, so difficult are they of analysis. We cannot doubt that practice, and the accuracy in the direction of the attention which practice brings, must always play an important part in their discrimination. But that these general factors are not the exclusive conditions of analysis is shown by the fact that a temporal separation of the constituents greatly facilitates their individual cognition.

(*e*) Lastly, there are certain other facts of fusion to mention in the department of auditory sensations. Considered as simultaneous impressions, the rustling of the wind, the hissing of steam, the roll of thunder, the roar of a salvo of artillery, the rumbling of a wagon, etc., must all be interpreted as fusions of simple noises (non-periodic vibrations) or of simple tones (uniting to form aperiodic vibrations) or of tones and noises.

3. (2) So far we have only spoken of connections of qualities within one and the same sense. We must now examine the simultaneous connections obtaining between qualities of different sense departments. Herbart proposed to call these connections 'complications' (§ 42. 4). They all seem to fall within the general meaning of the term fusion: *i.e.*, they give rise to a qualitative total impression, and are difficult of analysis into their individual constituents. The most favourable conditions are realised when the connection has become empirically associated to a definite idea, and when a single stimulus sets up simultaneous excitations in different sense organs. (*a*) Thus a gustatory substance often serves as a stimulus to the pressure sense of the buccal cavity and to the sense of smell, at the same time that it excites the organ of taste. This explains why the sense of taste is commonly accredited with so many qualities which reylal

belong to the sense of smell (§ 12. 1). Our customary foodstuffs (meats and many vegetables) are tasteless, and only obtain a gustatory value by the intermixture of salt, sugar, etc. Nevertheless, all these substances, which we actually discriminate by smell, are ordinarily regarded as possessed of special attributes for the affection of taste. The same holds of the 'taste' of a good cigar or a fine wine or a refreshing fruit. And the co-operation of the pressure sense is implied in many names for 'tastes': biting and burning tastes, mild and astringent flavours are certainly referable to its influence. In every case, the fusion is prejudicial to accurate analysis.

4. (*b*) Similar phenomena recur in the domain of cutaneous sensation. Pressure and temperature readily combine to a qualitative total impression. Light contact may be confused with a temperature stimulation, and *vice versa*. It has been inferred from these facts that the peripheral conditions of the origination of temperature sensations (heat or cold) must be identical with those of the production of pressure sensations. The conclusion is certainly incorrect. For (α) confusions of the kind are by no means uncommon elsewhere under similar conditions of stimulation; (β) recent investigations have proved that thermal sensations are excitable by simple mechanical pressure upon the skin; and (γ) there are many reasons for the separation of the peripheral apparatus of pressure and temperature (cf. §§ 10 and 11). To explain the observation we must rather suppose either that the sensations perceived are actually produced, or that the frequent connection of the two kinds of qualities prevents their cognition in the particular case. Another fact which might be alleged here is that cold weights seem heavier than warm weights of the same objective magnitude. But it is probable (§ 24. 3) that the wrong judgment can be adequately accounted for by the external conditions of stimulation.

5. The various 'qualities' of the sense of 'touch',—smoothness and roughness, bluntness and sharpness, hardness and softness,—may also be looked upon as phenomena of fusion. The components in every case are the sensations proceeding from friction of the articular surfaces, and sensations arising from pressure upon the skin. We have seen that these two classes of sensations are exceedingly similar in quality (cf. § 22), so that it is not surprising that their analysis dates from very recent investigations. We can best inform ourselves of the smoothness or roughness of an object by passing a sensitive portion of the skin to and fro upon it, *i.e.*, by moving over it at a uniform rate. If the movement is not noticeably obstructed, the surface is judged to be smooth; if contact is more or less often interrupted as the movement continues, the object appears uneven or rough.

In this case, the co-operation of the articular 'sensations of resistance' is at least as important for the accuracy of judgment as the succession of the stimuli affecting the particular cutaneous area. The articular sensations are of less importance for the apprehension of sharpness and bluntness, the discrimination of which depends for the most part upon the spatial characters of the pressure sensations aroused by the object. They are more important, again, for the estimation of hardness and softness.

6. The 'sensation of double contact' is also a combination of cutaneous and articular sensations. If we touch an object with a stick or other solid body, we seem to sense, besides the pressure of the stick upon our skin, the resistance which the object offers to its progress; and we can judge of the quality of the surface touched in this indirect way with extraordinary accuracy, when visual perceptions are excluded. This sensation of double contact is especially important to the blind man, who has only his stick to aid him in 'finding the way' which he has to travel. There can be no doubt that experience (association) plays a part in the sensation, and is one condition of the apparent transference of sensation from the hand to the farther extremity of the stick which it grasps. But it is equally certain that the duplication of sensation is based on a definite sensory fact,—the difference in the excitation of the cutaneous and articular sensibility by the object held in the hand. The distribution of pressure over the surface of the hand is fairly irregular, and takes various directions; but the articular surfaces are always stimulated from one and the same direction. Here, therefore, we are able to analyse two components whose separation under normal circumstances is exceedingly difficult. It would be well if this interesting phenomenon were made the subject of exact psychological investigation, and attention paid to the physical relations involved.

(c) In conclusion we may briefly mention that the common sensations are also to be regarded as phenomena of fusion (except where they are characterised by the succession of individual sensations; § 23. 3). This would explain the extreme difficulty of their analysis, and the apparent novelty and peculiarity of their total impression (§ 23. 1 : cf. clang colour).

Literature :

F. Hillebrand, *Ueber die specifische Helligkeit der Farben. Sitzber. d. Wiener Akad. d. Wiss.* Section III. Vol. 98.

A. Koenig, *Ueber den Helligkeitswerth der Spectralfarben*, etc. *Beiträge zur Psychologie und Physiologie der Sinnesorgane*, 1891.

Cf. the literature cited under §§ 21—23.

CHAPTER III. THE EMOTIONS AND IMPULSES.

§ 52. The Emotions.

1. Emotions and impulses are ordinarily classed together as *affective processes.* This phrase emphasises the feeling element of the fusion. And the emphasis is natural, in view of the current classification of the experiences in terms of affective quality—of the emotions as pleasurable and unpleasurable, of the impulses as desires and aversions, and of the passions (which are referred to the same psychological category) as love and hate. The systematic proof that all these terms cover definite sensations as well as feelings, and that it is the sensations which give the various impulses and emotions their characteristic colouring, is of quite recent date. Traces of such a view, however, are discoverable in certain other customary classifications. Thus the distinction of *exciting* and *depressing* emotions, and the analogous discrimination of *attraction* and *repulsion* among impulses, plainly contain a reference to definite differences in bodily posture and movement, and their attendant organic sensations.—The words 'exciting' and 'depressing', as applied to the emotions, are not strictly identical with 'pleasurable' and 'unpleasurable': we have seen that there are two stages of unpleasantness (§ 37. 3), so that the unpleasurable emotions may be either exciting or depressing. But this fact does not constitute a sufficient reason for the recognition of two new affective qualities (§ 35. 3).

2. Our own view of the emotions and impulses is, then, that they represent the fusion of sensations and feelings. This theory enables us to understand the lateness of the discovery and definition of the sensations which they contain. (i) The sensible components are more or less obscured by the vividness of the concomitant feelings. Even now, we have no adequate knowledge of their various combinations. (ii) Moreover, the sensations involved in an emotion or impulse are exceedingly numerous, and consequently fuse to a characteristic total impression. (iii) And lastly, there are some emotions, expectation and surprise, *e.g.*, whose affective tone, as pleasurable or unpleasurable, is hardly noticeable. It cannot be said, therefore, that their *differentia* is the affective quality of pleasantness or unpleasantness. A surprise may be agreeable or disagreeable: expectation pleasant or unpleasant. This fact, again, has been urged in support of the hypothesis that the emotions are peculiar affective processes, co-ordinate with the feelings of pleasantness and unpleasantness. But it can hardly be denied that processes like expectation and surprise owe their specific character

simply to certain complexes of organic sensations—however difficult
the description of these may be in the particular case. If we abstract
from the ideas which arouse the emotive reaction, their sole components
(the feelings of pleasantness and unpleasantness being ruled out as
characteristic constituents) are organic sensations, which, however, as
everyone knows from experience, wear a very different aspect in the
two cases. We thus obtain two classes of emotions: one in which the
organic sensations are so far preponderant that they appear to be the
sole determinants of the character of the total state, and another whose
essential characteristic is a feeling of pleasantness or unpleasantness.
Between these two extremes is arranged the long series of moderately
intensive emotions, in which the influence of feelings and organic sensations is approximately evenly balanced.

3. The discrimination of emotions from impulses, which always
involve definite feelings of pleasantness or unpleasantness, is only difficult in cases where the emotions themselves are characterised by the
presence of a similar affective quality. It is sufficiently obvious that
expectation and surprise are not impulses: but the classificatory position of such experiences as anger and rapture can hardly yet be stated
with any degree of certainty. Various characteristics have been taken
as distinctive of the two states. Thus (i) the emotions are passive,
the impulses active experiences. (ii) Or the emotion may be defined
as an affective process which is externally conditioned, the impulse as
an internally conditioned process of the same order. For the emotion
is evoked, as a general rule, by the action of external stimulation,
while the impulse is ordinarily originated by certain internal stimuli.
(iii) A third ground of distinction has been suggested by Lehmann.
The only certain criterion of emotion and impulse, in his opinion, is
the difference in the movements to which they give rise. It is characteristic of emotive expression that the muscles whose innervation is
independent of the will of the subject are thrown into contraction,
whereas in impulse the principal part is played by the activity of the
'voluntary' muscles. It is true that the voluntary muscles are also
demonstrably concerned in emotive expression; but the movements
here, Lehmann declares, have not the definite direction which they
take under the influence of impulse. They appear rather as irradia-
tory processes, the causes of which are to be looked for in the excitations widely diffused throughout the central nervous system during
a violent emotion. The difference between emotion and impulse is
thus reduced to a difference between the emotive and impulsive
movements.

4. It is evident that this last attempt to formulate the distinguishing

21

characteristics of impulse and emotion expressly renounces the appeal
to introspection which is, nevertheless, our one reliable means of
determining the qualitative nature of psychical states. At the same
time, the definition of the objective differences in emotive and
impulsive expression, if they are constant and well marked, may
prove very useful for the identification of the subjective experience.
And as a matter of fact, Lehmann's distinction seems to agree with
the first of the differences between emotion and impulse mentioned
above, the difference of activity and passivity. The most adequate
description of the two processes will accordingly run somewhat as follows.
Emotion is a connection of feelings and organic sensations, whose
sensible constituents are conditioned partly by the excitation of bodily
changes independent of the volition of the subject, partly by innervation
of the voluntary muscles, indefinitely directed, and also independent
of the will as such. Impulse, on the other hand, is a fusion of
feelings and organic sensations whose sensible constituents are conditioned by voluntary movements, ideated or executed, more or less
determinate in direction. These definitions, it will be noticed, furnish
the vindication or explanation of the positiveness of our recent
distinction between the emotions which have no noticeable affective
tone and impulses. The organic sensations in expectation and surprise
are entirely due to involuntary movement or strain.—The remaining
view, that external or internal stimulation is the characteristic condition
of the origin of emotion or impulse, must be rejected as inadequate.
The exceptions to the rule are so numerous that it certainly cannot
be made the basis of an exact definition of the two states.

5. There is no extant classification of the emotions which does
justice to their character as analysed in the foregoing discussion.
Spinoza's famous exposition (Ethics, Pt. III), is not conceived at all
from the psychological standpoint, and becomes rigidly schematic
under the influence of the writer's geometric method. The main
principle of classification of the emotions, as joys or sorrows, is the
distinction of a *transitio a minore ad majorem* and a *majore ad
minorem perfectionem:* a fact which shows at once how completely
unpsychological Spinoza's procedure is. In the popular classifications
there is a conflict of the two divisions by pleasantness or unpleasantness and excitement or depression. Some weight is also laid upon
the intensity and duration of the various states. Anger and rage are
exciting unpleasurable emotions; rapture and enthusiasm are exciting
pleasurable emotions. Sorrow, care, and dejection, on the other hand,
are depressing unpleasurable emotions; there are no nameable depressing
pleasurable emotions. Intensive series are formed by such states as

enthusiasm, admiration, and respect; rage, anger, and ill humour; rapture, joy, and content; despair, sorrow and melancholy. Duration discriminates emotions like happiness and rapture or fright and despair. Relatively permanent emotive states are often termed *moods;* we speak of a happy or despairing, a cheerful or sorrowful mood, and so on. No sharp line of distinction can be drawn between emotion and mood. The only point to notice is that there is no such state as an exciting unpleasurable mood, because the primary stage of unpleasantness, which is correlated with an abnormal increase of excitability, is too transitory to persist as a permanent affective tone (§ 37. 3).

6. A classification of the emotions, to be psychologically satisfactory, must take account both of the relative preponderance of the particular emotive constituents and of their special nature. No such classification is possible at the present time; the various emotions have not been subjected to exact analysis in either direction. We can, therefore, do no more here than select certain types for characterisation. We saw just now (2 above) that there are two extreme forms of emotion, between which all the rest may be arranged. One extreme is constituted by emotions in which the organic sensations are so completely predominant as to determine the actual character of the emotion. Emotions of this class we may term *objective.* Here belong the processes of expectation and surprise, instanced above, together with amazement, etc. We have already treated of expectation as a general condition of sensitivity and sensible discrimination (§ 5), of feeling (§ 39), and of tonal fusion (§ 47). In every case, it appeared to be a form of attention, an attentive preparation for a coming state, process, or content. The emotive constituent in expectation consists essentially in the complex of strain sensations, which appear as the result of this preparation for some more or less definite occurrence. The intensity of the emotion is ordinarily measured by the vividness of these strain sensations. Thus we speak of a strained expectation, and refer to the amount of strain as agreeable or disagreeable. The relation of these degrees of strain to the feelings is governed by the rules which we laid down in our discussion of the influence of stimulus intensity on feeling (§ 37. 7). The strain of expectation, that is, may be agreeable or disagreeable, according to its duration or intensity. The phenomenon is complicated by the feelings attaching to the ideas of the expected event, etc., which may also be of a pleasurable or unpleasurable character. Thus an agreeable strain of expectation may be connected with the idea of an unpleasant occurrence, or a painful strain of expectation accompany the idea of a very delightful experience. We attribute a different character to expectation itself,

according as one or the other feeling preponderates. 'Fear' suggests the expectation of an unpleasant event, often connected with vivid sensations of strain; 'confidence' the normal steadiness and evenness of strain sensation, which are maintained as long as the object of expectation remains indeterminate. We may say in general terms that the clearness of the really emotive constituents of expectation, the strain sensations with their attendant feelings, is proportional to the indeterminateness of the ideas upon which expectation is directed. This serves to explain the fact that the emotion plays a far more important part in the investigation of sensitivity and sensible discrimination by the procedure without knowledge, than in experiments made by the procedure with knowledge.

7. The origin of the strain sensations which occur in expectation can, of course, be more easily traced when the ideas of the expected event are determinate than when they are indeterminate. Expectation is never wholly undirected: some ideas will be present, however indefinite. Hence no sharp line of distinction can be drawn between the procedure with and the procedure without knowledge. The strain sensations seem in every case to be preponderantly localised in the sense organ whose stimulation is expected. Thus if the content of expectation is a visual idea, we can trace more or less distinct strains in and about the eye, caused apparently by the contraction of the muscles which keep the eyeball turned in a definite direction and by the accommodation for a definite distance. Expectation is characteristically expressed by arrest of bodily movement, steady and unflinching gaze, the turn of the head for listening, etc. All this points to an intensive strain upon muscles and tendons, appearing with peculiar distinctness in different parts of the body according to the quality of the expected impression.

The objective symptoms of surprise may be very fairly described as the precise opposite of those of expectation. And subjectively it is the antitype of expectation. There is no preparation for the coming impression. Indeed, the completeness of surprise is proportional to the unpreparedness of the whole course of thought, the adaptation of the sense organs, and the direction of the attention, for the entrance of the new process into the existent state of consciousness. The surprising event, therefore, produces a sudden interruption of the train of ideas and a relaxation of the processes of movement or contraction connected with precedent impressions.

8. It is evident that we must distinguish in surprise, as we have done in expectation, between the ideas which introduce or occasion the emotion and the organic sensations produced by the character-

istic motor disturbance. The feelings attaching to the two sets of processes are, here too, of quite different character, and language distinguishes between the two factors in the emotion in such phrases as 'pleasant agitation'. We mean by the expression an unpleasantly violent shock, occasioned by a pleasurable occurrence; a pleasurable occurrence may be as unpleasant, in this sense, as a sorrowful. It is difficult to define the peculiar organic sensations which we experience in surprise. Nothing more definite can be said, perhaps, than that they must be the conscious correlates of sudden changes in the motor condition of the body. Some part is played in the emotion, however, by the equally sudden diversion of the course of ideas, the more or less complete reversal of the thoughts and feelings of the moment. It is clear, therefore, that the surprise will be most distinct when the actual impression is the direct opposite of the expected. If we are expecting a weak stimulus, and an intensity is given for which we are absolutely unprepared, the resultant surprise is very great; and as the intensity of the emotion affords a certain measure of the magnitude of the difference between the expected and the real, our judgment is correspondingly deceived. Thus a strong stimulus which surprises us is taken to be stronger than it really is, and a weak impression seems weaker than it otherwise would appear. This deception of judgment is especially liable to occur in the course of the procedure without knowledge, when definite expectations have been involuntarily formed by the subject, at the suggestion of some incident in the progress of experimentation (§ 5. 6).

9. The other class of emotions contains the *subjective* states, in which the two affective qualities exert a determining influence. Language has done far more for this category of emotion than for the former. Perhaps the only objective emotion, besides expectation and surprise, is amazement or wonder, the constituents of which are very simular to those of surprise itself. Here, on the other hand, we have not only the fundamental forms of affective emotion roper, joy and sorrow, but the further distinction of excitement and depression, within the unpleasurable emotions. And there are all manner of degrees of the intensity and duration of these states, as we mentioned briefly just now. Since the pleasurable emotions are invariably exciting, the classification by joy and sorrow points at once to a certain contrast in organic sensations: the contrast of intensive innervation and movement, on the one hand, and greatly diminished and restricted motor excitability on the other. The violent unpleasant emotions, such as rage and anger, are also of an exciting character; but the primary stage of unpleasantness is too transitory for them to persist for any

length of time. The distinction between the feelings connected with organic sensations and the feelings attaching to initiatory ideas is again in place, but can hardly be carried through in practice, as the ideational contents tend strongly to predominate and the feelings attaching to them exercise a determining influence upon the affective character of the emotion.

§ 53. The Impulses.

1. The close relationship of emotion and impulse is universally acknowledged. The definitions in the foregoing Section (§ 52. 4) show how difficult it is to draw a hard and fast line of division between the two states. Emotion becomes impulse whenever the expressive movements are directed into a definite channel under the influence of the will. Thus anger passes over into impulse when there are added to the emotion determinate ideas (and the corresponding organic sensations) of the movements which would serve to restore contentment, and so to abrogate the emotive state: and rapture passes over into impulse when there are added to the emotion certain other ideas of movements, subserving the retention of the emotive state. This fact is of itself sufficient to show that impulses in general are far more closely connected with the affective qualities than are the emotions. It is frequently asserted that the end of an impulse is always either the retention of a pleasurable feeling or the removal of an unpleasurable feeling. And the content of the impulse is partly determined by the nature of its end, since the movements subserving the two opposite purposes take equally opposite directions. Again, the popular distinction of likes and dislikes, attraction and repulsion, love and hate, is also reducible to this fundamental contrast of feeling. Likes and dislikes, with their various degrees of longing, wish, aversion, repugnance, etc., are forms of impulse which border very closely upon emotion,—except, of course, as regards the definitely directed movements to which they give rise. In the passions (love and hate) we have, on the other hand, the most intensive impulses, *i.e.*, those which find the readiest and most direct expression in fully determinate movements.

2. The analysis of the elementary processes contained in impulse is exceedingly difficult, if only for the reason that so many different states are comprised under the one name. Indeed, all that can be taken for granted at the outset is the invariable relation of impulses to the affective qualities. But even this requires closer definition than it has yet received in the particular case. Some psychologists assert, *e.g.*, that the end of the impulse in hunger is the feeling of satiety,

others that it is the idea of food. We will ourselves, therefore, attempt first of all to discover the relation obtaining between certain ideas present in impulse and the organic sensations corresponding to the impulsive action, intended or executed. In impulse, as in emotion, both sets of processes play an important part, and the feelings attaching to each have their own special significance. (i) It is noteworthy that the feelings connected with the impulsive idea are ordinarily much more vivid, and therefore of more decisive influence upon the determination of the general character of the impulse, than those connected with the organic sensations as such. This is apparently due to the fact that the impulsive movements, executed or intended, are simply the result of the pleasantly or unpleasantly toned idea, and can, therefore, but rarely be of equal importance with it in the total impression. (ii) Again, we often find that the starting point of an impulse is a primary feeling of pleasantness or unpleasantness in connection with a definite complex of sensations. The course of the impulse is then widely divergent from the course of the emotion. Thus, the disagreeableness of hunger or thirst is the condition of origin of the nutritive impulse; the pleasure felt in a beautiful work of art arouses the desire for its possession, etc. These primary feelings, which constitute the first step towards the origination of an impulse, do not, *i.e.*, bear the same relation to it as the feelings attaching to certain ideas bear to emotion.

3. The characteristic factor in impulse, apart from definite feelings, is the peculiar complex of organic sensations arising from the impulsive movement. No description of longing would be adequate, *e.g.*, which did not contain a reference to the sensations aroused by ideation of the movements necessary to attain the desired end. This sensation complex is the real and universal characteristic of the impulse. It is true that the name is often applied to other than sensory processes, in which no definite ideas of movement are involved. But the application is either simply metaphorical, or illustrative of a common tendency of language,—the transference of terms with an original sensible connotation to abstract objects. When we speak, *e.g.*, of an 'ethical' or 'logical impulse', we are applying the word, out of its right connection, to processes which, in this general formulation, contain no reference to bodily movement. The reference is somewhat more concrete in the phrase 'charitable impulse' although here, too, the nature of the movements implied is altogether indeterminate. It is, therefore, necessary to set a definite limit to the use of the term 'impulse' in psychological terminology. We must refuse to regard every possible alteration of the existent conscious state, in any direction whatsoever, as due to an 'impulse'; or to consider every pleasantly or unpleas-

antly toned idea as the necessary starting point of an 'impulse'; or
to speak of 'impulse' even in cases where we find an intention to
act in accordance with a definite purpose expressed in abstract language.
We can only use the word 'impulse' where definite movements,
dependent upon the will, are ideated or executed at the instance of
affectively toned sensations. The vividness of the impulse is directly
proportional to the clearness of these ideas of movement and the
corresponding organic sensations. This explains the frequency with
which a particularly distinct impulsive idea leads to the execution of
the appropriate impulsive movements. An involuntary extension of
the arms and a forward inclination of the body, *e.g.*, are characteristic
of the impulse of longing.

4. Impulses have been classified as higher and lower, in the
sense in which the same terms were applied to feeling (§ 35. 1). We
cannot accept the classification, since it makes the character of the
whole process exclusively dependent upon the toned ideas which
constitute the end of the impulse, agreeable or disagreeable. Nor can
we attach any psychological value to the more detailed discrimination
of impulses according to their objects, which gives as many impulses
as there are ideas capable of serving as the objects of desire or
aversion. These contents or ends of impulse are not necessary constituents of it: in many cases they are altogether absent. The *instincts*
or instinctive impulses, which are more numerous in the animals than
in man, show us in particular that impulses need not be aroused by
any definite idea of their end. The impulse appears here before its
purpose has been learned by individual experience. There is absolutely
no foundation for the assumption that instincts depend upon unconscious
ideas, transmitted by inheritance. The newly hatched chicken does
not possess an unconscious idea of the grains which are to satisfy its
hunger; neither has the new-born infant an unconscious idea of the
mother's breast which is to furnish it with nourishment. We must
rather suppose that the chicken and the infant inherit a purposive
motor mechanism, which under the definite stimulation of internal or
external bodily organs is set in action in the accustomed way, *i.e.*,
in the form of a pecking at the ground, or a sucking with the lips.
The organic sensations connected with the movements are present in
these cases, but there is no definite idea which serves as the object
of the instinctive movements. Once more, therefore, we are led to
the conclusion that certain feelings and organic sensations are the
distinguishing characteristics of impulse.

5. We have now to consider the relation of these two essential
components to each other. We have already mentioned the current

view that impulsive movements are intended to retain (or intensify) a feeling of pleasantness or to remove (or diminish) a feeling of unpleasantness. This distinction certainly holds for the objective observer; but it is not equally valid for the experiencing subject. For the principal difference between impulsive movement and voluntary action is that the former constitutes a direct reaction, not initiated by consideration, reflection or choice, but an automatic consequence or expression of the given pleasantly or unpleasantly toned impression, while voluntary action implies the conscious intention to execute definite movements for definite reasons or purposes. In the impulsive action proper, *i.e.*, we know nothing of the end; we have not expressly inquired into the ultimate aim of the movements which we execute. If, therefore, the result of these movements is what it is described to be in the current view of the nature of impulse, at least it is not foreseen by the subject, but must be referred to a gradually perfected purposive co-ordination of toned sensations and movements. In the developed consciousness, of course, an impulsive action will often assume the character of a voluntary action; all that is needed is the connection of the idea of a definite movement (the movement to be executed in the given case) with the appearance of certain feelings. But this connection appears to be irrelevant for the impulse itself, which is wholly composed of the characteristic complex of organic sensations and the feelings of pleasantness and unpleasantness attaching to definite impressions. We cannot at present give any accurate account of the origin of these organic sensations. It may, however, be pointed out that in view of the great variety of possible impulsive movements, it would be difficult to bring definite muscle groups or definite forms of movement into any unequivocal relation with the affective qualities, with effort and reluctance, or with desire and aversion. The distinction of attraction and repulsion is certainly based upon such differences of direction or form of movement; but the implied connection between these and pleasantness or unpleasantness is simply customary, not universal or invariable. And there is even less justification for the assumption of a strict correlation of the flexors and extensors, the antagonistic voluntary muscles, with the two affective qualities.

§ 54. The Expressive Movements.

1. In our discussion of the simple feelings we found that there were certain bodily movements bearing a characteristic relation to their two qualities and, therefore, useful for the experimental demonstration and investigation of pleasantness and unpleasantness (§ 37. 1 ff.). The

more complex affective states,—emotion, impulse, mood and passion—are also correlated with definite bodily changes. But their visible expression is far more complicated than that of feeling, as might be expected from the number of elementary conscious processes contained in them (§ 52. 2). In expectation, *e.g.*, we have not only a definite complex of organic sensations, with their attendant feelings, but the more or less determinate group of ideas which constitutes the contents or object of the emotion. The expressive movements are influenced, of course, by both classes of constituents. Thus the eavesdropper and the scout have different characteristic attitudes, although both alike are in a state of expectation. Similar phenomena recur in every emotion. It is plain, then, that the conditions of expressive movement may be very different in different cases. The forms and laws which have been discriminated hitherto refer almost exclusively to the expression of the ideas which constitute the contents or object of the emotion—not unnaturally, as this is much more individual in its nature and delicate in its adjustment than is the expression of the emotive constituents proper. No distinction is drawn between the two in the language of everyday life. The blush of shame or joy and the paleness of fear or terror are regarded as expressive movements on the same plane with the clenching of the fist in anger or the clapping of the hands in pleasure. We shall not be far wrong in supposing that this confusion is responsible for the diversity of psychological opinion in regard to the simple principles which regulate expressive movement in general.

2. The application of the method of expression (§ 35. 7) to emotion has shown that its objective symptoms are essentially the same with those of feeling. In an unpleasurable emotion like fright, *e.g.*, we find the two distinctive stages of the expression of unpleasantness,—a violent inspiration, followed by a period of weaker respiration, with diminution of volume and reduced height of pulse. The pleasant and unpleasant emotions, *i.e.*, manifest the same objective symptoms as the pleasant and unpleasant feelings. Complication arises at once, however, if the bodily changes underlying the organic sensations begin to influence the results of the method of expression. In certain circumstances, *e.g.*, the curve of volume in fright is not the characteristic 'unpleasant' curve, but is heightened in consequence of the emotive 'start,' the general motor shock. In fear, again, the curves of respiration and pulse are not of the pure 'unpleasant' type, but show irregularities due to muscular tremor, the emotive 'quivering'. In anger, the curve of volume is very considerably heightened, probably by the involuntary movements which have combined with unpleasant-

ness to determine its course. Even in these comparatively simple emotions, therefore, we can trace the effect of a whole series of factors which co-operate with the character of the feeling to give individual form to the expressive movements. It cannot be said that these movements and the organic sensations connected with them are dependent upon the feelings as such: they occur in too great variety, and are too little parallel or proportional to the original pleasant or unpleasant elements of the emotion. Trembling and shaking are characteristic of chill and shivering as well as of keen anxiety or fear, while the feelings in the two cases may differ very widely, at least in intensity.

3. The variety of the movements expressive of definite ideational contents is inexhaustible. They have had free play in the course of generic and individual development; and they are the principal source of one whole department of human expression,—gesture language. We need not here enter upon the consideration of the phenomena in all their complication : the expressive movements are primarily objects of external perception, and from the purely psychological standpoint are simply illustrations of the various types of action—voluntary, impulsive or reflex. Any voluntary action which is apprehended and interpreted by an objective observer as a sign or symptom of an internal state takes rank at once as an expressive movement. It is evident, then, that the problem presented to psychology proper by the expressive movements is very much more restricted than the vast number of facts covered by the phrase might lead us to suppose. The psychologist is not concerned to interpret these external processes or to tabulate their physiological conditions, but merely to determine their relation to emotions, impulses, moods or passions. We have ourselves decided that the essential constituents in the affective fusions are organic sensations and feelings. We do not ascribe any considerable importance to the ideational contents which may connect with these, except in cases where the feelings dependent upon them modify or intensify the pleasantness or unpleasantness of the primary state or determine the direction of an impulsive expression. We may, therefore, confine ourselves to the two original factors, in our consideration of the expressive movements.

4. Many recent psychologies share the view that emotions arise from the expressive movements. James, *e.g.*, asserts that we do not cry because we are sorry, but are sorry because we cry. There is plainly so much of truth in this belief, that the organic sensations connected with the expressive movements contribute very materially to the total emotive impression. It would be difficult to explain in any

other way the extraordinary constancy of the expressive movements, and the emotive differences of which we have already spoken (§ 52). The objective emotions in particular,—the emotions of expectation, surprise, and wonder, in which the affective colouring is exceedingly weak,—must often be originated by the appropriate expressive movements. But the theory has overlooked two facts: (α) that reproduced organic sensations are possible constituents of an emotion, and (β) that the feelings in the subjective emotions cannot, in the majority of cases, be regarded as simple consequences of expressive movements, since the ideational contents play an important part in their determination (§ 52. 9). The view, therefore, contains no more than a fraction of the truth. The emotion is ordinarily initiated, in the developed consciousness, by certain ideational contents in connection with feelings.

5. Darwin brings all expressive movements under three principles, in which he attempts to do justice to their origination from general physiological conditions and to their development in the life history of the race. The first principle is that of *serviceable associated habits*. Certain actions which were originally of direct or indirect service for the satisfaction of definite needs are afterwards performed altogether automatically, even though they have entirely lost their primary significance. The second principle is that of *antithesis*. If definite psychical processes are habitually connected with definite actions, there is a tendency for mental processes of the reverse kind to accompany movements of the opposite character. The third principle is that of the *direct activity of the nervous system*. According to it, intensive excitation in the nervous centres gives rise of itself to certain motor phenomena which we recognise as expressive. Valid objections have been urged against these principles, and especially against the second. They are not wholly co-extensive with the facts, and cannot be separated with the rigour necessary for the arrangement and explanation of the phenomena. Piderit has formulated two very general laws of mimetic expression, according to which expressive movements refer partly to ideated objects, partly to ideated sense impressions, agreeable or disagreeable. Here it is obvious that exclusive attention has been paid to what we have termed the ideational contents in emotion or impulse, and its attendant feelings. Lehmann has laid special emphasis upon the individual development of emotive expression. He regards the connection between affective process and expressive movement as an association. Definite motor processes are constantly connected with definite ideas, and are therefore reproduced by these, directly or indirectly, on their subsequent occurrence. But the phenomena of movement differ far too widely in different emotions for this view to

be tenable. It is inadequate to explain the connection of emotion and expressive movement even in the most general outline. And in particular we may pause before we admit that the individual origination of emotive expression is so universal a fact as Lehmann supposes.

6. The most satisfactory analysis of expressive movement from the psychological point of view is that of Wundt. He brings all types of emotive and impulsive expression under three rules, which must be regarded as co-operating with one another in the great majority of concrete expressive movements. The first of these rules, the principle of *direct change of innervation*, lays it down that intensive affective processes are attended by a direct excitation of the motor centres. Here belong paling and blushing, laughing and crying, etc. The second rule, the principle of *association of analogous sensations*, expresses the fact that sensations of similar affective tone readily connect with one another. In this way, movements which are characteristic of the reaction upon definite sensory stimuli become indicative of emotions, etc., which resemble these sense impressions in their affective nature. The 'sour' face and 'bitter' smile are familiar illustrations of the rule. The third, the principle of the *relation of movement to sensory ideas*, includes gesture, etc. It is exemplified by the clenching of the fist in anger, the steady regard in strained expectation, etc. A detailed discussion of these three rules would have to show their reference to the different constituents of emotion and impulse. Thus, the first is principally concerned with the direct psychological concomitants of the feelings; the second serves mainly to elucidate the origin of the organic sensations; while the third comprises all those cases in which the movement is dependent upon the ideational contents.

We have at present no materials for the erection of a *theory* of emotion and impulse. It would presuppose not only a fairly assured theory of feeling and organic sensation, but also some clear idea of the process of fusion itself. We will here, therefore, merely call attention to the fact that the connections of feelings with other sensations must also be looked upon as instances of fusion. We cannot, however, say anything of their general laws, in the existing state of our knowledge. There remains the question of the interconnection of feelings themselves. We have already pointed out the difficulties which here bar the way to the simple ascertainment of the facts (§ 39. 7). In particular, we cannot decide with any degree of certainty for or against 'mixed' feelings. In our own opinion, there is no convincing evidence for the existence of a simultaneity of feelings in consciousness. On the other hand, a rapid alternation of different feelings is a phenomenon of common occurrence, and one which appears to stand in very close relation to the fluctuation of attention. This is yet another indication of the importance of attention for the origination of the feelings.

Literature :

Th. Piderit, *Wissenschaftliches System der Mimik und Physiognomik.* Second ed., 1886.

C. Darwin, *The Expression of the Emotions.* Second ed., 1890.

G. H. Schneider, *Der thierische Wille.* 1880.

C. Lange, *Ueber Gemüthsbewegungen.* 1887.

A. Mosso, *Die Furcht.* 1889.

W. Wundt, *Zur Lehre von den Gemüthsbewegungen. Phil. Studien,* vol. vi., pp. 335 ff.

Cf. the literature cited under § 41.

Section II. Colligation.

CHAPTER I. THE SPATIAL ATTRIBUTES AND RELATIONS OF SENSATIONS.

§ 55. Prefatory Remarks.

1. The psychological investigation of the idea of space has suffered very considerably from a metaphysical prejudice, for the introduction of which into philosophy Descartes is chiefly responsible. In the Cartesian system, thought and extension are the two essential characteristics of the psychical and the physical; and it seems as absurd to attach a spatial attribute to mental processes, as it is inconceivable that the physical world is the substrate of spiritual experience. Spinoza, it is true, regarded body and mind simply as *modi, i.e.,* as special expressions of the universal attributes of thought and extension, as different aspects or properties of one and the same existence. But the distinction of the two, whatever its limits, is again absolutely prohibitive of the attribution of space to mentality. Spiritualistic philosophers like Leibniz, Herbart, and Lotze, either attempted to explain at least the apparent space element in the spatial idea of the seeing or touching subject, or refused to predicate any kind of reality or objectivity of space in general. It is only quite recently that psychology has begun to free itself from this metaphysical prejudice, as epistemological views have been clarified and psychological investigation based upon empirical definitions.

2. We can ourselves have no hesitation (cf. the position taken up in § 1) in predicating spatial attributes of certain conscious processes. Psychology consists, for us, simply in the description and explanation of the facts of experience in their dependency upon an experiencing individual. And temporal or spatial definition is certainly just as much an attribute or relation of the fact of experience as its quality

or intensity. If, then, we can show that this temporal or spatial character is also definitely dependent upon the psychophysical organisation, its treatment in a work upon psychology becomes a matter of course. Now the existence of this dependency is proved by observations of everyday occurrence. We speak of the 'apparent magnitude' of an object, of 'apparent locality' and 'apparent movement', implying that our space ideas are more or less widely divergent from the facts of objective space measurement. Here too, *i.e.*, we have a distinction of subjective and objective, as we had a parallelism between the quality and intensity of sensation and certain attributes of stimulus.

The psychological space problem must not be misunderstood. We are not concerned to reduce the spatial predicate to any more general category; we made no attempt to explain the sensible predicates of quality or intensity. In particular, we cannot imagine that any material contribution will have been made to the explanation of the experiential data by the ascription to the mind of an original capacity of spatial ideation. The space predicate as such is, for psychology, a fundamental fact, as ultimate and irreducible as the experiences of which it is predicated, as attribute or relation, subjective or objective. The sole business of psychology, therefore, is to exhibit the dependency of the various spatial factors upon the psychophysical organisation.

3. Spatial attributes are ascribed only to certain classes of sensations, *viz.*, the visual and 'tactual',—the latter term embracing both cutaneous sensations proper and the articular sensations set up in the motile parts of the body. Spatial relations, on the other hand, are predicable of all sensations alike, since all alike are localisable. The localisation of unspatial contents, however, is mediate only: it consists in a reproduction of originally spatial sensations, of movements indicative of the place of origin of the given contents, or of judgments directly expressive of their local determination. Localisation in this sense is plainly altogether different from the localisation of an originally spatial process, and we may, therefore, speak of it as a 'transferred' spatial relation. A spatial relation *sensu stricto* can only obtain between contents possessed of the true spatial attribute. It seems best, however, despite this essential difference between the two kinds of localisation, to discuss the transferred here in connection with the direct, and not to deal with it separately as a special form of association or reproduction of ideas,—the rubric under which its general psychological significance would lead us to place it. We shall, therefore, treat in this chapter (*a*) of the space of tactual perception, (*b*) of the space of visual perception, and lastly (*c*) of transferred localisation with especial reference to auditory impressions.

4. There is, of course, a very great variety of possible spatial definitions. If our treatment is to be complete and systematic, we must endeavour to reduce them to certain fundamental forms. To this end we begin with the distinction between spatial *attributes* and spatial *relations*, the former attaching to a perceived content as such, the latter to the content only as related to other contents. Form or *figure* is the general term comprehending all the spatial characters that can be attributively predicated of an impression; *position* or locality is a similar term embracing all the spatial relations in which a content stands to other contents. Both determinations may be further analysed,—position into elementary relations, as a sum of distances; and figure into spatial elements, as a sum of extensions. To them must be added a more complex spatial determination, which also contains a temporal reference—movement. We understand by *movement* any continuous alteration of a spatial attribute or relation. Extension, then, is the elementary phenomenon in all spatial attributes; distance the elementary factor in all spatial relations. Spatially considered, of course, the two are but one; but they require special psychological investigation in cases where their apprehension or estimation is governed by different laws. We have already mentioned extension as one of the attributes of sensation (§ 4. 2); distance, as reduced to it, is the extension of the contents intervening between two given impressions. The *magnitude* of a figure is simply a quantitative determination of extension; and we speak in precisely the same way of the magnitude of a distance. *Direction* is, again, only a special form of extension or distance, indicative of the spatial interrelations of certain given extensions or distances.

5. Unfortunately, we have no systematic investigation of spatial attributes and relations on the lines here laid down. Philosophic prejudice on the one hand, and the limitation of special problems on the other, have prevented any thorough examination of the space idea. Hence there are certain factors which have hardly received any direct attention, while theories have been propounded which are valid only for one quite definite aspect or characteristic of the whole process. In particular, (i) the psychology of space, like the psychology of time (§§ 63 ff.), has suffered from the assumption that space must be regarded as something absolute and self-existent, given more or less independently of all the specific contents of perception. There can be no doubt that this view has been furthered by the notion of 'empty' space as employed in the natural sciences. From the psychological standpoint it is altogether erroneous. Again, (ii) the possibility of the intercomparison of the spatial characters of perceptions,

independently of their other attributes, has also in all probability helped to give the space idea an exceptional place among the contents of consciousness. It explains the tendency of psychologists to see the real object of investigation into the psychology of space, not in the spatial attributes, but in the spatial relations. This independent 'space' seems to be given in its purest form in distance, locality, etc. It also accounts for the definition of movement as change simply of locality. —The result has been an almost total neglect of the perception of extension and figure and almost exclusive regard of the perception of distance and position. This is the more regrettable as the former process is psychologically very much the more simple. The space character is always given with particular perception contents; there is no independent space content, which can be discriminated from other qualitatively determinate impressions. 'Empty' space is the spatial character of certain contents not defined. And as the other attributes of a content are of determining influence upon its spatial qualities (§ 56. 3; § 59. 2, *e.g.*), the simplest material for the investigation of the space idea is furnished by the extension or figure of a quite definite content. (iii) Lastly, the expressions 'sense of space' and 'sense of locality,' which have recently become current in physiology, betray a wholly inadequate realisation of the requirements of theory. The 'sense of space' is measured by the least noticeable distance between two impressions; the 'sense of locality' by the accuracy of localisation. Not only is the word 'sense' applied here in a very exceptionable meaning (§ 4. 10), but the spatial relations are given an unjustifiable preference over the spatial attributes.

§ 56. The Space of Tactual Perception.

I. The Spatial Functions of the Cutaneous Sensations.

1. The spatial estimation of an object brought into contact with the skin is mediated both by pressure sensations and by temperature sensations. We attribute a certain extension and figure to an impression of heat or cold, just as we do to an impression of smooth or rough, *i.e.*, to a pressure sensed as such. No thorough investigation, however, has as yet been made (cf. § 55. 5) into the cutaneous apprehension of extension and figure, although the experimental examination of the 'sense of space' or 'sense of locality' has been taken up again and again since the time of E.H. Weber. It is especially curious that no attention has been paid to the extension factor, as the method employed in these researches necessarily presupposes a

definite view as to the extension of the cutaneous pressure or temperature sensations. The method consists in the determination of the distance between two points of cutaneous contact at which the two impressions are still just apprehensible as two. (i) Now first of all there is involved here the purely logical assumption that a just noticeable twoness of cutaneous sensations is equivalent to a just noticeable distance between them. But twoness and distance are essentially different concepts, and the possibility of their identification requires special psychological proof [1] (cf. § 5. 1). (ii) Nor is this all. To explain the great diversity of experimental results obtained from different portions of the skin, recourse is had to the hypothesis of 'sensation circles' varying in magnitude, but alike in the peculiarity that any two points lying within a single circle are sensed only as one. The explanation plainly contains a reference to the psychological extension which we predicate of cutaneous stimulation. From this point of view also, then, investigation of extension seems essential.

2. We can say but little of the perception of figure as mediated by cutaneous sensations. It has been found that if objectively parallel lines are drawn with the 'dividers' (an instrument which gives all gradations of distance within certain limits between two metal points) from the elbow to the wrist, they appear gradually to diverge from one another in sensation. We imagine, *i.e.*, that the impressions are divergent and not parallel. A similar phenomenon is observed if the two lines are drawn from lobe to lobe of the ears, across the face. The lines appear to diverge towards the median line of the face, and to attain their widest separation in the region of the lips. Again, experiments have been made upon the sensible discrimination for the magnitude of circular surfaces, by the determination of the just noticeable difference of diameter of two objects applied to the skin. It was found that at the tip of the tongue, two circular surfaces were judged to be just different whose diameters were no more than 0.5 and 1 mm.; while on the back the two just discriminable surfaces had diameters of 2 and 25 mm. respectively. Where sight is normal, the ability to cognise figures by aid of the cutaneous sensations is present in very slight degree. In most cases, judgment stops short at the fact of difference, and nothing can be said of its character. The capacity is much more highly developed in the blind, who read without hesitation from an alphabet in which the number and arrange-

---

[1] Our suspicions of the validity of Weber's assumption become still stronger if we translate it into retinal terms, and think what it would mean for points on either side of the blind spot.

ment of raised points upon the paper constitutes the sole ground of distinction between the letters. Lastly, the importance of temperature sensations for the perception of figure is shown by the observation that cold surfaces appear larger than warm surfaces of the same objective extension (cf. § 24. 3; § 51. 4).

3. In all these cases, spatial perception is seen to be principally dependent upon the locality of the stimulated area. The same dependency has been noticed in the numerous investigations made into the just noticeable twoness of sensations. We will only mention the results recently obtained by Goldscheider on the basis of a discrimination of pressure spots, cold spots and heat spots. The values are considerably smaller than those found by Weber and other previous investigators. This is mainly due to the greater sensitivity of the cutaneous 'spots' (cf. §§ 10, 11). In deference to current usage—which, however, is not strictly correct—we may term the least distance between two points brought into contact with the skin, at which their separate sensation is still just possible, the *space limen*. The space limina determined by Goldscheider for pressure spots were 0.3 mm. upon the back of the hand, 0.5 mm. upon the forehead, 0.8 mm. upon the chest, and 4.0 mm. upon the back. The values for cold spots, in the same cutaneous areas, were 2.0, 0.8, 2.0 and 1.5 mm.; for heat spots, 3, 4, 4 and 4 mm. All these observations (with the exception of the various limina upon the back) agree in ascribing the greatest discriminative power to the pressure spots and the least to the heat spots. The result is borne out by the fact that an exploration of the skin with adequate stimuli shows the pressure spots to be most numerous, and the heat spots of least frequent occurrence. Previous experiments indicate that the tip of the tongue has the smallest space limen. Another phenomenon which belongs here is that of the dependency of the space limen upon the motility of the stimulated cutaneous area. This was made the subject of an elaborate experimental investigation by Vierordt and his pupils. The space limen was found to decrease continuously, *e.g.*, from the shoulder to the tips of the fingers. Vierordt has laid it down as a general rule, on the basis of his experiments, that the space limen at any point in the length of a limb is inversely proportional to the distance of the stimulated part from the axis of rotation of the limb.

4. The intensity of the impressions is also of influence upon the space limen. Up to a certain stimulus intensity the facility of separate cognition increases; beyond this intensity it decreases. A certain mean degree of intensity is, therefore, the most favourable condition

for the investigation of the space limen. But as the intensive sensibility varies very greatly with the locality of the stimulated area (§ 24. 3), only those space limina are comparable which are obtained with the same subjective intensity of pressure. The experiments made hitherto are extremely defective in this regard; neither the objective nor the subjective intensity of the impressions has been kept uniformly constant. Distraction of the attention has the same effect as diminution of intensity, *i.e.*, increases the stimulus limen. The influence of practice, too, is very marked. This is the principal reason why the space limen of the blind is noticeably smaller than the space limen where vision is normal. If the two points brought into contact with the skin are set down not simultaneously but successively, or differ in their relative intensity, judgment is rendered very uncertain,—as is not surprising, when we consider that simultaneity and equal intensity are presuppositions of the validity of the method.

Another method has been employed for the determination of the delicacy of localisation of impressions brought into contact with the skin. A simple stimulus is applied, and the subject indicates the place of stimulation with a pencil; the magnitude of the average error is looked upon as inversely proportional to the delicacy of localisation. A series of different degrees is thus obtained, which runs precisely parallel to the series of space limina. No systematic observations have as yet been made upon the cutaneous estimation of movement of the stimulus object. One fact, however, may be mentioned: that a point moved at a uniform rate along the resting arm seems to travel more quickly where the space limen is smaller.

5. The space limen has usually been obtained by the procedure of stimulus determination (methods of minimal changes and right and wrong cases). Recently, however, application has been made of the procedure of stimulus comparison, which undoubtedly gives more unequivocal results in the sphere of spatial estimation. Several of the observations made in this way are of especial interest, as throwing light upon the value of the space limen for the investigation of tactual space perception. (i) The first result of importance in this connection is the following. When two cutaneous distances are made subjectively equal to each other, the objective distances between the limiting points approach the ratio 1 : 1 when these points are set at all widely apart. This is clear evidence that the space limen is not adequate to inform us of the real value of a just noticeable distance. The longer the distances compared, the fewer will be the disturbing influences to which spatial estimation as such is exposed. (ii) Another result of importance is a seeming paradox. We should expect, on mathematical

grounds, that if two distances were made apparently equal to a third, they would appear equal to one another. But this is by no means the case. The fact, again, may be conjecturally referred to certain organic conditions of spatial estimation of the kind which prejudice the determination of the space limen. The first problem to be attacked in the future, therefore, is the problem of extension, which must be directly examined, with particular and constant reference to intensity, duration of stimulation, and other circumstances.

II. The Spatial Functions of the Articular Sensibility.

6. The articular sensibility appears to be be principally concerned (α) in the non-visual perception of movements. It mediates the judgment of the change of position of the moved limb. But (β) the position of a limb is also cognised by the articular sensations; and it has accordingly been proposed to term them 'sensations of position' (§ 23. 6). And (γ) arm movement affords a fairly accurate measure of space magnitudes, *i.e.*, of extension or distance. The articular sensibility is thus seen to have an equal range of spatial function with the cutaneous. No systematic investigation along all three lines has as yet been carried out (cf. § 56. 1), although a large number of special researches, bearing upon the general question of this Section, have quite recently appeared. There is plainly only one practicable method for the determination of the spatial functions of the articular sensibility: correlation of the angle through which the joint is rotated with the magnitude of the distance traversed in consequence by the moved limb. We do not measure the excursion of a pendulum by chords and tangents. And since the movements of a limb may be regarded as at least approximately circular, they too should be measured by the angle or arc described from the given point of rest. Only in this way can we obtain any unequivocal information with regard to the chief factor in the resultant judgment,—the articular sensibility. It has been usual, hitherto, where the distances traversed have been at all long, to employ a rectilineally moving car, which travels along a rail without noticeable friction; or to allow the arm free movement, but to measure the curves described in rectilineal projection. In the former case, however, the result is so ambiguous that the part played by the various articular surfaces cannot be made out with any degree of accuracy; while in the latter it is erroneously calculated. The laws which have been established in this way have accordingly a merely provisional importance.

7. Goldscheider has determined the just noticeable movements of different limbs, and expressed the results in angular magnitudes. He investigated both passive and active movement. The movement limen (if we may employ the expression for brevity's sake) was invariably larger with passive than with active. There seem to be two reasons for this fact. (i) Active movement, initiated by the will of the subject, necessarily involves the procedure with knowledge; passive movement implies the procedure without knowledge. And sensitivity and sensible discrimination are as a general rule (§ 5. 6) somewhat greater in the former case than in the latter. But (ii) the pressure upon the articular surfaces is more intensive in active movement. This will influence the result, since in articular as in cutaneous sensation an increase of intensity serves within certain limits to increase the accuracy of the spatial judgment.—Another interesting point is that the larger joints have, upon the whole, a smaller movement limen than the smaller. Thus the shoulder is more discriminative than the elbow, the hip noticeably more discriminative than the ankle, etc. The values obtained varied between the limits 0.3° and 3.0°.—Again, the rapidity of movement had a marked effect upon its noticeability. Other things equal, *i.e.*, the movement limen decreased as the rapidity of movement increased.. On the other hand, the cognition of movement proved to be independent both of its direction and of the sensibility of the moved limb; *i.e.*, it was irrelevant for the estimation of a movement of the shoulder whether (or how) the arm was extended or flexed, and whether its sensations of pressure and strain were normal or abnormal. Movement, therefore, or at least the determination of the movement limen, must be regarded as exclusively dependent upon the articular sensibility (cf. § 22). In one respect, however, a certain amount of influence seems attributable to the tendinous strain sensation. The indication which it gives of the weight of the moved limb facilitates the judgment of movement direction when the movement is actively executed.

8. Numerous investigations have been made (cf. 6 above) into the conditions of the comparison of movements of some length with one another. But their results have no claim to finality, owing to the defects of the methods employed. Thus it has been found that the degree of contraction of the stimulated muscles exercises a determining influence upon the estimation of movement; but the statement is, in all probability, to be ascribed to an erroneous evaluation of experimental results. Again, we cannot say at present whether the absolute or relative sensible discrimination is constant for all movements, or whether some other uniformity obtains, since the various joints have not yet been subjected to investigation by methods which

lead to unequivocal conclusions. Preliminary experiments upon arm movement (rotation in the shoulder joint; the arm being fully extended, and the body kept as steadily as possible in one position) appear to show that the absolute sensible discrimination is approximately constant. Once more, it is still an open question whether the overestimation of small movements and underestimation of large is a constant error, to which the judgment of space magnitudes is invariably subject, or whether the phenomenon, where it occurs, is not simply the consequence of rapidity of movement, *i.e.*, a phenomenon of temporal estimation as well. There can be no doubt of the fact that the duration and rapidity of a movement influence our estimation of its magnitude. As a general, rule the apparent magnitude of a distance is proportional to the length of time required for movement across it. It should be noted, however, that our judgment of the extent of arm movement is not based (in the author's observation) upon the temporal relations of the movement, but upon the reproduced visual image of the space passed through, and more especially of the extreme positions of the moved arm. No direct comparison of the rapidity of movements has as yet been instituted; and a recently published inquiry into their duration followed so crude a method that its results need not be discussed here. We will conclude this survey of the spatial functions of the articular sensibility with a reference to two points of interest: that movements are ordinarily more accurately estimated by the blind than by subjects whose vision is normal; and that the spatial discrimination of the articular sensibility (as of the cutaneous) is somewhat greater in children than in adults.

§ 57. Theory of Tactual Space Perception.

1. We have already defined the scope and meaning of a theory of spatial ideation (§ 55. 2). All that psychology can do is to elucidate the subjective conditions of space perception; it is not concerned to explain space perception as such. If we ask what these conditions are, we see that different answers are possible. (i) Where vision is normal, the tactual space perception will ordinarily consist in a visual idea of the cutaneous area touched, of the movements of the limbs, etc. (ii) But a judgment may also be formulated directly at the instance of the touch sensations themselves, which must accordingly (as some one has put it) be 'quasi-spatial'. This order of space perception is best illustrated in congenital blindness. (iii) And thirdly and lastly, the locality of an impression, the position of a

limb, etc., can be indicated by 'localising' movements. Hitherto, no sharp line of division has been drawn between these different modes in which the spatial peculiarities of the sense of touch may find expression, although their discrimination is necessary in the interests of psychological analysis and theoretic explanation. In particular, we are still in ignorance as to which of the three forms of spatial apprehension is the most accurate, and therefore possibly the most original in its application to the tactual data. The common element in all of them is the unequivocal relation in which the tactual sensations must be conceived to stand to visual ideas, direct judgments or movements. The first problem presented by the facts of tactual space perception is accordingly that of the origin of this unequivocal relation,—how it has arisen that a touch upon the back of the hand, when the eyes are closed, excites just the visual idea of this part of the skin and no other, just the particular name of this cutaneous area, or just the special movement of the other hand to the stimulated surface.

2. The first noteworthy attempt at a resolution of this problem is Lotze's *theory of local signs*. Its metaphysical origin need not delay us here, more particularly as we may neglect this without prejudice to the psychological constituents of the hypothesis. Lotze sets out to explain the inexchangeableness of impressions, *i.e.*, the fact that every impression is invariably referred to a definite locality. This reference would not be possible unless they somehow varied with their place of excitation. If the sensations from the skin of the hand, *i.e.*, were wholly similar to the sensations from the skin of the back, it is not conceivable that the mind could acquire the ability to localise each group correctly. Lotze accordingly ascribes to the locally distinct or distinguishable cutaneous impressions a specific qualitative colouring or shading which he expresses by the phrase 'local signature'. The local sign combines with the cutaneous impression dependent upon the quality of stimulus (*i.e.*, pressure or temperature) in the form of an association, in which neither constituent modifies the peculiar character of the other. Lotze gives us some idea of what he regards as the nature of the local signature by pointing out that the skin is very different in structure at different parts of the body,—now covered by a thick, and now by a delicate epidermis; now tightly stretched by its attachment to the bones, now elastic and displaceable within wide limits; now spread over a cushion of fat, now passing over bone or muscle or hollow space. Moreover, in some parts of the body the structural differences pass into one another by slow degrees, in others quite abruptly. It is plain that all these conditions can only

influence the intensity of the impression. The system of local signs would consequently consist simply in varying degrees of intensity, demonstrable for the same stimulus over different regions of the skin. But it is also possible to interpret local signature as a qualitative colouring, and this view is actually represented by certain psychologists, *e.g.*, by Wundt.

3. The thought upon which this whole theory is based is that the distinguishing characteristics which mediate the localisation of impressions must all be of a *conscious* nature. And here we see the influence of metaphysical prepossession. It was difficult to conceive that the unequivocal relation obtaining between tactual impressions and visual ideas, or other factors subserving localisation, could have arisen without conscious direction, by way (perhaps) of purely physiological connection. But there is no justification for the assumption of these conscious intermediaries in the facts of consciousness itself. (i) It has been found that a longer time is required for the discrimination of intensity than for the discrimination of locality (cf. § 71. 2). This is in itself sufficient evidence that the first cannot be the basis of the second. (ii) Moreover, we are able to graduate the intensities of two pressure stimuli at different parts of the skin until the impressions appear to be equally intensive. But provided that the absolute intensity of the sensations interposes no difficulty, the discrimination of locality is not affected in the least. (iii) And again, one of the most prompt and certain forms of localisation under normal conditions is reference to the right or left side of the body. Now if we take two entirely symmetrical areas, *e.g.*, the back of the right and the left hand, we have very great similarity of anatomical conditions. On Lotze's view, therefore, the discrimination of locality should here be very difficult, if not altogether impossible. From all these reasons we must conclude that the theory of local signature, at least in the special form in which Lotze has applied it to the sense of touch, is untenable. But neither does there seem any adequate ground for the assumption of a qualitative colouring, varying with the particular locally distinguishable cutaneous impressions. The hypothesis posits a very large number of discriminable qualities, of which we find no sufficient evidence in consciousness (cf. § 10. 4).

4. At all events, the connection of tactual impressions with localising movements is possible without any participation of consciousness. The decapitated frog which is touched with acetic acid at some point of its body, brings one or the other leg to the stimulated part with great accuracy of movement. In sleep, too, we brush aside unpleasant cutaneous impressions without knowing anything of our action. It is

an obvious conjecture, then, that the real basis of tactual localisation is to be looked for in the movement sensations aroused in us by these localising touches of stimulated regions. And the view is represented by Bain and others. Even where movements are not directly executed, we are supposed on the hypothesis to notice the impulses to movement, and to argue from their character to the locality of stimulation. But there are three objections to the theory. (i) In the first place, it is altogether unable to explain cases of wholly unconscious and reflex motor localisation. (ii) Moreover, it really does no more than push the entire problem one step further back, since the other question at once arises how the movement sensations have acquired this unequivocal relation to visual ideas or judgments. (iii) And lastly, the original problem remains unsolved. For the unequivocal relation obtaining between cutaneous impressions and localising movements still requires special explanation, *i.e.*, the hypothetical ascription of some kind of specific character to the former. Nothing is left, therefore, but to transfer the local signs to the sphere of anatomy or physiology. We must then demand either a special anatomical connection, or a physiological connection perfected by practice, in virtue of which locally determinate cutaneous stimulations give rise to wholly determinate movements or visual ideas or judgments.

5. The most original of these localising factors is, in all probability, the movement towards the stimulated part. For there can be no doubt that the connection between visual ideas or direct judgments and the different cutaneous impressions takes shape in the course of the individual development, while certain localising movements are almost certainly inherited. Moreover, we may suppose that the connection of visual ideas (under normal conditions of vision) with cutaneous stimulations is not only earlier than the formation of an immediate space judgment, but is also, as a general rule, more accurate in its indication of the locality of the impression. Hence it would follow that the direct space judgments,—the accurate employment of which presupposes, of course, the further acquisition of a system of special symbols,—were originally developed under the influence of the other two instruments of localisation, sight and movement, and are even now to some extent dependent upon them. We may, accordingly, confine our present investigation into the conditions of localisation to the discussion of visual ideas and localising movements. The question then arises, whether the local signs (we use the term 'local sign' in its most general significance as the equivalent of 'condition of localisation') are to be conceived of as anatomical or physiological in

origin. (i) An anatomical connection of peripheral and central con-
ductions is wholly improbable in the case of the visual ideas. The
connection is built up gradually, in the form of an association. It is,
therefore, impossible to believe that certain central cells, which are
excited by cutaneous stimuli, are given a priori in an isolated anatomical connection with certain other central cells, whose excitations are
the substrate of visual ideas. Nor is there any likelihood of an original anatomical connection between cutaneous stimulations and localising movements. For the transference of an excitation from the sensory
to the motor centres of the spinal cord may be very differently mediated, and take very different directions. (ii) We are thus forced to the
conclusion that local signature has been physiologically originated.
There then arises the further question, whether the unequivocalness
of the local sign is determined by the nature of the excitation as
central or peripheral. We may answer it by a reference to the
phenomena of localisation in cases of transplantation of fragments of
the skin. If a piece of the skin of the forehead is used to cover the
nose, *e.g.*, a touch upon the transplanted area calls up the idea of a
touch upon the original locality, and is consequently referred to the
forehead, for a considerable time after the performance of the operation. We can only interpret this fact by making the peripheral nervous terminations in the skin of determining importance for localisation.
Further evidence to the same effect is afforded by the gradual correction of the erroneous localisation, which comes with practice under
the changed conditions. We conclude, then, that the local signs
must be regarded as physiological peculiarities of peripheral excitation.

6. The spatial functions of the articular sensibility must be
explained in the same way, *i.e.*, by the hypothesis of a local signature in the form of physiological peculiarities of the peripheral
sensory excitations. But before we apply this principle in detail, we
must attempt to analyse a phenomenon of the articular sensibility
which has aroused the belief that there are specific 'movement sensations' in addition to the 'sensations of position' noticed above
(§ 23. 6; § 56. 6). It has been found that the judgment of 'movement' may be formed, before there is any knowledge of the direction
which the movement takes, or of the positions assumed by the moved
limb between its limiting points. An exactly similar phenomenon
occurs with movement of the eyes in the darkened field of vision,
and again, when an external object moves rapidly for a short distance
over the skin or in the field of vision. The question is, then,
whether we must assume the existence of 'movement sensations' of
a specific kind. Now the fact that the same result can be produced

in so many different ways is a sufficient indication that it is not due to definite sensory conditions, but is a phenomenon of more general psychological significance. And, indeed, we find it re-appearing in various other sensory judgments. Thus in the discrimination of sensation differences, there is a certain lower limit of objective difference, at which we can say that a difference exists, but have no idea of its special nature. Hence, if we assume movement sensations in the one case, we should assume a specific 'difference sensation' in the other. But neither assumption is valid. The real explanation of the facts lies in the character of the relation obtaining between the direct and indirect sensitivity and sensible discrimination (cf. § 4). In other words, not every sensation or sensation difference finds adequate expression in a judgment, but the formation of the judgment is subject to special conditions. These conditions come under the general rubric of association. The most important of them is expressed in the law that general or abstract names are more easily reproduced than concrete (§ 27. 5, 6). The judgment of 'movement' is certainly of more general significance than the judgment of 'movement in a definite direction' and 'of definite extent and duration'. Hence a movement of slight extent and high rapidity will reproduce the more general judgment, though it is unable to call up a more special definition. There remains the other point,—that the various positions of the moved limb are not separately remarked. This phenomenon, again, has many analogies: we are unable to discriminate the various degrees of intensity in the rise of a tone, in the growing brilliance of an illumination, and in an increasing pressure upon the skin. And we have seen that the estimation of any sensory impression requires a certain amount of time. Here again, then, is a phenomenon of general occurrence, referable to the fact that not every attribute or alteration of a sensation is expressible in a particular judgment. When it appears in connection with continuous change of intensity or quality, however, we do not at once set up a special class of sensations (sensations of rise and fall, *e.g.*). So here, we need not assume a specific 'movement sensation' in contradistinction to 'sensations of position'.

7. We may now pass to the consideration of the special form assumed by the local sign theory in its application to the facts of cutaneous and articular sensibility (§ 56). The delimitation of the local signature at different parts of the skin has been suggested, in particular, by the experiments on the space limen. The first theory to mention in this connection is Weber's hypothesis of *sensation circles* (§ 56. 1). It is based upon the valid assumption that a just

noticeable separateness of sensations is indicative of the relative dimensions of the area covered by stimuli at different parts of the skin. The sensation circle is simply an area of this kind, characterised by the indistinguishability of two stimuli which fall within its borders. Weber accordingly looks upon the skin as a mosaic of sensation circles, which differ in form and magnitude from part to part of its surface. Sensations originated in neighbouring circles differ very slightly; and their difference increases, up to a certain limit, with the number of separate sensation circles included between the two points of contact. The perception of an interval between these points requires the intervention of several unstimulated sensation circles. A vague recollection of their number arouses in the mind the idea of an interval, and this interval increases subjectively with the number of unstimulated circles. The specific sensitivity of the circles, finally, is due to differences in the distribution of sensory nerve trunks, whose peripheral radiations do not mediate spatially discriminable sensations.

Weber's theory, however, cannot be reconciled with Goldscheider's observation that a space limen is obtainable from two neighbouring pressure spots; for in this case it is impossible to suppose that a certain number of unstimulated sensation circles intervene between the just noticeably separate stimuli. Goldscheider accordingly substitutes for the sensation circles a system of radially disposed nervous terminations.

8. In one respect, however, Weber's whole idea needs revision — as regards the psychological relation between the just noticeable separateness of two points in contact with the skin, and the distance contained between them. The connection between separateness and distance can only be interpreted in one of two ways. Either we must assume (and this is the more obvious supposition) that the impression has a very different extension at different parts of the skin, so that the least noticeable distance always remains constant, and wears so different an appearance in objective measurement simply because the extension of the separate stimuli is very different in sensation: or we must imagine that the estimation of the spatial significance of different stimuli is essentially different in different places, so that, *e.g.*, a given distance upon the back has a quite different significance from the same distance upon the forehead. In the former case, *i.e.*, the difference of the space limen would be attributable to the different subjective extension of the stimuli; whereas in the second case, the difference would be reducible merely to a relative overestimation or underestimation of the stimulus distance. We can

hardly decide in favour of either view, until investigations have been made into the perception of extension. In all probability, however, both processes are concerned in the production of the observed result. The second explanation in particular finds distinct support in the fact that the subjective differences of extension with simple contact are not so large as we shoud expect them to be, if the first alone were cogent.

Still less can be said at present of the local signature of the articular sensibility. There is a certain connection between the number of cutaneous nerves within a given area and the delicacy of spatial discrimination. But nothing is known of a similar topographical distribution of sensory nerves over the articular surfaces, although the differences in sensitivity for extent of movement in the different joints seem to suggest it.

9. The space perception of the congenitally blind is almost exclusively mediated by the functions of the cutaneous and articular sensibilities,—apart, of course, from the very accurate localisation of auditory impressions. We cannot hesitate to identify the spatial attributes of cutaneous sensations, at least in principle, with those of vision. Extension is a common property of these two senses, just as duration or succession is a common predicate of sense impressions in general. We must believe, therefore, that congenital blindness is compatible with a real space perception. We have already remarked incidentally that the spatial functions of skin and joint are ordinarily more delicate in the blind than where vision is normal (§ 56. 2, 4, 8). The fact is probably referable simply to the greater share of the attention, and to the more constant practice which the sense of touch receives in blindness. But there is no evidence that the tactual space perception of the blind furnishes them with any new quality of sensation. Thus the 'feeling of distance', which often reaches a high degree of development, seems to depend entirely upon changes of pressure or temperature noticed by the peculiarly sensitive skin of the face as an object is approached. The space idea in normal vision is far richer in qualitative variety, far more comprehensive at each moment, and far more differentiated (owing to the greater refinement of the retina as an organ of space perception) than that of the blind. Hence we can understand that a congenitally blind patient, restored to sight by operation, accustoms himself slowly and with difficulty to the new world of visual space into which he is suddenly introduced. But his inability to name objects presented to him does not justify the conclusion that he has at first no visual space perception at all. The colligation of the familiar name with the absolutely new conscious

contents must be learned, as it had to be learned originally in tactual space perception.

10. Observations of the results of operation for congenital blindness are not adequate, then,—as has often been supposed,—to the settlement of a theoretical controversy, the controversy of *empirism* and *nativism*. The nativistic theory of space assumes that certain constituents of space perception are connate or given a priori. The empiristic theory declares, on the other hand, that the whole system of space perception is a product of gradual development. It is evident that the distinction becomes psychologically important only when an originally 'spatial' is opposed to an originally 'unspatial'; when, *i.e.*, the theories take the form (i) that certain spatial attributes attach to the very first visual or tactual idea which appears in consciousness, and (ii) that spatial attributes do not primarily attach to these ideas at all. A strict empirism in this latter sense seems tenable only as connected with some metaphysical view of the mind. Psychologically, it is imposible for us to conceive of a visual or cutaneous sensation wholly deprived of spatial character. It is sometimes urged that the auditory nerve might also have a spatial function, since its separate fibres are capable of isolated conduction. The objection overlooks the fact that a simple correspondence between the points in space and particular sensory terminations obtains only for skin and retina. Only the sensations excited in these two organs, *i.e.*, can be accredited with direct spatial attributes. The correspondence is not the same even for the articular sensibility, where it subserves the development of the idea of position or movement. An unequivocal connection between the local signs of articular impressions and the movements of the limbs is the presupposition of the great importance which they come to possess for certain space ideas. The controversy between nativism and empirism would seem, therefore, to be based upon misunderstanding.

§ 58. The External Conditions of Visual Space Perception.

1. The external conditions of tactual space perception are comparatively simple and readily distinguishable. Those of visual space perception, on the other hand, are extremely complicated, and we must consequently devote a Section to the consideration of the different factors which the spatial judgment involves. The spatial functions of monocular vision are different from those of binocular, and those of the resting eye from those of the moving. Moreover, the retinal image which corresponds to an object in external space is dependent upon the refraction, constant or variable, of the rays of light in their

path through the eye. We will, therefore, begin with a brief summary of the effects of these different conditions upon spatial vision.

I. Monocular Vision.

(a) *The Resting Eye.*—The rays of light which penetrate the eye are more or less limited in number by the small size of the pupil, and changed in direction by a series of refractive media. (i) The small size of the pupil sets a limit to the extension of the spatial field of the resting eye. The limit is variable, as the circle of the pupil varies,—reflexly constricted or dilated by the muscles *sphincter* and *dilatator pupillae* of the iris. The pupillar reflex bears no direct relation to the spatial character of the seen object. As a general rule, strong stimuli produce constriction and weak stimuli dilatation, though the reflex is also subject to organic conditions.

2. (ii) The media which change the course of the rays of light are as follows, in the order from without inward: cornea, aqueous humour, lens and vitreous humour. Each of these media has a different index of refraction, as has each layer of the lens. It is usual to discuss these influences under simpler conditions, in the 'reduced' eye of Listing,—an eye which has only one optical centre and, therefore, only one point of intersection of all unrefracted rays. This point is termed the nodal point of the lines of direction. It lies in the posterior curvature of the lens, at a distance of about 15 mm. from the retina. The construction of the retinal image of the reduced eye is exceedingly simple, since all the various conditions of refraction are conceived of as concentrated in the lens, which is then given a single ideal exponent. The lens itself acts as a converging lens, so that the retinal image of a visible object is inverted, diminished and real. This image will plainly be distinct in one case only,—when all the rays proceeding from a luminous point meet again in a single point upon the retina. If, therefore, the curvature of the refractive medium were invariable, as in an ordinary glass lens, distinct vision would only be possible at one definite distance of the object from the eye. The eye, however, possesses a *mechanism of accommodation*, by which the degree of curvature of the lens can be varied within fairly wide limits. The limits of accommodation are the limits of distinct vision, and are generally referred to as the 'near point' and the 'far point' of accommodation. Changes in lenticular curvature are effected by the contraction of the muscle of accommodation, which is attached to the choroid coat and pulls upon the zonula Zinnii, a membrane surrounding the edge of the lens. If the muscle is unstimulated, this

membrane is stretched taut, and so gives the lens a weaker curvature. If the muscle contracts, the choroid is brought forward, the zonula relaxed, and the lens forced into a stronger curve by its own elastic tension.

3. In the emmetropic (normal) eye, the far point of accommodation is infinitely distant, the near point 12 to 13 cm. from the eye. In the myopic (short-sighted) eye, the far point is brought to a finite distance and the near point also approaches the eye; in the hypermetropic (long-sighted) eye, the near point is abnormally distant. If the eye is wrongly accommodated, the object seen gives rise to dispersion images upon the retina, due either to the meeting of the rays proceeding from a luminous point in front of the retina or to the situation of their ideal meeting point behind it. The mechanism of accommodation thus secures a distinct vision of objects at very different distances and within wide limits of absolute distance.

The sensitive retinal units are the cones (cf. § 21. 2). These occur in the greatest numbers in the fovea centralis, a transparent depressed area at the centre of the yellow spot (macula lutea). At this point some 13,500 cones have been counted in 1 □ mm. The macula lutea is termed the *spot of clearest vision.* It is principally employed in the 'fixation' of an object. Hence we distinguish between direct and indirect vision: if the retinal image of an object is formed at the spot of clearest vision, it is seen directly; if it is formed at some point in the lateral portions of the retina, it is seen indirectly. The line of junction between the fovea centralis and the luminous point is named the visual axis. It meets the line of junction between nodal point and luminous point, the optical axis, at an angle of about 5°, whose vertex lies at the nodal point (point of intersection of the lines of direction). The different distances separating the cones correspond to the different distances between spatially discriminable pressure spots in the skin. The diameter of the point of a cone is about 0.6 μ ($1 \mu = \frac{1}{1000}$ mm.); and the distance between cone and cone seems to be not much greater than this diameter: it has been measured as about 2 μ. The resting eye is accordingly as well fitted for every kind of spatial function as is any not moving part of the skin. Extension and figure, distance and position and movement can all find representation on the resting retina in monocular vision. But besides this we have a definite empirical criterion for the distance from the eye of a visible object, in the strain of accommodation and dispersion images. The various degrees of accommodation may arouse sensation, and the dispersion images indicate the position of the object which gives rise to them as before or behind the object of distinct vision.

4. (b) *The Moving Eye.*—The eyeball is a sphere, moving with great ease and rapidity on the fatty cushion of the orbit. All its movements are movements of rotation, and the point round which they are made, the point of rotation, lies some 6 mm. behind the nodal point on the *line of regard*, the line of junction between the fixation point and the point of rotation. The angle formed by the rays which pass through the nodal point is the visual angle; the angle which the eye describes in movement the angle of rotation. The angle of rotation is, accordingly, always somewhat smaller than the visual angle, for a constant distance of two points in space. The eye is moved by means of six muscles, constituting three pairs of antagonists. The first pair, the internal and external recti, turn the eye outwards and inwards in the horizontal plane; *i.e.*, their axis of rotation lies in a vertical plane at right angles to the line of regard. The second pair, the superior and inferior recti, turn the eye up and down, but exert a slight pull inwards at the same time. Their axis of rotation is, therefore, perpendicular neither to the line of regard nor to the axis of rotation of the first pair. It makes an angle of about 70° with the line of regard. The rotatory movement in this case is consequently more complicated. We may regard it as composed of a rotation round a horizontal axis, cutting the eye at the point of rotation, and perpendicular to the vertical axis and to the line of regard, of a rotation round the line of regard, and of a rotation round a vertical axis. By the first component the eye is raised and lowered, while by the other two it is rotated inwards. A rotation whose axis is the line of regard is termed torsion or swivel rotation. Its magnitude is measured by the angle of torsion.

5. The movement produced by the third pair of muscles, the superior and inferior obliqui, is also a composite rotation. The superior obliquus lowers the eye and turns it outwards; the inferior raises the eye and turns it outwards. The axis of rotation of these muscles lies in the same plane with the horizontal axis and the line of regard, but makes an angle of 30° with the latter. The superior obliquus, *i.e.*, assists the inferior rectus to depress the line of regard, but is antagonistic to it as regards torsion; the inferior obliquus assists the superior rectus to raise the eye, but is similarly antagonistic to it with regard to torsion. There is only one movement which can be effected by a single pair of muscles,—movement outwards and inwards. Movement in any other direction requires the co-operation of four or of all six muscles.

The spatial functions of the eye which depend upon movement are (i) primarily indirect: movement changes the retinal image of the resting eye, under constant conditions of external environment. The spot of clearest vision can thus be brought into connection with different external objects over a fairly wide area, and the whole field of vision is considerably enlarged. Movement of the eye would in this respect be precisely analogous to movement of the head or of the whole body; and would be preferable to either of these movements simply in virtue of its greater facility and rapidity. But (ii) eye movement has also been held to exert a direct influence upon visual space perception. The muscular sensations produced by the contraction of the different eye muscles, it is said, furnish a delicate and accurate measure of spatial distances. We shall discuss the validity of this hypothesis later (§§ 59, 3, 8; 60, 3, 4; 61).

II. Binocular Vision.

6. (a) *The Resting Eyes.*—A portion of the fields of vision of the two eyes is coincident in binocular vision, while the remaining parts of the total field are seen only by a single eye. The luminous points in the common portion, the centre of the full field, are represented upon both retinae. They may, however, be seen as single; in which case their points of representation upon the retinae are termed *corresponding* or *identical* points. The position of these points is not anatomically determined, but is very largely dependent upon the special practice of the eyes in binocular vision. Thus they are differently situated in eyes which squint and in eyes whose movement is symmetrical. Only in the latter are they symmetrically arranged with reference to the fovea centralis. But their strict localisation is not possible at any time. Circumstances may always arise under which a unitary image of a luminous point is mediated by asymmetrically situated retinal points, although the possible variation from symmetry is not large. We cannot, therefore, correctly speak of corresponding 'points', but must rather say that each sensitive point upon one retina 'corresponds' to a small area upon the other. The sum total of luminous points which find representation upon corresponding parts of the retinae is called the *horopter.* The mathematical construction of the horopter has often been attempted; but the variability of the corresponding points deprives it of all practical importance. If a luminous point stimulates retinal points which lie beyond the limits of correspondence, we have two spatially separate sensations, or double images. This single or double vision of objects in space constitutes an important addition to the spatial functions of the resting eye in monocular vision; double images enable us to

measure distance in the third dimension with great accuracy, and
thus transform areal into tridimensional vision.

7. (*b*) *The Moving Eyes.*—The ends of vision are greatly furthered
by an automatic co-ordination of the movements of the two eyes,
which is perfected at a comparatively early stage of individual development. There are then, as a general rule, only two possible forms
of movement: (i) *parallel movement*, during which the lines of regard
of the two eyes remain constantly parallel to each other, and (ii) movements of *convergence*, in which the lines of regard of the two eyes
intersect at some point of objective space. Movements of divergence,
i.e., movements in which the two lines of regard would intersect at
a point behind the eyes, occur only in exceptional cases, as the
result of special practice or a pathological disability of certain muscles.
Parallel movements may be regarded as movements of convergence
in which the lines of regard intersect at an infinitely distant point of
space. Movements of convergence are further divided into *symmetrical*
and *asymmetrical*. In symmetrical convergence the lines of regard
make equal angles with the horizontal axis of the two eyes; in asymmetrical convergence these angles are unequal. Asymmetrical convergence is confined to movement from without inwards and from
within outwards; convergence of the eyes upward or downward is
always symmetrical. The *orientation* of the eye, *i.e.*, its position with
regard to objects in the field of vision, is by no means constant for
all movements. It has been found, more particularly in experiments
upon the apparent locality of after-images, that a constant orientation
of the eyes during movement is only possible under one condition,
that the movement be made from the *primary position*, in which
the lines of regard are parallel and inclined a little below the horizontal plane. *Secondary positions* are reached by simple movements
outwards and inwards or upwards and downwards, *i.e.*, by movements
in which either the plane of the primary position or the parallelism of
the lines of regard is retained. *Tertiary* positions are reached by
convergent movement of the lines of regard upwards or downwards,
i.e., by movements in which neither the parallelism of the lines of
regard nor the horizontal plane of the primary position is preserved.
The divergence of all these new positions from the primary position
is expressed by the magnitude of the ascensional angle or the angle
of lateral displacement or both.

8. The first secondary position can be brought about by the exclusive action of the external and internal recti. The second requires
the combined action of the superior rectus and inferior obliquus, or
of the inferior rectus and superior obliquus. A tertiary position can

only be obtained by the combination of all three pairs: movement outwards and downwards, *e.g.*, presupposes the co-operation of the exterior and inferior recti and the superior obliquus. All movements of this kind involve torsion of the eyes. We need not consider the forms and laws of these composite eye movements in detail, as their interest is purely physiological. But it may be noticed that the relation between orientation and direction of movement has evidently taken shape under the influence of visual experience. It may be regarded in essential as a purposive connection of the two eyes for common fixation. Hence movements of divergence, which would be unserviceable for this purpose, have not been developed at all. The two lines of regard can only move under the condition that a common fixation point is possible, and the displacement of the retinal image is intimately related to movements of regard. Another factor in the result is the preference accorded to the fixated parts of the field of vision by the selective function of the attention.

It is again questionable whether the movements of the eyes in binocular vision stand in a direct relation to visual space estimation, or are simply indirect aids to spatial perception, like movements of head and body (cf. 5 above). If the former view be held, it becomes necessary, in the interests of psychological theory, to take account of the muscular or other sensations arising from eye movement, and to consider the relative strength or weakness of the particular muscles, *i.e.*, the mechanical conditions of muscular action in the orbit. Otherwise, these questions need not detain us. Movements of convergence at all events furnish a means for the estimation of the distance of an object from the eye. The degree of convergence is a measure of the proximity of the object. There is a close interconnection of movement of convergence and accommodation, so that, as a general rule, the object of binocular fixation is clearly seen. Recent investigation has made it probable that this interconnection is connate.

§ 59. The Facts of Visual Space Perception.

I. The Estimation of Extension and Distance.

1. The just noticeable visual extension and distance are exceedingly small. Their determination is quite simple: two luminous points, white lines, etc., at a constant distance from the eye, are approximated or separated to the limit at which they are just noticeably distinguishable. Either the visual angle or the distance between the two retinal images may be used to express the *keenness of vision*, *i.e.*, the capacity of

discrimination of points in space. It has been found that keenness of vision is largely dependent upon the part of the retina stimulated. It is greatest in direct vision, and decreases continuously towards the lateral portions of the retina, so that its value at 30^0 to 40^0 from the fovea centralis is only $\frac{1}{100}$ of its value at the centre. The just noticeable distance of colours and brightnesses in direct vision is about one minute of arc (visual angle) or 0.004 mm. (distance between retinal images). It is probable, however, that this result is vitiated by irradiation, the diffusion of stimulation on the retina: at least, a much smaller value has been recently obtained by a different method. Two lines or slits were taken, one below the other, and their relative position altered until the change in direction became just noticeable. The visual angle was here only 10" to 12" (seconds of arc), and the corresponding distance between the retinal images only 0.00089 mm.

2. The accuracy of the eye for the comparison of spaces of some length, *eye measurement* as it is called, has been made the subject of frequent investigation. The chief points at issue have been the validity of Weber's law for the sensible discrimination of visual extension, the part played in comparison by eye movements, the influence of the quality of the estimated distances upon the judgment of their extent, etc. But no satisfactory conclusion has been reached, despite the number of experiments made. The outcome of the different researches has not always been the same; in some cases the method employed has been exceptionable; and there are various circumstances whose isolation, while necessary for certainty of result, is very difficult, if not impossible. The absolute sensible discrimination has always been found to decrease with the extent of the distances compared, both as regards magnitude (method of minimal changes) and delicacy (method of average error). The relative sensible discrimination appears from several investigations to be constant within certain limits, with a relative difference limen of approximately $\frac{1}{50}$. From others, however, it would seem at first to increase and then to decrease with increase of the distance, and to show no constancy over any particular region. The quality of the compared distances is of great importance for the estimation of their extent. We have evidence of this in our everyday experience: a life-size portrait appears smaller than it really is; if we try to draw the diameter of a half-crown we ordinarily make it too small, etc. Distances which are bounded by two points, 'point distances', are taken to be smaller than ruled lines of equal objective length; while interrupted lines, composed of a series of points or small dashes, appear longer than ruled lines. The position of the compared distances is

also of importance. Vertical distances generally appear larger than horizontal, and a distance to the left greater than a distance to the right. If two space lengths are compared at different distances from the eye, the more remote is relatively overestimated. Again, it has been shown that the sensible discrimination of the moving eye is greater than that of the resting, and that in either case it is somewhat greater with binocular vision than with monocular. Comparison is apparently most accurate when the eyes are allowed to move unconstrainedly to and fro over the stimulus distances, for a little time before judgment is passed. A purely successive estimation diminishes sensible discrimination, more especially if the distance of comparison does not simply replace the normal distance, but is shown in some other spot. The result in this case is further modified by the length of time elapsing between the perception of the two distances.

II. The Estimation of Position and Direction.

3. The most important element in the determination of the position of an object in space, apart from its distance from other objects in the visual field, is its distance from the body of the observing subject. The perception of this distance is the *idea of depth* or of the third dimension. This idea can only be formed by indirect means. There is no specific representation of distance in depth upon the retina, which can only reflect the extension or distance of objects in space in the horizontal or vertical direction. There are three indirect aids to the idea of depth in monocular vision: the degree of accommodation, dispersion images, and eye movement. The first of these has been experimentally tested, with the result that the difference limen was approximately $\frac{1}{10}$ of the compared distances. It possesses no great accuracy, therefore, and in any case its assistance is necessarily restricted to the limits of accommodation. Dispersion circles, again, give no definite information as to the distance of the object from the eye, since the object represented by the dispersion image might equally well be situated before or behind the object of reference (whose existence must be assumed), *i.e.*, the object of clear vision. And lastly, the reliability of eye movement is inversely proportional to the distance of the compared objects from the eye. In appealing to it, we make the length of the path traversed by the point of regard the measure of the distance of the object (the movement being supposed to begin from our own body, *i.e.*, from the feet). But the farther from us two objects really are, the smaller, of course, is the movement of the point of regard corresponding to the difference

in their distances.   On the whole, therefore, monocular vision is characterised by lack of perspective or of depth discrimination.

4.   There are two principal aids to the formation of the idea of depth in binocular vision, which enable us to estimate the distance of objects from our own body.   These are movements of convergence and double images.   Experiments upon convergence have shown that the difference limen is about $\frac{1}{80}$ of the distances compared, *i.e.*, that there is constancy of the relative sensible discrimination.   But the most important aid to the estimation of depth is the difference between the retinal images of the two eyes.   The right eye sees a depth difference of two points in space differently from the left eye.   This can easily be verified by observation (alternate closing of the two eyes) and by geometrical construction.   The third dimension of a single object, *i.e.*, or the depth distance between two objects, is always differently represented upon the two retinae.   Thus if a point *a* lies behind the point of fixation *b*, in the median plane (the plane which bisects the line of junction of the two points of ocular rotation or optical centres at right angles), its apparent distance from *b* is the same in both eyes, but it is seen with the right as far to the right of *b* as it is seen with the left to the left of *b* (*uncrossed double images*).   If it lies in the median plane before the point of fixation *b*, it is seen by the right eye as far to the left of *b*, as it is by the left to the right of *b* (*crossed double images*).   The idea of depth originates in the combination of these different individual functions of the two eyes (§ 58. 6; cf. § 51. 7): in other words, it is reducible to the difference between retinal distances.   And, as a matter of fact, it has been found in experiments upon the just noticeable change of depth, that the accuracy with which we estimate depth differences in the distance of an object from our own body or from a given object of reference is the same with the keenness of vision or delicacy of eye measurement.   This circumstance is of the very highest importance for perspective vision.   Under any other condition it would be absolutely impossible that the reverse effect should be produced, and superficial area seen as tridimensional reality.

5.   Our judgment of the distance of an object from our own body, however, is not wholly mediated by these visual factors.   There are a number of empirical criteria which are of importance here as they are for visual space perception in general.   One such criterion, *e.g.*, is the clearness of the distant object.   The more distinct it appears, the nearer do we take it to be: hence distant houses or mountains seen on a clear day seem nearer than they do when the air is damp and foggy.   The directions which we attribute to objects in space have already been referred to in our discussion of distance (cf. 2

above); but they call for special mention here because their determination stands in direct relation to the local quality of our own
body. Right and left, above and below, before and behind, are
primarily indicative of the position of the body with regard to the
objects of which they are predicated. As the reciprocal orientation
of the various parts of the body is ordinarily constant, the determination
of their position is an adequate criterion of spatial direction. This is
the key to the solution of the much discussed problem of the inversion
of the retinal image.

III. The Perception of Figure.

6. The perception of the figure of an object is reducible (§ 55. 4)
to the perception of a sum of extensions. Of determining importance
are the limiting lines or surfaces and their position in regard to one
another. We can estimate with great accuracy whether a line is
straight or curved, and whether two lines are parallel, divergent or
convergent. Visual estimation of the magnitude of the angle formed
by two convergent lines, however, is less accurate. The perception
of surface presents a special problem, since the discreteness of the
sensitive retinal units has to be reconciled with the continuity of the
areal field of vision. In particular, there is quite a large area in
either eye which is insensitive to light, —the *blind spot* at the place
of entry of the optic nerve, towards the nasal periphery of the two
retinae. The existence of this spot was not discovered until the
seventeenth century, and is only demonstrable by special experiments.
It cannot, of course, be remarked in binocular vision, since the nasal
portions of the monocular fields are coincident (§ 58. 6), so that what
is blind in the right retina corresponds to a sensitive portion of the
left, and *vice versa*. But neither is there any perception of it in monocular
vision as a gap or hole in the visual field: it is apparently altogether
filled out by the quality of its environment. An object which lies
exactly opposite to the blind spot in the field of vision is not seen,
its place being apparently taken by a simple continuation of its
surroundings. This effacement is greatly assisted by the indistinctness
of indirect vision. On the other hand, there is no real problem in
the relation of the discrete cones to the continuous field of vision.
Since the keenness of vision is hardly adequate to appreciate the
distance between cone and cone (§§ 58. 3; 59. 1), the discreteness of
the retina has no existence in space perception.

7. The perception of a body, of a tridimensional object, —stereoscopic vision, —involves a new factor, the idea of depth. Our previous

discussion of its formation (II above) also applies here. The most important factor in stereoscopic vision, especially if the visual objects are somewhat small, is the disposition of the double images, the distance of the retinal images from one another. Eye movement is certainly not of determining influence (§ 58. 8); for stereoscopic vision is possible when the object is illuminated by the electric spark, *i.e.*, when the duration of stimulus is so short that eye movements are entirely precluded. Moreover, the artificial combination of two areal images in the stereoscope proves that the real basis of the idea of depth is simply the different position of the retinal images in the two eyes. On the other hand, the tridimensional interpretation of a superficial representation, *e.g.*, of a drawing in perspective, is wholly dependent upon empirical criteria. The illusion of tridimensionality must be produced by shading, by the distribution of colour and brightness, by the omission of the farther side of the object represented, etc. And lastly, it is noteworthy that the discrimination of particular objects in space is the result of a development, principally conditioned by the constant interconnection of their various constituents through all other changes of spatial relation. The congenitally blind are wholly unable to distinguish particular things immediately after the operation. They see a single, comprehensive whole, made up of different brightnesses and colour tones; and they are subject to a whole series of illusions as to the nature of objects presented to them, which are referable to their inability to isolate the particular thing from its surroundings.

IV. The Perception of Movement.

8. Alteration of the position of an object is only determinable when the object can be brought into a constant relation with the perceiving eye. For there can plainly be no absolute determination of a continuous spatial alteration; it must be defined by reference to the spatial character of the moving object as previously known, or to other objects of ascertained position. The most important of these objects of reference is the observing eye itself, because the eye is capable of extensive movement, and an apparent movement may, therefore, be due to its own change of position, as well as to that of the object. Estimation of the movement of an object in external space, *i.e.*, necessarily presupposes an accurate determination of the movement of the eye, or of its position in steady fixation. It is to be noted, however, that when the field of vision is completely darkened, objective and subjective movements may be confused within quite wide limits.

In the author's experiments upon centrally excited sensations (§ 28. 2, 3) the subjects were not infrequently deceived as to the position and movement of the faint light stimulus employed. Movement of the objective illumination was entirely excluded by the conditions of the experiment, and the attitude of the body was also constant throughout. Nevertheless, the light was seen above or below, to the right or the left, and was not seldom accredited with a movement in various directions. Similar illusions have been noticed by other observers.

We are thus forced to conclude that our judgment of the position and movement of the eyes is extremely uncertain. Our cognition of the movement of an external object will only be accurate, *i.e.*, when we have some further object of reference by the help of which we may perceive the changes which it undergoes. This object of reference is chiefly useful as ensuring a constant orientation as to the position of the eyes: we can judge with very great accuracy whether or not an object is situated at the common point of regard (§ 58. 8).

9. A movement is completely defined by a statement of its direction, rapidity and extent. These factors have not been sharply enough distinguished in previous experiments upon the perception of movements (only partially, *e.g.*, in investigations into the articular sensibility: cf. § 56, 6-8). Attention has been attracted, however, to the characteristic differences in the visual perception of movement in different parts of the visual field, *i.e.*, over different portions of the retina. Both the magnitude and the rapidity of objective movement are far more adequately cognised in indirect than in direct vision. The limits of the perception of movement have also been ascertained. There are an upper and a lower limit of rapidity, beyond which its perception is impossible. The least rapidity of movement which is just perceptible is that of one to two minutes of arc in the second (= 7 cones per sec. at the centre of the retina). This value is greatly increased if there is no orientation of the moving object by points of reference in the visual field. It is also larger in indirect vision, though this increase is not correlated with diminution of keenness of vision. The determination of the upper limit is merely relative, consisting in the comparison of the just noticeable movement with the just noticeable time difference between the appearance of two visual impressions at different places. While this just noticeable interval or succession is 44σ ($1\sigma = \frac{1}{1000}$ sec.; cf. § 65. 1), a movement between two points at the same distance from the eye is noticeable when the time elapsing between beginning and end is no more than 14σ. The fact that a judgment of movement can be made before any precise judgment of the nature of the spatial change is possible has again led to the assumption of specific movement sensations. The assumption overlooks the fact that general predicates are

always more easy of reproduction than special (cf. § 27. 5, 6; § 57. 6).
Lastly, experiments have been made upon the sensible discrimination
for the rapidity of movement. Accuracy of determination, however,
was only possible for comparatively slow movements, where the difference limen was approximately one minute of arc in the second. At
higher rapidities of movement, the observations were disturbed by
movement after-images or metakinetic movements (§ 60. 5).

§ 60. Optical Illusions.

1. Nothing more need be implied in the expression 'optical illusion'
than that there is a discrepancy between vision and objective measurement. This discrepancy may obviously be due to very different
reasons. Hence the current view that optical illusion is referable to
one definite cause implies a limitation of the term in a definite direction. The ordinary explanation of the phenomena as deceptions of
judgment makes them altogether independent of the anatomical
structure or physiological function of the visual apparatus. If we
are not biassed in favour of this explanation, we cannot refuse to
recognise that optical illusions are produced by a great variety of
causes. At the same time it is noteworthy that visual perception in
particular, the perception to which we owe our most exact and comprehensive knowledge of the external world, is peculiarly susceptible
to subjective influences. We have had instances of this in the filling
out of the blind spot (§ 59. 6), in the idea of depth (§ 59. II), and
in other factors of the normal perception of visual space (*e.g.*, § 59. 5).
The causes of optical illusion may be divided under three general
headings. The first embraces all those conditions of the divergence
of subjective and objective spatial determination which are given with
the visual apparatus. The second includes those associative supplements of sense perception which lead to a discrepancy between a
judgment of the spatial qualities of the visible object and the actual
contents of the sensation or sense idea. And the third comprises
wrong interpretations of sense impressions in the strict use of the
phrase; *i.e.*, a judgment of the given perception which transcends
the visual contents of reproduction or peripheral stimulation on the ground
of certain indirect criteria. It is evident that only the second and third
of these three groups fall within the current definition of optical illusion.

2. We may note that the existence of an optical illusion presupposes the comparison of at least two visual space determinations. No
one would think of applying the term to a just noticeable distance
between two points of visual space. This is simply due to the fact

that we are ordinarily as incapable of an absolute estimation of spatial magnitudes, as we are of intensities or time intervals; and that absolute determination is only possible at all through a continued exercise of memory. We have, therefore, to revise the general definition of optical illusion given above, and to say that illusion arises, not from the discrepancy between vision and objective measurement, but from an error in the comparison of two visual perceptions, one of which is taken as standard. Direct vision, *e.g.*, gives the standard of visual space perception, in contradistinction to indirect vision. The choice of the standard of reference, however, is obviously wholly conventional, and we shall, therefore, pay it no more attention than seems necessary for an exact definition of optical illusion. Remodelling our original statement from this standpoint we may lay it down that optical illusion occurs whenever one and the same objective space character is judged in different ways under the influence of secondary circumstances. We need make no attempt to decide as to the relative correctness of the divergent judgments. The phenomena covered by the expression 'optical illusion,' as we employ it, thus reduce to subjective differences in the spatial estimation of the same visual objects. And we accordingly have to distinguish as many kinds of optical illusion as we found kinds of visual space determination; *i.e.*, illusory perceptions of extension and distance, of position and direction, of figure and of movement. We will give a brief summary of the most important phenomena under these four heads.

3. (*a*) *Illusions of Eye Measurement.*—We have already discussed most of the facts which belong here (§ 59. 2). Thus a square appears to be a rectangle which is higher than it is broad; and if we are required to draw a square we make the vertical sides shorter than the horizontal. As this fact seems to be practically independent of the part of the retina stimulated, we must have recourse to indirect criteria of judgment for its explanation. One theory refers it to the relative ease of eye movement in the two directions, another to subjective influences. But it might also be ascribed to the far greater accuracy of judgment (keenness of vision) in the horizontal direction. This single instance, therefore, shows how difficult it is to trace the real conditions of an optical illusion, and how wide a field is here still open for experimental investigation. Eye movement may be made to some extent responsible for the subjective difference in the estimation of distances, since upward and downward movements imply the activity of more than a single pair of muscles (§ 58. 5), and may accordingly be more difficult than the outward and inward movements mediated simply by the internal and external recti. And there is the further circumstance

that the visual field, whether monocular or binocular and whether for the resting or moving eye, has a less extension in the vertical direction than in the horizontal. No conclusion can at present be drawn as to the relative importance of the two factors.—Different reasons have also been alleged for the apparently greater length of dotted lines as compared with ruled lines. Some observers maintain that the dots serve (so to speak) as stations for the movement of the lines of regard. The eye is detained by them, its movement retarded, and consequently the distance passed through appears longer than when the line can be traversed without hindrance. Others bring the phenomenon into connection with the analogous estimation of time intervals: an interval which is occupied by a succession of separate impressions is taken to be longer than an empty (uniformly filled) interval. From this point of view the illusion would be explicable as an instance of the general type of indirect judgment in which the number of separate constituents in the filling of a duration or extension is made a measure of its length.—A very interesting and striking optical illusion, which has lately been the subject of much discussion, is represented in Fig. 9. The line which is bounded by the acute angles appears much shorter than the line bounded by the obtuse. Some psychologists explain this by the inhibition of eye movement in the former figure. Others refer it to a general rule of optical illusion,—the overestimation of acute angles. In all probability, neither of these views is correct: for the illusion persists both when the movement of the eyes in the opposite direction is artificially assisted, and when the angles are replaced by other figures, e.g., by arcs of circles. The illusion is, therefore, most probably a special case of a general form of indirect judgment, the criteria of which cannot at present be elucidated with any degree of precision.

Fig. 9.

4. (b) *Illusions of Direction and Position.*—Illusions of direction which involve the idea of depth are very common. One of the most familiar instances is the apparent flattening of the arch of the sky at the zenith, with its consequence that the sun and moon seem to be larger when on the horizon than when seen directly overhead. This difference of size may be partly due to the illusion of filled and open spaces, since in moving over the surface of the earth towards the horizon, the point of regard must rest upon a greater number of particular objects, and hence this interrupted distance will

seem longer than the empty distance toward the zenith. And it may be partly due, again, to the density of the atmosphere through which the object is seen. This latter hypothesis is confirmed by the fact that the illusion passes continuously through all stages from limiting value to limiting value. The criterion of distance from our own body would then be the relative clearness of the objects seen (§ 59. 5).— Wrong localisation of direction has been observed in cases of unilateral paralysis of the eye muscles. Thus, if it is impossible to turn the eyes toward the right, but the patient intends to make this movement, the objects in the field of vision seem to have suffered displacement towards the right. The same effect can be produced artificially if the eyes are turned as far as possible toward the left and two large pieces of wax or putty pressed upon the right side of the eye balls. An attempt to move the eyes quickly to the right is, of course, only partially successful, and we again have the illusion of a marked movement of the objects in the field of vision towards the right. This observation has led to the very curious theory that the will to execute movements of the eyes is the sensation of space itself. What the observation really proves is that our judgment of the movement which the eye actually makes

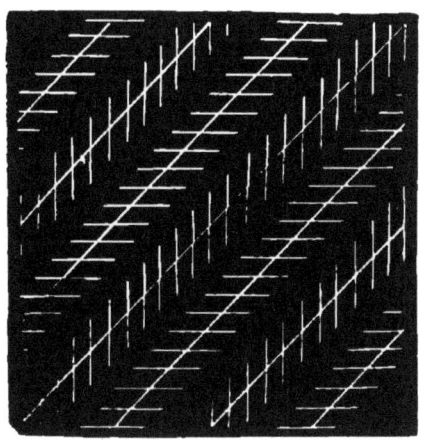

Fig. 10.

is extremely uncertain, and that the mere idea of it suffices under certain circumstances to bring about a very considerable deception with regard to change of objective space relations (§ 59. 8).

5. (*c*) *Illusions of Figure.*—Illusory perceptions of the form and direction of lines are of very frequent occurrence. Thus two parallel lines appear to diverge or converge when they are cut at an acute angle by cross strokes of opposite directions, as is shown in Zöllner's pattern (Fig. 10). The phenomenon is very striking, and has again been explained in various ways. It is usually referred to the over-estimation of acute angles (cf. 3 above), which would make the parallels diverge in the direction of the opening of these angles. The number of illusions under this head is exceedingly great, but they consist for the most part in repetitions of the simpler illusions of distance or direction which we have already discussed.

(*d*) *Apparent Movements.*—Certain apparent movements are due to a confusion of the movement of an object with the movement of our own eyes, or *vice versa.* Thus in railway travelling, where the eyes are passively moved with the whole body, near objects, which pass quickly across the field of vision, seem to move, while more remote objects whose movement across the retina is very slow seem stationary. The moon appears to move when clouds drift across it. This may be partly due to the fact that a change in the position of small objects is always more readily cognisable than the movement of large bodies. Many illusions are attributable to imperceptible eye movements. Thus the bank of a stream appears to travel backwards, because the lines of regard are involuntarily carried forward with the current. Stroboscopic phenomena (the composition of apparent movements from a quick succession of their separate phases) are caused principally by the rise and fall of retinal excitations (§ 24.6). But the recollection of the movement, if it be familiar, *e.g.*, the galloping of a horse, contributes very largely to the sensible reality of the whole phenomenon. There are an upper and a lower limit to the rapidity with which the representations of the separate phases may follow one another; and the apparent movement varies with the difference between these phases and the duration of each impression. Apparent movement may also arise as the result of a very intensive movement idea, perhaps in consequence of imperceptible rotations of the eyes. Thus a statue may seem to be alive, to open its lips, to smile, to nod its head. The chief reason of the illusion here is the associative supplementing of perception (cf. 1 above). Lastly, we may mention in this place the movement after-images or metakinetic apparent movements (§ 59.8). They appear after an objective movement of a certain duration, and consist in an apparently backward movement of stationary objects subsequently fixated. These phenomena may be confined to definite parts of the retina or field of view, so that movements of the eyeball cannot be made responsible for them. They are more correctly regarded as simple after-image phenomena.

§ 61. Theory of Visual Space Perception.

1. A theory of visual space perception must be based upon the epistemological presupposition that the spatial attribute as such is an original datum, and that only its subjective conditions can be made the basis of a psychological theory (§ 55). This was the position which we adopted in our explanation of tactual space perception

(§ 57.1). But the fact could not there be brought out in its full force, because in normal vision the data of touch are constantly referred to the space of sight, and the problem is thereby very greatly simplified. No such reference is possible in the case of visual space itself. The visual space idea is *the* space idea. Even the space of geometry and natural science is not of an entirely different construction, but is simply visual space objectively measured and calculated, *i.e.*, a visual space conceived of as independent of all subjective influences and discrepancies. Science knows no more of a space in itself than it does of a space which is a purely subjective form of intuition, and the metaphysical notion of the non-spatial mind is no more scientifically valuable than the notion of an arrangement of real existences in accordance with the appearance of spatial relations in the world of things. We cannot attempt to explain the inexplicable; we can only seek to assign the reason for the subjective variations of the space datum. But the limits of psychological theory have been constantly overlooked; and time and again the psychologist has set out on no less a quest than the discovery of the origin of the space idea. Now an empirical space theory in the strict sense of the term is altogether impracticable. If the originality of the space datum is once given up, there is not a single fact of visual space perception which any theory will be adequate to explain.

2. From this point of view we shall be unable to accept Lotze's local sign theory in its visual form. In Lotze's view, the local signs which dispose the primarily non-spatial sensations in an apparent space order are to be found in the movement sensations which arise from rotation of the eye. These movements are originally reflexes, which serve to bring an impression to the spot of clearest vision. The nearer the retinal image approaches the periphery, the more extensive is the corresponding reflex movement. All these movements arouse actual sensations, of indescribable quality, and the sensations are utilised by the mind for the arrangement of retinal impressions in visual space. Many objections may be urged against this theory, apart from the general charge of an incorrect epistemological foundation. (i) It overlooks the fact that the most original space determination, that of which the eye is capable, altogether independently of movement, is extension. The field of vision first seen by the congenitally blind after operation,—seen, *i.e.*, before the patient has learned to put a definite spatial interpretation upon his eye movements,—is extended, though the idea of depth is as yet unformed, and the various objects which the eye embraces are as yet unseparated from one another. (ii) It does not give any local sign at all to the spot

24

of clearest vision, although the spot is certainly not a simple point, and although it is capable of more exact local discrimination than any other part of the retina. (iii) It lays stress upon movement sensations; and the movement sensations of the eye are of especially doubtful significance. We have seen that they are extremely unreliable as indices of the position or movement of the eye itself (§ 59. 8); and assuredly we are but very seldom conscious of them under the customary conditions of vision. Besides which, the movements of the head and of the whole body also furnish means for the bringing of an impression upon the spot of clearest vision. This being the case, the complication of movement sensations would plainly be too great to allow of the maintenance of an unequivocal arrangement of visual space solely by the help of eye movements.

3. Lipps has attempted to meet these difficulties by substituting other local signs for the movement sensations. Neighbouring retinal elements, he says, are more frequently excited by similar stimuli, more remote elements by different stimuli. This fact is the basis of spatial arrangement and separation. The hypothesis, however, is not only unproved, but unproveable and improbable to boot. We can neither conceive of an original total impression in which there should be absolutely no separation of the various spatial constituents; nor understand how a connection should be formed between the qualitative difference of the visual impressions and their spatial disposition, so delicate in its adjustment and so reliable in the particular case as the facts demand. It is true that the datum is a visual total impression, whose separate spatial constituents are not cognised or defined as particular objects, *i.e.*, whose various qualities are not grouped together as individual things. But this does not prejudice their intrinsic spatial definiteness; indeed, it is wholly inconceivable that this spatial separateness should be simply non-existent. Moreover, if the connection between the qualitatively like (different) and the spatially proximate (remote) really existed, as it is supposed to exist in Lipps' theory, there would surely be some indication of it in the developed consciousness, and especially when unfamiliar objects are presented to perception. But we find nothing of the kind in experience (with the exception of a trifling effect in the sphere of optical illusion) and statistical theory lends no colour to the hypothesis.

4. Helmholtz practically accepts Lotze's view, but rejects the metaphysical constituents which are so necessary to its support. He is thus led into a wholly incomprehensible empiricism, which somehow makes the muscular sensations arising from eye movement represent the space of visual perception. Hering, on the other hand, holds a

nativistic view, in which spatial vision is referred to the familiar schema of antagonistic nervous processes, altered to suit the condition of tridimensionality (cf. § 21. 4). Every retinal point has three simple space values; a breadth value, a height value and a depth value. Its stimulation will, therefore, arouse three 'space feelings', each of which may be positive or negative in quality. The centre of the retina is the zero point of space value in all the three dimensions. A vertical line ('median longitudinal section') separates the portions of the retina with positive breadth and depth values from those with negative; and a horizontal line ('median transversal section') divides the parts with positive height values from those with negative. The theory is both unphilosophical and unpsychological, and we need not spend time upon its discussion. Movement sensations, again, play an important part in the theory of Wundt (§ 57. 2). But they are regarded as combining with a specific qualitative local signature of the retinal elements for the production of visual space, which is accordingly conceived of as the result of a synthesis or fusion of the two factors. Wundt thus obtains a system of complex local signs, and is thereby able to do fuller justice to the facts than was done by Lotze, with his simple local signature and its merely quantitative gradation. At the same time, when we remember the imperfection of our perception of eye movements (§ 59. 8), it seems impossible to allow them the great importance which they are given in these theories. However, a final judgment is impossible on the basis of the facts as at present known.

5. With this reservation the author would confess his inclination to regard visual space perception as sensibly and directly conditioned by the functions of the retina, and by them alone. The part played by eye movement in visual perception would then be analogous to the part played by movement of the head or of the whole body. It would not possess any independent function in space perception, but would serve to extend the field of vision, to secure the appropriate direction of regard, to effect a quick change of fixation, and in general to induce favourable external conditions. On the other hand, the unequivocal correlation of definite objects in space with definite retinal elements is fully guaranteed by the organisation of the eye, as we found a similar correspondence to be by the organisation of the skin (§ 57. 5). The essential importance of the separate retinal elements for spatial vision is clearly evidenced by the facts of *metamorphopsia*,— a distortion of spatial figure due to a pathological migration or separation of particular fragments of the retina, the phenomena of which are wholly similar to those observed after the transplantation of

fragments of skin. We have no choice, therefore, but to attribute a certain local signature to the various retinal elements,—certain peculiarities, in virtue of which they attach to themselves definite spatial judgments. Here again, the most obvious course is to look upon these local signs, not as conscious attributes of the particular visual impressions, but as physiological characteristics. Nothing more positive, however, can be said about them.

6. It cannot be denied that this hypothesis is sufficiently difficult of detailed application to the facts. One clear point in its favour is the dependency of spatial perception upon the place of retinal stimulation. We know that the cones, which in all probability are the sensitive units of the retina, occur in the greatest numbers at the fovea centralis, the spot of clearest vision, and are more and more sparsely distributed as the periphery is approached. Here we seem to have an explanation of the indistinctness of indirect vision,—the diminution of keenness of vision, the uncertainty of eye measurement, etc. And here we may refer the special facility of the peripheral retina in the cognition of change or movement. For if the intervals between the sensitive elements are comparatively large, changes in sensation (whether produced by movement of an object or by alteration of its luminosity) will presumably be remarked more clearly, owing to diminution of irradiation. Probably, too, the fall (§ 24. 6) of excitation in the lateral portions of the retina takes place far more quickly than in the central parts, and the peripheral after-images are less intensive than the central. At the same time, there are a whole number of facts of visual space perception which are very largely due to the operation of other than purely sensible conditions: the idea of depth, the continuity of the field of vision, a variety of optical illusions, etc. If a distinction may be drawn at all between sensation and perception (and we have made no attempt to distinguish them hitherto), it may be drawn within the sense of sight. Nowhere is the contrast of insignificant qualities and their significant arrangement impressed upon us so forcibly as in the domain of vision. Nevertheless, it would seem that the difference is always psychologically referable to the familiar phenomena of sensations as elementary conscious processes, and of the connections into which they are brought by their liability of reproduction, by fusion and colligation.

7. We have already remarked that the part played by eye movement in the formation of the space idea is still a matter of dispute. There are certain phenomena (the influence of the movements of convergence upon the estimation of distance in depth, the illusions arising from the intention to execute an impossible movement, etc.)

which seem to give it a direct significance for spatial vision. Against this is the fact that eye movements themselves are incorrectly and uncertainly judged. A complete theory of visual space' perception cannot be formulated until the question has received a final answer (§ 58. 5, 8).

It has sometimes been objected that if visual sensations really possessed an original spatial attribute, the insensitive areas between the sensitive retinal elements, and the blind spot in particular, would betray themselves in the character of the field of vision. The objection may be met in various ways. (i) The influence of associative supplementing (§ 60.1) is very great throughout the whole domain of visual perception. The filling out of the visual field may, therefore, very well be regarded as due to experience. (ii) Again, under particularly favourable conditions, we are able spatially to discriminate two luminous points whose images fall upon two contiguous cones in the retina. And (iii) it is not easy to see how movement sensations could be the instruments in the filling out of the field, since its continuity for perception is certainly not a continuity of movement.— There remains the view that the space of visual perception is the product of a fusion of retinal impressions and movement sensations, in which the separate constituents have combined to produce a new result, of an essentially different nature from their own. This hypothesis seems untenable, for the reason that the space of visual perception is given introspectively as a direct function of the retinal impressions, while movement sensations are entirely different in character from anything that we know as a space idea.—We must, therefore, conclude with Stumpf and James, that the retinal impressions are from the first endowed with a spatial predicate.

§ 62. The Localisation of Non-spatial Sensations. The Perception of the Position and Movement of the Body.

1. Localisation in the strict meaning of the word is only possible for sensations originally possessed of a spatial attribute, *i.e.*, sensations of touch and sight. At the same time, we speak of the localisation of impressions, *e.g.*, of smell and hearing. In these instances the term is evidently employed with a transferred meaning, to indicate the relation of the particular sensations to visual or tactual objects. This relation is not a relation of spatial contiguity, but an association, in virtue of which more or less definite ideas of sight or touch are aroused or reproduced by definite auditory or olfactory sensations, or at least a

certain judgment of spatial connection becomes possible.—An attempt has recently been made to accredit tones with spatial attributes. Deep tones are said to be more voluminous than high tones, and the sound sensations of the right ear somehow spatially different from the sounds produced by stimulation of the left. But the former statement translates a metaphorical characterisation into an objective attribute; and the observation that we can discriminate between excitation of the right and left ears by stimuli which are identical in all respects but localisation, merely proves that we can discriminate their position by some indirect means,—perhaps by aid of the cutaneous sensations aroused at the same time.

The problem which the localisation of these non-spatial impressions presents for solution is, therefore, simply that of the discovery of the relations obtaining between them and the space ideas (judgments) and movements which they excite, and, more especially, that of the determination of the particular attribute which serves as the incentive to the reproduction (§ 30) of their space references. The auditory sensations have received by far the most exhaustive treatment, theoretical and experimental, of all the localisable non-spatial sensations. We shall, therefore, restrict ourselves in the main to the discussion of their localisation.

2. There can be no doubt that the idea of massiveness and volume which is often aroused by deep tones is referable to the facts that they are ordinarily more intensive than high tones, and that their sound waves occasion a more intensive concomitant excitation in other sensitive and resonant parts. Thus a deep organ clang, struck with sufficient intensity, seems, as we say, to fill the whole church. The same facts serve to explain the less accurate localisation of deep tones. In this particular case, the auditory sensations excite ideas of extension or figure; but, as a rule, they also mediate ideas of their distance from our own body and of the direction from which they come. Here again, the spatial predicates do not belong to the sensations themselves, but to their exciting stimuli, the sources of sound. Experience is the determining factor in their localisation (= the combination of distance and direction; § 55. 4). The fundamental factor in the cognition of direction is the distinction of right and left. We do not yet know what the criteria of this distinction are; but we may conjecture that cutaneous sensations, concomitantly excited by the different sound waves, inform us whether the right or the left ear has been stimulated. Where both ears are concerned, the judgment of direction is certainly further dependent to a very large extent upon the relative intensity of the two stimulations. If we can distinguish whether a

sound is heard by the right or the left ear (and experiments have shown that we can do so with a fairly high degree of accuracy) we must also be able to say within certain limits whether a sound to the right is more intensive than a sound to the left, and *vice versa*. From this point of view it is possible to construct a field of audition, the discriminable directions in which are represented by the discriminability of the intensities to right and left. There must, however, always be two directions within the total field, in which these relative intensities are equal,—the directions straight before and behind us. These two directions will, therefore, be especially liable to confusion, except in the cases where the difference in the absolute intensity of the two sound waves (other things equal, the position of the pinnae is favourable to a sound coming from the front, and unfavourable to one coming from behind) is sufficient for their discrimination. Experience seems to show that a confusion is not uncommon. And experiments in which the pinnae were tied back against the head, and artificial pinnae, turned in the opposite direction, placed forwards from the external auditory meatus, gave the result that sound impressions coming from behind were localised in front of the face. Moreover, the importance of the relative intensity of binaural impressions is attested by the increased number of erroneous judgments of direction in unilateral hearing.

3. The influence of relative intensity is further evidenced by a number of observations upon the localisation of tones, with and without beats, when the two ears are simultaneously excited by tuning forks of equal or of somewhat different pitch held close before them, or by vibrating rods applied to the bones of the head, etc. A single tone is heard, and localised in the head, approximately in the median line if the tones to right and left are of subjectively equal intensity, and more towards the right or left if the right or left tone preponderates in the total impression. Another fact which belongs here is that we are able separately to localise two simultaneous sound stimuli of different quality with great accuracy. The sensible discrimination for direction was found by Münsterberg to be surprisingly well developed. The difference limen in his experiments varied on the average between 1 and 10 cm. for a source of sound 1 m. distant. It has been further demonstrated that noises are better localised than tones.

. We cannot estimate of the distance of a source of sound with any degree of confidence unless the intensity and quality of the sound itself are familiar. Other things equal, intensity of sound is taken as an indication of the proximity of the object which produces it. Thus the rumbling of a wagon, the clang of a familiar composition and the tread of an approaching step are all employed as criteria of distance. No systematic investigation has been made into the accuracy of the inference in these and similar instances; but we may conjecture that the sensible discrimination for distance is the same with the sensible discrimination for sound intensity. We ordinarily regard the judgment of distance in general as extremely uncertain, and as based upon purely fortuitous ideas in all cases where the normal intensity of the sound heard is unknown. Certain recent observations, however, show that it possesses a quite unexpected accuracy. In any event, the capacity of localisation is probably extremely different in different individuals.

4. The foregoing statements have laid down the lines upon which a theory of auditory localisation must be elaborated. The incentives to the reproduction of the spatial predicates of extension, direction and distance, whether by way of judgment or visual idea or movement, will be (α) certain peculiar attributes of deep tones as contradistinguished from high; (β) concomitant tactual excitations of the two ears; (γ) the relative intensity of the unilateral auditory sensations; (δ) a definite recollection of the character of the tones or noises heard; and (ϵ) the colour of the clang or noise (§ 14.4). This list of incentives to reproduction brings the problem of a theory of auditory localisation under the more general question of the conditions of the reproduction of ideas (cf. especially § 30).

We must, however, note before we leave the subject that a quite different theory of auditory localisation has been proposed by Preyer and Münsterberg. In the opinion of these authors we determine the direction of a sound by the help of the semicircular canals. Preyer regards the mediation of a 'feeling of the direction' of a sound as the specific energy of the nerve endings in the ampullae (§ 23. 5). The discriminable directions of sound correspond to differences in the intensive excitation of the individual canals. Münsterberg has modified this hypothesis : he does not posit 'feelings of direction' as the direct correlates of stimulation of the canals, but thinks that their stimulation releases reflex movements (or impulses to movement) of the head, which serve to turn it in the direction in which the source of sound is brought immediately before the eyes. The muscular sensations thus excited afford the means of localisation. But (a) this assumption seems to be altogether superfluous for the explanation of the facts, while (b) there is a positive objection to be urged against it,—that the assumed unequivocal relation between directions of sound and the relative intensity of particular stimulations of the canals is altogether inconceivable. As the sound waves are always propagated to the labyrinth in the same way, it is difficult to see how they can excite this or that ampulla, according to the direction from which they come. (*c*) Moreover, the theory cannot explain the different localisation of simultaneous auditory stimuli.

5. Not much can be said of the localisation of other sense impressions. Gustatory stimulation, *e.g.*, always occurs together with a stimulation of the cutaneous sensibility, so that we know nothing of the spatial character of gustatory sensations as such. It is noteworthy, however, that the space relations of the different gustatory stimuli are very differently interpreted in sensation. A bitter taste spreads with great rapidity over the whole of the buccal cavity; a weak stimulation of this quality at a definite point of the tongue radiates at once over the entire sensitive area. Stimulation by the other taste qualities seems, on the contrary, to retain its local distinctness for a comparatively long time.—No accurate observations have been made of the localisation of olfactory sensations. If we may judge by the conditions which govern olfaction, the cognition of the direction from which the olfactory stimulus comes will require the aid of movements of the head or body, and the only criterion of localisation will be the intensity of the sensation itself.—The organic sensations are ordinarily localised at the place of their peripheral excitation. Thus the muscular, articular, and tendinous sensations are referred to the different parts of the body at which their sense organs are situated; hunger is placed in the stomach, thirst in the pharynx, etc. Physiology brings all these phenomena under the law of *excentric projection*, which states that all cutaneous and organic sensations are localised at their peripheral source of origin. But it is evident that this is no exception to a general rule obtaining in other sense departments. Localisation of any contents consists in its associative connection with the visual image of the place of stimulation. Thus, auditory impressions are referred to points in objective space; cutaneous impressions to the visible cutaneous areas, subject to touch or pressure; organic sensations to the parts of the body (less definitely conceived of, because invisible) in which the excitatory process is set up, etc. Reproduced sensations are localised in the same way; and it is, therefore, not surprising that pain is sometimes sensed in an amputated limb. All these localisations take shape in the course of experience, unless the localised sensations possess an original spatial attribute.

6. We may conclude this Section with a few brief remarks upon the perception of the position and movement of our own body. We have already mentioned (§ 23) that the semicircular canals and vestibule of the labyrinth constitute an organ for the maintenance and regulation of the bodily equilibrium. But we were compelled to

leave it uncertain whether this reflex activity has a direct sensory correlate, and were unable to decide, in particular, whether giddiness may be looked upon as a common sensation originated in the internal ear. In the author's observation, the position of the body is inferred, when the eyes are closed, simply from cutaneous and articular sensations. Stimulation of the canals may possibly serve to determine the judgment of position indirectly, as implying the stimulation of particular muscles to more intensive function. The important part played by the head in orientation is natural, when we remember that it carries several sense organs, and more especially the eyes. The judgment of the position of the body is based upon a number of ideas of the position of its various parts. It is somewhat different with the perception of a passive movement of the whole body. Here the position of its various parts is constant, and we cannot, therefore, infer that we are moving, from the relative positions of the limbs. Now it is an established fact of frequent observation that movement is imperceptible as long as its velocity is uniform, or even if it is subject to uniform acceleration. On the other hand, the beginning or cessation of a movement, or a positive or negative acceleration of a given velocity, is remarked at once. It seems reasonable to explain these phenomena by the hypothesis that in every case there is either a change in the position of the limbs, caused by the inertia of the mass of the body, or (if that is not possible) a change in the pressure sensations produced by contact with surrounding objects. Thus, if the carriage in which we are riding is suddenly stopped, the upper part of the body falls forward; and if we are sitting with our back against the cushions, we receive an intensive pressure from behind when it starts again. Most of our ideas of the movement of the whole body will certainly be referable to similar changes of sensation in its different parts. Movement after-images like those which occur in visual sensation (§ 60. 5), are very distinct in these cases, and again take the form of apparent movements in the opposite direction, appearing on the cessation of an objective movement which has been continued during a considerable time. Judging from all these facts, we find no reason to believe that the organ which subserves the maintenance of the bodily equilibrium mediates spatially interpretable sensations. We do not as a matter of fact localise any such sensations within the labyrinth of the ear; and, in particular, there are no noticeable differences of sensation correlated with different positions or movements of the head. At the same time we freely admit that no final decision of the point is at present possible.

Literature:

W. Wundt: *Beiträge zur Theorie der Sinneswahrnehmung.* 1862.

F. Mach: *Beiträge zur Analyse der Empfindungen.* 1886.

G. Hirth: *Aufgaben der Kunstphysiologie.* Two parts. 1891.

E. Hering: *Der Raumsinn und die Bewegungen des Auges.* Hermann's *Handbuch der Physiologie.* III. 1. pp. 343 ff.

Th. Lipps: *Der Raum der Gesichtswahrnehmung.* In: *Psychologische Studien,* 1885.

H. Münsterberg: *Raumsinn des Ohres.* In: *Beiträge zur experimentellen Psychologie.* Part ii. 1889.

C. Stumpf: *Ueber den psychologischen Ursprung der Raumvorstellung.* 1873.

Cf. the literature cited under §§ 8. 8; 10. 1; 21; 23.

Chapter II. The Temporal Attributes and Relations of
the Elements of Consciousness.

§ 63. Prefatory Remarks.

1. With the modern advance of epistemology has come the conviction that time, like space, is an original datum of our experience. We have given this fact its place in psychology by predicating an elementary temporal character of sensations and feelings, and recognising *duration* as a universal attribute of both, co-ordinate with quality and intensity. To duration must now be added certain other definitions of the temporal relations of sensations or feelings. All these contents possess a *temporal position,* an earlier or later place in the succession of conscious processes, and recur at a certain *frequency,* i.e., bear, as particular durations of a series, a determinate relation to its total duration. To these might be added a predicate which stands to duration as spatial distance to spatial extension,—the *interval,* or temporal distance intervening between one process and others. As a matter of fact, however, this term is really identical with duration; it does not signify a temporal determination as such, an 'empty' time, but always the duration of something. The only difference is that when we use the word 'duration' in its strict sense we can refer to a definite process as the substrate of the temporal attribute, whereas the word 'interval' leaves it entirely indefinite what durations fall within the time limits. But the interval has been given the preference over duration in the psychology of time with as perplexing results as follow from the preference of distance over extension in the psychology of space (§ 55. 5).

2. To determine the quality, intensity and spatial characteristics of sensations we have to rely on the subjective methods of sensitivity and sensible discrimination. Duration, on the other hand, may be measured

by objective procedures. (1) The first of these, which is based upon the fact that duration always stands in a certain relation to frequency, and *vice versa,* we may call the *method of frequency.* If n sensations are given in succession, and T is the duration of the whole series, the duration of each separate sensation, t, may be calculated from the equation $t = \dfrac{T}{n}$. The use of this method presupposes (α) the similarity of the individual successive sensations, and (β) a sufficiently large number of terms to reduce the objectively incalculable time for the rise of the first sensation and the fall of the last to a negligible quantity. It might be urged against the method that it simply gives a certain minimal duration of sensation, since the temporal course of each impression in a series which stands upon the border-line between temporal separateness and qualitative fusion must always be represented in a more or less curtailed form in the results. But this circumstance hardly comes into account for the comparison of sensations from different sense departments, or of different qualities and intensities within the same sense department; and here the method of frequency has proved to be a valuable instrument of psychological analysis. (2) Another objective procedure for the determination of the duration of conscious processes is the *method of reaction.* The time elapsing between a sense impression and the execution of a definite movement, previously agreed upon, in direct response to it (reaction) is termed the 'simple reaction time'. The duration of the whole process can be accurately measured by the aid of appropriate instruments. If a further mental act (cognition, choice, association) is interpolated between impression and movement, this duration is increased. Provided that no extraneous cause interfere to protract the experiment, the duration of the particular act may then be obtained by subtraction of the shorter time of the simple reaction from the longer time of the 'compound'. —It is plain that the validity of this method depends upon the correctness of the implied assumption that all the part-processes of the simple reaction recur in the compound with their original temporal attributes unchanged. In the author's opinion, this assumption is not justified. The reasons for his opinion will be given in detail later (§ 70).

3. Many investigations have been undertaken into our estimation of intervals. (i) Attempts have been made to measure the least noticeable interval between two successive stimuli, *i.e.,* to determine the temporal sensitivity. But the results may equally well be explained as the values of a just noticeable succession of impressions. Indeed, since the object of the experiments is the simple discrimination of two impressions, and mistakes are often made as to their temporal

position, we may conjecture that in many cases the recorded judgment is not even a judgment of succession, but only of the separateness (twoness) of sensations. In other words, we have a recurrence of precisely similar difficulties to those which we found attaching to the determination of the space limen in the sphere of tactual perception (cf. § 56. 1). (ii) Numerous experiments have been made upon the sensible discrimination of intervals. But here again, the determining factor in the judgment of small intervals is in all probability the perception of succession, and not the perception of duration. Unfortunately, no comparison of the duration of sensations has as yet been instituted, despite its eminent desirability. The perception of temporal position has been investigated by experiments upon the apparent temporal displacement of disparate sense impressions. These experiments seek to trace the conditions under which simultaneity is apprehended as succession, and *vice versa.* Little has been done so far toward the explication of the circumstances under which the perception of frequency is possible. Here belong in particular certain observations of the 'range' of consciousness. Their purpose is to ascertain the greatest number of successive sound impressions which can be directly compared with other similar groups of sensations.

4. These remarks may suffice to indicate the range and character of the contributions made hitherto by the experimental method to the psychology of time, *i.e.*, to the definition of temporal attributes and relations. We proceed now to analyse the various forms of the temporal judgment in greater detail: the analysis will assist us in our criticism of these researches, and will bring into relief the problems which the subject presents. The duration of a process can only be defined by its *magnitude*, whether we are dealing with the least noticeable time or the comparison of longer times. The same is true of the perception of interval, in all cases where its direct determination is attempted. Temporal position, on the other hand, can not only be brought under the general categories of *simultaneity* or *succession*, but may be specially investigated under the heads of *direction* and *rapidity*. The judgment of direction of a succession takes the form of 'before' and 'after', 'earlier' and 'later'. Its rapidity is measured by the magnitude of the interval elapsing between the successive impressions and the duration of the impressions themselves. In the case of frequency, the most complicated temporal judgment, we have to determine the *number* of successive processes and the *period* in which similar sections of the total time recur, besides this total duration itself, the direction and rapidity of the succession, the magnitude of the interval between impression and impression, and the duration of the separate

impressions. It follows at once from this survey of the various temporal judgments that duration is the simplest temporal predicate. It may appear as the attribute of a single conscious process, while the judgment of temporal position or frequency presupposes the existence of two or more conscious processes. We do not mean, of course, that the judgment of duration must, therefore, necessarily be the most original in the psychology of time, i.e., that it is chronologically prior to all the others and is the foundation of any one of them in the particular case. We believe, on the contrary, that all the different kinds of temporal judgment which we have mentioned,—duration or interval, direction and rapidity of succession, number and period,—are capable of an equally direct or immediate application.

5. The most favourable conditions for the investigation of the various temporal judgments will obviously be those which best admit of their isolated formulation. Especial care is needed in the selection of such conditions, since the temporal judgments, as applicable to all contents alike, stand in the most diverse relations to the co-ordinate conscious attributes and to one another, and we are consequently only too liable to judge of temporal characters mediately or indirectly, by the help of certain empirical criteria. A particular reason for this liability is the fact that in everyday life we are ordinarily called upon to estimate or compare considerable lengths of time, which must, of course, be judged by reference to secondary criteria. The experiments published hitherto have unfortunately paid but little regard to the different possibilities of judgment; there has been a regrettably strong tendency to consider objective time relations as the natural objects of subjective apprehension. One of the consequences of this attitude may be mentioned, for the sake of illustration. Until quite recently it had passed altogether unnoticed that the basis of comparison in a quick succession of three sound stimuli is not the duration of the small intervals which they mark off, but the rapidity of succession of 1 and 2 and of 2 and 3 (§ 65. 3 *ff.*). We now know that the observations made with these small times cannot be compared with those of longer times, in which the duration of the interval as such affords the material of estimation. This and similar confusions render the task of exposition exceedingly difficult. In certain cases it is quite impossible to discover what the object of judgment actually was.

§ 64. The Duration of Sensations.

1. The method of frequency has been employed for the determination of the duration of cutaneous, auditory and visual sensations.

(*a*) *The duration of cutaneous sensations.*—Various forms of the method have been used in this connection. Intermittent stimulation has been given by means of a toothed wheel held during rotation against a fixed point of the skin, by the application of a tongue attached to a vibrating tuning fork, etc. At a high rapidity of succession, these stimuli fuse to a unitary sensation. The question is, at what limit of rapidity the separate impressions can be still just cognised as successive. Some observers place this limit at 20 to 30 contacts, others at 500 to 1000 in the 1 sec. The wide divergence of result is partly due to the different intensity of the stimuli employed,—a factor of very considerable influence. But another and yet more important reason is the utter discrepancy between the objects of the different investigations, the high numbers marking the limit between roughness and smoothness, the lower that between a perceptible and imperceptible succession of the separate impressions. The latter (20 to 30 stimulations in the 1 sec.) may perhaps be made the basis of a determination of duration. We should then have a duration of $\frac{1}{20}$ to $\frac{1}{30}$ sec. for pressure sensations of moderate intensity. The value seems to be much higher in the case of temperature. It has been found that temperature impressions are temporally just discriminable if they occur at the rate of about 2 in the 1 sec.

2. (*b*) *The duration of auditory sensations.*—A very simple musical experience serves to show that deep tones have a longer duration than high tones. In a trill upon two notes in the lower region of the scale it is quite difficult to distinguish the succession of tones; in the higher region they are very distinct. The trill is generally said to comprise some 10 to 12 impressions in the 1 sec.; but there can be no doubt that the number may rise to 20 in the case of a practised executant. Accurate experimental investigation shows that the duration of tonal sensations steadily decreases with rise of pitch. The *C* of 64 vibrations lasts $\frac{1}{25}$ sec.; the *c* of 128 vibrations $\frac{1}{45}$ sec.; and the c^3 of 1024, $\frac{1}{180}$ sec. This result is confirmed by observations on the rate of succession at which beats are still discriminable. In the lower portion of the scale they are imperceptible as separate impressions at 16 to 20 in the 1 sec., while in the higher region the limit is variously given from 60 to a considerably larger number. Here again, however, the discrepancy is probably due to the absence of any sharp line of distinction between just noticeable succession and just noticeable harshness or intermittence. As regards simple noises, we have the statement that two electric sparks are just distinguishable at an interval of $\frac{1}{500}$ sec. It is impossible to draw any reliable inference from this fact to the duration of the sensations themselves.

3. (c) *The duration of visual sensations.*—The numerous researches which deal with this subject differ so widely in object, method, and technique, that they do not admit of any strict intercomparison. In most cases, investigation has been carried out by the aid of rotating discs, composed of white or coloured sectors. But very little familiarity with the experiments is sufficient to show that the just noticeable succession is largely dependent upon the brightness of the stimuli employed for its determination and upon the difference between their brightness and that of the visual intervals which separate them. Thus a disc of black and white sectors must be rotated more rapidly by daylight than by lamplight, for the production of a subjective mixture of the two brightnesses. On the other hand, it has been found that while the brighter sensations have a longer absolute duration than the darker, they are subject to a more rapid decrease in brightness. Again, the duration of a sensation in indirect vision is longer for the same stimulus than its duration in direct vision; a fact which accords very well with the greater intensity which must be attributed within certain limits to peripheral retinal stimulations (cf. § 18. 6). Nothing positive can be said at present of the influence of brightness and saturation upon the duration of sensations of colour tone. The question of duration is further complicated in the sphere of vision by the vividness of the after sensations, whose duration is dependent upon the intensity, duration and extension of the stimulus, and upon the character of its surroundings (§ 20. 2). The after-image produced by an intensive excitation may last for several minutes. — It is clear, then, that no very certain statement can be made as to the duration of visual sensations. Putting the different results together, we may, perhaps, estimate it at $\frac{1}{10}$ sec. without negative after-image. We have already briefly referred to the numerous investigations into the rapidity of the rise and fall of visual sensations (§ 19. 5).

4. A theory of all these processes is evidently given with the assumption of a difference of physiological conditions for the different sensations. The transmission of stimulus will certainly be far more quickly mediated when the skin is subjected to a mechanical pressure, than when it is exposed to the influence of heat or cold; and we may reasonably suppose that the elastic tissue will show but little after effect of the impact, whereas thermal changes can disappear but slowly in such a bad conductor as the epidermis. The comparatively long duration of the visual sensation will not surprise us, when we remember that the process of stimulation is in all probability chemical in character (§ 21. 2); both decomposition and reparation of the sensitive substance will require a relatively long period of time. The

transmission of stimulus in auditory sensation, on the other hand, is again purely mechanical, and therefore, we may imagine, quickly begun and quickly ended. We conclude, then, that all these differences in the duration of sensations are the results of purely peripheral causes, brought about by the special conditions of stimulation in the various sense departments.—The rapidity of memorial images appears to be precisely similar to that of the peripherally excited sensations. In the voluntary reproduction of successive ideas, however, the rate of advance is more slow. This is probably due to the necessary oscillation of the attention between term and term. The rapidity of succession of the separate independent ideas in a train of thought (in which there is no reproduction of a totality of successive impressions as such) is similarly much more slow, and, therefore, the duration of each idea much greater, than in the series of simple sensations. Experiments give about $\frac{3}{4}$ sec. as the time required for the transition from one idea to the next.

§ 65. The Estimation of Intervals.

1. Investigations into the estimation of intervals fall into two series, the first dealing with least noticeable times, and the second with the sensible discrimination for intervals. We will discuss the former under the heading of 'temporal sensitivity,' and the latter under that of 'temporal sensible discrimination': the rubrics are conveniently brief, although the use of terms is not strictly accurate (§ 63. 3). (a) *The temporal sensitivity.*—The fact of most importance here is the dependency of the times found for the just noticeable interval upon the nature of the limiting impressions. Exner discovered that the just noticeable interval between two successive visual impressions (electric sparks) given at the spot of clearest vision amounted to 44σ. Experiments made under slightly different conditions in indirect vision put the just noticeable interval at 49σ. If the stimuli excited different parts of the retina, central and peripheral, they were temporally just discriminable with a separation of 76σ. If the light sensation was produced by electrical stimulation of the optic nerve, the interval fell to 16σ. The evidence furnished by these numbers of the dependency of the just noticeable interval or just noticeable succession upon peripheral stimulation is plainly parallel to that afforded by the values quoted in the previous Section of the same dependency in the case of duration (§ 64. 4). The lengthening of the interval with stimulation of different parts of the retina, however, seems to indicate that central conditions of apprehension are also

25

concerned in the results.—Similar relations are found to obtain in other sense departments. Thus Exner discovered that the least noticeable interval elapsing between auditory impressions was 2σ for a single ear, but rose to 64σ if the two stimuli were separately conducted to the two ears.

2. If the intervals are limited by disparate sense impressions, these two principles,—the duration of peripheral stimulation and the apprehension of the two sensations,—cross each other in various ways. Thus when a visual (electric spark) and an auditory stimulus (stroke of a bell) were given simultaneously, the auditory impression was sensed before the visual, in consequence of the more rapid transmission of the stimulus process in the labyrinth. When the same stimuli were given successively, the just noticeable interval was 160σ in the order visual-auditory, but only 60σ in the order auditory-visual. The difference was less if an electrical cutaneous stimulus was substituted for the bell stroke. All these observations are in complete accord with the experiments on the determination of duration by the method of frequency, as regards the relations of peripheral stimulation. Still further confirmation is derived from the occurrence of similar temporal differences in the simple reaction (cf. § 69). Other things equal, a reaction to auditory stimuli occupies about 110σ, a reaction to touch approximately the same time, and a reaction to sight about 200σ. The figures show, once more, that different times are required for stimulus-transmission in different sense departments.—The other influence which we can trace in the experimental results—the effect of local or modal separation of the impressions upon the cognition of an interval between them—is of greater psychological interest. This influence is so considerable and its manifestations so similar that we are able on the one hand to separate it sharply from the peripheral factors and on the other to refer it to a single psychophysical cause. It may be looked upon as a special instance of the general rule that our cognition or judgment of definite relations, differences or attributes is easiest and most certain when they are the sole objects of observation. Thus, it is very difficult to cognise a difference of intensity, as between two different qualities. We must leave it undecided whether the phenomena are due to an unavoidable distraction of the attention, or a simple inhibition of reproduction. In conclusion we would again emphasise the fact that the object of judgment in many of these experiments upon 'intervals' was very probably the just noticeable succession or even separateness (twoness) of the sense impressions (cf. § 63. 3).

3. (*b*) *The temporal sensible discrimination.*—It is customary at the present time to use the expression *time sense* with exclusive reference to investigations into the temporal sensible discrimination. Now in the first place this name is as misleading as the terms 'space sense' and 'sense of locality', and should, therefore, be discarded; and in the second, the implied restriction of the time judgment to one sharply defined problem is very undesirable (cf. § 55. 5). A more special objection is that the inclusion of all judgments of interval under the general rubric of sensible discrimination for temporal magnitudes has been a serious obstacle in the way of a thorough psychological analysis. (i) The temporal judgment has three essentially distinct forms; one with 'small' intervals up to about 0.5 sec., another with 'moderate' intervals between the limits 0.5 and about 3·0 sec., and yet another with 'larger' intervals beyond 3.0 sec. In estimating the very smallest times we do not compare the magnitude of pairs of two intervals, but the rapidity of succession of two impressions (§ 63. 5). In estimating moderate intervals we really compare the time-lengths themselves. Neither method is ordinarily applicable to large intervals, and we consequently make our estimation of them by indirect means,—by the help of a subjective revival of the limiting impression, or of the contents of the time as it passes (phases of respiration or what not), etc. It is plain that these three different cases are not by any means co-ordinate. (ii) Again, our estimation of small intervals in particular is liable to be modified by certain phenomena of rhythm, which give rise to definite temporal illusions and thus to definite variation of the temporal judgment. These various factors have not as yet been satisfactorily isolated; and the summarising of the experimental results is consequently attended with extreme difficulty.

4. The methods employed to test the temporal sensible discrimination are those of minimal changes (in the strict sense; § 7. III.), right and wrong cases (as applied to difference determination; § 8. I.), and average error (§ 8. II.). A determination of the constant error has been attempted, besides that of the absolute and relative sensible discrimination. This constant error is indicative of an overestimation or underestimation of the standard time. The investigation of sensible discrimination has usually been undertaken with a view to the formulation of its dependency upon the magnitude of the times compared. Auditory impressions have been almost exclusively used as limiting stimuli, owing to their short duration and rapid rise and fall. The dependency of our estimation of intervals upon the quality of the limiting stimuli, however, has also been made the subject of experimental inquiry.

The following facts appear to have been established. The absolute sensible discrimination reaches its maximum both of magnitude and delicacy at an interval of o·3 sec., where the absolute difference limen for a highly practised observer amounts to about 3σ. The decrease of the absolute sensible discrimination with higher time values seems to take the form of a constancy of the relative sensible discrimination; *i.e.*, estimation is made in accordance with Weber's law. But neither the fact itself nor the interpretation of the fact is as yet quite certain, since judgments beyond the o·3 sec. limit are not by any means necessarily based upon a pure duration estimate. The course of the constant error shows that, upon the whole, small times are overestimated and large times underestimated. The limiting value, an interval of o·5 to o·6 sec., has been termed the *interval of indifference*, and is, of course, characterised by an approximate o-value of the constant error. It has further been found that the underestimation of large times is subject to a peculiar periodicity; the constant error, while it increases with increase of the interval, sinks to a relative minimum at each simple multiple of the interval of indifference. We may remark that all these determinations of the constant error were made with the first interval as the standard time. And we must not omit to mention that the interval of indifference has been assigned quite different positions (o·5 to 3·5 sec.) by different observers.

5. It is only quite recently that an attempt has been made to formulate the various psychological conditions of the estimation of intervals. (1) Judgment of small times, where the real object of perception is the succession of the sensory impressions, is, of course, very largely dependent upon the character (quality, intensity, duration) of these impressions themselves. Two objectively equal intervals, limited respectively by visual and auditory stimuli, are differently estimated, the visual time (if we may use the expression) appearing smaller than the auditory. Again, a visual time in indirect vision seems considerably longer than the same time in direct vision. And again, an interval which is limited by two more intensive sound impressions is taken to be shorter than an objectively equal interval bounded by weaker stimuli. All these observations illustrate the dependency of the temporal judgment upon purely sensory conditions,—the relative apparent duration of the limiting impressions. They are in complete accord with the determinations of the duration of sensations by the method of frequency (§ 64). We must, accordingly, suppose that the difference of the subjective interval, with strong and weak sound impressions, with visual and auditory stimuli, and with

direct and indirect vision, is due to the difference of duration of the limiting sensations. In other words, the results are not to be referred to a 'deception of judgment', but to a simple incongruity between the objective times and the times given in sensation.

(2) Another factor in the comparison of intervals, of a different order from the foregoing, is the influence of rhythm. (α) It is a curious fact that the involuntary rhythmical apprehension of stimuli is confined to auditory impressions. (β) The rhythmical division can be effected in a variety of ways: by objective alternation of intensities or qualities of the impressions, by the temporal dissociation of two successive terms of a stimulus series, by their different localisation, or by a purely subjective emphasis or 'accentuation' of a particular impression. The general result of rhythmical division is the production of a *time fringe*, *i.e.*, a subjective lengthening of the intervals lying before and after the accented impression. There can be no doubt that the alteration of the temporal judgment in this case must be referred to some more general condition than that just discussed (cf. the factors which determine temporal sensitivity; § 65. 2).

6. (3) The judgment of time intervals appears to be further dependent upon their æsthetic impression. If this is the case, we must recognise an influence of agreeableness and disagreeableness upon the estimation of the temporal attributes or relations of sensation, which is only paralleled by their influence upon spatial judgments (cf. § 34. 3). (4) Again, the smallest times are apprehended directly, in a single act of perception, whereas two moderate times given in immediate succession are perceptible as distinct intervals. Time memory, *i.e.*, can play but a small part in the former judgment, while it is plainly implied in the latter. (5) And lastly, the estimation of intervals from moderate times onwards is in great measure dependent on the character of their contents. This is sufficiently shown by the empirical criteria of lapse of time employed in ordinary life. The greater the number of different occurrences which have taken place within a given period of time, the longer do we take it to have been. Our ordinary measure of the length of time, *i.e.*, is the number of impressions which it comprises. This fact stands in apparent contradiction to another fact of common experience,—that time passes more quickly (the given period is judged to be smaller) when it includes a variety of experiences than when it is 'empty'. But the contradiction is only apparent, and disappears when we remember that the contents of the period in the latter instance entirely divert the attention from the passage of time and draw it upon themselves. If the content processes are of a monotonous or uninteresting character the time seems to pass very much more slowly (the

period is largely overestimated). Here again, then, we have a condition of temporal estimation in general.

7. It follows from this discussion that a theory of the direct judgment of time interval must begin with a distinction between special and general conditions. The former need hardly be discussed further. We may sum them up in the general proposition that all the peripheral factors which produce a change in the duration of sensation serve at the same time to lengthen or shorten an interval limited by sense stimuli. The question of the nature and relative importance of the general conditions is more difficult to answer. (i) We may certainly give attention the first place in the list; but in doing so we are only setting a problem in psychological analysis, of which no satisfactory solution has as yet been given. (ii) Expectation and surprise have been suggested as the basis of the temporal judgments 'greater' and 'less'. But while there can be no doubt that these emotive states are to some extent involved in the formation of the judgments, it must be pointed out that their influence is at best of a purely secondary character, and that it is wholly inadequate to the explanation of a large number of the facts of temporal sensible discrimination. Thus (α) the attempt to reduce the overestimation of small and the underestimation of large times to terms of expectation and surprise (as appearing earlier in the first case and later in the second) has proved altogether unsuccessful. (β) Moreover, sensible discrimination reaches its maximum with the smallest times, *i.e.*, under conditions where it is admitted that the two emotions are hardly remarked at all. And lastly, (γ) there seems to be no unequivocal relation between them and the judgments 'greater' and 'less'. We may be surprised, *e.g.*, that an interval lasts too long; and we need not expect that the second interval will be similar to the first,—expectation is not necessarily directed upon (predisposed for) equality of the stimulus times. We are, therefore, led to the conclusion that these factors are not general conditions, but occasional and indirect criteria of the time judgment. (iii) Again, an exaggerated importance for temporal estimation has been attributed to strain sensations.—There is a fundamental objection to all theories of this kind: their holders regard the temporal character of conscious processes not as something originally given, but as superinduced upon them by muscular sensations, the adjustment of the sensory attention, etc. Such a view is as inconceivable and as epistemologically mistaken as is the strictly empiristic theory of the space idea (§ 57. 10).

8. It must be left to future investigators to define more specifically the processes which we have termed 'general conditions' of temporal estimation. The effect of attention upon the temporal judgment,

however, may be inferred with some degree of probability from its influence in other connections. Two points in particular may be mentioned. (α) Every attribute of a conscious process is enhanced in the state of attention; quality becomes clearer, intensity more vivid, extension and duration larger. And this enhancement is apparently proportional to the concentration of the attention, so that the degree of concentration is correlated with a certain degree of change of the four attributes. (β) Every relation between conscious processes is made closer, stronger, and more evident in the state of attention. The associability and reproductivity of sensations are increased, all kinds of difference between sensations become more distinct, etc. We may conclude from these facts (i) that, other things equal, the apparent length of an interval is directly proportional to the concentration of the attention upon it, and (ii) that the distinctness of a temporal difference in consciousness, *i.e.*, its apparent magnitude, increases with attentive observation of its own nature or of the nature of the impressions which constitute it. Any thing which hinders or diminishes the concentration of the attention upon an interval or a temporal difference must also reduce the apparent duration of the time, and decrease the delicacy of the temporal sensible discrimination. Now it is extremely difficult to hold the attention upon the time as such even in intervals of 3 to 4 secs., and almost impossible with longer times. The observation presupposes that consciousness is kept persistently empty of contents; and to effect and maintain the inhibition of incoming contents requires a very considerable effort. This effort manifests itself in an intensive common sensation, which can plainly be employed for purposes of temporal estimation,—its intensity affording a direct measure of the lapse of time. If the effort is relaxed (it is ordinarily shown in attentive observation in the general attitude of the body and the adjustment of the sense organs; cf. § 75. 2), *i.e.*, if exhaustion sets in, the attention is at once diverted from the exclusive object of perception, and other contents and relations begin to force their way into consciousness. This analysis is supported by the fact that the comparison of longer times than those mentioned (half a minute and several minutes) is not only characterised by an extreme fluctuation of sensible discrimination, but has also given a second reversal of the constant error, *i.e.*, an overestimation of the standard time.

We are able in this way to explain the underestimation of large times; but we have not yet accounted for the overestimation of small intervals. Nothing is gained from the analogy of the overestimation of small spatial distances, or from an appeal to the special (peripheral) conditions of rapidly recurrent stimulation. The comparison of sensations of corresponding duration will perhaps help towards the establishment of a definite theory.

§ 66. The Perception of Temporal Position and of Frequency.

1. Many of the experiments recorded in the foregoing Section have a direct bearing upon the determination of temporal position and frequency. Thus the observations of the least noticeable interval should in all probability be regarded as observations of just noticeable succession. The comparison of least intervals may be interpreted as the comparison of the rapidities of successive impressions. And the introduction of rhythm brings us to what we termed 'period' in our analysis of frequency (§ 63. 4).—The estimation of *temporal position* may, as we have seen, be either *general* or *special*. If we simply judge whether two impressions are simultaneous or successive, we are making a general estimation of temporal position. Just noticeable succession may, therefore, mean either just noticeable divergence from simultaneity, or the just noticeable distinction of 'before' and 'after'. The general fact of non-simultaneity is cognised more quickly and easily than its direction. The special estimation of temporal position includes the judgments of direction and rapidity. A direct estimation of succession is, of course, only possible at a certain rapidity of recurrent stimulation; just as the direct estimation of movement is restricted to a certain zone of movement velocity (cf. § 59. 9). The upper limit of rapidity at which succession is noticeable may, perhaps, be inferred from the observations on the least noticeable interval; the lower limit of rapidity, below which a direct perception of succession is impossible, has not been ascertained and is not in any case capable of accurate definition. No express experiments have been made, so far as the author's knowledge extends, upon the conditions of the judgments of 'before' and 'after'.

2. The general estimation of temporal position forms the subject of inquiry in a series of experimental researches upon the validity of an astronomical method, the 'eye and ear' method. It was formerly customary in astronomy to determine the time of the movement of a star across the field of a telescope by the aid of a number of fine parallel threads in the eye-piece of the instrument (eye) and the seconds strokes of a pendulum clock (ear). The basis of calculation was the coincidence of a definite position of the star with a beat of the pendulum. The differences in the results of different observers and of the same observer at different times gave occasion to a special investigation of the conditions under which the simultaneity of impressions was here estimated. Wundt constructed an apparatus, which combined the continuous movement of a visual impression with intermittent

auditory or tactual stimulation, and thus allowed of an accurate reproduction of the circumstances of astronomical observation ('complication pendulum'). In this instrument the rapidity of movement can be varied within wide limits, and the auditory or tactual impressions brought into different temporal relations with the visual series, so that the simultaneity of two or three given impressions can be estimated under very different conditions. The experiments show that the direction of the attention is of determining importance. If the attention is predominantly or exclusively directed upon the visual series, the auditory stimulus is referred to a later visual impression than that which it really accompanies; *i.e.*, two impressions are judged as simultaneous, of which the auditory is actually the earlier. If on the other hand (as usually happens when this apparatus is employed), expectation is concentrated on the auditory stimulus, the sound is combined with an earlier visual impression than that which it really accompanies; *i.e.*, two impressions are judged as simultaneous, of which the auditory is objectively the later. The time displacement in the latter instance cannot be exclusively due to peripheral conditions, *i.e.*, to the more rapid rise of an auditory sensation (cf. § 65. 2), since under certain circumstances it may reach the value of $\frac{1}{5}$ sec.

3. The foregoing arguments are confirmed by the fact that this negative time displacement (in which the auditory impression coincides in perception with an earlier visual impression than that with which it is objectively combined) is reduced by the introduction into the experiment of a second disparate impression. The new stimulus is taken to be simultaneous with the auditory: there is no secondary time displacement. If a third impression is added, whether disparate or of similar quality to either of the original impressions, the complex is referred to a later term of the visual series than that which it really accompanies. And the introduction of a fourth complication still further increases the value of this positive displacement. The plain conclusion from these observations is that the rapidity of apprehension of the complicating sensations (the sensations which are to be brought into connection with the visual impression) is greatly diminished by increase of their number. The same conclusion is required by the fact that complication by a number of impressions from the same sense department is much less effective for time displacement than complication by the same number of disparate stimuli (cf. also the results of Exner's experiments, mentioned above: § 65. 1, 2). Still further confirmation of our general theory is furnished by the possibility of arbitrary correlation of the visual and auditory impressions. The continuous series of visual stimuli is given by an index,

moving round a circle upon which its separate positions are marked in degrees. It is, therefore, not difficult for the observer to imprint upon his mind some definite position of the moving index, and to look for the occurrence of the auditory impression at that point. If the attention has been 'trained' to make this connection, displacement of the auditory impression is possible within wide limits.—If, then, we abstract from the sensory conditions of the time displacement, we may bring all these observations under the single principle, that the rapidity of the perception of a sense impression is essentially dependent upon the degree of attention which it receives.

4. The determination of the *frequency* of successive impressions involves (α) judgments of the direction and rapidity of their succession, and (β) judgments of the duration of the intervals between successive contents, of each content itself, and of the total series of intervals and contents. But it also implies two new judgments, (γ) the judgment of number, and (δ) the judgment of period or rhythm (§ 63. 4). Only the first of these two special factors has been subjected to thorough experimental analysis; the second has never been made the object of special investigation, in spite of its importance for music and discourse. (i) The question of the *number* of successive impressions has not been raised in this particular form, but certain of the phenomena have been examined in connection with the problem of the 'range of consciousness'. The method employed was that of the determination of the greatest number of successive auditory stimuli which could be cognised with any high degree of certainty. A series of successive metronome beats was compared with another group of similar impressions; and a limit of accurate comparison was found in terms of the number of stimuli and the rapidity of their succession. We need not attempt to decide whether or not it is necessary for the purposes of this comparison that all the members of the series should be conceived of as present in consciousness at different degrees of distinctness,—the first impression being just above the conscious limen when the last is given. We do not, *i.e.*, venture an opinion on the controverted question whether these experiments have really measured the range of consciousness. In any event, they furnish valuable material for the analysis of the judgment of number, with which we are here concerned.

5. The results may be summarised as follows. (α) The most favourable rapidity of succession was given with intervals of 0·2 to 0·3 sec. between the separate sound stimuli; *i.e.*, it was under these conditions that the longest series could be accurately compared. The maximal number of separate impressions was 16. Serial comparison became practically impossible at a higher limit of 0·1 sec. intervals, and at a

lower limit of 4 sec. intervals. (β) Comparison was considerably easier with an even number of impressions than with an odd number. This fact clearly points to the influence of rhythmical division of the stimuli, —which, indeed, was extremely apparent throughout the whole course of the experiments. Where the series could be divided into periods, the apprehension of the total number of impressions was very greatly facilitated. Abstention from rhythmical division would seem to be not impossible, but the tendency towards it is extraordinarily strong. The formation of simple periods of two impressions is almost inevitable, whatever precautions are taken, and very possibly accounts for the greater range of judgment with even numbered series. The maximal number of 16 impressions is probably reducible to 8 double impressions. If periods of 8 stimuli are formed, the limit of accuracy of comparison rises to 40 separate impressions, which are thus arranged in five periods.—When we ask for an explanation of this comparison of groups of successive stimuli, the hypothesis at once suggests itself that accustomedness to a definite number leads to an involuntary tendency on the part of the observer to reproduce the succession of sounds in its original length and at its original rapidity. If, therefore, the second series is an exact repetition of that to which the subject has grown accustomed, its likeness to the standard would then be vouched for by the absence of any expectation of further stimulation and of the surprise which would be aroused by its premature conclusion. But it is undeniable that these indirect criteria may quite well be dispensed with, and that the actual comparison of the series is often directly made. We are thus forced to the conclusion that the interconnection of a number of successive stimuli represents a relation of conscious contents no less original than that of simultaneous stimuli, and that series may be compared as directly as time intervals, intensities, etc. Expectation and surprise, whatever part their predisposition may play in the determination of a given number of successive impressions, are no more the necessary conditions of serial comparison in general than they are of the intercomparison of numbers of points or lines simultaneously presented in the field of vision. Before any more definite statement can be made, however, further experiments must be instituted, and in particular the conditions of judgment varied and their effects noted. In all probability, these observations of simultaneous groups or successive series constitute the first psychological beginnings of the concept of number. The elementary discrimination of visible or audible contents in terms of number, when all other attributes or relations are given equal, cannot possibly be referred to any more fundamental phenomenon.

6. (ii) The great importance of _rhythm_ in any kind of auditory sequence has suggested the hypothesis that it is the specific time sensation. It is certainly true that series of very different quality may be heard in the same rhythm, and that precisely similar impressions may be given very different rhythmical division in perception. The impression of a particular rhythm, again, may be due to widely divergent causes; any difference of regular recurrence in successive pairs of auditory stimuli, whether it be intensive, qualitative or temporal (difference of interval), can give rise to one and the same rhythmical division. The 'times' of musical rendition are not by any means necessarily identical with particular rhythms. Musical 'time' marks the value and the mutual relation of the separate notes; while rhythm may take on the most different forms, according to the nature of the regular intensive changes, pauses, etc., within the time. The great variety of musical effect is, therefore, due to the possible variation of rhythm under a constant time rubric. The same applies to poetic composition, where again the prescribed metre is not the exclusive determinant of rhythm. It is noteworthy that the typical rhythmical forms appear to be restricted to three successive impressions. Beyond this limit we simply have repetitions of the various types possible with two and three impressions. In bimembral rhythms, either impression may be accented. But only two forms of trimembral rhythm have been developed, those in which the accent falls upon the first and third term. These rules are illustrated in the four common metres,—the iambic, trochaic, dactylic and anapæstic. A rhythm of four impressions is always reducible to two bimembral rhythms, one of which (usually the second) has a weaker accent than the other. A seximembral rhythm is analysable in the same way into periods of two or three impressions. Nothing definite can be said at present of the conditions of the various rhythmical phenomena, as the necessary investigations have not been carried out.

Literature :

S. Exner, _Experimentelle Untersuchungen der einfachsten psychischen Processe._ Pflüger's _Archiv f. Physiol.,_ vol. xi., pp. 403 ff.

C. Vierordt, _Der Zeitsinn,_ 1868.

F. Schumann, _Ueber die Schätzung kleiner Zeitgrössen. Zeitschr. f. Psych. u. Physiol. d. Sinnesorgane,_ vol. iv., pp. 1 ff.

E. Meumann, _Beiträge zur Psychologie des Zeitsinns. Phil. Studien,_ vol. viii., pp. 431 ff.; vol. ix., pp. 264 ff.

W. von Tschisch, _Ueber die Zeitverhältnisse der Apperception,_ etc. _Phil. Studien,_ vol. ii., pp. 603 ff.

CHAPTER III. SPATIAL AND TEMPORAL COLLIGATION.

§ 67. The General Phenomena of Colligation.

1. Nothing shows more plainly the peculiar character of spatial and temporal colligation than the separate treatment which time and space have received, altogether apart from the conscious contents of which they may be predicated as attributes. The intensity of a sensation or feeling is known and rated simply as the intensity of a particular process of the particular kind: but rhythm and figure, extension and duration, locality and number seem to indicate contents *sui generis*, which, however regarded—whether from the objective standpoint of natural science, or under the conditions of a purely formal inquiry, or from the point of view of psychological experience— are something more than mere attributes of an underlying reality. This is undoubtedly the reason of the special position accorded to space and time in psychological treatises. But there is one observation in particular which seems to give a reason for their isolation: the fact that the temporal and spatial attributes of conscious contents are always and everywhere easy of combination into total impressions. A simultaneous presentment of different colours takes rank at once as a spatial whole: a successive presentment of different tones as a temporal whole. This independence of the temporal and spatial total impression has helped more than anything else to obscure the psychology of space and time, and to raise them above their true level as attributes and relations of conscious contents to the dignity of specific and elementary qualities. It must be emphatically stated that the observation quoted just now is not without its analogues in the sphere of intensity and quality; it merely shows us a familiar phenomenon in an extreme form. We are already acquainted with the qualitative total impression and the total intensity of the fusion; and we know that it is possible to compare the intensities of two contents within the same sense department, even if they are different in quality. On the other hand, there are limits to the independence of the spatial and temporal attributes: their variation with the nature of the sensations to which they attach is a fact which we have frequently had occasion to note in the two preceding Chapters.

2. It is not only in the nature of the total impression, however, that spatial and temporal colligation differs from fusion. The connected contents themselves possess a distinct character in the two cases. Analysis is made more difficult by fusion, easier by colligation. The

apprehension of the tones contained in a chord is a very different matter from their separate perception in a *motif* or a melody; and while it is difficult enough to distinguish colour tone and brightness in a colour impression, it is relatively easy to discriminate the various colours and the distribution of light and shade in a picture. It might seem, therefore, as if the title of temporal and spatial disjunction were more applicable than that of colligation. But that the proximity of different impressions in time and space renders really important service for analysis, better service than any given degree of disjunction, is shown by the fact that their difference is brought out with especial clearness under the conditions of temporal and spatial contiguity. Whatever we are accustomed or inclined to regard as a unitary object, we endeavour to make as uniform as possible in quality. Thus, we furnish our rooms upon a single colour scheme, and avoid the juxtaposition of gay tints in our clothing. And if we wish to bring out the effect of a figure in all its purity, we have it copied or represented in a substance of homogeneous quality. Thus a statue or a building makes the most direct impression upon the mind when it is left in monotone and not painted over and particoloured [1]. But, again, it is not only the quality of conscious contents that is thrown into stronger relief by spatial or temporal colligation; intensities also become more vivid under its influence. In any series of experiments upon the intensive sensible discrimination, the best results are obtained with a temporal succession or spatial collocation of the compared impressions. And the same rule holds, of course, for the spatial and temporal attributes of the conscious elements.

3. This brings us to a third point of difference between fusion and colligation. In the former case a content cannot be said to be adequately defined by a simple enumeration of the qualities with which it is connected at the moment. For fusion itself is not an unequivocal term; the connections as well as the terms of connection are capable of variation within wide limits. On the other hand, a conscious content is individually characterised and completely defined by its position within a temporal or spatial colligation. We have already had occasion to mention this fact: it helped us to explain the exceptional importance ascribed by psychologists to the 'law of contiguity' in the doctrine of association of ideas (cf. § 30. 4). 'Position' is used, of course, in both its meanings: temporal position constitutes the individual definition of a content in respect of time, and spatial position or locality gives it

---

[1] I once saw a house in South Germany the part-ownership of which by two persons was sufficiently indicated by a simple difference of colour; the line of junction of the paints running up the middle of the front door.

an unmistakeable characterisation with regard to space. It is in this property of colligation that memory finds its chief support; and in practical life it furnishes the most effectual means for the intelligible communication of experience by mind to mind.—All these influences react upon one another. The independence of the separate contents in spatial and temporal colligation prevents the formation of any but a temporal or spatial total impression; and, on the other side, the general interconnection of all determinations of space and time gives each particular content an entirely individual significance. Again, the idea of a single object, of a thing as such, is best secured by the uniformity of its quality. We have referred to the distinction which has been drawn between sensation and perception (§ 61. 6). One of the principal arguments alleged in favour of the distinction is that perception implies a delimitation of separate objects, which is only possible by the help of spatial or temporal disjunction. From the psychological point of view, however, we must insist that the reason for this disjunction cannot be looked for in the spatial or temporal determinations themselves. On the contrary, nothing is more probable than that tracts of space and time, as originally given, mediate total impressions exclusively, and that the differentiation of these is only effected by the aid of definite contents or content complexes.

4. We have already said something of the special forms of spatial and temporal colligation (§ 42). (1) The phenomena of spatial colligation fall into two groups. (α) The first comprises colligations within the sphere of touch and vision, *i.e.*, under circumstances which admit of a direct space judgment. The phenomena of visual *contrast* in particular furnish a striking illustration of the various properties of spatial colligation which we have just been discussing. There is, of course, no tactual contrast in this meaning of the word, for the simple reason that the cutaneous sensations do not exhibit any considerable number of qualitative differences. On the other hand, something analogous to visual contrast is found in the interrelation of tactual intensities. And in both sense departments we have what is called contrast of magnitude, *i.e.*, an enhancement by colligation of a given difference between two spatial determinations. (β) Contrast phenomena of more indirect origin are observed when there are differences in the localisation of two non-spatial contents.

Visual contrast is the only one of all these processes which has been discussed and investigated in detail; and we shall, therefore, devote a special Section to its consideration. Two forms have been distinguished, a *simultaneous* and a *successive* contrast. The latter appears when the visual sensations are given in temporal succession, *i.e.*, implies temporal as well as spatial colligation. We have briefly noted its influence upon the sensible discrimination of tones (§ 14. 4), and of cutaneous intensities (§ 25. 3). The serial order of the separate qualities is an important aid to their clear apprehension, as well as to their accurate discrimination. The stimuli, however, must not be given in immediate succession, or the after effect of each precedent excitation will interfere with the cognition of the following. If the sensations are to reap the full benefit of their temporal colligation they must be separated by intervals adjusted to the conditions of stimulation in the different sense departments (§ 64; § 65. 1, 2; cf. 2 above).

5. (2) Temporal colligation is co-extensive with consciousness: it is the most general form of interconnection of conscious processes. But its laws and conditions have only incidentally been made the object of special inquiry. It is true that two types of temporal colligation,— reproduction and action,—have been recognised and investigated as independent processes. But even here the observer's interest has been principally centred upon secondary phenomena; in the case of reproduction, upon the conditions of colligation, the different 'associations'; and in the case of action, upon the variation of the total duration with variation of determining influences. We shall, therefore, spend no more time here upon the process of reproduction, but will refer the reader to the discussion in Pt. I, Chap. 4. The rules which hold for the fusion and colligation of peripherally excited sensations can be easily applied to centrally excited contents. The same differences exist between the two types of connection in both spheres, though naturally altered in absolute amount by the wide divergence of peripherally and centrally excited sensations. Hence we did not hesitate, when we were considering centrally excited sensations as such, to extend our investigation beyond the separate contents to their interconnections (*e.g.*, § 31. 6).—We give the name of *reactions* to those types of action which are accessible to scientific examination, *i.e.*, which are initiated by a peripheral impression. Both simple and compound reactions will be considered in the present Chapter. The mention of reactions concludes the list of colligation processes of which we have any exact knowledge at the present stage of psychological inquiry.

§ 68. The Contrast of Brightness and Colour.

1. The law of contrast holds within both of the great divisions of visual qualities, and the phenomena of contrast itself accordingly fall into two main classes. If two different brightnesses are observed simultaneously or in succession, each seems to throw the quality of the

other into higher relief; and two different colour tones act and react upon each other in a precisely similar manner. But curiously enough, no such result is produced by the juxtaposition of colour tone and brightness. The purity of a white is not enhanced by coloured surroundings, and a precedent or simultaneous brightness has no direct effect upon the saturation of a colour. There is, *i.e.*, no such thing as a *contrast of saturation*, in the strict meaning of the word. Where the term is employed, it usually denotes the influence of the degree of saturation of the separate colours upon a resultant colour contrast. Besides the distinction of brightness and colour contrast, we have those of *simultaneous* and *successive*, and of *monocular* and *binocular* contrast phenomena. These expressions, however, do not designate new facts of contrast, but only different conditions or circumstances under which the processes of brightness and colour contrast appear. Again, a distinction has been drawn within the sphere of simultaneous contrast between *contrast of margin*, which arises when the contrasting surfaces are in direct contact, and *contrast of distance*, which occurs when the two fields are separated by a considerable interval. Here too, however, the expressions merely call attention to the dependency of contrast upon the distance which separates the interacting qualities. The colour or brightness which influences another by way of contrast is commonly known as the *inducing*, and that which is changed by contrast as the *induced;* while the normal appearance of the latter, previous to its induction, is termed the *reacting* quality. As a matter of fact, contrast is always reciprocal, consisting simply in an alteration or enhancement of the normal difference between two qualities. But the terms just defined are exceedingly useful in experimental investigation, for the unequivocal specification of the objects compared.

2. (*a*) *Contrast of brightness.*—The general rule of brightness contrast is that when two brightnesses of different quality are seen simultaneously or in succession, the difference between them is apparently increased. If we have before us a small white square upon a white surface of the same quality, a similar square upon a gray surface, and a third square of the same kind upon a black background, the first will appear darker and the last lighter than the other two. The conditions of brightness contrast are general and special. Under the former head fall attention, fatigue, etc.,—all the processes which we found to have a general influence upon sensible discrimination (§ 5). There are four special conditions: the absolute brightness of the contrasting qualities, their brightness difference, their extension and their distance from each other. (*α*) The *absolute brightness* of the impressions is

26

of importance because a noticeable enhancement of its quality is only possible within certain limits. If either of the stimuli approaches the upper or lower limit of brightness sensation, no noticeable brightening or darkening can be expected to result from its contrast with the other. Moreover, the constancy of the relative sensible discrimination for brightnesses (§ 18. 5) means that the absolute amount of difference necessary to produce a noticeable change of quality is directly proportional to the degree of brightness of the reacting surface. Contrast effects between brightness sensations will accordingly be noticeable only within certain limits. It will not be found, *e.g.*, that a clear sky is noticeably brightened if we hold some small dark object before the eyes as we look at it.—It follows from these statements that we can distinguish different degrees of contrast, and that each must be capable of quantitative expression. To obtain a measure for the magnitude of a contrast effect, it is only necessary to compare the induced brightness with a brightness of the same quality as the reacting surface, and to vary the latter until the two are apparently equal. The amount of change which the reacting brightness undergoes gives the measure required.

3. (β) The second special condition is that of the *brightness difference* of the two surfaces. It is found that the degree of contrast reaches its maximum with a moderate difference between the inducing and the reacting surfaces. If the difference is too small or too great, no contrast effect is noticeable. Within certain limits the most favourable relation between the two impressions appears to remain constant, *i.e.*, to be independent of their absolute brightness. It is expressed by the proportion 1 : 4·76. (γ) No systematic investigation has been made into the influence of the *distance* which separates the contrasting brightnesses. As a general rule, contrast of margin, which appears at the line of division between the two adjacent qualities, is more intensive than the contrast produced when the reacting and inducing surfaces are placed at some little distance apart. But the exact rate of decrease of degree of contrast with increase of distance has not yet been determined. (δ) On the other hand, the dependency of contrast upon the *extension* of the inducing surface has been very thoroughly investigated. Kirschmann has discovered that the degree of contrast increases in direct proportion to the linear extension of the inducing stimulus or to the square root of its areal contents. The law is only valid within certain limits. It suggests at once the influence of extension upon apparent brightness, of which we have previously spoken (§ 18. 7). Increase of extent, *i.e.*, has the same effect, under certain conditions, as increase of brightness.—The same rules probably hold for the brightness contrast of colour impressions.

4. (*b*) *Contrast of colour.*—The general conditions of colour contrast are the same with those of brightness contrast. There are three sets of special conditions: the quality of the colour tone, and the difference between the inducing and reacting colours; the saturation and saturation difference of the particular colours; and lastly, their extension and distance from each other. (α) The only specific influence which can be attributed to *colour quality* as such is that it tends in every case to tinge the surrounding surface with the complementary quality. No noticeable effect is produced, however, unless the reacting quality stands at a very low level of saturation. The complementary colours are those which show the widest subjective divergence in the colour series (cf. § 17. 4). Here again, therefore, contrast consists in an enhancement of the normal difference between two qualities. The dependency of contrast upon the *difference* between the colour tones is twofold. In the first place, it reaches an upper and lower limit at a certain maximal and minimal degree of difference. Thus, no change is produced in a red object whether we place it against a background of its own quality or on a bluish green surface; whereas it is slightly altered in the direction of purple if its surroundings are green, and takes on a weakly bluish tinge if they are yellow. It follows that the highest degree of colour contrast is produced when the two qualities lie fairly near each other on the colour scale. In the second place, it is important to note that the strongest contrast effects are obtained under conditions which exclude a simultaneous brightness contrast, *i.e.*, when the brightnesses of the reacting and inducing colours are subjectively equal.

5. (β) The *saturation* of a colour tone militates against the effect of contrast; *i.e.*, the more saturated the colour, the less is it liable to apparent alteration by its surroundings. As we may regard gray or white as the lower limit of the saturation of any colour, it is clear that an inducing colour will produce its maximal contrast effect upon a colourless surface of equal brightness. It has been experimentally shown that the induced surface, under these circumstances, takes on a distinct complementary tinge. Here again, the magnitude of the contrast effect can be measured by the amount of colour of the same quality with the inducing which is required to cancel the complementary tone of the induced surface. The degree of saturation of the inducing colour itself is of considerable importance for the result. It seems probable from Kirschmann's investigations, that simultaneous contrast between a colour impression and a gray of equal brightness increases in logarithmic proportion to its saturation, *i.e.*, in accordance with a rule whose formulation is identical with that of Weber's law (cf. § 26). As regards

the influence of *saturation difference*, contrast is maximal when the two colours possess a moderate degree of saturation. This fact may be deduced a priori from the consideration that each of two given colours induces the other, and that the inverse variation of their induction with increase or decrease of saturation does not proceed in the same numerical proportion. (γ) The influence of *extension* and *distance* upon colour contrast is probably the same with their influence upon brightness contrast; but the question has not been definitely investigated. The contrast of margin is again especially vivid. But it is noteworthy that distinctness of outline or steady fixation of the margin of the colour surfaces diminishes the degree of contrast. The same result is produced by the introduction of a narrow strip of different quality between the adjacent borders of the reacting and inducing surfaces.

6. Both kinds of contrast are in great measure dependent upon the duration of the brightness or colour stimulation. One quite recent experiment is of peculiar importance for the theoretical explanation of the contrast effect. It was found that the duration of the electric discharge of a Holtz machine (calculated at about $\frac{1}{10000000}$ sec.) is fully sufficient to produce a distinct impression of contrast, which cannot be destroyed by any previous suggestion which may have given a wrong direction to expectation. The impression arises instantaneously, and remains unchanged during the course (approximately $\frac{1}{2}$ sec.) of the subsequent after-image. In all probability contrast reaches its maximum very soon after the beginning of the observation; then decreases; and finally, if the surface is persistently fixated, changes to an induction of the same quality with the reacting light. The effect of *successive* contrast is precisely similar to that of simultaneous, but is difficult to distinguish from the after-image phenomena, to which it bears a very close general resemblance. Observations have also been made upon *binocular* contrast, *i.e.*, the transference of the contrast effect from the stimulated to the unstimulated eye. It must not be supposed, of course, that the processes described hitherto are only set up by monocular fixation. The difference between them and binocular contrast is simply this: that they are the result either of monocular perception or of a simple co-operation of the two eyes, whereas binocular contrast (in this special sense) presupposes a separate functioning of either eye (cf. the 'direct' and 'crossed' after-images: § 20. 1). It may be laid down as a general rule that the after effect of monocular stimulation in the unstimulated eye is altogether similar to that produced under ordinary conditions, except that it is weaker and less sharply defined. But even when the two fields of vision are not completely separated, and more especially in experiments upon

the stereoscopic combination of objects of different spatial position, we sometimes have the occurrence of phenomena which are referred to binocular contrast, and which are intimately related to the phenomena of lustre, of reflection, and of retinal rivalry. All these binocular effects require for their origination a sufficient difference between the impressions perceived by each eye, in conjunction with an approximately equal degree of clearness or vividness. A very important part is played in the rivalry of contours by voluntary or involuntary movements of the point of regard, and by the momentary direction of the attention, which may give either of the images a temporary advantage over the other.

7. The theory of the phenomena of visual contrast constitutes a corollary to the theory of vision in general; and the forms which it has taken have been as different as the different theories of visual sensation (cf. § 21). Helmholtz interprets the contrast effect as a deception of judgment. A dwarf looks shorter than he really is, if he stands beside a giant; and the giant looks taller than he otherwise would, when the dwarf is by his side. In the same way, a light object on a dark background is taken to be brighter, and a dark object on a light background to be darker, than their qualities really are, as represented in perception. But this theory meets with very considerable difficulties as soon as ever it attempts the explanation of colour contrast. It is difficult to see why the deception of judgment should always change sensation in the direction of the complementary quality. And there are other objections. The hypothesis cannot account for the actual magnitude of the contrast effect; and the demonstration of its existence with a minimal duration of stimulation would seem absolutely to preclude the possibility of a deception of judgment. Wundt holds that the phenomenon of contrast, like Weber's law (§ 26. 4), is a particular expression of a general law of relativity. This view, again, seems untenable, at least as an explanation of colour contrast. There can be no doubt that the apprehension of a sensation is dependent upon the character of the other conscious contents of the time; but this fact does not enable us to understand the magnitude of the contrast effect, and the specific direction which colour contrast follows. We do not mean to deny that the phenomena of visual contrast point to conditions of a general or central nature. These are necessary to account for the universality of contrast,—which obtains between intensities and tracts of space or time as evidently as it does between qualities; and the magnitude of contrast is most certainly influenced by all those conditions of sensible discrimination which lead to the results formulated in Weber's law. But the close relationship of contrast phenomena

to after-images shows with equal plainness that they must be referred in part to definite peripheral conditions. Hering has proposed an exclusively peripheral theory of contrast, or as he phrases it, of simultaneous and successive light induction. On this hypothesis, the stimulation of any part of the retina by way of dissimilation (*i.e.*, by white, red or yellow) disposes the contiguous parts to processes of assimilation (*i.e.*, arouses a tendency to sensations of black, green or blue), and *vice versa*. A similar reason is alleged for the effect of successive excitation by the same stimuli. It is clear that every peripheral theory of visual sensation which can give account of the phenomena of after-images will also be able to furnish a plausible explanation of the conditions of contrast effects. But even a peripheral theory meets with a whole number of difficulties and disputed points, the final resolution of which is not possible in the present state of our knowledge.

Literature:

G. T. Fechner: *Ueber einige Verhältnisse des binocularen Sehens. Abhandl. d. Kgl. Sächs. Ges. d. Wiss., math.-phys. Classe*, vol. v., pp. 339 ff.

A. Kirschmann: *Ueber die quantitativen Verhältnisse des simultanen Helligkeits- und Farbencontrastes. Philos. Studien*, vol. vi., pp. 417 ff.

Cf. the literature cited under § 21.

§ 69. Simple Reactions.

1. A reaction (§ 63. 2) is a movement made in response to a sense impression. If it follows directly upon the reception of the impression, we have a *simple* reaction; if some further conscious process is interpolated between sensation and motor innervation, a *compound* reaction. The simple reaction, therefore, is very similar to the physiological *reflex*, in which a movement of definite muscle groups results from the direct transmission of a sensory stimulation to motor centres, without the participation of consciousness. Indeed, no sharp line of distinction can be drawn between the reflex and the simple reaction. The reaction experiment consists in the measurement (by an electric clock or by graphic registration) of the duration of the whole chain of processes from the moment of stimulation to the execution of the movement. The experiment is useful in two ways. (α) The differences in the times obtained serve to express the quickness or slowness of the part-processes contained in the reaction, and indicate the direction and magnitude of the various influences to which it is subject. (β) And the frequent repetition of the same act enables us to analyse with some degree of certainty the various factors which compose the reaction itself. This analysis is of especial importance in view of the high degree of com-

plexity which actions ordinarily exhibit. The reaction is simply the exact type of all actions, as they are called in the psychology of everyday life, which are initiated by an external stimulus. The reaction experiment, therefore, presents many points of interest aside from the question of its duration. It helps us to understand the nature and conditions of our practical relations to the external world. And it has contributed largely to our knowledge of the sensory conditions of sensation, of association, of the connection of conscious elements, etc. The wide range of its results has naturally rendered it a favourite object of investigation in experimental psychology. But physiology and astronomy are also interested in the measurement of reaction times : physiology, because it supplies a method for the determination of the rate of propagation of a sensory nervous excitation; and astronomy, because the registration of observations of stellar transits consists simply in the execution of reactions.

2. The duration of a simple reaction is dependent upon *external* and *internal* conditions. (i) The most important external condition is the *quality* of the initiatory sense impression. Reaction to light lasts about 80σ longer than reaction to sound or pressure; reaction to taste is also comparatively slow, and reaction to smell and temperature slowest of all. The *intensity* of the impressions is undoubtedly of importance in the sphere of vision and temperature: the stronger the stimulus, within certain limits, the shorter is the reaction time. On the other hand, there is no certain proof of a parallel influence of intensity when the stimuli employed are auditory or electrical-cutaneous. All these phenomena are referable to purely physiological causes, and present a complete analogy to the phenomena of the duration of sensations (§ 64). (ii) The changes which are due to the influence of internal conditions are of greater psychological importance. Besides altering the duration of the whole act, they usually imply a qualitative modification of its contents. Especially important in this connection is the *preparation* of the subject for the reaction. If the stimulus is given unexpectedly, the reaction time is considerably lengthened, and in many cases an emotion is produced (the reactor is surprised or, in extreme instances, startled), which is directly inhibitory of the requisite motor innervation. Even when the expectation is adequately adjusted to the experiment, the results differ very widely with its direction and intensity. It is customary to distinguish two types of simple reaction; the *sensorial* or complete and the *muscular* (motor) or abbreviated forms. The reaction is sensorial, when expectation is directed on the sense impression, and no special preparation is made for the movement. It is muscular, when expectation is concentrated as exclusively as

possible on the answering movement, and no particular preparation is made for the sense impression. The psychology of these forms of expectation differs very widely in actual experimentation; capacity of reproduction varies in different individuals, and the degree of preparation does not remain constant for the same subject. Thus, if the reactor is unable to ideate a sense impression with sufficient vividness, he will give the prescribed direction to his expectation by the help of judgments of an appropriate kind, or of the organic sensations aroused by the strain in sense organ or organ of movement, or perhaps of visual ideas of the stimulus or of the movement to be made in response to it. These different forms of sensorial or muscular preparation still await accurate analysis. In all probability, certain differences in the determination of reaction times are largely due to differences in the form of expectation.

3. The objective result of this difference in preparation is that the sensorial reaction lasts some $\frac{1}{10}$ sec. longer than the muscular. But the qualitative course of the two processes is also different. In the muscular reaction, the sense impression acts merely as a stimulus to the release of the movement, which is quick and spasmodic; in the sensorial reaction, there is not only a clear perception of the stimulus but also a conscious innervation of the movement. This difference accounts for certain characteristic reaction types, the *premature* and *erroneous* reactions, which not infrequently occur with muscular preparation. The premature reaction consists in the execution of the prescribed movement before the sensory stimulus has been given; the erroneous reaction in the execution of the required movement in answer to some other stimulus than that which is employed in the experiment. In either case, the subject is often ignorant that he has reacted wrongly. There can be no clearer evidence that the muscular reaction is essentially physiological in nature. In its extreme form it has, as a matter of fact, been interpreted as a practised brain reflex. Neither of these divergences from the normal type occurs in the sensorial reaction.—It is further noteworthy that the mean variation (cf. § 6. 7) of the sensorial type is twice or three times as large as that of the muscular. This is not surprising when we remember that the reflexes possess extraordinarily constant time values. We may, therefore, lay it down that the participation of consciousness in the muscular reaction is restricted to the intensive preparation for the movement, and a somewhat uncertain and indistinct sensation of the initiatory stimulus. Oftentimes this sensation does not become fully clear until after the reaction has been performed. The sensorial reaction begins with a similarly intensive expectation, which is realised by a

clear apprehension of the sensation; and ends with a movement, made with more or less conscious intention, and with or without the intervention of a movement idea. The indefiniteness of this description indicates the greater variety of the processes contained in the sensorial reaction, and the impossibility of the reduction of all its forms to a single comprehensive schema.

4. It is not difficult to discover analogies between these forms of the simple reaction and certain activities or actions in everyday life. Everyone must have had experiences which recall the premature or erroneous reaction; and everyone knows the difference between two actions, one of which is continuously directed by the idea of its end, while the other is accomplished step by step, as it were, each stage in its execution requiring special preparation. When the series of factors involved in an action has become familiar by long practice, there can be no doubt of the advantage of a constant idea of its ultimate conclusion. The predominance of the one idea makes it quicker and more accurate, and effects a saving of energy as well as of time. The sensorial reactions, when they have been thoroughly practised, bear a very close resemblance to the *habitual* actions of ordinary life. The connection which has grown up between a sensation and a movement is brought about in the particular case without any special impulse of will,—without any reflection at all. A vast number of our daily actions are performed in this way, except that the process is usually initiated by connections of sensations and concluded by combinations of several movements. The term 'association' would seem to be as applicable to this process as to the interrelation of sensations; for the laws and conditions which obtain for the reproduction of movements by ideas are the same with those for the reproduction of sensations by sensations. Actions of this kind have also been named *ideomotor*.

5. The reaction time is taken up (α) with a purely physiological process, consisting in the peripheral stimulation and the propagation of the excitation to the cerebral cortex. This is followed (β) by the psychophysical process of central sensory stimulation, with its corresponding sensation; and this again, (γ) by the conscious or unconscious transmission of the sensory excitation to the motor cortical centre, with its purely physiological consequences of the centrifugal stimulation and resulting contraction of definite muscle groups. The better the whole course is prepared, or the more it is disposed to correlated function, the shorter will the time of reaction be. This explains the difference of duration between the two forms of the simple reaction. Thus, the additional $\frac{1}{10}$ sec. in the sensorial time is accounted for by two principal facts: that the sense impression is apprehended or

apperceived with maximal distinctness before the movement is performed, and that the transmission of a stimulation to the motor centre takes place more slowly than in the muscular type. The essential dependency of the whole process upon the intensity of preparation is shown by the marked influence of the time allowed for concentration of the attention upon the rapidity of the reaction. It is customary to give a signal at about 2 secs. before the sensory stimulus, this interval having been found most favourable for the simple preparation which the experiment requires (§ 5. 4). *Practice*, of course, shortens the reaction, and *fatigue* lengthens it. *Distraction* of the attention, too, naturally exerts an influence upon the rapidity of reaction. All these general conditions, however, seem to be of far less importance for the muscular than for the sensorial form, provided only that the motor preparation is not seriously interfered with. The reason probably is that we can more easily dispose ourselves for a definite movement, whose performance is under our own control, than keep ourselves prepared for any length of time together to receive a definite sense impression. Distraction is most readily produced by an impression of the same character with the reaction stimulus, though diversion of the attention by disparate stimuli, when it occurs, is probably the more effective of the two (cf. § 75. 5). This difference helps us to explain the divergent results of investigations into the dependency of reaction upon distracting stimuli. We have no space here to discuss further the many observations of detail which have been made in the measurement of simple reaction times. We will simply give in conclusion the rough average time of the muscular and sensorial forms in different sense departments. Auditory stimuli give times of $\frac{1}{10}$ and $\frac{2}{10}$ sec.; visual stimuli, $\frac{2}{10}$ and $\frac{3}{10}$ sec.; and tactual (pressure) stimuli, $\frac{1}{10}$ and $\frac{2}{10}$ sec.

§ 70. The Analysis of Compound Reactions.

1. Psychologists have been principally interested in the compound reactions, in which (according to the current hypothesis) the execution of the movement is delayed by definite mental acts performed at once on the reception of the sense impression, in accordance with a prescribed rule. Donders was the first to attempt a determination of the rapidity of judgment, choice and discrimination by a subtraction of the simple from the compound reaction time; and his example has been followed by many subsequent investigators. Now it is clear that the result is only valid if the interpolation of the mental act constitutes the sole change in the course of the reaction, *i.e.*, if preparation, sensory stimulation and movement are precisely identical in both the simple and the compound form. We must, therefore, separately examine the

various types of compound reaction with a view to ascertaining whether or how far this requirement is fulfilled. The investigation of compound reactions will, however, lose nothing of its importance, even if we find reason to mistrust these particular calculations of the duration of different mental activities. For the real value of the measurement of compound reactions (cf. § 69. 1) consists (α) in the furtherance of an accurate analysis of the individual components by the frequent repetition of the same process, and (β) in the illustration of the influence of different conditions upon the course of the action. And these objects of inquiry are not touched at all by the possibility or impossibility of a separate statement of the duration of definite mental acts. The interpolated processes have been those of cognition, discrimination, choice, reproduction and judgment. We will, therefore, begin with an analysis of these particular acts.

2. (*a*) *Cognition* is the simplest term of the series. As employed here, it means that the precise character of the sense impression to be used in a given experiment is left indefinite, and that the subject must, therefore, cognise its quality, intensity or other attributes before he can execute the reaction movement. The actual occurrence of the act of cognition is secured either by the requirement of conscientious introspection on the part of the reactor, or by the restriction of the reaction to one definite impression. The former procedure is to be preferred, since in the alternative case practice will very quickly lead to the formation of a simple ideomotor colligation between the particular sense impression and the movement of the reactor. The idea of an objective check, which here takes the form of a limitation of the reaction to a sense impression previously defined, is correct in itself; but the only method for its realisation would consist in a frequent variation of the sense impressions employed, since only in this way could the danger of an ideomotor colligation be avoided. It is always the sensorial form of the simple reaction which is subtracted from the compound in the calculation of the time of the interpolated act, whether of cognition or of discrimination, etc. This type of the simple reaction is undoubtedly more nearly related to the different complex actions than is the other; for the interpolated act is in every instance associated to the sense impression, and it is, therefore, most appropriate to give a sensorial direction to expectation. An attempt has been made to obtain compound reaction times with muscular preparation; but it can only be successful if the subject is not thinking exclusively of the prescribed movement, but is at the same time bringing sense impressions and movements into more or less close connection in consciousness. This latter form of preparation has been termed

associative, as contradistinguished from the sensorial. The effect of really muscular preparation is either to lengthen the compound reaction, or to rule out the mental acts required, and so to make the whole reaction dependent upon automatic practice or mere accident.

3. The question now arises whether the cognition reaction is simply the sensorial reaction, *plus* a new mental act. There are two reasons for a negative answer. (i) Preparation is essentially different in the two cases. In the sensorial reaction, expectation is directed upon a perfectly definite sense impression, and the observer may be disposed solely for its special reception. In the cognition reaction, the direction of the attention is indefinite, and the preparation for the stimulus incomplete: the most that the subject knows is the sense department, or the range of variation of the impressions from which the initiatory stimulus will be selected. When we find, therefore, that the cognition time is from 30 to 50σ longer than the sensorial, we have still to ask how much of this additional time is due to the more imperfect preparation, and how much to a particular act of cognition; and there is no way of obtaining an answer. (ii) Again, it is difficult to see what the act of cognition would be, as distinguished from the perception of the sense impression which occurs in the sensorial reaction itself. [1] Distinct perception is, as a general rule, a sufficient reason for the origination of definite judgments, *i.e.*, of judgments which give accurate expression to the familiarity of the observer with the perceived object; although the effectiveness of a clearly perceived impression for central excitation may also be of a quite general character, and the judgment simply state its familiarity without closer definition (§ 27. 4 ff.). It follows that the only difference between the apprehension of the sense impression in the cognition reaction and in the sensorial is the disposition of the reactor (usually remarked by himself) to give utterance to judgments expressive of the character of the perceived stimulus. As this disposition must change with every change of impression, we cannot speak of the act of cognition as though it were one and the same throughout. If we attempted to determine its real nature, we should find that it was primarily a phenomenon of reproduction. But the time difference between the cognition and sensorial times of a practised observer is in all probability referable to the difference of preparation, rather than to the interpolation of this reproductory process. We have seen that the direction of expectation is the chief factor in the time difference between the muscular and sensorial reaction, which is practically as large again.

---

[1] The only difference that I can discover in my own case is a slower apprehension of the sense impression.

4. (*b*) The same arguments apply to the measurement of *discrimination*, as the term is ordinarily employed in reaction experiments. In the discrimination reaction, any one of a limited number of impressions may be selected; the reactor knows their number and nature, but not which of them will be given in the particular case. Thus, we should have a discrimination reaction, if the subject knew that one of two definite sounds of different intensities would serve as stimulus, but was uncertain to which of them he would be required to react in each individual experiment. It is evident that the process here is essentially the same as in the cognition reaction. The reader should notice in particular that these discrimination reactions do not imply any exercise of the sensible discrimination, as he might infer from the similarity of the names. Sensible discrimination would imply the simultaneous presentation of at least two impressions, or the persistence in consciousness of a centrally excited sensation with which the peripheral might be compared.

What we actually observe in the reactions is, again, the clear perception of the given impression, and a more or less noticeable reproduction of judgments subserving its precise definition. We do not mean to deny that a true discrimination reaction could be carried out. That would be possible if the subject were required, *e.g.*, to cognise the difference in magnitude and direction between two simultaneously presented stimuli.

(*c*) The *choice* reaction presupposes a co-ordination between a number of impressions and movements; the reactor has to respond to the impression *a* with the movement *α*, to the impression *b* with the movement *β*, etc. He does not know which of these impressions will be given in the particular case. The preparation for the experiment is, therefore, precisely similar to the preparation for the discrimination reaction. And it is indisputable that the state of expectation *may* be precisely the same in the two experiments. This is the basis of the assumption that the subtraction of the time of a discrimination reaction from the time of a choice reaction obtained under exactly analogous conditions gives the duration of the act of choice. Ordinarily, however, the necessary co-ordinations are specially practised; and expectation, despite its indefinite direction, is not wholly free (as, indeed, it is better that it should not be) from the idea of the individual connections. We have spoken of this kind of preparation as *associative* (cf. 2 above). It is plain that the subtraction cannot give us any reliable information as to the duration of the act of choice, if only for the reason that the precedent state of consciousness, which we have found to be of first importance in all reaction time experimentation is essentially different for the minuend and the subtrahend.

5. We have now to ask whether choice itself constitutes a specific independent mental act. This question would seem to take us to the heart of the problem of the freedom of the will, and to involve an analysis of resolution, *i.e.*, of decision in face of different possibilities. But our present inquiry is really much more simple than appears from its formulation, inasmuch as the incentives to decision, the reasons for choice, in the choice reaction are perfectly definite. Any oscillation between the different possibilities of movement—which, moreover, are always limited in number—must, therefore, be ascribed to a failure of memory, *i.e.*, to an uncertain recollection of the prescribed co-ordination. For a thoroughly practised subject the course of the choice reaction may be precisely the same with that of the sensorial: clear perception of the sense impression reproduces the appropriate movement. A very striking illustration is afforded by the playing of a practised musician; the sight of the score calls up at once the corresponding movements of arm and fingers. It follows from this extraordinary power of practice to modify our actions that choice reactions in the strict sense of the word do not occur beyond the first beginnings of experimentation, and that the reaction times taken at different stages of practice are less comparable here than in any other department of reaction work. Before the subject has perfected the simple ideomotor action, however, the rapidity of which seems to be independent of the number of possible sense impressions and movements, the time of the reaction is lengthened by the introduction of the act of choice. The result may be explained as due (α) to the uncertainty of recollection, which may render it necessary that the judgment formulating the particular co-ordination be specially reproduced, and (β) to the rivalry of a number of relatively intensive movement ideas, which inhibits the reproduction of the right idea. This stage of practice is characterised by the frequent occurrence of concomitant movements of the hand, on either side of the reacting finger, and of erroneous reactions. It is clear that all these processes are merely familiar phenomena of reproduction, and that they do not constitute a specific act of choice, interpolated in the course of the experiment, and separably measurable.

6. (*d*) In the *association* reaction, the prescribed movement is not to be executed until the given sense impression, of whose quality the reactor is ignorant, has reproduced a second idea. This form of the compound reaction, *i.e.*, presupposes a single movement and an unlimited number of possible sense impressions, and consequently approaches the type of the cognition reaction. Hence the duration of the cognition

reaction is used as the subtrahend in the calculation of the 'association time'. The precedent state of consciousness certainly *may* be the same in both cases; but, as a general rule, the knowledge that he must 'associate' will serve to modify the disposition of the reactor. Apart from this possible discrepancy, the association time would seem to admit of the simplest interpretation of any of the subtraction times, as it may very well be accredited to the reproduced idea. However, it does not only represent, and does not wholly represent, the duration of the reproduced idea. Some time, more or less, may elapse before the appearance of the second idea in consciousness, and the movement may be innervated at very different stages of its development. This would account for the great divergences in the association times of different subjects. The term 'association time', therefore, proves in its turn to be not free from ambiguity.

The higher forms of the compound reactions, the choice and association reactions, may be still further complicated. Thus we may co-ordinate general categories with definite movements, and require the reactor to wait for the execution of a particular movement until he has subsumed the sense impression under a given category.

(*e*) The association reaction may be extended in a similar way by the requirement that a *judgment* be passed upon the reproduction aroused by the sense impression, before the reaction movement is made. These experiments take us into the domain of the activity of thought, in the strict sense of the phrase, and raise a large number of interesting problems in the analysis of thought processes and their conditions. The exact comparability of the experiments in all but the one respect is here, as everywhere, the prerequisite of the evaluation of their quantitative results. The method of measurement is precisely the same for the compound as for the simple reactions.

It is hardly necessary to point out the analogies which obtain between compound reactions and actions of our everyday experience. Our attitude to external objects very commonly takes the form of the cognition or choice or association reaction. With the exception of the voluntary action, which is an independent activity of the subject arising from internal incentives, there is no type of conscious movement which cannot be reduced to one or other kind of simple or compound reaction.

§ 71. The Principal Results of the Measurement of Compound Reactions.

1. We attempt in what follows to give a summary of the most important facts which have been brought to light by the measurement

of compound reactions. It follows from the discussions of the fore-going Section that we shall lay no weight upon the absolute duration of the time of cognition, discrimination, etc. All our statements of reaction rapidity will be relative. The cognition and discrimination reactions may be bracketed together, as the professed discrimination reactions are not strictly what their name would indicate them to be (§ 70. 4).

(a) *Cognition reactions.*—Different methods have been employed for the measurement of these times (§ 70. 2). The method of reaction to an indefinite number of impressions with purely subjective (introspective) guarantee is ordinarily termed the *d-method* (Wundt); the limitation of reaction to definite selected impressions, which is intended to serve as an objective check, is the cardinal point of what is called the *c-method* (Donders). It is evident that the *c*-method itself may take two different forms. The subject may attain by associative preparation (§ 70. 2, 4) to a wholly automatic reproduction of the movement by the sense impression, or he may be expressly required to avoid association, and be given the choice between movement and no movement. These differences in the execution of the cognition reaction are accurately reflected in the time differences obtained. The shortest times are those of the *c*-method with associative preparation; the times given by the *d*-method are somewhat longer; and the reactions taken by the second form of the *c*-method are longest of all. Associative practice in a definite connection of sense impression and movement puts the cognition times midway between those of the muscular and sensorial reactions. This is not difficult to understand, when we remember that the preparation consists in a simultaneous expectation of sense impression and movement, *i.e.*, that it is really an intermediate form between the extreme sensorial and extreme muscular dispositions. Similar transition forms occur in simple reactions to stimuli whose precise nature is known to the subject, and are also characterised by a mean duration. Hence, for a thoroughly practised reactor this form of cognition reaction is in reality merely a simple reaction with mixed preparation, and the fact that other stimuli are or may be presented is either without influence of any kind or simply serves in a general way to divert the attention.

2. The cognition reactions taken by the *d*-method are on the average longer than the sensorial times. The result is probably referable to the influence of an indefinite direction of expectation. The further extension of the reaction time by the necessity of choice between movement and no movement is obviously due to the oscillation of reproduction.—The relative differences of cognition time obtained

with the different methods will naturally be independent of the method itself in the great majority of cases. We may, therefore, proceed to tabulate the most important results without reference to the form of the method.

(α) As a general rule, the cognition of intensities of sensation occupies a longer time than the cognition of qualities. This result is of importance as illustrating the lack of an absolute memory for the intensity of impressions (§ 26. 6), and the poverty of language in specific names for intensive differences. Our estimation of intensity is almost always comparative, whereas we possess an elaborate system of symbols, by the help of which we are perfectly well able, within certain limits, to make an absolute determination of quality.

(β) The cognition of direction (visual, tactual and auditory localisation) requires a less average time than the cognition of the corresponding quality or intensity (colour, strength and weakness of cutaneous stimulation, tone); the cognition of distance (from our own body) by means of sight requires the same average time as the cognition of visual qualities. This result renders the time of localisation surprisingly small, and it seems reasonable to make the method employed (the first form of the *c*-method) at least partly responsible for it. In all probability, the reaction movements enter especially easily into associative connection with definite directions in space. Nevertheless, there appears to be sufficient ground for the inference drawn from the experiments that local signature cannot be interpreted as a conscious intensive variation (cf. § 57. 3). The length of time required for the cognition of distances from our own body is fully explained by the relativity of the determination. In this respect it resembles the cognition of intensity.

(γ) The cognition of different qualities of the same sense and of disparate senses increases the times of the simple reaction to the same impressions by different increments. Thus, colours are more quickly cognised than tones, pressures more quickly than tastes, high tones more quickly than deep tones, black more quickly than white, etc. It is difficult to reconcile these facts with the assumption of a specific act of cognition. On the other hand, they speak very definitely for differences in the stability of the associative connections.

3. (δ) The cognition of more complex impressions requires a longer average time than the cognition of more simple stimuli, and the duration of the discrimination reaction by the *d*-method is dependent upon the number of possible sense impressions. The difference between simple and complex stimuli has received special attention in the domain of vision (letters, words, numbers, pictures). Within

certain limits, increased complexity of the initiatory impression makes no difference to the length of the reaction: indeed, short words are cognised even more quickly than single letters, and numbers of two or three places hardly less quickly than simple numbers. A further increase in the number of constituents is required to produce a distinct increase of reaction time. This shows that the conditions of the sensory apprehension of complex impressions remain the same with those of the apprehension of simple stimuli up to a certain point of complexity, and that practice in the reproduction of the name of the complex object may cancel the advantage which the simple stimulus possesses for perception. Similar conclusions may be drawn from the fact that the time of the discrimination reaction is dependent upon the number of impressions. This dependency is most pronounced where the stimuli differ in intensity: the conditions of reproduction render it exceedingly difficult to discriminate even between three different intensities of sound. But it is also observed with qualitative impressions, when their number exceeds the number of names comprised in the subject's ordinary vocabulary.

The results which we have described and explained so far are wholly confirmatory of the analysis of the previous Section. They point more particularly to the importance of reproduction, and consequently of association, for the process of cognition. As a matter of fact, the word 'cognition', in whatever context it is employed, always means the description of an experience by the help of symbols, which relegate it, in accordance with its essential attributes, to its appropriate place in the general interconnection of concepts and judgments which constitutes our system of reflection or knowledge. So that cognition, in its psychological significance, is simply a more or less distinct reproductory phenomenon (§ 70. 3). In the present connection it is especially interesting to note that the effectiveness of an impression for central excitation may be observed in the absence of definite reproduced ideas or sensations from consciousness. Everyone who has taken part in cognition reactions will know that he may be positively certain of having cognised the visual or auditory impression, before the name which designates it has appeared in any form above the conscious limen. This fact serves to illustrate and confirm our original analysis of recognition (§§ 27 ff.).

4. (*b*) *Choice reactions.*—Our estimate of the relative duration of these reactions can only be based upon their comparison with cognition reactions taken by the *d*-method. At the same time, the course of the choice reaction is very similar to the associative preparation of the *c*-method, if practice in the prescribed co-ordinations has been

carried to any great extent. We have, therefore, a large number of actual choice reactions lying between the two extremes of an automatic co-ordination of sense impression with movement and the mediation of their connection by a special reflective process. It will be readily understood that under these conditions it is exceedingly difficult to summarise and interpret the experimental results. The following facts seem to be well established.

(α) The average duration of the choice reaction increases with the number of possible co-ordinations. Reaction with simple choice between two movements is only some 60 to 80σ longer than reaction with cognition, but the difference rises to 300 or 400σ when the reactor has to choose between ten movements (movements of the ten fingers). The result is easily explained, if we may presuppose equal conditions of practice in every case. The degree of liability of reproduction and the quickness with which it is realised by connection in the particular instance are certainly dependent upon the number of equally possible connections,—and the greater their number, the greater will be the inhibition or retardation of the individual reproduction.

(β) All differences in the facility and certainty of the separate co-ordinations are reflected in corresponding differences in the rapidity with which they are brought about. The certainty of the association between impression and movement may be (i) originally given as a result of previous individual development, or (ii) consciously effected by practice, or (iii) involuntarily produced by repetition in the course of the experiments. (i) The first of these possibilities is fulfilled in all cases of 'natural' co-ordination, *e.g.*, in the connection of printed words with the corresponding movements of speech, or in that of the numbers 1 to 5 with the fingers of the right hand in the order of thumb to little finger, etc. If the spoken word is employed as the reaction movement, the experiment must usually take the form of an ideomotor colligation of the perceived object and its name, and not of a choice between equally possible activities. It has been found that short words, printed upon cards and shown to the reactor, arouse the corresponding speech movement most quickly; that separate letters require a somewhat longer time for their naming; and that a considerably longer time still is needed for the reproduction of the appropriate words by pictures and colours. The result is interesting and readily intelligible. The reproduction of spoken by printed words is especially direct and exceedingly common; while pictures or colours may arouse very different ideas according to the individual disposition of the subject, and are by no means so universally reproductive of names as are printed words. Moreover, the names for what is seen in a picture or a colour may vary within certain limits, whereas printed words give a single definite direction to the reaction movement.

5. Cognition reactions to the objects just mentioned give different and partly contrary time values. Colours and pictures are cognised rather more quickly than letters and words. It plainly follows that the rapidity of the choice reaction is really conditioned by the stability and exclusiveness of the natural co-ordinations. We have already noticed that short words are more quickly cognised than separate letters (cf. 3 above). This shows (what is evident from other considerations) that we do not read letter by letter, and that the 'word method' which is now followed in elementary schools is better adapted to the psychological conditions of the apprehension of printed words than the older '*a, b, c* method.' (ii) The connection of sense impression and appropriate movement is purposely strengthened by associative preparation and may, of course, be further established by more or less obvious associations. (iii) Lastly, liability of reproduction is involuntarily and unintentionally increased by the repetition of the experiments; so that care must be taken that definite co-ordinations are not rendered overeffective by their relatively more frequent application,—unless, of course, the influence of repetition is the subject of the special investigation.

(γ) The same phenomena recur in the more complex choice reactions. The co-ordinations employed in these experiments are those of definite categories, *e.g.*, of five parts of speech or forms of inflection, with a corresponding number of movements. The sense impression, perhaps a word called out by the experimenter, must then be subsumed to its appropriate category before the co-ordination can be completed. The only difference is that complication arises from variations in the connection of sense impression and category. The rapidity of the connection is again dependent upon all the conditions which determine the permanence and strength of liability of reproduction.

6. (*c*) *Association reactions.*—Reproduction with all its conditions has played an important part in our analysis and explanation of the times both of choice and of cognition. Its place in the association reaction, however, is somewhat different. It is there, so to speak, embodied as a whole in the course of the experiment. The cognition reaction times again furnish us with a basis of comparison. The most important results are as follows.

(α) Unequivocally definite reproduction is most quickly effected; ambiguously defined reproduction requires a longer time; and free reproduction is slowest of all (§ 30. 6). The different degrees of limitation are set to the reproductory activity by its direction in a more or less definite channel previously to the experiment. Thus, the movement of ideation is unequivocally determined when the stimulus consists in the title of a familiar poem, and the subject is asked to reproduce the author's name. Reproduction is equivocally determined, on the other hand, when the name of a season is employed to call up the name of a month which falls within it. Free reproductions, in which the nature and direction of the centrally excited processes are left altogether indefinite, are simply equivocally determined reproductions of the highest order; a certain limitation is still imposed upon the movement of ideation, by the character of the selected impression. Other things equal, we may account for the rapidity of the unequivocally determined reproductions by the fact that in their case the reproduced idea is least liable to inhibition. The more indefinite, the less characteristic the centrally exciting stimulus, the more difficult is the reproduction of a completely definite idea (cf. *loc. cit.*). Moreover, the unequivocally and equivocally determined reproductions are further assisted by the limited number of the sense impressions and the relative concreteness of expectation.

7. (β) Any circumstance which serves to increase liability of reproduction, in accordance with the laws of centrally excited sensation, serves also to accelerate the association reaction. Hence the commonest ideational connections, *e.g.*, are also the quickest. This is perhaps the reason why the reproduction of the idea of a means by that of its end requires less time than that of the reverse reproduction, and the idea of a part by that of the whole less time than that of the whole by that of its part. Again, we can reproduce the name of the month immediately following a given month much more quickly than the name of the next preceding month. And a large number of individual differences may be referred under this rubric to differences in the stability of associations in individual minds.

(γ) The rapidity of the association reaction is dependent upon the significance (whether accidental or as the result of education) of the materials of reproduction. This is what we mean by saying that ideas stand at different levels of *preparedness* in consciousness. The preparedness is influenced not only by the degree of liability of reproduction at the moment, which is a matter of chance, but also by the conditions of fidelity of reproduction (§ 31). Here would seem to belong the fact that the reproduction of the general by the particular takes less time than that of the particular by the general. We have referred to it on more than one occasion (cf. § 27. 5, 6; § 57. 6, etc.). The principle also explains the great proportion of recollections of elary life in the minds of elderly persons. Galton made a collection of free reproductions, and found that 85 p. c. were associations of childhood and early manhood, while only 15 p. c. were suggested by experiences of the immediate past. We cannot here enter into further detail with regard to these experiments, which, as the reader can see, may be extended in very many directions. We will only mention in conclusion that more complex forms, obtained by the interpolation of logical or æsthetic judgments of the presented ideas, naturally give very much longer average times; and that the fluctuation of subjective estimation and appreciation has led to extremely divergent determinations (i.e., makes the mean variation of the times exceedingly large).

Literature:

K. Fricke: *Ueber psychische Zeitmessung. Biologisches Centralblatt*, vol. viii., pp. 673 ff.; vol. ix., pp. 234 ff., 437 ff., 467 ff.

S. Exner: *Experimentelle Untersuchungen der einfachsten psychischen Processe. Pflüger's Archiv für Physiol.*, vol. vii., pp. 601 ff.

J. von Kries und F. Auerbach: *Die Zeitdauer einfacher psychischer Processe. Du Bois' Archiv f. Physiologie*, 1877, pp. 297 ff.

Cf. a long series of experimental researches by Tischer, Trautscholdt, Cattell, Merkel, L. Lange, Martius, etc., in the *Philos. Studien*, vols. i.-viii.

§ 72. The Attention as State of Consciousness.

1. The description and explanation of the facts comprised under the familiar term 'attention' constitute one of the most formidable difficulties which the psychologist encounters in the whole course of his inquiry. In certain psychological systems attention is regarded as identical with consciousness, and is thus made to appear susceptible of none but a metaphysical treatment. But as early as the eighteenth century empirical psychology had awakened to the importance of a discrimination of the two concepts, and modern experimental psychology and psychophysics have laid still greater emphasis upon the necessity of their separation. This unity of standpoint, however, has not led to unity of explanation; and every psychologist of any independence at the present time analyses and derives attention in his own way. Some reduce it to a specific class of sensations, sensations of muscular contraction or of strain; others regard it as an emotion, which exercises an especial influence upon the motor side of our activity. Another, psychophysical theory makes it the primary office of attention to reinforce excitation in the sensory centres; and a fourth hypothesis characterises its positive function as a process of inhibition. In popular thinking attention, like feeling and will (§§ 34. 1; 40. 1), is looked upon as a purely subjective activity, as a mode of the self's behaviour in face of external impressions. So we are said to 'direct' our attention upon something; and even when a change of direction is involuntarily produced, we do not relinquish our belief that it is in our own power to be attentive to one thing or another. From this point of view we can understand Leibniz' identification of the attention with the self-conscious assimilation of an impression, or, as he termed it, apperception.—Now we found in our consideration of feeling and will that popular opinion, schooled as it has been by the experiences of countless generations, contained no small measure of the truth. So here the common view of attention, however deficient its analysis and inaccurate its method of expression, is undoubtedly worthy of psycho-

logical respect. Hence, all those theories which contradict the verdict
of general experience, and resolve attention into a complex of certain
sensations, must be judged from the outset to possess but little
probability.

2. The first business of a careful psychological investigation into the
phenomenon of attention is to distinguish between its manifestations
and its conditions. We must begin by defining the nature of attention,
as discovered by introspection. Hence the question at once arises,
whether we have in the process of attention something above and
beyond the elementary conscious contents described in the preceding
Parts, or whether the term simply indicates a special state in which all
these contents may be presented under certain conditions. It seems
that the second alternative is the correct one; for introspection disco-
vers nothing really new in attention, nothing which is characteristic
of the process as such. Those who maintain the contrary have
nothing to allege but a sum of sensations, which occur just as well in
other contexts, or a change in the contents given in the state of attention, or a general judgment of the origin of the process. (i) Strain
sensations, *e.g.*, are ordinary concomitants of attention, and are referred
to in the phrases 'strained' and 'relaxed attention'; but they are
neither necessary constituents of attention nor attention itself. (ii) So
again, when we find the increased clearness of a perception or the
increased vividness of a sensation or conscious concentration upon one or
two definite ideas, interpreted as functions of attention, we must reply
that while all these changes regularly appear in the attentive state,
they are always changes in the conscious contents, and cannot be
conceived of as separated from them. It is, therefore, altogether impossible to add all these changes together and account them a specific
process, and to give this process the name of attention in contradistinction to the particular contents. For every item in the sum proves,
when accurately analysed, to be no more than an enhancement of
the given attributes of sensations or ideas or of the given relations
between them, or a limitation of their number—in a word, nothing
more than a purely quantitative process, which may be set up in
consciousness by other means than that of attention. The reader
may incline to find a possible exception to this statement in the clearness of the quality, difference, etc., in the state of attention. For clearness or distinctness is certainly not identical with the intensity of an
impression: weak stimuli may be more distinct than intensive. Now distinctness is partly referable to conditions in the sense organ (cf. the mechanism of accommodation or the *fovea centralis* of the retina in the
eye). But, this apart, we mean by the term simply the relatively

most favourable apprehension of an impression, as expressed in a relative maximum (α) of its discriminability from other contents, and (β) of the liability of reproduction of its attributes. It follows, of course, that clearness or distinctness is not a new character, which can be detached from the particular contents to which it is ascribed, and constituted the predominant factor in attention.

3. (iii) Lastly, we have a general judgment of the origin of attention in its description as an internal activity, concentrated in various degrees upon the particular ideas in consciousness. For this description only applies to attention, as given to introspection, on the assumption that we are able to perceive the internal activity as such. And this would mean, in its turn, that we are conscious of an internal activity above and beyond the contents upon which it is concentrated, and above and beyond the concomitant sensations to which its functioning gives rise. The author is unable to discover any such distinct act of consciousness in the state of attentive observation. Either a sum of organic sensations (cf. the experience of 'effort': § 40) has been described, and its interpretation attempted, by this term ; or 'internal activity' is merely an inexact expression of the popular view of attention mentioned just now. We shall see later (§ 74) that there is really a very close connection between attention and organic sensations; but we have already rejected the hypothesis that the two are identical. In the same way, we believe that the popular view of the origin of attention is correct; but we do not believe that this view requires the assumption of a special conscious content, 'internal activity', or that internal activity is demonstrable by introspection. If we consider that all classes of conscious contents, without distinction of origin or of value, may be the object of attention, and that the alterations which they undergo in consequence of attention are all of one nature and capable of formulation in the same terms, we have no alternative but to regard attention as a state of consciousness in general,—though its conditions, of course, must be sought aside from the different contents which enter into it at different times. The psychological problem of attention may, therefore, be stated somewhat as follows. (α) The psychologist must describe the changes which the simple and compound processes of consciousness undergo in the state of attention. (β) He must depict the secondary phenomena which ordinarily accompany it. (γ) And he must tabulate the conditions which determine its appearance and its degree in the particular case.

4. It is one of Wundt's services to modern psychology that he has recognised the unique nature and the general and fundamental importance of attention, and has given expression to both in his doctrine of *apperception*. The English *association* psychology, with the

German and French schools which have adopted its tenets, refers all the phenomena of conscious mental life to the mechanics of sensations and ideas, and more or less completely ignores the significance of the attentive state. Wundt has realised that the 'having' of an idea is not identical with its attentive experience, and that the conditions of attention are not given with the internal and external stimuli which we regard as the physical counterparts of centrally and peripherally excited sensations. He accordingly distinguishes between perception and apperception,—the former denoting the appearance of a content in consciousness, at the instance of external and internal stimuli, the latter its reception into the state of attention. This accurate analysis of the facts of consciousness has been altogether wrongly interpreted as a metaphysical construction: Wundt's definition of apperception, though recognised as different from that of Herbart, having been confused with Kant's transcendental apperception, or the doctrine in its entirety relegated to the region of pure metaphysics (§ 32. 5). In the Herbartian psychology, apperception is the reception of a new impression into an already existent ideational complex, and a distinction is consequently drawn between the perception mass (the impression which awaits reception) and the apperception mass (the receiving ideas). The practical importance of this process is undoubted: it typifies the course of every perception. At the same time, we cannot find a place for the Herbartian definition of apperception in our psychological system, since it merely covers the action of familiar laws of association and reproduction. Wundt's definition, on the other hand, is wholly adequate to the requirements of a systematic psychology, and we shall, therefore, frequently employ his phraseology in what follows. It has the additional advantage of being more convenient and more precise than the other modes of expression in current use.

5. Many writers emphasise the distinction—in what appear to the author to be exaggerated terms—between *sensible* and *intellectual* attention, although the meanings which they attach to the two words are not always identical. Thus, some find the criterion of sensible attention in the circumstance that an external stimulus draws attention to itself in virtue of some attribute or attributes, while they conceive that intellectual attention originates in the preference accorded to a particular impression by the "presentation auxiliaries" or apperception masses, in the Herbartian sense. Others again, speak of sensible attention when the object or content of the process consists of peripherally excited sensations, and of intellectual attention when it embraces centrally excited sensations. The first of these distinctions obviously rests upon the division of the conditions of attention into

external and internal (cf. the parallel distinction in the sphere of feeling: § 35. 2); the second employs a difference in the character of the sensations which form the objects or contents of attention as the basis of a classification of the forms of attention itself. On neither principle, however, is the assumption of specific kinds of attention justifiable, unless it can be shown that the process as such is essentially different in the two cases. And it would seem as a matter of fact that the changes which contents undergo in the state of attention, and the nature of its concomitant phenomena, are so constant and uniform alike under the sensible and the intellectual rubric, that there is no reason for the recognition of different kinds of attention. The various conditions of attention will, of course, fall within the scope of our own inquiry (§ 75). But to separate the conditions from one another is surely a more correct procedure than to derive different forms of the attention from them.

Another current distinction makes attention *voluntary* and *involuntary*, according as the will does or does not participate in its direction upon particular contents. This classification, again, is a classification by conditions, though it is not the same with that discussed above. Wundt names the two forms *active* and *passive* apperception; but remarks that the process of attention is the same in both cases, so that the only point of divergence is to be found in the character of the conditions. He supposes that passive apperception is an unequivocally determined, and active apperception an equivocally determined act of attention; *i.e.*, that the sole difference between them is that of the number of incentives (§§ 30. 6: 71. 6). We need not decide at present for or against the validity of the hypothesis. It is intimately connected with Wundt's belief that apperception and will are ultimately one and the same process. We may, therefore, postpone our criticism, until we come to inquire into the relations obtaining between attention and will (§ 77. 7).

§ 73. The Effects of Attention.

1. The first of the three problems which attention presents to psychological investigation is a description of the changes which conscious contents undergo in the attentive state. We term these changes 'effects of attention', for the sake of brevity, although we found ourselves obliged to reject the hypothesis that they really add anything new and specific to sensations or ideas. The expression is not intended to arouse or to betray any theoretical prepossession as to the factors involved in the production of the state. We shall, therefore, employ it without hesitation, after this express caution to the reader

not to confuse the conditions of attention (§ 75) with the changes in the contents attended to, which we are now to discuss.

We have already spoken in various passages of the first and second Parts of the dependency upon attention of sensitivity and sensible discrimination, of liability and fidelity of reproduction, of the feelings, of fusion and analysis, etc. (cf. §§ 5; 32; 39; 47, etc.). Experimental psychology has begun the quantitative measurement of the degree of influence exerted in these different cases. The undertaking is beset with very considerable difficulties, and we can hardly say that an unexceptionable method has as yet been devised for the accomplishment of the desired end. In principle, of course, the influence of the attention in any given instance may be taken as the measure of its degree or effect. But results obtained in this way have only a relative validity: (α) because we are unable accurately to determine either an absolute zero point or an absolute maximum of attention; (β) because its function would seem to be exceedingly different in individual cases; and (γ) because the efficacy of the means employed to diminish the attention for particular contents is very uncertain and very difficult to check or regulate.

2. Our subjective estimate of the degree of attention is based partly upon the result achieved under its influence by the activity of thought or perception, and partly upon the intensity of the strain sensations, which are especially apt to arise if we are continuously occupied with a single topic. But the result achieved may depend upon entirely different conditions; and there is no simple or necessary proportionality between the intensity of strain sensation and the degree of attention. Recourse must, therefore, be had in the experimental investigation of attention to objective and less equivocal means of measurement. These are found in *distracting* stimuli. The attention to a definite content is regarded as inversely proportional to the magnitude of the distraction, the quantitative gradation of which is ordinarily secured by alteration of the intensity or number of the distracting stimuli. But the relation of the particular means of distraction to the mental disposition of the experimentee is also of extreme importance. Thus, it was found in an examination of the dependency of the sensible discrimination for intensities of sound upon the degree of attention, that the application of very intensive electrical stimulation (the intensity was so great as to be painful, and as to cause tetanic contractions of the muscles) to the arm of the observer during the experiments scarcely produced any noticeable decrease of sensible discrimination, as compared with that shown by the results of experiments in which the attention was not distracted at all. On the other hand, the running through of a piece

of music in thought during the comparison of visual distances was
sufficient to effect a relatively considerable reduction of sensible discrimination. The introduction of a specific intellectual operation
(addition, intelligent reading, etc.) is still more effectual for the distraction
of attention from the observation of definite impressions. It is clear
from these illustrations, that the mere employment of distracting stimuli
of a certain intensity or number is absolutely no guarantee that a
corresponding distraction of the attention has actually been accomplished.
The discovery of a reliable measure of the attention would appear to
be one of the most important problems that await solution by the
experimental psychology of the future.

3. It only remains for us here to give a general statement of the
various effects of attention. (1) We find in the first place that attention
increases sensitivity and sensible discrimination, both in their direct
and indirect forms (§ 4. 6, 9). Its influence upon sensitivity has been
determined principally in experiments upon the sensation limen. The
relatively small difference produced under these circumstances by an
increased activity of attention is certainly referable to the fact that
the distraction employed was not very effective: for our everyday
experience teaches us that quite considerable intensities, times and
spaces rebound from consciousness, so to speak, without making any
mark upon it, if the attention is intensively occupied with other
contents. This is of itself sufficient evidence that we regard its influence
as co-extensive with the apprehension of all the four sensation attributes.
But we also believe, in particular, that the indirect sensitivity and
sensible discrimination are always far more liable to modification by
the attention than the direct. A change in the attributes and relations
of sensations themselves is necessarily confined within certain narrow
limits, whereas there is hardly any restriction upon change of judgment,
i.e., of reproduction. At the same time, we cannot admit,—what has
often been maintained,—that a change of the former kind is wholly
impossible. Thus, the statement that attention is incapable of inten-
sifying an impression, and that the observed change is really an increase
of distinctness only, is contradicted by the fact that the sensation of
a loud sound, inattentively experienced, may seem equal (such, at
least, is the author's experience) to that of a faint sound, attentively
experienced. Again, it is interesting to note that the alteration of
judgment by inattentive observation is always precisely the same with
the alteration produced by a reduction of the intensive, spatial or
temporal values of the impressions, except that it is somewhat more
uncertain (*i.e.*, the mean variation is larger). This fact requires further
investigation.

4. No less important is the influence of attention upon sensible discrimination, whatever the particular method employed for its determination (§§ 6 ff.). Here again, the effect of attention can certainly be traced in both directions, upon sensation differences themselves and upon our judgment about them. An exact discrimination between these two effects, though eminently desirable, is at present out of the question. But it is necessary to emphasise the extent of the influence of attention in this connection, in view of the current tendency to explain all the facts of sensible discrimination without reference to it. There is really hardly any difference which may not pass unnoticed, if apperception holds aloof. At the same time, this general condition must not, of course, be called upon to explain any special set of experimental results.

(2) The effect of attention upon the indirect sensitivity and sensible discrimination brings us to the consideration of its influence upon liability and fidelity of reproduction. For the application of certain judgments to sensations or sensation differences consists psychologically in a reproduction of the names subserving these judgments by the contents of perception. When we remember the magnitude of the influence of attention upon reproductory phenomena in general (§ 32. 1), we shall find it difficult to decide whether reproduction in the state of inattention is possible at all. In any case, attention produces its maximal effect in the reproductory sphere. Liability of reproduction would seem to show more marked traces of its influence than material of reproduction. But, once more, further investigation is required before any positive statement can be made.

5. (3) The effect of attention upon the feelings is of a quite different kind (§ 39. 1, 2, 3). While pleasure and pain are brought far more vividly to consciousness by the concentration of attention upon their concomitant sensations, they disappear entirely when we succeed (and we can only succeed for a moment) in making the feeling as such the object of attentive observation. This difference of result led us to adopt a particular interpretation of the feelings,—that which they receive in Wundt's theory (§ 41. 8, 9). The feelings, therefore, form an exception to our general rule of the effect of attention upon conscious contents (§ 72. 3). All the 'changes', in the strict sense of the term, which conscious contents undergo in the state of attention presuppose its concentration upon sensations or sensation complexes or their interrelations. But the feelings are the products of the interaction of contents and attention.

(4) We found in our examination of fusion that attention was of great assistance for analysis. Indeed, the singling out of a tone from

a simple or compound clang by help of the attention constitutes a fundamental experiment in the cognition of auditory complexity (§ 47. 6, 7). (5) And we meet with quite similar phenomena in the sphere of spatial and temporal colligation. Thus the perception of certain details of a picture or a melody is one of the most familiar functions of the attention. In all these cases, consciousness undergoes the characteristic change which we term *concentration*, a more or less definite restriction of the attention to a certain number of contents. What has been called the *narrowness* of consciousness (cf. § 66. 4) is essentially conditioned by the inability of apperception to comprehend any considerable number of discriminable contents at one time.

6. It is plainly this peculiarity of the attention which has led to Wundt's metaphorical distinction of a conscious fixation point and field of regard. The apperception of a content is its appearance at the fixation point of consciousness; the perception of an impression is its appearance in the conscious field of regard. The metaphor is suggested by the constant relation of fixation point and attention in the field of vision (§ 58. 8). Wundt does not mean, of course, that apperception is restricted to a single object, still less to a single conscious element. The narrowness of consciousness has a certain, if limited, range of variation.

An attempt has been made to determine the number of impressions which are simultaneously apprehensible by an act of visual attention. The number is dependent upon the duration, intensity and extension of the stimuli; but also, as can be readily understood, upon the interconnection of the separate impressions. This latter condition is very difficult of elimination. It obviously depends upon the liability of reproduction of a complex whole as such (§ 30. 4). Hence the fact that words of four or five letters, *e.g.*, can be apperceived almost as easily as single letters simply proves that the attention may be concentrated upon a complex almost as intensively as upon its separate constituents, provided always that the complex is definite and familiar and, therefore, liable of reproduction in its entirety. On the other hand, if the letters presented together do not 'make sense', *i.e.*, if the liability of reproduction of each separate impression is approximately equal and the complex has hardly any value of its own as an incentive to reproduction, the number of letters which can be simultaneously apperceived in the time required for the apperception of a single impression is reduced to two. Again, if we have had some practice in the analysis of chords, we find it comparatively easy to pass an accurate judgment upon the particular tones or clangs which they contain. Here too, the total impression has become associated with a knowledge of the elements which are required for its production; the judgment is not based upon an equal distribution of apperception to all the individual constituents of the chord. So that if the degree of concentration of the attention is to be measured by the number of contents upon which it is directed, care must be taken to select impressions which are equally liable of reproduction and whose juxtaposition does not give rise to a complex which may reproduce or be reproduced as such. Our principal criterion of concentration in everyday life, however, is the relative inaccessibility of consciousness to other ideas than those which are placed directly at the conscious fixation point. *Absentmindedness, i.e.,* is simply a sign of intensive concentration.

7. Lastly, we have to consider the influence of attention upon the temporal course of conscious contents. (α) The quickness with which an impression is perceived is proportional to the concentration of expectation, of voluntary attention upon it. We have already had many illustrations of this rule (§ 66). If a visual and an auditory impression are given simultaneously, the visual sensation normally comes later, owing to peripheral conditions; but its retardation may be more than counterbalanced under certain circumstances by the preference accorded to it by apperception. (β) The rapidity of reaction is essentially dependent upon the direction of the preparatory attention. Here again, it is in reproduction that the effect of attention is manifested.

After this hasty survey of the effects of apperception, we may attempt a brief summary of the more important phenomena. It must be admitted that the element of hypothesis cannot be wholly eliminated. But it seems proper—the feelings being ruled out, for reasons already given—to distinguish between a change of sensations and sensation attributes and a change of their reproductory activity. All the effects of attention appear to fall under one or other of these rubrics. Its principal function in the former case is that of intensification, in the latter that of increase of liability of reproduction. This statement must not, however, be interpreted to mean that attention is a creative principle, capable of increasing the intensity of given sensations by a certain definite amount, or of qualifying them for reproductory functions to which they would otherwise be inadequate. The determination of either kind of change is purely relative; and the result is, therefore, necessarily ambiguous. That is to say, the facts may be explained on the theory that apperception simply removes obstacles which prevent the maximal functioning of the contents in consciousness, as well as by the assumption that it positively enhances the attributes or activities which are normally predicable of these contents. The former view gives the attention a directly inhibitory function, the latter ascribes to it a direct reinforcement of perception. The phenomena can be explained in either way,—except that the second view requires to be supplemented by the first, whereas this latter furnishes of itself a comprehensive and consistent theory. We will postpone our decision between them to a later Section (§ 76).

§ 74. The Phenomena which accompany Attention.

1. No systematic investigation into the concomitants of attention has as yet been instituted. The more physiological processes which appear in the train of attention stand in especial need of accurate experimental observation and determination. There can be no doubt that a long list of involuntary bodily changes of varying origin bears a characteristic relation to the direction and vividness of attention, as it does to the course of the feelings. We have already mentioned one curious fact: that the acceleration of pulse which is connected with the dominance of the feeling of pleasantness in consciousness decreases when the attention is directed upon the feeling itself; and that the slowing of the pulse due to unpleasantness becomes still more marked under similar circumstances (§ 39. 3). The stimuli employed in these experiments for the production of pleasantness and unpleasantness were of very different character, so that the results may be assumed to possess general validity. Again, we all 'hold our breath' when we are trying to be more than usually attentive. This phenomenon, it is true, is very closely connected with that of listening, *i.e.*, with the attentive expectation of auditory impressions; and we might, therefore, be inclined to suppose that it simply indicated a desire to rid the ear of disturbance by the sounds of expiration and inspiration. But similar phenomena recur in other sense departments. Wherever apperception is rendered more than usually difficult by the faintness or brief duration of the impression, or the simultaneous presentation of distracting stimuli, the observer does his best to inhibit respiration. A pneumographic investigation of this correlation showed that the breath was always taken more quickly and less deeply when the attention was exclusively concentrated upon definite sensations or intellectual operations. The change became more apparent with increase of effort, and was greatest under the influence of distracting stimuli. Another involuntary consequence of attentive concentration is the arrest of movement of the body or limbs. When we fall into a 'brown study' we slacken our pace, or even come to a standstill. If an idea suddenly seizes upon us with full force, we interrupt whatever movement we

28

may be making, quite automatically. All these processes point to inhibitory effects, brought about by intensive concentration of the attention, upon the motor innervation of muscles whose activity is not implied in the attentive act.

2. Besides these concomitant phenomena of motor inhibition, which obviously assist in securing the maximal concentration of the attention upon the object to which it is directed, there are others which possess the character of adjuvant processes. In the first place we may mention the probable local hyperæmia of definite brain areas whose activity is implied in the presence of the apperceived contents. This functional hyperæmia, which is due to arterial dilatation, must certainly serve to increase the excitability of the region over which it occurs. And peripheral phenomena of the same kind have also been recorded. If we hold our attention for some time together upon a particular part of the skin, there arise sensations of pressure or temperature, of pricking, and even of pain, which are localised at the exact spot which has been the object of continued energetic and exclusive observation. The substrate of these sensations might possibly be looked for in the weak excitations constantly set up at all parts of the sense organ, and now brought to consciousness by concentration of the attention. But it has been more plausibly conjectured that they are correlated with the vasomotor changes which this concentration incidentally produces. In all probability the remarkable phenomena which have been noticed in hypnosis and, under similar conditions, in cases of mental 'stigmatism' should be referred to the same cause. In principle, at any rate, it is not more incomprehensible or enigmatical that an innocent piece of paper should induce reddening and inflammation of the skin to which it is applied with the suggestion that it is sticking-plaster, or that scars should make their appearance at uninjured parts, than that definitely localised cutaneous sensations should be aroused with a far less intensive engagement of the attention. We should then have to suppose that centrifugal excitations are propagated from the sensory regions primarily concerned in the attentive act to the peripheral organs with which they are connected. These centrifugal effects would naturally show themselves in certain sensory changes, as well as in motor. The recent demonstration of the existence of centrifugal sensory paths removes the only real difficulty in the way of the hypothesis (§ 9. 9).

3. Several trustworthy observers have stated that they are able to call up at will visual sensations of definite quality and of equal vividness with those of external perception.[1] These visual qualities are

[1] I have often succeeded in making colours, which I tried to bring vividly to mind,

as a rule quite clearly distinguishable from ordinary memorial images. And as in certain extreme cases they have been found to give rise to after-images, there can be absolutely no doubt that the peripheral organs are concerned in their origination. But the mechanism of the whole process is obscure, and it is impossible to decide between the various theoretical explanations. In any event, associative interconnection must be an important factor; for the effort to see a particular colour is at first upheld simply by certain judgments,—spoken, heard or merely ideated words, which are adequate to excite the sense organ by virtue of their liability of reproduction, as reinforced by an appropriate direction of the attention. It is clear that voluntary attention must reap a very special advantage from the working of this mechanism. For if continued concentration of the attention gives rise to actual sensations, the physiological sense apparatus must obviously be rendered at the same time peculiarly susceptible to external impressions. Hence we can readily understand that vividness and concreteness of expectation constitute the most favourable conditions of perception (§ 5. 6).

4. Among the motor processes which subserve the concentration of the attention upon a particular object, the *adaptation* of the sense organs occupies a place of especial importance. In a very large number of cases this adaptation appears to be altogether involuntary. Thus the twitching of the skin which has been observed in experiments with pressure stimuli upon the cutaneous sensibility of the blind is probably to be interpreted as a movement of adaptation, leading to a more exact perception of the impression. Again, we often speak of 'straining the ears', when our expectation or attention is intensively directed upon auditory stimuli. It is uncertain how far the muscles tensor tympani and stapedius are concerned in this state (§ 16. 1), though it would seem that the tensor is strongly contracted for the hearing of high tones. But the most familiar phenomena are those of ocular adaptation. Not only are binocular movements and positions apparently dependent upon their serviceableness for attentive vision (§ 58. 8), but the mechanism of accommodation secures the most favourable conditions for attention both by voluntary and involuntary function. Similar phenomena recur in the departments of taste and smell. The rhythmic movements of respiration, of the limbs and of the whole body, which have often been noticed as concomitants of attention, are of more secondary importance. When we are listening to a particular rhythm, *e.g.*, we are apt to 'keep time' by involuntary movement, and our apprehension of the time relations of the stimulus

flash out upon the darkened field of vision. Several of my observers in the experiments described in § 28. 2 were able to call up colour sensations in any required order.

seems to be facilitated by this accompaniment. Lastly, certain recent investigators have spoken of a *predisposition* of the sensible attention, which they regard as partly motor and partly sensory in nature, and as manifested in the formation of a disposition in lower centres to the correct continuation of repeated movements or sensations (cf. § 5. 7). This phenomenon must certainly be interpreted as an effect of attention which stands upon the same plane with the adaptation of the sense organs. As such, it necessarily acquires considerable importance in all cases where the reaction upon definite kinds or forms of movement or sense impression tends to become automatic by continued practice.

5. There were two alternative theories of the effects of attention (§ 73. 7); and there are similar alternative theories of its concomitant phenomena. All the motor processes of which we have spoken in this Section can be regarded either as adjuvant or as inhibitory. The former view finds its chief support in the direct reinforcements of the attention, whose discussion begins in our second paragraph. On the other hand, the phenomena enumerated in the first paragraph must be classed as inhibitory effects, whatever ideas are entertained as to the nature of attention itself. Whether the inhibition hypothesis alone is adequate to the facts, or whether their explanation requires a combination of the two theories, can only be decided in the light of introspection. We shall return to the question when we attempt to give a theory of attention (§ 76).

With the motor concomitant phenomena are conjoined certain sensations, which thus constitute a characteristic factor in every process of attention. They are for the most part strain sensations, arising from the adaptation of the sense organs and the position of the body or limbs; and they are indicated in the phrases 'strained' attention, 'intent' expectation, etc. They form one of the chief aids in our subjective measurement of the intensity of attention and expectation (§ 73. 2); and they furnish a sensory background for 'intellectual' attention,—localised, in this case, principally in the head (forehead or back of the head). In view of the great variety of sources from which they are derived, they must, of course, be regarded not as constitutive, but only as consecutive characteristics of the state of attention. They stand guard over attention, so to speak, to prevent its too persistent occupation with a single object; and their growing unpleasantness is a warning signal of excess of function in some particular part of the nervous system, which must ultimately prove harmful to the organism.

§ 75. The Conditions of Attention.

1. We must not be understood to mean by the 'conditions' of

attention the conditions of the state as such. We use the word simply to denote the incentives which lead to the appearance of particular contents in the attentive state. The question which we have to answer here is, therefore, that of the circumstances which attract the attention upon these particular processes. For attention is always alert and busy during the waking hours of consciousness; it is the higher court of consciousness, as someone has said, to which comparatively few of the processes in the lower consciousness have access.—But we also distinguish different *degrees* of attention, according to the intensity of its concentration or the steadiness of its hold upon the various contents. We must, therefore, as far as we can, elucidate the conditions of these degrees of attention.

We can distinguish two different classes of conditions, using the term as defined just now: *external* and *internal* conditions. The former consist of different motor and sensory characters, which give a content the advantage over other contents; the latter in the affective value of an impression, and in its relations to phenomena either actually given in consciousness or contained in its past history. All these conditions are primarily valid for the phenomenon of involuntary attention. But they are also of influence upon the voluntary form of the process, as is shown in the increased ease or rapidity with which the attentive act is accomplished under their direction. And they enable us at the same time to explain the relative vividness, the greater or less degree of attention in the individual case.

I. External Conditions.

2. (*a*) *Motor Conditions.*—The interest of psychologists in recent years has largely centred in the motor processes, and a theory has been proposed which makes them the essential factors in attention. Such a view is plainly onesided and inadequate to the explanation of all the phenomena. At the same time, its elaboration has led to a thorough investigation of what we might call the expressive movements of attention, as well as of the motor processes which help to induce and maintain it. It is with the latter that we are concerned in the present connection. We include under the rubric of 'motor conditions' every kind of predisposition of the motor apparatus, whether purposed or accidental, for the reception of definite sense impressions. These conditions, therefore, border very closely upon certain of the concomitant phenomena of attention,—more especially the adaptation of the sense organs (§ 74). The difference is, that in the previous Section we meant by this 'adaptation' a motor phenomenon produced naturally, by way of reflex movement, or voluntarily, by a definite attitude of

expectation, as a concomitant or consequence of attentive perception;
whereas here it specifies a condition of the preferential direction of the
attention upon particular impressions. Other things equal, *e.g.*, the
attention is more liable to be attracted by the object which accident
or intention has brought under the motor conditions of clear vision
(fixation and accommodation). Some part is also played by the position
of the body and by other adaptive processes. It may be doubted,
however, whether these motor phenomena are really to be regarded
as a special class of conditions, over and above the sensible effects
to which they give rise. We shall, perhaps, be more correct in supposing
that they are only indirectly conducive to the apperception of particular
contents, as determining the attributes of the contents themselves.

3. (*b*) *Sensory Conditions.*—Under this title we include all those
attributes of peripherally or centrally excited sensations which give them
an influence upon apperception, apart from the relations which they
bear to other contents simultaneously present in consciousness. The
first to be mentioned is of a purely negative character; it consists in
the absence of other impressions. The more completely isolated a
sight or a sound, the more powerful is it to attract the attention.
This observation must obviously be brought into connection with the
facts of the 'concentration' of the attention and the 'narrowness of
consciousness' (§ 73. 5); and it probably gives the explanation of
contrast effects (§ 68. 7). For an isolated visual or auditory impression
can receive a measure of attention which is altogether impossible when
it is accompanied or surrounded by a number of other objects of perception. And (internal relations apart) a contrast effect, which shows
itself in an especial facility of apperception of an object standing out
against its environment, consists simply in the relative isolation of the
particular impression.—The most prominent of the positive attributes
is intensity. Relatively intensive impressions attract the attention, in
all sense departments alike. It is as if the intensive stimulus
had power to enter the magic circle which surrounds the upper consciousness. In view of the early appearance of a relation between
intensive sense impressions and reflex movements in the course of
individual development, we can hardly question its biogenetic character.
All the equivalents of intensity have a similar influence upon apperception. Thus the attention is readily aroused by a stimulus of
considerable extension or duration, even though it be of but slight
intensity. In the adult consciousness the effect of all these external
conditions is greatly obscured by the overwhelming importance of the
internal. Hence it can obviously be traced most directly in the minds
of children or animals, where it is least liable to inhibition from within.

II. Internal Conditions.

4. (a) *The Affective Value of the Impression.*—'Interest' is so constant a condition of the apperception of a particular conscious content that it has often been identified with attention itself. Hence we sometimes find it said that attention is simply a feeling. But as an agreeable impression holds our attention as strongly as a disagreeable impression, from which we cannot escape, while the state of attention may be the same in both cases, we must evidently draw a sharp line of distinction between it and the feelings. Moreover, 'interest', as ordinarily understood, implies that it is a pleasant feeling which attracts the attention to the special content. But there can be no question that an unpleasant or painful stimulus, from which we are unable to free ourselves, forces its way to the conscious fixation point and keeps the attention directed upon it. Both facts are sufficiently accounted for by their relation to the maintenance and furtherance of life.—It may be that the effect of intensity upon apperception, which we mentioned above, is also explicable by its influence upon the feelings (§ 37. 6, 7).

(b) *The Relation of the Impression to the Psychophysical Disposition.*— This heading covers the most important conditions of attention in the adult consciousness. We include under it (α) the associative relations of the impression to the ideas already present in consciousness; (β) its relations to the materials of reproduction; and (γ) the relative vacancy of consciousness.

(α) The greater the liability of reproduction which an impression possesses, the more readily does it attract the attention. The careful observance of this law is one of the chief conditions of pedagogical success in education and instruction. The matter to be assimilated must be brought into connection with the store of past experiences, whether by its similarity to what is already known or by some other incentive to reproduction. The whole course of thought is largely regulated by the same principle.

5. Voluntary attention also makes use of these associative relations for the apperception of particular impressions or ideas. And another fact which belongs here is that impressions which repeat or resemble ideas already present in consciousness are especially liable to attract the attention. For as they possess an equal liability of reproduction (§ 30. 10), they are very likely, other things equal, to oust the given contents from the conscious fixation point (cf. § 69. 5). (β) In speaking of the relation of the perceived impression to the materials of reproduction, we mean that identical or similar contents have been

previously experienced, and have thus set up functional dispositions (cf. § 9. 8), which facilitate its entry into consciousness and into the state of attention in the particular case. 'Spontaneous' ideas (§ 30. 9, etc.) fall under this head. They come to attention by virtue of the persistence and vividness of their materials of reproduction, quite apart from any other attributes or relations. More important is the fact that the power of a centrally excited sensation to attract the attention varies with the level of preparedness (§§ 31. 3; 71. 7) to which it has been raised by its psychophysical disposition. This explains why it is that we can single out an overtone in a clang with especial facility after we have previously heard it in isolation; or that the histologist finds in his preparation a number of interesting details which altogether escape the unskilled eye, etc. The rule can also be pressed into the service of the voluntary attention, as when we arouse the materials of reproduction of an expected impression as intensively as possible, *i.e.*, raise them to the highest possible level of preparedness. The time required for this maximal preparedness in simple cases appears to be approximately constant. It has been found in reaction experiments, and in special investigations into the dependency of attention upon time interval, to be 2 to 2·5 secs. (§ 69. 5). (γ) The relative vacancy of consciousness is a pendant to the absence of rival stimuli, cited under the head of external conditions. The less occupied attention is at the moment, the more likelihood will there be of the apperception of the impression. All these internal conditions combine and conflict with the external in the most various ways. But it is owing to the relative preponderance of the internal, that distracting stimuli, at least as employed hitherto, do not afford a reliable measure of the degree of attention (§ 73. 2).

6. It would seem that the state of attention cannot be prolonged beyond a certain time limit. It is a matter of common experience that if an apperceived stimulus persists for any length of time, our susceptibility to it soon becomes blunted. Quantitative expression has been given to the time relations of attention in a number of experimental researches. These have always employed the stimulus or difference limen, since in their case decrease of excitability must mean disappearance of impression or difference, and can thus be most easily remarked. The results are exceedingly interesting. It is found that if attentive observation is prolonged beyond the first disappearance of the stimulus or stimulus difference, there is a return of it to consciousness; this is again followed by disappearance, and so on,—noticeableness alternating with unnoticeableness as long as the experiment is continued. In some cases the phenomenon is approximately periodic, *i.e.*, appear-

ance and disappearance succeed each other at approximately equal intervals of time; but ordinarily there is no evidence of periodicity. The phenomena recur in different sense departments, and may also be observed when apperception is continuously directed upon centrally excited sensations. Hence it is probable that they are due to central and not to peripheral causes. The observer's belief that the degree and direction of his attention remain unchanged throughout the experimental series can hardly be taken as a decisive argument to the contrary. Moreover, the central hypothesis is confirmed by the observation that the experimentee can discriminate very positively between the subjective disappearance of a persistent stimulus and its objective cessation. The rhythm of respiration does not appear to exert any considerable influence upon these *fluctuations of the attention,* as they are called; and the changes of accommodation and eye movements, which have been made responsible for their origination in the sphere of vision, are in all probability of merely secondary importance. It is hardly possible, as things are, to give an adequate theory of the phenomena. It seems reasonable to suppose that the exclusive direction of the attention at a constant intensity upon a particular impression cannot be maintained for any length of time, owing to the necessary inhibition of the other contents which are crowding in upon consciousness; and that it is, therefore, interrupted by intervals, in which the inhibited processes secure some measure of recognition.

§ 76. The Theory of Attention.

1. The explication of the special conditions under which a content enters into the state of attention does not carry with it the determination of the essential factors in attention itself. In the foregoing Section we assumed that there was a general difference between the conscious fixation point and field of regard (§ 73. 6); but we made no attempt to explain it. It is conceivable, of course, that attention is nothing else than an increased intensity of sensation; and this view has actually been held, more especially by the English psychologists. But its refutation does not require many words. (α) According to Weber's law, the absolute difference limen of intensive sensations is greater than that of weaker. If attention consisted in an increased intensity of sensation, therefore, the absolute sensible discrimination would be less at a high degree of attention than it is at a lower degree or in the state of complete inattention. The facts are absolutely opposed to this conclusion. (β) Moreover, it is a matter of familiar experience that the vividness or degree of attention is itself capable of

quantitative gradation, and that the differences may be distinguished from differences in the intensity of sensations. (γ) Lastly, while we freely admit that contents are really intensified in the state of attention, we have already pointed out (§ 73) that the intensive change is only possible within certain narrow limits, and is not adequate to explain the passage from unnoticeableness to its subjective antithesis, noticeableness. Indeed, it may be said in general, that any mere statement of the changes produced by apperception, and of the empirical conditions under which a content is apperceived, fails to explain two essential facts: that the internal conditions, though very much less intensive for consciousness, exercise so preponderant an influence upon apperception; and that inhibition of motor and sensory processes may be so complete and far reaching.

2. Another recent theory of attention, of which Ribot is the principal representative, distinguishes 'spontaneous' from voluntary attention, as the genetically earliest form of the attentive state. This rudimentary attention is the outcome of the natural impulses and desires; and its essential elements are the motor processes which we dealt with in our Section upon concomitant phenomena (§ 74). "In a word, the attention is simply an emotive state translated into terms of motor energy." The voluntary form does not differ in kind from the spontaneous: it is simply later in the order of development, and depends upon the emotions or impulses acquired by education. It is a 'sociological phenomenon', developed by the needs and exigencies of social life. It is plain that the distinction is different from that of voluntary and involuntary attention discussed above (§ 72. 5). Apart from this, however, the theory attaches far too much importance to accidental conditions and secondary phenomena. 'Emotion' means in it what we have termed the 'affective value' of the impression (§ 75. 4). We do not, of course, dispute the influence of this factor; but we are unable to understand how Ribot can make it the exclusive and ultimate condition of the state of attention. The importance of the motor phenomena is also exaggerated by the theory. As a matter of fact they are either simply expressive movements, of generic or individual development, on the same level with the analogous processes in emotion and impulse; or they serve a subordinate purpose, as reinforcing or maintaining the changes set up by the attention. And lastly, it is difficult to see how we should distinguish a phenomenon of impulsive or emotive expression from the process of attention, if these factors were the sole criteria of difference. Ribot, it is true, makes the further statement that monoideism, a characteristic intellectual process which corresponds to what we have called 'concentration' (§ 73. 5), is the

differentia of attention. But if this shows that he realises that attention is not simply emotion or movement, it throws his failure to provide a real theory of its origin into still stronger relief.

3. An explanation of the attention in purely psychological terms, such as has been attempted, *e.g.*, by Herbart, obliges its adherents to ascribe a determining influence to the unconscious as a psychical process, if not to make it the one primal force in mind. For there can be no doubt that the most essential conditions of the origin and maintenance of attention must be sought outside of consciousness. The evidence on this point is overwhelming. The force of the attention is wholly unintelligible on any other hypothesis; it is a frequent experience that the incentive to the preference of a content by apperception does not come to consciousness; and individual variation of the capacity of attention in normal subjects, as well as the differences observed in pathological cases, put the assumption of definite physiological conditions of a central character beyond the range of question. We cannot derive apperception itself from any of the conditions, known or assumed, of the origination and determination of sensations or ideas. For the characteristic differences of attention displayed by different individuals and in different forms of mental disease appear to be in a certain measure independent of the peripheral or central excitations which we look upon as the conditions of sensation. Idiots and dements, *e.g.*, show an abnormal weakness of attention in all directions, a general incapacity of concentration and insusceptibility to external and internal stimuli. In other cases, consciousness is always in a ferment of change,—ideas come and go in inextricable confusion, and the patient has no power to direct his thoughts or regulate his actions. This state takes on its most pronounced form in delirium and mania; but it also occurs in a less marked degree in imbecility. Indeed, it is the difference in the attitude of attention which has led to the distinction of imbecility from idiocy, as a special type of mental disease. Lastly, we have instances of abnormality of attention in the shape of an insistence of particular contents, which have practically undisturbed possession of the conscious fixation point. Hypochondria, melancholia, and the well-defined illusions of paranoia, furnish familiar illustrations of the pathological concentration of the attention upon a single object. As all these phenomena are compatible with the utmost variety of mental furniture, and there is no necessary interference with the ordinary conditions of ideation, peripheral and central, we cannot resist the conclusion that they must be referred to some specific cause.

4. The first systematic investigation in which the necessity of a

special psychophysical theory of the attention is recognised was carried out by G. E. Müller. According to Müller the process of attention consists primarily in a centrosensory reinforcement of peripherally excited or centrally prepared sensations or ideas. It is not clear whence this reinforcement is derived; but it serves either to intensify a present excitation, or to increase the disposition or preparedness for a future or expected excitation. It may perhaps be conjectured that a special central organ is the centre of the reinforcing influence. But apart from the indefiniteness which attaches to this particular point, the question arises whether a reinforcement, *i.e.*, a positive alteration, is really to be regarded as the fundamental phenomenon in attention; and it is a strong objection to Müller's theory that it fails to discuss, what is certainly not less important, the phenomenon of inhibition. We have had occasion to remark in more than one connection that the changes which conscious contents undergo in the state of attention, and the motor phenomena which follow in its train, admit of two interpretations, one of which accredits attention with functions both of reinforcement and inhibition, while the other attempts to explain all the facts in terms of inhibition alone (§§ 73. 7; 74. 5). On the former view the sensory and motor changes which we find in attention cannot be wholly derived from the nature and attributes of the contents themselves. On the latter, the peripheral and central excitations and their relations, if they can secure free and unimpeded recognition in consciousness, produce all the phenomena which characterise the state of attention, of their own power and by their own laws; and the function of apperception consists simply in the suppression of competitive activities. There seems to be no valid objection to this second hypothesis, which is certainly the simpler of the two; and we may, therefore, follow it in regarding the psychophysical process in attention as a process of inhibition. The phenomena of voluntary attention might, perhaps, be cited in favour of the alternative position. For there, it may be urged, we surely find a positive preference accorded to particular contents,— everything is prepared on the sensory side for the furtherance of their underlying excitations, and motor arrangements are expressly made to facilitate the reception of the expected impressions. But it will hardly be supposed that this motor adjustment has not originated by way of associative co-excitation; and it will hardly be denied that expectation, even when voluntary and definitely directed, has been determined by incentives to reproduction. There seems no reason, therefore, for the assumption that the associative relations, which are certainly involved in voluntary attention, are not able of themselves to produce all the observed effects.

5. If we combine the view that the functions of the attention require the existence of a specific central organ with the hypothesis that all these functions may be regarded as inhibitory processes, we obtain Wundt's theory of apperception in its most recent formulation. Since a weakening of the attention implies a weakening of the intelligence, and intellectual derangement is correlated for the most part with an abnormal state of the frontal lobes, Wundt conjectures that the organ of apperception has its seat in the frontal area of the cerebral cortex. The theory finds further support in the growing importance of the frontal brain as we rise higher in the scale of organic evolution, and in the fact that it stands in anatomical connection not only with all the sensory centres of the cerebral cortex, but also with the motor region, and with the central organ which ranks next below the cortex in general importance, the thalamus opticus. No other part of the brain can lay claim to such universal significance. And so far, physiological investigation has not resulted in the ascription of any special function to the frontal lobes. On the other hand, there is strong physiological evidence of inhibitory processes, originated in a supreme central organ: evidence which long ago led to the hypothesis that the will is an organ of inhibition. It is true that the mechanism of the interconnection of all these different centres is at present capable of no more than schematic representation. But the important point is, that the idea of a physiological, functional inhibition is nothing new or unusual; that similar ideas of the inefficacy of certain peripheral or central excitations are suggested by the phenomena of mental deafness and mental blindness (§ 27. 7); and that there is no difficulty in imagining the process of inhibition translated into physical and chemical terms.

Literature:

G. E. Müller: *Zur Theorie der sinnlichen Aufmerksamkeit.* 1873.

T. Ribot: *Psychologie de l'attention.* 1889.

L. L. Uhl: *Attention: a Historical Summary.* 1890.

A. Bertels: *Versuche über die Ablenkung der Aufmerksamkeit.* 1889.

Cf. the experimental investigations of N. Lange, Eckener, Pace, Marbe and Lehmann, in the *Philos. Studien*, vols. iv., viii. and ix.

§ 77. Will and Self-consciousness.

1. It is usual to describe the activity of will as *external* or *internal*, according as its aim or result is a bodily movement or a change in the course of ideation. Will, *i.e.*, is regarded as a subjective power or capacity to exercise a determining influence upon conscious processes or movements of the body. It is plain that a capacity of this kind need not be conscious. At the same time, we do not ordinarily speak of 'will',

except when we may assume that there is consciousness at least of the result of its activity. Indeed, it is this fact of consciousness of the result which furnishes the chief ground of distinction between voluntary action and automatic or reflex movement. Some psychologists maintain, however, that the capacity as such, the power by which the willed result is achieved, is a conscious process. Such a view is more especially suggested by the phenomenon of choice: and hence we find will regarded as a selective activity, which decides or resolves upon some one of various possibilities. There thus arises the further distinction of selective and impulsive action. Impulsive action follows directly at the hest of a dominant incentive: but the characteristic power of the will is manifested only when a number of actions are suggested by reasons of equal weight, and a decision must be made in favour of one particular course. Lastly, the discussion of the will is rendered still more complicated by the question whether the process of internal or external voluntary action anywhere contains a third qualitatively irreducible element, a specific 'voluntary act', in addition to the familiar contents of sensation and feeling, the elementary nature of which is universally admitted.

2. This last question may be ruled out of our present inquiry without hesitation, as we have devoted a previous Section to its answer (§ 40). It will be remembered also that when we were speaking of choice in connection with reaction times (§ 70. 5) we found no reason to postulate a specific conscious act to account for it. There is, it is true, one great difference between the choice reaction and the selective actions of our practical experience. The reaction movements depend upon an equal number of simple and well defined conditions; while choice, as an experience of ordinary life, and an experience which not seldom involves distressing anxiety, either requires a certain amount of reflection, or is partially determined by unconscious incentives. But reflection, psychologically considered, is nothing else than a more or less complicated series of reproductions, associatively originated, and possibly abbreviated by the exclusion of intermediary terms (§ 31. 6). We have already had a primitive instance of it in one of the complex forms of choice reaction (§§ 70. 6; 71. 5). Moreover, the co-operation of unconscious incentives to reproduction is nothing unusual; it is often appealed to, *e.g.*, as an explanation of spontaneous ideas (cf. § 29. 2). So that the differences between the act of choice in common life and the choice of the compound reaction experiment are not such as to necessitate the hypothesis that decision or selection is a new and qualitatively irreducible process. And, consequently, there seems to be no reason for the identification of will with choice, or of voluntary

with selective action. Hence we may say in conclusion, that as the incentives to voluntary activity may be of exceedingly different kinds, and as any other internal or external change may be set up at the instance of conscious or unconscious incentives, the one phenomenon which is characteristic of will is the consciousness of the result, the end or aim, of its activity.

3. This hypothesis, however, seems to require further and more accurate definition. For we may be conscious of the results of an action, though we have neither the power nor the will to contribute anything to its execution. We will accordingly define voluntary action as the internal or external activity of a subject which is conditioned and sustained by the conscious idea of its result. This idea, like every form of expectation, may be more or less determinate; *i.e.*, we may ideate the result quite concretely and unequivocally, or in a more suggestive and general way, which simply outlines the sphere of activity by which it can be attained. We have an expectation of the latter kind in equivocally determined association reactions (§ 71. 6). We do not know what stimulus will actually be given in the individual case, but we have had named to us some general category under which it will fall or within which its reproductory effect is to be confined. So, too, when we are trying to remember an occurrence, or are meditating over a problem, the conditions are often the same,—the result of the internal activity of the will is given only in the abstract. And similar differences in the definiteness of the idea of the result may be traced in cases of external voluntary action.

These considerations help us to answer the question of a psychological content of will, *i.e.*, of what will appears to be in introspective analysis (§ 32. 5). The idea of the result, which is so important as exercising a regulative and determinative influence upon the course of reproduction or the execution of co-ordinated movements, can only be regarded as an apperceived content. Hence, the internal and external voluntary actions differ simply in the special quality of the idea of their end, and of the processes which follow in its train. We speak of an external voluntary action, when the object of apperception is an idea of movement. This relation of will to apperception serves at the same time to explain the 'power' which is ordinarily attributed to it (cf. 1 above).

4. The internal voluntary action is most familiar to us in the form of *thought*. Here again we find an anticipatory apperception, which covers a more or less extensive circle of individual reproductions, and differs from a group of accidental incentives to reproduction only in the consistency with which all ideas outside the circle are checked

or suppressed. Wundt has made this difference the ground of distinction between associative and apperceptive connections (§§ 29. 1 ; 42. 6). Associative connections are formed by the contents themselves, apperception being concerned merely in its passive form: apperceptive connections imply the co-operation of the active apperception, which acts upon the peripherally or centrally excited sensations by way of connection or of disjunction. This distinction is intimately connected with Wundt's discrimination of passive and active apperception which we have noticed above (§ 72. 5). Passive apperception is unequivocally, active apperception is equivocally determined. Now there can be no doubt that the apperceptive connection may be due to incentives which find but fragmentary representation in consciousness, i.e., which are determined by character, habit, mood, and other resultant influences of the whole of the past course of individual development. But we can discover no good reason for regarding it as a really new form of connection, as incapable of subsumption (at least in principle) to the familiar laws of reproduction. Thought would seem to be differentiated from the automatic interplay of ideas not by the appearance of a specific kind of connection, but simply by the fact that anticipatory apperceptions assume the conduct of the course of ideation. Wundt himself sees no essential difference between the unequivocally and equivocally determined apperception in external voluntary action; and we can find no justification for its assumption in the domain of internal voluntary activity.

5. We can touch but lightly here upon the vexed question of the freedom of the will. The problem centres round two points: the fact that we can decide between possibilities, when the various incentives are apparently of equal strength; and the judgment, which follows upon decision, that we could have decided otherwise than we actually did. The fact of decision presents no great difficulty to psychological explanation. We have only to remember that the reasons which introspection or memory can discover for a psychophysical phenomenon are but a small fraction of its actual conditions; and that, consequently, a decision may seem to lack incentives, or at least to be inadequately conditioned, when it is not so in reality. And the subsequent judgment is partly explicable in the same way, since our estimate of the possibility of an action is based upon an experience which includes these apparently unconditioned decisions. There is also the simple logical consideration that the statement of (or argument from) the possibility of a phenomenon involves nothing more than the statement of (or argument from) its general conditions; and that constancy of general conditions may very well consist with the utmost

variety of special. So that the judgment is not by any means incompatible with the existence of special incentives to the process forming the object of judgment, adequate to exclude other special conditions in the particular case.—The distinction between self-determination and influence from without we do not regard as an essential part of the problem. For this distinction, which depends upon a clear differentiation of the ego and the non ego, may co-exist with adequacy of conscious incentives; and need not, therefore, imply any real choice, such as is always presupposed by the supporters of the doctrine of freedom.

6. The development of *self-consciousness* has often been depicted, and its close relation to that of will rightly emphasised. But the state has also a sensible root, in the visual or tactual demarcation of the subject's own body form the external world, which comes with the gradual delimitation of objects in space. Everything which can be brought into connection with the visual or tactual image of the body, as its attribute, activity, etc., is then ascribed to the self as attribute or function. These facts have been greatly obscured by philosophical speculation, which makes the self appear as an abstract potency, practically independent in its final constitution of the sensible factors concerned in its origination. But the language of daily life, and a whole number of pathological derangements of self-consciousness, furnish conclusive evidence that the visual and tactual idea of the body forms one of the most essential constituents in the idea of the self. It is not the sole constituent, of course: there is a mental content besides the sensible. The mental content varies in character and importance with the course of individual development, being largely determined by the scientific, moral and religious beliefs of the subject. It is on this side that self-consciousness is so closely connected with will. The experience that we are not wholly at the mercy of external influences and impressions, but can hold our own against them by choice and action, *i.e.*, the fact of apperception or will, is one of the most important incentives to the differentiation of the ego and the non-ego. And the same fact underlies the epistemological distinction of subject and object. We have seen that this distinction, in the form of the twofold dependency of experiences upon external and internal factors, furnishes the criterion by which psychology is separated from natural science (cf. § 1).

7. Various suggestions towards a *theory of will*, along very different lines, may be found in the different psychologies. As a rule, however, the object of investigation has been not the will as such, but the voluntary action,—and more particularly the external voluntary action. The genetic method is most commonly followed, *i.e.*,

29

voluntary action is derived from accidental movements and their consequences. Thus a child cannot 'will' to eat a particular kind of food,
until it has tasted this same food and executed all the movements
which subserve the act of eating. Only then can it have any idea
of a result, the attainment of which necessitates its own activity.
This view appears in Herbart, and has found its chief modern representatives in Lotze and Bain. It is doubtless correct in its description of the origin of the mechanical connection between idea of result
and movement; the arousal of definitely co-ordinated movements by
an anticipatory apperception implies a liability of reproduction which
can only be due to long continued practice. But it overlooks one
essential point,—apperception itself. If we do away with the inhibitory power of apperception, it is difficult to see how any single idea
of result can lead to a voluntary action. Hence we shall prefer to
adopt Wundt's view, which considers apperception and will as ultimately one and the same function. For the characteristic energy which
we attribute to will, the energy which makes it the supreme power
in our conscious life, would seem to flow from one single source,—apperception. All the peculiar attributes of apperception are also predicable
of will; so that will, we may say, is only a special mode of manifestation
of apperception. The phenomena of will are thus seen to be referable
partly to the laws of reproduction, and partly to apperception.

Literature:

T. Ribot: *Les maladies de la volonté.* Fifth ed., 1889.

„   *Les maladies de la personnalité.* Second ed., 1888.

G. T. Schneider: *Der menschliche Wille.* 1882.

H. Münsterberg: *Die Willenshandlung.* 1888.

§ 78. Sleep and Dreams. Hypnosis.

1. Consciousness does not present a continuous series of contents,
but is always interrupted at more or less regular intervals; and an
experience once had is relegated, on the cessation of external or
internal stimulus, to the sphere of the unconscious, from which it can
return only under certain special circumstances. Empirical psychology
has no occasion to endow this unconscious with any but a purely
physiological existence. We have only found one case which seems
to contradict the rule: the case in which an unconscious state exerts
a perceptible influence on consciousness. But here we really have a
conscious process, whose sole difference from the other conscious
processes of the time is its impossibility of separate perception. There
are two connections in which these unconscious components are especially
important: those of fusion and attention (cf. § 45. 6). The constituents

of the conscious field of regard in the state of attention generally form an unanalysed total impression; though any alteration or disappearance among them is remarked at once. The 'unconscious' in this sense is, therefore, in reality something conscious, something which contributes in noticeable degree to the psychical processes of the moment. It is essentially different from the 'unconscious', in the strict meaning of the term, of which we can only say that it may possibly serve as an incentive to the reproduction of the experience with which it was once correlated. In the process of apperception in particular, the number of unconscious constituents in the total sum of incentives to reproduction may be very considerable. From this point of view, therefore, we may lay it down that the whole past history of consciousness is implied in every mental act, while we can understand the extent of the power wielded by apperception.

2. But apperception is also intermittent. The state in which consciousness appears to be altogether blotted out we term *sleep*, in contradistinction to the activity of the waking life. The fact of sleep raises the question of the conditions of consciousness, *i.e.*, of the special psychophysical factors which determine the entrance and continuance of sensations and feelings in the conscious field of regard or at the conscious fixation point. Of these conditions we know practically nothing. Observations have been made upon sleeping persons; and the physiology of sleep has been investigated, and in some cases an activity of the brain in certain directions made out. But the results obtained appear to be of a purely secondary character, and do not furnish any information as to the actual conditions of consciousness. This is obviously due to the imperfect state of nervous physiology. All that we can do, then, is to mention the most important characters of sleep, as at present known.

The depth of sleep has frequently been measured, in terms of the intensity of the impression required to produce waking. It has been found to be a general law that sleep reaches its maximal depth very soon (about three quarters of an hour) after its induction, and then grows lighter by very slow degrees. It has also been observed that the blood supply and, therefore, the volume of the brain are relatively small in sleep, and are immediately increased by any sudden sense stimulus. This is confirmed by the fact that the relative weight of the upper and lower parts of the body is different in sleeping and waking. If the body is balanced in the horizontal position in the waking state, the feet fall when sleep sets in, and the inclination appears to be proportional to the depth of sleep. Sleep can hardly be regarded as a special instance of the general phenomenon of fatigue, as it is often impossible under circumstances of extreme exhaustion. A theory of sleep must, therefore, include a reference to the attention, the importance of which for its induction or prevention is well known. There is no surer means of producing sleep than to tire the attention. The effect would seem to consist in a universal reciprocal inhibition of the psychophysical processes.

3. But conscious processes are not altogether abrogated even in sleep. They appear in the form of *dreams*, and are most frequent in the lighter stages of sleep, *i.e.*, shortly before waking. Recent statistical observations and experimental researches have served to throw some light upon the origin and character of dreams. The older theories looked upon them as the result of a spontaneous ideational activity and attempted to wring some deep meaning from them by all manner of symbolical explanations. The more sober methods of modern inquiry have traced the origin of dreams to the intensive action of external or internal stimuli upon definite sensory centres. All ideas which are not directly related to the particular excitations remain inhibited. This is the principal reason why the connection and interpretation of the dream consciousness are so essentially different from those of the ideas of the waking life. There is no will to direct and regulate the train of thought; and hence the activities of the sleeper whether internal (dreaming) or external (sleep walking, *e.g.*) possess the character of accidentally incited reproductions. It is a primary symptom of pathological excitability that the dream consciousness retains the attributes of coherent voluntary thought. It is plain that laws of the formation and course of the dream ideas can hardly be laid down in any detail. We can say, however, that their vividness, *i.e.*, the nearness of their approach to hallucinations, is dependent upon the absence of other impressions, which might orientate or still further confuse the sleeping consciousness; and that there seems to be no departure in dreaming from the laws of reproduction which we have found to hold in the waking life. Lastly, it is a common experience that dreams have but a slight effect upon the waking consciousness. This is mainly due to the fact that apperception is involved to a very slight extent, if at all, in their origination.

4. We cannot enter here into the detailed results of dream observation. But we may devote a brief space to the consideration of a cognate phenomenon, the practical importance of which has given it a prominent place in recent scientific investigation,—the phenomenon of *hypnosis*. Regarded from the purely physiological and psychophysical point of view, hypnosis presents so marked a resemblance in all essential characters to the normal states of sleep and dreaming, that theory and interpretation must certainly follow the same lines in all three cases. All the influences which serve to bring on sleep are also

adapted to induce the hypnotic state: whether uniform and monotonous sensory stimulation, or a repetition of assurance or command. It is the latter kind of influence, the 'psychical' method of induction, which is now chiefly employed for hypnotisation, (α) because it is more convenient and less dangerous than the other, and (β) because it paves the way for the subsequent reaction of the hypnotised subject to orders given in the same voice, with the same inflection, etc. There are different degrees of hypnosis, varying between the lightest and the deepest forms, just as there are different degrees of depth of sleep. Light hypnosis resembles a gentle slumber; the sleeper wakes quickly and easily, and remembers practically everything which he has experienced during the continuance of the state. The deeper forms are characterised by phenomena which can be but rarely observed or produced during sleep. (i) The first of these phenomena is *catalepsy*, a muscular rigidity either of particular limbs or of the whole body. In this state, the arms or legs remain immovable in any position in which they are placed, and the subject will continue for a long time together in the most constrained attitude. (ii) The second is what is called *somnambulism*. In this stage, consciousness recovers its functions, and movements are performed with great accuracy, but thought and action are entirely dependent upon the commands of the hypnotiser.

5. To the psychologist, somnambulism is obviously the most interesting of all these phenomena of hypnosis. The control which the hypnotiser possesses over the somnambulistic consciousness is termed *suggestion*. Recent theories of hypnosis make it the principal factor in the origination and subsequent direction of the state. It is undoubtedly of primary importance for somnambulism. Its effect may persist after the abrogation of the hypnotic state, a circumstance of which advantage is taken in the application of hypnosis for therapeutic purposes. If the subject is naturally excitable, or has become especially susceptible by frequent hypnotisation, the efficacy of suggestion is practically unlimited. Every organic function, motor and sensory alike, is subjected to its influence; and the personal resistance which would be offered in the waking life by character, judgment or will gives place to an unconditional subservience to the invading power. The wildest illusions of sense and the most absurd actions are evoked with equal ease, and the whole individual seems reduced to a machine, which can only be set in motion from outside, *i.e.*, at the command of another. Curious as these phenomena are, they have many analogues in less extreme processes of the normal consciousness. The authoritative influence which certain persons exercise upon those around them, the force of persuasion, etc., are illustrations of facts of the same order

with somnambulistic suggestion, and differ from it only in intensity and extent. The mechanism of all these effects is again simply the familiar mechanism of association and reproduction. What the theory of hypnosis is called upon to explain, therefore, is not the existence of suggestion, but simply the abnormal range and power of its influence.

6. We cannot here attempt to discuss the various theories of hypnosis. The older view, of which Charcot was the chief representative, was that only hysterical subjects were liable to fall into the hypnotic state. But with the recognition of the general significance of suggestion, it has been replaced by a more correct hypothesis (Bernheim, Delboeuf, etc.), which regards everyone as hypnotisable, though not by any means with the same facility. The physiological conditions of the hypnotic state are still obscure; though here again the observations make it probable that we have in the first instance a derangement or functional paralysis of the organ of apperception. The will of the hypnotised subject takes no independent part in the actions which he performs. The exaggeration of motor and sensory activity is probably to be explained by the fact that the excitability of the elements which are roused to function under the influence of suggestion is especially great owing to the inhibition of all other excitatory processes. Wundt speaks in this connection of a neuro-dynamic interaction, in virtue of which the energy of the inactive nervous elements serves to reinforce the function of the active parts of the system. In any event, it cannot be wrong to suppose that the more exclusively predominant a psychophysical process is, the greater will be its clearness and intensity. Looked at in this way the efficacy of attention furnishes an analogy to the power of suggestion. Under normal circumstances the attention is hardly ever found to hold sway over a definite group of ideas for so long a time together. It may be that the phenomena which appear under the influence of suggestion show us of what it is capable, if permanently directed with complete and exclusive concentration upon particular contents.

Literature :

P. Radestock: *Schlaf und Traum.* 1879.

H. Spitta: *Die Schlaf- und Traumzustände der menschlichen Seele.* Second ed., 1882.

M. Giessler: *Aus den Tiefen des Traumlebens.* 1890.

E. Michelson: *Untersuchungen über die Tiefe des Schlafes.* 1891.

W. Weygandt: *Entstehung der Träume.* 1893.

A. Moll: *Der Hypnotismus.* Second ed., 1890 (trs. in Contemporary Science Series).

W. Wundt: *Hypnotismus und Suggestion. Philos. Studien,* vol. viii., pp. 1 ff. Published separately: 1892.

INDEX OF SUBJECTS.

(The more important references are indicated by italicised figures).

INDEX OF NAMES.